ROBIN

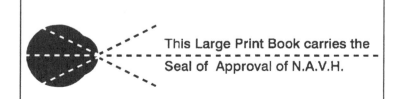

This Large Print Book carries the
Seal of Approval of N.A.V.H.

ROBIN

DAVE ITZKOFF

THORNDIKE PRESS
A part of Gale, a Cengage Company

Farmington Hills, Mich • San Francisco • New York • Waterville, Maine
Meriden, Conn • Mason, Ohio • Chicago

Thorndike Press® Large Print Biographies and Memoirs.
The text of this Large Print edition is unabridged.
Other aspects of the book may vary from the original edition.
Set in 16 pt. Plantin.

LIBRARY OF CONGRESS CIP DATA ON FILE.
CATALOGUING IN PUBLICATION FOR THIS BOOK
IS AVAILABLE FROM THE LIBRARY OF CONGRESS

ISBN-13: 978-1-4328-5367-9 (hardcover)

Published in 2018 by arrangement with Macmillan Publishing Group, LLC/Henry Holt and Company

Printed in Mexico
1 2 3 4 5 6 7 22 21 20 19 18

For Max, who opened my eyes

The creative adult is the child who survived.

— provenance unknown

his mother called him "WILD THING!" and Max said "I'LL EAT YOU UP!" so he was sent to bed without eating anything. That very night in Max's room a forest grew and grew — and grew until his ceiling hung with vines and the walls became the world all around.

— Maurice Sendak,
Where the Wild Things Are

CONTENTS

PROLOGUE

It is the late summer of 1977, and no one in the Great American Music Hall feels like laughing anymore. For hours now, this old, ornate San Francisco theater, which even its admirers have been known to compare to a Barbary Coast whorehouse, has been filling with cigarette smoke. The fetid air has been baking under the lights supplied by a camera crew. The crowd, some six hundred locals dressed in leisure suits and floral prints, are gathered around oak tables, at balconies, and beneath electric chandeliers. They have been sitting here all evening, lured by the promise of free entertainment and the spectacle of a television taping. These are culturally adventurous people in a freethinking city that has lately exploded with comic talent; they've seen and heard a lot of stand-up already, over the years and on this particular bill, packed with performers whom some of them recognize from the nearby clubs. But the electricity at the top of the show has dissipated as the sweltering night has dragged on. No one has been permitted to leave their seats, not even to go to the bathroom; the atmosphere has gone from stuffy to insufferable in this vast and windowless auditorium. It's hard to imagine a room less receptive to another stand-up comedy act.

Onto the stage strides a handsome, compact man of twenty-six, unfazed by either the steamy temperature or the irritable audience. Dressed in a brown suit, he is a bizarre sight against the gold velvet curtain of the music hall; a battered white T-shirt is visible beneath his suit jacket, its collar barely holding back a generous tuft of chest hair similar to the shaggy patches spreading up his arms and over his hands. He wears an uncomfortable-looking Russian fur hat on his head, and he is dabbed with sweat as a wide, earnest smile unfurls across his face. To anyone watching, he might as well *be* Russian, a suspicion seemingly confirmed when he speaks for the first time, over the diminishing applause, and says to the audience in a heavy accent, "Thank you for the clap, thank you very much." A roar of laughter erupts from the still-puzzled crowd. The comedian's act has not even started, and he already has them in his hands.

Over the span of his set, this young man, Robin Williams, will transform himself into any number of characters: in one moment, he is a fidgety, eager-to-please Soviet stand-up comic; the next, a stoned-out Superman, flying backward and upside-down while under the influence of drugs; in still another, the contorted Quasimodo, as portrayed by Charles Laughton in *The Hunchback of Notre Dame.* He pauses briefly to talk in his natural speaking voice — its cadence so oddly formal that it sounds like he is playing another role — so he can introduce a mid-act commercial in which he is Jacques Cousteau. Peeling off his coat to expose a pair of well-worn rainbow suspenders, Robin is soaked in his own perspiration by the end of his four-minute presentation. Like the needy alter ego he adopted at the start of the routine, he just wants this audience to like him so badly, and he will assume as many identities as it takes until he has achieved this goal. It is a mission he has certainly accomplished by the end of his act, when every member of that exhausted audience is standing on his or her feet, clapping, whistling, and cheering for more. Many of them ask themselves the same question that millions of TV viewers will wonder when this strange, silly, sweaty man's performance is broadcast a few weeks later: *Who was he?*

No one knows quite how to describe what they have just seen, and the precise words will elude them for months to come. Sure, it was a comedy routine, but the performer didn't tell identifiable jokes with setups and punch lines. He wasn't a monologist or a put-down man, an impressionist or a close observer of quotidian detail. He was more like an illusionist, and his magic trick was making you see what he wanted you to see — the act and not the artist delivering it. Behind all the artifice, all the accents and characters, all the blurs of motion and flashes of energy, there was just a lone man facing the crowd, who decided which levers to pull and which buttons to press, which voices and facades to put on, how much to reveal and how much to keep hidden.

But who was he? Except for that one stray moment when he had spoken a few tentative words in his surprisingly stately voice and then metamorphosed into a French undersea explorer, Robin had never let the audience see his true self. Some part of him would be present in every role and stand-up set he would play over the next thirty-five years, but in their totality these things did not add up to him. The real Robin was a modest, almost inconspicuous man, who never fully believed he was worthy of the monumental fame, adulation, and accomplishments he would achieve. He shared the authentic person at his core with considerable reluctance, but he also felt obliged to give a sliver of himself to anyone he encountered even fleetingly. It wounded him deeply to think that he had denied a memorable Robin Williams experience to anyone who wanted it, yet the people who spent years by his side were left to feel that he had kept some fundamental part of himself concealed, even from them.

Everyone felt as if they knew him, even if they did not always admire the work he did. Millions of people loved him for his generosity of spirit, his quickness of mind, and the hopefulness he inspired. Some lost their affection for him in later years, as the quality of his work declined, even as they held out hope that he'd find the thing — the project, the character, the spark — that had made him great before, as great as he was when he first burst into the cultural consciousness. And when he was gone, we all wished we'd had him just a little bit longer.

■ ■ ■ ■

PART ONE:
COMET

■ ■ ■ ■

1
PUNKY AND LORD POSH

The house, on the northeast corner of Opdyke Road and Woodward Avenue, was unlike any other. The giant old mansion, nearly
seventy years old, stood lovely and lopsided
in its asymmetrical design, with its roofs and
lofts of varying heights and chimneys that
reached into the sky. Here in Bloomfield
Hills, a wealthy northern suburb of Detroit
where top executives of the automobile
industry spent their evenings and weekends
in rustic comfort with their wives, children,
and servants, the unusual dwelling was more
home than a family needed. It sat on a
country estate that spanned some thirty acres
of former farmland, with a gatehouse, gar-
dens, barns, and a spacious garage that could
hold more than two dozen cars. It even had
its own name, Stonycroft, a harsh and daunting moniker for a tranquil, out-of-the-way
setting. There were few neighbors for miles
around and no distractions to disturb its
residents from their serenity, aside from the

occasional slicing at golf balls that could be heard from a nearby country club. More often, the chilly residence echoed with its own emptiness while its current tenants left many of its forty rooms mostly unoccupied, unheated, and unused. But on its highest floor, spanning the vast width of the house, was an attic. And in the attic there was a boy.

The sprawling manor was one of several places where Robin Williams had lived before he became a teenager, just the latest stop in an itinerant childhood spent shuttled between Michigan and Illinois as his father worked his way up the corporate ladder at the Ford Motor Company, and there would be more destinations on this lifelong tour, each of which would be his home for a time, but never for good. He and his parents would leave Stonycroft after a few years, but in a sense Robin would never leave its attic. It was his exclusive domain, where he was left by himself for hours at a time. Given this freedom, he shared the space with fictional friends he created in his mind; he made it the staging ground for the massive battles he would wage with his collection of toy soldiers, a battalion that ran thousands of men deep and for each of whom he had created a unique personality and voice. He used it as his private rehearsal space, where he taught himself to masterfully mimic the routines of favorite stand-up comedians he had preserved by holding a tape recorder up to his television set.

The attic was the playground of his mind, where he could stretch his imagination to its maximum dimensions. It was his sanctuary from the world and his vantage point above it — a place where he could observe and absorb it all, at a height where nobody could touch him. It was also a terribly lonely refuge, and its sense of solitude followed him beyond its walls. He emerged from the room with a sense of himself that, to outsiders, could seem inscrutable and upside down. In a room full of strangers, it compelled him to keep everyone entertained and happy, and it left him feeling utterly deserted in the company of the people who loved him most.

These fundamental attributes had been handed down to Robin by his parents long before the Williams family arrived at Stonycroft. His father, Rob, was a fastidious, plainspoken, and practical Midwesterner, a war hero who believed in the value of a hard day's work. His approval, awarded fitfully and begrudgingly, would elude Robin well into his adulthood. His mother, Laurie, was in many ways her husband's opposite: she was a lighthearted, fanciful, and free-spirited Southerner, adoring of Robin and attentive to him. But with her frivolity came unpredictability, and her affirmation, which was just as vital to Robin, could prove just as hard to come by.

On some level, Robin understood that he was the perfect blend of his parents, two drastically different people who, after earlier missteps, had found their lifelong matches in each another. As he later acknowledged, "The craziness comes from my mother. The discipline comes from my dad."

But in the melding of their traits, behaviors, quirks, and shortcomings, they laid the foundation for a son whose life was filled with paradoxes and incongruities. As an adult, Robin would describe himself as having been an overweight child, only to have Laurie knock down this disparaging self-analysis, sometimes straight to his face and with photographic evidence to the contrary. He grew up aware of the luxury he was raised in, and even made humorous grist of it — "Daddy, Daddy, come upstairs," he would later joke, "Biffy and Muffy aren't happy. We have only seven servants. All the other families have ten" — yet when pressed on the subject, he could not always bring himself to admit his family was wealthy. He would describe himself as an only child, yet he had two half brothers, both of whom he loved and received as full siblings. He would call himself isolated, even though he had friends at every school he attended and in every city where he was raised.

For all the loneliness he experienced as a child, and the unsettled emotions that came from a youth spent in a state of perpetual transition — in an eight-year span, he attended six different schools — Robin concluded that his upbringing had been blithely uncomplicated. "It's the contradiction of what people say about comedy and pain," he would say many years later. "My childhood was really nice." As he had spent his whole life learning, he could define himself however he wanted, picking and choosing the pieces of his history that he found useful while discarding the rest. Not all contradictions had to be detrimental. Some of them could even be productive.

In a portrait photograph of Rob and Laurie Williams taken early in their relationship, the two make for a deeply contrasting pair: "Picture George Burns and Gracie Allen looking like Alastair Cooke and Audrey Hepburn and that's what my parents are like," Robin later said. His father's facial features are handsome but sharp, severe, and angular; he is clean-shaven and his dark hair is close-cropped and precisely set in place. His mother's face is round, warm, and inviting, and even in this black-and-white image, the soft sparkle of her blue eyes is unmistakable. Her dimpled smile reveals a gleaming top row of teeth; his pleasant expression is thin and tight-lipped, giving away nothing. They are clasping each other, his arm wrapped around hers just below the lower border of the image, and for all that sets them apart, there is also plainly love between them.

Robert Fitz-Gerrell Williams, who was known as Rob, came from a background of privilege and had been taught the repeated lesson that adversity could be overcome through labor and perseverance. He was born in 1906 into a well-to-do family in Evansville, Indiana, where his father, Robert Ross Williams, owned strip mines and lumber companies. The younger Rob had a covert streak of playfulness, and he sometimes teasingly told people that his mother was an Indian princess. While he studied at prep school, his father would go on what Laurie would later describe as "periodic toots," taking a suite at the Blackstone Hotel in Chicago where he'd grab a chorus girl or two and "just whoop it up." Sometimes it fell to Rob, when he was as young as twelve, to travel the three hundred miles north to Chicago with the family's black servant, get his father sober, and bring him home. Rob later enrolled at Kenyon College in Ohio, but when a stock market crash in 1926 nearly wiped out the Williams family business, he had to quit school, come back to Evansville, and take a job as a junior engineer in the mines. A few years later, when Robert Ross became gravely ill, Rob unquestioningly offered his blood for transfusions, until his father finally pulled the needle out of his own arm and told his son, "I don't want you to do this anymore — you've done enough." Robert Ross died a short time later.

Rob and his first wife, Susan Todd Laurent, had a son in 1938; they named him Robert Todd Williams, and he would be known as Todd. But by 1941, Rob and Susan had separated, and Susan took Todd to live with her in Kentucky. Rob was working for Ford as a plant manager when the United States entered into World War II, and he enlisted in the navy, eventually becoming a lieutenant commander on the USS *Ticonderoga,* an aircraft carrier in the Pacific. On January 21, 1945, while at sea near the Philippines, the *Ticonderoga* came under attack from Japanese kamikaze pilots, one of whom crashed through the carrier's flight deck and managed to detonate a bomb in its hangar, destroying several stowed planes. More than one hundred sailors were killed or injured in the attack, and Rob was wounded when he leapt in front of his captain to protect him from an explosion, taking shrapnel in his back, legs, and arm.

Rob could not be redeployed in combat because of his injuries, so he reluctantly took a government desk job in Washington. But he soon returned to work at Ford, gaining a management position and eventually ascending to national sales for the company's Lincoln Mercury division in Chicago. It was there in 1949 that Rob met an effervescent young divorcée named Laurie McLaurin Janin on a blind double date at an upscale restaurant. Laurie arrived with Rob's receptionist while Rob showed up with the man who was supposed to be Laurie's date, but it was very quickly clear that Rob and Laurie had eyes for each other. Rob told his receptionist to take some wild duck from the restaurant's freezer and go home, while Laurie similarly dispatched her intended suitor. "I figured, hey, let the fun begin," she said.

Laurie was attracted to Rob physically, drawn in by his confidence and captivated by his intense, understated charisma. As she described him:

He could walk in a room, anywhere, and the minute he walked in, people were at attention. We could go to any restaurant, anywhere, the finest. The maître d' would come and up and say, "Sir, do you have a reservation?"
He would say very politely, "No, I don't."
"Right this way."

"He definitely had 'IT,' " Laurie said of Rob. "With a capital I and a capital T." He also had a darker side that was activated by alcohol. When the couple miscommunicated over a canceled date and Rob thought he had been stood up, he was devastated. He told

Laurie, "I went out and got so drunk." She responded, "What are you talking about? You had drinks every night." Perhaps the biggest fight they had, Laurie said, occurred when they were drinking at a restaurant and Rob leaned across the table to tell her: "You know what? My imagination is better than yours."

"Oh man," Laurie recalled. "The stuff hit the fan."

Laurie was born in 1922 in Jackson, Mississippi, and raised in New Orleans, where she was immersed in the city's epicurean culture and the lively parties thrown by her parents. Her parents' marriage was mildly scandalous in the largely Catholic Crescent City: her father, Robert Armistead Janin, was Catholic, but her mother, Laura McLaurin, was Protestant. The couple had separated by the time their daughter was five years old and divorced soon after, leaving Laurie to live with her even more ostracized mother.

The McLaurin family was descended from the MacLaren clan of Scotland, and Laurie's great-grandfather Anselm Joseph McLaurin had served as a captain in the Confederate army during the Civil War and was later elected a US senator and governor of Mississippi. But Laurie was essentially cut off from this aristocratic heritage when her mother remarried in 1929; her new husband, Robert Forest Smith, adopted Laurie and nicknamed her "Punky," to her dismay. "Doors that would have been open to Laurie McLaurin Janin were slammed shut to Punky Smith," said Laurie, who would nevertheless take ownership of the nickname and ask friends to call her Punky in her adult years.

Looking back on her childhood, she would recognize a strain of alcoholism that ran through her family, which made her mother volatile and her own life unstable. "Growing up," Laurie said, "I never knew when I woke up each day whether I was going to be Queen of the May or Little Orphan Annie." Her natural father, too, had a drinking problem: "It made me realize that we cannot drink," she said. "There were people in the family who rose to great heights and then BOOM! just like that, and it was from alcohol. If you can't handle it, just stay away from it. . . . It's poison for our family."

When the Great Depression nearly wiped out Robert Smith, it led to more than a decade of wandering for Laurie's family, a time they spent shifting back and forth between New Orleans and Crowley, Louisiana. At one point, her stepfather considered running an ice-cream business, and, "for the first time in my life," she said, "we didn't have a colored servant. I thought that was the end." In her late teens, she moved to Pass Christian, Mississippi, then back again to New Orleans, and in 1941 Laurie took up residence in a boarding house there while her parents went on to Mobile, Alabama. For a time she performed as an actress in the French Quarter. At the start of World War II, she was working for the Weather Bureau in New Orleans when the Pentagon inquired if she spoke French. "Fluently," she lied, and she was transferred to an office in Georgetown. There in Washington she met a young naval officer named William Musgrave, and the two were married shortly before he shipped out to the South Pacific.

Now known as Laurie McLaurin Musgrave, she spent part of the war living in San Francisco, taking lithography classes and crossing paths (by her account) with the likes of Frank Lloyd Wright and Henry Miller. When the war ended and William Musgrave returned home, the couple lived briefly in San Diego and then moved to Chicago, where he found work as an electrical engineer. In 1947, Laurie gave birth to their son, Laurin McLaurin Musgrave, who would later be known as McLaurin. In his infancy, he developed pneumonia, and Laurie was fearful of the effects that a worsening Chicago winter might have on the child. So she sent the baby McLaurin to live with her mother and stepfather in Mobile. Laurie and William separated and divorced soon after. She was on her own, but she was unbowed and excited for all that lay ahead of her. "I just married too young," Laurie would later explain. "I just thought I wanted to go out and try my wings."

Two years later, Laurie was working as a model for the Marshall Field's department store when she met Rob Williams, who touched her nonconformist's heart to such a degree that *she* bought *him* an engagement ring and proposed that they get married. On June 3, 1950, they were wed by a justice of the peace in Omaha, Nebraska, and they took their honeymoon at a fishing lodge in Hayward, Wisconsin. Afterward, Laurie told Rob, "That was the lousiest honeymoon I ever had."

The newlyweds moved into an apartment on Chicago's north side, and on July 21, 1951, Laurie delivered their son, Robin McLaurin Williams, at Wesley Memorial Hospital. Though Robin would later joke that his mother's concept of natural childbirth was "giving birth without makeup," Laurie recalled his arrival as an easy one, nearly occurring in the hospital's lobby. While the medical staff there peppered her with questions and requests for personal information, Rob scolded them: "Get this woman to a room. She's going to have the baby right here." As Laurie told the story, "They finally got me up to the room, gave me a shot, and, when I woke up, they said, 'You have a wonderful baby boy.' That was it."

Unlike the difficulty Laurie had experienced

following the birth of her son McLaurin, she had no such trouble with Robin, who was joyous and healthy, and who was raised principally by a black nurse named Susie. (Decades later, Laurie would still unhesitatingly describe Susie as "colored.") "She wouldn't put up with anything — wouldn't take it," Robin later said of Susie. "If you try and go, 'I won't do that.' 'Mm-*hmm,* I think you will. I think you'll get your sweet self UPSTAIRS!' She was a very strong force."

Shortly after Robin's birth, the family moved from Chicago to a rented house in Lake Forest, a suburb about thirty miles north of the city, beginning a migratory pattern for the Williamses that would persist for many years. Rob, an astute negotiator, would usually find the family's homes, while Laurie was responsible for decorating and entertaining; these were crucial skills while Rob worked for Ford, which still considered itself a family business whose executives expected to be invited to frequent dinner parties.

After spending her days shopping and attending society luncheons, Laurie approached these formal, sit-down dinners as exciting opportunities to exercise her creativity. They required the careful planning of menus and seating charts, and the hiring of large numbers of household staff, including a seamstress who would sew fresh napkins and tablecloths for each gathering. Laurie was immersed in these events while Rob was consumed by his work; the family almost never took vacations, and the only indulgences Rob permitted himself were an occasional round of golf or a fishing trip. It seemed not to leave them very much time for child rearing at all.

Still, Robin grew up enthralled with his parents, captivated by their moods and desirous of their attention. In many family photographs from this period, his gentleness and humility radiate right off the page; he was a small boy, often with a crew cut, a ruddy complexion, his father's pointed facial features and his mother's iridescent blue eyes. (Aptly, one of his childhood nicknames was "Leprechaun.") If Laurie is in the picture with him, she is usually beaming at her baby boy, mirroring his ear-to-ear smile as they share an embrace or, in at least one such photo, she faces off against him in a mock-combative pose while Robin, in a martial arts outfit, appears ready to deliver a devastating finishing move.

Robin was deeply enamored of Laurie, with her picaresque tales from New Orleans and unsqueamish sense of humor, exemplified by a beloved sight gag for which she would cut apart a rubber band, wad it up inside her nose, pretend to sneeze, and let it dangle flagrantly from her nostril. She also delighted in telling her son of a book, supposedly written by an English princess of the nineteenth century, about the many parties she had organized, titled *Balls I Have Held.* And she shared with Robin her affinity for strange poems that did not quite rhyme and which were not quite jokes, but which dared him to figure out the mystery of why they were funny. As one ran:

Spider crawling on the wall,
Ain't you got no sense at all?
Don't you know that wall's been plastered?
Get off the wall, you little spider.

Another one went:

I love you in blue,
I love you in red,
But most of all,
I love you in blue.

Wherever their power came from, Robin understood that these verses could make his mother laugh, and he became determined to do the same. "At that point, I went, okay," he said. "And then I tried to find things to make her laugh, doing voices or anything that would get a response out of her."

"What drives you to perform is the need for that primal connection," he later explained. "My mother was funny with me, and I started to be charming and funny for her, and I learned that by being entertaining, you make a connection with another person."

But where Robin saw Laurie as a convivial and essentially optimistic figure — "my mother has never met a stranger," he would later say — Rob was enigmatic and impenetrable. He regarded his father as ethical but stern, and the nicknames he had for Rob, like "Lord Stokesbury, Viceroy to India," "Lord Posh," or simply "the Pasha," reflected his respect for his father and the authority he wielded, his aura of infallibility and the distance between them. Needless to say, Robin did not call his father these names to his face.

In one emblematic story from his upbringing, Robin recalled returning home from school with an envelope that he presented to his father. "What's that, my boy?" Rob asked.

"My report card, sir," Robin answered.

Rob opened the envelope and ran his eyes down a list of As, smiling as he reviewed the grades. "Well done, son," he said. "Now let's get ready for dinner." Robin was eight years old.

As Todd, Rob's older son, later described his father, Rob's reticence obscured an ability to quietly scan a room, observe the people around him, and retain everything he heard them say. "It all went in and stayed there," Todd said. "He never forgot anything anybody told him, unless, selectively, he did so."

Todd knew of one other person who shared this apparent modesty and also possessed this faculty: his half brother Robin. He "can be in a room full of people where there are ten conversations going on," Todd said. "He will be talking to you and focused on you, but everything around him goes into that file." It was a trait that Todd said Robin took with him into adulthood: "He's very shy, very quiet. A lot of folks can't believe that, but you have to recharge those batteries or you're going to wind up in the loony bin."

At a very early age, Robin noticed that alcohol could get his father to lower his protective shell. After "a couple of cocktails," he later said of Rob, "he got very happy. He would just get very much, 'What do you want, a car?' I'm five."

There was at least one other activity that could pierce Rob's defenses and reach him at his soul, and one that he allowed Robin to share in. On those late weekday nights when Rob was looking for a way to unwind, he turned on Jack Paar's *Tonight Show*. And when the droll, sophisticated host was joined by Jonathan Winters, the chubby-cheeked, rubber-faced deadpan comedian, Robin was allowed to stay up past his bedtime, join his father in the consoling glow of their black-and-white TV set, and watch Winters's latest unpredictable routine.

In the first such appearance that Robin

could remember, Winters came strolling onto Paar's stage dressed in a pith helmet and declared himself a great white hunter. "I hunt mostly squirrels," he said.

"How do you do that?" Paar asked.

Winters replied, "I aim for their little nuts."

In a rare moment of father-and-son synchronicity, Rob and Robin burst out laughing. The effect on the child was galvanic: "My dad was a sweet man, but not an easy laugh," Robin explained. "Seeing my father laugh like that made me think, 'Who is this guy and what's he on?' "

Robin said he was also watching Paar some months later when Winters gave his legendary performance in which the host offered him a stick (after slapping him on his shin with it) and Winters proceeded to fill the next four minutes relying solely on his improvisational instincts, metamorphosing from a fly fisherman to a circus animal trainer to an Austrian violinist; the stick became an oar in the grip of a chanting native canoeist, a spear in the chest of an unfortunate United Nations parliamentarian, and a golf club in the hands of Bing Crosby, whose trademark croon the showboating Winters could reproduce flawlessly.

Other TV comedians thrilled Robin, like Danny Kaye, the maestro of seemingly a million nonsense songs and a million more invented foreign accents. But no one lit him up quite like Winters, who concealed an impish sensibility in a seemingly button-down package. Winters did not apologize for his squareness, and instead made it a part of his stage persona. ("I like to fish, that's one of my hobbies," he joked. "The rest of them I can't discuss.") Also, like Rob, he had served in the Pacific during World War II. When Winters, a US Marine, returned from combat, he discovered his mother had given away his prized collection of toy trucks. "I didn't think you were coming back," she told him.

Unlike most stand-up comics, who wanted to stand out for having a particular persona, routine, or shtick, Winters was the rare performer who didn't play by those rules. In Robin's eyes, he was a master comedian who could make any stage his canvas, needing nothing more than a microphone and his boundless ingenuity. "He was performing comedic alchemy," Robin said later. "The world was his laboratory."

Before Bloomfield Hills and Stonycroft, the Williams family lived on Washington Road in Lake Forest, not far from Lake Michigan, in "a big house, in a neighborhood of fairly big houses," said Jeff Hodgen, one of Robin's school friends. "The house was set back, off a shared driveway from another road, so it was almost mysterious. You would walk through the trees and get to his house and go, 'Wow — you live here?' "

Robin had the usual penchants for mischief. He became known around the neighborhood for possessing an enviable collection of toy soldiers — not the cheap plastic type, but the costlier kind made from metal — and for delighting in their destruction. "We'd go up on the garage roof with a book of matches and hold these soldiers over a match, and the lead would melt and drop off," said Jon Welsh, a classmate. "I am amazed that neither one of us fell off the garage roof and broke an arm or a leg, or set the garage on fire."

Other real-life implements of combat, like a silk parachute that his father had brought home as a war souvenir, became toys in Robin's hands. "We'd take it out on the lawn and tunnel under it," Welsh said. "And being silk, it would collapse around you. We would get in at opposite sides of the parachute and try to find each other, play games of tag or hide-and-seek. You couldn't see underneath it, so you would be completely isolated. Anybody with claustrophobia would just freak out."

In the presence of his parents, however, Robin suppressed his rebelliousness. "He always had an almost artificial, squared-up, shoulders-back thing" when Rob and Laurie were in the house, Welsh said. "It was 'Yes, sir,' and 'Yes, ma'am.' They weren't martinets, as far as I saw. They were always very pleasant and social. But their rules in the house were, you call us sir and ma'am. And he was like, 'Yes, sir,' and 'Yes, ma'am.' Straight spine and shoulders back, son."

Around the age of ten, Robin was introduced to his half brothers. Both had very different upbringings from his, and though their lives would intersect only intermittently, they would have a profound impact on Robin's understanding of what constitutes a family. Todd, who was Rob's older son, was now twenty-three years old and living in the Chicago area. He had grown up with his mother in Versailles, Kentucky, then ran away from home at the age of fifteen, making his way through Florida and working as a busboy in Naples. ("I was a dumb kid," he later explained.) Todd's rowdy streak did not dissipate after he returned to Versailles to finish high school, so he moved to Chicago to be nearer to his father and attend college at Lake Forest. It did not stick. "I played too much," Todd said. "So much for higher education."

Todd may have had a strained relationship with Rob, but he enjoyed an unexpected kinship with Laurie, his father's new wife. "I was determined not to like her out of loyalty to my mom," Todd said. "Laurie had married my dad and who did she think she was? But in a short period of time we became pretty good buddies." When Todd misbehaved — which was often — Laurie looked after him. "I'd do something bad, Pop would be mad, and she would always manage to get in the middle and keep me out of too much trouble," Todd said.

Todd believed he was held up to Robin as a living illustration of how he should not want to grow up. "He was reserved," Todd said. "I was the other way and just full of hell. My father raised Robin saying, 'Don't do that. Your brother did that. See what happened to him?' "

But Todd became for Robin a model older sibling that he'd lacked until now, a rowdy harbinger of what adulthood might look like, as well as an occasional tormentor. As Robin recalled, "Todd always extorted all my money. He'd come into my room and say he needed some beer money, and I'd say, 'Oh, gosh, yes, take it *all.*' My mother would get furious, because Todd would get into my piggy bank and walk out with $40 worth of pennies."

Meanwhile, McLaurin, who was Laurie's older son, had been living in Alabama with Laurie's mother and father, believing that they were his own parents. When Laurie would visit from time to time, they let him think that she was his cousin. However, when McLaurin was around thirteen or fourteen, they shared a startling truth with him: "They tell me that my very beautiful and drop-dead gorgeous cousin, Punky, is not my cousin," he said. "She's their daughter and my mother." McLaurin could now decide whether he wished to live up north with Laurie, Rob, and Robin or to stay in Alabama and let his grandparents adopt him. Rob invited him to spend time with the Williams family while he weighed these options.

The discovery that he now had Robin in his life was one that McLaurin had longed for and welcomed wholeheartedly. Before this point, McLaurin said that he had been "growing up as a quote-unquote only child, and always hoping to have a brother. And then, all of a sudden — oh, boy, I do! I do have brothers, that's wonderful. All our personalities seemed to blend very nicely together."

McLaurin identified with Robin in a particular and meaningful way. "We were both very private, solitary-type individuals," he said. "Both of us had this thing where we sometimes just liked to be in our own heads. And he was very much that way. He was a wonderfully kind, gentle, sweet soul." He was also impressed with Robin's vivid imagination, and how he expressed it through his collection of toy soldiers.

McLaurin admitted to some tensions with his mother, having been brought up by the same people who had raised her. But he was fascinated with Rob, who regaled him with stories about the reputed Chicago mobsters who would come to his old Lincoln dealership to buy their cars entirely in cash. "Two weeks later, they'd fish the car out of the river full of bullet holes," Rob would claim. Where others regarded Rob as cold and uncommunicative, McLaurin was impressed with the tough but fair way he meted out his discipline. "He had a very strong personality and he would have his own way," McLaurin said. "But if you messed up, the next day, you'd hear, 'Well, bub.' Uh-oh — okay, what did I do? And then he'd always explain the reason to you why this or that should have been done differently. He was a wonderful, wonderful gentleman." In the end, McLaurin chose to remain in Alabama with his grandparents, who then legally adopted him. "It was kind of the devil you know versus the devil you don't, as far as my decision to stay," he explained. "But I deeply, deeply loved Rob."

Todd and McLaurin met each other, too, and they and Robin all accepted one another as brothers. "It used to amaze Rob," McLaurin recalled. "He said, 'They all get along so well. I don't understand it.' I'd say, 'Well, we didn't grow up together — that's why.' "

Yet it remained something of a bewilderment that, throughout his life, Robin seemed to acknowledge the existence of his siblings inconsistently. As Todd's wife, Frankie Williams, said many years later, "Robin would say, occasionally, that he was brought up as an only child. And then, of course, we would have to deal with somebody saying, 'Well, Todd, we heard that Robin's an only child.' And it's like, no, he has two half brothers. And Todd would spend time with him and his dad and his stepmom, for holidays, summer vacations, that kind of thing."

As an adolescent, Robin had little difficulty expressing his interest in girls — one that was happily matched by their interest in him — though his earliest relationships were largely chaste affairs. Christie Platt, a neighbor of his in Lake Forest, became one of his first girlfriends, when she was thirteen and he was twelve, and she remembered him as a conspicuously handsome boy. "I always thought he looked a little British," she said. "He had that thatch of thick hair, and long legs and a husky little body."

Their affection at this age was expressed by trading dog tags, "which was the thing to do," Platt said with a laugh, "or you wrote the other person's name all over your notebook. I'm pretty sure we never kissed each other or did anything like that. I think we just stood and talked shyly to each other and then went home." On nights and weekends, they might ride their bikes together through the woods, or engage in Kick the Can or Capture the Flag with other friends. Occasionally she would see Robin playing with his toy soldiers with other boys, but she stayed out of such pastimes. "Those looked like very serious games," she said. "They looked extremely boring to me."

And then their brief entanglement unwound: Robin was a sixth grader at the Gorton School, but Christie, a year older, was a seventh grader at the Deer Path School, and knew she, a junior high student, risked social oblivion if she admitted to dating a younger, elementary school admirer. "I was kind of shy about it," she said. "You've got people going, 'I don't know him. Does he go to Deer Path?' And I'd go, '*Welllll*, he goes to Gorton.' Try to make it sound cool. But it was completely uncool. There was nothing cool about that."

While Robin was still in the fifth grade, his classmates started becoming targets for bullies, usually older children they encountered on the playground, although Robin himself proved more adept at escaping their attacks. His friend Jeff Hodgen recalled that "the bullies wanted to put me in my place, because I was as big as the sixth graders if not bigger, a lot of them. So they would actually hold me and hit me in the stomach, to knock the breath out of me. Robin was the one saying, 'When the whistle blows, get back in the classroom.' I think he was just being smart. 'You want to avoid this pain? Get in quicker.' "

Between the fifth and sixth grades, friends saw a subtle difference in Robin. Hodgen said he noticed "just a year later, just the change in him, the maturity and the look on his face. He went from smiling and kind of shy in fifth grade, to almost — not a sneer, exactly. Almost like he's ready to say something."

As a seventh grader at Deer Path Middle School, Robin found it necessary to speak up, if only to save his own skin. "I started telling jokes in the seventh grade as a way to keep from getting the shit kicked out of me," he said. By now, at school, many kids there "were bigger than me and wanted to *prove* they were bigger by throwing me into walls. There were a lot of burly farm kids and sons of auto-plant workers there, and I'd come to school looking for new entrances and thinking, if only I could come in through the *roof.* They'd nail me as soon as I got through the door." Robin dismissed the notion that he might have been singled out because his family was wealthy. "How could they know I was rich?" he said. "Just because I'd say, 'Hi, guys, any of you play lacrosse?' They thought lacrosse was what you find in *la* church."

But Robin did not have much time to hone his social skills. A few months into the school year, the Williams family was gone, having moved from Lake Forest to Bloomfield Hills. As best as Robin's friends could tell, there was no forewarning that he was about to leave; one day, Jon Welsh said, "He just wasn't in school. 'Where's Robin?' 'Oh, his family moved.' He was just gone. You get used to it, because in that time, people did come and go, just like anyplace else."

"He left without much of a ripple," Christie Platt said.

Perhaps, wondered Welsh, the children of executives learn to be resigned about their transient way of life and avoid getting attached to their surroundings, just like army brats — "the kids who've been moved from one military post to another," he said. "It's sort of like an early intimation of death. Here today and gone tomorrow. We all internalize it, one way or another."

In fact, Robin had been hurt by his family's relocations, and had to train himself to be ready for whenever the next move might come. Each time he arrived in a new city or a new school, he felt awkwardly on display. "I was always the new boy," he once said. "This makes you different."

This latest move to Bloomfield Hills, and to the peculiar and secluded Stonycroft mansion, was particularly tough on Robin. It ushered in the beginning of a strange period spent partly in freedom and partly in banishment in the third-floor attic, searching for ways to stimulate his ravenous imagination. It wasn't that he was unpopular with other kids in the neighborhood — "there *were* no other kids in the neighborhood," he said. "I made up my own little friends. 'Can I come out and play?' 'I don't know; I'll have to ask myself.' " He spent his time with Susie, the nurse and maid who had helped raise him as a baby back in Chicago and who continued to work for the Williams family at Stonycroft; with John and Johnnie Etchen, a black husband and wife who also worked as servants on the estate; and with their son Alfred, who was a few years older than Robin and would sometimes play with him there.

Robin endured long periods of heartache while Rob traveled for business or relaxation, and Laurie went with him, not appreciating how this detachment was affecting their son. "I didn't realize how lonely Robin had been," Laurie said many years later. "But I had to be with Rob. I didn't trust him. Come on, don't be stupid. But Robin suffered and I didn't realize that. He had some very lonely years. You think you're being a wonderful mother, but maybe you aren't."

Robin was not entirely alone in his upstairs exile. His inexhaustible collection of toy soldiers had made the move to Stonycroft with him, and now that he had vast new amounts of space in which to deploy them, and no one else to judge or dictate how they were to be used, his fantasy battles became more byzantine and ornate. In his third-floor hideaway, Confederate generals could take on GIs armed with automatic weapons, and knights on horseback could do battle with

Nazis. "My world," he said, "was bounded by thousands of toy soldiers with whom I would play out World War II battles. I had a whole panzer division, 150 tanks, and a board, 10 feet by 3 feet, that I covered with sand for Guadalcanal."

He also found refuge in the routines of his favorite late-night comedians, which had become much more than a shared source of entertainment between his father and him. By holding a cassette recorder up to the television set, Robin had hit upon a rudimentary method to preserve these performances and make them portable. He diligently listened to these tapes, teaching himself to imitate the stand-up sets, paying close attention not only to their content but also to tone and tempo, to cadence and inflection. Comedy was a science to be studied, like chemistry; from some calculable combination of language and technique, an audience's explosion into laughter could be guaranteed. If Robin had no one else to share these pleasures and insights with, he didn't need them. "My imagination was my friend, my companion," he said.

By day, Robin was enrolled in the Detroit Country Day School, an elite multicampus institution that had been founded in 1914. It was the most rigorous school he had attended to this point, with a dress code that required its students to wear sports coats, sweaters, ties, and slacks in the school's navy and gold colors; it had an austere Latin motto, *mens sana in corpore sano,* meaning "a sound mind in a sound body."

The school allowed only male pupils in its upper grades, which created some tensions for the postpubescent boys who roamed its halls. To placate the surging tides of testosterone, Robin said, "They'd bring in a busload from an all-girls' school and dangle them in front of us at a dance. Then, just when you were asking, 'Was that your *tongue?*,' they'd pack the girls back up on the bus. I'd be chasing it, shouting, 'Wait, come back — what are *those* things? What do you *use* them for?'"

The school was engineered to groom its students for prestigious colleges and future leadership roles, and Robin thrived on the rigor. He even started carrying a briefcase to class. His grades were good and he blossomed as an athlete, trying his hand at football for about a week before turning to soccer and wrestling. With his dense, compact, and hairy body, Robin proved an especially proficient wrestler and went undefeated in his freshman year — until, by his own account, he reached Michigan's state finals and was pitted against "some kid from upstate who looked like he was twenty-three and balding."

A dislocated shoulder eventually required Robin to withdraw from the squad, but he came away transformed by the overall experience, having finally been allowed, as he put it, "the chance to take out your aggressions on somebody your own size." He was also grateful for his interactions with the team's coach, John Campbell, an outspoken iconoclast at Detroit Country Day who was also the chairman of its history department and adviser to its Model United Nations and Political Simulation teams. As his daughter Sue described him, John Campbell was an unapologetic liberal — "really idealistic, really left-leaning, really believed in democracy" — who loved to tangle with his students and force them to scrutinize their unexamined beliefs.

"Republicans especially," Sue Campbell said. "A lot of his students were coming from families that were super-conservative and he just loved to needle them and challenge them. 'Are those your views or your parents' views?' " Though they might not manifest themselves in Robin right away, the values that Campbell espoused — and the confrontational manner in which he taught them — would reveal their impact in time.

At Detroit Country Day, Robin continued to slip one-liners into the otherwise sober speeches that students were required to give at lunchtime, a strategy that worked until he added a Polish joke into one such oration, to the displeasure of the school's Polish American assistant headmaster. And it was where he — a not-especially-observant member of an Episcopalian family — attended as many as fourteen bar mitzvahs a year and made some of his first Jewish friends, whose funny customs and fatalistic attitudes would imprint themselves on his mind, and whose crackling, phlegm-filled Yiddish words, instantly hilarious in their enunciation, would live forever on his tongue. "My friends made me an honorary Jew," he said later, "and used to tell people I went to services at Temple Beth Dublin."

As he approached the end of his junior year at Detroit Country Day in the spring of 1968, Robin was flourishing. He was a member of the school's honor roll; he had served on its Prefect Board, an elected student council; and he had been voted class president for the following senior year. "I was looking forward to a very straight existence and was planning to attend either a small college in the Midwest or, if I was lucky, an Ivy League school," he recalled. But none of this would come to pass.

For many years, Rob Williams had prospered at Ford. He was a military veteran with a high school diploma who relished the chance to go toe-to-toe with a management staff that was increasingly younger, more educated, and less experienced than he was. As he once told his son Todd, "When I pull up to that building in the eastern suburbs and drive into the parking lot, I look up and I know there are fifteen young hotshot kids in there, all with MBAs, and they want my job. I'm the big boss. They know I don't have a college degree and they really want to show me up. When I walk in the door, I take a big, deep breath of fresh air and it's just like stepping into the Coliseum."

But by the late 1960s, Rob could no longer fight this generational change in the company's operations. As he saw it, Ford was ignoring his recommendations on its most prominent product lines, and it was time for him to leave. He parted ways with the company in 1967 at the age of sixty-one and took a pension; though Robin would later characterize his father's departure from Ford as an early retirement, the arrangement, according to Laurie, did not allow her husband to collect the full benefits he would have received if he'd stayed on a few years longer. Rob wanted to move to Florida, but Laurie said she had no wish to live in "an elephants' graveyard" with "a lot of old rich people." Instead, she steered the family to California, and the town of Tiburon, on the San Francisco Bay. Rob accepted a job at First National Bank, a Detroit bank for which he was named western region representative.

Once more, Rob's career choice was going to uproot the Williams family, and his decision would require that Robin leave behind the home and the school he had gotten to know, the friends he had made and the identity he had created for himself, to live in another part of the country that was thousands of miles away and utterly unknown to him. The relationships that Robin had started to develop here, the achievements he had earned, the coping mechanisms he had pieced together, and the sense of self-worth that had taken years to accumulate — all of that was gone, and he would have to rebuild them from scratch, as he'd done before, when they arrived on the West Coast. It was time to start all over again.

2
THE ESCAPE ARTIST

In the summer of 1968, as Rob and Laurie Williams were nearing the end of their cross-country car ride to California — they were still, after all, an automobile family — their seventeen-year-old son looked out the window to behold something he had never seen before, and it terrified him. A gray mist was tumbling down the hills and across the San Francisco Bay, and it was coming directly for his parents and him. It was only fog, but to his inexperienced eyes, Robin was certain it was poison gas. "It scared the piss out of me," he said later.

When the fog cleared, Robin got his first glimpse of the bay and of Marin County, its mighty redwood forests and its mellow network of interconnected suburbs. Tiburon, the prosperous peninsula town where the Williamses had relocated, sat safely on the northern side of the Golden Gate Bridge, far enough from San Francisco, where the bohemian circus that was the Summer of Love had pulled up its stakes and left town. Rob and Laurie acclimated easily, taking a home on Paradise Drive, a looping stretch of road that snakes along the town's rangy coastline. Outside his duties for First National Bank, Rob started a management consulting business and amused himself with fishing trips. He even bought a couple of Monterey Clipper fishing boats, one with a noisy Hicks engine whose rumbling report delighted him so much that he made recordings of it so he could listen to it on land. Laurie began to attend services at a Christian Science church in the nearby island city of Belvedere. "I'd go to church on Wednesday night," she said, "and when I'd get home, my husband would say, 'How were the "smilies" tonight?' " The church's most famous tenet, which teaches reliance on prayer rather than modern medicine, did not dissuade Laurie from using doctors from time to time, nor from getting a facelift at a later age. As an adult, Robin would affectionately describe her as a "Christian Dior Scientist."

The teenage Robin, however, was utterly baffled by the transition from a regimented and comfortably conservative Midwest upbringing to this calm, coastal haven where everything seemed permissible. "It probably would have been easier for me to move to Mexico," he later said. "I had *total* cultural shock." Nowhere were these differences more striking for him than at Redwood High School, where he enrolled as a senior that fall. Redwood may not have appeared much different from Detroit Country Day at first: it was a public school, but its students were mostly affluent and mostly white, its athletics department was well funded, and its aptitude for placing its seniors at top-tier colleges was estimable. (One significant difference, however: Redwood was coed.) Beneath the surface was a student body that, like much of the country, was in conflict with itself, a generation fighting for the right to decide its destiny while struggling to figure out what it wanted to be.

When Robin began attending classes at Redwood, he arrived each day dressed in a blazer and tie and carrying a briefcase, just as he used to at Detroit Country Day. Only now his formal manner and attire drew stares and teasing from his classmates, who called him a geek and told him he was "creating negative energy." Several weeks went by before he let go of his old school's dress code and allowed himself to wear blue jeans. Soon after, someone gave him a life-altering article of clothing: his first Hawaiian shirt. At that point, he said, "I was *gone;* I got into a whole wild phase and I learned to totally let go."

Unlike the straitlaced school he came from, Redwood offered courses in psychology, 16-millimeter filmmaking, and black studies, despite having no black students in its senior class. Encounter groups, a form of sensitivity training that flourished in the 1960s, still held sway here, and, as Robin recounted, it was not uncommon for his seminars to end in a group hug or with other unconventional rituals. "One teacher would sometimes just stop what he was doing and then a few kids would start pounding out a beat and everybody would get up and dance around the room," he said.

Robin was not quite the class cut-up, as he had been at Detroit Country Day, but he was not a total outcast either. Despite his fellow students' lack of familiarity with him, he boldly ran for senior president at Redwood and drew a respectable second-place showing, with sixty-one votes. He continued to immerse himself in athletics, playing for Redwood's varsity soccer team and running cross-country. Sports were, perhaps, "his only thing that brought him into the groups," said Douglas Basham, who was one of Robin's track coaches and a math teacher at Redwood.

Like his classmates, Robin began to experiment with drugs. Although he was at first too timid to try smoking pot, fearing that it would affect his performance as a runner, he said that he did eventually try it on "an astrological scavenger hunt," where "people who had the same astrological sign would pile into a bus and they'd drive all over the country searching for things like lost mandalas." He would later say he felt that marijuana made him feel too sleepy and he "didn't get into it," but he continued to use it recreationally, even on a training run with other members of his cross-country team. While under the influence on that run, Robin said he saw a turkey vulture and tried to shoo it out of his path. "When I got close, it went *hsssssss* and spread its wings, and I turned to the rest of the guys and said, 'Oh, Jesus, I *knew* this would happen if I got stoned. I can't *deal* with it!' "

The cross-country team was an important social hub for Robin and a place where he felt he genuinely fit in. He and a friend and teammate, Phil Russell, would sometimes pretend that they were the Olympic long-distance runners Frank Shorter and Jack Bacheler. The squad's outdoor exercises strengthened his sense of inclusion, and the exposure to San Francisco's natural beauty offered him an atmosphere of peacefulness and well-being. On another training run, Robin remembered ascending the heights of Mount Tamalpais and looking down onto Stinson Beach, where he once again saw the fog. Only this time, the now-familiar sight did not fill him with dread but rather with "a beautiful Zen-like feeling of *satori*" that compelled him to run down the hillside and into the waters of the Pacific Ocean.

The athletes at Redwood were not spared from the social turmoil sweeping through the school. That year, Redwood's head track coach, Gary Shaw, instituted a rule requiring that male runners keep their hair at a "reasonable length" or else be dropped from the team. "Everybody that was rather conservative thought, 'These are communists that are doing this, just to screw us up,' " said Basham, who did not agree with Shaw's decision. "How that got related to the length of hair, I'll never know." Many students objected to this arbitrary exercise of authority, including Robin — who nonetheless kept his hair short — and nearly all members of the Redwood track team signed a petition objecting to the rule. The dispute roiled the school for months. "We went through a period of time where people were throwing things at the kids running at the track and shouting, 'Get those hippies out of there!' " Basham recalled. "Some of the guys on the football team beat up a couple of the track guys, caught 'em after a dance and beat them up pretty badly. A lot of stuff like that went on and it was pretty hard to do anything about."

Robin was no stereotypical jock: he was a diligent student and a member of the school's honor society, a performer in its satirical senior farewell play, an individualist who kept an eclectic coterie of friends, and a sensitive person for whom this sort of unrest weighed on his conscience. As his classmate Phillip Culver saw him, Robin "was not really extroverted — he was quite shy, and he felt very uncomfortable around large numbers of people."

When Culver hung out with Robin in his basement-level dwelling in the Williams family home on Paradise Drive, Robin's formidable collection of toy soldiers was there, too. "He would tell me the conversations that were going on in each little section of the battlefield, like he could hear it," Culver recalled. "For me, I'm just seeing these toy soldiers on a huge board. But for Robin, he was hearing the voices in his head and putting them into the minds of these soldiers on this really large battlefield board. I thought, 'This guy is really interesting.' "

Robin's half brother Todd was back in his life again. Todd had recently been discharged from the air force, where he had spent four years bouncing around posts in Greenland, Panama, Oklahoma, and Mississippi; he then worked as a soil engineer in Ohio and had now come to California to become a proprietor of bars and restaurants. "I drank," Todd explained, "and having a saloon was the easy way to handle that."

When Todd revived a San Francisco nightspot called Mother Fletcher's, he had assistance from seventeen-year-old Robin, who, for minimum wage, helped him tear down the old club and set up its new incarnation. Robin also spent part of the summer after his high school graduation working at the Trident, a restaurant and music club in Sausalito that was owned by the members of the Kingston Trio, decorated in kaleidoscopic murals and staffed by servers who were as esoteric as its menu of organic cuisine. The waitresses there, Robin said, "wore spray-on two-piece macramé outfits that looked like a pair of socks. It was like, 'Sonja, your *nipple's* hanging out.' And she'd say, 'I know; I'm trying to get tips.'"

That fall, Robin began his freshman year at Claremont Men's College, on the eastern edge of Los Angeles County, where he planned to study to become a foreign-service officer. The occupation neatly split the difference between Robin's desire to do something exotic and his father's insistence that he choose a respectable profession. Claremont was a school whose students were expected to follow traditional white-collar career paths.

"Anybody that went to Claremont was expected to go into business or law or politics," said Dick Gale, a friend who was two years ahead of Robin. "That was the raison d'être of the Claremont Men's College. You were expected to take that shit seriously, and do something with it. If you weren't a political-science or econ major, somehow you were missing the boat." Few students saw Robin as a quintessential candidate for Claremont; no one believed that his path would bring him to a law firm, a chief executive officer's office, or the governor's mansion. The wider assumption was that he did not quite have the courage to tell his father that his true ambitions lay elsewhere. "It was a time when everyone was being told: question authority," said Mary Alette Davis, who knew Robin at Claremont while she studied at Scripps College, an affiliated school. "Everyone was on that wave. And Robin wasn't in rebellion."

But an invisible revolution was taking place in Robin's mind, allowing him to see, for perhaps the first time in his life, that he had the ability to choose his own path. "It was this weird catharsis," he later said of Claremont. "Total freedom. Like going from Sing Sing to a Gestalt nudist camp. Everything opened up. The whole world just changed in that one year."

At Claremont, Robin played soccer and lived in Berger Hall, whose residents proudly identified themselves as Sons of Berger — abbreviated, by design, as SOBs — and where he found himself among lusty, likeminded young men who were not too sophisticated to appreciate a good dick joke. Across the hall lived his friend Bob Davis, a sophomore who was one of several members of an intramural squad that called themselves the Nads so that during various sports competitions, Davis explained, "We could yell 'Go Nads!' "

Here Robin also reencountered Christie Platt, his former middle school girlfriend, who was now a sophomore at Pitzer College, another affiliated school. "I saw this really cute boy in the stairwell," she recalled, "and he had these sun-bleached blond eyebrows, and he was really tan because he had been running a lot in high school. He goes, 'Christie!' And I go, 'Yes?' He goes, 'Do you know who I am?' And I go, 'Oh my God — Robin.' "

The two resumed dating, but Robin never made any promises of exclusivity. He was discovering just how much he liked women and how much they liked him, and he was enjoying every moment of it. "I had one or two steady girlfriends in high school, but then in college, it was three, four," he later explained. "I went crazy. At one point I had three separate girlfriends, running around mad. 'Let's make love in a car! I've got to have a bed with a stick shift right here!' " Women, he said, were "amazing creatures": "You can never learn enough! They're addicting in the most amazing sense."

Perhaps the most significant decision that Robin would make at Claremont was undertaken without much forethought, almost impulsively. As one of the eight freshman classes he was required to take, Robin chose a theater elective offered at Scripps, "and after my first day," he said, "I was hooked." This was no traditional stage-acting seminar that he had signed up for: the course was for improvisational theater, and it was taught by Dale Morse, who had previously trained at some of the leading improvisation groups that had come to prominence during the 1960s, including The Committee, a San Francisco spin-off of Chicago's Second City.

Morse's students felt she provided them with more than just a new way of looking at the stage — she was teaching them how to engage with their lives. Her lessons, Bob Davis said, were "not only a way to do theater, but a way to channel your energy, a way to think about the universe."

Among the basic principles of Morse's instruction, which were used to construct comedic as well as dramatic scenes, was the improv imperative of the "yes and": the directive to always affirm the choices made by your onstage partners and build upon them rather than negate them. As Paul Tepper, another friend who studied with Robin in Morse's class, explained, "It's actually quite a good life theory. When someone says something to you — 'When did you get here from Mars?' — you don't say, 'I don't know what you're talking about. I've never been to

Mars.' You say, 'Yes, and.' You say, 'Wow, I just got here three days ago, and I've been drunk ever since I arrived.' "

Eventually, Morse told her students that it was not enough to take her class as an academic exercise; they had to form a company of their own and start performing for audiences. Thus, Robin and eighteen of his classmates came together to create Claremont's earliest improv group, known as Karma Pie. Twice a week, the group would gather at the Strut and Fret Theater on the Scripps campus and put on free shows whose unscripted contents were built from simple improvisational games.

"We'd stand in a line in the back, and if you had an idea you would step out and start, or maybe you'd try to save the other actor," Bob Davis said. "It made for such a camaraderie, because you were out onstage with absolutely nothing to help you except the other person. It's high-risk theater. We weren't necessarily like other companies, where it's all about finding a funny bit and then repeating that funny bit. We might go for twenty minutes, all unified around a question from the audience or some kind of theme. We disdained being funny, in a high-tone way. 'We're doing art here.' "

A local newspaper critic who attended one of their performances in January 1970 was not entirely amused. He described the troupe as "a gaggle of talented and imaginative youngsters zealously tackling the problem of 'What will we do when the curtain goes up and we've forgotten our lines?' " The review glumly observed that, for the performers, "It generally seems that they are having more fun than the audience," comparing the experience to "watching football practice."

Yet to several members of the company, it was soon clear that Robin was funnier — and just plain better at this — than the rest of Karma Pie. "He was doing it the same way all of us were doing it," Bob Davis said. "He wasn't looking for a place to try out comedic material. I don't think he looked at it as developing into a career." But the experience seemed to unlock something in him that had previously gone untapped. "He discovered that you could make something of this energy he had," said Davis. "And he had a *lot* of energy. I used to say I knew him for six months before I found out what his real voice was."

Robin's talent did not always mesh well with the communal spirit of improvisational theater. As Mary Alette Davis recalled, "I remember Dale saying once, 'You guys think Robin is amazing, but I've got to say that he doesn't really follow the rules of improv. He's not always going out there and supporting people.' " The advantage of having Robin in your scene, Davis said, was that "he could take it to so many places that you weren't imagining. But if you weren't on that particular journey, you just sat in the back and you figured out how to fit in."

Around the Claremont campuses, Robin started to become a kind of minor celebrity, renowned for his sense of humor and quick onstage wit. Some friends began calling him Ralph Williams, after a shifty, almost incoherently fast-talking used-car pitchman whose TV advertisements were ubiquitous in Southern California at the time. (Naturally, Ralph Williams ran a Ford dealership.) When he and Christie Platt would go to parties, she said, "People would just start clapping when we came in. It definitely wasn't because of me — he just had charisma and an original sense of humor." Occasionally, his motor-mouth charm could be too much: "When he came to my dorm, people went a little nuts," Platt said. "They'd go, 'Can't we get him to be quiet?' I used to have a blanket that I'd put over his head to tell him to be quiet. And of course he was completely irrepressible and it didn't work at all."

Outside of Karma Pie, Robin honed his stage skills by performing in campus productions of *Under Milk Wood,* playing the blind sailor Captain Cat in Dylan Thomas's drama about a fictional Welsh fishing town, and *Alice in Wonderland,* playing a hookah-smoking Caterpillar. He also came to the attention of some upperclassmen, including Al Dauber, a senior who was organizing a college comedy show. Though Dauber and Dick Gale had spent several weeks preparing jokes and sketches for the event, Gale felt the show might benefit from the addition of a particularly funny freshman he knew from his improv theater class. "We were trying to build the audience," said Gale, who had previously performed with Dauber at some campus antiwar rallies. "Robin brought a bunch of the people that he knew. But more importantly, he brought the kind of certifiable talent that Al and I probably lacked."

When Dauber and Gale sat down with Robin in their dorm room one night, over a lengthy period of what Gale later described as "much libation, inhalation and conversation," they found someone with a unique creative spark. He had in his possession a whole arsenal of comic accents and voices that included the squeaking title character from *The Fly* — *"help meeeeee, help meeeeee"* — and although their act already included a send-up of *The Ed Sullivan Show,* Gale said, "when Robin came in, all of a sudden, we had Topo Gigio."

They began to wonder if there was any character Robin could not play on the spur of the moment. "We started challenging him," said Dauber. " 'Do a bohemian priest. Do an orthodox rabbi. Do a peasant out on the farm with his crops.' " Robin came through every time, he said: "You couldn't keep up with his mind, it was going so fast. He was going off on all these tangents."

On the evening of February 21, 1970, the trio put on what was officially billed as "An Evening with Al Dauber, co-starring Dick Gale & Rob Williams," as a free show at the McKenna Auditorium. The ninety-minute program opened with a parody of *To Tell the Truth* and featured a sketch called "How to Remove a Rhinoceros from Your Bed" as well as the parody of Ed Sullivan and Topo Gigio. "When Robin came," Gale said, "it brought about a holistic change — this became actual entertainment."

But all the hours that Robin devoted to this newfound interest were adding up. For perhaps the first time in his educational career, he was flunking, and in spectacular fashion. Classes (other than his improv theater elective) went unattended, coursework was neglected — he would later claim that his final paper in a macroeconomics course contained the single sentence "I really don't know, sir" — and his own teachers did not recognize him. According to Robin, when one professor asked at the end of the term, "Who is this man?" a second professor replied, "If I *knew* who he was, I could give him a failing grade."

Robin could not hide his academic failure

from his father, and Rob made little effort to conceal his disappointment. "I'm not paying all that tuition for this," he told his son bluntly. Once more, Robin was forced to withdraw from a school he was just getting accustomed to, and so abruptly that few of his friends knew what had happened — so rapidly that the legend still endures at Claremont that Robin was kicked out of the school for driving a golf cart through a dining hall.

What would he do now? Robin was nearing eligibility for the military draft, but he had little reason to worry that he would be conscripted into the Vietnam War. The draft number for his birthdate was a comfortable 356, meaning, as Robin later put it, "the Viet Cong had to be coming from Kansas for me to be drafted." Nor did Rob, a World War II veteran, suggest that he seek a career in the armed services. "At some point," Robin said, "my father sat me down and said, 'Listen, war is not *dolce et decorum est,* it's really quite brutal. War isn't like the movies portray it. People die alone and miserable.' He was honest with me, because he wanted me to be safe."

In fact, Robin told his father, he'd already discovered his calling. "I've found what I really love to do," he said to Rob. "I've decided I want to be an actor."

The response from his father was hardly inspiring. "It's fine to have a dream," Rob told his son, "but you'd better learn a skill, like welding, just in case."

It is a tale that Robin would go on to tell about himself many times after — so frequently that one might wonder if his telling it was an act of self-mythologizing. But the story appears to be truthful. According to his half brother McLaurin, Rob did more than give this piece of advice to Robin. "He made Robin go down and sign up for a course at the local trade school to learn how to weld," McLaurin said. Robin attended a first class, where a trained technician demonstrated how the process worked, and he found it more interesting than he expected. Then, at his second class, the instructor discussed safety guidelines and warned that, without proper precautions, you could accidentally blind yourself. As McLaurin recalled, "He said he heard the word 'blind' and he was out of there. He never came back."

Laurie was more enthusiastic about Robin's desire to become an actor. "Mom said, 'Your grandmother would be very proud,' and wished me good luck," Robin said. But Rob, who had just paid amply for Robin to indulge in what he felt was a fruitless year at a private university, did not want to repeat this mistake; as a compromise, Robin lived at home while he studied at the College of Marin, a public community college not far from Tiburon.

Though the school did not possess brand-name status, its drama program, which it had only just established in 1964, had nimbleness and innovation on its side, and it was already drawing favorable comparisons to the American Conservatory Theater in San Francisco. It also had an unlikely program director in James Dunn, a San Rafael native and Marine Corps veteran who had served as a drill instructor during the Korean War. Despite those daunting credentials, Dunn took a playful and broad-minded approach to the stage, casting students in offbeat productions of classic texts, like *Twelfth Night* set in a California hacienda, and *The Comedy of Errors* recasting Shakespeare's mismatched twins as the Marx Brothers.

Dunn was well aware of the other forms of exploration going on around him; though the school had a no-tolerance policy for drug or alcohol use during its productions, he said, "You couldn't walk across our campus in the daytime without getting a contact high." He also believed in orderliness and applied boot-camp tactics when needed. The actor Dakin Matthews, who worked professionally as a guest artist at the College of Marin during the 1960s and '70s, recalled Dunn directing him in a production of *Othello* that emphasized soldierly obedience. "We had to march," Matthews said. "We had to learn how to salute. And he would get in our faces and scream at us, just like a good D.I. would."

Dunn's military training and desire for discipline made him a powerful influence on Robin. "Knowing that his own talents tended to the nondisciplined, that was exactly what Robin loved about him," Matthews said. "And after a couple of years there, he was clearly the star of the program. He was something special, absolutely."

When Robin arrived in the fall of 1970, he discovered that a production of *A Midsummer Night's Dream* had already been cast. But he was determined to participate and talked his way into a minor part as a spear-carrier. "He said, 'I would really like to get into the play — is there anything I could do?'" Dunn recalled. "I said, 'Well, I've already cast it. But I need some walk-ons.' He said, 'I'll do that.'"

As his roles and stage time grew, Robin stretched the boundaries of his characters without violating the sanctity of his texts. When he played the Reverend Canon Chasuble in *The Importance of Being Earnest,* "every night it was a different Chasuble," said Ronald Krempetz, a theater instructor and set designer at the college. "He didn't change the words, but sometimes it was accents, or how he emphasized a line or two, the looks, the facial expressions." And as Malvolio in *Twelfth Night,* imprisoned alone in a cell with only a wooden staff, he only had to remember the TV teachings of Jonathan Winters. "He just had his hands and his staff, and the staff became a second character," Krempetz said.

Robin received many of his earliest professional reviews in the *Daily Independent Journal,* a local newspaper in San Rafael, and over a three-year span they grew increasingly appreciative. His first notice came in December 1970 with a college production of Ionesco's absurdist play *The Bald Soprano,* for which the paper observed, "Most enjoyable of the hard-working cast was Robin Williams as Mr. Martin, whose timing was almost perfect." The paper also gave him strong marks for his work as Banquo in *Macbeth,* and in *You in Your Small Corner and I in Mine,* a melodrama by Carol Roper, for which he was described as "really one of the fine young talents in the college's theatrical stable." Even in a mixed review of *Fiddler on the Roof,* Robin was described as being among the cast members who "add strength to the musical, playing the progressive intellectual Perchik."

Robin's breakout role came at the end of 1972, when he was cast as the master pickpocket Fagin in the college's Christmastime production of *Oliver!* The days leading up to its opening had been a slog, Dunn said, "because we had a new lighting board and it was doing all kinds of strange things, and it had held up the rehearsals." One particular run-through had stretched all the way to midnight, and "everybody was very uptight, especially me," he said. Then Dunn noticed Robin offstage: "He was standing by the piano, and he had a baton in his hand, like a drum major's baton, and he began talking to it. And it began talking back." For what felt like twenty minutes, Dunn said, Robin and the baton conversed, kidded, and argued with each other — with Robin providing both of the voices of course, and a crowd of actors and crew members supplying a grateful audience. When Dunn at last got home at two a.m., he woke up his wife to tell her, "I saw a young man do something tonight that I have never seen before. And this kid is going to go somewhere."

In its own assessment of *Oliver!,* the *Daily Independent Journal* wrote, "The big star of the evening is Robin Williams as an unforgettable Fagin. It's a real tour de force performance. . . . It's been a great pleasure over the past year to watch this young collegian develop his talents into such a professional status."

While he lived with his parents, Robin always seemed to be broke and asking to borrow money from colleagues. "It was a running joke, whenever you'd see him," Krempetz said. " 'Hi, Robin. How are you? Where's my five dollars?' "

Not everyone was entirely won over by his unruly magnetism. As Joel Blum, an actor and classmate of Robin's, described him, "He was such a nice guy, such a sweetheart. At the same time, he was a total show-off, but in a very endearing way." Overall, he said, "It was hard to tell who he really was."

To Blum, Robin appeared to lack some basic social skills, whether making simple chitchat or engaging in "the bullshit that everybody would talk about when they were stoned." "When I would talk to him," Blum said, "I'd try to have a conversation with him and it would go okay for about ten seconds. And then he would go into a character voice, he would do a bit. He would almost literally bounce off the walls with craziness. And then he would be gone."

In 1971, he and Robin were among the College of Marin students invited to perform Dunn's Western-style production of *The Taming of the Shrew* at the Edinburgh Festival Fringe, where it won a first prize and played a command performance for Princess Margaret, the sister of Queen Elizabeth II. On the flight from San Francisco to Scotland, Blum said he and Robin were seated next to each other, "and we didn't say a word to each other the whole time. Like twelve hours of it. It's not that he didn't like me or I didn't like him. He was just a quiet guy, personally. There wasn't much to talk about."

In his summers off, Robin returned to Southern California, where he performed at the Pacific Conservatory of the Performing Arts in Orange County. He appeared in a production of Bertolt Brecht's *The Caucasian Chalk Circle* and in *The Music Man,* playing the reformed con man Marcellus Washburn as he sang and danced his way through the nonsensical crowd-pleaser "Shipoopi."

Shelly Lipkin, an actor who also performed in these shows, said that Robin's audition for *The Music Man* was a notable near disaster that nonetheless showcased his talent for ad-libbing his way out of dire situations. Prior to the tryouts, Lipkin said, a prideful James Dunn had told the other directors at the program to pay particular attention to Robin, "that this is a guy to watch out for — this guy is talented." Each prospective player had been told to prepare a monologue and a song, and Robin began with some of his Malvolio material that he'd previously recited in *Twelfth Night.* But when it came time to sing his song, Robin was stumped; he had nothing he felt confident in, so he began to sing a portion of Danny Kaye's "The Lobby Number," from *Up in Arms:*

When it's cherry-blossom time in Orange,
    New Jersey,
We'll make a peach of a pear
I know we cantaloupe, so honeydew be
    mine . . .

77

"Sitting way in the back of the audience," Lipkin said, "you saw a little figure, which was Jim Dunn, starting to shake. And then he stood up and was shaking a little bit more." Afterward, Dunn angrily confronted Robin, believing that his star pupil had made a mockery of his endorsement. "How could you do that to me?" he demanded to know. "You did this silly, stupid number." Robin was chastened and believed he had thrown away his audition. But instead he got the role and, Lipkin said, "He walked away with the show. He was the best thing on that stage."

Yet for all of Robin's growth as an artist, it was not clear that his accomplishments had earned him any further esteem at home, particularly with his father. When Bob Davis, one of Robin's former classmates at Claremont, came with some friends to stay with him in Tiburon, he said that they had to keep their visit a secret, so that Rob would not know his son was hanging out with other actors. "We had to sneak into the house," Davis said. "We slept in his bedroom but we came in through a back window or something, because we were theater people and that was forbidden."

After nearly three years at the College of Marin, a school from which most students moved on after two years, Robin was craving further instruction. Dunn had a next step in mind. Some summers earlier, Dunn had befriended John Houseman, the distinguished British-American actor and collaborator of Orson Welles, who was now in charge of the newly established Drama Division of the Juilliard School in New York. At Dunn's recommendation, Robin performed an audition for Houseman and two colleagues from the Juilliard faculty, Michael Kahn and Elizabeth Smith, as they evaluated candidates in San Francisco in 1973. His father reluctantly gave him $50 so that he could take part in the tryout.

Robin's audition consisted of two monologues. One was Malvolio's famous soliloquy from *Twelfth Night:* "Some are born great, some achieve greatness, and some have greatness thrust upon 'em." The other, adapted from John Knowles's *A Separate Peace,* was spoken by Elwin "Leper" Lepellier, an emotionally fragile prep-school student who enlists in the army during World War II. In the forceful and unsettling scene that Robin chose, Leper recounts how he lost his mind during basic training and, in doing so, he starts to go mad all over again.

Smith, a voice and speech teacher, recalled Robin's tryout as somewhat clumsy but also irresistible. "I remember thinking he didn't speak very well," she said. "By that, I mean sort of carelessly. But he certainly had a personality. He seemed funny and very bright." Most important, his audition was

79

successful, and Robin was offered a place at Juilliard that fall. He was also provided a full scholarship, which meant that, for once, he would not have to rely on handouts from his father to advance his education. But Rob would not bankroll Robin, either, while his son continued to pursue a passion Rob didn't support.

Living in New York required a whole new series of readjustments. Robin had spent the past five years attuning himself to California's alternating currents of tranquillity and intensity, and now he had landed in a city that moved only at maximum velocity. New York's grit, its indifference, and its ruthless fervor for self-preservation were yet more unfamiliar conditions to which he had to adapt, but there was also an allure he could not deny. "I'd been in danger of becoming terminally mellow," Robin said, "and it peeled away that layer very quickly." When he arrived in the city in September 1973, he still dressed in Hawaiian shirts and yoga pants and walked around in thong sandals that proved a sartorial mistake for sidewalks spattered in dog shit.

During his first week in Manhattan, he was riding a public bus, when, a few rows ahead of him, he saw a man slump over onto the woman he was sitting next to. "Get *off* me!" she shouted as she changed seats. But the man was dead. The driver stopped the bus and told everyone to exit the vehicle. Robin, still an altruistic transplant from the West Coast, said he wanted to stay and help out, but the driver replied: "He's *dead,* mother-fucker, now get off! You can't do *shit* for him, so take your raggedy California ass and get outta my bus!"

Like the city that provided its home, Juilliard had its own complicated profile. It was revered, it was feared, and it was fearsomely competitive; on some days it took what was good about you and made it better, and on others it did not care whether you flourished or floundered. Its Drama Division had been established in 1968, and in its first five years the program had helped launch rising stars like Kevin Kline, Patti LuPone, and David Ogden Stiers. The students who followed them at Juilliard could not help but get swept up in the romance of the institution and the possibilities that awaited them. "It had a very monastic, religious feeling about it," said Richard Levine, who was a student there with Robin. "That had partly to do with the structure itself, which was white stone, very precious and secluded. It had a certain forbidding toughness about it, but you were very protected from the temptations of com-mercialism and it really did encourage you to just delve into the training."

The heady atmosphere could also give students an inflated sense of their self-worth.

"Juilliard actors were considered first-rate," said Paul Perri, another of Robin's classmates. "They were also considered pains in the ass, and snooty — which was a wonderful edge if you were a young actor. The business is the business, and the business is horrible. Being thrown to the wolves is how you get out of drama school."

Days generally started at eight or nine a.m. and could go until as late as ten or eleven p.m., and the long working hours, spent almost exclusively in the company of classmates, gave rise to many passionately forged, rapidly depleted relationships over the span of a semester. "We were completely under each other's butts and we were completely involved with each other, and everybody slept with everybody else, which happens in college anyway," Perri said. "It's very incestuous."

Like Juilliard's music and dance programs, its Drama Division operated as a conservatory. The four-year curriculum emphasized long days of studio training in its first two years (the "discovery" and "transformation" years), with upper-class students (in their "interpretation" and "performing" years) going on to audition for and act in stage productions that they performed throughout New York. It was understood that of the twenty-five or thirty pupils who entered as freshmen, only half would still be enrolled by the time they were juniors, having dropped out or been cut systematically by the school's staff. This Darwinian system operated under the auspices of Houseman, who emphasized the classics — ancient Greek drama and Shakespeare plays — while he basked in the glow of late-career celebrity. In 1973, when Robin arrived at Juilliard, Houseman, at the age of seventy-one, was starring in *The Paper Chase* as the imperious law professor Charles W. Kingsfield Jr., a role for which he would win an Academy Award.

To his students, Houseman could be a pleasing, perplexingly contradictory figure, at once avuncular and austere. As Robin recalled, "He gave a speech one day in which he said, 'The theater *needs* you. Don't be tempted by television or the movies. The theater needs new plasma, new blood.' And then, a week later, we saw him in a Volvo commercial."

Robin, who came to Juilliard with undergraduate training and stage experience, was admitted as an advanced student. The expectation was that he would graduate in two years, and he was considered a member of Group IV, rather than Group VI, as other incoming students were ranked. (As the *New York Times* has said of Juilliard, "Classes are designated not by year but by Roman numerals, like royalty and the Super Bowl.")

Other students training at Juilliard at this time included Mandy Patinkin, the future Broadway and television star, who was a member of Group IV; the film actor William Hurt, who was in Group V; and Kelsey Grammer, who would have a decades-long sitcom career, in Group VI. One peer in particular would become an important confidant and source of moral support for Robin: a staggeringly tall, boyishly handsome young man who had recently come from Cornell to enter Juilliard as a member of its advanced training program. His name was Christopher Reeve.

Reeve, who was raised in Princeton, New Jersey, had, like Robin, spent some formative years in the cloistered world of suburban prep schools, then continued to try his hand at regional theater companies and had traveled to Europe to sample its stage productions before he arrived at Juilliard. When the two met — Reeve said Robin was the first student he encountered there — all Reeve saw was "a short, stocky long-haired fellow from Marin County, California, who wore tie-dyed shirts with track suit bottoms and talked a mile a minute." But like others before him, he found himself swept up in the force of his new friend's vitality. "I'd never seen so much energy contained in one person," Reeve said. "He was like an untied balloon that had been inflated and immediately released. I watched in awe as he virtually caromed off the walls of classrooms and hallways. To say that he was 'on' would be a major understatement."

In classes, Reeve occasionally saw Robin baffle and bemuse his orthodox instructors. When they studied with Edith Skinner, the venerated speech and voice teacher, Reeve said, "She had no idea what to make of him." While Skinner worked methodically to teach them about the phonetic alphabet and vowel changes that occur from one dialect to another, and Reeve diligently annotated his texts to teach himself each new accent, "Robin didn't need any of this," he said. "He could instantly perform in any dialect — Scottish, Irish, English, Russian, Italian and many of his own invention."

Some courses seemed to connect with Robin at a visceral level, like a class led by the French English acting teacher Pierre Lefèvre on the use of masks, requiring students to focus on body language and sometimes work without speech entirely. As Margot Harley, the Drama Division administrator, explained the training, "There were neutral masks, which covered the face — they were young, middle-aged, and old; male and female — and you couldn't speak. Then you graduated into comedy masks — character masks — and you could speak."

The purpose of the masks, Harley said, was that "they changed your body, and actors should have bodies that transform and change, and tell you something about the person that you're playing. Those masks helped you to transform your physical self, which is something so many actors can't do. I would imagine that was the most valuable class that Robin took."

But other instructors felt that Robin was bumping up against his limitations as an actor and trying to use his sense of humor to skirt around them. In her speech class, Elizabeth Smith said, "I used to give him big, heroic poems to make him breathe and open up. I remember thinking how absurd it was that I was asking this young man to do this. Because it was obviously so far removed from anything he would end up doing. There was no question that he had a future. But it certainly wasn't in speaking heroic verse." With a laugh, she added, "He used to try very, very hard not to send it up, not to make fun of it. But he couldn't do it straight. He just couldn't."

Within his first few weeks, Robin clashed with Michael Kahn, another of his acting instructors. Asked to perform a monologue for the class, Robin presented a rambling, satirical sermon delivered by Alan Bennett in the British comedy revue *Beyond the Fringe.* Reeve would say later that Robin's delivery "was even funnier than the original" and that his "characterization, timing and delivery were impeccable," earning applause from the other students. But Kahn was unimpressed. In front of the class, he told Robin, "It looks like *you* were enjoying yourself." He waited for a moment, then said, "It's like someone who peed into their corduroy pants." And just to twist the knife further, he added, "You feel fabulous. We see nothing." (As Kahn later explained, "You can't see pee in corduroy pants. He didn't like me very much.")

The Juilliard faculty began to question whether Robin was equipped for its advanced program. "He didn't have a basic foundation of how to approach acting," Kahn said in reflection. "It was coming from a kind of manic intuition, and it was, finally, an act of imitation rather than an act of creation." Before his first year was out, Robin was asked to give up his place in Group IV and pursue a customary four-year track as a member of Group VI, and he agreed to the arrangement.

Through good news and bad, Robin came to depend on his friend Reeve. They affectionately called each other "brother," and they would sit together on the roof of Reeve's building to indulge in cheap wine and war stories about the women they had pined for. "Many of our classmates related to Robin by doing bits with him, attempting to keep pace with his antics," Reeve later said. "I didn't even try. Occasionally Robin would need to switch off and have a serious conversation with someone, and I was always ready to listen."

But at the end of his first Juilliard term, Robin found himself at an emotional ebb, feeling alone and abandoned, and he experienced what he would later characterize as a mental breakdown. Robin was unable to afford a trip home to Tiburon for Christmas, and as the school emptied out, he stayed in New York for the holiday, in a cold and unfamiliar city that felt more deserted than usual. "New York seemed unbearably bleak and lonely," he said.

> One day, I just started sobbing and I couldn't stop, and when I ran out of tears my body kept going; it was like having emotional dry heaves. I went through two days like that and finally hit rock bottom and realized I had a choice: I could either tube out or level off and relax. At that point, I became like a submarine on the bottom that blows out some ballast and gets back up again.

"Once all my anxieties were behind me," he said, "the rest of that year was easy."

Robin made other friends among the classmates he lived with in a low-rent floor-through apartment on the Upper West Side of Manhattan. Its open space was partitioned with curtains that did not quite reach from the ceiling to the floor, creating more bedroom areas but not much privacy. "Whatever you were doing in your room, you could easily share it with the world if you weren't careful," said Frances Conroy, who inhabited one of these subdivisions. The building was walking distance from the Lincoln Center campus, though not always an easy stroll. "You would have to walk with someone else to get home safely," said Kevin Conroy, another student who lived there.

When Richard Levine and Paul Perri, the apartment's original tenants, first met Robin, he was still a California bohemian striving to fit in with the crowd. "One time, Paul and I had to sit Robin down and tell him that he couldn't use the word *funky* anymore, that it was driving us crazy," Levine recalled with a laugh. "We said every third word out of your mouth is 'funky' and you have to stop."

His penchant for letting his girlfriends stay with him in the tiny, exposed compartment he rented did not endear Robin to other residents. "He did have some long-term girls in his life," said one person who lived with him. "He had one girl come and I think she stayed for six months. In a room without walls going to the ceiling. So as his roommates, we were not pleased."

At other times, Robin was absent from the apartment for long stretches and it wasn't clear where he was staying. As far as Frances Conroy could tell, she said, "He may have

89

even slept in the school some nights when he didn't have a place to live. You could easily do that, because you could find a couch onstage, and have a place to sleep for the night. And there were showers, and then if you wanted to, you could go down to the cafeteria and get some food once the school opened."

"Everybody got by however they could," she said. "Everybody's private life was whatever it was."

"I didn't know there were times that Robin was desperate to eat," she added.

Just as at the College of Marin, Robin quickly ran through what little cash he possessed and was in debt to nearly everyone. He could always depend on the kindness of administrators: Margot Harley said that she would often find Robin at the building with empty pockets and an empty belly, and she would take mercy on him. "I used to bring him breakfast," she said. "He came from a family that certainly wasn't poor. But he was always short of money." By night, Harley said, Robin was helped by a similarly charitable cleaning woman who brought him dinner.

The thought that Robin could be having trouble with food, money, or basic personal maintenance was totally alien to his Drama Division peers. "We were all baby boomers, raised in one of the fattest times in American history," said Paul Perri. "And Robin's parents probably had more money than some, but there were some people with a ton of money that went to Juilliard. The rarity was on the other side, of people who were lower middle class or working class, or outright poor. You didn't see that much in a conservatory."

None of these problems diminished Robin as a performer. In his first student production, while still a member of Group IV and the advanced training program, Robin was cast in *The Night of the Iguana,* the gothic Tennessee Williams drama about a disgraced priest reduced to working as a tour guide and the unusual cohort of characters he encounters in a Mexican hotel. Robin played Nonno, a wheelchair-bound ninety-seven-year-old man who spends the play trying to compose a poem from memory.

Despite the drubbing Robin had taken in class from Michael Kahn, Reeve said that this performance "immediately silenced the critics." "His portrayal of an old man confined to a wheelchair was thoroughly convincing," Reeve said. "He simply *was* the old man. I was astonished by his work and very grateful that fate had thrown us together."

In a later production of *A Midsummer Night's Dream,* Robin brought a delightful physicality to the role of the fairy Mustardseed, and even helped to fine-tune the character's costume for a few extra laughs. As

Harley recalled Robin's performance, "He was on the floor, projecting himself along with his bottom, and he had rigged up a hat, so that when he spoke, the hat popped up. It was so funny. It was perfectly clear that he was incredibly creative and that he was a very special talent, from the very beginning, even though he didn't have any acting technique. He was clearly, wildly talented, but he just didn't have a technique yet. It's something you have to learn — you don't just get up there and act."

Not that Robin needed anything as elaborate as a stage or a script or even a hat to enthrall onlookers. Paul Perri said they once found themselves passing time together in a hallway, when Robin was invigorated by the sight of a soda vending machine. "And out of the blue, he decided to just fuck around," Perri said. "He did five minutes of just imitating a Coke machine. It was funny, but of course everything's funny when you're young. The thing that stayed with me about it was the five-minute part. It had a beginning, a middle, and an end. It wasn't just a concept. It was fully realized. It was beautiful and it was physically adept. And it was hilarious. Robin could think faster than anybody I ever saw."

However, Perri could not say with certainty that Robin had made up the routine on the spot. "Things that would be extemporaneous in anybody else, he might have been thinking about for a long time," Perri said.

Kevin Conroy also suspected that the voices and characters that appeared to spring spontaneously from Robin had been previously workshopped in other settings. "Everything you saw, the facile ability to jump from character to character, it looked like he was creating in that moment — he wasn't," Conroy said. "He had honed those characters for years and years. He studied people."

"The emotional turmoil in him was about a quarter-inch beneath the surface," said Conroy, who was nonetheless envious of Robin's ability to make it look easy and extemporaneous. "He was head and shoulders above any of the rest of us in that group — and it was a *good* group," he said.

Other classmates regarded Robin as a hardworking, quietly bookish artist in training. The author Kevin Sessums, who started at Juilliard two years after Robin as a member of Group VIII, remembers seeing him in a student workshop of Pirandello's *Six Characters in Search of an Author,* playing the Boy, a mute and mournful character who ends his life by suicide. At a rehearsal break, Sessums noticed that "many of the students broke off into little groups to gossip or giggle and go over their lines," but Robin "sat in a chair all by himself and retrieved a book from his backpack." When he saw that it was *Ragtime,*

E. L. Doctorow's sweeping historical novel about New York at the turn of the twentieth century, Sessums, who had also been reading the book, approached Robin and asked who his favorite character was. Robin replied that it was Harry Houdini, the master stage illusionist and escape artist, who appears throughout the novel as a recurring motif of fame and celebrity. Saying so, Robin pointed to an early page and began to read from a pored-over passage:

His life was absurd. He went all over the world accepting all kinds of bondage and escaping. He was roped to a chair. He escaped. He was chained to a ladder. He escaped. He was handcuffed, his legs were put in irons, he was tied up in a strait jacket and put in a locked cabinet. He escaped. He escaped from bank vaults, nailed-up barrels, sewn mailbags; he escaped from a zinc-lined Knabe piano case, a giant football, a galvanized iron boiler, a rolltop desk, a sausage skin. His escapes were mystifying because he never damaged or appeared to unlock what he escaped from. The screen was pulled away and there he stood disheveled but triumphant beside the inviolate container that was supposed to have contained him. He waved to the crowd.

Transported by Doctorow's evocations of

that bygone era, Robin offered a brief comment. "It doesn't get much better than this," he said.

Still, there were lessons that Juilliard could not teach Robin, desires it could not fulfill, and itches it could not scratch. For those, he would turn to mime. The strange, silent theatrical technique — one that needed no equipment or props, other than black-and-white face paint, and required no formal stage or scenery — was one he indulged in from time to time with Todd Oppenheimer, an acting student at the Neighborhood Playhouse and a fellow émigré from the Bay Area. Oppenheimer had struggled as a solo mime performer in Central Park and other public spaces around New York, but his prospects improved when a mutual friend introduced him to Robin.

As he was speaking to his friend on a Manhattan sidewalk, Oppenheimer recalled, "Bouncing down the street comes this guy in painter's overalls and a Dutch boy cap, bounces right up and says hello in this beautiful, stentorian voice. Then he turns in my direction and says, 'It's great seeing somebody doing mime again in the park.' Something that suggested he knew it or had done it himself." When Oppenheimer asked him if he performed it himself, Robin demurred: "Oh, not really," he answered. "I've played with things." But, Oppenheimer continued,

"Having nothing better to think of, I said, 'Well, you want to do it with me? I'm looking for a partner.' What I realized is that I had to have somebody for support, so we could at least commiserate with each other when people walked away."

They practiced their ad hoc mime partnership on days off from their formal education, when Oppenheimer would head over to Robin's apartment around eleven a.m. to wake him up and get their makeup on. "He was just so undisciplined, and there was always a different girl over there," Oppenheimer said. Then, in striped shirts and painter pants — which Robin would wear held up by a pair of rainbow suspenders — they would walk to Central Park or the plaza in front of the Metropolitan Museum of Art, using those several blocks to warm up and get into character.

Robin was "not the kind of guy who had much patience for rehearsal," Oppenheimer said, "but we planned a few things," many of which were routines they copied from established mime artists.

Among them, Oppenheimer said, was the character of a mask maker, a piece that he had previously seen performed by Marcel Marceau. "It's a guy sitting on a bench making masks," he explained, "and he keeps trying them on. There's an angry face, and a sad face and a laughing face. He eventually gets one stuck on, and it's the smiling face. And as he realizes it's stuck, he goes through a whole sequence of emotions — but his face has to remain smiling."

In another routine, either he or Robin would play the role of a small child being led around a store as his mother holds his hand. "He's getting in trouble and he's reaching for candy and his mom's reaching down and slapping him," Oppenheimer said. "You get this whole visual sense of this tiny person, because he's always looking up and his hand's up in the air. And eventually he has to pee, and he tries to get his mom's attention but she's busy shopping. It gets worse and worse, and she will not listen to him, and the more he bothers her the more she thinks he's bothering her. The kids just love it, because they've all been there."

Sometimes a bit would consist of nothing more than a wicked imitation of a bystander he or Robin might spot in their audience. "If you did your job," Oppenheimer said, "the person you were imitating wouldn't even know you were there. They would look at the crowd, and they would see the crowd looking at them. And they wouldn't know why every-one was staring at them. They'd look down at their shoes, they'd check their zipper, they'd do whatever. Then they'd think, is there something behind me? Then they'd look, and if you were agile enough, you'd

97

move with them so they couldn't see you. It would just get funnier and funnier, and worse and worse."

These free-form forays in front of unsuspecting and occasionally hostile audiences were also formative experiences in rejection. Once while he was doing a mime routine in front of an apartment building, Robin was doused from above with a sudden splash of water — he looked up in time to see someone pouring it on him from an upper floor. As he later described the experience, "It was like getting slapped in the face." It became a war story he later shared with friends, not to boast about how far he'd come but to illustrate how vulnerable and exposed performers are. The sudden, painful shock of getting doused like that was one that Robin would reenact for years to come, often recoiling as he acted out the moment — one of many small battle scars he'd bear forever.

Robin's Juilliard classmates felt he was straining at the margins of a system designed to break students down and put them back together like new. "The school did have a tendency to want to strip you of your own personal idiosyncrasies," Richard Levine said. "In time, you gain a little bit more choice and have more options available to you, as you reinstate your idiosyncrasies, but you're not glued to them if a part required something else. I understand the philosophy and it had a real intelligence to it. But I think for Robin, it was very stultifying. He really did need to spread his wings and do his thing."

Oppenheimer, his mime partner, thought he saw Robin growing disenchanted with Juilliard, too. But then again, he said, "You never had a serious conversation with Robin."

In the summer of 1974, his friend Christopher Reeve was cast in the popular CBS soap opera *Love of Life* and was given permission to take a leave from the school. The role led to other roles and set him on a path to stardom, and he would never complete his Juilliard training. Meanwhile, Robin fell in love with a woman he'd met who, like him, had recently moved to New York from California. Though he never gave her name publicly, he described her as "a free spirit who thought nothing about walking through tough neighborhoods wearing white lace gowns. I told her that if she kept it up, she'd get killed, and she said, 'No, my aura will defend me.' "

In the summer of 1975, between Robin's second and third years at Juilliard, he and his girlfriend returned to California, where the love affair became even more passionate. But when Robin returned to New York in the fall, she did not come with him, and their separation badly brought him down. "I really *missed* my lady friend and I began running up $400-a-month telephone bills — and at the time I was having trouble just making the rent," he said. "The tension of a long-distance romance was such a drain."

Shelly Lipkin, Robin's friend from the Pacific Conservatory of the Performing Arts, said his angst about the relationship was sincere and overwhelming. "He would call me, sometimes at one or two o'clock in the morning, really heartbroken, because he wasn't sure if she was seeing someone else," Lipkin said. "What was going on? She didn't call back right away. He was really upset about it."

On February 10, 1976, Robin and the Juilliard faculty came to the mutual agreement that he should withdraw from the school. Though a persistent urban legend has endured that John Houseman dismissed him with his congratulations for having outstripped the school's ability to educate him — he is supposed to have said in one telling of this tale, "There's just nothing more we can teach you" — this is almost certainly untrue. Such departures from the Drama Division were routine occurrences, and the wayward students would find their way in the wider world or they would not. "John was very good about letting people go and not saying, 'Oh, you have to finish the whole thing,' " said Margot Harley. "He was right to let Robin go at that point."

Other Juilliard instructors who worked with

Robin were even less sentimental about his exit from the school. "I think we all felt it was fine that he left," said Michael Kahn. "It was clear that this particular kind of training wasn't necessarily what he needed or wanted. He got out of it what he wanted to get out of it, and he didn't get all of it. There are people who really don't need the four years, or it's not the right thing for them. And I always understand that. It's never upset me, ever, when people say I don't think this right for me, or I don't want any more of it."

For Robin, though, it was yet another plan that didn't come to fruition, and another three years of education that did not result in a degree. It was time to come home, but at least this time he knew where home was, back in San Francisco, where his parents and his girlfriend would be waiting for him.

3
LEGALIZED INSANITY

Not long after Robin's return to the Bay Area in the winter of 1976, he and his girlfriend broke up. "She fell into this Marin County thing and just went crazy, got really drugged and crazed out," he later explained, adding the sound of a crashing rocket. "Things went whoooosh." Robin was stuck living with his parents in Tiburon, a young man sleeping in a teenager's bedroom, and he fell into what he considered a massive depression. The only place he could find salvation was on the stage, and so he began to explore the local theater scene.

San Francisco, which seemed so strange and foreboding in his senior year of high school, was a diverse, liberal metropolis with a complex ecosystem of theaters, clubs, and nightlife. Performances were happening not only at dedicated playhouses but also at storefronts, restaurants, basements, and almost anywhere you could string up a set of curtains and point a spotlight. Robin's half brother Todd had set up shop in the Marina District at a bar he called Toad Manner, where the regulars nicknamed the proprietor "Toad," like the giant top-hatted amphibian whose extended tongue spelled out the bar's name, and he in turn called them his "Marina maggots." The clientele ran the gamut from doctors and lawyers to firemen and policemen, to bikers and cross-dressers, to the editorial staff of *Rolling Stone* magazine. "There was one guy named Beefy, who wore a pillbox hat and a black housedress and had a big black beard," Robin later recalled. "In San Francisco, that's kind of like day-wear."

Robin dabbled in an improvisational comedy group run by The Committee, the institution where Dale Morse, his drama teacher at Claremont, had trained. On Monday nights, when regular sketch shows and classes were not being offered at The Committee's performance space in the North Beach neighborhood, Del Close, the renegade improv virtuoso from Chicago's Second City, taught a more serious-minded approach to the art. "We were working on improvisation as — how can I express this? — as a serious investigative form," said Joe Spano, an actor who studied there. Close eventually left The Committee, but the splinter group lived on as The Committee Workshop, then the Experimental Wing of The Committee, and then simply the Wing.

This was when Robin showed up, but he did not stick around for long. "It was immediately apparent that the form we were using was too restrictive for Robin's imagination," Spano said. "He couldn't work in our format, which was much slower. None of us had wits as quick. We weren't really doing that kind of comedy. We were trying to work as a team, but I don't mean he wasn't a team player. His speed, his wit, and his acuity were cramped."

It wasn't ambition, either, that got in the way of Robin's work with the Wing, Spano said: "I don't think it was a matter of his aspirations. It was a matter of his nature. His talent was to be Robin."

In March 1976, Robin made his professional San Francisco theater debut in Harold Pinter's *The Lover,* about a husband and wife in a role-playing relationship, at the Gumption, a fringe theater in the city's Haight-Ashbury district. When its director, Cynthia "Kiki" Wallis, first encountered Robin, she found him so destitute she gave him $100 for his wardrobe. As an actor, he seemed to care more about making the role interesting for himself each night than delivering a consistent performance from show to show. "Serious was very difficult for Robin; to remember what it was he had just done and repeat it, wrenching," Wallis said. "He did it every performance beautifully, differently — close enough, but fresh." And sometimes he took it too far: "He had gotten used to getting a laugh and one night he didn't," she said. "So then he did a Tarzan thing with his voice, and he got the laugh. I told him after, 'You got the laugh, but you broke the show rule.' "

Still looking for direction and mentorship, Robin began training with Frank Kidder, who ran a workshop for would-be stand-up comedians in North Beach. Kidder was another former military man, an air force enlistee who ran his program in the basement of the Intersection, a café and arts space established by a three-church coalition. The Intersection took an open-minded approach to programming and offered cabaret, vaudeville, vintage movies, and spoken-word acts, sometimes all on the same bill. The space had started to develop a small following of comedy fans who came to see performers like "Freaky Ralph" Eno, a local fixture who specialized in stream-of-consciousness prose pieces and slightly off-key punk-and-surf-rock pastiches. Don Novello, a recent transplant from Chicago who had grown tired of his advertising copywriting job, came here to try his hand at stand-up, drawn in by the receptive crowds and the promise of even modest compensation.

"Admission cost a dollar and we would split the door," said Novello, who would later become known as the comedic clergyman Father Guido Sarducci. "You usually got,

105

like, two dollars. The bridge at that time was seventy-five cents. So you could end up making fifty cents. It was no money, but it was all hippies and it was very easy. I was doing a lot of stuff about Watergate and Nixon, and they were on your side. It was talking to the choir."

Robin's formative efforts here were character pieces, quaint and juvenile. They included a tongue-in-cheek takeoff on Lawrence Welk, full of the bandleader's familiar German-accented malapropisms: "Tank you, tank you. Now let's all get down and get fonky. The boys in the band will now play for you a luffly melody, *Chumping Chack Flash.* Play that fonky Muzak, white boys. Folks, I want you to know that efery one of the boys in the band is a real motherfocker in his own right."

Another early bit was a quarterback tripping on LSD, who, instead of calling traditional plays, tells his teammates in a loopy California accent, "Well, hike when the energy's right."

It was too early for Robin to be thinking about developing a voice; he was simply trying on the role of the stand-up comedian and finding that he enjoyed it. "It was such a rush the first time I did it," he later said. "The fun thing was being out there on stage in the total silence. The performance was yours. If you died, it was yours too."

With his San Francisco peers, Robin was helping to develop a mode of comedy called the "riffing style": as opposed to organized stand-up routines that proceeded in a logical sequence, this anarchic approach meant that any impulse could be explored at the moment that it occurred, without the need for setup or context, and it could be tossed aside as soon as the next good idea popped up. He took inspiration from more experienced local comics like Jeremy S. Kramer who, he said, "would just go on and do loud, wonderful characters. People would love him or it would drive people out of the room. There was no middle ground."

Robin's theatrical training had given him a voice loud enough that he did not need a microphone to project himself, and he used this to his advantage. "If people started heckling you, you just wade over into the audience and go near their table," he said. "Or move away from them, and use the other side of the room, and fuck the loud people over here, the drunks at the bar." Sometimes he would wander into his audience, establishing a trademark move that helped distinguish him from his competitors. "If you were on mike, you did the standard thing where people could kind of lose track," he said. "So if I didn't go on mike, they were immediately listening."

Comedy offered Robin a personal outlet, a release valve that could help him get past his demoralizing breakup. And it paid just enough that Robin felt he could support himself; if he pushed himself and hustled hard, he could scrape together as much as $25 a night. "I was self-sustaining," he explained, "and I could say, 'No, Pop, I don't need that check, but thanks.' "Yet he couldn't seem to gauge for himself how naturally he took to this strange new discipline. Lorenzo Matawaran, another aspiring comedian who also studied with Kidder and became a friend of Robin's, recalled, "Robin got up and blew everyone away, but he was meek. . . . He'd do a monster set and then come sit down and ask us in that little voice, *'Did I go over?'* "

Robin had come into comedy at an auspicious moment. Stand-up was entering its awkward adolescence; it was growing like crazy and definitely not concerned with being polite. Record albums like George Carlin's vulgar confessional *Class Clown,* Robert Klein's erudite and nostalgic *Child of the Fifties,* and Richard Pryor's raucous and unsparing breakthrough *That Nigger's Crazy* had all been best sellers in recent years. Each of these artists had gained a following with a sensibility that was intensely personal and unconcerned with traditional notions of propriety.

San Francisco had been a comedy town before, and it was becoming one again. In the 1950s and 1960s, it was famous for nightclubs like the hungry i, where Mort Sahl and Bill Cosby held court; Ann's 440 Club, where the volatile Lenny Bruce grew into a force of nature during his lengthy residencies; and the Jazz Workshop, where Bruce was arrested for obscenity after using what the abashed local newspapers could only refer to as a ten-letter word. (It was *cocksucker.*) Now as the city rode a larger wave of artistic renewal, it was ready to supply fresh faces and new venues. And in the span of about six months, one performer seemed to find his way into all of them.

Robin turned up at the Savoy Tivoli and the Old Spaghetti Factory, a pair of interconnected North Beach cabarets that had been beatnik magnets in the 1950s and now offered their space to acts like the improv troupe Spaghetti Jam. Debi Durst, a young comedian who was training with the group, saw Robin perform with them, and she came away impressed, envious, and motivated. "He would take your breath away," she said. "I realized, this guy's got more than improv — he's had real training. Because he had a *voice.* With *enunciation.* He could do all these characters and pull all this stuff out of nowhere. From everything else I had seen, it was like, 'Ah, this looks too easy. I could get onstage and destroy these people.' But playing with him would be a challenge."

During one Spaghetti Jam show at the Savoy Tivoli, the group's director, John Elk, put Durst together with Robin, because they each had high-pitched little-kid voices in their comic repertoires. "He took both of us by the hand and led us out onstage," she recalled. "He goes, 'All right, your mother and I are going out to dinner, and we want you kids to behave. We'll be back in a little bit.' That's all he had to say. He just left the stage, and I looked at Robin. It was like, here we go. It's a free-for-all."

Other comedy novices found Robin's prowess intimidating. "The first time I did improv with him, I couldn't keep up," said Mark Pitta, who first encountered Robin in Spaghetti Jam. "I turned out to be his audience, onstage. It was very embarrassing. He used to sweat, and he reeked. So I wanted to get offstage for two reasons. One is, he stinks, and the other is, I'm not doing well."

When Durst found out that Robin had recently studied at Juilliard, she said it "just totally boosted his esteem in my eyes. I thought, whoa, that's like saying you studied with God or something." But his elite education and his family's wealth did not alienate him from the other members of the group. "It was all about who was going to buy a pitcher of beer at the Savoy after the show," Durst said, adding that Robin would never be that person. "He had like one pair of pants, two pairs of pants. And he was constantly borrowing money because he didn't like to carry money with him. We were always like, 'Okay, I got the buck-fifty, I'll pop for the pitcher. If you don't have any money, that's fine.' We had the rest of our lives to be crazy."

Meanwhile, Robin was also appearing frequently at the Other Café, a storefront and onetime pharmacy built into the corner of a Victorian house, where he performed with an improvisational comedy group called Papaya Juice. The group often went on the road to Bay Area colleges and was willing to appear at just about any room where a crowd could be assembled. "We just wanted to play, just to practice the art, so to speak," explained Tony DePaul, one of its members. "Somehow or other, we got booked into doing a show for the YMCA, practically for nothing. We go down there and it's all Chinese people who don't speak English, so you can't really do improv. Robin started running around the room, making funny sounds and voices, and they liked him, so we just watched him for fifteen minutes and then we left." On another occasion, DePaul said, the troupe performed at a Department of Motor Vehicles office, "because people are waiting in line and that meant we could tell them jokes. You've just got to learn to do it."

Dana Carvey, then a college student at San Francisco State, had been harboring his own secret dream of becoming a stand-up — one that he felt too introverted to act on — when

111

he happened to catch Robin performing a solo set as part of a comedy show at a Berkeley café called La Salamandra. "The fourth guy up blew the room away, and it was Robin," Carvey recalled. "It was so free-form, I'd just never seen anything like it. His voice didn't need amplification. He had kind of a British accent. He was very shy and quiet, until he wasn't."

"People always said he could get away with anything," Carvey said. "He'd do an improv and touch a woman's breasts — 'Oh, titties' — and somehow it was fine when he did it. That was his explosive thing. Off-stage, in a small group, he'd be so shy and so quiet. One side of you is just a monster onstage — the other is painfully awkward, really. The charisma of Robin came from these battling forces."

San Francisco comics could also get exposure at the Boarding House, a music club in Nob Hill, whose owner, David Allen, allowed Robin to open for the rock bands booked there, and at dedicated stand-up spots like the Punch Line, which Bill Graham would establish in the Financial District. At the Open Theater, a performance space on Clement Street frequented by magicians, jugglers, and belly dancers, Robin opened for Rick and Ruby, a comedy rock-cabaret group.

But for authentically in-the-know joke-slingers, there was only one place — one lovingly well-worn, lived-in, beer-stained malodorous shithole — that they regarded as their true home and hangout, and that was the Holy City Zoo.

A claustrophobic performance space of about ten feet by one hundred feet, which at its official seating capacity of seventy-eight was frequently packed with twice or three times as many people, the wood-paneled venue took its name from a sign that its original owner had found in a small community in the Santa Cruz Mountains, called Holy City, where its wildlife preserve was going out of business. Once a jazz and folk music club, the Zoo now offered frequent comedy nights. John Cantu, who programmed its Sunday night open-mic comedy shows and gradually colonized the rest of its schedule, had served in the army during the Vietnam War, and he took a blunt but enthusiastic approach to promoting his shows: when he needed to drum up business he would walk along Clement Street bellowing "Comedy! Comedy! Comedy!" at passersby.

Cantu's personal tastes determined who received the choicest time slots at the Zoo, but just about anyone who wanted to play on its stage was given the opportunity. "If you signed up by eight thirty, they would guarantee you a spot," explained Don Stevens, a comedian and house emcee. "It might be at one thirty in the morning in front of the staff, but you were guaranteed a spot."

As one night's bill wore on until about two a.m., Robin was onstage trading quips with Michael Pritchard, a hulking former army medic, for an enthusiastic audience while a lone performer waited in the wings. Because the Zoo had guaranteed this eager humorist a spot, Stevens said, "I asked him, 'Do you want to go on?' And he said yes, because he was convinced, wow, what a great crowd. I had to actually kick Robin Williams and Michael Pritchard offstage. They left, and the guy got up to perform to people's backs as they walked out of the club. I went to Robin afterward to apologize, and he was quite gracious about it. Those were the rules. He was fine with it."

Here, as in so many of the clubs he passed through, Robin became one of its most exciting prospects, a whiz kid who could make you wait for hours on the chance that he might make an appearance. His routines seemed entirely off-the-cuff and different each time you saw him, but as those who worked closely with Robin knew, his true gift was not necessarily in being purely spontaneous but in creating the appearance of spontaneity.

"Robin just did a hundred little different pieces, as opposed to most of us that had one character that ran throughout," said Tony DePaul. "Then he would start doing the improv and making stuff up, and as long as they kept laughing, he kept doing it. But as soon as it hit a snag, he'd go back and do joke number three and joke number four, and get 'em back. This way, he constantly was building his act."

DePaul said that when he would do his own stand-up at the Zoo, "I didn't have enough time to rehearse, so I would write all my stuff down on a napkin and take it up onstage with a drink. I'd pretend I'm going to get a drink, and I'd look at what I had to do next. Robin almost perfected it. He could go out and they would not even know he was looking at a napkin with a clue on it. You just need one or two. When you jump around like he did, I don't think he ever did the same act twice. He might have done the same material but not in the same order. You've got to mix and match stuff because you're making it up as you go through."

Yet many comedians who performed with Robin at the Zoo did not feel they'd gotten to know the man on the stage. "He was not an easy person," said Don Stevens. "He was either very quiet, or he was in a monologue. There was really no discussion. I'm sure he had friends he could talk to, but he was just on."

Bob Sarlatte, a comedian and broadcast announcer who often worked alongside Robin in this era, said he could not tell which stand-ups Robin regarded as true confidants and which he considered mere acquaintances. "I don't know who was his best friend," he said. "Everyone claims to have been, because they're sort of smitten with his success. But I came up with him and I knew him. I liked him and he liked familiar people. But he wasn't a guy I could even talk much with, without him being distracted."

Many of the relationships forged in these clubs had been facilitated by the steady flow of alcohol they provided. Though the Zoo served only beer and wine, the club offered irresistible incentives to stick around for hours on end. "If you were a comic you pretty much drank for free there," said Will Durst, a comedian and humorist who later took ownership of the club. "They might charge you for one out of every three or four drinks. Which was one of the reasons why it went under."

Those willing to make the slightest extra effort could obtain even more potent diversions. Cocaine had taken up residence in San Francisco's booming nightlife scene, and it was not yet stigmatized like the marijuana and psychedelics with which the city had already gratified itself. "You could turn on a faucet and cocaine would come out," said Steven Pearl, a fellow comic and friend of Robin's. "It was everywhere. We were having fun. We were locally famous. We were making money. Why not spend some of it on something you shouldn't have, really? Everybody did more than they should if you did it once."

Dana Carvey, who started performing stand-up a few months after seeing some of Robin's shows, did not use the drug but agreed it was ubiquitous. Of all the drugs available to comedians in this era, Carvey said, "The only thing I remember is cocaine. I don't remember anything else, really. But it was even kept from me, because I was clearly not in the club. Like, 'Hey, we're back there, if you want, we're doing a line.' I just was out of that loop. It wasn't in my wheelhouse. But I know it spoke to Robin."

Still, other colleagues of Robin's felt certain he had not been turned on to cocaine at this time. "He wasn't doing drugs in those days," said DePaul.

And not everyone agreed with the generous word of mouth his comedy act was generating. "You could see his acting skill, more than his being anything revolutionary as a stand-up," said Joshua Raoul Brody, a pianist and musical director who performed with Rick and Ruby. "He didn't tell jokes — he did bits. And his characterizations were absolutely crisp and spot-on. His transitions didn't hold the viewer's hand — he just went to the next thing and trusted that the viewer was going to follow you. That was exciting to watch. But the things that you were laughing at were things that you had laughed at in other people's acts. It wasn't that original."

In one of the first major reviews of his stand-up comedy, Robin was hardly greeted as the standard-bearer for a new era. In an August 1976 review, John Wasserman of the *San Francisco Chronicle* chided him for a dirty mouth and a juvenile mind. "Motherf — can be funny if used in the right place at the right time," his assessment read, "but there is nothing amusing about the word per se, and the sooner Williams perceives this, the more effective he'll be with any audience old enough to dress themselves."

Robin would later acknowledge that being described as a "scatological pubescent" got deeply under his skin because he felt it was true. "It hit me right on the nose," he said. "In the beginning, you're imitating everybody you've ever seen. . . . But all of a sudden, you get to a point where you go, 'Ah, I can be *me.* I can develop my own stuff.' And you *do.*"

In April 1976, Frank Kidder, Robin's comedy tutor at the Intersection, held a rudimentary stand-up contest in which a dozen amateur performers faced off in a single night, vying to meet the benchmark of three to four laughs per minute, with a "laugh" defined as "three seconds of sustained laughter and/or applause." The $50 prize for first place went to Lorenzo Matawaran, with second place a three-way tie among Robin and the comedians Mark Miller and Mitch Krug. That September, Kidder organized a more ambitious version of the tournament, establishing the first annual San Francisco Comedy Competition and inviting about twenty comics to perform over a nine-night span at four different clubs, where eighteen judges would rate them in seven different categories. At the final round, Robin, Krug, Miller, Bob Sarlatte, and a fifth comedian, Bill Farley, were all still in contention. With one conclusive, fifteen-minute set standing between each man and his destiny, Robin was in first place by a narrow margin, and "that's probably how it should have ended," Sarlatte said.

"At that time," Sarlatte said, "people didn't know that much about stand-up." Robin, he said, "didn't have a very traditional kind of act. It was a little hit-and-miss. It wasn't like it was *that* great. He was still developing, just doing little bits and sketches that were funny and could tear the house down, but they didn't have a lot of symmetry to them."

Paul Krassner, the counterculture journalist and editor of the *Realist,* who was one of the jurors at the competition's final round, said that he remembered Robin's set for "his energy and his obvious presence. He wore a cowboy hat, had a hairy chest and sweated a lot."

But when Farley came up for his final set, Sarlatte said, "he gets about five minutes into his act, and all the lights go out." The club had suffered a momentary power outage and no one knew quite what to do, but Farley, still onstage, made the most of his opportunity. "While the lights are out," Sarlatte recalled, "Bill Farley–with no live mic — says, 'Okay, now when he comes in, let's all sing 'Happy Birthday.' Which was a tremendous ad-lib. And that's what turned it to him. So he ended up finishing in first, Robin was in second, and I was in third."

That, at least, was the story that the judges' scorecards told, and Sarlatte said he could respect the outcome. "Robin's act was so different than everybody else's," he said. "He hadn't become the fawning phenomenon yet. But based on the happenstance of Bill Farley's remarks, it probably ended up the way it should've ended up." But as Krassner recalled it, "People in the audience were angry he didn't win." It was perhaps the last time Robin Williams would be deemed second-best to anyone for a very long time.

One night when Robin was not scheduled to perform at the Holy City Zoo, he was working behind its bar, serving drinks and sneaking a few on the side for himself, when his attention was suddenly consumed by one particular patron. Valerie Velardi, a dancer and movement instructor, was on a break from a nearby tavern where she worked as a cocktail waitress when she stopped into the raucous neighborhood comedy club she had heard so much about. Robin was transfixed by this self-assured woman, who stood a couple of inches taller than he was, and by her classical features. He later explained that what he experienced in this moment was not so much love at first sight: "More like lust," he said. "She was this Italian woman, a Napoletana girl. She wasn't dressed especially sexily; she just looked . . . hot. *Caliente.*" Valerie, for her part, was charmed by this small, stocky, animated man in a striped shirt and rainbow suspenders. Robin, whether trying to amuse her or to hide some undesirable part of himself, decided to talk to Valerie in a feigned French accent.

"He kept it, all night," said Valerie, who never thought to wonder if she was being duped. "No, I thought he was French." With the self-deprecating laugh of someone who should have known better, she added: "I know. I know."

While maintaining his false front, Robin asked Valerie for a ride home at the end of the night, and she, intrigued, took him in her car across the Golden Gate Bridge, around the bay, and into Tiburon. Throughout the ride, Valerie said, "He was very funny. My goodness, he just made me laugh. We got on really well and he was enjoying himself immensely." When they reached a familiar house on Paradise Drive, she said, "I thought I was driving him home, but he said, 'Drop me off here,' which was not his home, it turned out. He said he was living with his parents."

The next time Robin ran into Valerie after this encounter — which the couple would later regard as their first date — he walked up to her and addressed her in a Western twang: "Hi, honey, how are ya?" The two began to see each other regularly after that, and Valerie would soon discover what he really sounded like. "He continued to be delightful in many ways," she said. "I didn't make any distinction between him and his voices. He would just pull them out, and always did."

Valerie, who was a year older than Robin, had grown up in an Italian family in New Haven, Connecticut. She was the oldest of four children and became a de facto parent to her three younger siblings after her mother and father divorced when she was twelve years old. As she learned about Robin's upbringing, she saw the contrasts in their experiences and believed she understood his psychology. "Since he didn't grow up with other children, he was an only child, as far as I'm concerned," she said. "The result is that he has a very rich private life and it's hard to filter in. It's hard to get in deep with someone who's used to taking care of himself only. It's such a cliché, but they make their own worlds."

After attending Goddard College in rural Vermont, Valerie had moved to the Bay Area to study for a master's degree at Mills College in Oakland. By day she attended classes, and by night she went out with Robin and learned about his history in Marin, his frustrations at Juilliard, and his latest, hazy dreams of becoming a stand-up comic. Within weeks the two had fallen in love.

"He always had that tinge," Valerie said. "I had come from that way of thinking, that anything is possible and the world is bright and beautiful. And he made it even brighter and more magical. We were living a lovely existence. We were very young."

When Valerie attended Robin's stand-up shows, she was stunned by how zealously he committed to his craft and how naturally he fit on a stage. "This really was his passion," she said. "And I noticed, immediately, that he was very facile. He had the gift of mimicry. I'd never really seen anything quite like that, and I was quite delighted by that. It was clear that he was quicker than his peers, and it became very apparent, the more I hung with him."

The couple soon came to wonder if Robin had reached the limit of what San Francisco could offer him. To the south there was Los

123

Angeles, which not only had a stand-up circuit of its own; it also had pathways for progress and ladders to ascend — television networks, movie studios, and platforms for national exposure like *The Merv Griffin Show* and *The Tonight Show.*

Robin felt he had to convince Valerie to make the move with him, fearing that she would find fewer opportunities outside of San Francisco to perform and teach modern dance. "There isn't too much of a call for that in Los Angeles," he said. "I mean, Twyla Tharp doesn't choreograph the June Taylor Dancers."

But Valerie believed that she had been the more enthusiastic advocate for their move. "It was very clear to me," she said. "I might have been a bit of a *noodge* on the subject. He was game, certainly, and I just thought, let's go down and see what happens."

When Robin and Valerie entered into this plan, they had no specific ambition, no timetable, and no set date to take stock of whether it was working. Soon they'd have results faster than either of them could have imagined was possible.

Robin arrived in Los Angeles in the fall of 1976, finding an amplified version of everything he had experienced in San Francisco. The talent was more plentiful and more polished, and the opportunities were greater;

the competition was more formidable and the distractions were more seductive. No other city, it seemed, could beat L.A. for the irresistible promise of its rags-to-riches stories or for the rock-bottom devastation of its cautionary tales.

Los Angeles had been an entertainment capital for decades; amid the constellation of comedy clubs that stretched across the city, there were just two where Robin needed to break through, both situated in the boisterous crucible of West Hollywood. The Improv was the marginally more polished establishment of the pair, having already helped launch the careers of performers like Jay Leno, a relentless Boston comic with a rapid-fire delivery and a thick mane of black hair; Andy Kaufman, a Long Island transplant who encased his authentically shy, soft-spoken self in the armor of outspoken, over-the-top stage characters; and Freddie Prinze, the half–Puerto Rican, half-Hungarian sensation from New York who, within a year of moving to Los Angeles, had been snapped up to star in his own NBC sitcom, *Chico and the Man.*

The Improv's rival, the Comedy Store, sat a few blocks north on the rowdy strip of Sunset Boulevard. With multiple showrooms offering more capacity and more debauchery than the Improv, the Comedy Store was the dominion of Mitzi Shore, its booker and owner. All but a few of her favorite performers played the club in return for free drinks and exposure but no money, and those who she felt did not deserve even that much compensation she made work as receptionists, parking attendants, or ushers until she deemed them ready to appear on one of her stages.

As frantic and competitive as the Los Angeles comedy scene could be, its most promising participants found it oddly endearing, and they bonded over the strange aspirations they shared. "It was a hugely romantic period," said Leno. "You had a bunch of outcasts, people who didn't fit in their own communities, converge in one place, where they finally met people like themselves." Comedy, Leno said, is an unusual discipline where "the affirmation of strangers is more important than that of friends or family members. No comic wants his friends or his family in the audience. They're either going to laugh too hard or they're not going to laugh at all. You want complete strangers. They're the only ones that count."

When a new performer entered into this system — a circuit that tired rapidly of the familiar and hungered for anything fresh and unseen — he was quickly sought out and evaluated. As this process was explained by Mark Lonow, a comedian, actor, and business partner at the Improv, "Word spread in the comedy community — we're talking about performers, but we're also talking about a large section of the audience — within hours. Days was a long time. If people came in and they discovered a new comic, all of a sudden, within weeks, they could sell out the room. It was a small, incestuous — in every definition of that word — community. Now, it did comprise probably tens of thousands of people. But you'd be surprised how quickly word spread."

Robin started at the West Hollywood studios of Off the Wall, a small, year-old improv comedy troupe, arriving in shabby clothes that looked slept in: a rumpled brown suit, a beret, and his rainbow suspenders. The other performers assumed, reasonably, that he was living out of the car he'd driven down from San Francisco. Off the Wall had been started by DeVera Marcus, an early advocate of improvisational theater from Northern California, who chose the members of the troupe from a workshop of improv students she taught. The shows, in which the performers rattled off spontaneous sketches based on audience suggestions, were usually break-even affairs done for fun rather than profit. Even so, Marcus offered Robin a place in the group as well as a small stipend while got himself set up in L.A., because, as she would be among the first in the city to learn, he was just that good.

Wendy Cutler, one of the charter members of the troupe, recalled that Robin immediately brought a sense of clarity to this group of young people who were similarly brimming with spirit but unsure how to focus it. "I remember Robin bouncing in," she said, "and he was brilliant from the get-go. He was fun and interesting and fast and surprising. He brought a sense of being able to build something completely unexpected, which was really, really exciting."

Andy Goldberg, another company member, thought Robin was a foreigner at first. "The guy just showed up, wearing the brown suit and the beret, and he was talking in a Russian accent. And because of the suit and the Russian accent, I thought, oh, he's Russian. He had this little book in his hand — I don't know if it was notes that he jotted down for his act — and he opened the book like it was a Russian-to-English dictionary or something, and did a line that I've heard him say a billion times since: 'Get down. Get back up again.' "

In addition to his ability and goodwill, Robin had a magnetic charisma. "I remember being very attracted to Robin's energy," Cutler said. "And everybody else in the group, too. He was so committed and his mind was just so wild. You wanted to just go up there and play with it."

Robin took his gig with Off the Wall seriously enough to have business cards printed up, with the group's name in big hand-drawn letters meant to look like they were made out of bricks, and his own name in small type, just above the misspelled description, "IM-PROVISTIONAL COMEDY THEATRE." In the program given out at Off the Wall performances, he provided one of his first professional biographies, in which he described himself as follows:

ROBIN WILLIAMS, born in Chicago, spent his prepubescence bouncing back and forth between Detroit and Chicago before finally moving to San Francisco. It was there he discovered his imagination and women. He graduated high school most funny and least likely to succeed. To avoid terminal mellowness Robin left paradise to study in New York at The Juilliard School of Drama. After three years he returned to San Francisco to begin a career in the legalized insanity of stand up comedy. The rest is history. His hobbies are swimming, cross country running and bondage.

Just as he did in this short bio, in which he tried to strike a balance between a proper amount of modesty and pride in his accomplishments, Robin strained in his Off the Wall performances to temper vanity with restraint — to juggle the communal spirit of improv theater and the solitary impulse of stand-up comedy.

In one scene they created together, Goldberg recalled, "We were little kids playing baseball, and he went behind the audience and played the scene from there — which none of us had ever done before. We kept our performance on the stage, because that's where the lights were and that's where the audience was looking. So then the whole audience turned around and they're watching him riff behind them.

"There were times like that," Goldberg said. "I'm not saying it was malicious or intentional or anything like that. That's just who he was."

As he worked to situate himself in Los Angeles and had little to call his own, Robin was also capable of acts of kindness, compassion, and charity. Jamie Masada, who would later establish the Laugh Factory comedy-club franchise, was a young recent immigrant from Iran when he first encountered Robin at the Bla-Bla Café, a restaurant and nightspot in Studio City. Masada, who was living out of a garage while he tried to earn a steady income, had recently stumbled his way into a few stand-up and hosting spots; he spoke Farsi and Hebrew but was still learning to master English, and when he saw Robin was having his lunch, he was too ashamed to ask if he could join him.

"He was eating a tuna sandwich on whole wheat, and I was starving," Masada recalled. "He said, 'Come on,' and I sat down with him and he ordered me one. He said, 'What are you doing with your act? You should do this.' He gave me the name of a teacher, I should call him and study with him for acting." In exchanges like these, Masada said Robin never talked down to him or treated him as an inferior. "He said hello and how are you, like he genuinely cared for you," he said. "And I genuinely connected with him."

On another night at the Bla-Bla Café, Masada was emceeing a show where Robin was on the bill. "I brought him on the stage," Masada said, "and he went, 'Did you ever do Shakespeare?' I didn't know Shakespeare. Who the fuck is Shakespeare? What's Shakespeare? He's trying to describe it, and he starts teaching me the lines. 'To be, or to not be. That is the question.' I said, 'What is the question?' And people, they start laughing. I didn't know what I was doing right. People are rolling because I'm fucking it up, and I'm not doing it purposely. But I felt secure being around him."

By now, Robin's routine had grown into an overstuffed grab bag of outrageous voices and exaggerated characters, drawn from people he'd encountered in his travels, facets of himself, and his far-reaching imagination: the haughty aristocrat and the Southern good-ol'-boy; the mumble-mouthed codger, the TV evangelist, and the heavily accented Russian; stray impersonations of pop-culture figures familiar and obscure, whether a *Wizard of Oz* Munchkin or the whining protagonist of *The Fly*, the sinister, mewling Peter Lorre, or the folksy vaude-villian George Jessel; and, perhaps closest to his heart, a classically trained actor who speaks in a seamless blend of elevated Elizabethan language and crude anatomical references.

Robin began to draw comparisons to the eccentric Andy Kaufman, who seemed to be perpetually leaping from one persona to the next, even when he wasn't performing. As Robin would later recall, "I only had one conversation with Andy where he wasn't talking to me as a character. He just went, 'Hi, Robin, how are you?' I went, 'Good, Andy, how are you?' 'Really good, I'm just here buying something.' It was at some health-food store. Then by the end of the conversation" — he switched into Kaufman's soft-spoken Foreign Man accent — "slowly but surely *he went back to theees*. And I went, 'I'll see you. Take care.' "

Bennett Tramer, an aspiring screenwriter, heard from a friend that he'd seen a comic at the Improv who was even better and more nimble than Kaufman. With some skepticism, Tramer went to the club a few nights later and was astounded to see Robin riffing in his Shakespearean voice with a cocktail waitress who had unknowingly become part of the act. "Whatever she would say or do, he had the ability to incorporate that as if they'd rehearsed it earlier in the day," Tramer said. "He asked her for a drink: 'My lady, I hear yon Perrier sparkling in a bottle.' Someone heckled him and he said, 'First time heckling?' Just destroyed the guy."

When Robin got his chance to audition for the Comedy Store and the mighty Mitzi Shore, he did not squander the opportunity. Appearing in performance one Monday night at the chain's principal location on Sunset Boulevard, he took the stage in bare feet, a T-shirt, and a pair of overalls and delivered a line in the sassy persona of his ribald Shakespearean thespian: "Now, a reading from *Two Gentlemen of Santa Monica,* also known as *As You Lick It.*" Then, while his ecstatic audience was still recovering, he hit them with another punch to the gut: "Hark, the moon, like a testicle, hangs low in the sky." Shore immediately called Argus Hamilton, a comedian who hosted her shows at the Comedy Store's satellite club in Westwood, and told him: "I'm coming over right now with this new comic so he can do there what he just did here."

As the newest hire of the Comedy Store, Robin was given a rare salaried position that paid him $200 a week and an elevated status at one of the city's most visited venues for stand-up talent. The gig conferred on him an aura of legitimacy, and it ensured that anyone in Hollywood looking for employable, exploitable new performers would be seeing his show in the months to come.

Other comics had to check out Robin, too, and they came away from his shows feeling awestruck and — if they were being honest — jealous and unnerved. David Letterman, an acerbic stand-up and writer who had recently arrived from Indiana, and a friend, the comedian George Miller, watched Robin play several sets at the Comedy Store in Westwood, where they developed a kind of masochistic obsession with him. "We were just guys who stood behind the microphone and told jokes," Letterman said. "Robin comes in, and my memory of him is that he actually flew in — the energy gave one the impression that he was levitating. He seemed to be hovering above the stage and the tables and the bar. George and I would discuss Robin Williams endlessly, like, What did we just see? How did he do it? Because he didn't seem to have an act. And George and I would think, well, now, does that mean things have changed and we should leave the business?"

Robin became a member of the Comedy Store Players, the club's in-house ensemble of improv performers, who delivered a mix of ad-libbed sketches and character pieces, as well as more experimental fare, like late-night sets that were accompanied by a blues band. "We were trying to be pure," said Jim Staahl, another member of the Comedy Store Players. "The rules of improvisation were sacrosanct: Give and take — it's the scene that's important. And then Robin came in and was a bull in a china shop. He was doing six jokes and the audience is wetting their pants by the time the other person speaks. And then when they say something, he'd switch the location. He'd Pirandello on it: 'Now I'm in a bank.' I thought I was in a car wash!"

Robin continued to play with other groups he belonged to; on some nights he would go directly from an Off the Wall show to a stand-up set at the Comedy Store or the Improv, with some of his troupe members in tow. Valerie would often sit in the crowd at his stand-up shows, helping to catalog his material and to steer him if he got offtrack. As audiences were first getting to know Robin and his unfamiliar style, Valerie acted as an audience plant, helping him and the crowd adjust to one another. When she saw Robin hesitate in his stampeding delivery, she would call out to him: "Robin, what's going on in your head?" Hearing this familiar voice, he would make a slow, creaking noise and pretend to lift off the top of his cranium, giving him a moment to catch his breath before letting a new stream of insanity pour forth.

The Comedy Store also offered Robin a conduit to Richard Pryor, one of his idols, whom he studied and later befriended. Pryor was a regular performer at the club, and he came there to lay everything on the line, to joke about his brutal upbringing in Peoria or his recent battles with cocaine abuse. Multiple times a week, Robin would watch Pryor slip into the slurred Mississippi patois of his inebriated alter ego, Mudbone, or riff on the latest misfortune to befall him in real life. "He would go on last," Robin said. "Everyone would come and watch. It was like an audience for the pope. I saw him do stuff that he would never do again. People would yell out, 'Do Mudbone!' and he'd say, 'You do Mudbone, motherfucker. You know it better than me.' It was a kind of a transformative thing, seeing him just trying stuff and going so far out, the most personal, painful stuff you could ever see."

One of Pryor's routines that stuck with Robin was a bit about God coming back to earth to pick up his Son, only to find out that Jesus has been crucified. "You could see the entire audience going, *What?*" Robin said. "The most strangely beautiful piece. That wasn't a character. That was just him." And then there were the evenings when you just couldn't predict Pryor at all.

"There'd be these weird nights where you'd

just watch him," Robin said, "and then sometimes you'd get to go on after him, once in a while, like he would have people come on stage with him, and then there would be people in the audience, like Willie Nelson would play music at the end, after everyone split. It was like jazz, it was pretty wonderful."

Pryor did not disguise his rampant drinking and drug use — not from his audience and not from the comics who sought his guidance — and Robin saw the effects that substance abuse had on his performance. "Coke would get him going," Robin said, "but alcohol would give him just enough buffer between him and the audience to kind of let it out. You could see when he was off of it. Then it was hard because he was getting too much feedback. The fear would kind of take over. But when he had a couple of Courvoisiers, he was like fuckin' flyin'."

Drugs had begun to insinuate themselves into Robin's life, too. Cocaine had already gained acceptance in Hollywood, earning a reputation as the "Champagne of drugs" for its powerful but "clean" high, without the messiness or apparatus of harder drugs like heroin. Cocaine was in the city's bloodstream and it was traded like currency, especially by those who wanted access or proximity to fame, who wanted to keep that night's party going just a little bit longer.

When Bob Davis, one of Robin's friends from Claremont College, came to see him at the Comedy Store, he was stunned to find his old classmate after the show, casually doing cocaine with other people in the parking lot of the club. "Some guy just walked up to him with a spoon full of cocaine, and held it up to his nose, and — *whoosh,*" Davis said. "That's the way it was. It seemed startling to me." Davis did not use cocaine himself but said he expected to find it around the comedy scene. "Even so," he said, "that just seemed like, that's not what you did. This wasn't a friend of his — this was a fan who just walked up. It was such an odd thing."

Davis had not seen Robin much in recent years, but he could tell that some of the people who orbited him, drawn into the gravity of his nascent celebrity, were not intimate confidants either. When one of Robin's stand-up sets ended, Davis said, "Instead of just four or five of us, there'd be like twenty. Mostly people I didn't know. They were just sort of glomming onto him."

Later in his life, when Robin was open about his drug habit, he said that cocaine was so readily available to him that he almost never had to pay for it. "They give it to you for free," he said. " 'You have a drug problem?' 'No problem. Everybody's got it.' Everyone will pump you up if you're ready, because it also gives them some control over you. You'll tolerate conversations with people you wouldn't even talk to in daylight."

Robin's acceptance into the Comedy Store crowd ushered him further into a tight-knit community of stand-ups and industry figures who also drank heavily and did cocaine, and who then brought their revelry back to Mitzi Shore's house for further hours of closed-door depravity. If the night did not end there, it might take Robin and his fellow performers on a sweeping party circuit — to Canter's Deli on Fairfax to swap sandwiches and war stories, or to an out-of-town club like the Show Biz in the San Fernando Valley, the Ice House in Pasadena, or the Comedy & Magic Club in Hermosa Beach, where there would be more antics onstage, followed by more drinking and drugging behind the scenes. At a formative moment in his career, Robin was establishing what would become an enduring pattern of behavior, where an evening's performance at a club did not end with a handshake at the exit door and a car ride home. One set somewhere would be followed by drinking and drugs, or it would lead to more sets at more clubs, followed by more drinking and more drugs. Once the night began, there was no way of knowing how it might end and no clear signal, not even the rising sun, that indicated it was over.

The Los Angeles comedy community received a shocking wake-up call on the morning of January 28, 1977, when Freddie Prinze, the dazzling young comic and star of *Chico and the Man,* put a loaded .32-caliber pistol to his head and fired a bullet into his temple. He never regained consciousness and died at a Los Angeles hospital the following afternoon, at the age of twenty-two. Prinze, who had only a week earlier performed at the inaugural ball for President Jimmy Carter, seemed to be on top of the world, but within the stand-up scene it was known that he had been keeping himself steady by taking quaaludes, which he washed down with cognac, and then perking himself up with cocaine. Prinze suffered from depression and had recently learned that his wife had filed for divorce; though a coroner initially declared his death a suicide, a jury would later rule that it had been an accident.

Hollywood's comics should have taken the lesson that substance abuse posed a perilous threat to them. But the conclusion that many drew from Prinze's death was that he had gone too far in his decadence, while they might be spared if they just reined in their excesses, even slightly. For this fraternity of performers that Robin was now a part of, drugs and alcohol were a means of celebrating success and prolonging the uniquely exquisite ecstasy of a good night on the stage. They were also a last line of defense against that most terrifying fear of failure — the dreaded sense of uncertainty that came with every stand-up set.

Valerie, who had started teaching modern dance classes at Pepperdine University, was hardly oblivious to what Robin was getting up to in his after-hours antics. But at the time she felt it was something she had to allow him — a toll to pay so that he could be doing what made him so genuinely happy.

"He wanted to be with his friends, and he wanted to be with like-minded souls who could keep up with him," Valerie explained. "He sought them out. His incentive was to play. And he liked playing in front of audiences — the bigger the audience the better. So in that respect, he was happy that he was moving forward, because he was getting the audience in prime time with the prime people."

There are some disagreements about their relationship in this period. Both Robin and Valerie have said that they arrived in Los Angeles together. But some friends who knew the couple at this time say that it was Robin who came first, alone, and Valerie who followed sometime after, once Robin had gotten himself established. Wendy Asher, who met Robin as a young employee of the William Morris Agency and remained a friend for decades after, said that Robin had already pursued another romantic relationship, waged from start to finish, before Valerie came to town. "One of my friends was going out with him, because he had broken up with Valerie," Asher said. "He had been dating her, and he broke up with her."

The comedian Elayne Boosler had been seeing Andy Kaufman when the two of them moved to Los Angeles from New York; after their amicable breakup, she began dating Robin. "I had never been so pursued," Boosler said. "Even though he had an apartment, which I never saw in all that time, he came to my place every night." Robin called her "Punk" or "Punky," just as his mother, Laurie, had been called since her childhood. When Boosler asked him if she was the first girlfriend to whom he'd given this affectionate nickname, she said Robin told her, "Just the last 14."

On top of his relentless stand-up schedule and his involvement in the professional improv troupes, Robin also trained at instructional comedy workshops to keep his edge and to schmooze with other strivers. One of these classes was taught by Harvey Lembeck, a Brooklyn-born actor who had appeared in *Stalag 17,* played the conniving Corporal Barbella on *The Phil Silvers Show,* and co-starred in a series of 1960s teen comedies that included *Beach Party, Bikini Beach, Beach Blanket Bingo, How to Stuff a Wild Bikini,* and *The Ghost in the Invisible Bikini.* Despite his whimsical résumé, Lembeck

142

was a stern master of his studio and did not admit students without at least a few serious professional credits. "You had to have a lot going for you, to just get in there," said Joel Blum, one of Robin's classmates at the College of Marin, who was also enrolled in one of Lembeck's seminars. "You had to be in something to be in the class." Lembeck was officious in dictating the scenes his students would play in class and the punch lines they were expected to arrive at, but Robin, as always, found ways to innovate. At one session, Blum recalled, Lembeck instructed Robin and another student to play out a very specific scene: "Two people who don't know each other, watching a movie sitting right next to each other. Robin wound up doing this homeless person who was rubbing his armpits and smelling them. It was just outthere, crazy stuff."

The class was populated with an assortment of actors already in their first flushes of stardom, including Penny Marshall, who was starring in the ABC sitcom *Laverne & Shirley*, and John Ritter, who played a lucky bachelor living with two female roommates on *Three's Company*, another ABC comedy. Ritter, whose own comic sensibilities were considerably less ribald than those of his TV show, became a fast friend to Robin, whom he regarded as a delightfully perverse virtuoso.

"I saw the way this dude was dressed," said

Ritter, "in baggy pants, suspenders, a beaten-up tux over high-topped sneakers, a straw hat with the brim falling off, John Lennon glasses with no glass in the frames, and I thought, 'Well, this guy is definitely going for the sight gag.' I was almost a bit suspicious. So I watched carefully and he turned out to be the funniest guy I've ever seen."

As Ritter recalled, "The first bit I ever saw him do was a kiddie-show host, and it was the most *demented* thing you can imagine. He brought these puppets onstage and did these weird voices, and wound up doing an S&M routine with the puppets that's indescribable.

"He took care of me onstage, because I'd never try to top him," Ritter said. "I headed right for the straight-man role."

Another student in the class was the singer-songwriter Melissa Manchester, who was then the wife and client of Larry Brezner, a partner at the talent firm of Rollins, Joffe, Morra & Brezner. He would often visit these workshops to scout for new prospects, and Robin was an immediate standout. "I watched this one kid get up, and no matter what situation was thrown at him, he never got lost," Brezner said. "In an improv, right before the blackout, you've either won or lost; you either hit the big line or it lays there. I watched two hours of this kid never losing, reacting off the top of his head, working off nerve impulses — not intellect at all." Comparing him to the disillusioned and achingly sincere young protagonist of *The Catcher in the Rye,* Brezner said that Robin was "like Holden Caulfield, a guy walking around with all his nerve endings completely exposed."

Robin had tried working with other management firms before, with little to show for it. Earlier in his Hollywood apprenticeship, he had been handled by three different managers in a two-week period, one of whom sent him to audition for a role in *CHiPs,* the TV drama about a pair of motorcycle cops on the California Highway Patrol. "They wanted a strapping six-footer who could ride a Harley-Davidson," Robin said. "I'd never ridden a motorcycle and I stood five-eight, maybe 135 pounds. . . . I realized: 'This is no good. This man is not for me.' "

For any comedian, the representation of Rollins, Joffe, Morra & Brezner was all but a guarantee of prosperity and fame — the key to the very best opportunities that the entertainment industry could provide. In exchange for a 15 percent commission of a performer's earnings, the firm offered the cachet of an unparalleled client list that included Woody Allen, Dick Cavett, Robert Klein, and Mike Nichols — not to mention the services of one of the craftiest and most adaptable management teams around.

Jack Rollins, the firm's founder, was an

archetypal Brooklyn *macher* with a love of harness racing and a cigar perennially dangling from his mouth. His earliest clients had included Harry Belafonte and Lenny Bruce as well as Allen, whom Rollins and his partner, Charles H. Joffe, had helped elevate from an intellectual stand-up to a triple-threat actor, writer, and director. Rollins and Joffe produced Allen's brainy, lucrative comedies — Joffe himself accepted the Academy Award that *Annie Hall* won for best picture — and even employed Allen's father, Martin Konigsberg, as a part-time messenger in New York. Their company, which for the first decade of its existence had been based out of a Manhattan duplex, took on Larry Brezner as a third partner and Buddy Morra as a fourth, and established a satellite office in Los Angeles that, over time, would become its epicenter.

By the time Robin appeared on the radar of the Rollins Joffe firm, it had started working with two other comics whom it was grooming as its next generation of talent. One was David Letterman, who had become a favorite guest on Johnny Carson's *Tonight Show* and was now starting to fill in occasionally as a host in Johnny's absence. The other was Billy Crystal, an amiable, rib-poking New York comic and actor with an omnivorous cultural appetite and a repertoire of celebrity impersonations that somehow included both

Howard Cosell and Muhammad Ali, as well as Sammy Davis Jr. Crystal had missed a possible big break when he was cut from the 1975 debut episode of *Saturday Night Live;* he was now enjoying national attention as one of television's first openly gay characters on the ABC sitcom *Soap.*

Robin had been brought to the firm for a meeting, and was later evaluated in performance by Stu Smiley, a young new employee who had been hired as an assistant to Brezner and Morra. Jack Rollins's initial assessment of Robin was mixed, to say the least: "The talent is endless; the discipline is nil." But Smiley, who was much closer in age to Robin than any of the partners at the company, was impressed when he saw one of Robin's sets at the Comedy Store. "He would do his Shakespearean actor character and he would walk on the tables," Smiley said. "He was so fearless that *you* were afraid."

Smiley, who had just come off a job as a production assistant on *Annie Hall,* knew Robin was a special individual, and the many months he was about to spend shadowing him would show him just how special. "I knew he could pirouette on a needle," Smiley said. "I didn't know that no one else could."

Robin signed on with the firm, preferring to remain happily in the dark about how it handled his affairs. As Joffe would later boast, "Robin is a neophyte. . . . That doesn't interest him. What interests him is his work. That's what gives me great hope for his growth. What interests me is that twenty years from now, people still care about Robin Williams."

The managers saw almost unlimited potential in Robin, and they had no hesitation about expressing this to him, and to Valerie. "They wanted him, and that was exciting," she said. "It's the next level. You hear that they're Woody Allen's managers, and that's pretty terrific. They took me out to lunch, and I'll never forget this. They said, 'You are going to be very, very rich. You are not going to have to do anything anymore. You can lunch and shop.' I'll never forget that. *Lunch and shop.* And I have manners, and I'm polite, and I listened and nodded. But I was so upset afterwards."

Valerie was happy to see Robin's career begin to bloom and had no desire to help guide or run it. But she could see that lines were being drawn between what she could and could not be a part of — where she belonged and where she was not wanted. "I wasn't aspiring to anything," she said. "I was dancing and enjoying my boyfriend, my life with him. Not that I really wanted any particular role, but now it's like, okay, this is big and you don't get to be a part of it. And I really felt shut out."

Robin had an energy that had turned on the town, a growing reputation that signaled he was going to do something big, and the people who could make it happen for him. Now all he needed was a role.

4
MY FAVORITE ORKAN

In early 1977, before Robin had any noteworthy Hollywood representation or credits, he met with Howard Papush, a talent coordinator at *The Tonight Show Starring Johnny Carson.* A successful five-minute set on the program moved you to the front of the line for better stand-up gigs, and for film and TV auditions; an invitation from Johnny to sit on his couch was a crowning accomplishment and a signal to millions of viewers that you had just been inducted into an exclusive pantheon.

Robin knew how vitally important *The Tonight Show* was to advancing comedy careers, and he had sat in its storied Burbank studio when friends like Jay Leno made their debuts. As Leno later recalled, every time one of his punch lines landed, "you could hear, in the audience, 'Huh-HAAH!' " he said, imitating Robin's telltale laugh. Robin seemed destined for such a spot when Papush spotted him at a club in San Diego, where he was "flinging props all over the stage and he was hilarious, and the audience was going nuts," as Papush described the scene. A longtime talent producer, Papush had helped comics like Steve Martin and Freddie Prinze get on *The Tonight Show,* and it seemed unthinkable that someone so clearly poised for his breakthrough had escaped his attention. "I just couldn't believe it," he said. "It's like, where did he crawl out of? From under what rock? How come I didn't know who he is?"

Papush had some apprehensions that Robin's vulgarity would not be suitable for NBC. "He was saying 'motherfucker' and things like that, but not just to say it — the context of how he was doing it was extraordinary," he observed. But what worried Papush more was whether Robin could only deliver the same set over and over again, or whether he could vary and update his material from performance to performance. At *The Tonight Show,* Papush said, "We had an unspoken rule — sometimes it was spoken — that we would not put a new comedian on the show until they had what we deemed was fifteen minutes of good material, so we knew they'd have three spots on the show. Somebody could have five dynamite minutes and then bomb the second time if their material wasn't up to what it had been the first time. My belief was that likability was a very important factor. It couldn't be just telling jokes — the audience really had to like you."

A few weeks after seeing Robin in San Diego, Papush laid out this larger concern to Robin. "I told him that I really wanted to put him on the show, but it was not going to happen right away, because there were issues with the material," Papush recalled. "At some point I said to him, 'You know, Robin, you're a big star already. We just have to work on your material.' And he looked at me very quizzically." The idea that his stand-up set was a body of work that needed to be updated and refined simply had not occurred to him. "There are people who have their eye on their career and making it," Papush said, "and then there are true artists who just do their art, and what happens, happens. When I said to him, 'You're a big star,' he looked at me like, what are you talking about?"

Robin did not get on *The Tonight Show* this time, though he was determined to take his act to the next level, whatever that meant. But his desperation to make good on the promise others saw in him, combined with a naïve attitude about the entertainment industry, sometimes led him to make poor decisions. As Stu Smiley, his friend and minder at Rollins Joffe, said of Robin in this period, "He would take any job. If he got a call for a birthday party, he would do it." It was one of the firm's responsibilities, going forward, to keep him from repeating these mistakes.

152

Robin's screen debut could hardly have been less glamorous or auspicious. It was in a film called *Can I Do It . . . Til I Need Glasses?*, which happened to be the sequel to *If You Don't Stop It . . . You'll Go Blind;* both were low-budget, R-rated features consisting of short reenactments of dirty jokes that any borscht belt comedian would dismiss for being too obvious. The poster for the original, released in 1974, was illustrated with a dastardly man in a top hat flashing his body to two buxom, possibly naked women; the sequel, released in the summer of 1977, billed itself as "the nuttiest, naughtiest, looniest, gooniest, *funniest* madcap comedy of the year."

Robin appears in two segments in the film. In one, he is seen pacing outside a doctor's office, wearing his rainbow suspenders and a kerchief tied around his head. As a man in a suit starts to unlock the front door, Robin declares in a Southern yokel's accent, "Thank goodness you're here, Doc — I'm new in this town and this tooth is killing me." "I'm afraid you made a mistake, young man," the doctor replies. "I'm not a dentist, I'm a gynecologist." Perplexed, Robin asks why the doctor has hung a picture of a tooth above his office entrance, and this time the doctor answers more forcefully: "Schmuck, what did you expect me to hang up there?" (For completeness, the gag is punctuated with the sound of

153

a slide whistle and the ringing of a bell.)

For his second scene, Robin, dressed in a bow tie and a pair of round John Lennon spectacles with his hair slicked back, plays a courtroom attorney interrogating a large-breasted woman in a low-cut top. In a voice that starts off evenly and grows louder over the course of his inquiry, he asks her, "Is it true, Mrs. Frisbee, that last summer, you had sexual intercourse with a red-headed midget during a thunderstorm, while riding nude in the sidecar of a Kawasaki motorcycle, performing an unnatural act on a Polish plumbing contractor, going sixty miles an hour, up and down the steps of the Washington Monument, on the night of July 14th? Is that true, Mrs. Frisbee? Is that *true*?"

Having delivered those lines with more craft and thoughtfulness than they deserve, Robin is rewarded with the punch line: the witness looks up at him and asks, "Could you repeat that date again, please?" (At this point, Robin stares balefully into the camera while a trumpet blares a sad wah-wah refrain.) His brief appearances in the film were not worth what little energy he invested in them, and if he thought they were harmless, he would later come to regret them.

Robin followed with his first television roles, many just as ephemeral, but at least not nearly as embarrassing. His stand-up performances had brought him to the attention of George Schlatter, the veteran television producer who had helped make *Rowan & Martin's Laugh-In,* the kooky, counterculture comedy-variety show of the Vietnam War era. Schlatter remembered a performance he had seen at a small club in Santa Monica, where a barefoot Robin, wearing long hair and a long beard, overalls, and a straw hat, hung his microphone stand out over the audience and said, "I'm fishing for assholes." At that point, Schlatter said, "I became absolutely enamored of this young man and explained to him that if he could clean up his act, I had a job for him."

When they met again a few days later at Schlatter's office, Robin was neatly dressed and groomed — in a suit, his hair cut, and his beard trimmed. "Here I am, boss," he declared. Schlatter marveled to himself at how crude and how cultured Robin could be at the same time. "I wondered, where did this come from?" he said. "Because he knew drama. He knew Shakespeare. And he knew the street. It was impossible for that much knowledge and talent, professionalism, and ability to be all piled up into this one little guy."

What Schlatter had in mind for Robin was a role in a new incarnation of *Laugh-In,* one in which a house team of performers and a rotating lineup of celebrity guests would act out comedy sketches in a rapid-fire style. In a cast of thirteen rookie comedians (as well as two puppets), Robin spent part of the summer of 1977 on the MGM Studios lot near Culver City, recording as many as thirty or more segments a day, on sets that looked like leftovers from a bygone age of protest, decorated in polka dots and psychedelic designs. The new *Laugh-In* offered an awkward juxtaposition of corny setups and knock-downs ("Do you feel that pay TV will catch on?" "I wouldn't watch TV no matter how much they paid me") with earnest efforts at topicality and social relevance. In one segment, the cast sang a backhanded tribute to Anita Bryant, the beauty queen and pitchwoman turned antigay activist, set to the tune of "Carolina in the Morning": "She's the missionary / Who can sock it to a fairy / In the morning." Another sketch cast Robin as the cultlike leader of a religious movement not unlike Sun Myung Moon's Unification Church ("We believe in life after death — in other words, there's a sucker reborn every minute"), whose broadcasts evoke children's shows like *The Mickey Mouse Club.*

The skits were often banal, but they allowed Robin to share the screen with some of the biggest stars of the day. He sang a duet with Tina Turner and serenaded a visibly impressed Joan Rivers with a spontaneous tune about her movie *Rabbit Test.* ("Went to bed last night with hair upon my chest / I woke up this morning with a couple of beautiful breasts / You know I'm changing.") Afterward, Rivers found Robin hard to forget, if only because he never seemed to know when to turn himself off. "You know how it is: You're struggling, you want to be noticed, and the only way is to be the funny boy," she later recalled. "We took a picture together — and he never stopped mugging. You wanted to tie him down and say, 'Stop.' "

In one surprisingly rebellious skit, Robin tried to convince Jimmy Stewart to get with the times and smoke a joint; in another, he managed to elicit some approving chuckles from the sullen Frank Sinatra, who shared his bawdy sense of humor. "When Frank Sinatra looked at him," Schlatter recalled, "Robin said, 'I'm so excited I could drop a log!' Well, when he heard 'drop a log,' Sinatra almost fainted. We all were in shock, disbelief, and a bit of awe."

Robin wasn't sure the joke would work, either. "I was afraid they'd want to fire me and that I'd have to explain that I'd never meant to upset Uncle Frank," he said. "Thank God he laughed."

Bette Davis, another of Robin's illustrious scene partners on the show, had a brief bit of advice for him: "The one word you'll need is *no.*" What Robin took this to mean, he later explained, is that "the secret is to be able to turn things down, to not take on projects . . .

just because they say they want you. If they can't get you, they'll get anybody, so wise up."

That same summer, Robin was cast in another sketch show — one that, unlike *Laugh-In,* did not try to find a safe middle ground and instead embraced a provocative sensibility. NBC had offered Richard Pryor his own prime-time variety series and gave him free rein to cast and write the program — its latest effort to adapt Pryor's proudly defiant comedy for a mass viewership. From the outset, the temperamental headliner had one particular demand for what would be called *The Richard Pryor Show:* according to John Moffitt, who directed the series, "Richard says, 'For my cast, I want all my friends from the Comedy Store.' Pause. Beat. Beat. Beat. I asked, 'But how many of them can act?' He said, 'I want them.' So we went to the Comedy Store and we got the cast."

Robin was one of those disciples that Pryor selected for his team, along with Sandra Bernhard, Paul Mooney, and several other young comedians. Building upon Pryor's fearless stand-up act, *The Richard Pryor Show* focused on comedy sketches — usually with Pryor as their central character — that satirized issues of race and bigotry in America. In one segment, he is cast as the first black president of the United States, fielding questions at a White House press conference. ("I feel it's time that black people went to space," he tells one reporter. "White people have been going to space for years.") In another, he plays the only person of color on an archaeological team that discovers proof that humanity's earliest ancestors were black people, brought to Earth by extraterrestrial black gods. The punch line is that Pryor's character is left behind in the tomb along with these revelatory artifacts.

Robin was sufficiently unfamiliar to the staff at *The Richard Pryor Show* that some early call sheets and script drafts mistakenly refer to him as "Robert Williams," and he was not even given a speaking role in the pilot episode. But later installments provided him with extensive opportunities to shine, particularly a twelve-minute sketch satirizing a trial similar to the one depicted in *To Kill a Mockingbird,* where Pryor plays a rural Southern district attorney prosecuting a black man accused of attacking a white woman and Robin plays the man's Atticus Finch–like defense lawyer.

Dressed similarly to the attorney he played in *Can I Do It . . . Til I Need Glasses?,* Robin gives a closing argument on behalf of his railroaded client and what he unhesitatingly calls "the colored species": "How soon we forget what the Negro has done for you," he intones. "Who picked your cotton? Who tied their hair up in neat little bandannas and sang softly as they wet-nursed your little miserable children? Who taught you the meaning of *doo-dah*? How soon we forget, but I'm not going to let you forget." It is an uncomfortable speech, one aimed at the well-intentioned liberals of the 1920s as well as those of the 1970s, but Robin's delivery is stirring and sincere; for his troubles, he succeeds in freeing the defendant, but the jury finds the "carpet-bagging, Communist pinko Jewboy lawyer guilty of getting him off," and he is hauled out of the courtroom to be hanged.

In another satirical bit of button-pushing, Robin plays one of several passengers on a lifeboat from the *Titanic*, and the only one who defends Pryor's character from his fellow survivors who assail him with racial slurs — that is, until Robin learns that the overweighted lifeboat is sinking, at which point he declares, in his most dignified tones: "Ah, I see. Well, throw the nigger overboard, then."

The sketch mirrored a toxic behind-the-scenes environment at *The Richard Pryor Show*, where its volatile leading man was in danger of being tossed into the icy deep. From the moment that Pryor and NBC struck the deal that created the program, there was disagreement as to whether the comedian was going to star in an intermittent series of specials (his belief) or a weekly show (the network's); Pryor was further frustrated that the show would be broadcast at eight p.m., when it would have to be more family-friendly, and he was incensed that NBC made him eliminate the opening sketch from the first episode, in which he would have declared to the audience, "I'm on TV — *me,* Richard Pryor — and I didn't have to give up a thing," at which point the camera would pan down to show him nude below the waist (while actually wearing a body stocking).

In his anger, Pryor descended further into alcohol and cocaine abuse, and it amplified his paranoia and wrath. "It was a fraught setting," Sandra Bernhard said. "Fun, but there was drama going on every five minutes. Pryor would go to his dressing room, and because we were young, that was exciting and glamorous to see such a superstar talented person be in that state of mind. It wasn't boring. We would quickly do as much shooting as possible before we lost Pryor for the day, or he just went home, got in his Bentley and drove off."

As the program imploded, NBC allowed Pryor and his cast one final episode that featured a Friars Club–style comedy roast of Pryor. "Richard was relapsing and NBC just betrayed him and all of us, and so it didn't go that well," John Moffitt said of the overall experience. "But in terms of Robin, he got a chance to do his stand-up." When it was his moment at the lectern, Robin began with a few familiar jokes: "Look at me, I'm on national TV," he said in his fake-yokel accent. "I'm so happy I could drop a log." In his own voice, he added, with seeming solemnity, "This man's a genius. Now, who else can take all the forms of comedy — slapstick, satire, mime, stand-up — and turn it into something that'll offend everyone. No, this man doesn't want any frills on his show. All he wants is a loose director, a tight script and a warm place to rehearse."

Thus ended Robin's time on *The Richard Pryor Show,* along with the program. Its first episode was broadcast on NBC on September 13, 1977, pitted against ABC's unstoppably popular comedies *Happy Days* and *Laverne & Shirley,* and its last installment was shown three weeks later, on October 4. "It was sad," Robin said of the whole experience, "because he went into it with so much hope. That was the first chance I ever had to uncork on TV."

Laugh-In, which had debuted on NBC just a week earlier, on September 5, fared no better, never capturing the zeitgeist the way its predecessor did. However, under Robin's contract with George Schlatter, he was featured in *The Great American Laugh-Off,* an NBC comedy special that Schlatter produced later that fall. Recorded at San Francisco's Great American Music Hall and shown on

October 20, the special was largely a clearing-house for the performers who had never gotten their due on *Laugh-In*, and it became one of the first places that TV viewers got to see Robin perform his full stand-up act.

As Robin spins and sweats his way through his repertoire of characters and voices, at one point he gets tangled up in his own microphone cord, but without flustering, he ad-libs, "It likes me." (He also points to a sweat stain under his armpit and describes it as a "Soviet no-pest strip.") Then he flips through a notebook and, in his ersatz Russian accent, reads what he says is a love poem, but it is in fact a familiar and personal piece of family verse:

I love you in blue,
I love you in red,
But most of all,
I love you in blue.

Pivoting off the crowd's laughter he says, "I take you this way, then that way. Is old Soviet custom!" Then, before adopting the persona of his lewd Shakespearean actor, he adds, in the voice of a far-out California dude: "I know, wow, reality, what a concept."

In no time at all, Robin had already been involved with two failed television shows, and while *The Great American Laugh-Off* brimmed with tantalizing potential, it had not done much to further his career. In the weeks that followed, Robin's only other TV roles were a nonspeaking part on an episode of the ABC comedy-drama *Eight Is Enough,* as a member of a punk-rock band that considers buying the family home of Dick Van Patten and his children, and a nebbishy college student in a failed TV pilot called *Sorority '62.*

By this point, Robin had signed with Rollins Joffe, where one of the firm's responsibilities was to rein in some of this wildness. But Robin didn't make it easy for his managers. When they began dispatching him to auditions, they would sometimes get quizzical responses asking why they had sent a Welshman for the role; Robin was putting on foreign accents for his own amusement in these casting sessions. "Sometimes in those days I would sound almost English or Scottish," he later recalled. "Maybe after coming from Juilliard, my voice had a certain precision about it." When Stu Smiley prepared a short biographical summary that was kept in his client file, Robin told him that he was originally from Edinburgh; the Associated Press once reported unskeptically that Robin was "an Edinburgh, Scotland native whose folks moved to the United States when he was a tot." All his high-powered representatives could do was laugh and shrug.

And then, unexpectedly, Robin was handed the biggest break of his life — one that would call upon every skill he had developed and would require the alignment of all the planets in our solar system and beyond.

Midway through its fifth year, *Happy Days,* the second-most-popular series on television, was running low on ideas. The nostalgic ABC comedy about a wholesome group of friends in the 1950s had started the season with a clumsy multipart story line about Fonzie, its leather-jacketed rebel, traveling to Hollywood and accepting a dare to put on water skis and jump over a shark. And now, with just the slightest bit of desperation, Garry Marshall, the series creator, was turning for inspiration to his nine-year-old son.

Marshall, the avuncular TV mogul whose portfolio also included *The Odd Couple* and *Laverne & Shirley,* had reached the conclusion that the Fonz lacked worthy adversaries, and he sought the counsel of his son, Scott, who like most boys of the era was a rabid fan of the blockbuster science-fiction film *Star Wars,* which had opened the previous summer. "When I asked him, he wanted space people," Marshall said. "I remember going to the writers and saying, 'Let's get Fonzie an alien.' They mostly stared at me and rolled their eyes, but I was the boss. When I told my son that I couldn't have space people — there's no space people in the '50s — my son, because he watched a lot of TV, said, 'You'll make it a dream.' And that's what I told the writers. Make it a dream. And that was the episode."

As its title suggests, "My Favorite Orkan" was less a tribute to the intergalactic dogfights of *Star Wars* than an homage to the simple charms of bygone shows like *My Favorite Martian*. The episode, credited to the writer Joe Glauberg, tells the story of a friendly humanoid alien named Mork, from the planet Ork, who possesses supernatural abilities and is repeatedly confused, to comic effect, by Earth customs, language, and technology. His search for a perfectly average human specimen to take back to Ork initially leads him to Richie Cunningham (played by Ron Howard), but he is sidetracked into a series of contests with Fonzie (Henry Winkler), which Mork wins. As Mork prepares to claim the Fonz as his prize and kidnap him to outer space, Richie wakes up and realizes he has dreamed the whole incident.

The teleplay was not particularly beloved on the *Happy Days* set. When it was first reviewed at a table read in January 1978, about a week before production was to begin, costar Anson Williams said, "We got this script that was horrid. Horrible. . . . We were all embarrassed. We were used to great material. Garry says, 'Don't worry, don't worry — we got a week to fix it. It'll be better.' . . . So the next week we come in, we got the new script. It's worse. And we're going, all right,

166

gotta do it."

The show was also having trouble finding an actor to play the role of Mork. Marshall himself had wanted either John Byner or Dom DeLuise, both of whom passed on the role. Jerry Paris, the episode's director, had reached out to Jonathan Winters, but he was about to leave for a tour of Australia. Instead, the actor Roger Rees, an alumnus of the Royal Shakespeare Company, signed on for the part, only to withdraw early in the week. ("I can't do this role," he said. "He's not a real person.") With the show set to tape at the end of the week, Marshall visited the set and asked his cast: "Does anyone know a funny Martian?"

Al Molinaro, who played the show's kind-hearted diner owner, had studied in the Harvey Lembeck workshop, and he proposed Robin as a candidate. Robin was also familiar to Ronny Hallin, a producer and casting associate who was Garry Marshall's sister, who had heard about him from their other sister, Penny Marshall, who was one of Lembeck's students as well.

When Garry Marshall asked Hallin what kind of work Robin did, she told him, "He stands on a street corner, does a lot of voices and impressions, and passes the hat."

Marshall was unconvinced. "Are you kidding?" he said. "This is who you want me to hire?"

167

"Well, you've got to understand, it's an *awfully* full hat," Hallin replied.

"I thought that was a great line," Marshall recalled. "So I said, all right. Bring in the guy with the full hat."

That Wednesday, Marshall and Paris auditioned Robin in a marathon casting session of about fifty actors to fill the Mork role. On his way into their office, Robin encountered the comedian Richard Lewis coming out: "I told them I don't speak Norwegian," a dejected Lewis told him.

Robin didn't make any small talk when he came into the room. "He didn't say, 'Hi, you play golf?' or any of the nonsense most actors talk to you about," Marshall recalled. "He just was there to audition." But when he was asked to take a seat, Robin unexpectedly planted himself face-first on the couch and stood on his head. Then he reached for a nearby glass of water and pretended to drink it through his finger. "It went past where the script went, and he was quiet," Marshall said. "He was only loud when you said go. Before that, he didn't talk. We hired him."

On Thursday, January 19, Robin showed up to the Paramount lot to begin work on "My Favorite Orkan." Bobby Hoffman, the casting director, introduced the shy young stand-up comedian to the actors he would be working with, and they quickly said hello as rehearsals began for an episode that would begin shooting at seven p.m. on Friday night.

Robin carried with him a script that he had marked up with brief notes and pointers. On its ninth page, the stage directions described Mork's arrival at the Cunninghams' home and his entry into the pop-cultural consciousness:

The door opens and Mork, a spaceman wearing a very ominous-looking black helmet with face mask and silver space suit, is standing in the doorway. Richie doesn't look at him. Mork makes some rapid, high-pitched noises. He's speaking in his native tongue.

In his scribbly cursive handwriting, Robin wrote: "close encounters." The stage directions indicated that Mork "speaks in a weird, high-pitched voice whenever he's alone with Richie and a normal voice when other people are present," and following his brief opening lines — "I am Mork, from Ork" — Robin noted: "hand shake (vulcan)." That was his reminder to himself to extend a split-finger greeting, à la *Star Trek*'s Mr. Spock, to Howard. In the take used in the episode, he went a bit farther, adding in an adenoidal, rapidly spoken *"¿Qué pasa?"* then locking his hand with Howard's as he babbles alien-sounding gibberish.

Robin was going beyond the boundaries of

what had been written for him, but Marshall said these contributions were welcomed. "What helped matters was that the *Happy Days* actors were very secure," he said. "Henry Winkler and Ron Howard, they were not flibbertigibbets. So when they saw this talented man, who they didn't know from Adam either, they both gave him plenty of room to work."

Winkler, a graduate of the Yale School of Drama who had become one of television's best-known stars, said that there was no jealousy from him or Howard if Robin happened to be commandeering the spotlight. "It didn't matter," Winkler said. "That wasn't even in my mind. It was: if the show was successful, we have a job. If it's not, we're back on the unemployment line. So it never dawned on me that it was anybody's show. No one talked about fan mail, or fame, or status. We were an ensemble, and if you just gave yourself over to what he was doing, you would be where you were supposed to be."

From what he and Howard saw of him, Robin — who had been outfitted in a red jumpsuit with a silver triangle on the chest, silver gloves, and silver boots — was very clearly running away with the episode. "You would say something, no matter what the script said, and he absorbed it," Winkler said. "It was almost as if he sucked it in like a sponge. And then he would spit it back out, but then it would have been Robin-ized. It's an intangible. All of a sudden, you're amazed. You're amazed by the speed. You're amazed by the clarity. You're amazed by the originality."

Marshall, too, sensed that Robin was different from the other guest stars who came and went on Stage 19. "I'm not deaf and I'm not blind," he said, "and at the end of the show, when I introduced the cast, and I brought out Robin, who was the day player, the audience — three hundred people — stood up and gave him a standing ovation. I saw that and I heard that, and I said, 'Ooh, he's pretty good.' "

"My Favorite Orkan" was broadcast on February 28, 1978, and it was as popular as *Happy Days* had been all season; it was seen in about 23.8 million households, making it the second-most-watched show of the week, just behind the latest episode of *Laverne & Shirley.* It had been a great showcase for Robin, putting him in the guise of a character who shared his endearing innocence and his curiosity about a planet that its inhabitants took for granted.

At first, the episode's success seemed to pay no further dividends to Robin, beyond the satisfaction of a job well done. After the show aired, he resumed his stand-up comedy club work and appeared on *America 2-Night,* the TV talk-show parody with Martin Mull and Fred Willard, to whom he'd pitched many outlandish characters (including Edsel Ford Fong, the master of a cowardly form of kung fu called the "School of Flaming Chicken"; Rev. Oral Satisfaction, a Hollywood evangelist from the "Church of the Multiple Comings"; and an automated joke-generating robot called Comediatron) before being cast in the role of Jason Shine, a professional escort.

But behind the scenes, Robin was about to be rewarded by a serendipitous convergence of events he didn't even know was taking place. It started that spring, when ABC's programming team looked at the new shows being developed for the coming fall season and concluded that the cupboard was bare. "They look at all their pilots, and after they look through all the pilots, they say, 'We got nothing!' and they panic," Marshall said. "This is the modus operandi of television."

Marshall was getting ready to leave for a vacation when he was contacted by Michael Eisner, the top executive at Paramount, the studio that produced *Happy Days* and *Laverne & Shirley.* Eisner told him that ABC hated what it had for the fall and wondered if Marshall had anything new in the works. (As Marshall recalled the conversation, Eisner said, "They like you, so what else you got? Make up something.") In fact, Marshall had nothing in the pipeline, but he remembered

Robin's performance on "My Favorite Or-kan," and the audience's euphoric response to it: "I said, well, we had a kid on the show — and of course Eisner and the network never watched the show. It's been on for years. Why would they watch *Happy Days*? It's a hit? Good, fine, enough — this kid was on, who was really brilliant, and deserves his own show. He says, 'Good — it's a spin-off.' "

Making up the show on the fly, Marshall decided to set it in Boulder, Colorado, where he had a niece who was attending the University of Colorado. Asked for a title, Marshall said he wanted to call it *The Mork Chronicles,* "because he comes to Earth and he observes and he reports back." The response he received from ABC was, "Nobody knows what *chronicle* means." But, Marshall said, "There was a rule of thumb that they liked shows that you could name your pets after. So I said, I know what you want. You want *Mork & Mabel. Mork & Somebody,* right? Finally I said, how about *Mork & Mindy*? They said, '*Mork & Mindy*! We love it.' "

Out of nowhere and through no further effort of his own, Robin was being sought to star in his own network sitcom. As remarkable a prospect as this was for a young actor who'd never had a gig for more than a few weeks, his managers were unsure if they wanted him to take it. "We felt it would be a mistake to put him on television at that point," Larry

173

Brezner recalled. "I said, 'Garry, we really think this guy has a film career." But Marshall had a persuasive way of getting what he wanted, telling Brezner: "Look, we're just doing Robin. He's gonna wear his clothing. It will be him." Sensing that Brezner was coming around to the idea, he added, "This is television, Larry. We're not doing Greek theater."

Buddy Morra, Brezner's partner, was tasked with telling Robin he was being offered a TV show on the number one television network, produced by the studio responsible for the number one and number two sitcoms, with a guaranteed order of twenty-two episodes, rather than the thirteen that most first-season shows customarily receive. When Morra told him he'd be paid $1,500 a week, Robin, in his innocence, screamed excitedly on the other end of the phone, "Wow!" To which Morra, the old showbiz hand, replied, "Schmuck, it's $15,000 a week — I was just teasing you."

One question remained for *Mork & Mindy:* Who is Mindy? As Marshall saw it, she had to be a counterbalance to what Robin would bring to Mork: "It needs a Waspy, all-around, very American girl to go against this lunatic," he said. And the first actress who came to his mind was Pam Dawber, who had recently starred in *Sister Terri,* a failed TV pilot about a young nun who teaches and coaches gym at an inner-city parish while trying to raise her teenage sister. With no time to write or produce a proper pilot episode of *Mork & Mindy,* Paramount created a five-minute presentation reel combining footage of Robin in "My Favorite Orkan" with scenes of Dawber in *Sister Terri* and submitted it to ABC. Marshall was on vacation in the Virgin Islands when he got the call from Gary Nardino, the head of television production at Paramount: "Whatever you said to them, you sold it."

This was all news to Pam Dawber, who had no idea she had been cast in anything. Dawber, a twenty-six-year-old actress and former model with the prestigious Wilhelmina agency, was living in New York and had only just started breaking into television and film: she had played one of the guests in *A Wedding,* the Robert Altman ensemble comedy, and her exclusive TV deal with ABC had so far led to little more than an audition for the title role in *Tabitha,* a short-lived spin-off of *Bewitched.*

On Friday, April 28, Dawber received a call from her agent telling her that *Sister Terri* had not been picked up as a series, and she assumed that her ABC contract was over. That following Monday, May 1, Dawber's agent called her again: ABC had just announced its primetime schedule for the fall, and in the eight p.m. slot on Thursday nights was a show called *Mork & Mindy,* starring Robin Williams and Pam Dawber. An initial report in the *New York Times* tepidly described *Mork & Mindy* as "a comedy about a being from the planet Ork who meets an attractive earth person." "I never heard about it," Dawber said. "Now it's in the press, and when my agent reads me what this show's about, I was pi-*issed.*"

Dawber was somewhat placated by a conversation with Marshall, who told her about the making of "My Favorite Orkan." As he told her, "This guy doesn't stay on book. It's going to be totally different. It's going to be wonderful. 'See this, it's *fah*ny.' " And when she saw the episode for herself, Dawber was completely won over by Robin. "It was like, Sign. Me. Up," she said. "He was cu-*ute.* He was sexy. He was funny. He was so different. Not that I was anybody. But you hadn't seen anything like him. He was just shot out of a cannon."

Dawber did not met her screen-partner-to-be until she traveled to Los Angeles later that spring to shoot their first publicity photographs for a series that still had not filmed its first episode. "I'm in hair and makeup," she said, "and the hair and makeup person tells me that this Robin Williams guy is right next door. 'You've got to meet him. He's nuts.' " Dawber went in to introduce herself: "I said, 'Hi, Mork. I'm Mindy.' And

Robin was, on a real, soul level, a very shy guy. So he feigned this broken Russian accent — 'Oh, it's so nice to meet you. I don't know what to so say' — Only I didn't know he was feigning. I went back in and I said to the makeup person, 'Where's he from, is he Russian?' And she said, 'He's not Russian! He's nuts!' "

Later that night, Robin invited Dawber and a friend of hers to see him perform at the Comedy Store. By the end of the set, she was no longer worried whether she could stand to work with him and instead wondered whether she could keep up. "Oh ho ho — he was so brilliant," she said. "It was so smart. It was so sophisticated and warm and hysterical. I could hardly believe my luck, watching this guy onstage, and thinking, this is my partner — I hope I know what *I'm* doing and I don't get fired!' "

There was one more hurdle that Robin had to clear before he could begin work on *Mork & Mindy.* It was discovered that the contract he had signed with George Schlatter, the executive producer of *Laugh-In* and *The Great American Laugh-Off,* was so comprehensive that, under its terms, Robin could not permissibly work as a regular cast member in another TV comedy while it was still in effect. Though this deal predated his becoming a Rollins Joffe client, the firm now had to help him pursue a legal remedy that would allow his career to move forward. "He had signed an all-purposes contract with George Schlatter," Stu Smiley said. Before shooting began on *Mork & Mindy,* he said, "Robin went to court, every day, to get out of it."

For one of the first times, Robin would have to use the services of Gerald Margolis, an entertainment lawyer who would represent him for years to come. "The deal he was under with George Schlatter was very oner-ous, and Gerry got him out of it, so that he could do *Mork & Mindy,*" said Cyndi McHale, who would later become Margolis's girlfriend and then his wife.

Schlatter disputes that he did anything to stand in Robin's way or that the termination of his contract was anything other than amicable. "We had an agreement with Robin," he said. "We had done six shows, and we had an option for six more shows." But when Robin made his guest appearance on *Happy Days,* Schlatter said, "it was just obvious what was going to happen with him. They offered him a series. So we let him out to go do *Mork & Mindy.* You just can't hold on to people forever, you know? But I loved him. I just loved him."

Robin returned to the Bay Area in the spring to participate in a fund-raising concert for the Boarding House, a local venue that had featured him as a novice stand-up comedian and was now having financial difficulties. He was hardly the best-known name at this four-hour show, held at the San Francisco Civic Auditorium on May 17. But it was an opportunity for him to play in front of one of the biggest live audiences he'd ever had, about seventy-five hundred people, and to share a bill with performers like Steve Martin, Martin Mull, and Billy Crystal. Crystal had previously seen Robin perform improv with John Ritter in Harvey Lembeck's acting workshop and knew Robin was a promising talent. "When they went toe-to-toe, John was hilarious, but Robin was fearless," he said. "You could see right away, who's this guy?"

Robin saw things in a slightly different light: "We were very competitive at first," he said. "It was like two elks spraying musk. We were both marking our territory."

Crystal delivered a well-regarded routine of character pieces: a former boxer who now sells peanuts at the arenas where he used to fight; a weathered old black jazz musician who's working his way down the nightclub ladder, but still takes pride in his old lady, his music, and his horn. He thought he'd done fine that night, but when Robin came out a few performers later, he felt he was witnessing something monumental. "It was electric, and we all just sat there and went, 'Oh my god, what is this?' " Crystal later recalled. "It was like trying to catch a comet with a baseball glove."

In his twenty-minute set, Robin delivered a characteristic cross-section of the jokes he told to adult audiences: a mixture of drug humor, ethnic accents, and a monster-movie parody called *Attack of the Killer Vibrators.* But as the frenzied routine neared its end, after he had recited a few lines from his Shakespearean actor character, he transitioned to a self-doubting bit in which the different parts of his consciousness grapple with his fear that his act is falling apart as he is performing it. Or, as Robin put it: "Come inside my mind and see what it's like when a comedian eats the big one."

Beginning, in his own voice, with a confident declaration — "That piece was incredible! I'm fantastic" — he switches to a serpentine Peter Lorre character, who retorts, "No you're not, you fool. You're just using pee-pee ca-ca. You're nothing. You liar. You're not doing an act. No material. No substance. No truth." There are further assessments offered by his rational mind, his subconscious, and his intellect, which, as if it were a panicked radio dispatcher, calls out: "Mayday! Mayday! Mayday! All systems overload, anything goes now! Try anything! . . . Career over! Eating the big one! All alerts! Try Vegas ending!"

"Hey, you've been fantastic," Robin says as himself.

The intellect responds frantically, "Not buying the bullshit, you're over! Release honesty response!"

Robin desperately cries out, "Well, fuck you, what do you want from me anyway?"

Here, the crowded auditorium applauded, cheered, and hooted its approval.

Crystal was blown away by what he had just witnessed. "The audience knew him from performing in the clubs there, so he already had a following," he said. "But it increased, at least by one, from when I saw him. The closest I could make to it was Jonathan Winters, but it was at warp speed. He could say things that weren't really funny, sometimes, but there was a commitment to the mania that they would go nuts for. And you'd go, That's not really funny. But it would go over huge because *he* was doing it."

Crystal, who was about to return to Los Angeles for the second season of *Soap,* knew that Robin was preparing for his starring role in *Mork & Mindy,* and he envied Robin for it. "There was a level of jealousy, but it wasn't about his gifts," Crystal said. "It was that I was going to be confined to one character, and he walked around with a million in his mind, and had a character that would let him do all of them."

With the opportunity of a lifetime awaiting him, Robin and Valerie decided to get married that summer, just a few weeks before

Robin had to report to work. "It was just like, of course we were going to be together," Valerie said. "Now there's money and I didn't have to work, and he was starting to support us. He had managers and I get to lunch and shop. The next step is, what do people do in their twenties? They get married."

Robin held his bachelor party on the night of June 3, an evening that culminated at the Holy City Zoo, where several of his friends and fellow comedians performed long-form improvisational sketches for his entertainment. In a rare tranquil moment, one of the guests, Don Stitt, an actor and playwright, turned to Robin and asked him, "Hey, what's happening with your career?"

Robin replied, "I've just signed on for six weeks with a show that may be the *end* of my career." Stitt, who was headed to New York to pursue work on Broadway, told Robin that if he ever needed a job, he would get him a gig as a stage manager.

The next day, June 4, 1978, Robin and Valerie were married in an outdoor ceremony on a hill near Tiburon, overlooking the San Francisco Bay. Robin's half brother Todd served as his best man, and all the members of the wedding party dressed in white, including the bride, the groom, their parents, and their families. Rick and Ruby, the musical comedy act for whom Robin had occasionally opened in San Francisco, performed at the reception. Then the newlyweds traveled to Kauai for their honeymoon. For at least a couple of weeks, it felt as if the whole world belonged only to them.

Though Valerie had known Robin and his family for just a short while, she could see the influence that his parents exerted on him. "He had both of them very strongly implanted in him," Valerie said. "He was always delighting his mother, who adored him. His father was stern — he was a very serious, serious person. And I loved the Rob in him so much. I think that acceptance is what bonded us. I allowed and accepted him to be Rob. When he came home, he would sit and be quiet. He was very quiet, a lot, with me. And I liked that. I like a quiet person around the house. He was percolating."

When it was just the two of them, Valerie said, "We had a very rich life together, alone. I was his family life."

Robin went to Los Angeles in July to start work on the first episode of *Mork & Mindy.* The story, set in the present day of 1978, begins with Mork on his home planet of Ork, dressed in a slightly upgraded version of the red jumpsuit he wore on *Happy Days.* Standing in a barren, vaguely futuristic room and speaking to a blinking, egg-shaped beacon, Mork receives orders from his commander, Orson, to travel to Earth — "an insignificant planet on the far side of the galaxy" — to learn about its primitive societies and to rein in his own impulses for mischief-making. "These constant displays of humor are not acceptable here on Ork," Orson tells him in a booming monotone. "Emotions have been weeded out of us for the good of the race, and you constantly make jokes. I'm afraid that won't do."

Accepting his assignment, Mork rolls his eyes back in his head, twists his earlobes, and offers a strange alien salutation: "Nanu, nanu."

Mork pilots his egg-shaped spaceship to Earth, where he crash-lands on the outskirts of Boulder (followed by a second egg containing his luggage). There, he encounters Mindy, who is breaking up with a boyfriend who has gotten too frisky with her. Mindy mistakes Mork for a priest — he is wearing a suit and tie on backward — and walks back to town with him. By the time they have reached her house, she realizes that he is from outer space. At first, Mindy is fearful of her interstellar visitor, then excited to learn that alien life exists.

But Mork discourages her from revealing his secret to the wider world. "You see," he tells her, "my mission is to observe Earth, and the only way I can do that is by being one of you, a face in the crowd, which is easy because I fit right in."

"Not really," Mindy answers.

Together they forge a pact to teach each other about their cultures, and Mindy helps Mork argue his way out of a legal hearing where a prosecutor and a psychiatrist are attempting to have him declared insane. "While it's true that the defendant may add a new dimension to the word *eccentric,*" a judge finally rules, "there is no law against that."

Dale McRaven, the comedy writer who created *Mork & Mindy* with Garry Marshall and Joe Glauberg, and who wrote its debut episode, said that the appeal of the show rested in its promise of unrestricted creative freedom — a spirit that was embodied in Robin's portrayal of Mork and extended to nearly every other part of the program.

"Garry basically said, 'Look, if you do the show, do whatever you want to do,' and that was very intriguing, so he wasn't putting any limits on me," McRaven explained. "I came up with the idea of him being sent to Earth as a torture, basically for having a sense of humor. And I realized it was a good opportunity to make fun of ourselves."

Howard Storm, who directed the first episode and became the director of the series, said in the first week he worked with Robin, "I was frightened to death.

"We shot on Friday," Storm explained, "and we used to block cameras on Thursday and Friday morning. Wednesday, Robin didn't say a sentence that was written. I didn't hear a word of the script. And I thought on Thursday: 'This is it. I'm finished. It's over. What are we going to do? He doesn't know the lines. It's my responsibility.' And Thursday morning, he walked in at nine o'clock and he knew every line. Knew all his marks. What I realized is, he finally read the script that night. He had a photographic memory. He just looked the script over and had it. When he did, I thought, 'Oh, thank God, my job is safe. I don't have to become a shoe salesman.' "

At a time when nearly all of TV's top comedies were about friends or families who lived together — *Laverne & Shirley, Happy Days, Three's Company, All in the Family, One Day at a Time* — the notion of a sitcom where one lead character was an extraterrestrial with paranormal powers was genuinely daring. And, astonishingly, the earliest critical assessments of the show were enthusiastically positive. Reviewing the pilot, the *Los Angeles Times* wrote that it was "nothing less than uproarious" and "a prime contender for best new comedy of the season."

"The reason," the review continued, "can be summed up in two words: Robin Williams. . . . He's fantastic — wild, inventive, unpredictable. He's a major comedic talent with an arsenal that includes crazy voices, credible imitations, excellent timing and a zany spontaneity that makes him refreshing and immensely likable." The *Hollywood Reporter* wrote that *Mork & Mindy* was "this season's most innovative comedy, shedding a new spotlight on that old chestnut — human nature — and allowing it to glow in its own built-in comedy. Because Mork isn't human, our frailties are as much a subject of curiosity as anything else. Not knowing enough himself to be critical, Mork accepts what he sees on face value and turns the whole shady business of living into a series of misunderstandings which aim right for belly laughs, and hit the target." And the *Boston Globe* wrote that Robin "soon may be known as the funniest man on television."

On September 11, *People* magazine published a modest feature on Robin, accompanied by a photo of him wearing a feathered headband and spoons over his eyes; captured in mid-jump, he almost seemed to be levitating. And he was a sufficiently hot prospect to ABC that the network flew Valerie and him to New Orleans on Friday, September 15, so that they could be in the audience at the Superdome for the much anticipated boxing rematch between Muhammad Ali and Leon Spinks. While Ali was winning his championship belt back from Spinks, Robin was mingling in the stands with celebrity guests like Tony Curtis and Sylvester Stallone and appearing in an interview with the sportscaster

187

Frank Gifford, who seemed baffled by Mork's strange Orkan slang and generally unclear of who Robin was or why he was talking to him.

At eight p.m. the following Monday, September 18, *Mork & Mindy* made its debut on ABC. It was watched in 19.7 million homes, making it the seventh-most-popular show of the week and an instant nationwide hit. Robin was no longer just another striver peddling his comedy act at the Los Angeles clubs; he was a bona fide star, and soon everyone in the country would know exactly who he was.

5
THE ROBIN WILLIAMS SHOW

A fledgling comic with ruffled hair and shim-
mering eyes, wearing a pair of rainbow
suspenders to hold up his baggy pants,
wandered around Stage 27 on the Paramount
studio lot, where a set had been built to look
like the living room of a home in Boulder,
Colorado. This was his personal comedy
laboratory, a space for him to riff and ramble, and to mock everything that crossed his
field of vision. Maybe he'd pick up a stack of
bologna sandwiches and pretend to feed
them to a coleus plant — so that, he said, it
will "grow up strong and have hairy pistils
like its father." Or maybe he'd pick up a bric-
a-brac statue and speak into it like a microphone, singing an extemporaneous song he
called "The Beverly Hills Blues": "Woke up
the other day / Ran out of Perrier / I've really
paid my dues / Had to sell my Gucci shoes."
The cameras weren't even rolling, but the
studio audience was there, and he wanted
them to have fun.

189

Robin Williams was twenty-seven years old, and he hardly carried himself like a young man who had just won the Hollywood lottery. He still lived in the same modest apartment, decorated with oversize Japanese sci-fi posters, that he shared with Valerie and their parrot, Cora, who spoke three phrases: "Hello," "Buzz off," and "Birds can't talk." He still shopped in used-clothing stores, dressed himself in silk-striped tuxedo pants that he'd bought for fifty cents, a Brazilian *figa* charm, and a 1940 "Win with Willkie" button, and glided around the Paramount campus in a pair of black roller skates.

Though he tried to hang on to the bohemian life he'd been living, Robin was the biggest success story that the 1978–79 television season had produced. *Mork & Mindy* was on its way to becoming the third-most-popular program on the air — even more popular than *Happy Days* — and it was largely due to Robin's irresistible performance as the cosmically naïve title character.

"It was a good show because we were so unlimited," said Dale McRaven, *Mork & Mindy*'s cocreator. "Somebody would come in with an idea that they wouldn't dare pitch to another show — because they'd just be thrown out of the office — and they could pitch it to us and it would work fine, because the character and the situation were so unorthodox."

Most story lines focused on Mork's misunderstandings about Earth society, giving him a chance to comment on human nature and Robin the opportunity to show off his range as a comic actor. Mork might fall in love with a mannequin, accidentally get drunk on ginger ale, or use his Orkan abilities to shut off his emotions, only to have them come surging back with greater intensity. He would share a few meaningful moments with Mindy, her father, Fred (played by Conrad Janis), and her grandmother, Cora (Elizabeth Kerr), before ending each episode with a thinly disguised comedy routine, presented in the form of a dialogue with Orson where he'd share a newly learned lesson about life on Earth.

The formula was gentle enough that *Mork & Mindy* could be considered a family show, befitting its eight p.m. time slot, yet porous enough for Robin to slip in a few adult innuendos each week. When, after returning from a party, Mindy asks Mork why he described one of the guests as a hide-and-seek champion, he replies, "Isn't hiding in a closet for twenty-six years some sort of record?"

Robin believed that *Mork & Mindy* was a hit because of its simplicity. "It was about this cheerful little man doing very simple things — 'Mork buys bread' or 'Mork deals with racism,' " he explained. "Mork and Mindy were both very straitlaced and the charm of the show, I think, was in having Pam Dawber deal with me in normal, everyday situations — to which I would react in bizarre ways." Comparing it to the classic 1950s sitcom *The Honeymooners,* Robin said, "You know who Ralph Kramden was and you know who [Ed] Norton was; they were at their best in everyday situations and the simpler the better." If the stories ever became too complicated, he went on, "the show wouldn't have been nearly as effective."

Robin's reputation as a one-of-a-kind talent was spreading around the country and throughout the Paramount lot, where other stars would visit Stage 27 just to watch him rehearse and tape the show. One day it might be Henry Winkler and Ron Howard from *Happy Days* or Melissa Gilbert from *Little House on the Prairie;* another day it might be Ginger Rogers.

Whether or not Robin understood it or was willing to acknowledge it, he was the center of this universe. As Howard Storm, the director of the series, explained, "The other actors on the show were chosen for their abilities to respond to his improvisations and not be thrown by them. Everybody here is aware that this really is *The Robin Williams Show.* My job is to make sure Robin doesn't go so far off the wall that only seven people in the audience understand what he's doing."

Pam Dawber understood that her responsibility was to play the straight woman, a cheerful, smiling springboard for Robin to bounce off of. And she was happy to do it for Robin, she said, because he never behaved arrogantly toward her and they genuinely got along. "It was the greatest acting class I'd ever had," she said. "Because, lucky for me, Robin was such a nice person. He had such a gigantic heart. And I really loved Robin, and Robin really loved me. We just clicked."

But Dawber found it difficult to find her own place on the program. "I was hanging on by my fingernails at the beginning," she said. "I don't think they even understood where I fit into that show, probably until the fourth or fifth episode, when I realized the formula: I had to be the sane person. I was the eyes of the audience. And I need to be real, because he's so *un*real. You've got to have some place, a platform where the audience can view the craziness. So I calmed down and figured out how to memorize lines and not get eaten alive. Not that I ever felt that he would, because he was so kind."

"We could be in the middle of doing a take," she said, "and if he thought I was upset or lost, he would chase me all over the set, going, 'Dawber, are you okay?' 'Dawbs, are you okay?' 'Dawber-dog, Dawber-dog, what's going on?' He'd improvise stuff for the audience that never would end up in the show. But a couple times he burned me, and he didn't mean to, but he did. He'd toss me a ball all of a sudden and I didn't know what to do with it. He once made a comment, saying, 'What, do I have to improvise everything around here?' And I just shot him a look, and he chased me all over the set: 'Dawbs, are you all right? What's wrong, are you mad?' Shut up, leave me alone!"

Like Robin, Dawber had grown up in the Detroit area, and though she was three months younger, she became the big sister he never had, who scolded him when he showed up late to work (which was often) and berated him for his poor hygiene and crass behavior.

"He would just fart," Dawber said. "He would just sit on me and fart. 'God, Robin!' And it makes me sound like an elitist to even admit that I said this — but I did, because I was in my twenties, too — I said, 'God damn it, didn't anybody teach you manners? Were you raised by the help in the kitchen?' And he went: 'Yeah.' "

By and by, Dawber came to understand the alienated life Robin had led and how significantly it had been shaped by his parents. "He definitely was buttoned-down," she said. "They were very wealthy: He was a big executive and his mom was a socialite, and she was a lot of fun. I'm quoting Robin: 'She had her ladies' things.' And she was out and about.

And Robin was this little genius boy in this big house in Bloomfield Hills."

Howard Storm understood that he would never be completely in charge of Robin at *Mork & Mindy*. "You couldn't harness him totally," he said. "It's like a great horse, and you can't just run that horse at top speed all the time. You've got to somehow pull it back. With Robin, that's basically what happened."

Storm, a former stand-up comedian who had directed sitcoms like *Laverne & Shirley*, recalled that when he would give Robin a note or a suggestion for a scene, "He would take it twenty times further than you'd expect. 'Robin, to fill that moment, why don't you pour yourself a drink of juice?' Forget about that. He would juggle the juice, pour it from a distance, whatever. Something that no one else would do."

Viewers were left with the impression that Robin was making up whole portions of episodes — on the spot, while the cameras rolled — a false perception that Robin was often all too happy to indulge. During a press conference early in the show's first season, he led reporters to believe that each script contained large sections that were blank save for a single instruction: improvise. "It's about one-third of each show," he said at the press conference. "On Mondays and Tuesdays we work out all the shticks, and then we have to spend Wednesday trimming it all down because we have too much material." All that ingenuity, Robin explained, created a lot of pressure — on him. "Going from standup to situation comedy was no problem," he said. "But after a while I realized that falling into the same pattern each week could be a danger. So I had to work harder at keeping my material fresh and different."

Storm said that it was "not true at all" that *Mork & Mindy* writers would simply provide their star with generic stage directions like "Robin does his thing." "The show was scripted," he said. "His brilliance added to it." There were, of course, instances where he and Robin would work through a scene as written and then revise it to better suit their needs. While watching one sequence in which Mork was called upon to portray five different poker players sitting around a card table, Storm said Robin "would jump from seat to seat, and I realized that it was going to be too confusing for the audience, in a two-minute span, to remember who the characters were." Instead, Storm suggested to Robin, "Why don't we try doing an old Wasp and an old Jew, sitting in a park, playing chess? And so he loved that."

When Robin wasn't pleased with what was written for him, he found it hard to express his opinion constructively. Pam Dawber observed that when Robin was frustrated, he would mutter, under his breath, "This sucks!

This sucks!" But the realization that he was unhappy could tear him in two, between a person who felt legitimately dissatisfied and one who felt guilty for simply feeling that way.

Storm said that in those instances when he offered Robin a note that he didn't agree with, "he was so shy and childlike that he wouldn't question me. But as he walked away, out of the side of his mouth he would always say" — here Storm imitated Robin's clenched voice — " 'A bullshit note. Who gives a shit about that?' "

One day, Storm pulled Robin aside and told him, "Listen, Robin, I know there are two of you, and I don't like the other guy. I don't like him at all. So from now on, when I give you a note, if you do the other guy, I'm going to stop giving notes. If you don't like the note, just tell me. Or I'll give you notes in private. Or if you don't want any notes, I won't give you notes." The response he got from Robin was, "Oh, okay, Papa, I'm sorry." ("Papa" was Robin's nickname for the director, who had a woolly beard like Ernest Hemingway's.)

"All sitcoms do changes," Dale McRaven explained. "The script is a starting point. If they come up with something that works better, we always include it. Robin would always try something. And if it worked, we used it. Unfortunately, Robin's publicity people made it sound like Robin was just ad-libbing the show and there was no script. And that just wasn't true. Other people have to know what's being said so they can do their lines."

In one instance, McRaven recalled, "Robin came out and he adlibbed a joke in front of the audience. The joke died. And he said, 'Stop, I want to do that one again.' And he ad-libbed another joke, and that one died even worse. I've got to say this didn't happen often, but it happened this time. So he said, 'I've got to do that again, that was just dreadful.' And he came out the third time and he did the line that was originally in the script. And it got screams. Everybody thought he made it up."

The mythology of Robin's improvisational skills began to grate on the *Mork & Mindy* writing staff. When they could no longer hide their annoyance, they delivered a symbolic message to Robin, to remind him that he needed them as much as they needed him. "One week the writers sent down a blank script that said 'Robin does his thing,'" Garry Marshall said. "Robin quickly came up to the offices to say, 'That wasn't me! I don't say that!' A big fuss. We always gave him a script."

Often, Robin's improvisations were of a sexual nature, directed at the women in the cast. In one episode, Mork takes pity on Mindy's grandmother, Cora, who is growing old and seeing her close friends die, and he decides to turn himself into an elderly man so he can provide her with companionship. As Storm recalled the scene, "He goosed her with the cane. Now I'm standing there, watching this, and I'm thinking, oh, my God. And I just laughed. I thought she was going to turn and say, 'How dare you?' If I did that, the grips would probably come off the set and beat the shit out of me. 'How dare you stick a cane in a woman's ass? That sweet old lady.' There was nothing lascivious about it, in his mind. It was just Robin being Robin, and he thought it would be funny. He could get away with murder."

Pam Dawber was the most frequent target of these sexualized outbursts. "He would get bored," Storm said. "He'd be doing a whole paragraph, and in the middle of it, he would just turn and grab her ass. Or grab a breast. And we'd start again. I'd say, 'Robin, there's nothing in the script that says you grab Pam's ass.' And he'd say, 'Oh, okay' "

"When he would finish his moment and he'd go offstage, she would be there, continuing the scene," Marshall said. "He would take all his clothes off, he would be standing there totally naked and she was trying to act. His aim in life was to make Pam Dawber blush." In the service of that goal, Robin would sometimes blurt out risqué riddles instead of his scripted dialogue. On one occasion, Marshall and his writers found out in advance what riddle Robin was going to pose to Dawber and secretly supplied her with its solution.

"The riddle that Robin was doing that week was, 'What do you get when you cross an onion with a donkey?' " Marshall said. "The punch line was, 'You get a piece of ass that makes your eyes water.' So we told Pam the punch line. So Robin goes, 'What do you get . . .' And she slammed him. She delivered it perfect. And he just stood there, startled. 'You had help!' All the writers applauded her. One of the first times I saw him totally startled. And Pam loved that."

Dawber said she was never bothered by Robin's dirty behavior, and considered it his way of acting out gentle feelings of affection for her. "I had the grossest things done to me — by him," she said. "And I never took offense. I mean, I was flashed, humped, bumped, grabbed. I think he probably did it to a lot of people. But he certainly did it to me, because I was with him all the time for eight months out of the year. But it was so much fun. Somehow he had that magic. Even though, if you put it on paper, you would be appalled. But somehow, he had this guileless little *thing* that he would do — those little sparkly eyes. He'd look at you, really playful, like a puppy, all of a sudden. And then he'd grab your tits and then run away. And somehow he could get away with it. It was the seventies, after all."

Just weeks after *Mork & Mindy* went on the air, Robin was the subject of major profiles in *Time, TV Guide,* and the *New York Times,* among other publications, and in the spring of 1979 he appeared on the cover of *Time,* giving an odd wink to the camera while he sat with a small TV set in his lap, one with his own face on its screen. (When he joked that the only publications that had not yet featured him were *Popular Mechanics* and *Ebony,* a friend, Ernie Fosselius, created mock-ups of those magazines with Robin on their covers.) He and Valerie moved into an eight-room, $200,000 house in Topanga Canyon, joined by a menagerie that included Cora the parrot, an Alaskan malamute named Sam, some Polish chickens, and two iguanas named Mr. I and Truman Capote. For convenience, Robin continued to keep an apartment in Hollywood to be near the Paramount lot, and he bought himself a vintage Austin-Healey sports car to drive around Los Angeles, until it was stolen, at which point he replaced it with a silver BMW. Told by his landlord that he had witnessed the theft in progress, Robin asked why he had done nothing to stop it. The landlord replied, "Well, I saw them pushing the car down the street and I thought it was your comedian friends just borrowing it."

Any time Robin ventured beyond the Paramount lot, he was reminded how his celebrity had exploded. At a celebrity charity softball tournament held near the studio, he and his *Mork & Mindy* colleagues were making their way onto the field, while the stars of *Happy Days* were coming off. Fans were running up to Henry Winkler, seeking photos and autographs, until they noticed Robin getting out of his car and heading into right field.

"Everybody in the stands ran to right field," said Storm, who was playing for the *Mork & Mindy* team. "It was frightening. There were forty or fifty people at the most, but they started to run at him. And we all ran to right field to protect him, because we didn't know what the hell was going on. And then we had to beg them to please stay on the other side of the foul line and let him play. I kept thinking, Don't hit to Robin. Or if it is, make it a simple pop-up or whatever. Then when the game was over, we had to make a wedge around him and get him back to his car. We literally ran him back to his car, like the police make a wedge around somebody they're protecting."

Dawber was also getting her first taste of fame, and she felt that her life was not all that thrilling when she stepped outside the studio. "It was really a happening place," she said, "and so you got used to that. And then you'd go home. I wasn't even dating. I was so lonely. I was there, really, just to do *Mork & Mindy.* I didn't even have a boyfriend."

"Honestly," she added with a laugh, "I'd go home and watch TV. It wasn't all that cool."

But any time she looked at a magazine rack, she saw Robin's face smiling back at her, often in photos that did not include her. "Listen, I was just fighting for my life," she said. "Robin had management and I just had an ABC contract. So I realized I'm going to get pushed off of things. They were trying to build Robin, and we weren't a comedy team. I was the girl. It got real ugly there for a while. We'd hear: '*People* magazine wants to do a cover of you and Robin!' And then: 'Robin doesn't want to do it if you're on it.' *TV Guide:* 'No, it's got to be Robin alone.' Fortunately for me, people said, 'No, it's called *Mork & Mindy,* it's got to be both of them."

In those times when she learned she'd been denied a significant publicity opportunity, Dawber said, "I'd go to Robin, just absolutely distraught. And he'd go" — in his muttered voice — "Ah, those motherfuckers. I don't know anything about this."

But Robin found it unbearable to think that he might upset Dawber. "Oh, he couldn't stand it," she said. "My personal opinion of it was that he probably didn't get enough of his mother. We all are scarred growing up, and in high school. He blossomed once he got to

203

the West Coast and became this wonderful crazy person. But a lot of damage is done to all of us. Kids are mean. And so he probably saw himself as this little nebbishy boy. He'd make jokes about himself, like that. Women were very important in Robin's life, on many levels."

As Dawber saw him, Robin tried to portray himself as unconcerned about his emerging celebrity, when in fact he was desirous of it, and, on some level, certain that it would come his way. "Somewhere in his soul, he knew he had this destiny," she said. "He knew where he was going. He would talk about, 'When I get my star on Hollywood Boulevard . . .' I didn't know how that worked anyway. But I remember thinking, he knows he's really going somewhere. Did Robin ever go fight for me, that I'm aware of? No. But not because he was a bad person. Robin was just hyperactive and everywhere, and didn't like conflict. He didn't want to be in trouble with me. He didn't want to be in trouble with anybody. But he wasn't going to go lobby for me, because he'd probably forget ten minutes after he walked away from me."

While *Mork & Mindy* was enhancing Robin's status as a gifted comic actor, his reputation as an equally inventive stand-up comedian was boosted by a television special called *Live at the Roxy,* recorded at that Sunset Boulevard nightclub and shown on HBO, a pay-cable network that had only recently become available on a nationwide basis. Unlike his ABC sitcom, which had to play to viewers of every age and where Robin's every ad-lib or errant gesture got scrutinized by a standards-and-practices department, he faced no such constraints on this hour-long broadcast, which made its debut in October 1978.

In a pre-taped opening segment, Robin played every role in a parody of *To Tell the Truth,* a game show where celebrity panelists try to pick out a noteworthy contestant from a group of imposters who also claim to be this person. One by one, each character — a redneck in a cowboy hat; a Hispanic man in a mustache and fedora; a Russian in a blazer and T-shirt — makes an identical and mutually contradictory assertion: "My name is Robin Williams." That is, except for the Russian, who at first accidentally identifies himself as Hank Williams.

His routine proper commences with Robin striding through the audience and onto the stage, making a few startled remarks of wonder and gratitude ("Everyone I've ever known! There are people here I've slept with twice!") and throwing out one-liners that the dedicated fans of his comedy were starting to recognize as familiar — "I'm so happy to be here I could drop a log" and "reality, what a concept" among them.

After climbing up into the theater's balcony

and back to the stage, Robin settles into a series of oddball celebrity impressions — George Jessel on acid; Laurence Olivier delivering an endorsement for Ripple fortified wine — while the cameras in the theater show his famous friends in the audience, including Henry Winkler, Tony Danza, and John Ritter. These are followed by several of his well-honed character pieces, including the faith-healing televangelist Reverend Ernest Lee Sincere; the Soviet stand-up Nicky Lenin; and his Shakespearean actor, who does not miss a beat when a clubgoer, loudly and for no apparent reason, yells out the name "Mork!" Remaining in character, Robin answers, "Nay, not Mork. Nay, speak not to that TV or not TV. Whether it is nobler to do crazy shit at eight o'clock, and take up arms against the god Nielsen who will dare to put down taste, or sweat your ass off in a small club."

Late in the special, Robin steps offstage and returns as his old man character, wearing a beret and a pair of glasses while he pretends to be feeding some unseen pigeons. "I give the pigeons my methadone so they come back," he explains in a quavering voice. But by and large, this is not really a comic routine; it is a bittersweet character piece in which Robin plays a geriatric and enfeebled version of himself, some forty years in the future, when space aliens who are not as kind as Mork have overtaken the planet and have driven humanity into hiding. Addressing his audience as if they are fellow survivors of this invasion, he offers them some advice on how to live through incomprehensible times:

From me to you. You got to be crazy. You know what I'm talking about? Full goose bozo. 'Cause what is reality? You got to be crazy. You got to! 'Cause madness is the only way I've stayed alive. Used to be a comedian. Used to, a long time ago. It's true. You got to go full-tilt bozo. 'Cause you're only given a little spark of madness. If you lose that, you're nothing. Don't. From me to you. Don't ever lose that, because it keeps you alive. Because if you lose that, *pfft.* That's my only love. Crazy.

Then in the show's final segment, Robin pulls John Ritter onto the stage for what is supposed to be a round of Second City–style improv; an audience member shouts out a suggested scene about a waiter serving a lonely man in a restaurant, but the bit gradually degenerates into Robin and Ritter exchanging dick jokes and platonic ass-grabs.

That November, on the kind of whim that occurs to someone who can suddenly have his every whim fulfilled, Robin decided to fly across the country and attend a broadcast of *Saturday Night Live* in New York. Traveling with Valerie and Stu Smiley, he was there to take in the performances of cast members like John Belushi, who were starting to become his friends; the deadpan comedy star Buck Henry, who was hosting that episode; and the Grateful Dead, that week's musical guest. But there was a complication: along with the Dead's mellow vibes and meandering guitar solos came members of the Hells Angels, the outlaw motorcycle club that revered and looked out for the band. This created a problem for Robin, who in his stand-up routine had been known to ask his audience, "Are there any Hells Angels here tonight?" And then, when that line invariably yielded no response, he would add: "Those pussy-whipped faggots."

So it was not entirely surprising that a posse of Hells Angels, including their brutish, barrel-chested New York chapter president, Vincent "Big Vinny" Girolamo, confronted Robin backstage, crowding around him and Smiley and preventing them from leaving. Smiley, who was morbidly transfixed by the tattoos running up and down Big Vinny's arms, got a leather-clad finger buried squarely into his sternum and could just barely stutter out the words, "Can I help you?" The bikers made clear, in varying tones and degrees of bluntness, that they had heard Robin's joke about the Hells Angels in his recent HBO appearance and wanted him to take it out of his routine. Then the horde dispersed, leaving Smiley quaking while Robin was seemingly unaffected. Back in Los Angeles, Robin excitedly related the story to his lawyer, Gerry Margolis, chuckling at the narrowness of his escape. Margolis didn't find the tale funny; he explained to Robin that one of the gang members who had accosted him was also charged with and later acquitted of murdering a concertgoer at the Altamont Speedway Free Festival. The Hells Angels joke was excised from future showings of the HBO performance.

Though Robin tried not to take his increasing visibility too seriously, he could not avoid giving in to certain fundamental rules that governed Hollywood media. He hired a prominent publicist, Estelle Endler, who also represented Rodney Dangerfield and Andy Kaufman, to help manage and cultivate his press coverage. Her memos to him were often methodically detailed do-and-do-not lists of behavior for his interviews. Just before he sat for a *New York Times* profile, she instructed him, "Please bring some toys and improvise. PLEASE try to stay *in* your clothes and *out* of your glasses. When the interview itself starts at 1 P.M. in your trailer, I'm not allowed in. This does not mean that you forget you're being interviewed. The Times is the best newspaper because their reporters are the roughest. If you don't want to see it in print don't say it."

That December, Robin signed up to record his first comedy album with Casablanca Records, a label that was flying high from the success of acts like Donna Summer, Kiss, and the Village People. Buddy Morra, at Rollins Joffe, oversaw the record project and decided to pair Robin with Bennett Tramer, a screenwriter who had previously helped Robin write the parody of *To Tell the Truth* that had played at the start of *Live at the Roxy.*

"Normally, he wouldn't have needed me," Tramer said, "but his schedule was such that he was doing *Mork & Mindy* all the time, and his material was so visual, they were worried he needed someone to make the act more verbal. In terms of a club performance, it was great how all over the place Robin was. But on a record album, you're so used to beginnings, middles, and ends. So I was there to do that. We'd sit in my apartment and work stuff out, and go right to the Comedy Store or the Improv and do it."

Tramer and Robin bonded over their love of vintage Hollywood and character actors like George Jessel and Peter Lorre; repeated listenings to a bootleg recording of Jonathan Winters improvising a brutally ribald coupling between his characters Maude Frickert and Lenny the Hired Hand; and a shared passion for toy soldiers. "When I said I had a collection, he really freaked out," Tramer said. "He came to my apartment, and said, 'Where are the toy soldiers?' I had to dig out these boxes that I hadn't opened up — big bags of soldiers, cowboys and knights, and he really got off on all that stuff. You're so powerless as a kid. The adults have power, and you're told children should be seen and not heard. But his imagination was so great."

From their discussions about Robin's stand-up material, Tramer learned that there was often a thought-out structure underpinning what looked like his scattershot and impulsive actions. "Even someone like him, where you think it's just lightning-fast, there was a real logic to it," Tramer said. "It seems scattered and grab-bag, but it's very coherent, organized thinking."

He also noticed the way that stock characters and voices crept into Robin's act — caricatures of blacks, Jews, gays, Asians, and others, that were not meant to be derogatory but were caricatures nonetheless — as throwaway accents that would occasionally supersede his own natural, elegant intonations. So far as Tramer could tell, Robin's attraction to these groups seemed to stem from their marginalization — his understanding that in the upside-down hierarchy of comedy, their otherness gave them power he would never possess. "So much of comedy is standing on the margins, looking at the majority and poking fun at them," Tramer said. "He was a

Wasp, and he was a wealthy Wasp. It's not that funny being a Wasp. That might be the fascination, not only with Jews, but with black culture, which he would love to do."

On January 27, 1979, Robin won a Golden Globe Award for Best Actor in a Comedy Series, besting a field that included his friend John Ritter from *Three's Company,* Alan Alda from *M*A*S*H,* and Judd Hirsch from *Taxi.* Though that year's ceremony was not broadcast on TV, the *Los Angeles Times* reported that Robin accepted his trophy "by turning to the audience and grabbing himself."

In the spring, as *Mork & Mindy* was hitting number one in the Nielsen ratings and reaching nearly twenty-six million homes nationwide, Robin set out on a series of short tours to record and perform material for the album, accompanied by the members of Rick and Ruby, the comedy music act for whom he had previously opened in the avant-garde clubs of San Francisco and which was now opening for him. The tour started at San Francisco's Boarding House and reached its zenith with a five-day run at the Copacabana in New York. Robin would take home about $35,000 from these shows, which were immediate sell-outs.

The Copa was no longer a top-flight venue for live performance — one writer described it as a backdrop of "chrome-and-plaster palm glitz" against which Robin himself played like a "hilarious sight gag," dressed in a Hawaiian shirt, ill-fitting pants, and his trademark rainbow suspenders. By now, the identities of the characters he played, the trajectories of their monologues, and the divisions between them had been cleanly worked out: Nicky Lenin, the Soviet stand-up; the televangelist Reverend Ernest Lee Sincere; the postapocalyptic old man, who now had a name, Grandpa Funk. In between these longer bits were Robin's freely associative non-sequitur scenarios: Truman Capote as a first-grader, offering a savage assessment of *See Dick Run* ("This isn't writing, it's typing"); "Goldilocks and the Three Bears" as told by William F. Buckley Jr. ("Goldie, an Aryan stereotype, and Lox, a Jewish soul food, combined to form a bourgeois archetype, who in time comes in contact with three bears, dark bears, maybe brown bears, maybe black bears, let's just call them Third World bears").

Anyone who had seen Robin's stand-up would have been familiar with these routines, and those who watched him do it in successive shows were becoming well versed in how the magician assembled his illusion. "It wasn't a work of improvisational genius — 90 percent of the show was the same from night to night," said Joshua Raoul Brody, a band member with Rick and Ruby. "His genius was making it seem fresh and having a catalog of one-liners to respond to just about any situation, and made it look like he was making stuff up on the spot."

The reviews for his Copacabana shows were almost universally ecstatic, but more crucially, they articulated how Robin Williams was a different person from Mork, who was by far the better known of the two. Robin shared Mork's sweetness and his compassion, but behind the character was a man of estimable intelligence and a full understanding of the power it gave him. As one critic observed, "I get the feeling that if Williams were to let it all out, his audience would need a scholastic aptitude test to get in the door."

These themes were picked up in the *New York Times'* review of Robin's opening night:

It's extraordinary that anyone as funny as Robin Williams can also create the impression of being so nice. . . . Mr. Williams doesn't need sex, malice or self-deprecation to round out his repertory. He doesn't even need real experience, or even real jokes. Mr. Williams simply assumes the manner of a small boy impersonating a stern, grown-up hero and whizzes from one crazy proposition to the next with cheerful aplomb. When the crowd responds appreciatively . . . he seems to beam with sweet, uncomplicated pride.

As Robin was enjoying the embrace of the

critics, he was also being accepted into an elite society of celebrity. Following his opening night at the Copacabana, at an after-party at the Sherry-Netherland Hotel, he was welcomed by the *Saturday Night Live* stars Bill Murray and Gilda Radner, Dick Cavett, Andy Kaufman, Gene Simmons, Robert Klein, Lucie Arnaz, Peter Allen, and Andy Warhol. (As Bennett Tramer recalled, "I remember Bill Murray delivering one of the all-time great lines: 'Mom, meet Andy Warhol.' ") The following day, Robin and Warhol went shopping at thrift stores. The comedy tour continued through the Midwest, where Robin's shows in Detroit drew the likes of Diana Ross and the Jackson 5, before concluding at the Universal Amphitheatre in Los Angeles.

The itinerary was not always an unending procession of glamour. Brian Seff from Rick and Ruby said that after many performances, they were likely to be welcomed by "this complete throng that was hanging around Robin, of press and media and hangers-on. They're all bothering Robin who, incidentally, when he would get offstage, you could smell him from twenty feet away. He had the world's worst b.o. of anybody I've ever encountered. Because he's hairy, and he'd work up such a sweat onstage. You could not get anywhere near him. But that didn't seem to bother the people that were just wanting to hang. They didn't really want to give him time to freshen up. It was just like, we want to see him as soon as he gets offstage — don't allow him a moment to just chill for a minute or two."

Other distractions abounded as well. "He was famous, so women were throwing themselves at him," said Seff. "But also, every drug dealer was giving him stuff."

The adulation, coming so quickly at Robin and from seemingly every direction, was not always easy for him to process. A few months into his run on *Mork & Mindy,* Robin was in Beverly Hills, where Jack Lemmon stopped him on the street and told him, "I think you're the most talented guy to come along in the last five years." When Robin later told Tramer about this encounter, he was plainly torn between wanting to accept the compliment and worrying that he could not meet such outsize expectations. "It was part, 'Isn't that fantastic?' and part, 'Do I really deserve that?' " Tramer said. "His reaction was not self-deprecating, necessarily, but, 'How do I live up to that?' 'This is happening too fast.' Not, 'Isn't that the greatest thing?' It threw him a little."

Later, during the live tour, Robin met Bruce Springsteen, expecting that the young rock musician would share his secrets to navigating fame and its pitfalls, and finding that Springsteen hoped to hear the same from him. "Robin went out in Bruce's Corvette," Tramer said, "and he asked Robin, 'How do you handle it?' — meaning, how do you handle stardom? Like they had a disease or something."

Many people who had been close to Robin before his upsurge of fame were realizing that their relationship with him could never be the same as it was before. "It really changed," said Sonya Sones, a friend who had started dating Bennett Tramer. "It's like the Big Bang, when a universe suddenly springs into being." If she and Tramer happened to be out on a date together with Robin and Valerie, Sones said, "People were completely starstruck. They were coming at him, asking for autographs and saying, 'Nanu, nanu' and wanting pictures taken. But as a result of his meteoric rise, other people who were also meteors in their own right began seeking him out. It's as though people who are at that level of talent and fame, they're almost like in a club together. Only they can understand what it's like to have that happen to you."

Often these fellow celebrities seemed to have no use for Robin's civilian friends. "Since Bennett and I were not famous, some people would just look through us and move on," she said. How Robin was adjusting to this abrupt elevation of status wasn't clear, either. "I think he was loving it," she said.

"But I think it was in some ways overwhelming."

Robin's first album, titled *Reality . . . What a Concept,* was released in the summer of 1979. It was sloppier, less intimate, and less personal than the routines he had delivered onstage and on TV. His now familiar lineup of characters had been steered hard toward delivering punch lines and eliciting laughter, at the cost of their underlying humanity. There was nothing sentimental anymore about Grandpa Funk, who is no longer implied to be an aged version of Robin himself, and who says things like, "Come here, I'll gum you. Because that's about all I can do with this." The televangelist, now called Reverend Earnest Angry, offers this homily: "You know, friends, comedy can help you. You know, life's like a big fan. And sometimes the ca-ca hits it. But comedy can be your shield. It can help you laugh it away."

The only time that Robin is really heard speaking as himself is when he is setting up his Shakespearean actor routine and asks his audience to suggest a topic from the news that he can improvise off of; someone is heard shouting out, "Robin Williams!"

"Robin Williams? Who's he?" he asks.

"Mork," comes the reply.

"No, no, no, my child," Robin answers. "We are not doing that tonight, man. No, no, I'm free from that now, Massa Bob. No, I don't have to 'nanu' for a while. We're doing something different. Five months ago he couldn't say his own name. Thanks to your dollars, he's learned to go 'nanu, nanu.' And you could have your very own series."

By now, audience members are heard chanting, "Mork! Mork! Mork!"

"An angry mob!" says Robin. "Shh, wait, time-out. I have to explain one thing. I ain't doing Mork, because this is why I perform here. To do something different." The crowd applauds and he continues with the routine.

The cover of *Reality . . . What a Concept* was a fuzzy portrait photo of Robin, caught in mid-expression, with a seeming smirk or a look of surprise on his face, while the interior record sleeve offered multiple depictions of him as his various alter egos: the reverend, in a seersucker suit with a Bible in hand; Nicky Lenin, in a Soviet T-shirt with a duffle bag at his feet; Grandpa Funk, wearing a trench coat and eyeglass frames with no lenses. The sleeve also carried a modest personal inscription from Robin: "This album is dedicated to Laura Berry Smith," though he gave no indication that this was his mother. He was equally cryptic about the series of people he offered thanks to by their first name only, including "Rob, Miss V., Todd, Laurin." More explicitly, he offered special thanks to Jonathan Winters "for giving me the spark."

Like the live shows that had spawned it,

Reality . . . What a Concept received glowingly positive appraisals. *People* magazine declared, "If nothing else, this LP of live nightclub routines proves that Robin Williams is like a butterfly in harness on a network sitcom. For while he is a delight as Mork, TV inevitably constrains his dizzyingly bountiful imagination. It's no loss that he doesn't do Mork here." The review added, "Comedy LPs are frustrating — Williams' 'Death of a Sperm Ballet' is obviously a visual bit and he takes easy laughs by imitating a drunk or just mentioning the word 'drugs.' That doesn't prevent his stand-up stuff from being as good as the best of Hope, Bruce, Cosby, Carlin or Pryor." By that fall, Robin's album was in the Billboard Top 10 (alongside rock albums like Led Zeppelin's *In Through the Out Door* and Supertramp's *Breakfast in America*) and had sold more than half a million copies.

Everything seemed to be going Robin's way; there was almost nothing to which he applied himself that did not result in immediate, staggering success. When Robin got his *Time* magazine cover, his friend Bennett Tramer extended his congratulations to Robin's publicist, Estelle Endler, telling her, "Isn't this great?"

To Tramer's surprise, Endler answered, "Not really."

"Why?" Tramer asked.

"I helped get him there," she replied.

"So why isn't it great?"

"Well," she answered, "don't you realize you have to build up these big stars so they can tear 'em down?"

6
MORK BLOWS HIS CORK

It was just another night at the Improv in Manhattan until Robin dropped in for a guest set. He liked to come to the city when he could get away for a weekend, to catch that fix he could find only in the New York clubs. The crowds there were unforgiving and the possibility of failure felt like a dangerous proposition, not like in Los Angeles or San Francisco, where audiences had been conditioned to anticipate his surprise performances.

Rich Shydner, a friend and fellow comedian, was emceeing when Robin made his unannounced appearance, and it was one he would always remember. "Of course the place goes crazy," Shydner said. "He just destroyed for like forty minutes. Everything he did got a laugh." Afterward, Shydner was backstage with Robin, watching other performers get washed away in his wake — "The next two acts just died, it was a wasteland to have to follow that, it was nuclear" — when Robin said something unexpected. "He didn't say it to me, in particular," Shydner recalled. "He just said it to himself. He had this worried look on his face. He just went, 'I don't even know what's funny anymore.' I'd never experienced that. There might be some guys that would go, 'I'll just take whatever I do for a laugh, and just run with it, and that's great.' He was concerned that he was losing a grip on what's funny and what's not. Which is, I think, every true comic's concern."

For nearly a year it seemed as if Robin could do no wrong. His sitcom was a smash hit and his record album had become a best seller. His beaming face adorned all kinds of *Mork & Mindy* merchandise, including T-shirts, trading cards, board games, and action figures. He had become so recognizable that he no longer went out in public wearing his rainbow suspenders — a formerly inseparable piece of his personal identity that had been commandeered by his TV alter ego — so that children would not approach him to ask if he would take them into space with him. His outsize stature did not make him invulnerable; instead, it forced him to confront a range of problems on a scale he had never previously experienced. And there were very real problems for him to worry about.

In the March 1979 issue of *Los Angeles* magazine, atop a gossipy column called The Insider, there appeared a one-paragraph item alleging that Robin had plagiarized some of his material from other stand-up comics. The item said that a "group of young L.A. comedians" — no names were given — claimed that Robin had been coming to their shows at the Comedy Store and stealing their lines for later use on *Mork & Mindy*. Some of these comedians, the item said, would not play at the club if Robin was there, and one unnamed performer was said to have thrown Robin against a wall and ordered him to pay him $300 for the parts of his routine he believed had been lifted, a shakedown that Robin supposedly agreed to. The item concluded by saying that this group of comedians was too intimidated to defy Robin's powerful managers at Rollins Joffe but added that they "also realize that national air play can kill their best jokes."

A few days later, this story was carried to the East Coast when it was picked up by Liz Smith in the New York *Daily News*. Again, no names or specifics were given, though Smith's account repeated the story of the anonymous accoster who "threw TV's brightest talent up against a wall and demanded payment for some bits," adding that "club regulars claim that Williams paid up."

Then in April, the *Chicago Tribune* weighed in with a lengthy feature story that explored these claims in greater detail, and the picture it painted was deeply unflattering. While it noted the enviable challenges that Robin faced for having a massive television audience, an army of fans, and a lexicon of signature lines that "are thrown back at him like half-eaten jelly beans," the paper said that he had a more significant problem: "In the close-knit West Coast comedic community, he is becoming known for 'borrowing' lines and concepts from other performers — stealing material, to put it bluntly."

The *Tribune* cautioned that, historically, performers like Milton Berle, Lenny Bruce, and Freddie Prinze were also "notoriously light-fingered," and it revisited some possibly apocryphal stories about W. C. Fields, who was said to have had a vaudeville rival's legs broken for stealing one of his routines, and Shecky Greene, who refused to play a Las Vegas show until a thieving comedian was thrown out of his audience.

The story went on to catalog several jokes that Robin had used, either in his live act or on *Mork & Mindy,* that were the likely property of other comics. The recurring bit in which Robin would announce, "I'd like to show you something I'm extremely proud of," and then start to unzip his fly, was said to have originated with Charles Fleischer; and the line "Reality, what a concept," which became the title of Robin's landmark record album, supposedly belonged to Biff Manard. The article

225

also made the case that one of Mork's lesser catchphrases, "What's happening, plasma?" — a line he would often address to his young friend Eugene (Jeffrey Jacquet), and a deliberately comic misinterpretation of "What's happening, blood?" a bit of black slang — had been taken from John Witherspoon, an actor and comedian who had appeared with Robin on *The Richard Pryor Show,* and who had a years-old routine about a friend who had moved to Beverly Hills and started saying, "What's happening, plasma?"

Witherspoon told the *Tribune* that he had confronted Robin about the alleged theft. "His answer was, 'Well, I ad lib a lot. If I used your line, I'll pay you,'" Witherspoon recalled. "And I said, 'You can't pay me because 40 million people saw that show. If you gave me a dollar for every one of those people, that would be great. But otherwise it's not even worth it.'" The story also quoted veteran comics like Tom Dreesen, who vouched for Witherspoon's authorship of the line, and Tim Thomerson, who said he had been threatened by Robin's managers for performing a bitingly satirical impersonation of Robin in his stand-up act. ("I took his stance, with my hand on my hip, and said, 'Oh, I'll use *that,*'" Thomerson explained. "It got a big laugh from the comics in the audience who knew what I was referring to.")

Robin, while wounded by these personal

indictments, flatly denied them. "There's no truth in it," he said. "Those are all my friends and I don't want to bad-mouth any of them." Several of his colleagues rallied to his defense. Howard Storm, his director at *Mork & Mindy,* said the less prosperous comedians were jealous of Robin's accomplishments. "When you're a success, it's the same old charge," he said.

Other performers who knew Robin in this era say there is no easy answer to these allegations. Few if any of them believe that he acted with malice or that he ripped off other people's jokes with the deliberate intention of trying to pass off their original work as his own. However, several say that they saw a pattern of behavior that, if it did not amount to outright plagiarism, still resulted in his repeating bits, lines, characters, or tropes that previous performers had originated, sometimes without his realizing that he was doing it.

Some comedians say that Robin's borrowing fell into a gray area that was considered tolerable by the ethical standards of the industry. "Robin would see something and he'd appreciate it for what it was and how good it was," said Jim Staahl, who performed with Robin in the Comedy Store Players and joined the cast of *Mork & Mindy* in its second season. "And then he would incorporate it and do it his way, and add something to it.

We used to call it the 'sweet steal.' You'd see somebody's bit and you'd go, 'They're doing it wrong. Here's my variation of it.' There were times he could do a variation of somebody else's material and the audience wouldn't know."

Not everyone agrees that even this much replication is permissible. Richard Lewis, a friend and fellow comedian, said he could understand if some comics considered this unforgivable. "Robin could take a premise or a joke and then go off on it and make it better, because he was a genius," Lewis said. "But a premise is gold. If a young comic has four, five minutes and he's going to go on *The Tonight Show,* and all of a sudden, Robin does three of his jokes, he's fucked. So yeah, there's real reason for some of these people to have tremendous hostility."

But there was also a part of Robin, friends said, who repeated other people's words and ideas unknowingly and unconsciously — the result of a rapidly firing mind that absorbed nearly everything and resurfaced old ideas that he believed were his own inventions.

There would be times when Robin realized, after the fact, what he had done, and he would be filled with regret and a desire to make amends. "Something would be in his head, and then it was like, *pop,* his synapses would go so fast," said Staahl. "Something would come up. And later he would go, 'Oh, crap, that was so-and-so's line. I swear to God, it was innocent.' "

While Robin was performing at the Copacabana in New York, he went shopping one afternoon with Monica Ganas and Joshua Raoul Brody from the Rick and Ruby band, then got in a cab to head back to the theater. "It was rush-hour traffic, so it was a slow cab," Brody recalled. "As they were getting into the cab, Monica told Robin a story about something that had happened to her cousin. And by the time they were getting out of the cab, Robin was telling the same story back to Monica, as if it had happened to somebody else. In the course of a cab ride, he had forgotten where he had heard the story." As to any accusations of misappropriation that Robin may have faced, Brody said, "I offer guilty with an explanation, your honor. It was a disease, it wasn't theft."

Much later in his career, Robin would take a more defiant stance on these allegations. "If you hang out in comedy clubs, when I was doing it, almost 24-7, you hear things," he said then, "and then if you're improvising, all of a sudden, you repeat it, going, 'Oh shit.' My brain was working that way." For a time, he said he simply stopped going to clubs, for fear that he would be accused of trolling for other people's material. "I was also like the bank of comedy," he said. "I went, 'Oh shit, here, here you go, here's money, I'm sorry. I didn't know that. Oh shit.' . . . And then after a while, I went, 'I bought that line already. I'm sorry.' And then you have to pay again."

But as long as he was giving audiences something that no other comic could provide, Robin felt he had nothing to worry about: "The truly unique guys don't give a fuck," he said.

Whatever Robin may have done deliberately or accidentally, Jamie Masada, the owner of the Laugh Factory, said he was motivated by a worthwhile goal that eventually got out of hand. "He had an addictive personality," Masada said. "He became so addicted to laughter. Sometimes he wanted to make everybody laugh so bad. He didn't need to steal material."

But now that Robin had been labeled a joke thief, he was going to find that, whether he fought back vehemently against the accusations or did not respond to them at all, a cloud was now hanging over his head and there was nothing he could do to make it go away.

Home could still be a refuge for him, when Robin was there. In a *TV Guide* profile from this period, he tenderly declared that he had Valerie to thank for whatever he had accomplished or amassed to this point. "Valerie is my inspiration," he said in the interview. "She is my grounding point to keep me centered."

But friends who knew the couple could see that they were struggling with the rapid acceleration of Robin's fame. "He was young, and it's a strange thing to go from being known as this real funny guy in the clubs to being a huge star," said Bennett Tramer. "And you can imagine, it's a strain on a marriage. You just get married, and then literally, two or three months later, your husband is the biggest star in the country: 'It was just my husband and me, and now the whole world wants a piece of him.' Marriage is a great thing, but you don't want to have it exposed to the whole world a month or two after it happens. They were great together, but she certainly paid her dues."

At times, Robin could be unexpectedly cutting or callous in how he spoke about Valerie. At a press conference for *Mork & Mindy,* when he was asked how his wife was handling his "skyrocketing success," Robin answered, "Pretty well, I think. She lives in Louisiana now — but she keeps in touch by mail. 'Our boy is growing up,' she writes."

One night, Valerie was in the audience at the Comedy Store with Brian Seff, their friend from Rick and Ruby, as they watched Robin finish up a set. Robin was holding forth on the strangeness of being famous, and he said to the audience, "There's girls that just come up to me. I've never seen them before, and they're like, 'Excuse me, would you — ?" At this point in the riff, Robin pointed at his crotch.

"He's saying it like it's a hardship," Seff recalled. "And Valerie yells, 'Oh, you love it.' " There was no question that Robin had heard her remark from the audience because he reacted to it: "Oh, now my wife's heckling me," he responded.

Robin could be a good husband when he focused on his marriage, but he was an easily distractible person, and his occupation provided him with an unrelenting succession of pleasurable distractions. "Robin was like a giant puppy: 'Let's play. Let's goof around. Let's do something,' " said Jim Staahl. It didn't help matters that his work schedule at the show offered plenty of downtime and allowed one form of misbehavior to blend seamlessly into the next.

"We would get the new script on Monday, do the table read-through, do lunch, and then in the afternoon, maybe block a couple scenes, knock off for the day," Staahl said. "Monday night, Robin and I would go to the Comedy Store. We would do the show, and then somebody would say, 'Hey, let's go to the beach' " — meaning Hermosa Beach, where they would perform at the Comedy Magic Club, and hang out at the home of Molly Madden, a model and agent who was a friend of Dawber's and a girlfriend of Christopher Reeve's.

Staahl, who was going through a divorce at the time, said the crowd at Madden's house was "people who just showed up at the beach and wanted to have fun," and that he would go there to "meet the models of her agency. I would go home early — Robin would party hearty." Whatever the night and whoever the crowd, Robin seemed up for anything, and his appetites and his endurance far exceeded anyone else's. "He would do our show at the Comedy Store and then he would go across to do the Improv," Staahl said. "Or he might break with us and wind up in Hermosa Beach. Or he might do two other clubs. More and more and more."

Taylor Negron, an actor, comedian, and fellow member of the Comedy Store Players, was also a frequent companion on Robin's decadent itineraries. Negron said that the scene following a performance by the Comedy Store Players was reliably dissolute. The group's dressing room would fill "with Lou Reed lookalikes named Hercules and Raquel, all shaking tiny bottles of cocaine." Then, he said, the search continued for more party fuel: "Robin loved cocaine and we loved Robin, so we went with Robin to parties with sniff in the air. I did not enjoy cocaine. It made me want to vacuum every hallway in every apartment building in the world."

Anyone who was a friend of Robin's, or even on the periphery of his social circle, was a potential source to the *National Enquirer* and other celebrity tabloids that were scouring Los Angeles for tawdry tales about him. "People were forever looking for stories and angles," said Staahl. "It would be weird. We would go out, do something, and then a couple days later, I'm reading about stuff in the *Enquirer* like, yeah, that happened. How did they get that? I'd come to learn that the *Enquirer* did pay a bounty. You could make five hundred bucks, a thousand bucks if you had firsthand information, and they could somehow vet it. Or you would verify another source, if you said, 'Yeah, that really happened.'"

To prevent these misdeeds from going public — ideally, to keep them from happening at all — Valerie was sometimes put in the awkward position of having to ask Robin's friends to run interference on her behalf. In one instance, Staahl said, Valerie approached him at the Comedy Store and inquired: "You're not dating anyone right now, are you?" When he said no, she asked him if he would go out with Candy Clark, the actress and model, "so that I can get her away from my husband." Staahl said he came away from the encounter thinking to himself, "Oh, really, is it like that? Is their relationship that bad?"

But there was only so much that Valerie could do to conceal their secrets. In July, the

New York Post claimed that she and Robin were preparing for a legal separation and a divorce, amid allegations that Robin was "openly running around Hollywood with model Molly Madden." Valerie was quoted on the record as saying, "I've had enough. It's very embarrassing when your husband is seen all over the place with another woman. I hate the thought of losing him forever but what else can I do?" A few days later, the New York *Daily News* caught up with Robin and Valerie at Studio 54, where they were attending a birthday party for Andy Warhol and appeared to have reconciled. Robin told the paper that their trip to New York was "a four-day honeymoon," and, its report observed, "not even the early-hours arrival of Cheryl Tiegs could lure him before the camera with another woman."

When Robin appeared on the cover of *Rolling Stone* that August, he was photographed bare-chested, with tufts of brown hair spreading across his torso and along his upper arms. "Sexuality figures in the Williams appeal," the rock 'n' roll magazine observed in its profile. "Not only does he get a huge volume of perfumed come-ons and childishly scrawled invitations in the mail, but he also gets away with more naughty jokes and gestures than anyone I've ever seen. . . . Like Mork, Robin seems to defuse sexuality of its threatening aspects, until lust appears merely to be cuddly raised to the second power. There's a warmth to his sex humor that keeps it from turning smutty." The following section of the story described Robin conducting an imaginary conversation with his penis, whose voice he provided in a Señor Wences falsetto. In the interview, Robin rejected the scandalous tabloid coverage of his private life as "nonsense."

But at the end of October, Robin was on the cover of *People* in a story that asked, "Has MORK blown his cork? Success shook his life and marriage, but both are solid now." The accompanying feature recapitulated the accounts linking Robin to Madden, as well as rumors that during this time Valerie had left Robin to spend time alone in Italy, but Valerie knocked them down as "completely false."

Robin dismissed any friction in their marriage as the result of their acclimation to the Los Angeles A-list — "The social ramble ain't restful," he said — adding that he and Valerie had to make different adjustments: "They should give courses in Hollywood parties, A and B. Valerie would bristle, 'Get me out of here.' But now she's learned a certain diplomacy." The lesson Robin said he had to learn for himself was how to slow things down: "It's like slowly turning off an engine," he explained. "When you've been going at high speed, it'll keep idling." But, he added, "We're not becoming monks."

As hard as she tried to put on a diplomatic face, Valerie had no illusions about Robin's escapades: he was drinking, he was using drugs, and he was committing acts of infidelity. But as surely as she felt honor-bound to keep her husband's confidences, she also believed that she had to allow him these indulgences, in the hope that his waywardness was somehow providing him with something that he needed as an artist and performer, and that when he sobered up and saw what he'd done wrong, he would do the right thing and come back to her.

"I just loved that man to pieces," Valerie said many years later. "And I wanted him to be happy and this was making him happy, so I moved over a lot. And the more I moved over and created space, it left a vacuum. And you know about vacuums. There were a lot of people who really jumped in to fill that vacuum."

To see Robin receiving a level of recognition and acclaim that they believed he deserved had been thrilling at first. "That was the adventure, and we were really bonded in that," Valerie said. But as Robin became increasingly famous, Valerie did not; she felt that she was not welcome in the same social settings, and it drove a wedge between them. "I didn't get respect, no," she said. "People wanted him, on his own. It's unfortunate, but it happens in L.A. There were certain people that were taking him off on rides that I didn't think were serving him. It didn't serve us as a couple, and it certainly didn't serve his health or his talent. He was being dummied down by the drugs and the women. And that was a problem."

It was impossible for Valerie to keep tabs on Robin when he was away from her. "L.A. is very spread out, and there were no cell phones," she said. "We had two cars. And two homes. And he was running wild. And enjoying it."

Mork & Mindy, the source of so much of Robin's good fortune, was not spared from the changes rippling through his life. In the spring of 1979, Robin's managers renegotiated a doubling of his salary, to $30,000 an episode, as part of an overall deal that was expected to pay him roughly $3 million over the life of the show. But when the series returned in September, it was not the same wholesome comedy it had been in its first year. Several important cast members had been written off the show, including Conrad Janis and Elizabeth Kerr, who played Mindy's father and grandmother, and Jeffrey Jacquet, who played their young friend Eugene. They were replaced by new characters like a nosy next-door neighbor (Tom Poston) and Mindy's pompous cousin (Jim Staahl), as well as a bickering brother and sister (Jay Thomas and Gina Hecht) who ran a New

York–style deli.

In observance of a long-standing television tradition, ABC executives saw that they had a hit show and determined that the best way to preserve it was to change it, making alterations based on the advice of focus groups as well as their own unfathomable caprices. "Basically, the network felt that the older people were dead weight, that they weren't adding to the show," said Dale McRaven. "I thought that was a terrible idea. You just don't get rid of your dad, or your grandmother. And they did. We had to go along with it, and they ate their words and brought some of them back, but it was a little late and the damage had already been done."

To make matters worse, ABC had moved *Mork & Mindy* from Thursday to Sunday, where it was expected to hold its own against *Archie Bunker's Place,* a new CBS spin-off of its acclaimed comedy *All in the Family.* But there was still plenty of life left in the character played by Carroll O'Connor, who later prevailed over Robin at the Emmy Awards for Best Actor in a Comedy Series. *Archie Bunker's Place* emerged as the new ratings champion of the night, while viewership for the retooled *Mork & Mindy* began to decline.

These changes were dispiriting to the show's staff, and Robin felt their impact with a particularly personal intensity. The goodness and integrity that audiences perceived in

Mork were fundamental to the role, giving Robin the license to be innocent and unsophisticated. But when he was set against new sparring partners who were more knowing and worldly, Robin had to change how he responded to them. Mork became less virtuous, more self-aware, more overtly libidinous and attuned to his own double entendres.

Pam Dawber noticed this change in course, too, though she felt it was ultimately the fault of the ABC executives and their unwarranted interference. "That screwed up the gist of the show the second year," she said. "They gave him a whole different agenda and therefore he started leaning into it in a different way." Eventually ABC realized that the lovable Mork had gained some sharp edges. But by now the network was too intimidated by Robin to tell him to do anything differently, and so they asked Dawber to deliver the note. "They were all, 'Talk to Robin, he's not playing the character naïve anymore,' " she said. "They just double-whammied it. They destroyed it themselves and then were mad that Robin was playing it a little differently."

Robin himself was mystified as the *Mork & Mindy* scripts veered into sexualized territory — an episode where Mork becomes a member of the Denver Broncos cheerleading squad; a two-part story line where Mork meets a race of lustful, bikini-clad aliens whose leader was played by Raquel Welch —

and the series devolved into what he described as "a T&A show." Still, he wasn't sufficiently worked up to take action, and watched these events unfold with frustrated resignation. "Shows like those changed us during the second year, and they weren't a help," he later said. "I think people who'd always watched the series just looked at this stuff and said, 'Jesus, what's *this*?' It didn't piss me off as much as make me wonder why."

At the same time, Robin's managers had been trying to move him beyond a television career and establish him as a film star. To that end, they had been fiercely defensive of their client, and went so far as to threaten legal action against the producers of *Can I Do It . . . Til I Need Glasses,* the bawdy, low-budget bomb of a comedy that Robin had briefly appeared in when he was still breaking into the Los Angeles scene, and which had recently been rereleased to capitalize on his surging fame. Robin's team contended that it was "an invasion of privacy" and "misleading advertising" for the producers to promote the film as Robin's first screen role, and a court later ruled that any banners or ads that mentioned Robin's name had to include at least three other cast members, and could not mention *Mork & Mindy.*

In their protectiveness, Robin's managers also discouraged him from cultivating future projects that did not fit with the future plans they imagined for him. Ever since he and Bennett Tramer had worked together on *Reality . . . What a Concept,* the two of them had been discussing ideas for movie screenplays that Tramer would write and Robin would star in. Robin dismissed early on the possibility that he could write anything for himself. "To be funny in print is a real hard thing for me to do," he said. "I can do it in performing, because it's straight out, *ka-boom.* But when I sit down at the typewriter, I feel like an autistic child."

Tramer's stories included one where Robin would play multiple characters, like Peter Sellers in *Dr. Strangelove* or Alec Guinness in *Kind Hearts and Coronets,* in a story about quintuplets — or possibly sextuplets — who had been separated at birth and grew up unaware of one another, only to be reunited as adults. "I think it ended at the United Nations," Tramer said of the concept. "The last line was something like, 'We believe we're all brothers — in our case, literally.' "

In another possible script, one that Tramer wanted to call *Achoo,* Robin would have played a shy, discombobulated chemist who invents a cure for the common cold. And in a third, Robin would play the role of a ten-year-old boy who, inexplicably, becomes thirty years old overnight. This one, Tramer said, would have had a transformation scene like in *The Wolfman,* "with his hair coming in and thunder cracking and everything."

Yet each of these ideas had a fatal flaw that caused it to be turned down: Tramer received some development money from Paramount for *Achoo,* but the studio pulled out when it learned that Paddy Chayefsky, the dyspeptic, Academy Award–winning screenwriter of *Network,* was also working on a project about the pharmaceutical industry. The other concepts were dismissed out of hand by Robin's managers, who considered them untenable, somewhat contrived, and too similar to the character he was already playing on *Mork & Mindy.* Rejection is a natural and commonplace occurrence in the entertainment industry, but Robin was lately unaccustomed to the phenomenon; he seemed stunned by the rejections and resigned to their outcomes.

"That was a little depressing," Tramer said. "Robin's a very, very sensitive guy. He didn't take rejection well. Not in terms of throwing furniture around or slashing furniture, but it would dishearten him. And this is normal; you have to pitch a lot of stuff. But he was so used to everything going his way, not in a selfish way, not in a babyish way. To get resistance, I wouldn't say that ended his wanting to do it. But that was kind of hard."

The film that Robin's managers had in mind for his debut as a leading man was a movie musical version of *Popeye,* the comic-strip and cartoon sailor, which they had been pursuing for him for more than a year, ever since its original star, Dustin Hoffman, dropped out. *Popeye* had been the brainchild of the producer Robert Evans, the slick raconteur behind *Love Story, The Godfather,* and *Chinatown,* who had lined up the singer-songwriter Harry Nilsson to create the music, and Jules Feiffer, the cartoonist and screenwriter (*Carnal Knowledge*), to provide the script. Rather than presenting the slapstick sailor seen in animated shorts and TV cartoons, Feiffer wanted to bring the character back to his ornery roots, as he was depicted in the original E. C. Segar comic strips of the 1930s. John Schlesinger, the Oscar-winning director of *Midnight Cowboy,* had been Evans's first choice to direct, but he wasn't interested; Hal Ashby, the laid-back director of *Harold and Maude, Coming Home,* and *Being There,* had briefly been recruited but also departed when Hoffman left. So the project was instead entrusted to Robert Altman, the idiosyncratic filmmaker of *M*A*S*H* and *Nashville,* who had no experience with big-budget franchise movies.

Evans, who was being encouraged to cast *Popeye*'s lead role with an established star like Jack Nicholson or Al Pacino, later acknowledged that he'd chosen Robin somewhat impulsively. "Now, I didn't even know who Robin Williams was, frankly," Evans said. "But I knew he'd just come out with a series and was the talk of the town. So I said, 'We could use Robin Williams.' The name just popped off my tongue."

Robin had some misgivings about the role of the muscle-bound mariner, worrying that his unique attributes would get lost in the trappings of a familiar cartoon character. He had also shared the *Popeye* script with Tramer, who was not impressed. "I said, 'Unless you talking like Popeye is enough to sell a movie, there's no story here,' " Tramer recalled. "He said, 'Yeah, I don't know.' But how do you turn down Robert Altman on your first movie?" On the other hand, among those encouraging him to embrace the challenge was his friend Christopher Reeve, who had recently triumphed in the hit film adaptation of *Superman.*

Robin agreed to take the role, and when he did, he committed to it fully. He trained in dance and acrobatics, learned to sing the songs, got a close-cropped, dyed-blond hairdo, and convinced himself that this was going to be his cinematic breakthrough. "I also had that dream of getting up to thank the Academy," he said. "I thought, this is it, this is *my Superman,* and it's gonna go through the fuckin' roof! After the first day on *Popeye,* I thought, Well, maybe this *isn't* it, and I finally wound up going, Oh, God,

245

when is it going to be *over*?"

In January 1980, Robin traveled to the Mediterranean island of Malta to begin the six-month shoot for *Popeye.* The $20 million film was jointly produced by Walt Disney and Paramount Pictures, and Robin was paid a salary of $500,000 plus a small percentage of any potential profits. Shelley Duvall, a frequent actor in Altman's films and a dead ringer for Olive Oyl, was cast as Popeye's love interest, despite Evans's preference for Gilda Radner.

When Robin arrived for work, wearing oversize forearm prosthetics that cut off his circulation, and saw the ramshackle set for the seaside shantytown of Sweethaven, it struck him as a decidedly inelegant operation. ("Imagine San Quentin on Valium," he would later say.) And it was all overseen by a director who had never handled a film of this scale — let alone a musical — and who felt little obligation to help get his leading man acclimated. "Altman loved organized chaos," said Feiffer. "That's what he was comfortable in. It was quite a brouhaha."

Almost immediately, Robin and Altman clashed over Popeye's dialogue, which, even as it was written, was a complicated mouthful of malapropisms and mispronunciations. In an early soliloquy, the character recounts a sea journey spent with "nuttin' on board t'eat but carroks":

After six weeks o' carroks me eye sike got so good I could see through walls. See the fishes on the bottom o' the oceang. After ten weeks o' carroks I could see through flesh — look a man through to his bare bones. Ya can go too far wit' a good t'ing. Even eye sike.

Robin would deliver these lines out of the side of his mouth, sometimes with a corncob pipe clenched in his teeth; he wanted the flexibility to improvise from time to time, but Altman wanted everything performed as written in the script. Feiffer said he had no strong preference: "While I loved the improvisation, I thought I had written this as a Popeye and Olive Oyl romance, thinking of Tracy and Hepburn in *Adam's Rib* and things like that." But as Altman saw it, Feiffer said, "Robin was kind of trashing the character by making jokes here and there. We got past that. It was his first movie, working out some kind of nervousness, which he got under control."

"Bob said I could ad lib the mumbles — they'd be for me," Robin explained. "On one or two occasions when I went too far, they simply lowered the sound."

When night fell on Malta, the collaborative spirit of the *Popeye* cast and crew gave way to something darker and more primal. Feiffer, who had come there alone, was living out of a motel and indulging in the melancholy of a collapsing relationship he'd left behind at home.

"I was deeply gloomy and drinking just a little bit," Feiffer said. "And I got awakened in the middle of the night by somebody in the company, saying, 'Robin's coming to beat you up. He heard you're sleeping with Valerie, his wife.' "

Still in a groggy state of disbelief, Feiffer asked his caller to repeat himself. "He told me again," he said. "And I said, 'That's nuts.' And he said, 'Well, you'd better get out of here. He's going to beat you up.' And I got up, in my pajamas, and I walked down the street."

He came out of his room to find Robin standing in the road, gradually making his way toward him, as if preparing to challenge him to a duel. Feiffer stood his ground, holding out his arms, and crying, "Robin!" And when Robin had shambled up close enough to him, he reached out his arms and hugged him. "We announced our love for each other and that was the end of the evening," Feiffer recalled with a laugh. "I know what *I* was on, but I don't know what he was on. He was doing a lot of stuff." ("Besides which," Feiffer added, "I was a hundred years older than everybody else there. That notion of me sleeping with his wife was nuts.")

Beneath its bluster and roughhousing, *Popeye* was ultimately a tender film, providing an origin story for his romance with Olive Oyl, a score filled with off-kilter musical tributes to daily rituals ("Everything Is Food") and oversize boyfriends ("He's Large"), and presenting its hero as an introspective existentialist who's just looking for a family wherever he can find it.

But bit by bit, the production began to fall apart. Feiffer had a falling-out with Altman over a musical number called "I Yam What I Yam," which the screenwriter had wanted to be staged like "Singin' in the Rain." "I wanted it to be his announcement of self, this take-charge number for Robin to just dominate the screen," Feiffer said. But when he saw the lackluster version that Altman had shot, he said, "I was in a state of horror. Because this number essentially made Popeye an extra in his own song." Feiffer left the set and did not return.

Then, at the conclusion of the shoot, in the midst of a grand finale where Popeye and Olive Oyl fought a giant octopus, the production ran out of money. "That was literally where they pulled the plug," Robin later recalled, "at a point where, if ever we needed special effects, it was like, now!" Some of his last days on Malta, he said, were spent watching Shelley Duvall "in a pool, going, 'Oh, help!' with an octopus with no mechanical devices inside, because the special effects guys had left. At the end it was like *Ed Wood.*"

So dire were the circumstances that just about any suggestion for how to finish the movie was taken seriously. As Robin recalled, "I joked to Robert Evans, who was coked out of his tits, and I said, 'Maybe I should walk on water.' He said, 'Yes!' " Thus, *Popeye* ended with its title hero dancing atop the sea to the tune of "I'm Popeye the Sailor Man."

When Robin returned to the United States that summer, he came home to the Grammy Award he had won in absentia for *Reality . . . What a Concept,* and to steep expectations for the movie that he sensed would not be fulfilled. Still, he tried to put a good face on the experience and spoke about Popeye as if he were a kindred spirit. As he said in one interview, "He's a simple man. He's kind of bittersweet, he's got a lot of pain, and he's been through a lot. He's kind of an outsider — nobody you'd notice until he turns on his talent when he really has to prove himself." Robin also began wearing a button on his pants that read EXPECT A MIRACLE.

But it was clear at the film's gala premiere, which was held at Mann's Chinese Theatre in Hollywood and which Robin attended wearing a top hat and a boutonniere of spinach, that the movie was not going to be well received. Audiences could hardly make out Robin's garbled blow-me-down dialogue, let alone much of what anyone else was saying in the murky audio mix, and Altman's shambling directorial style was not well suited to musical comedy. "People didn't know what to make of it," said Tramer, who attended the premiere with Robin. "It was an unusual movie, because it was very stylized, and people were like, 'I don't quite get it.' "

The major film critics were similarly dubious, neither praising it nor condemning it entirely when it opened on December 12, 1980. Vincent Canby, in the *New York Times,* said that *Popeye* was "a thoroughly charming, immensely appealing mess of a movie, often high-spirited and witty, occasionally pretentious and flat, sometimes robustly funny and frequently unintelligible. It is, in short, a very mixed bag." Gene Siskel, in the *Chicago Tribune,* called the film "an apparent big-budget bomb in a year full of overproduced stinkeroos," but he did hail Robin for "a performance that only a major artist could bring off," comparing him to a "young Peter Sellers."

Audiences saw the movie in large numbers, and it sold nearly $50 million in tickets for its US release, making it the twelfth-highest-grossing film of the year. But there was no sense that viewers were enjoying *Popeye* or embracing Robin's performance, and the film did not become his springboard to motion-picture stardom. Though in time he came to admire it as "a nice fairy tale with a loving spirit to it," Robin carried the wound of *Pop-*

eye with him, as if its failure to become an out-and-out blockbuster were his fault alone. It would sting him even to hear its title called out at his stand-up shows, though eventually he crafted a couple of one-liners for when he got heckled about it:

"For your information, it's playing in Hollywood on a double bill with *Heaven's Gate.*"

"If you watch it backward, it really *does* have an ending."

Other concerns were weighing on Robin's mind, more immediate than his box-office results. A few days before the film's opening, John Lennon was shot and killed by a disturbed fan who had waited outside his home in New York. Robin did not personally know Lennon, but the shooting left him feeling shaken and vulnerable. "When that happened, I saw a change in Robin," Brian Seff recalled. "There was some paranoia." One night that winter, Robin was coming off the stage at the Comedy Store when he was approached by a member of the audience. "And he says, 'Hey, man, I know where you live, because I've seen you coming out of there,'" Seff recalled. "I never saw him be so paranoid. Really, he just thought, okay, here's a stalker who's going to shoot me."

Robin worked through some of these feelings in an unusual episode of *Mork & Mindy* that aired at the start of 1981, in the middle of the show's third season. The episode, titled "Mork Meets Robin Williams," double-cast Robin as himself, the superstar comedian, who is visiting Boulder for a solar-energy benefit concert, where Mindy is tasked with obtaining an interview with him. The story treats it as a given that Robin is chased by adoring fans wherever he goes; one of its running jokes is that Mork is frequently mistaken for Robin, though neither of them can quite see the resemblance. Mork, in his alien naïveté, cannot understand why Earthlings prize celebrity or this Robin Williams person. "Don't you understand that a star is just a big ball of glowing hot gas?" he asks Mindy at one point. "He's just an ordinary human being that's been hyped by an advertising campaign."

When he and Mindy finally meet Robin in his dressing room — "You're not from the *Enquirer,* are you?" Robin asks them — he is soft-spoken and mildly ashamed of the status afforded him. With a mixture of self-deprecation and surprising truthfulness, he explains that he got into comedy as the result of a lonely childhood — "You see, my dad used to have this job where he had to move around a lot, and sometimes he'd leave the forwarding address" — and that he created his outrageous voices and characters as a way to keep himself entertained. "Then it got to the point where I realized that the characters

253

could say and do things that I was afraid to do myself," he says.

This Robin confesses to them that he has a hard time saying no to people, whether friends who ask him to spend time with them or strangers who ask him to participate in their benefit shows, for fear of letting anyone down.

"You know," Mindy tells him, "if you learned to say no, you'd probably have a lot more time to yourself."

"Maybe that's the last thing I want," he answers quietly.

The episode ends with Mork delivering his regular weekly report back to Orson. Standing in total blackness, dressed in his red spacesuit, Mork explains what he has learned about the cost of fame and the loss of privacy that comes with it. "When you're a celebrity, everybody wants a piece of you, sir. Unless you can say no, there'll be no pieces left for yourself," he says. "To get that, you have to pay a very heavy price. You have responsibilities, anxieties, and to be honest, sir, some of them can't take it."

The unseen Orson responds, "I'm not buying it, Mork. It sounds to me like they have it made."

"Most of them do, sir," Mork answers in a quavering voice, "but some are victims of their own fame. Very special, intelligent people. People like Elvis Presley. Marilyn

Monroe. Janis Joplin. Jimi Hendrix. Lenny Bruce. Freddie Prinze. And John Lennon."

By now his eyes are visibly full of tears. There is no laughter, nor any other response from the audience as the screen fades to black.

7
BUNGALOW 3

At every step of his Hollywood career — the one that had started not quite three years earlier — Robin was reminded how fantastically rapid his rise had been. *Things just did not happen this way.* Now he would have to agree this was true: things didn't happen this way, and things were no longer happening for him the way they used to. Maybe it was already over for him. He tried, of course, to laugh it off, applying an unsentimental and sardonic humor to the wild whiplash of his up-and-down trajectory. "A god at twenty-seven, a washout at twenty-eight," he said of himself in the spring of 1980, not long before he turned twenty-nine. "After you hit thirty, you're just flab, failing hair and old drug flashes." "Besides," he added "there's the future." But with his once popular television series running out of steam and his marriage in peril, what kind of future could he hope for?

New and valued friends were still coming

into his life, and a barnstorming trip to London, just after he finished filming *Popeye,* turned into a chain of unexpected encounters with several of his British comedy idols. When he visited London's Playboy Mansion to immerse himself in cotton-tailed models, he ran into Peter Cook, the pioneering screen satirist, who introduced himself and hailed Robin as a hero before Robin had the chance to do the same; by the end of the night they were watching films together back at Cook's apartment.

On that same vacation, Robin spent another evening sweating through a performance at a London venue called the Comic Strip — so named because it sat above a Soho strip club — fearing that the locals wouldn't appreciate his riffs on Ronald Reagan, the Republican presidential candidate. ("This is Ronald —," he would say, pausing as someone whispers the name "Reagan" into his ear, "— Reagan!") Eric Idle, of Monty Python, was in the audience that night, and he said it was "a ruthless crowd. Quite funny people were being booed off and howled off within seconds of going on. And then Robin came on, and he was just breathtaking. He was being heckled and got the whole audience to pray for the death of the heckler. He was merciless, the way he went after him. And it was just great to see a real professional, totally comfortable at dismissing these drunken louts who thought they had something to say."

When Robin finished his set (which included a spontaneous one-man interpretation of a furious Wimbledon championship match between Björn Borg and John McEnroe), Idle gave him a standing ovation. "I haven't laughed this hard in years," he told Robin after the show, then rewarded him with an outing to a private gentlemen's club, where they spent the night in the company of even greater luminaries like Michael Caine and Sean Connery.

Idle, who was about eight years older, was a creative hero to Robin; they both loved a style of incongruous comedy informed by a wealth of intellectual and literary references. Idle had little use for banal euphemism; he was a rare ally who could cut through the bullshit and say, in his own unsparing but humorous way, exactly what he was thinking, even when it came to assessing Robin. And while he was impressed by his new friend's unparalleled ability for improvisation, he also suspected that it was in some way compensating or covering up for other ways in which Robin was unable to share himself with his audience.

"It was just a simple, effortless thing," Idle said of Robin's most identifiable talent. "I've always felt that Robin's blinding speed and flash of wit was an effort at concealment, rather than revealing. He would ostensibly be talking about something personal or sexual, but it was always not close to him. He would be general."

Later that summer, Robin made a spur-of-the-moment trip to Toronto, following through on an invitation he'd received a few weeks earlier from Martin Short, a cast member of the Second City comedy troupe and the *SCTV* program. During a brief strike by the Screen Actors Guild, Short had told Robin he planned to spend his downtime performing with the Toronto company of Second City; when Robin asked if he could drop in for a set or two, Short answered, "Absolutely," never expecting that Robin would take him up on the offer.

But then, one August night at the Old Fire Hall, there was Robin, by himself, carrying no money and bearing no luggage. He and Short riffed their way through a series of improvisations, playing "Shakespearean father-and-son haberdashers, competing drunken choreographers with a bitter interpersonal history, and a two-headed man from Newfoundland singing gaily about the glories of Canada," as Short described the set. He also said that, at one point in his exuberant routine, Robin, "being unfamiliar with the dimensions of the stage, tumbled right off and onto some delighted patrons."

Short and his wife, Nancy, let Robin stay

over at their home; Nancy even washed Robin's linen pants while he slept late the following afternoon. When Robin discovered that Nancy had accidentally shrunk his pants to the size of culottes, he said he'd tell Valerie, "I swear, I didn't fuck anybody! I have no idea why my pants are four inches shorter!" Robin spent a week at the couple's house, sometimes doing nothing more than sitting at the window and looking longingly at children playing hockey in the street. Then he'd turn to his host and say — in what Short described as a "vaguely Irish-sounding, wonderment-tinged lilt" — "*Ohhh,* they're so *won*-derful, Marty. So utterly carefree. I wish I could stay here and watch them all day!" As Short would later observe, "He reminded me of Saint-Exupéry's Little Prince: wistfully surveying a world to which he felt he didn't quite belong."

There wasn't much waiting for Robin back in Los Angeles. *Mork & Mindy* had taken a precipitous tumble in its third season, falling to forty-ninth place in the ratings, even though the show had reinstated banished cast members like Conrad Janis and Elizabeth Kerr and had moved back to its eight p.m. Thursday night time slot. "The third year was groping," Garry Marshall said. The character of Mork could no longer pretend to be baffled by a telephone or a toaster or otherwise uninitiated in the ways of human-

260

ity, nor could the show's writing staff disregard that he and Mindy had lived under the same roof for three years and only ever conducted a platonic relationship. In the fourth-season premiere, Mork proposed to Mindy and the following week, in defiance of a two-million-year-old Orkan ban on weddings, the two of them were married. (As punishment, Mork was temporarily turned into a dog by Orson.)

The TV couple clearly waited no time in consummating their nuptials, because two weeks later, they were pregnant: Mork gave birth, through his navel, to an egg that then grew massively in size and hatched a fully grown (if not fully mentally developed) man he and Mindy named Mearth. To play a character with the physical makeup of an adult but the mind-set of a child, the producers of *Mork & Mindy* cast Jonathan Winters, a truly inspired choice. Robin had idolized Winters since childhood, and he was an even more unpredictable and unruly improviser.

Winters had been briefly considered to play Mork in the *Happy Days* episode that introduced the character, and he had guest-starred in the third season of *Mork & Mindy,* playing Mindy's uncle Dave, a domineering multimillionaire. Even then, the show's staff knew he did not always play according to the rules. As director Howard Storm recalled, "When he's introduced to Pam, he looks at her and he says, 'What a pretty little girl you are.' Well, Johnny looked her up and down and he was so lascivious. 'What a *pretty* little girl *you* are.' I said, John, she's your niece. You can't come on with her like that. It's not like you want to jump her bones. I don't know whether he didn't want to or he just couldn't, but he would never say a line in the script. He would change it all the time."

At the end of the episode, Mork has his revenge on Uncle Dave by feeding him an Orkan dessert that causes him to hallucinate that he is in the middle of a comical war scene. In this moment, when Winters and Robin were given the freedom to riff and play with each other, something special happened. "Johnny goes wacko and starts doing everyone in the war," said Storm. "He was a general. He was a sergeant. He was a private. He was a gunner. He was behind the couch, with an imaginary machine gun, shooting everything, and Robin was feeding the belt of bullets into the machine gun. This is how much in tune they were with each other: Johnny decided that the gun jammed, and Robin knew it, 'cause Robin made believe his finger got caught inside. He yelled, 'Ouch!' " With Robin at his side, Winters improvised twenty-two minutes of material. "And the show only ran twenty-two minutes," Storm said. "So we had to cut it down to about six or seven minutes."

It had not been Robin's idea to bring Winters back to *Mork & Mindy* in an ongoing role, but the producers thought it might help lift Robin's spirits. "I don't think Jonathan had been doing much at that time," said cocreator Dale McRaven. "We were asked if we wanted to use him, and Jonathan was my hero growing up. And Robin's even more so. So when Robin heard about it, he said, 'Get him in, please.' "

Sure enough, casting Winters as Mearth gave the program and its besieged leading man a new burst of energy. "Having him on the show was one of the main reasons I stayed with it," said Robin — who was contractually obligated to continue, whether he liked it or not. "For me, it was like the chance to play alongside Babe Ruth." It also paired him with a costar who was almost pathologically unable to stop playing characters, who might suddenly decide he's a building inspector checking for code violations, a guard who's been working the Paramount gate for decades, or the emcee of a telethon to keep Lucille Ball off the air.

Winters, now in his mid-fifties, still had an impeccable comedy reputation earned from films like *It's a Mad, Mad, Mad, Mad World* and his many TV appearances. But he was also a tragic, wounded figure who was open about his struggles with bipolar disorder and had been institutionalized for nervous breakdowns in 1959 and 1961. Whatever blithe expression crossed his face and whatever character he imagined himself to be playing, he always carried in his wallet a meaningful Ralph Waldo Emerson quotation: "Humor is the mistress of sorrow."

So the crew at *Mork & Mindy* tended to forgive Winters if he occasionally forgot his lines or ignored his cue cards; they knew that if he started to stumble, Robin would help prop him up. And Winters gave Robin tacit permission to rescue him when he needed saving; he regarded Robin as a kindred spirit who understood, as he did, that comedy could be as light as a feather or as heavy as a suit of armor, and who used it defensively, to protect his personal space.

"I think what Robin and I have is a quality that forces us, when in doubt, to lash out by capturing someone else's personality when we become threatened," Winters said. "We are blessed with an extra lens to see with and an extra transistor to hear with. . . . Robin once said our madness is organized to a finely honed edge over wildness. When we're performing, we've got to get out there and paint a picture. If nobody gets the paintings, then we're in trouble."

Yet anyone who was able to glimpse them goofing around — and people on the Paramount lot went out of their way for the chance — did not necessarily see two deeply hurting comedians using their humor to help them work through the pain. They seemed to be a pair of like-minded jokers for whom the whole world was a proving ground to practice their work. As Henry Winkler, who was filming *Happy Days* a few stages away, described their antics, "He and Jonathan Winters are walking down the street to the commissary. Now all of a sudden, they stop in the middle of the street and start doing bits. And now people are congregating. Now you've got two dozen people standing in the street, at lunchtime, watching these two men riff. Sometimes it worked, sometimes it didn't. But it didn't matter. Because they were still better than what was happening in the world."

  That same fall of 1981, just a few days into the fourth season of *Mork & Mindy,* Robin made his long-awaited debut on *The Tonight Show.* On October 14, he got to bypass the tryout process that many of his stand-up peers had been subjected to and went straight to the couch to sit by Johnny Carson's side as his leadoff guest. Following an introduction from Carson, who acknowledged with some astonishment that Robin had never previously appeared on the program, he came onto the stage wearing a tuxedo jacket and vinyl pants but no belt or tie. Appearing nervous and eager to please, Robin quickly cycled through many voices and bits, speaking first in his preacher's voice — "Believe that comedy can heal you! Praise the power" — then leaping and clapping at the boom microphone as if he were Flipper.

Carson got few sincere answers to his questions and asked few that could have been answered seriously ("Where is home for you? Or did you come from a home?") but one of Robin's responses stood out.

"People see you," Carson said to Robin, "they probably think you" — he paused here to consider the right word — "experiment with, uh, foreign substances in your body."

"Medication, you mean?" Robin said teasingly as he began to play with his nose. "What makes you say that, in any way?" By now, he was swiping at his nose and mouth more furiously. "No!" he answered emphatically, adding a line that had recently become part of his act: "Because I believe that cocaine is God's way of saying you're making too much money." As the audience cheered and Johnny laughed at the quip, Robin continued, "No, I wouldn't take any medication. You couldn't. You see the girls at the Rainbow Bar & Grill taking one too many quaaludes, going, 'Is my lipstick on?' " Here he mimed the act of encircling his entire face with a lipstick tube.

Robin's customary position in his interviews from this time was to say that he did not really use recreational drugs. As he told the permissive readership of *Playboy,* "I never will. I mean, someone once gave me a Valium and it stayed in my blood for a couple of days. . . . Most times, anything I try, I have the opposite reaction to what I'm supposed to have." He claimed he avoided cocaine in particular, because it did not deliver its promised invigorating effects and instead, he said, "I get passive and just hold back. . . . I don't like doing any of the heavies, because normally my energy is just up when I'm performing."

But none of this was true. By now, Robin's cocaine use had become an ingrained part of his nightly post-work routine at *Mork & Mindy,* as much a part of this ritual as his stops at the Hollywood comedy clubs. "I'd go from doing the show," he later explained, "and then come to do the Comedy Store, and then go to the Improv, and then you'd go hang out at clubs, and then end up in the Hills, at some coke dealer's house. [Knocking on a door] 'Angel, it's Robin.' And then you'd wake up the next morning, going, 'Ohhh.' Not even wake up — you haven't gone to sleep. You're like a vampire on a day pass, going, 'How are you?' *Hisssssssss.*"

Robin never seemed to take pleasure in the stimulative properties of cocaine, and it certainly did not make him a more social person. "I did cocaine so I wouldn't have to talk to anybody," he said. "For me it was like a sedative, a way of pulling back from people and from a world that I was afraid of."

Around the *Mork & Mindy* set, it was no secret that Robin had been abusing drugs and alcohol to the point where it was interfering with his work on the show. "He was running like a mad man," Dawber said. "And of course drugs were playing into it. And I'd get mad at him and he'd deny it. It was just classic. But he'd still be at the Comedy Store at two in the morning and just running all over when he had to be at work the next day. He was exhausted. We'd be sitting on the couch at noon while Howard's giving us notes, and Robin would be asleep on the couch."

Storm, too, saw through Robin's deceptions and knew what was causing him to take multiple midday naps and miss his morning call-times. "When he would show up an hour later, he'd look like a wreck," said Storm. "He hadn't slept all night. He was snorting coke, and if you snort coke, in order to come down, you drink booze. He was out all night and screwing everybody in town. It was like a smorgasbord for him. It was all laid out there."

Robin realized his weak attempts at feigning sobriety weren't fooling anyone. "You'd come in the next day," he said, "and people would say, 'Oh, pardon me. Refried shit?' Looking like, you know, a big human tostada walking around."

But even when he was recovering from a round of carousing, he could skate by on his extraordinary memory skills. "I remember after one night of partying, he was late," recalled costar Jim Staahl. "The stage manager actually called Robin's manager and said, 'Where's Robin?' 'I dunno.' Robin came stumbling in, unwashed, tired, blown-out-looking. And they said, 'Did you get the script?' 'Script?' " His revised script for the day had been left at his Hollywood apartment, but because Robin had never come home that night, he had not received it.

"We're doing the run-through for the network," Staahl said. "It's a lot of pressure, because it's Wednesday and we're trying to lock the script. They hand him the script, Act I is completely rewritten. I'm sitting there going over my lines, Robin reads it through, hands it to Marty Nedboy, who was our dialogue coach. And then he goes, 'Okay, guys, let's do it.' We do the run-through and Robin does it without holding the script. I'm like, 'Huh? How did you do that?' "

"He was so good that he could just phone it in, and the audience bought it," said Storm, who eventually confronted Robin about his out-of-control conduct. "I said to him, 'You know you're not working at 100 percent, Robin. You're probably at 75 percent. But I know you, and I know what you can do. You're not really working full-out, and consequently the show becomes mediocre, and my work becomes mediocre.' So I said to him,

'Either you start to give 100 percent or I'm out of here. I don't want to be around someone who's not working full-blast.' "

Robin hung his head and gave Storm a meek reply of regret. "Okay, Papa. Okay," he said. But Storm eventually did leave *Mork & Mindy* to become a director on *Taxi.*

Some colleagues suspected that Robin was chasing not the high of cocaine so much as the comforting sense of belonging he got from being around other working comics. "He was addicted to performing," said McRaven. "And he would go out every night after work and go to all the clubs and stay out late. If a place was open till four o'clock, he'd stay there till four o'clock. And in the mornings, he was always hungover." But his drug use was not the problem, per se — "that was just something he did when he was performing," McRaven said. "I think he was also trying to prove to the other comics that he hadn't changed. He was just trying to be one of the guys."

The problems created by Robin's misconduct spilled out of his private life and into his workplace, eroding the boundaries between them. The gossip columns were again taking note of Valerie's public feuds with other women, and Robin's coworkers found themselves in the awkward position of having to cover for him. "When we'd find out Valerie was coming to the set, we'd hide the woman that was dating him," Storm said. "We'd have to say, 'Get her out of here.' To protect Robin."

But Valerie knew what was going on, and the couple's friends were warning them that a greater reckoning was coming if they did not act soon to salvage their relationship. "We got hit hard by the drugs and the women," Valerie later recalled. On one night when she and Robin were out together, Valerie was taken aside by Richard Pryor, who warned her that they were headed for serious calamity. "You've got to get out of town," Pryor told her. "You guys are not like this. You're not *them*" — here Pryor indicated the revelers not only in their immediate vicinity but anywhere they went in Los Angeles. "You are disintegrating. This is not good."

Pryor, who two years earlier had barely survived a horrible incident in which he'd badly burned himself after a days-long period of freebasing cocaine, delivered a similar lecture to Robin. He gave Valerie the watch he was wearing, for some reason, and he later presented the two of them with an unusual gift: a pair of wooden African fertility statues. At this point the couple decided to heed his advice: "We went and got out of town," Valerie said. A few days later she and Robin were flying in a helicopter above Napa Valley, looking for land to buy, and for $750,000 they purchased a ranch on a 640-acre plot in what Robin called the "rose-smelling, deep-breathing, waterfall country" north of San Francisco. The ranch became their gated getaway, where they could fish, swim, ride horses, or water plants. It was a place of solace and relaxation but also a fortification to keep Robin away from Hollywood, where he would habitually be tempted into bad behavior or feel pressure to further his career. Or, as Eric Idle would put it to him, "Look, that's a flower, asshole. You don't need to talk into a microphone when you can smell a flower." But the couple did not give up Hollywood altogether.

In January 1982, Robin welcomed the latest celebrity visitor to the *Mork & Mindy* set: John Belushi, the husky, hell-raising star of *Saturday Night Live, The Blues Brothers,* and *Animal House.* Belushi had been talking to Paramount executives about a new film project, and in his downtime he dropped by Stage 27 to watch Jonathan Winters ad-lib a scene about a World War II veteran who realizes the Japanese soldiers who shot at him at Okinawa are now tending his garden back in America.

Belushi had hung out with Robin a few previous times in New York, where Robin sang backup to his peerless Joe Cocker impersonation at Catch a Rising Star, and Belushi took him on a tour of the city's punk rock clubs. Robin said the experience was "like being on a tour with Dante, if Dante were James Brown. I was like Beaver Cleaver in the underworld." When Belushi was in Los Angeles, the two of them sometimes got their drugs from some of the same people.

On this visit, Robin was mourning the loss of Harvey Lembeck, the influential Los Angeles improvisation teacher who had helped him find his way to sitcom stardom, and who had died of a heart attack after falling ill on the *Mork & Mindy* set, where he'd been filming a role. Robin was still hurting, too, from his experience with *Popeye*, racked with self-loathing about the declining fortunes of *Mork & Mindy* and questioning whether he was anything more than a one-hit wonder. Even a throwaway item in a local magazine's In and Out column, which decreed that being at a party attended by Robin Williams was henceforth Out, had gotten under his skin. He thought frequently of the giant billboards and posters along Sunset Boulevard that advertised the hot new movies and albums, which elevated the stars featured in them to the status of gods. But Robin had never been depicted in one of these promotions, and it ate at him. "They're fifty feet tall and I'm only five foot eight," he thought. "I'm nothing."

Robin was lifted out of his funk when he watched Belushi observe Winters on the set; Belushi's quiet admiration for this legendary comedian seemed pure and sincere, to the point where he would shush anyone who tried to talk to him while Winters was playing his scene. Robin and Belushi did not say much more that day, but they made vague plans to see each other again soon.

On the night of March 4, Belushi was staying in Bungalow 3 at the Chateau Marmont, the shadowy gothic hotel that loomed over the Sunset Strip, while he continued to negotiate with Paramount about his next film project. Around midnight, Belushi ran into Robert De Niro and Harry Dean Stanton at On the Rox, an elite nightclub above the Roxy Theatre, and at two a.m. Robin, having wrapped up another therapeutic early-morning set at the Comedy Store, came by to find that the club had just closed. A bouncer told him that De Niro and Belushi had been looking for him, so Robin drove over to the Chateau. At the hotel, Robin first phoned De Niro, who told him he couldn't make it down from his room. So he headed over to Belushi's bungalow, where he was let in by Derf Scratch, the bassist from the punk band Fear, and waited for its primary resident to return.

When Belushi came back, he was joined by Cathy Evelyn Smith, a singer and drug dealer who had dated musicians like Levon Helm and Gordon Lightfoot, and her presence made Robin deeply uncomfortable. She seemed gaunt and worn down, and the room itself was disheveled and strewn with empty wine bottles. Belushi took out a guitar and strummed a few chords; subsequent accounts of the evening would later state that he and Robin did some cocaine, though Robin himself denied this.

As Belushi grew groggier — he said he'd taken some quaaludes earlier — Robin realized it was time to go. He told Belushi he was welcome to visit him at his new ranch in Napa Valley, then he made the drive alone to his home in Topanga Canyon, where Valerie was waiting for him. He told her that he'd just been to see Belushi but could not put the image of Cathy Evelyn Smith out of his mind. "God, man," he told Valerie. "He was with this lady — she was tough, scary."

Sometime later that morning, Smith prepared two speedballs — powerful mixtures of cocaine and heroin — injecting herself with one and Belushi with the other. He complained of feeling cold, so she turned up the thermostat and tucked him into bed, where he fell asleep. In his sleep, he died of an overdose, from the toxic quantity and combination of drugs he had taken. His physical trainer discovered his lifeless body just after twelve noon. He was thirty-three years old.

That morning, Robin had come to work a little late and a little bleary, as usual, and he told Dawber about his unusual night. "He said, 'Wow, I was with Belushi last night, and *boy,* ' " Dawber recalled. "First of all, Robin never had judgment, because he was doing a lot of the same stuff, but certainly not what Belushi was doing." He recounted for her his missed connection with De Niro, his uneasy visit to the bungalow, and how magnificently Belushi had played his guitar, as stoned as he was. " 'He could hardly stand up, and yet he could play the guitar to perfection,' — that's what he was saying," Dawber said. "There was some girl there and John was just so stoned. That's what Robin told me about that, and I went, 'Wow. Okay.' "

Just as the cast and crew were preparing to break for lunch, they received the news that had been rippling across Hollywood that day: Belushi had died in his bungalow at the Chateau. The producers knew that someone had to tell Robin, but fearing that the information would devastate him, they felt that it was best delivered by a trusted friend like Dawber. "They said, 'Will you tell Robin?' " she recalled. "I said, 'Oh, God, Robin was with him *last night.*' And they said they knew. I don't know how they knew."

Dawber waited for a discreet moment when she and Robin were walking back from the Paramount commissary: "I said, 'I've got something really terrible to tell you, Robin. He went, 'What? What?' And I said that John Belushi was found dead last night." Robin

276

found it incomprehensible to hear this about someone he had seen only a few hours earlier. "He went, 'What? I was with him last night! *I was with him last night!*' " Dawber said. She could see that Robin was in pain but wanted to make sure he did not ignore the larger lesson in all of this. "I said, 'Robin, if that ever happens to you, I will find you and kill you first.' "

By now, she and Robin had made their way back to Stage 27, and they could hear the growing clamor of the studio audience being let in for the taping of that night's show. Dawber started looking for her script when she saw Robin standing with his hands cupped over his crotch, which for him was a sign of pensive contemplation. He was looking down at the ground, still processing the ultimatum that she had just given him. In a soft, solemn voice, he answered, "That's never going to happen to me, Dawbs."

As he grieved for a friend who could have had decades of great work ahead of him, Robin did not need any assistance to see how Belushi's death communicated an unmistakable message, addressed directly to him and all but hand-delivered to his doorstep.

Robin later described Belushi as "a powerful personality and a powerful physical being, too. When someone like him takes the cab, it wises your ass up really quick. . . . John was on the frontier; he was out there pushing it."

After his death, Robin said he could not help but look at himself and realize that a drastic change of lifestyle was needed if he wanted to avoid the same destiny: "It was like, 'Look at you, you little frail motherfucker. You're small change, Jack.' "

With the understanding that he seemed "to be running, if not as intense a circle" as Belushi, then at least he was motivated by "the same type of drive in terms of 'be out there,' " Robin made a personal vow to spend even less time in Los Angeles. "I think that was pretty much the bottom rung," he later said. "You don't get much lower than that. It was time to leave this unhappy watering hole — time not to wander down this canyon any longer."

But Robin's decision to rethink his life, to cut back on drugs and keep himself away from the city that was the single greatest source of these seductions, was not motivated solely by altruism and a desire for personal improvement. It was something he needed to do now that he had been exposed to the world as a cocaine user; first, by the widespread media reports that placed him in Belushi's bungalow prior to his death, and then in the *National Enquirer,* where Cathy Evelyn Smith confessed to all the debauched details of Belushi's final hours (at a reported fee of $15,000) for a feature story published that summer under the lurid headline, "I Killed

278

John Belushi." Following the tabloid report, the Los Angeles District Attorney's Office reopened its investigation into Belushi's death, and the city's celebrities lived in fear that their own drug use might draw the attention of law enforcement.

"It was a huge wake-up call," said Dawber, who did not partake in this aspect of show business. "There was so much investigation going on, that whole crowd had to pull it together. I don't think people really understood what a devastating drug it was. But it was everywhere. It was like, whoa — you're at a dinner party, and suddenly someone that you didn't know would hand you a little vial, like, 'It's your turn. You can go into the bathroom.' It's like, Ohhhh, okay."

That fall, Robin testified before a Los Angeles grand jury looking into Belushi's death, and though he did so voluntarily, it drew more unwanted attention from the tabloids and the paparazzi. ("Your lens is not properly focused," he wisecracked to one photographer who caught him outside the courthouse.) The ongoing inquiry hobbled his ability to promote *Mork & Mindy* — a responsibility he did not particularly mind — and in interviews he either backed away from questions about Belushi's death or gave combative answers.

The scene in Belushi's bungalow that night, now a permanent and notorious part of

Hollywood lore, "was nothing that exciting even then," Robin later said. "I was there for ten minutes and split. There was no great, wild madness. Nothing there. . . . I've talked about it very openly, and still, people keep going, 'But what happened that night at the Chateau Marmont?' Nothing happened. Wanna give me a lie detector test? They keep making it into something else, and it's not. I don't know what else they'll find out." He even suggested the possibility that the invitation he had been given at On the Rox to seek out Belushi was part of an attempt to entrap him. "Someone sent me there," he said. "No one seems to know who this guy was who was working the Roxy who said, 'Go over there. They're looking for you.' I got over there, and no one wanted to see me. I have a feeling it was some strange set-up, that they wanted to catch a whole bunch of people and that it didn't come through."

Soon he faced the very real risk that there would be nothing for him to promote at all. Despite the highly touted addition of Winters to the *Mork & Mindy* cast and a brief return to the effortlessly charming story lines that had first made the show a hit, its ratings declined even further, all the way to sixtieth place. Naturally, Robin's first inclination was to blame himself for its collapse. "For a little while," he said, "I thought, God, maybe I'm not goosing up like I used to; maybe the old mad energy is gone. But I decided that wasn't true, because people still liked my performance. I think the show just had a confused base. The combination of that and going up against *Magnum P.I.* was finally too strong."

Mork & Mindy had been pulled from ABC's schedule for the month of March, a sure sign that the network was considering canceling it. In the final episodes of the season, Mork and Mindy are pursued by a malevolent Neptunian named Kalnik who blows up their tranquil home in Boulder and forces Mork to reveal to the world that he is an extraterrestrial; he and Mindy then use a pair of magic ruby slippers to escape Kalnik, but they are accidentally beamed back in time to the dawn of man, where they introduce a tribe of cave people to the invention of fire. For good measure, a portion of this story line was also filmed and broadcast in 3-D.

This abrupt and ill-conceived change of direction was part of a larger, last-ditch plan to persuade ABC to save *Mork & Mindy.* Its cast and creators hoped to turn it into a children-oriented comedy show, one with some nominal educational value, where the title characters would travel through time and meet famous figures from history. In April, Robin, Dawber, and Garry Marshall recorded a presentation video that was meant to sell this new concept to the network's executives. But it also called for some supplication on

Robin's part, requiring him to poke self-deprecating fun at his insecurities and deflated self-image. "I know why the show's shaky," the script had him say at the outset. "It's my fault. I speak too fast and they can't understand me. I should talk more like you — like a Walkman with dead batteries."

With more desperation, Robin added, "I know we're not doing well in the ratings, but I'm not going to beg! I may wear baggy pants, but I have my dignity. I'm not going to get down on my knees to these people. Besides, they hate me. I know it." Strangely, the presentation script also called for Dawber to undo the top button of her blouse, and say — "sexily," as the stage direction indicated — that "the body is educational, too." At its end, Robin was to drop to his knees with his hands clasped in front of him and beg outright: "Please, please pick us up. We'll do anything!"

The misbegotten pitch was not successful, and in May ABC canceled *Mork & Mindy* after four seasons and ninety-one episodes, replacing it in the fall with a new *Happy Days* spin-off, *Joanie Loves Chachi.* The show had already wrapped production, so there were no farewell parties or send-off speeches thanking everyone for their hard work and dedication. On some level, Robin already sensed that the ax was about to fall and he attempted to avoid his representatives' efforts to inform him that it had happened, as if that could somehow keep the show on the air. "I think they tried to call me the day before," he said. "I just didn't return the call, because I kind of knew what it was about. I knew it was coming."

He learned it for certain when the story made its way into the industry trade publications and daily newspapers, at a time when he was filming an episode of *Shelley Duvall's Faerie Tale Theatre*, a Showtime children's series hosted by his *Popeye* costar. Playing the lead role in an adaptation of "The Tale of the Frog Prince" for an installment directed by Eric Idle, Robin was in full costume when the news was offhandedly relayed to him, and despite his lack of surprise, he did not handle it well.

"I was so angry and hurt," Robin said, "and I was dressed as a frog. It hit me hard."

As Idle described his reaction: "The end of that show wasn't unexpected, but you don't think you'll find out by having someone hand you a newspaper when you're on a set. Robin gathered the technicians around him and did a routine about TV executives. Everyone was on the floor, and it was behind him. I thought that was the most *useful* example of comedy I'd ever seen."

While ABC was dithering over its decision on *Mork & Mindy,* Robin missed out on the plum opportunity to play Hamlet for Joseph

Papp in a Public Theater production of the play — one that would have also starred Carol Burnett as Gertrude. The network still had one more year on its five-year contract with him, which was burnt off by naming Robin a coproducer and consultant on its new fall series *Star of the Family,* a blue-collar comedy starring Brian Dennehy and produced by Robin's managers at Rollins Joffe. Robin's involvement with the show was largely cosmetic, and *Star of the Family* was canceled after ten episodes.

Robin tried to play off the demise of *Mork & Mindy* — and the loss of the character that was his most personal creation — as if they were everyday Hollywood setbacks, but Dawber said his reaction was quite the opposite. "No!" she said. "Of course not. Oh, no, Robin was hurt to the quick over that.

"That was typical of show business," she said. "They just pull the plug. He was so personally offended. I think he felt like he was being abandoned, and we were. Not because of anything the cast did wrong. It was all network idiocy. They just blew a huge opportunity. But he was very, very mad. And really saddened by it. His representation, of course, was thrilled, because now he's available to go do all these fabulous movies."

But Robin knew that he was losing the most secure, welcoming work environment he had ever known. "It was a family," Dawber said.

"You're working with these people every day. He had a place to be. It was a certain stability for him. And then, it was gone. It was very personal for him."

The only relationship Robin could turn to now was with Valerie, and though their marriage had been neglected for some time, neither of them considered it hopelessly beyond repair. In a *Rolling Stone* interview, Robin was asked whether the sheer volume of tabloid coverage about his hard-partying ways meant that at least some of it must be accurate. He answered, "Obviously there has to be some truth to it and there probably is. . . . I was just being an all-around fuckup, which may include other things. I admit it myself. To the charge of Asshole, I plead guilty. To the charge of intent to snort and fuck and cheat — no. I plead Asshole, and cheat — no. Asshole, and leave it at that, my lords."

Valerie, by way of explaining her side of things, cited her education at Goddard College, which she regarded as a shrine to liberalism and tolerance. There, she said she was taught "that you can guide people; you can make yourself interesting enough and important enough in your lover's life so that he'll always come back to you if you just keep growing along with it. If you just be part of their rhythm and give them a lot of freedom and be part of their growth instead of pulling them back from what is titillating and exciting."

"Let's face it," she added, "Robin is a stimulus junkie."

Valerie was glad to have stood by her husband. "If I had jumped the gun and divorced him," she said, "I would have lost the most precious thing in my life and it would have curtailed our experience together, which is a lot richer than anything he can get off the street." After John Belushi's death, their lives became more complicated but their objectives were clarified; Valerie said the rules by which she and Robin operated from there on could be reduced to a single word: "Enough. Enough. Enough."

Robin Williams, center, as a sophomore at Detroit Country Day School, the elite preparatory school he attended in Michigan. He wore a sport coat and tie to classes, carried a briefcase, and occasionally slipped one-liners into the otherwise sober speeches that students were required to give at lunchtime.

Robin as a senior at Redwood High School in Larkspur, California. In 1968, Robin and his family moved to Marin County, north of San Francisco, and Redwood was the most liberal school he'd seen so far. There, Robin ditched the formal attire and acquired his first Hawaiian shirt.

Robin's parents, Laurie and Rob Williams, at their home in Tiburon. Rob was a fastidious, plainspoken, practical Midwesterner whose approval would elude Robin well into his adulthood. Laurie was a lighthearted, fanciful, free-spirited Southerner, adoring of Robin and attentive to him.

Robin as a student at Claremont Men's College, where he went in 1969 to fulfill his father's wishes and pursue a respectable, white-collar career path. Instead, his almost impulsive choice to take an improvisational theater course would change his life forever.

After dropping out of Claremont and studying theater at the College of Marin, Robin was accepted into the Juilliard School's recently established Drama Division in 1973. Here he is seen rehearsing for a student production of *A Midsummer Night's Dream*. Robin was once again bewildered by his transition to a new city and a prestigious, fearsomely competitive school that did not necessarily care whether he flourished or floundered.

THE ESTATE OF DIANE GORODNITZKI

DANIEL S. SORINE

Robin, right, performing as a street mime in New York with Todd Oppenheimer. Straining at the margins of Juilliard's system, Robin sought unconventional outlets for his creative energy. Wandering Central Park or the plaza in front of the Metropolitan Museum of Art, he and Oppenheimer would deliver short routines, often copied from Marcel Marceau or other established mimes.

RON GALELLA / WIREIMAGE

Robin and Christopher Reeve speak with John Houseman at a benefit in New York. At Juilliard, Reeve was drawn in by Robin's boundless vitality, and the two became fast friends. "He was like an untied balloon that had been inflated and immediately released," Reeve later said of him. Houseman, who ran the Drama Division, was their mentor and taskmaster.

Robin outside the Comedy Store in Los Angeles. Following a quick ascent in the comedy scene of San Francisco, Robin moved to Los Angeles, where his wild, improvisational style made him a talent to watch. If other stand-ups "were just guys who stood behind the microphone and told jokes," David Letterman said, Robin "seemed to be hovering above the stage and the tables and the bar."

When Robin first laid eyes on Valerie Velardi, a dancer and movement instructor, he said that what he experienced was not so much love at first sight. "More like lust," he explained. "She just looked . . . hot. *Caliente*." Even before he and Valerie were married in 1978, she offered crucial organizational help for his comedy and boundless forgiveness for his misdeeds.

Robin with Ron Howard and Henry Winkler on *Happy Days*. In a whirlwind process completed just days before the taping of "My Favorite Orkan," Robin was cast to play Mork from Ork, an intergalactic miscreant with supernatural powers and a comical misunderstanding of human customs. When ABC aired the episode on January 28, 1978, it proved hugely popular, showing that Mork—and Robin—had greater potential.

Robin and Pam Dawber as the title characters on *Mork & Mindy*. To the series' co-creator Garry Marshall, the show needed a straitlaced co-star to rein in Robin's unruliness—"a Waspy, all-around very American girl to go against this lunatic." Behind the scenes, Dawber came to accept that the show was Robin's platform and not hers. "I was hanging on by my fingernails at the beginning," she said.

Directed by Robert Altman and pairing Robin with Shelley Duvall, *Popeye* was ultimately a tender musical comedy (with a screenplay by Jules Feiffer and songs by Harry Nilsson) about the cartoon sailorman's search for a family. But the cluttered production and Robin's clenched dialogue confused viewers when the movie was released in 1980, and it did not advance his leading-man ambitions.

The arrival of Robin and Valerie's son, Zachary Pym Williams, in 1983 was a life-altering experience, providing Robin with a powerful incentive to stop his substance abuse and to reevaluate his priorities. As Robin would later write to Zak, recounting his birth, "Suddenly there was a focus, a meaning, a continuity. My newborn baby who looked like Churchill and Gandhi . . . you. You opened your eyes, and mine!"

Following *Mork & Mindy*'s cancelation in 1982, Robin was torn between the need to have commercial hits and his desire to make "strange films" that didn't align with his audience's expectations. "I hope I can keep doing more," he said, even as he felt gravity tugging him back to familiar settings: "I'll probably end up, next day you'll see, 'Look, it's *Mork & Mindy*! He's back and he's crazier than ever!'"

Robin on *Saturday Night Live* in 1984, playing William F. Buckley Jr. in a parody of *Firing Line* with Eddie Murphy. Murphy's phenomenal success, in stand-up, on *SNL*, and in hit movies like *Trading Places*, was not easily received by Robin, who saw comedy as something of a zero-sum game: for one comic to rise, another comic had to fall. Murphy, he said, "knows exactly what he does and how to get it out on film perfectly. I don't."

The selection of Robin, Whoopi Goldberg, and Billy Crystal as the hosts of HBO's *Comic Relief* telethon in 1986 was a somewhat ad-hoc assembly. Robin and Crystal were now fast friends with an easy give-and-take in their improvised sets, while Goldberg was the wild card of the group and an outsider due to her gender and race. But the trio's relentless riffing and the success of the first broadcast, which raised nearly $2.5 million in donations, established them as the nation's ambassadors of improv comedy.

Robin with his half-brothers McLaurin Smith-Williams, left, and Todd Williams, center. Though Robin sometimes spoke of being raised as an only child, Todd (his father's son from his first marriage) and McLaurin (his mother's son from her first marriage) were constant presences in his life. Each had a strong influence on him, and the three regarded one another as full siblings.

In this sketch from a 1988 episode of *Saturday Night Live*, Robin plays a bitter, curmudgeonly, sixty-year-old version of himself, after his talents have dissipated and his fans have forgotten him, while Dana Carvey plays his grown son, a nightmare version of Robin who pathologically riffs on everything he sees. The fear of what would happen to him in his later years was a persistent theme in Robin's work.

■ ■ ■ ■

PART TWO: STAR

■ ■ ■ ■

8
Mr. Happy

On the sunny lawn of a suburban New York home, Robin battled playfully with two small boys. He was dressed in a hard hat, a garbage can lid, and a welcome mat that, looked at with the proper imaginative spirit, could pass for a medieval hero's armor. Wielding two plastic swords, he dodged and parried the attacks of the children, who were wearing wrestlers' chin straps and fought with floppy toy blades of their own. As Robin leapt out from behind a tree, the boys charged at him: he received a stab on his side, through a gap in his armor, and was turned from a heroic champion into an evil warrior; then, with a second slash, he was slain, falling to the ground in mock slow motion, flailing his arms to simulate the gushing of blood from his open wounds.

The scene seemed so real to him: the simplicity of it all, the wonderment of being a parent, the nobility of taking responsibility for children and guiding them through life.

After all the extravagant ambitions he had chased in show business and all the self-indulgent itches he had been able to scratch, none of which had led to his finding fulfillment, maybe this was what he truly wanted in life — maybe becoming a father is what would finally make him happy.

It was all an illusion, of course — just another cinematic reverie that he'd been allowed to indulge on the set of *The World According to Garp,* the director George Roy Hill's adaptation of the best-selling John Irving novel. The project was only the second feature film that Robin had starred in, having shot it before what turned out to be the last season of *Mork & Mindy.* When it finally hit theaters in the summer of 1982, it still would not do what he hoped it would for his career. But the experience of getting to live out the entirety of an on-screen life had helped him identify a desire he realized it was now time to satisfy. "One really good thing about this film was tapping into that, working with all those children," he said. "After doing this movie, I want a family — real bad."

When the last few episodes of *Mork & Mindy* came and went in May 1982, Robin, having no other pending commitments, began another cross-country stand-up tour. As he had done with *Reality . . . What a Concept,* this latest set of dates was meant to prepare material for a record album and to take his mind off the slow suffocation of his TV show. It had been some time since Robin had taken on a stand-up obligation this ambitious; making even occasional, unannounced club appearances had become exceedingly difficult in the weeks since John Belushi's death. To get himself back into fighting shape, he had assistance from David Steinberg, a new junior member of his management team at Rollins Joffe, who traveled with him to his shows and collaborated with him on his material.

Steinberg, a former publicist, brought some much-needed structure to Robin's scattershot process of assembling and refining his material. In typewritten pages, Steinberg helped Robin wrangle the untamed ideas that roamed free on the range of his mind and steer them into a traditional outline. At the top of the hierarchy, in Roman numerals, were generic subject headings; they said little individually, but taken collectively, they suggested the trajectory of what could only be a Robin Williams routine:

I. Animals
II. Drinking
III. Cocaine
IV. Ethnics
V. Hats
VI. Mork/Performing
VII. Music

VIII. Politics

IX. Sex

The first entry under the topic of (I) Animals was (A) Cats, which was further split into possible jokes like:

1. on valium, cant remember "Meow"
2. LA cat says "MeWow"
3. Ethnic cats: Jewish cat says "Meoy" New York cat says "Me-fuckin'-ow"
4. Cat attacks erection in the morning: "At least I woke you up"
5. Cat disturbed in a litter box
6. Cat impressions (including cat in a blender, cat on puree and the catapult)

and so on. Naturally, the next major subheading to follow (A) Cats was (B) Dogs.

This outline was dated May 12, 1982, and Robin had completely assimilated it by the time he played the Royal Oak Music Theatre in the Detroit suburbs one week later. There, he riffed on the Falkland Islands crisis, Carl Sagan ("Mr. Rogers on Valium"), and Julia Child ("Margaret Thatcher on quaaludes"). He was careful, however, to never let the act get too introspective or reveal too much about himself; when a fan in the crowd offered up a plastic egg — an affectionate tribute to the iconography of *Mork & Mindy*

— he joked that he was no longer that person, saying, "Mr. Mork? Oh, he took a hike." And when he delivered his four-minute bit about cocaine use, he concluded it with a disclaimer that was meant to make clear he was not talking about his own personal experiences, telling the audience, "I've heard it happened to somebody just like that."

The World According to Garp was released in theaters two months later. Irving's strange and sizable novel had been a best seller at its publication in 1978; it told the tale of T. S. Garp, an aspiring writer and the son of a proudly feminist mother, a nurse who conceived him by forcing herself on a comatose World War II airman with a permanent erection. The novel had been hailed for its unbridled imagination and criticized for its perceived misogyny and lurid fixations on sexual violence and castration. There was wide agreement that it could never be adapted into a movie.

Robin had been contemplating the project ever since he read the book while making *Popeye* in Malta; once again, he was the beneficiary of the caprices of Dustin Hoffman, who passed on the role. As Robin saw it, *Garp* was an ideal vehicle to show off the full range of his classical training, to finally play a flesh-and-blood human being, and pivot away from the weirdness of Popeye and most especially Mork. "It was like going from

Marvel Comics to Tolstoy," he said. "The hero, T. S. Garp, is like another side of me — the nonperforming side. It was a process for me of mentally stripping away, getting back to what I was doing six years ago when I was an acting student at Juilliard."

Hill, a former marine pilot and the cantankerous, Academy Award–winning director of *The Sting* and *Butch Cassidy and the Sundance Kid,* initially had no interest in casting Robin. "I'd seen him as Popeye and didn't understand a word he said," Hill explained. "I'd seen him once as Mork and didn't understand him either." But after a face-to-face meeting, Hill said, "I felt he had a sense of decency that was important. Garp is an abrasive man, but his underlying decency is a key part of the character, and I felt Robin was the sort of actor who could provide that."

Hill kept a tight leash on Robin's ad-libbed shenanigans; the first time he tried to go off-script, the director simply called a wrap for the entire set. "I thought, okay, you've made your point — I won't do *that* again," Robin said. In another scene where Garp learns from his wife, Helen (played by Mary Beth Hurt), that she is pregnant and celebrates by drawing a baby's face on her belly, Robin began to go too far: "I wanted to say, 'Oh, looky, our baby has a beard,' " he recalled. Instead, Hill snapped at him: "Hold it, jerk." But when Robin's improvisations made him laugh, Hill would encourage him to go deeper. "Okay, that's a joke," the director would say. "Let's go back behind to the next level and find out what's behind it."

For Robin, who was paid $300,000 to make *Garp,* the movie was an introduction to many Hollywood filmmaking traditions, like shooting his first nude love scene. He later described it as "seventeen lights and fifteen guys and a big boom mike going almost up your ass." Some similarities between him and the character — the fact that both he and Garp were student wrestlers — were too good to pass up. He even shaved his arms to play the younger incarnation of the character.

But he also found resonance in the story of a man held in thrall by a trailblazing, idiosyncratic mother (Glenn Close, in her first film role), trying to stand outside her shadow while perpetually seeking her approval. There were whole lives inside of Garp that went well beyond anything Robin had experienced: in a narrative threaded through the movie's second half, his marriage to Helen is nearly destroyed by a series of events set in motion when Garp has an affair with the family babysitter, who considers him a literary celebrity. At its core, *The World According to Garp* was about how the things we fear most in life are determined at an early age and amplified, not overcome, as we grow older. Robin liked how the character tested him.

"Garp was like an oil drilling," he said. "I had to dig down and find things deep inside myself and then bring them up. Heavy griefs and joys, births and deaths."

The film performed well enough at the box office and had its share of positive notices. Some reviewers felt, as one put it, that Robin was "an appropriate choice for the sometimes bewildered Garp," but many others remained convinced that a complex dramatic role was still beyond his grasp. Jack Mathews of the *Detroit Free Press* wrote a particularly devastating pan of the film, blaming Robin for its artistic failure. "I won't say a thing about the rubbery nature of Robin Williams' face," Mathews wrote, "other than this":

> It is so hard to watch in dramatic close-ups that it spoiled for me *The World According to Garp,* a movie I would have otherwise placed among the year's best. . . . It is hard to look beyond such miscasting when the sympathetic nature of a character is as vital as it is with Garp. He represents the hopes and innocence in each of us, and in a story of such soaring literary ambitions . . . it must have that central credibility.

Glenn Close would receive an Oscar nomination for her performance as Garp's mother, as would John Lithgow, who played a transgender woman who befriends Garp. But

Robin would go unrecognized.

By that time, his life had been radically altered by a far happier piece of news: Valerie was pregnant. The couple learned in the summer of 1982 that they were going to have a child the following year, and they shared their good fortune with the world in September, putting out a press release that stated they had "waited this long to have a baby because Robin felt that while he was doing the series *Mork & Mindy,* he would be unable to give the attention he should to Valerie and a baby." The announcement also mentioned that Robin and Valerie were relaxing at home in Napa before he went back out on his comedy tour, and that *The World According to Garp* had grossed $26 million at the box office so far.

That announcement did not tell the entire truth. Robin and Valerie's volatile relationship had been the biggest impediment to starting a family, and their decision to have a baby was made in the hope that it would help reduce friction and inspire them to rededicate themselves to each other and to their child. And that was precisely the effect it had. Asked later if her pregnancy brought a much-needed measure of stability back into the marriage, Valerie said, "It did change, it did. No question. The actual pregnancy was beautiful." Once his tour was over, Robin became an attentive and dedicated husband, spending less time on the road and more with his wife, doing chores, running errands, and going with her to Lamaze classes in preparation for the birth.

Impending fatherhood also inspired Robin to recommit himself to sobriety; if Belushi's overdose and its fallout had not been enough to scare him straight, now he had a truly compelling reason to stay off cocaine and alcohol. And not just a little bit — he had to kick both habits completely. As far as Valerie could see, that was exactly what Robin did: "He was totally sober," she said. "He stayed totally sober from the minute I got pregnant. No more drugs." And, she said, Robin didn't need any form of rehab, twelve-step regimen, or other recovery program to excise these substances from his life; he did so through sheer force of will — "just dry drunk," Valerie said.

Robin's temperance was not achieved all at once. That October, he was in Gainesville, Florida, to perform at the University of Florida's "Gator Growl" homecoming event for more than sixty-four thousand students and alumni. In his routine, he told the voluble crowd of football worshippers that he did not expect much sympathy after the cancellation of *Mork & Mindy:* "It's hard to go around saying, 'Pardon me, can you spare $40,000 a week?' " he joked.

His manager David Steinberg, who joined

Robin on this trip, said that the raucousness was not restricted to his public appearance, and there was drinking and drug use after the show. "It was the biggest crowd Robin had ever worked with, and we were just out of control," Steinberg recalled. "We were all abusing everything at the time. At some point they said, 'It's for the parents and the kids, so if you can watch what Robin's going to do —.' We said, we can't do that. If that's what you're interested in, call someone else. And he just did what he normally feels like doing. Which was great. The kids loved it." When he and Robin later showed up at a formal dinner after the game, Steinberg said, "We were totally out of control. We were nuts."

Two weeks later, Robin was back in San Francisco, appearing at the Great American Music Hall to perform the stand-up set he'd been refining since the spring. The show was recorded as a ninety-minute HBO special that would air the next year under the title *An Evening with Robin Williams;* his top managers at Rollins Joffe were credited as executive producers, and Steinberg was cited as a creative consultant. As with *Live at the Roxy,* the special opened with a pre-taped character piece: here, Robin played a newsstand vendor who works outside the Great American Music Hall, telling passersby that he has known Robin Williams since he kicked off his comedy career in this city, then leads the camera into the venue for the show.

For all of Robin's preparation, the first forty-five minutes of his performance feel restless and devoid of structure or content. He spends most of that time riffing on members of the audience and the clothes they are wearing, or equipment he notices onstage (he puts a large amplifier on his shoulder and calls it a "Polish Walkman"), falling back on his stock accents of black and Japanese people. There is a noteworthy section on nicknames for the penis — it can be "a throbbing python of love" for some, he says — and he tells the audience he likes to call his own organ "Mr. Happy," explaining that "if something's going wrong, you can go, 'Oh, look, he's pouting.' "

Then, gradually, the show takes a personal turn, almost as if by accident. Robin mentions that his mother, Laurie, is in the theater tonight, and retells her treasured "I love you in blue" poem. He goes into a riff on conception, slipping in and out of the voices of Carl Sagan and an infant delighted by its mother's breasts, before telling the crowd, in his own voice, "I have good news for you." Then he slips back into another of his character accents, the Russian man, to tell the audience something truthful about himself: "I am going to be a father," he says meekly. Before the consequent applause subsides, Robin is once again addressing his penis: "Do you hear that, boy? Yay! He aimed straight and true! I feel like William Tell now." Then, back to the crowd: "I don't know who the mother is, but hey, it's wonderful."

Robin mentions that he and Valerie are thinking about naming their baby Christopher (for a boy) or Christina (for a girl) and jokes that its first words will probably be "trust fund." Then he goes into a bit that imagines what his future relationship with his child will be like. It starts with a scene at the child's first birthday party, where a somewhat desperate Robin is trying to teach the young guests how to perform stand-up comedy. "No, Father, no!" the child screams, in Robin's high-pitched kiddie voice. "I don't want to do any comedy! . . . Let me give it a break, Father, give it a break!"

"Come on, now, what do you want for your birthday?" Robin asks as himself.

"Power of attorney," the child responds.

In mock despair, Robin pleads with the child, " 'Ninny-ninny' isn't good enough for you? *Popeye* isn't good enough for you?"

The child screams, "*Popeye* wasn't good for anybody! Who are you kidding?"

The scene then flashes forward to a time when the child, now twenty-one years old, has rejected comedy and is leaving home to pursue a respectable career as a scientist (in order to cure herpes). Robin, in his rage and frustration, goes on a drinking spree, requiring the child to come rescue him from his incapacitated stupor.

"Pop," the grown child says, "I've come to take you home." He then adds, "Hey, Dad" — and grabs his own crotch as he makes a squeaking sound, proving once and for all that he is a loving, attentive chip off the old block.

His set continues with a bit about cocaine — "the devil's dandruff, the Peruvian marching powder" — and its tendencies to induce impotence and paranoia, but never with an explicit acknowledgment from Robin that this wisdom might have been gleaned from his own experiences. And in a pre-taped conclusion, the newsstand vendor from the opening of the show comes face-to-face with Robin (as himself). The two men talk as the Great American Music Hall is being cleaned up, and the newsboy gives Robin a personal memento: an autographed picture of Albert Einstein — a man, he explains, who used to say, "My sense of God is my sense of wonder about the universe." The newsboy asks Robin to pass it on to his unborn child. "It's yours now," the newsboy says. "You're going to be the keeper of the flame. . . . You're a crazy bastard. Good to see the lights are still on."

One more professional obligation stood between Robin and the reality of becoming a parent. He was committed to making *The Survivors,* a farcical comedy about a dental-equipment salesman who is fired from his job and drifts into a series of increasingly absurd misadventures: he accidentally blows up a gas station with a lit cigarette; finds himself at the same diner as the gas-station owner, where the two of them foil a stickup man; then enrolls at an outdoor survivalist camp in Vermont as his newfound enemies are converging on him for a final showdown.

Directed by Michael Ritchie (*The Candidate, The Bad News Bears*), the project showed potential but was beset by casting changes and production problems. Weeks before filming was to begin, the film lost its potential costars Jack Nicholson and James Caan, who were replaced by Joe Bologna and Jerry Reed. Then, at the start of 1983, Bologna dropped out and was replaced by Walter Matthau. Making matters even more challenging, the movie needed several days of filming in the snow for its outdoor survival-camp scenes, but the production showed up in rural Vermont just as the state was experiencing a wave of unseasonably warm weather. On one of the rare days that the temperature dropped to five degrees, Reed was hospitalized for accidental carbon monoxide inhalation in his trailer and Robin's mouth was so frozen he garbled his improvisations.

With the delays costing the film some $70,000 a day, the production was forced to move to Lake Tahoe to finish the snow scenes

— a relocation that was itself delayed when Vermont was blanketed in a blizzard on the day of the planned move — dragging out Robin's shooting schedule as Valerie's delivery date drew closer. Matthau passed the chilly downtime listening to football games on a portable radio he stashed in his parka, but Robin was miserable. "Now I know what it's like to be a dog," he grumbled, as filming lumbered on into February.

Even after *The Survivors* wrapped, Robin found time in April to squeeze in one more TV appearance, on an HBO special celebrating the Comedy Store. In front of a celebrity crowd that included Kris Kristofferson and Mr. T, Robin was introduced by his friend Richard Pryor, who said, with a kind of affectionate animosity, "He asked me to come up and do improvs with him, and I watched him for an hour." Robin performed for only a few minutes this time, reminding viewers that his wife was about to have a baby — "She's at home, going, 'I'll hold it, I'll hold it.'" He held forth a bit on deep-breathing exercises and amniocentesis. ("My God, it's a boy and he's hung like a bear. The doctor drew me aside: 'Mr. Williams, that's the umbilical.'")

Then he added, somewhat more sincerely, that he had been thinking about the strangeness of being a carefree and sometimes irresponsible young man who got paid to pretend for an audience, and that reflecting on this subject had a lasting impact on how he planned to behave going forward. "It really does sober your ass up," he said, "when you realize, you'll have to — six years from now — be going, 'Daddy doesn't really know what he does for a living.' "

Three days later, on April 11, 1983, Valerie gave birth to a boy she and Robin named Zachary Pym Williams, a name chosen for no other reason than that they thought it sounded good and "kind of Welsh." The child, who would come to be known as Zak, was delivered by cesarean section when it was discovered he was wrapped up in the umbilical cord, leaving Robin mildly annoyed that he and Valerie had devoted so much time to natural childbirth training that turned out to be unnecessary. "It was like going through flight training and ending up in a glider," he said.

The jokes would come later. In the immediate moment, seeing his son in front of him and holding him in his own hands — even before Valerie had the chance to do so — was profound and life-altering in a way that births tend to be. Robin fully understood now that there was a piece of him inside this little human, and the years-long process of nurturing him to become his own person was going to be an enormously satisfying undertaking. As Robin would later write to Zak, this was when it occurred to him that "suddenly there was a focus, a meaning, a continuity. My newborn baby who looked like Churchill and Gandhi . . . you. You opened your eyes, and mine!" Then, as Robin held him up, his infant son peed "a long, perfect arc" that landed right on him, almost as if it had been aimed at him on purpose. Simultaneously, Robin burst out laughing and broke down in tears of joy.

The surge of euphoria that Robin felt at Zak's birth was something he could share with Valerie, too — a development in their relationship that was so purely positive it seemed to cancel out the mistrust and regret that they had once felt toward each other, and allowed them to start over as father and mother. For so long, they had lived in a state of constant surveillance and anxiety, knowing that their most intimate difficulties were bound to be splashed across the tabloids and shared with millions of strangers — an atmosphere due in no small part to Robin's own indiscretions and recklessness. Now they had news they wanted everyone to know about, and they joyously proclaimed it wherever they could, in newspaper and trade-publication articles and in personal birth announcements they mailed to family members and close friends, featuring a photograph of the infant Zak dressed up in a baby-size tuxedo, a handmade gift sent to them by one of Robin's fans.

Parenthood offered Robin the added benefit of distracting him from the decadent Hollywood party scene that had been the source of so many of his troubles. A few months after Zak was born, Robin and Valerie took him to New York, so that Robin could work on his next film, *Moscow on the Hudson.* As he liked to do while he was in town, Robin used his free time to make unannounced appearances at Catch a Rising Star, and in these shows, he started bringing Billy Crystal with him as a surprise stage partner.

For many years he and Crystal had moved on parallel career paths, and they shared the same managers. While Robin was blasting off in *Mork & Mindy,* Crystal was gaining national attention on the ABC sitcom *Soap.* Their breakthrough shows had ended within a year of each other, and Robin had made a guest appearance on one episode of *The Billy Crystal Comedy Hour,* a short-lived 1982 NBC sketch program, playing Ed Norton to Crystal's Ralph Kramden in a punk-rock update of *The Honeymooners.*

But there was something more fundamental that drew them together. Crystal, a Jewish Long Islander and New York University graduate whose grandfather had founded the independent jazz label Commodore Records and whose father helped run the specialty music shop that had spawned it, had an authenticity that Robin could never duplicate. No matter how Robin tried to distort his own personal history, cover up his Waspishness, or compensate for his affluent upbringing by incorporating ethnic accents and characters into his routine, Crystal came by his outsider's perspective honestly, for the simple fact that he'd been born into it.

Crystal felt that Robin's fascination with him was even simpler, rooted in the fact that Robin, who led a chaotic, unpredictable life, saw Crystal as a paragon of stability: his marriage was secure, his life was free of vices and addictions, and his family was paramount. "We were a close-knit group," Crystal said of his relatives. But he also felt a kinship with Robin. "I lost my dad young; he lost his dad younger" — metaphorically speaking. "Even though his dad was still alive, there was a distance there," he said.

Their attachment grew stronger over many more sessions of improv at Catch a Rising Star, which Robin believed could cure all woes and rinse the gloom out of any bad day. On one such night, Crystal was in a dour mood, having whiffed a Broadway audition earlier in the day. "I'm done," he said. "I'm nobody. My career is over. I'm not any good. I'm going nowhere."

"C'mon," Robin said, "let's go play" — his invitation for Crystal to come with him to

Catch a Rising Star. They were joined on their walk to the club by Greg Phillips, Robin's saxophone instructor on the film, who feared for Crystal's safety that evening. "All he needs, when the guy is so down in the dumps, is to get up there with Robin Williams," Phillips said. "Nobody can stay with Robin. He'll be blown off the stage, he'll be an entire failure and he'll take his life. He'll jump into the Hudson River." Instead, Robin hit the stage to his usual applause and acclaim, which grew even louder when he brought out Crystal as his guest, and the pair joyously ad-libbed a scene pretending to be old Russian men in a cemetery. After that, Phillips said, "We walked back across town and Billy was feeling better. And I was thinking: wow, he dodged a bullet."

After one such show, Robin invited Crystal back to the Upper East Side brownstone where he and Valerie were staying so he could meet Zak for the first time. When they arrived, the baby was crying inconsolably and Robin, still a rookie parent, found himself unable to calm the child. But Crystal, who was the father of two daughters, was undeterred and had a battle-tested soothing strategy ready to deploy. "I said, 'Robin, let me,'" Crystal recalled. "I was a Dr. Spock fan, and I remembered it said, like on page seventy-eight or somewhere: 'Use your index finger to *effleurage*' — which is a fancy word for massage — 'the base of the baby's skull to calm it down.' Within a few minutes it worked, and Zak stopped crying. And Robin started. 'You're a miracle man.' And the three of us hugged."

This marked a new phase in their friendship where, whenever Robin and Crystal could stop goofing around long enough, their silliness gave way to more meaningful conversations, often about Robin's concerns about fatherhood. "Once we stopped making each other laugh and playing whoever we were going to play, it was always about the kids," Crystal said. "He would ask me, 'If this happened, what would you do? And then what would you do?' I already had footprints in the snow, you know?"

By now, Robin had withstood the release of *The Survivors,* which received a very subdued reception. Those reviewers who hoped, as the *Los Angeles Times'* critic did, that the film might generate heat from the friction of its two comic stars, "Walter Matthau's soulful deadpan against Robin Williams' Gatling-gun bursts of improvisation," found instead that the film "does not so much disappoint our hopes as dissipate them. Both actors are at the top of their form, but the comic premise of the first 15 minutes begins to come apart."

Others were brutal in their scorn; Gene Siskel, in the *Chicago Tribune,* called *The Survivors* "one of the most confused and repellent films of the year." Robin, he wrote, was "exhausting — not because one laughs so hard but because he runs on and on unchecked." *The Survivors* was crushed at the box office, too, and closed after a month.

In the summer of 1983, Robin was well into the shooting for *Moscow on the Hudson,* a film that was the brainchild of Paul Mazursky, an iconoclastic director who specialized in closely observed character studies (*Bob & Carol & Ted & Alice, An Unmarried Woman*), not blockbuster smashes. Mazursky, who wrote the screenplay with Leon Capetanos, wanted to tell the story of an émigré from the Soviet Union who defects to America on a visit to New York; the idea had come to him while riding in taxi cabs around the city. ("I met rear admirals from Leningrad driving taxis," he explained.) The film's protagonist, who announces his change of allegiance in the middle of Bloomingdale's, was originally supposed to be a ballet dancer, and Mazursky had hoped to cast Mikhail Baryshnikov in the role. But when Baryshnikov passed, Mazursky rewrote the lead as a saxophonist in a Moscow circus, making it a better fit for Robin. "There's not a long list if you decide to go with somebody who's 30 to 35, with a sense of humor, who can act and is willing to learn Russian," Mazursky said.

Robin threw himself into his preparations, in a way that went beyond the character work he had done for his previous movies. He let his hair and beard grow, and spent five months studying Russian through a Berlitz language course. The subterfuge was not totally convincing, however. When he traveled to Munich, which stood in for the portion of the film ostensibly set in Moscow, he found that most Europeans were unconvinced by his accent. "They said I sounded Czech," Robin explained. "I sounded Polish. I sounded Georgian. A lot of Russians see the film and go, *'Who iz ze Polish boy in ze lead?'* "

But Mazursky understood why Robin was so attracted to this immersive character work, and why he sought opportunities to create entirely new identities, just as he had done in his stand-up act: it was so much easier for him to be other people than it was to be himself. "He's really very modest," the director said. "He really hates talking about himself or his background. He doesn't like strangers to get too close. He protects himself by adopting this disguise."

Before he left California to start filming, Robin had Greg Phillips teach him to play the saxophone for scenes like the one where his character performs "Take the 'A' Train" for a stable of circus animals. For hours each day they would practice at the Napa ranch, in a small concrete pool house away from the main residence, where baby Zak was sleeping. Phillips was astonished at how quickly Robin took to it.

"He had never played a musical instrument at this point," said Phillips, who also traveled with Robin to Munich and to New York. "The only thing he'd ever done was dabble on the harmonica."

Like many of his colleagues, Phillips believed that Robin had a photographic memory. "Even though I insisted that he learned to read music," he said, "his mind was so fast that we would — I thought — be reading a piece, and he would memorize it as quickly as we had played through it. So then, when I would say to Robin, why don't we go back to Bar 15 or 16, he would go, 'Uh, yeah, where's that?' Because he had it in his head, but he couldn't tell on the music where it was."

During the New York portion of the shoot, Robin and Mazursky went to see the documentary *Unknown Chaplin,* in which Charlie Chaplin's movie outtakes and other personal footage had been carefully compiled to give a unique and detailed window into the silent comedy master's filmmaking process. Robin was blown away by a simple scene where Chaplin wordlessly illustrates to the camera that he has eaten an apple with a worm in it by taking a bite out of the fruit and then ever-so-slightly wiggling his index finger. After the three-hour screening, this was all he could seem to talk about: "Boy, can you believe that thing with his finger? Half a second, and he shows you there's a worm in the apple, and the look on his face?" This, to him, was the essence of comedy — the subtlety, the precision, the warmth — a Platonic ideal that he sensed was still miles away from his talkative, high-energy approach.

Robin's expressive, fragile character in *Moscow on the Hudson* — who speaks almost no English for the film's first half-hour, and who suffers a breakdown in an American supermarket when he sees the sheer number of coffee brands he can now choose from — may have seemed to viewers like he was outside the spectrum of what Robin was known for, possibly even beyond the realm of his capability as an actor. But Robin said he felt compelled to make more "strange films," as he called them — motion pictures that didn't align with his audience's expectations and seemed unlike anything he'd done before — for those precise reasons. "I hope I can keep doing more," he said. "I think I chose them because I didn't want to do what was easy." Then, almost immediately, he added: "I'll probably end up, next day you'll see, 'Look, it's *Mork & Mindy*! He's back and he's crazier than ever!' "

Robin sensed that a running tally was being kept of the ticket sales generated by his movies; there was an exact number that could be assigned to the worth he provided, which could be used to measure him against the value of other actors, and if that number dropped below a certain threshold, he wouldn't be able to make movies anymore. "If I have a couple more that don't do too well," he said, "they go like, 'Robin, you're so daring. . . . We'll get back to you.' 'A very daring movie you did — and a little stupid. But we love ya!' "

This was not some imaginary scenario that played out only in Robin's head; it was reinforced to him by his managers, who reminded him that, at some point soon, he needed to make a picture that added substantially to this bottom line. Yet he felt he had their support to pursue unconventional opportunities, too. "Sometimes my managers get worried, but they're sort of like parents saying, 'Well, if you really want to do these we'll stand with you,' " he said. "Which is nice. Sometimes you do feel that pressure. 'You haven't made a film that made any money. There's no big box office yet.' I say, 'Yeah, I know. I know there's not a lot of *Survivors* dolls around.' "

He was especially unnerved by the success of *Trading Places,* a hit comedy from that summer of 1983. Directed by John Landis, it starred Dan Aykroyd and Eddie Murphy as a wealthy commodities trader and a streetwise beggar who swap stations in life. The comedy marketplace, as Robin saw it, was a zero-sum game: for someone to rise, it meant that someone else had to fall, and if Aykroyd and Murphy were in ascendance, what did that mean for him? Murphy, in particular, seemed to be making the transition from television to movies so effortlessly, with an ease that eluded Robin. "Eddie is ideal — he knows exactly what he does and how to get it out on film perfectly," Robin said. "I don't — I keep trying different things."

Late one night that summer, Bennett Tramer, his friend and collaborator, got a phone call from Robin. As Tramer recounted the conversation, "He said, 'It's Robin — have you seen *Trading Places*?' And I said, yeah I have. And he said, 'How is it?' I didn't know what to say. And I said, I think it's Landis's best movie, it's much more sophisticated than his other stuff. And he said, 'How's Danny in it?' I said, he's good, it's good. It's hard to compete with Murphy but they're both good. He said, 'All right, just wondered.'"

Though Robin did not come out and say it, Tramer knew what he was really asking. "It wasn't like he rooted for other people to fail — he was a classy guy," Tramer said. "But it was kind of weird. Maybe not weird. Maybe it makes total sense. He was very happy for them and really liked them, but it was like, When's my turn coming? When's my turn going to come to have a hit movie?"

When Robin's second comedy album had been released earlier that spring, there was a similar sense that, for all its feverish energy and ingenuity, the performer at the heart of it was oddly absent. The album, defiantly titled *Throbbing Python of Love* as a sort of preemptive rebuke to anyone who might dismiss his dick jokes as juvenile, had been recorded during the same San Francisco club dates that yielded the HBO special *An Evening with Robin Williams.* It consisted of mostly the same bits in a different running order, and with more of his off-the-cuff interactions with audience members. When one person in the crowd is heard calling on Robin to do some improv, he teasingly shouts back, "What do you think the fuckin' last thirty minutes has been?"

Reviewing the album for the *Los Angeles Times,* Lawrence Christon wrote that "of the three major comedic talents who matured in the '70s" — the other two being Steve Martin and Richard Pryor — Robin was "the only one to get out alive as a stand-up." (Martin, the perception went, was more focused on his film career now, and Pryor was struggling to make the transition in this new decade.) Undoubtedly, Robin had "the fastest timing and the sharpest improvisational skills of anyone on the scene these days — there's probably never been anybody who has brought more pure theater to stand-up comedy." But Christon also felt obliged to acknowledge that Robin was "not a sympathetic performer." In those moments when Robin did share personal details about himself, like the fact that he was going to become a father (and already had by the time the album was released), they were "delivered in the spirit of comic outburst" rather than some act of intimate confession.

Unlike *Reality . . . What a Concept,* which had been a Top 10 hit, *Throbbing Python of Love* did not have the engine of a popular TV sitcom to keep Robin visible and drive its sales. It debuted at number 180 on the Billboard sales chart, peaked at 119, and dropped off the charts after nine weeks. Still, it was among the nominees for the Grammy Award for Best Comedy Album the following winter, along with *Eddie Murphy: Comedian,* the second stand-up record from that upstart twenty-two-year-old star of *Saturday Night Live* and *Trading Places.*

As it happened, Robin was invited to host *Saturday Night Live* for the first time on February 11, 1984, a little more than two weeks before the Grammys ceremony. He and Murphy acted opposite each other in only one sketch, a parody of the public affairs show *Firing Line,* in which Robin played the erudite William F. Buckley Jr. and Murphy played an academic type discussing why black entertainers were suddenly so hot. ("Because of pigment," he explains, the "black man is becoming more flammable every day.") In this brief confrontation of language and tone, the contrast between their two styles could not be sharper: Robin, in a gray-haired wig, getting wound up in the nuts and bolts of Buckley's upper-crust stammer and the racial provocations scripted for him ("N-n-n-now surely you're not implying the phenomenon i-i-is more prevalent among entertainers than a-a-among other blacks, ah, Afro-Americans, ah, whatever phrase is current among you coloreds"); Murphy, coolly gliding his way through the segment, even when his character begins to spontaneously combust. Naturally, it was *Eddie Murphy: Comedian,* not *Throbbing Python of Love,* that would win the Grammy.

Moscow on the Hudson was not to be the movie that elevated Robin's artistic or commercial standing when it was released in the spring of 1984. In the *New York Times,* Vincent Canby wrote that though Robin and his alter ego were "most engaging characters — spirited, skeptical, but still capable of wonderment," the film itself "doesn't seem to know what to do with them. They are men without a movie."

New York magazine was more appreciative;

319

David Denby wrote that Robin was "securely grounded; he has a real character to play, and he's extraordinarily touching. Bearded, and hairy as a Russian bear, he's a small, nearly innocuous figure in the Moscow scenes, clutching himself against the cold, grimacing at the sight of a three-hour waiting line for toilet paper." Commercially, *Moscow on the Hudson* had a respectable run but, once again, it was not a star-making turn.

Amid all the work he was doing, Robin always tried to find ways to acknowledge Zak and celebrate the newly happy home he and Valerie had created. He claimed that the opening of *Moscow on the Hudson* had coincided with the day that Zak took his first steps, and he used his closing minutes on *Saturday Night Live* to wish a special good night to his son: "He's at home right now going, 'Get off! You've done too much. Go home, take the money, let's go back to California.' "

Back in Napa, Valerie was considering bringing in more help at home to raise their rambunctious one-year-old son. Though the Williams family had previously employed a nanny, she had left the job, and in their search for a replacement they reached out to their friend Taylor Negron, who in turn suggested they consider a candidate named Marsha Garces. Marsha, who was in her late twenties, was practically overqualified for a

320

caregiver's position; having grown up in Milwaukee, she had studied art at the University of Wisconsin there, and after moving to the Bay Area she continued to take art classes at San Francisco State College while working as a waitress by night.

"I interviewed her at a fish restaurant," Valerie said of Marsha. "And she took the job."

9
TOUGH LOVE

"Lust!" Robin Williams intoned with an evangelist's fervor, speaking to nearly four thousand people in the vast orchestra and far-flung balconies of the Metropolitan Opera House in New York. Over the years, this opulent theater had been the setting for any number of tales about the irrevocable consequences of our human passions. On this night it was as good a place as any for Robin to get a few things off his chest, too.

"Men," he said to the crowd, "you know you have a tiny creature living between your legs that has no memory and no conscience. You *know* that. You know you have no control over this tiny beast.

"We have lust," Robin continued. "Lust permeates our soul sometimes. Men, we are so driven by this lust that we have a violent streak that comes along with it. If we can't fuck it, we'll kill it, you know what I'm saying?"

As he moved on to a bit about a penis being called to testify as a witness in a divorce trial, Robin had just offered an oblique glimpse into his own life — an accounting, of sorts, of what had happened in the months leading up to this performance. It was a window into his own personal shortcomings, in what would be his most personal routine to date. But few watching him knew just how honest he was being.

For a time after Zak was born, it seemed that Robin and Valerie had finally set their relationship on the right path. "The first year and a half, couple of years, it was beautiful," Valerie said. "And then it just started again, the same old thing." The alcohol and drugs that Robin renounced had stayed out of his life, but these were not the only temptations he wrestled with. He could not completely stay away from Los Angeles, the throbbing heart of the entertainment industry and the town whose approval he was determined to win. He could never resist the lure of the stand-up stage, the adulation of a crowd that came just to see him — or better yet, had no idea he would be there — and the satisfaction of sweating for an hour to live up to their every expectation. And he could not completely kick his desire for all the attendant pleasures that, in his mind, went hand in hand with a successful show.

One night in 1984, Robin showed up at the Improv in Los Angeles, where he caught the attention of Michelle Tish Carter, a cocktail waitress there. Carter, of course, knew who Robin was and considered herself a fan, but she was too starstruck to strike up a conversation, so she asked a friend to introduce them. Though she was only twenty-one, Carter was more accomplished than her age and job might have suggested; she was a skilled musician who had toured the country in her teens and earned a college degree before coming to Los Angeles to further her own dreams of stardom. She and Robin hit it off and began an affair. Robin did not bring Carter to his premieres or other industry functions, did not invite her to spend time among his friends, and likely did not consider their relationship anything more than a fling, but it would continue for nearly two years.

Valerie could never quite bring herself to condemn Robin for his infidelities; she seemed to accept them as an occupational hazard of stardom. "Very attractive women throw themselves at men in his position," she said. "You'd have to be a saint to resist." But now that they were parents it was not so easy to look away; after they had Zak, she said, "neither of us was prepared for the sudden life shift. I admit the other women were harder to take after I'd had a child."

Professionally, Robin's reputation as a viable leading man was faltering, laid low by two movies that were made, released, and dismissed in quick succession. The first was *The Best of Times,* a comedy in which he and Kurt Russell played former teammates on a high school football squad who are still smarting from their loss, years ago, in a championship game. Robin's character, now a buttoned-down bank executive with wide-rimmed glasses and a sensible haircut, still can't forgive himself for bobbling what would have been the winning pass, and he has become obsessed with re-creating the fateful match, to the exclusion of everything else in his life. Eventually, he is thrown out of his house by his wife (Holly Palance), who no longer has the patience for his boyish fixations.

Directed by Roger Spottiswoode, an editor for Sam Peckinpah and a screenwriter of *48 Hrs.* (as well as Palance's husband), and written by Ron Shelton (the future filmmaker of *Bull Durham* and *White Men Can't Jump*), *The Best of Times* was filmed at the start of 1985 in Taft, California, just outside Los Angeles. Its themes of youthful glory and athleticism had some appeal to Robin, harking back to his days as a high school and college wrestler and track runner, and to Russell, who'd been a child actor and a minor-league baseball player before establishing himself as a film star in adulthood.

When *The Best of Times* was released in

January 1986, Robin acknowledged that he needed it to be a hit. Though the reviews were positive if polite, the film's box-office receipts were abysmal. Robin was becoming the kind of celebrity who got written about in the where-are-they-now newspaper columns that filled space alongside TV listings and word jumbles. As one reader wrote to ask around this time, "What's happened to Robin Williams? I haven't heard much of him since *Garp.*" The column's scolding reply read that perhaps Robin's recent films "didn't fare too well because even fans like you missed them."

He followed *The Best of Times* with *Club Paradise,* a farcical comedy in which he played an injured Chicago firefighter who uses his disability money to buy property on a Caribbean island and set up a shabby resort. The movie had a promising pedigree, beginning with its director and cowriter, Harold Ramis, who was coming off the runaway success of *Ghostbusters* in the summer of 1984. (The project had initially been intended for Bill Murray, who turned it down.) Its impressively eclectic cast included Peter O'Toole as the island's elegantly dissipated governor, the fashion model Twiggy as Robin's love interest, the reggae star Jimmy Cliff as his partner in the resort scheme, and a smattering of *SCTV* cast members including Rick Moranis, Eugene Levy, Andrea Martin, and Joe Flaherty.

Ramis, whose own estimable comedy résumé included *SCTV* and films like *Animal House, Stripes, Caddyshack,* and *Vacation,* seemed like an ideal filmmaker to take advantage of Robin's improvisatory gifts. "I felt that Robin has never been seen as himself in films," Ramis said. "He's not as quirky as he was in *Garp* or *Moscow on the Hudson,* nor is he a schlemiel, as in *The Survivors.* In *Popeye* he was hidden. Trying to get an actor to be himself is tough. They much prefer to play other roles."

On location in Jamaica, Ramis struck a deal with Robin: if Robin shot one take as it was written in the script, he was then allowed to ad-lib in his further takes. When Robin told O'Toole in rehearsal that he planned to deviate from the script from time to time, the *Lawrence of Arabia* star replied, "Dear boy, go ahead. This is a *bizarre* way to make a fortune."

But an uneasy air seemed to hang over *Club Paradise.* In the midst of filming, a Jamaican soldier who performed in a parachute jump scene disappeared from the set and was presumed killed in a shark attack. Before the movie was released, Robin's costar Adolph Caesar died of a heart attack. And when *Club Paradise* opened in July 1986, the reviews were withering. As one critic wrote, "Robin

Williams' latest movie, *Club Paradise,* was shown exclusively in some cities last week; it should not be run again. It should be turned in to the Better Business Bureau for deceiving Williams' fans into thinking this is a funny movie." Another said: "Like a vacation during which everything goes wrong, the movie fizzles. There are funny moments, but they're all too few and this is another case of jokes looking better in a script than on screen."

Robin later acknowledged that the film had not been what he hoped for and that he'd taken it on for the wrong reasons. "They waved a lot of money at me," he said. "And then I tried to convince myself it would really be a political film. But slowly and surely it turned into just another beach movie." The one-two punch of *The Best of Times* and *Club Paradise* was a bitter lesson that he could not make a movie good all by himself, no matter how much improv he was allowed to do. "I took on slight projects, thinking, 'I can fix this,' " he said. "I got suckered into a couple films like that. . . . I thought, 'Well, they'll give me the freedom to do my thing,' but it turned out they didn't."

What he needed was for someone to write him a movie character that was madcap in moderation — the film equivalent of *Mork & Mindy* — but after so many misfires, it had become increasingly difficult to imagine what that role was. "God. It's out there some-where," he said. "It's got to be. Something with spirit, a character who doesn't drive people crazy. Mork was like that — Mork had total freedom, and yet people still found him sweet enough that they could tolerate the madness. It's a fine line. There has to be a story that's simple enough and strong enough to keep people going."

His stand-up was still the one part of his life where Robin could have control over every element, and by reinvesting himself in his craft, he was about to have a year of extraordinary creative fulfillment, one that would help make up for his cinematic disap-pointments. The past few years had seen a rapid increase in the number of stand-up clubs across the country, and the explosive growth of cable television gave stand-up comedy a national platform.

The 1980s had also witnessed a faddish rise in large-scale celebrity benefit events, where seemingly all the artists in a given field as-sembled to raise money for a charitable cause. It started in Great Britain with the hit 1984 Band Aid single "Do They Know It's Christmas?" to benefit starving children in Ethiopia. Then 1985 was the year of well-intentioned behemoths like USA for Africa, which gathered some fifty musicians and singers to record "We Are the World," and the Live Aid concerts, where dozens of bands

played at simultaneous concerts in Philadelphia and London. Now, in 1986, it was
comedy's turn to get into the act.

That January, HBO committed to broad-
casting a benefit concert, one that would
gather top comedians to raise money for
organizations that helped the American
homeless population. The event, called Comic
Relief, would be held at the end of March at
the Universal Amphitheatre in Los Angeles
and aired as a four-hour telethon, encouraging viewers to call in with donations. At a
press conference in Beverly Hills, HBO announced that Comic Relief would be hosted
by Robin Williams, Billy Crystal, and Whoopi
Goldberg.

There was not too much rhyme or reason
behind HBO's choice of headliners for the
event; as John Moffitt, an executive producer
of Comic Relief, later explained, "Basically,
they were under contract or they were people
that they had relationships with." But there
was a certain ad hoc logic at work. Robin
and Crystal were now fast friends who dis-
played an easy onstage give-and-take in their
improvised sets, though their shenanigans
had not been widely seen beyond the clubs.

Goldberg was the wild card of the group.
Born Caryn Johnson and raised in a New
York housing project, she had fleetingly
crossed paths with Robin at the Comedy
Store in San Diego when they were trying to

establish themselves as stand-ups in the 1970s. It had taken her nearly another decade to break through, time she spent raising a daughter as a single mother, working in the avant-garde theater scene in Berkeley, and developing a one-woman act she called *The Spook Show.* Playing a variety of imaginative and deeply felt characters — a pregnant Valley girl who gives herself a botched abortion; a Jamaican nurse who attends to an elderly white American man; a junkie with a PhD in literature who visits the Anne Frank house in Amsterdam — she certified her comedic and dramatic talents all at once. In 1984, she brought her show to New York's Dance Theater Workshop, where it was seen by Mike Nichols, who brought it to Broadway, where it was seen by Steven Spielberg, who cast her as Celie in *The Color Purple.* She had recently won a Golden Globe and was nominated for an Academy Award for her performance.

As a black woman, she brought some diversity to the top of the Comic Relief bill, though her reasons for wanting to participate in it were more personal: as recently as two years earlier, she had been on welfare and living with friends, and she never wanted anyone to fear homelessness as she did. "I want to cover my back in case I need help," she said. "It's hands across the street, boys and girls. It could be me tomorrow. It could be you tomorrow. It could be Mr. R." — by whom she meant Ronald Reagan.

The founder of the Comic Relief USA organization was Bob Zmuda, a veteran stand-up performer and a friend and former roommate of the HBO programming executive Chris Albrecht, a relationship that was crucial to setting up the benefit. Zmuda was best known as the long-time collaborator of Andy Kaufman, having occasionally played the role of the comic's disagreeable alter ego Tony Clifton — thus helping to perpetrate the ruse that Kaufman and Clifton were two different people. Zmuda's own sense of humor could sometimes be brusque: at the press conference announcing the HBO broadcast, a reporter asked if homeless viewers would have their own opportunity to watch the program. Zmuda bluntly answered, "No." After a few seconds of stunned silence, he told the room he was making a joke. Crystal rescued the awkward moment by wisecracking, "They get to see it only if they're subscribers to HBO."

Robin's involvement in Comic Relief was a natural outgrowth of his blossoming political consciousness, one that was unapologetically left-leaning and philanthropic. Of all the values he had been exposed to in the wanderings of his youth, he had embraced the altruistic liberalism of San Francisco, his adopted hometown, rather than the conservatism of the wealthy suburban automobile enclaves where he'd been raised. Robin made no secret of his revulsion for the presidency of Ronald Reagan, whom he mocked relentlessly in his stand-up, and the tone-deaf, inhumane lack of empathy that the Republican government represented to him.

It was a philosophy that put Robin at odds with his own upbringing, which was prosperous and comfortable, not to mention his newfound wealth from show business. He had begun to look for ways to give back, not only through outright donations but also with contributions of his time and comedy at benefit events. These took the form of appearances at well-intentioned if wonkish events like *The Night of At Least a Dozen Stars,* a 1984 fund-raiser for the National Committee for an Effective Congress, a political action group that had been founded decades earlier by Eleanor Roosevelt. This might have been an otherwise unremarkable night, if not for the fact that it was where Robin and Whoopi Goldberg first reencountered each other as established performers and faced off in an improvised routine of "dueling Valley people."

Comic Relief had the potential to reach further and to do more good, and Robin seemed genuinely touched by its purpose. At the press conference announcing the telethon, he explained how his coast-to-coast travels had opened his eyes to the burgeoning problem of homelessness and its harmful effects on families in particular. In a constant, nearly quavering voice, he said, "You ever see people, like a family of eight, living in a station wagon, have you seen that? Have you seen a sixteen-year-old wino wandering around Venice Beach? Have you been to Chicago and seen, like, a guy living in a paper box? Have you been wandering around New York and seen some of the people from the mental institutions that have been turned out, wandering around there? Guys talking to themselves? [leans into his shoulder and speaks gibberish] Just walk around any city, you'll have a good time. You'll catch it."

That winter, he began visiting homeless shelters around the country, partly to educate himself about the cause he would be supporting and partly to help promote the telecast the following month, though these appearances did not always lead to positive press coverage. When he and Tom Bradley, the mayor of Los Angeles, showed up together at a mission in the city's destitute downtown area, their news conference had the unintended effect of delaying meal service for about three hundred people who relied on the facility. Robin, it was reported, "smiled and waved as the homeless men waited patiently for the news conference to end so they could receive a free lunch." But when he, Crystal, and Goldberg appeared together at a shelter in Washington and then later at a press conference with Senator Ted Kennedy, there was a sense of a budding camaraderie among the three comedians, a playfulness that in time would grow into total, anarchic freedom — an unpredictability that could be thrilling and even dangerous.

On their trip to Washington, the hosts were warned not to make any wisecracks to Kennedy on one particular topic: Chappaquiddick. As Goldberg recalled, "We're on the plane and they say to us, 'Look, no jokes, you three. No jokes about cars. No jokes about driving off — nothing.' We all go, 'OK.' We're not going to mention anything. And we got off the plane, and we weren't going to mention anything." Upon arriving at his office, they were told by Kennedy: "Okay, I'm going to drive you to the next building." The three hosts could only gasp quietly and shake their heads at each other.

While the clock was ticking down to the big show and its organizers were racing to book as much talent as they could find, Robin was presented with another prominent opportunity: he was asked to cohost the Academy Awards, which would be held on March 24, only five days before the Comic Relief broadcast. He could hardly turn down this invitation, coming from the ceremony's producer, Stanley Donen, the venerated director of *On the Town* and *Singin' in the Rain,* in a rare instance where a comedian other than Bob Hope or Johnny Carson was invited to be an emcee of the Oscars. This year, Robin would share the stage with two more traditional co-hosts, Alan Alda and Jane Fonda.

Yet Robin was oddly underutilized during the Oscars broadcast. In its opening minutes, he appeared in a brief comedy sketch that kicked off the program, where he teasingly tried to persuade two accountants from Price Waterhouse that they should open their envelopes right away and reveal the night's winners so that everyone could get to their after-parties. Soon after, he turned up along-side Alda and Fonda, translating their intro-ductory remarks into what was supposed to be Chinese, Hindi, French, and "Filipino." Then he vanished for nearly two hours, returning at the program's midpoint for a brief routine of more ethnic jokes. Imagining viewers watching the show in China, he quipped, "Quick, Bing-Wa, Irving Thalberg award. We can't miss that."

He got off one good ad-lib on the night, after accidentally describing the Harrison Ford thriller *Witness* as being the story of "an Amish cop": "Oh, that wouldn't be too good," Robin said, chuckling at his own er-ror. " 'Dost thou know thy rights?' " By the following morning, all that anyone could seem to remember about the show was that *The Color Purple* had won none of the eleven

Oscars for which it had been nominated.

Two days later, Robin was in rehearsal for Comic Relief. Along with Crystal, Goldberg, and himself, the lineup included up-and-comers like Howie Mandel, Bobcat Goldthwait, and Paul Rodriguez; stars like Garry Shandling, Martin Short, Madeline Kahn, George Carlin, and Gilda Radner; and enduring legends like Jerry Lewis, Carl Reiner, Sid Caesar, and Minnie Pearl. The stage had been built to look like a shantytown of cardboard boxes, and the full script, encompassing ninety-five different comedy sketches, ran a total of 227 pages. Cuts were being made constantly, for time as well as sensitivity: a bit where the three hosts would have performed an advertisement for a product called the Sony Poorman — essentially a group of homeless singers who perform for people who can't afford a home stereo — felt in the end like it was not in the spirit of the evening. As Robin explained, "You can't make fun of the thing you're trying to help. So it was that fine line of, how much are you using it for humor, and how much were you helping it with it? It was a dangerous line."

The other members of the creative team were wary to ask the hosts to cut down their own material, largely out of respect for their talents and their stature. The show's opening routine had been budgeted at nine minutes in the script but ran nearly thirty minutes in rehearsal; it came down to seventeen minutes for broadcast. "They each made an entrance, individually, and then they played off each other," said Moffitt, the executive producer. "At that point we were so happy to have them do it, we weren't going to mess around with them, by saying, oh, you've got to cut that. You've got to cut that. We basically let them do what they wanted to do." As Crystal explained it, "We'd make these pretty interesting playbooks, and then not do them, because something else would pop up."

Comic Relief commenced with the trio's rotating character bits: Goldberg emerged from a cardboard box as a homeless character and observed, "I did a little time, got caught in another neighborhood. This is like a real hip place to live." Robin came out of the next box, dressed in a trucker cap and denim jacket, and delivered a familiar line: "I'm so happy to be here I could drop a log." He said he'd lost his farm but built himself a new home from government cheese with "a little brie for windows, gouda doorknobs. . . . Up came spring, phew, you didn't want to stand downwind from our little home. I miss it, though. Casa Velveeta." Crystal entered as an old black jazz musician; Goldberg returned, now as a window-display designer for Bergdorf Goodman; Robin played a street flasher and then Ronald Reagan inside the frame of a TV set: "I understand what it's like to be homeless because many of my friends are in escrow right now," he said. "Won't you please help little Baby Doc Duvalier and Ferdinand Marcos? Because we're trying to establish a thing called Club Fled." When the three hosts finished their opening act and went backstage for the first time, Pat Tourk Lee, one of the show's executive producers, told them, "The phones are ringing." At that moment, Crystal said, "We all started to cry. We knew we were doing something good."

And on and on and on it went. They riffed between the stand-up sets and the pre-taped segments; at times they even riffed on top of each other. When Robin and Crystal caught themselves talking over each other for the umpteenth time, Crystal joked, "Oh, in stereo." In another transitional segment, Robin appealed to the viewers for their contributions: "You'll feel great, we'll feel great, and the homeless will feel grateful, because you cared," he said, slipping inexplicably into the basso voice of a stereotypical black man: "We know where you live, man." Goldberg, in her own self-parodying patois, said to Robin, "I like the way you do them colored people." There was not much Robin could say in response, except for a deeply chagrined "a-ha."

Throughout the night, the three hosts were learning how to work together as a group — even Robin and Crystal, who had performed together many times before but continued to discover new dynamics in their partnership. "We're testing our abilities against each other," Crystal said, "feeling out, How can I work with him? How could he work with me? And I realized, don't compete — set up, let him do his thing, and then counterpunch. We'd be sparring, and he'd have a look in his eye, like, I'm going to throw a left, a right, a right, and a left, and you're not going to see it coming."

In their final sketch of the night, Robin and Crystal played "Betty's Boys," the two backup singer-dancers to an unspecified, aging former theater star as they rehearse their Las Vegas show in her absence. It was mostly an excuse for the two of them to sing, dance, and clown around in aerobics outfits and mincing gay voices while poking impish fun at each other. ("What's happening under your arms there?" Crystal asked Robin, who as usual was glazed in his own sweat. "It smells like Eau de Alex Karras." "I like to call them my little Smith Brothers," Robin answered.) Then the show — which ran so long, it would have to be rebroadcast in smaller ninety-minute chunks — concluded with all its cast members singing a "We Are the World"–style anthem of their own.

> There comes a time, when the world is
>   split in half

And you seem to be knee-deep in grief
There comes a time, when you sure could
   use a laugh
That's the time when we call for Comic
   Relief

It was not, perhaps, the funniest number, but at least it was over. A few days later, the *New York Times* wrote that the show had "faced and never quite surmounted, a split-personality problem. . . . But comedians are notoriously resilient performers, always determined to triumph over seemingly impossible odds. And the evening, while uneven, did manage to salvage a respectable quota of invigorating laughs, most of them from predictable sources. The three hosts did their turns capably, singly and together." Much more than that, the program had helped establish Robin, Crystal, and Goldberg in viewers' minds as the nation's ambassadors of improv comedy, a unit so tightly interwoven (if not always on the same page) that it would soon become impossible to see any two of them together without wondering where the third team member was. And the broadcast had raised nearly $2.5 million in donations, an outright success that would make Comic Relief an ongoing HBO tradition. The experience had helped fan the flame of a humane ember that was already inside Robin, and for years afterward, he would even try to find jobs for homeless people on the sets of his films.

No sooner had Robin finished Comic Relief than he was back on the road, undertaking another stand-up tour that would take him to twenty-three cities, from New Haven to Los Angeles, in a ten-week span over the spring and summer of 1986. His manager David Steinberg, who had become a valuable collaborator in the process of shaping and editing his material, traveled with him on this trip, as did Marsha Garces, whom the Williamses had hired as Zak's nanny and who had now been promoted to the position of Robin's assistant for the itinerary.

The relationship between them was strictly professional, Marsha said. "He was too screwed up and I wasn't interested in being sucked dry," she explained. So she mostly gave him tough-love pep talks: "You've got two great careers, you're really intelligent, you're healthy, you're strong, you're handsome, you have a great son — and you're totally depressed. You're an adult, Robin; pull it together!"

Whatever he had left in him after the Oscars and Comic Relief, Robin poured all of it into this tour: he played his scheduled, sold-out performances, of which there were one or two each night, then hit a local comedy club in each town for an additional after-hours appearance. By his own reckoning, he was getting about three to five hours of sleep a night, but at least he could now say honestly — and publicly — that the alcohol and cocaine benders that once figured prominently in these nocturnal sprees had been eliminated from his life.

That past era, Robin said, "was just a madhouse. A time when you didn't want to stop. It got to the point where people said I'd go to the opening of an envelope. I felt like the top of a roulette wheel." The drinking had made him bloated and overweight, and the drug use had inhibited his hallmark quickness. "It's a nerve deadener," he said of cocaine. "You totally withdraw yourself. It basically removes your ability to make connections, your synapses are frying. . . . Now I realize it was the most boring time in the world. I was doing so many things I could never really stop and enjoy one moment."

"Cocaine is one of the most selfish drugs in the world," he said. "The world is as big as your nostril."

There was almost nothing else for Robin to focus on but his work, because his personal life was in tatters. He had ended his extramarital relationship with Michelle Tish Carter, the waitress and musician he had met at the Comedy Store, but with considerable acrimony. She had told him initially that she was carrying his child and that she expected him to help support her financially. But when her pregnancy claim turned out to be false, Robin refused to pay her anything. Carter also said she told him the previous fall that she had contracted herpes from him, a contention that Robin said was impossible since two separate blood tests had shown he had no sexually transmitted diseases. She then sued Robin for more than $6 million, and though it would take many more months for this case to play out fully in the courts, this was time that he spent afraid that Carter's lawsuit would be discovered by the press.

When Robin was asked, in an interview from this period, what kept Valerie interesting to him, he answered, "The accountant." Then he laughed and added, "She's tried to support me as much as possible. She finds the public aspect very hard." But in truth, his marriage to Valerie was all but finished, done in not by any one particular betrayal or transgression but by the erosion of trust between them that occurred each time she forgave him for an act of wrongdoing. "I'm not a controlling person," Valerie said. "I wanted him to be free, and he wanted me to be free. And in that process, I think we got more separated than I would have liked."

As Robin explained it, "Ultimately, things went astray. We changed, and then with me wandering off again a little bit, then coming back and saying, 'Wait, I need help' — it just got terribly painful." He started seeing a therapist, as a way to help him come to terms with their separation without writing it off as a failure. "It's not disappointing," he said of their breakup. "That's why therapy helps a lot. It forces you to look at your life and figure out what's functioning and what isn't. You don't have to beat your brains against a wall if it's not working. That's why you choose to be separated rather than to call each other an asshole every day."

Through this difficult time, it was important to Robin that he continue to have a strong presence in the life of his son, Zak, who had just turned three and was becoming more attuned to the real person submerged within all the characters his father played. "You suddenly have a malleable little creature that picks up on everything you do," Robin explained. "If you are not together, he'll notice it very quickly. I don't get too manic or crazy around him. I've learned that I can turn off the voices very easily. It's becoming more comfortable to stay a few more seconds as myself. You have to be somewhat straight with your son so that he recognizes your voice as the 'basic Daddy voice.' "

In the eyes of his lifelong friend Christopher Reeve, the bond between Robin and Zak was crucial in helping Robin reconnect to his own childhood. "When you see Robin play with *any* child, you see the child immediately understand him," Reeve said. "The child in

Robin is so open and approachable and immediately apparent." As Reeve observed, Robin's humor was rooted in his youth, the sense of solitude he felt and the voices and stories he created to entertain himself. "He's very aware, real grown up, but still in touch with the child in him," Reeve said. "Throughout his life, he's always felt alone with his imagination."

But Robin was not entirely ready to give up on his family. Even in the midst of a tour stop in Orange County, California, he flew back to Napa to plead with Valerie that they stay together. By night his frustrations were spilling over into his stand-up act. "Maybe that's why there's a certain vehemence in my show, an intensity," he said. "One of the foundations of your life is about to change and you're going, 'Yeah, let's play, ladies and gentlemen, let's have a GOOD TIME!' " He said he had even cut back on the amount of spontaneous interaction he allowed himself with his audience members, for fear that he might accidentally snap at people. "I'm just going to have to try and stay very calm," he said. "The tendency is to overact at this point and just get crazy. It's a pretty raw time for me."

Still, he felt as if something was holding him back in his stand-up — that he still could not be completely honest about himself in front of an audience and tell them what was happening in his life. "Maybe that's the next step, to talk about really personal things," he said. "Soon I think I'll be ready to do that. Because I've never been able to do that in my life. I'm in a transitional phase. I feel like I'm like sixteen or seventeen in terms of the way it's about to mature."

It was against this turbulent emotional backdrop that Robin prepared for the most important stop of his tour: two nights at the Metropolitan Opera House on August 9 and 10, where he would be the first solo comedian to perform there. By this point in the trip, he was raring to open up a vein and engulf an audience that included celebrity guests like Robert De Niro, Sean Penn, and Madonna.

The concerts, which were taped for an HBO special and a record album, began with Robin speaking over the Met's public address system to say, "There'll be a minor change in the program tonight. Tonight, the part of Robin Williams will be played by the Temptations." Then, wearing a Hawaiian shirt, he rushed into the concert hall and said, in a Western twang, "Howdy!" After the laughter subsided he added, "Wrong opera house."

He approached a large *La Bohème*–type stagecoach that dominated the set and serenaded it with the song "The Wells Fargo Wagon" from *The Music Man.* Then he imagined how the Dallas Cowboys coach Tom Landry might fare as a ballet coach before settling into a bit about drinking. It was subject matter he had previously covered in *Throbbing Python of Love,* only this time Robin made clear he was not making broad jokes about the familiar plight of overindulgence; he was talking about himself and his own decision to go sober. "I had to stop drinking alcohol," he said, "because I used to wake up nude on the hood of my car with my keys in my ass. Not a good thing."

Not that this choice had made him a fundamentally better person, he explained: "I realized when I became a reformed alcoholic — I said, hey, 'I'm the same asshole. I just have fewer dents in my car.' And then there are your friends who smoke marijuana, going, [stoner voice] 'Yeah, man, alcohol's a crutch.' Really, Captain Herbalife? You just macramé-d your ass into the couch and you're giving me shit?"

Robin returned, too, to the topic of cocaine, though here he did not acknowledge his personal expertise on the matter. ("Here's a little warning sign if you have a cocaine problem," he said. "First of all, if you come home to your house, you have no furniture and your cat's going, 'I'm out of here, prick'? Warning.") Then came riffs on gun control, the Reagan presidency, and other political topics, followed by Robin's sermonizing on lust, sex, and the male libido. His long speech about sex culminated, as such acts often do, in childbirth. "You've just created a tiny creature that'll eventually quit college on you, too," he said. "And now that you have a child, you have to clean up your act."

Then Robin uncharacteristically opened up and started talking about his life with Zak. "My son is three years old," he said. "It's an amazing time. . . . It's an outrageous time, when they ask you about everything. It's like, [child voice] 'Why is the sky blue?' Well, because of the atmosphere. 'Why is there atmosphere?' Well, because we need to breathe. 'Why do we breathe?' WHY THE FUCK DO YOU WANT TO KNOW? A year ago, you were sitting in your own shit — now you're Carl Sagan?"

He went on to tell a story about how the impressionable young Zak was already learning some dubious lessons from his unmannerly dad:

I was driving in traffic, someone cut me off, I went, "Fuck it." From behind me, in his little rocket seat, a voice went, "Fuck it." All day long, he followed me around the house, going, "Fuck it." [smiles] "Fuck it." [waves] "Fuck it." "Fuckfuckfuckfuckfuckfuckfuckfuckfuckit." A sweet little old lady walked up and said, "Oh, what a beautiful child." "Fuck you!" "Oh, it's the Williams boy."

Then, after a brief aside about Jack Nicholson running for president, Robin revisited this idea at the end of the set:

There are times my son looks at me and gives me that look in the eyes, like, "Well? What's it going to be?" Hey, Zak, uh. Hey, it's, um, I don't know. But maybe along the way, you take my hand, tell a few jokes and have some fun. Hey, how do you get to the Met? "Money!"

Extending his hand as he would to Zak, Robin said, "Come on, pal. You're not afraid, are you?" In Zak's voice, he answered himself: "Nah. Fuck it." Then he raised up his hand, as a child might to a parent, and toddled off the stage.

Years later, Zak would say he was proud to be portrayed this way in his father's routines. At the time, he said, "I wasn't too aware of it." But as an adult considering what the material meant to Robin, he said, "It was good for him and it was cathartic for him, so that's what was important."

More immediately, the Metropolitan Opera shows were greeted euphorically, as a return to form for Robin, perhaps even the best stand-up set of his career. Reviewing the HBO broadcast for the *Village Voice,* Andrew Sarris called it a "virtuoso comedy hour" that put Robin "on a different planet from every other stand-up comedian." "I doubt that any other mere mortal can think and perform with such machine-gun rapidity and still be on target so much of the time," Sarris wrote. "Whenever anyone is that good, nobody but nobody should tamper with the inspired ravings of his unconscious."

The TV critic Tom Shales, who attended one of the shows in person, wrote, "If the HBO cameras only capture a modicum, a vestige or a semblance of the actual performance, it's still likely to be a night in comedy Mecca. Watching Robin Williams do his phenomenal and incomparable act is like riding to the moon in a Waring blender. You leave the show spent and exhausted and wonder what poor Robin must feel like."

It had been a grueling tour and a punishing final set of shows, but Robin had taken some encouragement from Marsha Garces, who was typically the last person he would see each night before going out onstage, and, as was her custom, gave him a hug and a message of affirmation before the curtain went up at the Met. "I told him, 'You can do it. You're okay. I love you' — which is what I say to my friends all the time," she explained. For Robin, the inspiration that her words provided could not have come at a better, more necessary time. "Marsha used to tell me I was a good person, and finally I believed it," he said.

Over the course of these shows, Marsha

said, "Robin was complaining, in a joking way, about the bimbettes who knocked on his door at the hotel. I asked him, 'Why are you so surprised? If I weren't working with you and I didn't know how screwed up you are, *I'd* be interested in you!' And he said that gave him a feeling that he could be really loved."

Robin could surely use the moral support. At the end of the year, he and Valerie reached a private agreement, handled out of court, that would allow them to split custody of Zak and live separately from each other. The longest loving relationship of his adult life was likely over, and it was time to pick himself up and begin again. What else could he do except say "Fuck it" and move on to the next stage of his life?

10
GOOOOOOOOD MORNING

Back when he could still allow himself to contemplate passion projects — the sort of work he did not because it would pay him particularly well or because it would advance his career in some strategic way but simply because it was what he wanted to do — Robin had committed to starring in a film adaptation of Saul Bellow's *Seize the Day.* In that 1956 novel, Bellow chronicled the unraveling of Tommy Wilhelm, a failed actor turned salesman who has lost his wife, his family, and his job and over the course of a dire day in New York is subsequently parted from his money, his sense of purpose, and his sanity.

The film was made for a meager $1.6 million, with a grant from the National Endowment for the Humanities, and could not afford to halt filming even when the city was hit by a hurricane. But it offered Robin an opportunity to pour his heart and soul into the Wilhelm character, to work with the director Fielder Cook and costars like Jerry Stiller and Joseph Wiseman. Wiseman played Wilhelm's wealthy, overbearing father, who chides him for having given up college to pursue his Hollywood pipe dream and demeans him for not having chosen a career that would make him financially secure.

"You want to be proud?" the father snarls at him in one brutal confrontation. "Have enough money in your checking account. . . . Let me tell you something, Wilky. You know what you are in this world without money? Nothing. Absolutely nothing."

When his father demands to know what he wants from him, Robin, as Wilhelm, breaks down: "What do I want from you?" he says, nearly in tears. "Help. Affection. When you see me suffering, doing all this. . . . Please, Pop."

Acknowledging that his father will surely die before he does, he says soberly, "It isn't fair, is it sir? The better of us, the more useful, the more admired is going to leave this world first."

For Robin — who felt an obvious kinship with Tommy Wilhelm and his existential crisis — *Seize the Day* provided an emotional cleansing, a place to work out unresolved conflicts with his own father. "I think there's that incredible feeling that, when you tap into those things, you can't get down any further," he said. "You really appreciate life when you finish a really cathartic scene where you examine a relationship and look at your own life. My own father, I'd go home and call him and say, 'Dad, I love you. Let's play football.' "

The film was meant to be shown on PBS, though throughout 1986 there were sporadic efforts to show *Seize the Day* at film festivals and bring it to distribution marketplaces in the hope that it might get a proper theatrical release in the United States. That never occurred, in part because its shoestring budget and dated production values were evident in every weather-beaten frame, and in part because of abiding concerns that Robin could no longer open a movie. When *Seize the Day* made its PBS debut in April 1987, the *New York Times* called it "a miscasting fiasco." From its very first scene, Robin was "a man falling apart, whimpering pathetically when not screwing up his face into odd contortions. There is no disintegration. He is virtually certifiable from the outset. There is no drama. Tommy is a foregone conclusion."

By now, Robin had come to his own conclusion that he no longer ranked among those actors who could command their choice of projects. He had recently learned, after a series of auditions, that he had lost out on a costarring role in the buddy comedy caper *Midnight Run* with Robert De Niro; the part had instead gone to Charles Grodin. He was certain he had further to fall, and he was making his peace with what came next. "You simply slip down the comedy food chain, that list of people who get scripts," he said. "It exists. From the top there's Eddie Murphy and Bill [Murray] and Steve [Martin]. I guess on the next level there's Tom Hanks, myself, John Candy — there's a lot of us." And if he were to sink any further, he said, "You have to work your way back up again or do character parts — or you fall back and punt."

He had been a hot commodity once. "That was nice," he said. "But this is nice, too, not being hot. Now I prefer the quiet."

And then, a project that had taken years to put together for Robin was about to come to fruition. Starting in 1979, Adrian Cronauer, a veteran of the US Air Force, had been trying to sell a TV sitcom about his experiences as a disc jockey on the Armed Forces Radio morning program *Dawn Buster,* which he had hosted in Vietnam in the mid-1960s. Imagining a hybrid of *M*A*S*H* and *WKRP in Cincinnati,* Cronauer sought to depict a version of Saigon, and of the Vietnam War, before they both went utterly to hell.

"When I got there, Saigon was still a sleepy little French colonial town, but by the time I left, it was a nightmare," Cronauer said. "It was this massive influx of troops and equipment and money. By the time I left, the economy was in ruins. The traffic was unmanageable. The black market was flourishing.

But it was an interesting experience to see all this happen within one year's time."

A later treatment by Cronauer, written as a TV movie, had been optioned by Robin's manager Larry Brezner, who essentially stripped it for parts and had it reassembled to better suit the needs of his client. Mitch Markowitz, the screenwriter assigned to rework Cronauer's premise and turn it into a feature film for Robin, said he was given little in the way of direction. "There wasn't really very much about this idea," said Markowitz, who had previously written for *M*A*S*H* and other sitcoms. "I remember telling Larry, I said, 'I really can't get hemmed into some story here that you have. I need to know all your preconceptions about this thing, just tell me what you absolutely need to have. And I will go and I'll write a script.' He said, 'Okay.' He said, 'Disc jockey, Vietnam, and a girl. And a romantic thing with a girl. And a brother — her brother is like, a Viet Cong, something like that.' I said, 'I have it.' "

In Markowitz's script for *Good Morning, Vietnam,* a fictional version of Cronauer arrives in Saigon. At his first appearance, as he deplanes from a flight from Greece, he is described as "dazed," with "a crazed, anesthesia-oriented smile, and wears mirrored sunglasses, sandals, a jacket with a name tag that reads, 'Hiya,' a scarf knitted by a grandmother, not necessarily his, Jamaican flour sack pants, a USAF hat, and a Greek peasant shirt stained with juices of many lands." In what was to have been his first scripted line of dialogue, after gazing up at the sun and seeing that he and everyone around him is sweating, he would toss aside his scarf and say, "Guess I won't be needing this."

The rowdy but likable Cronauer character upends the monotonous military radio station where he has been posted and falls in love with a Saigon native, only to learn that her brother is a Viet Cong operative, a development that forces Cronauer to resign his position and take an honorable discharge. The screenplay included several scenes that would show the character in his element at his DJ booth, spinning records and spouting comic commentary for his listeners. These scenes would presumably be showcases for Robin's improvisatory talents, even if they did not accurately reflect the real Cronauer, a mellifluous and even-tempered broadcaster who was not exactly a desperado of the airwaves.

"He's a very straight guy," Robin said of Cronauer. "He looks like Judge Bork. In real life he never did anything outrageous. He did witness a bombing in Saigon. He wanted to report it — he was overruled, but he said okay. He didn't want to buck the system, because you can get court-martialed for that shit. So, yes, we took some dramatic license.

"But he did play rock & roll, he did do characters to introduce standard army announcements, and 'Goooood morning, Vietnam' really was his signature line," Robin explained. "He learned whenever soldiers in the field heard his sign-on line, they'd shout back at their radios, 'Gehhhht fucked, Cronauer!' "

Good Morning, Vietnam had been set up at Paramount, but executives there wanted it to be a comedy from beginning to end, without any dramatic elements or political commentary. So it was shopped from studio to studio before it landed at Disney, where it was picked up by Jeffrey Katzenberg, a former Paramount executive, who believed it had potential for the company's new adult-oriented Touchstone Pictures division.

The director Barry Levinson was finishing his film *Tin Men* for Touchstone when he was offered *Good Morning, Vietnam* as his next project. Levinson had once been a stand-up and improv comic himself, and he was an early member of the Comedy Store Players in the years before Robin joined the ensemble. He and Robin also shared the services of Michael Ovitz, the powerful co-founder of Creative Artists Agency, who packaged their movies and negotiated their paychecks. (The Rollins Joffe team would continue to manage Robin's day-to-day career and develop new material for him.) Though he and Robin had not previously crossed paths, Levinson could easily imagine him dominating the screen with his voice and his imagination.

"My intention was to play around with the radio," Levinson said. "This is one of the things he could be so great at, even though he's never done it in a movie, but he's got the perfect persona for it."

Levinson knew that this was not necessarily how the rest of the industry regarded Robin. "At that moment in time — and I know this is going to sound crazy — but that's the nature of the business," he said. "It was: 'He has these movies. They didn't do well. It would be crazy to put Robin Williams in the movie.' That's what I would hear. 'Why would you do a movie with Robin Williams? That doesn't work. What's wrong with you?' I'd hear that a lot."

"And sometimes you've got to say, all right, I hear you," Levinson continued. "But I just can't buy into that. You say, 'This is an immensely talented person. We've just got to find a way to make him really work for what we're going to do.' "

As a proof of concept for what the film would be, and a way for Robin to try out the Cronauer role before there was no turning back, he and Levinson shot some test footage in Los Angeles, with the aim that it could be used as an early trailer if they were satisfied with the results. The sequence opens on a black screen, and a title card that reads:

VIETNAM 1965

Every morning military D.J.
Adrian Cronauer went on-the-air.

His mission:

To send the troops
to work laughing.

We first hear the hand claps and high-pitched refrain of the Four Seasons' "Walk Like a Man," followed by Robin's boisterous voice: "Goooood morning, Vietnam! That was a little song by Frankie Valli and the Four Seasons, 'Walk Like a Man.' Thank you, Frankie. [responding to himself in a high-pitched voice] 'Thank you, Adrian.' Wow, walk like a man, sing like a girl. An incredible thing to do. Hey, we're coming at you right now, it's 0600. Woo hoo. Not a bad time of day if you're a chicken. Weather today: Hot. Tonight: Hot. Tomorrow: Hot. Guess what? Big surprise tomorrow night: Hot."

The picture fades in on a darkened studio, where the camera circles around one corner and then another to find Robin alone at his broadcast booth, wearing a headset and a US

Air Force jacket bearing a name tag that reads CRONAUER, while a small American flag sits on his console.

Robin runs through a few more riffs — "Also, we have an interesting coincidence here. Ho Chi Minh. Colonel Sanders. Possibly the same person? Whoa. You be the judge. The lines are open. Call in." — and offers his impression of Ethel Merman singing "Silent Night" before the brief scene closes with a recording of Aretha Franklin's "Respect."

The trailer that Levinson quickly cut and rushed into theaters that summer of 1987, even before principal photography had begun on the movie, added one final title card in blue military-style lettering on a black background:

ROBIN WILLIAMS

GOOD MORNING

VIETNAM

Then, in smaller white letters, an ambitious promise: COMING THIS CHRISTMAS.

This was an aggressive timetable for a movie that did not yet exist, even one that had been budgeted at just $14 million and would be filmed over a span of about three and a half months, but Levinson had total confidence in Robin as soon as he saw him perform this scene. "Right then and there, it occurred to me that he's going to be fine," he said.

That summer, Robin and the production team began filming *Good Morning, Vietnam* in Bangkok, which would stand in for Saigon. Summer temperatures there could reach 110 degrees or higher, and bicycle traffic shared the streets with impromptu military processionals. Robin found himself fascinated with Bangkok's enduring and ageless way of life, the ornate Buddhist temples that seemed to be everywhere, and the children who would run up to him on the streets and call him *ling* — meaning monkey — as they grabbed at his hairy arms. For the portions of the film that were set in rural environs, the cast and crew would travel to the rain forest province of Phuket, using hand-drawn maps with helpful advisories like "last half of this road is dirt" and "Animals: Goats, Cows, Water Buffalo on location 07.00."

Still, some negative stereotypes about Bangkok persisted, enough to dissuade Robin from bringing Zak with him for any portion of the shoot. "They told us all these horror stories," Robin said. "I was afraid for him. Bangkok itself is pretty sanitary for a city with 300,000 prostitutes."

He did, however, travel with Marsha, who was now his full-time assistant and an indispensable partner as he planned for the movie. In the weeks before they went to Thailand, Robin had begun to study up on the events of the Vietnam War and the popular culture and vernacular that would have been familiar to military personnel of the time. As Robin started to think about the Cronauer character, a historical consultant created a research file for him, comprised of photocopied pages from history textbooks, lists of period-appropriate television shows (*Bonanza, The Beverly Hillbillies, Gomer Pyle U.S.M.C.*) and movies (*Mary Poppins, Goldfinger*) that Robin could crib from, and tables that translated the crude, hilarious lingo used by US servicemen, in which "Ho Chi Minh's revenge" meant "the shits" (as you'd experience from an antimalarial pill), "white mice" were the Vietnamese police, and the first rule of the Saigon bar girl was, "No tea, no talk; no money, no honey."

His preparations continued each day after filming, when he and Marsha would return to his hotel room and develop the material he would later deliver in his disc-jockey monologues. These scenes needed to look spontaneous, as if Cronauer were making things up as he went along, but doing so required Robin to be equipped in advance with dozens and dozens of one-liners that he'd already written and road-tested, as well as countless more jumping-off points for further riffs that might occur to him in the moment. There were no comedy clubs for him to do this in Bangkok, so Marsha became his audience of one, as well as his coach and cowriter.

Together they filled the pages of his notebooks with Robin's own loose and just-barely-legible handwriting, as well as Marsha's more careful and controlled mix of cursive and print; these represented the records of their efforts as they worked back and forth on a joke and she attempted to transcribe his stream of consciousness. Sometimes these notes were simply Robin's reminders to himself ("No psychedelic or soul . . . Kinks, Beatles, CCR, DC5, Top 40s") or names of characters he was starting to develop for Cronauer to banter with ("Hanoi Hannah," "Marvin the ARVN"). In other instances he or Marsha would write out an authentic news headline that Cronauer might read on the air, filled in by a gag playing off of the announcement ("the Mississippi River broke thru a protective dike — when asked, she said . . . ," "Pope Paul 6 named 27 new cardinals raising college to a record of 103. 'I hope one day to field my own football team' "). Titles of songs that Cronauer was likely to play on the air were also pored over and paired with jokes, usually about the unattractiveness of President Lyndon B. Johnson's daughters. ("Mrs.

Brown, You've Got a Lovely Daughter" —
Lady Bird if you want to beautify America
stop cranking out those ugly daughters; "Crying in the Chapel" — dedicated to anyone
who marries a Johnson girl.)

Of course, having all this material at his
disposal, Robin still had to perform it.

Cronauer's radio patter, which makes up
about twelve minutes of the movie, was
filmed over a span of a few days at a studio
in Bangkok. The general approach to these
scenes was that Robin would perform a take,
he and Levinson would confer and evaluate
it, and then Robin would deliver another take
based on those adjustments. "I might say,
'Well, that thing you did, it was really good,
but I wonder if we could just make it a little
shorter,' " Levinson recalled. " 'What about
if you want to try that?' Let's try this, let's
try this, let's try this. Then he would throw in
some new thing — say, that's pretty good! —
and out of that kind of playing around, it just
kept evolving."

Robin could wind himself up and go without very much guidance. In just a single take
seated at the microphone, running about four
and a half minutes, he either recited or ad-
libbed bits about the pope delivering his mass
in Yiddish (performed in his customary
George Jessel accent); the Vatican offering its
own line of bath products (he tries both "soap
on a rope" and "Pope on a rope" as punch

366

lines); the discovery that Liberace has been found to be Anastasia, the lost princess of the Russian imperial family; LBJ declaring his daughters an endangered species; Ethel Merman's music being used to jam Russian radar; the first Puerto Rican player in the National Hockey League; Gomer Pyle returning to Vietnam after an R&R trip to Thailand; the Ku Klux Klan suing Casper the Friendly Ghost; LBJ declaring his wife an endangered species; Great Britain recognizing Singapore ("Hey, wait a minute — didn't we meet last year at the Feinberg bar mitzvah?"); and Walter Cronkite working as a fill-in meteorologist ("Today's weather: hot and shitty").

He was almost always disappointed with his delivery of these monologues, to an excessive degree. "He so wanted to please and for everything to work," said Mark Johnson, one of the film's producers. "Sometimes, he would, first thing in the morning, come to me and say, 'Look, I want to redo yesterday's work. I'll pay for it.' And there was no reason to redo yesterday's work. It was spectacular."

Part of the problem, the filmmakers found, was that Robin was improvising in a comedic vacuum; he was performing to largely silent rooms where no one could respond to what he was doing, and he was missing the crucial, real-time feedback to his performance. "He's doing all this free-form spontaneity but he doesn't have an audience," Levinson said.

"It's not like you're doing a scene and there's humor to it. Here, he's doing one-liners and characters and no one can laugh. And that was a little difficult."

The impediment wasn't simply that an errant, offscreen laugh could ruin a take. As Mark Johnson explained, "Our crew was primarily British and a lot of Thai. Robin would do some extraordinarily funny bits, many of them specific to American culture, and of course, the crew didn't get it. So Barry would call cut and they would go back to doing what crews do, and Robin was devastated because he was sure the stuff wasn't funny, because no one was laughing." When Robin would joke, for example, about the Highway Beautification Act forbidding LBJ's daughters from riding in convertibles, Johnson said, "Barry and I would go crazy, and the rest of the crew would sit there. They had no idea that Lyndon Johnson had daughters."

Levinson once tried bringing in a live audience, seating people in a separate room from the radio studio and transmitting their laughter to the headset that Robin wore in his broadcast booth. This worked for Robin's first attempt at a particular joke but did not hold up in repetition. "The problem was that once you did it again, they had already heard it, so it wasn't as much fun as the first time," Levinson said. "And then he thought maybe he's not doing it well. So we go, All right, that idea's not going to work. So we gave up on that."

While Robin was putting it all on the line in his DJ sequences, Levinson was especially proud of the careful, quieter work he was doing in the scenes where Cronauer commandeers a classroom full of Vietnamese civilians learning English, and starts teaching them American slang and swear words. For these portions of the film, in which the classroom was populated with Thai locals of various ages dressed in their own street clothes, Levinson determined it was all but impossible to generate authentic-seeming interactions between them and Robin by sticking to a script. "We started to play around," the director said, "letting them just talk around what we were supposed to talk about, but trying to say the lines specifically." Rather than slate a scene — that is, formally announce that it was starting by banging a clapboard and calling action — Levinson would instruct Robin to go up to one of the students and just start talking. "I would give a hand signal, and the camera operator would get up, and the sound guy, and everybody would suddenly know that this is what we're going to do," Levinson said. "And it became very natural. There was a real honesty to it all. Robin was really good at just talking with them. And his spontaneity and excitement would kick their spontaneity, and that was very influential to the movie."

Robin felt engaged and inspired by every aspect of the filmmaking process, and along the way Marsha was becoming an increasingly vital component of his life. She was so much more than his secretary or transcriptionist; she was his constant companion to and from the set, at meal breaks, and at after-hours dinners with Levinson, Johnson, and their wives. She was his surrogate, with a keen understanding of his voice, helping to refine his dialogue and to speak up for his day-to-day needs when he was too shy to do so himself. "He relied on her," Johnson said, "and we in turn relied on her when she would let us know that there was something else that needed help or attention."

Marsha, who turned thirty during the making of *Good Morning, Vietnam,* was vivacious with long dark hair and exotic features. Her mother was Finnish, the youngest of seven children in an immigrant family that had settled on a farm in rural Wisconsin. Her father was Filipino, and he had completed two years of medical school before emigrating to the United States; he served (as Robin's father did) in the US Navy in World War II. Marsha, the youngest of four children, considered herself a loner, even among her siblings. "I grew up in a German community, where all the other kids were blond, and we were dark, so I know what it feels like to be what is considered different," she said. "I was different even from my brother and sisters. They were very social. I was always by myself."

By her own account, Marsha was four years old when she taught herself to read by studying the label on a shampoo bottle, and by the age of nine she was taking on voluminous classics of fantasy literature like J. R. R. Tolkien's *The Lord of the Rings*. As an adult, before she came to work for Robin and Valerie as Zak's nanny, she had had two past marriages that ended in divorce. Through all the service jobs she had worked — waitress, bank teller, caregiver — she said she had discovered something about herself: "I learned that I had an instinct for making people feel comfortable."

It was hardly a secret to their colleagues on *Good Morning, Vietnam* that Robin and Marsha had become romantically involved. But Robin was careful about how he talked about this blossoming relationship to the outside world, trying to temper his excitement with discretion. As he said to one reporter on the set in Bangkok, Marsha had become "my assistant, friend, confidant — and some other titles we can't talk about until she leaves the room."

When Robin returned to the United States that fall, his father, Rob, had become gravely ill with cancer. Knowing that their time together was running out, Robin spent many weeks traveling from San Francisco each afternoon to see Rob in the Tiburon house where he had moved the Williams family some twenty years earlier, and the two men began to open up to each other in ways they had waited their whole lives to do. Observing Rob now, at the age of eighty-one, Robin contemplated the enigmatic taskmaster who had instilled in him his values for hard work, diligence, discipline, and propriety; he saw past his father's reserve and recognized him as human and vulnerable. "I saw that he was funkier, that he had a darker side that made the other side work," Robin said. Up until that point, he said, "I kept distance out of respect. Then we made a connection. It's a wonderful feeling when your father becomes not a god but a man to you — when he comes down from the mountain and you see he's this man with weaknesses. And you love him as this whole being, not as a figurehead.

"He'd had operations and chemotherapy," Robin said. "It's weird. Everyone always thinks of their dad as invincible, and in the end, here's this little, tiny creature, almost all bone. You have to say goodbye to him as this very frail being."

Alluding to *The Wizard of Oz,* Robin added, "There was this little man behind the curtain, going, 'Take care of your mother and I love you and I've been very worried about certain things. And I'm afraid, but I'm not afraid.' It's an amazing combination to exhilaration and sadness at the same time, because the god transforms to a man."

With nothing to hide and no reason to hold back, Robin opened up to his father about the disintegration of his marriage to Valerie, and his fears that the livelihood he'd worked so hard to establish as an actor was slipping away. "I don't want to lose my family or my career," he said.

Rob, for the first time, told Robin of the challenges, disappointments, and failures he had faced in his own life: how he'd had to give up his youthful aspirations to work in the family coal business when it was nearly wiped out; his deployment on the USS *Ticonderoga,* where he'd taken shrapnel in a kamikaze attack; the collapse of his first marriage; the regret that he'd felt, in his last years at Ford, about wanting to devote more time to Robin and Laurie but feeling that he could not tear himself away from his responsibilities to the company, and then retreating to the Bay Area when he could not take it anymore. "I loved what I did, but all they wanted to do was churn out as many cars as they could," he told Robin. "The companies were losing their sense of pride in their product. I couldn't stand by and watch it happen. I had to get out."

Though the pain still lingered for Rob,

Robin found inspiration in these stories and the courage he felt his father had shown. The lesson he took is that he had to decide for himself what kind of life he wanted and then claim it for himself. "He gave me this depth," Robin said of his father, "that helps with acting and even with comedy, saying, 'Fuck it. Do you believe in this? Do you really want to talk about it? Do it. Don't be frightened off.' Somewhere in his early life, he had to give up certain things, certain dreams. And when I found mine, he was deeply pleased. He was working his tits off to make this life and he had been screwed over by too many people in the automobile industry, which uses you and discards you just like the movie industry. He had seen that my life was in transition and that I was starting to take control."

Rob Williams died in his sleep on October 18, 1987, in his Tiburon home. Laurie called Robin that Sunday morning and told him, calmly and evenly, "Robin, your father's dead." "She was a little in shock," Robin recalled, "but she sounded happy in a certain way, if only because he went without pain."

Amid the sadness, Rob's death reunited Robin with his half brothers Todd and McLaurin — who was not Rob's blood relative but regarded him as a father, and who had changed his name from Smith to Smith-Williams as a Father's Day gift to Rob. "It kind of melded us closer as a family than we've ever been before," Robin said. Rob was cremated, and his family gathered on the Tiburon coast to scatter his ashes into the water.

"At one point I had poured the ashes out," Robin recalled, "and they're floating off into this mist, seagulls flying overhead. A truly serene moment. Then I looked into the urn and said to my brother, 'There's still some ashes left, Todd. What do I do?' He said, 'It's Dad — he's holding on!' I thought, 'Yeah, you're right, he's hanging on.' He was an amazing man who had the courage not to impose limitations upon his sons, to literally say, 'I see you have something you want to do — do it.'"

By the time of his death, Rob had embraced Robin's artistic ambitions, and he had watched his son achieve extraordinary success in pursuit of them, but he had never seen him fully realize the potential of his gifts. It was now up to Robin to utilize his talents to their fullest possible degree, if only to prove to himself that he was worthy of them.

As postproduction continued on *Good Morning, Vietnam* and its promised Christmas release date drew closer, Levinson and his team began to sense that the distribution executives at Touchstone Pictures were growing nervous. It had been only a dozen years since the fall of Saigon; the Vietnam War and its aftermath were still raw subjects for many moviegoers. Thus far, Hollywood had addressed the war in motion pictures like *Coming Home, The Deer Hunter,* and *Apocalypse Now,* which were serious-minded and dealt unflinchingly with the human toll of its brutality; only a few months earlier, *Platoon,* Oliver Stone's semiautobiographical drama about a US infantry company decimated in battle after battle, had won four Academy Awards, including Best Picture.

The concern at Touchstone was that *Good Morning, Vietnam* might be seen as making fun of a subject no one was ready to laugh at, a worry that Levinson had shared when he was initially approached about the film. "Vietnam means soldiers fighting," he said. "It's a bad war, a negative war. That's why, when I first heard about this script, I thought I didn't want to do it. Then I read it and I went, 'Oh my God, how naïve, how narrow-minded I am.' "

"You forget," Levinson said, "that the thing spanned twelve years and there was an everyday life that went on that didn't relate directly to the soldiers fighting."

Touchstone did not put a halt to the film or ask for substantive changes to it, but the release plan for *Good Morning, Vietnam* was scaled back to just four theaters on December 25. That way, the movie could still make the deadline for the Oscars, and the studio could test the waters to see if wider audiences were ready for it. The print campaign, which emphasized a photo of Robin in an airman's uniform and an Uncle Sam pose, holding a microphone and pointing a finger in front of an American flag, emphasized in its text that Adrian Cronauer had been sent to Vietnam "to build morale," and described him as "The wrong man. In the wrong place. At the right time."

In the days just before this limited opening, Robin seemed punchier than usual, clearly understanding that the stakes for this movie were different from any of his other films. As he introduced a clip from *Good Morning, Vietnam* to Johnny Carson and the audience of *The Tonight Show* on December 18, Carson remarked offhandedly, "I think it's going to be good," to which Robin responded, in a mocking basso voice, "I hope so, and if not, I'll be on a game show."

Later, in a newspaper interview, Robin dismissed a reporter's gently flattering notion that he was America's premier comedian. "I don't like that title," he said. "It's too much. There are a lot of other funny people out there." Robin's modesty did not prevent him from suggesting that he had many unnamed enemies in the comedy world who "take a lot of shots" and would love to see him knocked down from his lofty perch. "You have your friends and then you have people who aren't that friendly," he said elliptically. "You're in a position where people are gonna fire at you and, in a certain way, you have to accept it. You can't make fun of other people and then go, *'Stop! Don't you understand? I'm sensitive!'* "

That fog of anxiety began to lift with the first reviews of *Good Morning, Vietnam,* which were effusive celebrations of Robin's performance. They not only suggested that the movie would be a hit but that this was the revolutionary film role he had been searching for. Look at Robin's motion-picture résumé up to this point, Vincent Canby wrote in the *New York Times.* "Each film has had its endearing moments, but there was always the feeling that an oddball natural resource was being inefficiently used, as if Arnold Schwarzenegger had been asked to host *Masterpiece Theater.* Just how much of the fresh, cheeky Williams brilliance was going up the chimney can now be seen in *Good Morning, Vietnam.*"

Praising the delirious Adrian Cronauer monologues, Canby wrote that Robin "floats down the stream of his own manic consciousness. He talks about sex, the drama inherent in weather forecasts in the tropics, body functions, Army regulations, politics and Richard Nixon, then the former Vice President. At frequent intervals, he conducts interviews with characters inhabiting the dark side of his brain, including an Army fashion designer who's distraught about the material used for camouflage uniforms. ('Why not plaids and stripes?' asks the petulant designer. 'When you go into battle, clash!')"

Levinson, he said, had succeeded "in doing something that's very rare in movies" by bringing to life "a character who really is as funny as he's supposed to be to most of the people sharing the fiction with him." Most importantly, Robin had given a performance that, "though it's full of uproarious comedy, is the work of an accomplished actor. *Good Morning, Vietnam* is one man's tour de force."

Michael Wilmington of the *Los Angeles Times* was less taken with the film as a whole, calling it "good-hearted but shallow." But he was every bit as abundant in his praise for Robin, who he said was

so blazingly brilliant that he detonates the center, exploding it in berserk blasts of electronic-age surreality. When he does Cronauer's anarchic broadcasts — screeching "Goo-oo-oood mornin', Viet-*nam!*" and launches into bursts of giddy, wildfire free association, punctuated with Motown and '60s rock — he's transformed. . . . Williams at the mike is like a man possessed, purified, liberated.

These early reactions were encouraging, but

for Levinson the success of the film did not seem tangible until he and his wife, Diana, were driving on Sunset Boulevard one night and found themselves in front of the Cinerama Dome, the one theater in Los Angeles where *Good Morning, Vietnam* was playing.

"My wife said, 'Why don't we just check and see how the movie's doing?' " Levinson recalled. "I saw like a dozen people in line for the eight o'clock show, I thought. I didn't want to go in, so Diana went in and I waited. And she came out and she said, 'Well, the eight o'clock show is sold out. And the ten o'clock show is sold out.' I said, 'Really? Who are these people in line, then?' 'They're lining up for the midnight show.' And suddenly, we went, 'Oh my God.' We saw some people that had some tickets and people were trying to get tickets. You could hear all this on the street: How do you get the tickets? It's sold out. This buzz was going on. It was on its way."

Good Morning, Vietnam went into wide release three weeks later, on January 15, 1988, in about eight hundred theaters, grossing more than $16 million that week. For the first time in his career, Robin had a number one movie at the box office.

"It was a huge relief for him," Levinson said. "He had never made a movie that had done well. He was feeling like, 'Well, this is it. Am I just going to be a television guy and a stand-up comic? Is that it?' All those things are going on in his head. And all of a sudden, there's this gigantic opening and the movie explodes, and he's a darling in Hollywood. That was a huge moment for him. He was just beside himself. He had broken through."

"For a guy who always had these insecurities," he added, "to finally be praised and all of a sudden to have made it, that was a great moment for him."

When it was clear that the film was going to be a commercial smash, it was like an artery of feeling and emotion, clogged for years, had finally burst open. Robin did not have to wonder any longer about which face he had to show in order for the public to accept him; he now had proof that he would be embraced if he just acted like himself. He could relax, open up, and share parts of himself that he had previously held back, without fear of what an audience might think.

In interviews, Robin talked about the real benefits he'd been seeing from psychotherapy — "open-heart surgery in installments," he called it — which he'd now been enrolled in for a year, and how he believed it had helped his performance in *Good Morning, Vietnam.* "It allowed me to show more vulnerability," he said, "and I think the camera can catch that. I think therapy has helped me to bring out a deeper level of comedy."

He was cagier, however, on the question of

whether the process was making him feel more sane — "They bought it," he said through a grin — and doubted that he'd ever achieve something akin to inner peace.

"I don't think I'll ever be the type that goes, 'I am now at one with myself,' " he said. "Then you're fucking dead, okay? You're out of your body. I do feel much calmer. And therapy helps a little. . . . I mean, it helps a lot. It makes you reexamine everything: your life, how you relate to people, how far you can push the 'like me' desire before there's nothing left of you to like. It makes you face your limitations, what I can and can't do."

Still, Robin had been here before, and he wondered how long this latest surge of interest in him would last. When his first flirtation with fame had evaporated to his surprise and disappointment, he had learned that he was at the mercy of external forces that could take it away a second time. He realized now that he was also susceptible to bouts of bad judgment that could halt his current ascent. "The secret is to be able to turn things down, to not take on projects like *The Best of Times* or *Club Paradise* just because they say they want you," he said. "If they can't get you, they'll get anybody, so wise up. They'll take Gary Coleman."

When Oprah Winfrey asked him, in an interview on her daytime talk show, if he had any insecurities, Robin became quiet and contemplative. "Oh, why do you ask?" he said, to laughter from the studio audience. Then he got serious: "A few things. That the muse will leave. All of a sudden, that you'll sink back and" — his voice grew slower, lower, and less coherent — "Just. Become. Almost. Just. Like. This. And eventually run as a Democratic candidate."

On January 23, 1988, when Robin could have been in Los Angeles, receiving the Golden Globe he won for Best Actor in a Motion Picture Musical or Comedy for *Good Morning, Vietnam,* he was instead in New York, hosting *Saturday Night Live* again. In a curious sketch that aired late in the show, Robin was cast as a future, sixty-year-old version of himself, with white hair and a matching mustache. This senior Robin is a bitter curmudgeon who lives alone in a threadbare apartment, sitting in a Barcalounger and yelling at his TV set. He is visited by a grown son played by Dana Carvey — the sketch takes pains to make clear that the character is not meant to be Zak — who dresses in a variation of Robin's old *Mork & Mindy* costume and minces around the room, pathologically riffing on everything he sees.

"Where did it all go wrong?" the elderly Robin asks as he bemoans his fate. "Maybe it was all those sequels to *Good Morning, Vietnam.* Maybe *Bon Jour, Beirut* was too much."

"I don't have it anymore," says sixty-year-old Robin. "I just can't do it like I used it to. I'm too old. Besides, nobody cares. Nobody remembers me."

Carvey, as Robin's fictional son, can muster up only a thin encouragement. "That's where you're wrong, Father," he says. "They do remember you. *Popeye*'s still the number one film in Budapest."

11
O Captain!

The praise for *Good Morning, Vietnam* kept coming and coming. In the days and weeks that followed its opening, Robin received effusive notes of congratulations from Michael Ovitz, his powerful agent at Creative Artists Agency, hailing his Golden Globe nomination ("Your film is creating an unusual amount of word-of-mouth excitement and critical acclaim. . . . PS Do you ever stop? I couldn't stop laughing when I watched you on the Tonight Show") and eventual win ("It was your week, and this will be your year"). Friends from every corner of his life were reaching out to express their admiration, including his old comedy mentor, Jonathan Winters ("Now you know . . . it pays to be a disc jockey. Stay away from John Houseman and listen to me. Have I ever steered you wrong? It's your turn now for me to be your Lewis Stone. Okay Andy Hardy?"), and the science-fiction writer Harlan Ellison ("Paul Muni and I are delighted you got nominated.

He told me so today, in a burning bush. I'd tell you myself, but whoever hears from you? Don't let the guilt make you crazy. Go, be a star.") When Steven Spielberg wrote to thank Robin for impersonating him in a video made to celebrate the director's fortieth birthday, he opened the letter, "Hey, movie star!!" adding that he was "available to sub for you on HBO, Showtime, the Comedy Store and *Good Morning Vietnam II* (which I haven't seen but will once the lines go down sometime in 1989)."

While these tributes were uplifting, the financial success of *Good Morning, Vietnam* was staggering. It remained the number one motion picture at the box office for the first nine weekends of its wide release, and by the end of March 1988 it had grossed over $100 million. When its national run came to an end that June, it had taken in more than $120 million, making it the fourth-highest-grossing movie of the year. The film also yielded a companion soundtrack album, containing short excerpts of Robin's DJ routines from the movie as well as some of the period songs played on Cronauer's show, and that became a hit, too: it spent thirty-five weeks on the Billboard chart, put the Louis Armstrong single "What a Wonderful World" back in the Top 40 for the first time since its original release in 1967, and sold more than one million copies, before winning Robin another

Grammy Award for Best Comedy Album the following year.

These were great windfalls for Robin, and also for Rollins Joffe, where an important generational shift was taking place. Charles Joffe decided to retire from the business he helped create, and Robin's comanagers Buddy Morra and Larry Brezner became partners in the company, now called Rollins, Morra & Brezner. They were younger, hungrier, and savvier than their predecessors, and eager to leverage their ability to produce and package movies that showcased their clients. They and Jack Rollins were credited as producers on *Good Morning, Vietnam,* assuring them substantial fees paid up front, and further royalties paid later as the movie continued to rake in profits. These were strong incentives for them to create more of their own films for Robin, and for Robin to keep working steadily on their behalf.

On February 16, Robin secured one of the greatest honors of his career. The nominations for the Academy Awards were announced that morning, and the five contenders for the Best Actor trophy were Jack Nicholson for *Ironweed,* Michael Douglas for *Wall Street,* Marcello Mastroianni for *Dark Eyes,* William Hurt for *Broadcast News,* and Robin Williams for *Good Morning, Vietnam.* This was the only Oscar nomination that *Good Morning, Vietnam* would receive, and a rare distinction for a performance in an essentially comedic film (though the same could be said of Hurt's role in the satirical *Broadcast News*). The distinction vaulted Robin into the first rank of film actors and ended any lingering concerns about his meandering artistic compass.

There was not much opportunity for Robin to revel in his good fortune. In the same week that his Oscar nomination was announced, he was the subject of a feature article in *People* magazine in which he spoke candidly about his personal life, revealing the full extent of his relationship with Marsha and describing her as "the one who makes my heart sing." But the magazine's cover told a different story. A small photo of Robin and Marsha appeared beneath a dramatic block of text that described him as caught up in "the emotional challenge of his life" and "entangled in a love affair with his son's nanny that has left his wife embittered — and Zachary, 4, in the middle." It was clear that *People* intended to present this story in a salacious light.

The article, titled "A Comic's Crisis of the Heart," began by commending Robin for stand-up skills that were as sharp as ever and for resuscitating his career with *Good Morning, Vietnam.* But it then took an abrupt turn, going on to say that Robin was "caught up in a private turmoil of passion and anguish," torn between Valerie, "the wife of nine years he deeply respects but no longer wants to live with," and Marsha, "the mistress he madly adores." It described Marsha as "sloe-eyed" and "elegantly slender," and having become a part of Robin's life "when Valerie (as she grimly acknowledges) hired her as a live-in nanny for baby Zachary."

Marsha declined to be interviewed for the story, and the *People* writer was unable to turn up much information on her ("When did their affair begin? Nobody's talking"), though the story spent a paragraph describing Robin backstage at *Saturday Night Live* as "he cupped her buttocks and pulled her in close for the kind of kiss usually exchanged in a bedroom."

Robin was open about the shared custody agreement he and Valerie had made for Zak and said that their son had been handling it well. "He's amazingly adaptive," Robin told the magazine, "and we all try hard to make the arrangement work. We all love Zachary, and Zachary loves us all. Also, we're all in therapy, and that's helped a lot — Jesus, I should get a discount! Valerie and I have a good understanding too. The separation was difficult, but it was also gentle. Better to do that than to go at each other's throats."

Valerie, who acknowledged that she was now in a relationship with another man, said that this arrangement was best for all of them.

"Robin has been conducting himself very well," she said. "We're acting together in Zak's interest. We separated to reexamine our lives. It's a time for personal growth for both of us. . . . I live alone, and I like it that way."

Though Robin had given the magazine his full and honest cooperation, the article had the overall effect of scandalizing him and Marsha. Through implication, omission, and misunderstanding, as well as the use of loaded words like "mistress," it suggested that their relationship was inappropriate and something they should be ashamed of. Robin and Valerie had made it clear that their marriage was over and had been over for some time when he and Marsha became involved, but the *People* feature seemed to suggest that Marsha was a home wrecker who had used her position as Zak's caregiver to infiltrate the Williams home and seduce Robin away from his loving wife. That could hardly have been further from the truth, but millions of readers didn't know that. Robin and Marsha found the article embarrassing and hurtful, and it left a misperception about their relationship that would linger for a very long time.

"I was so angry and horrified that the interview turned this way, it was like being mugged," Robin would later explain. "I sat down and talked to the reporter very personally and said, 'This is what's up, this is the truth.' And they didn't put any of it in. They made it seem exactly what they wanted to do from the very beginning: Marsha broke up the marriage. Which is total horseshit."

"It was really a hatchet job, a setup, an ambush. A very low blow," he said.

Robin and Marsha's friends ignored the *People* article, while other unexpected allies emerged to offer them words of comfort and support. Gene Siskel, the *Chicago Tribune* film critic and cohost of the television program *At the Movies,* who was hardly a reliable admirer of Robin's movies, wrote to him and encouraged him to put the incident out of his mind. "In case you are feeling low about the *People* magazine cover," Siskel said, "realize that I saw the magazine — they send it to me — and I was so disgusted by the invasion of privacy that I tossed out the issue without reading it. It wouldn't surprise me if other fans of yours and other journalists did the same. Your talent and love for your family remain unscathed in the real world."

On April 1, Robin and Valerie publicly announced in a statement that they were ending their marriage and that Valerie had made the initial filings that would begin their divorce process. Days later, on April 11, Robin made his first visit to the Academy Awards ceremony as a nominee, bringing Marsha with him as his date. But when Marlee Matlin stepped up to the lectern to reveal the winner of the Best Actor trophy, she announced Michael Douglas's name. At that instant, on the television broadcast, Robin could be seen tensing up ever-so-slightly and exhaling; it was as if, until then, he was still holding on to the belief that he could prevail in a highly competitive category, and against Douglas's searing performance as the morally compromised Gordon Gekko. As a consolation prize of sorts, Robin got to take the stage later in the show, to humorously bemoan his loss — "That award was so close! All those calls to *Entertainment Tonight* at fifty cents a pop, damn!" — and to bestow the trophy for Best Director. Addressing the nominees, none of whom were American, he said, "The Academy, along with the Oscar, this year is giving out a green card," before proclaiming Bernardo Bertolucci the winner for *The Last Emperor.*

Later that spring, Robin and Marsha relocated to New York so that he could begin work on a series of projects there. The first was a Lincoln Center Theater revival of Samuel Beckett's *Waiting for Godot* in which he and Steve Martin would play the existentially beleaguered hobos Estragon and Vladimir. The play, directed by Mike Nichols and with a cast that also featured F. Murray Abraham and Bill Irwin, was Robin's first major theater piece since achieving fame; it was sometimes billed as his professional stage debut, over-looking the handful of plays he had performed in San Francisco before turning to stand-up comedy. Though not technically a Broadway show, *Godot* was as highly anticipated as a New York theater production could be — one that would put Robin right back in the same storied arts complex where he had studied at Juilliard more than a decade earlier, and in a work that could take full advantage of his comic gifts and show off his intellectual heft.

The previous summer, Nichols had met with his two lead actors at Martin's house in Los Angeles for a private reading of the play. Satisfied with what he had seen, Nichols wrote to Robin a few weeks later to tell him, "Our hours with *Godot* were as happy as any I have spent around the theater. Thank you for your talent and your generosity. This is just to say count on it."

As a dutiful drama student, Robin devoured the *Godot* script, poring over its contents and filling his copy with enthusiastic annotations. On the first page he jotted down his initial thoughts on how Estragon would be presented: "real life! (make up: bruises, cuts, dried blood) beaten, no sleep." Underneath the character's famous first line, "Nothing to be done," which accompanies his fruitless effort to remove a boot, Robin added a few thoughts on how he might deliver it: " 'Ah well.' To audience? Throw away to self. (it's hopeless)." A few lines down, beneath a bit of dialogue — "Not now, not now" — spoken to Vladimir, he wrote, "Pity me. Help me!" Robin continued on like this for the entirety of his script, as if he had been assigned a term paper.

Robin was fascinated by the play's willful abstraction and its indifference to efforts to make it comprehensible. As he'd been told about its original 1956 Broadway production, in which his role was played by Bert Lahr, "they asked him, 'What are you doing in this play?' And he said, 'I don't know.' And then I heard that Beckett was real happy with that." He loved the rhythms of his give-and-take with Martin (who was appearing in his first play in twenty-five years), inventing all kinds of evocative similes to describe it: "It's like having sex in a wind tunnel." "It's like water skiing in quicksand." "Or putting together a jigsaw puzzle in a hurricane."

Of course the play came with a certain risk. What risk? "Of never working on the stage again!" he said. "Oh, no! You're ruined! It's like you're ruined socially in Tustin. Oh, no! You'll never be allowed back there again!" And more seriously, the fear of failing in a live setting, in the medium that drew him to acting in the first place.

But, as Robin was accustomed to asking for and receiving, Nichols gave him permission to improvise during the show and to update Beckett's text; not extensively, but even in small doses these ad-libs added up and helped contribute to the downfall of the play. Robin would sometimes deliver a line in the voice of Rod Serling, John Wayne, or Sylvester Stallone; he would pretend to wield an imaginary remote control or a microphone, and ask Irwin's character to "thank the Academy"; when Irwin spoke the strange phrase "Essy-in-Possy," an invention of Beckett's, Robin interjected with a line that was most assuredly not the author's: "Did he say *pussy*?"

Not every critic regarded Robin's taking of liberties as a literary felony; "the play has not been abused," the *New York Review of Books* said of the production when *Waiting for Godot* opened in November 1988. George Roy Hill, Robin's no-nonsense director on *The World According to Garp,* wrote to him to tell him, "I have seen any number of productions of *Godot* including the one with Lahr, and for me this was the best by far. It was also the most accessible and as a result the most moving of all of them, not in the least because of your work in it."

But other reviewers were aghast at what they felt was Robin's lack of respect for Beckett's masterpiece. In the *New York Times,* Frank Rich chided Robin for his "frenetic horseplay": "A brilliant mimic, the actor never runs out of wacky voices, but where is his own voice?" he asked. "As *Good Morning, Vietnam* seemed to evaporate whenever Mr. Williams had to forsake comedy routines for love scenes, so his Estragon vanishes whenever he has to convey genuine panic or loneliness or despair. There's more humor (and heartfelt agony) in the famous Richard Avedon photographic portrait of Bert Lahr's Estragon than there is in a whole night of Mr. Williams's sweaty efforts to keep us in stitches."

Steve Martin felt that theatergoers lost their appetite for the production after a series of negative critiques were published. "Before the show opened, during previews, everybody loved us. Ate us up. Cheers, bravos, the whole bit," Martin said. "Then as soon as the reviews came out, the audiences started sitting there without reacting — no laughter — nothing. It was chilling.

"I thought I had had every kind of experience on stage," he added, "but this was sheer torture. And yes, you might say we hadn't expected this. To put it mildly, we were surprised."

Waiting for Godot played its final performance on November 27, after just six weeks, and Robin regarded the production as an instructive failure. "We were a little shell-shocked when we were finished," he said. "*What was that?* Very strange sensation."

Describing the process as "painful," he said: "We put our ass out and got kicked for it."

That experience was further marred when details of Michelle Tish Carter's lawsuit began to seep out into public view. Carter had originally filed her suit in 1986, in Modesto, California, hoping that the matter would stay quiet while her lawyers and Robin's tried to reach a settlement. But in April 1988, her counsel moved the case to San Francisco Superior Court and it was discovered by the news media. The first reports about their two-year relationship, their breakup, and Carter's claim that Robin had given her herpes — she alleged that he had known since high school that he was infected with the virus — were published soon after.

That October, Robin filed a legal cross-claim of his own, contending that Carter had used "duress, coercion and fraud" to try to obtain money from him. His suit said that Carter had demanded $20,000 and a new car from him when she believed he had gotten her pregnant, and it stated that medical tests had shown that Robin did not have a sexually transmitted disease. His complaint charged her with extortion, conspiracy, and intentional infliction of emotional distress, and it asked for an unspecified amount of damages.

Robin knew that fighting for his name and

reputation would grow ugly and uncomfortable, and that there would not be an immediate or speedy resolution. And then, just when he needed some uplift and inspiration in his life, he found it.

It was delivered to him by a screenwriter named Tom Schulman. As a teenager growing up in the South in the 1960s, Schulman had attended Montgomery Bell Academy, a prep school in Nashville that was rigidly formal in its values; its all-male student body was taught to aspire to four pillars of conduct: to be a gentleman, a scholar, an athlete, and a Christian. (This despite the fact that Schulman was Jewish.) There he studied with a literature teacher named Sam Pickering, who was known for his unorthodox approach to classroom instruction: antic, adoring of his students, teasing them constantly but filling them full of great, lively stories and fundamental information for adulthood.

Then, one year, Pickering did not return to the school, leading his former pupils to spin all sorts of absurd and scurrilous rumors about what might have led to his departure. "Nobody ever bothered to ask," Schulman said, "because if we had, we would have found out that he just got a better job." (Pickering eventually became an assistant professor at Dartmouth College, and then a professor at the University of Connecticut.) "If I had known what happened to him," said

Schulman, "I might have never written this thing. But not knowing allowed my imagination to go to work."

The screenplay that Schulman wrote was about a group of students — some based on friends, others invented from his imagination, and one who wanted, as he did, to grow up to be an actor — and about John Keating, the unconventional teacher who steers them toward a life of individualism and self-reliance with his exuberant lessons about Shakespeare, Byron, Tennyson, and Thoreau. Keating stirs the boys' souls with an apt citation from Whitman's *Leaves of Grass:*

Oh me! Oh life! of the questions of these
    recurring,
Of the endless trains of the faithless, of
    cities fill'd with the foolish . . .
What good amid these, O me, O life?
                    Answer.

That you are here — that life exists and
    identity,
That the powerful play goes on, and you
    may contribute a verse.

In the film's final act, Keating disappears — at which point the boys learn he has been hospitalized. "It turns out he has non-Hodgkin's lymphoma," Schulman explained, "which you can live with for twenty, thirty years. So he's in the hospital to get some kind of infusion, and basically says, 'I'll be back tomorrow, so don't worry about it.' For me, that was the explanation of why he had this *carpe diem* — this extra kick about living to the fullest."

After Schulman wrote the script in the mid-1980s and found an agent who would represent it, *The Dead Poets Society* was picked up by a series of producers, each of whom shopped it to various Hollywood studios, all of whom passed on it. It then landed with Steven Haft, a novice producer who was inspired by it and determined to get it made. "It did more than it was supposed to do," Haft said. "It not only impressed me with the writing, but caused me to lose sleep."

When Haft was at last able to get Disney's Jeffrey Katzenberg to commit to the film for the studio's Touchstone Pictures division, it was with a catch: Katzenberg wanted to add some comedy shtick and have it directed by Jeff Kanew, who had made the bawdy college fraternity farce *Revenge of the Nerds.* In other words, as Haft called it, he wanted to make *Dead Funny Poet Guy.*

The filmmakers spent several months trying to assemble a cast and ran a nationwide search for the rebellious young clan of students known as the Poets, but they found it difficult to land the right star to play the all-important role of Mr. Keating. "It takes a Peter O'Toole in *Goodbye, Mr. Chips* — it takes a terrific actor to pull this off," Haft said. "And unfortunately, the *Nerds* director can't get a great actor." With just days before filming was scheduled to begin in Georgia, the few leading men willing to commit to the part included Alec Baldwin and Liam Neeson, who were considered too unknown at the time to carry the film, and Christopher Reeve, who was regarded as a risk outside of the flagging *Superman* franchise.

Robin was also approached, but he was ambivalent about the project. He sought advice from Dana Carvey, who had worked with Kanew on the comedy caper *Tough Guys,* and found little clarity. "I don't know, I might wait on that one," Carvey told him.

Disney persisted, with calamitous results. "Robin wouldn't say no, but he wouldn't say yes," Schulman said. Nevertheless, preproduction continued, sets were built, and a first day of filming was scheduled at which it was hoped Robin might appear. He did not. "He never said he would," Schulman said, "but Disney kept trying to pressure him by moving forward. After the first day he didn't show up, they canceled the production and burned the sets." Kanew and the actors he had recruited were let go.

The film started to regain momentum when Disney offered it to Peter Weir, the Australian director of haunting and abstract films like

Picnic at Hanging Rock and *The Last Wave,* and who'd recently had his first American hit with the Harrison Ford thriller *Witness.* While growing up in Sydney, Weir had attended the Scots College, a boarding school not unlike the one in Schulman's script, which permitted corporal punishment and bore the Latin motto *Utinam Patribus Nostris Digni Simus* ("May we be worthy of our forefathers"). It was not an experience he romanticized: "As soon as the gates were open in the last year, I just ran out," Weir said. "I was glad to get out of it." Later, at the University of Sydney, he'd had a formative, negative experience in a literature class, where a lecturer dismissed one of his favorite poems, William Blake's "The Sick Rose," as "inferior."

"That's how bad school can be," Weir said. "The joy of education is surely to give you the tools to communicate, to handle yourself in the world, and read on so you go into your life." On a plane ride back to Australia, Weir thumbed through a script that Katzenberg had given him, with its intriguing title. *"The Dead Poets Society,"* he said. "What is it? What are they? Who are they? I have to read it to find out."

With a highly regarded director now interested in the film, Robin saw it in a new light. It evoked his own time as a high school student at the conservative Detroit Country Day School and called to mind freethinking teachers like John Campbell, his history teacher and wrestling coach. It touched on themes of innocence and experience, and the power of art to break through the barricade of tradition. "It talks about something of the heart and of pursuing that which is a dream — and in some cases, to a tragic end," Robin said. And, though he did not explicitly acknowledge this, it also told the story of a young man who yearns to become an actor, and the stern father who wants him to pursue a more reliable career.

Now he wanted to make the movie, but just when all the pieces seemed to be in place again, Haft said, "It all started going wobbly." Dustin Hoffman became interested in the John Keating role — but only if he could also direct the film, a momentary crisis that resolved itself when the actor instead signed on to make *Rain Man* with Barry Levinson and Tom Cruise. There was uncertainty as well about whether Weir could tolerate Robin's well-established preference for creative wanderlust. "If you gave Peter a choice between being president of any country in the world, or being pope, he'd pick being pope," Haft explained. "Peter was a spiritual leader on his sets. Robin, in his view, had too much business — too many things going on, other than delivering the scene. Robin talked to outer beings, in Peter's mind. And the idea that you weren't just channeling Peter's inner thoughts made it very challenging for him to work with that actor."

Mark Johnson, who had produced *Good Morning, Vietnam* for Touchstone, had advice for Weir on how best to work with Robin. "The first thing you do is, you shoot the script," he said. "Word for word. Then, once you have the script, you just let the shackles off and say, 'Just go do it.' And you let him go do it. And then you sit with him, and you craft it from the material that you never saw but he found, and the stuff that you may have known was there but that he raised to a level you never imagined."

With Robin now on board, Weir worked with Schulman to fit the script to the strengths of their leading man, and to the director's own tastes. The time frame of the story was moved to the late 1950s, when Weir was in school, and the plot point about Keating's illness was removed. "Peter Weir said to me, 'That's got to go,' " Schulman said. "He said it's easy for the boys, at the end, to stand up for someone who's dying. But if he's *not* dying, then they're standing up for what he taught them, and that's much more powerful. And I went, eh, okay, you're right. But I still harbored the hope that somehow we were going to keep it." When Schulman and Weir had their first script meeting with Robin, the director told him that only one major change was coming. " 'We're going to take out the dying scene,' " Schulman recalled. "And Robin went: 'Good idea.' So out it went. And I'm glad it was out."

The casting of the Poets was started over from scratch, although some performers who had been seen for Kanew's canceled version of the film were revisited, including Ethan Hawke, who would play the painfully shy new pupil, Todd Anderson; and Josh Charles, as the love-struck Knox Overstreet. Robert Sean Leonard would play Neil Perry, the student driven to suicide by his father's denial of his artistic fantasies; Dylan Kussman, a high school senior, was chosen as the turncoat Richard Cameron; and Gale Hansen, a baby-faced twenty-eight-year-old who was asked to keep his age a secret from his costars, would play the reckless Charlie Dalton (who redubs himself Nuwanda). Filming was set for the late fall in Delaware, principally around the campus of St. Andrew's School in Wilmington, which would stand in for the fictional Welton Academy.

Robin was playing his final performances of *Waiting for Godot* in New York, which meant that he would not be available to start shooting his scenes until December. There was only time for him to participate in a quick table read of the *Dead Poets* script before the rest of the cast went to Delaware to begin filming. The young Poets were largely new-comers to film acting who admired Robin's work — this was their introduction to him, and many of them were intimidated, until he made individual efforts to put them at ease. Hansen, who had studied acting at some of New York's prestigious studio schools, re-called that when the reading was over, Robin strode right up to him and shook his hand "even though clearly he didn't need to."

"He was like, 'We have a lot in common,' " Hansen said. "I was like, 'There's no way we have anything in common' — I didn't say that, but that's what I'm thinking. I was serv-ing hot meals yesterday. And he was like, 'You studied with Sandy Meisner, I studied with John Houseman at Juilliard. We both come from the same background.' He did that with each boy. He had that one thing to make you identify with him. It was so smart to go, 'You can trust me. We can play.' "

In Robin's absence, the Poets spent their first days in Delaware in mid-November get-ting close-cropped, Eisenhower-era haircuts and breaking in their student uniforms. Weir encouraged them to spend time with each other, to form friendships and imagine back-stories for their characters; he forbade them from using contemporary slang words — "cool," "wow," "man," "shit" — and in-structed them to use period-appropriate lingo. For a couple of days, Weir himself played the role of a teacher he called Mr. Quern, requiring the boys to report, in costume, to his classroom (a rehearsal space that had been outfitted with desks), where he addressed them as their characters and instructed them to organize a school play. "It was a way of deconstructing my own position as director, to relax everything," he said. "I made a fool of myself. I became an actor myself."

Robin started filming on December 12, day 23 of the planned fifty-two-day production, and his scenes as Keating were shot largely in script order. The interior of his classroom was created on a soundstage installed at a former middle school in Wilmington, a few doors down from the ersatz cave where the boys would perform the late-night rites of their secret society. As a succinct set of stage directions describe the first classroom scene, "The boys take seats and settle in. Keating stares out the window a long time. The students start to shuffle uncomfortably. Finally Keating stands, picks up a yardstick, and begins slowly strolling the aisles. He stops and stares into the face of one of the boys."

As written, the scene also called for Keating to jump up on his own desk and address the boys, and Robin performed it as directed. But both Weir and Schulman felt it did not work. "We looked at each other and just went, 'Uh-uh, this is too much,' " Schulman said. (In a later scene, Keating would stand on his desk and invite his students to do the same, to "look at things in a different way.") Instead, Weir and Schulman decided to have Keating make his entrance walking through the room, whistling Tchaikovsky's *1812 Overture* and striding out the door into the hallway, where the perplexed students would follow him. Robin rolled with these changes; he stuck to the script and knew every line of his dialogue. Yet to the filmmakers he appeared somewhat stiff. "We were going, 'What the hell?' here. How is this?" Schulman said. What they felt he needed was some space to improvise.

"We were able to get about a half day ahead of schedule, and one afternoon, we basically just let Robin do some ad-libs," said Alan Curtiss, the film's first assistant director. "Peter is very spontaneous. Not in an irresponsible way — within the day's work. He would come in and change our plans slightly. But Robin really trusted Peter, and they had a very good communication." For an afternoon, the classroom and its students were turned over to Robin while two cameras rolled. Weir encouraged him to riff on the sorts of authors Keating would be teaching — Shakespeare, Dickens — knowing that Robin did not have any time to prepare material, but that this likely would not be a problem for him. "He's a kind of writer, without a pen," Weir said of Robin. "He just writes in the air."

To Robin, the exercise was a brief, blunt lesson that his ad-libs were largely incompatible with the spirit of the film. "It just didn't work," he said. "It was teaching, teaching, teaching, *shtick,* teaching, teaching. It was like Saran Wrap on Velcro. *Didn't stick. . . .* And it was sad. I got very hurt. It was a battle, sometimes, between the comedian and the actor. *Dr. Jessel and Mr. Jolson.* This strange thing of wanting it to be funny and realizing that this ain't going to be that."

In fact, only a couple of the bits that he whipped up in this session, some of which bore a passing resemblance to jokes that he told in his stand-up routine — Marlon Brando and John Wayne delivering lines from *Julius Caesar* and *Macbeth; American Bandstand* reviewing the poetry of Byron — would make it through to the completed movie. And Robin would have few other opportunities over the course of shooting to extemporize at length; even some of the more modest tweaks that he scrawled in his script — changing a phrase like "utter dreck which you must avoid like the plague" to "which you must wade through like a yak," or trying to slip in a reference to the dirty limerick "There once was a man from Nantucket" — either never got performed or were left on the cutting room floor. But just an afternoon of free play seemed to loosen Robin up and helped set the tone for the days that followed.

In a scene shot soon after, Keating and his charges look at a trophy case filled with photographs of students from past generations — an authentic artifact found on the St. Andrew's campus — and he urges his boys not to squander their potential.

"They're not that different from you, are they?" he asks them.

Same haircuts. Full of hormones, just like you. Invincible, just like you feel. The world is their oyster. They believe they're destined for great things, just like many of you. Their eyes are full of hope, just like you. Did they wait until it was too late to make from their lives even one iota of what they were capable? Because you see, gentlemen, these boys are now fertilizing daffodils. But if you listen real close, you can hear them whisper their legacy to you. Go on, lean in.

As the boys dutifully follow his instructions, Keating whispers to them, "*Carpe diem.* Seize the day, boys. Make your lives extraordinary."

The sequence called for quiet contemplation, and Robin knew just how to play it — not over-the-top but understated. "He's not playing on obvious emotions," Weir said. "He's a rather good storyteller, or mood-invoker, in that scene. He gets you in."

Around the set, Robin could be his usual, playful self — on days when paychecks were handed out, he would tell the young actors, *"Carpe per diem"* — but he was also a figure of immense power and inspiration. His presence alone was often enough to inspire his young costars to take chances and improvise in their own performances; if he could do it, why not them? When Keating brings his students out to a school courtyard and encourages them to walk around at whatever pace they wish, Robin happened to catch sight of Gale Hansen standing still, and he quipped, "Mr. Dalton — you be joining us?"

In that moment, Hansen said he decided, "I'm going to challenge him — see how well he's paying attention. And I was like, 'Exercising the right not to walk.' It was an improvised line, which I didn't do much of." Hansen was standing behind the camera as he delivered the line, and Weir, from behind the camera, shot him a glare that seemed to say, "What? *What?*" But when the take was completed, Weir turned the camera around so he could film Hansen's side of the exchange.

"It was very liberating for the rest of the shoot," Hansen said. "As long as I was behaving truthfully, working off something that existed in the moment between us, there was a little leeway there to catch fire. And that was Robin — Robin going, 'Let's play. Bring me what you have.' He wanted everything, and he could handle anything. The guy was a lion. He lay down with all these young actors and just let you play all over him."

During their time together, the Poets bonded over hang sessions and pool parties at their hotel, and took a group field trip into New York when several of them were asked to audition for the same role in *Dad,* a comedy-drama with Ted Danson and Jack Lemmon. (The part would eventually go to Hawke.)

Robin, who continued to employ Marsha as his assistant on the film and who stayed with her at a separate hotel, in some ways lived up to the cast and crew's anticipation of him. When there were large audiences available to him — say, a field full of actors and extras for a scene set at a soccer game — he often liked to break away and entertain the crowd. "The only times he acted up were when he was bored or a little nervous," said Andy Weltman, who was Weir's assistant on the film. "And when I mean act up, I mean not in a bad way. He'd start spinning off his thing."

But to these young men, Robin seemed very different from the persona he had cultivated in his acting work and stand-up appearances. "I expected him to be completely manic and all over the place and funny, a little edgy," Weltman said, "and he wasn't that way at all on our film. He was very quiet and self-effacing and generous. I remember there was one time he said to me, 'I'm just here to introduce the world to these boys.' "

Though his relationship with Marsha was now public, the two of them could be protective of each other, which sometimes made them seem aloof when they did not intend to be. "Robin and Marsha at that point were pretty hot and heavy," said Schulman, "so he spent all of his time with her. Not necessarily a comfortable fact." When she was not assisting Robin on set, she kept to herself, though Hansen, who was closer in age to her than any of the other Poets, found ways to connect with her; he discovered that they were both reading *The Dancing Wu Li Masters,* Gary Zukav's best-selling book about quantum physics, explained with the language and symbolism of Eastern spirituality. "We started talking about stuff like that, rather than other things," Hansen said. "She was a sweet, generous person, and their relationship was very open and loving and inclusive."

Lisa Birnbach, a coauthor of *The Official Preppy Handbook* and a consultant on the film, also became friendly with Robin and Marsha. Then married to the film's producer Steven Haft, she and her husband spent time with them as a couple and got to see them in a different light. "He and Marsha were very private while they were there," Birnbach said. "Let's say I'd be talking to Marsha, and suddenly Robin would come up and start really kissing her. 'I think I gotta go.' There was a lot of public demonstration of great affection for her." As the four of them grew closer, they became regulars at an old-fashioned Italian restaurant in Wilmington, where each after-hours dinner, following a shoot or a review of that day's footage, customarily ended with the waitstaff making a showy display of the dessert options, including a beverage they called "Café Diablo — coffee of the Devil."

"That was intoned every night," Birnbach said. " 'Café Diablo — coffee of the Devil.' And we always wanted to say, 'Hey, don't you remember us? We were here last night and you did the presentation. And we were here Tuesday also? We were here last Sunday?' Not because it was so fancy, but because the food was good and it was open late. Every night, 'Café Diablo — coffee of the Devil.' Robin never stopped saying that to me, ever. By the way, never once did any of us order it."

While the making of the movie proceeded smoothly, the filmmakers found themselves waging an unexpected battle with Disney to preserve the integrity of its title, which Schulman had given it at its conception. During shooting, Haft got a call from David Hoberman, a Disney executive, to tell him that they had market-tested *The Dead Poets*

414

Society and were concerned about the results. As Haft recounted the conversation, "*Dead* was a bummer, *Poets* was too effete, and nobody knew what *Society* meant, actually." When he conveyed this to his director and his leading man, neither of them was willing to change a word. Haft said, "Peter's lips are pursed and Robin's jaw is jutting out, as close as you can find to a cat ready to leap. There was a moment they talked about whether to stop shooting that day. They just wanted to send the strongest possible message." If their side had any leverage in this fight, it was the conviction that they were making a good movie, and that Disney was impressed with the dailies they had seen thus far. "They must have liked the footage, too," Haft said. "If they hated the footage, they've had told us to go stuff it. But they must have liked what they were seeing as well."

In the middle of a winter snowstorm, Disney dispatched its head of worldwide marketing, Robert Levin, to Delaware to meet with the insurgent *Poets* squad and negotiate a truce. Over a dinner with Robin and Marsha; Peter Weir and his wife, Wendy; and Steven Haft and Lisa Birnbach, all gathered in matching unisex parkas, Levin reiterated the results of the studio's testing, which further frustrated the group. "You watched Peter backing away from the table, as if he wanted enough room to jump over it," Haft said. "Robin adored working for Disney. But he knew words like 'Mauschwitz.' That stuff started coming out. And it was getting ugly."

Pressed further, Levin revealed that the studio had already registered several other possible titles, all benign and Disney-fied: *The Amazing Mr. Keating. Keating's Way. The Unforgettable Mr. Keating.* "If they had anything we thought they would actually go forward, it would have been such a different response," Haft said. "But they were such stupid ideas that we just concluded this was never going to happen." He, Weir, and Robin broke into a round of laughter at the suggestions, and told Levin, "Call us when you have something better. We're a unit."

Schulman was not part of this argument, but he feared that his screenplay had an Achilles' heel that could have allowed Disney to give it any name it wished. "I thought, 'Oh, if somebody realizes all they've got to do is change the name of the club, they can retitle the movie,' " he said. "But I didn't tell them that." Disney gave in to the protests of the creative team and left the title mostly intact, removing only the word *The,* so it stood as *Dead Poets Society.* ("They took that off — like Facebook," Schulman said.)

"It was a tremendous bonding experience for us all," Birnbach said. "Because we all hung tough, and obviously prevailed."

Days 28 and 29 of the shoot, on December 16 and 17, were devoted to Scene 138 of the film: the concluding moments when Keating, who has been dismissed from Welton, makes a last appearance in his former classroom, where the Poets pay him a final tribute by standing atop their desks and proclaiming to him, "O Captain! My Captain!" As Schulman described it in the script, the introverted Todd is the student who initiates this demonstration. The stage directions read:

> Keating turns to look at Todd. So does everybody else. Todd props one foot up on his desk, then stands up on it. He stands atop his desk, holding back tears, facing Mr. Keating. . . .
>
> One by one and then in groups, many others in the class follow suit, standing on their desks in silent salute to Mr. Keating. . . . Keating stands at the door, overcome with emotion .

Keating stammers out his final line — "Thank you, boys. I . . . Thank you" — and looks into each boy's eyes before giving a nod and exiting. The film's final shot is of Todd "holding back tears but standing proud," as the screen goes black.

Weir often played music on his set before the cameras rolled, to establish atmosphere and to get his actors in the corresponding

417

frame of mind. Throughout the shoot, he'd been piping in his selections on a small boom box, but for this occasion he chose Ennio Morricone's main theme from *The Mission,* the Roland Joffé film about a Jesuit evangelist in eighteenth-century Central America. It is a gentle and elegiac score, with an oboe at its center; a fitting accompaniment for Keating's farewell. Though a handful of shooting days still remained before the Christmas holiday and after the New Year, it felt like the right way to say good-bye to a character who everyone already seemed to know would never entirely leave them.

12
DREAMLIKE PARTS, WITH PHANTASMAGORIC ASSOCIATIONS

For more than two years, Marsha had been Robin's companion and ally, his love, his fan, and his advocate. She was his guarantee of comfort, stability, and security wherever he traveled — and there had been a lot of traveling in these past months. He had a home as long as she was with him. And now, finally, she could become his wife. Following the completion of his divorce from Valerie, Robin and Marsha got married on April 30, 1989, in a small ceremony in Lake Tahoe. Robin and Marsha exchanged rings shaped to look like wolves, animals chosen for their mythical reputation of mating for life. About thirty people attended the wedding, all close friends of the couple, including Billy and Janice Crystal; Barry and Diana Levinson; the *Good Morning, Vietnam* producer Mark Johnson and his wife, Lezlie; and the comedian Bobcat Goldthwait.

Among those who did not come to the ceremony was Zak, who was six years old at the time. Marsha was six months pregnant, and this was her and Robin's opportunity to start fresh and establish very clear boundaries between what had existed before the marriage and what they wanted their lives to be going forward. Robin also felt the wedding might be too perplexing for Zak to understand. "He kept that marriage very separate," Zak later explained. "I wasn't at the wedding, by design, so as not to get confused for myself. I think the idea around it was to keep me apart from those types of ceremonies, as a way of not confusing me."

Deep down, Robin trusted that there was love among all his family members, that the bonds of old relationships would be preserved and new ones would be created. "Zak loves Marsha and Marsha loves Zak," he told an interviewer two years later. "So for Valerie, along with the feeling that Marsha took *me* away, there was the threat that Marsha might replace *her* in Zak's affections. But that won't happen. Valerie's a very good mother, and nothing would shake Zak's love for her. . . . A relationship as long and close as ours can't be brushed aside. I expect to have Valerie in my life until I die."

Robin and Marsha went back to New York, where they had stayed following the run of *Waiting for Godot* and the filming of *Dead Poets Society.* Through the spring. Robin continued to play unannounced one and two

420

a.m. stand-up sets at Carolines and Catch a Rising Star, where at the end of the night Marsha and her growing belly would be waiting in a limousine to whisk him off to bed.

The approaching summer movie season was filled with big-budget franchise entertainments: a third *Indiana Jones,* a second *Ghostbusters,* a fifth *Star Trek,* another *Lethal Weapon,* another *Karate Kid,* and another James Bond movie. Looming over it all was the release of *Batman,* the gothic comic-book blockbuster, for which Robin believed he'd been offered the plum role of the Joker only as an enticement to force Jack Nicholson to commit to making the movie. "I replied, but they said I was too late," Robin later explained. "They said they'd gone to Jack over the weekend because I didn't reply soon enough. I said, 'You gave me till Monday, I replied before the deadline.' But it was just to get Jack off the pot."

Into this thunderous carnival of bullets, laser beams, and bat-shaped boomerangs, Disney opened *Dead Poets Society* in limited release on June 2, 1989. The initial reviews were respectful if occasionally bemused. In the *New York Times,* Vincent Canby called it a "dim, sad" movie in which "although John Keating is the most vivid, most complex character in it, he is not around long enough." He nonetheless praised Robin's "exceptionally fine performance." A largely positive review in the *Los Angeles Times* said that Robin "may be the most exciting performer in American movies, perhaps less for what he does than for what the audience, by now, knows he can do. *Good Morning, Vietnam* soared when it used his genius for the maniacal, cross-media, multi-referential spritz. In *Dead Poets Society,* he spritzes only occasionally." Roger Ebert gave the film just two stars in the *Chicago Sun-Times,* calling it "a collection of pious platitudes masquerading as a courageous stand in favor of something: doing your own thing, I think." He acidly remarked, "When his students stood on their desks to protest his dismissal, I was so moved, I wanted to throw up."

For the film's opening weekend, Disney brought the Poets and Tom Schulman, the screenwriter, to New York for an appearance on *The Phil Donahue Show* and other promotional opportunities. That Friday night, they gathered at a midtown restaurant with Robin and his close friend Christopher Reeve, who wanted to take a walk to some of the nearby movie theaters after dinner to see how *Dead Poets Society* was faring. Robin, out of nervousness, tried to beg off.

"I don't want to do that," he said.

"Come on," Reeve persisted. "We'll just stand in the back. They won't recognize you."

"I don't want to do it," Robin maintained.

"I'm just going to stay here."

So Reeve and Schulman went without him to find a theater, where they were let into a screening of *Dead Poets Society* and they waited at the back.

"It was the last scene of the movie," Schulman recalled, "and after the boys stood on their chairs, when the music started, the audience got up and applauded, gave it a standing ovation. And I went, 'Whoa. I've never seen this before.' Chris turned to me and was crying. He said, 'I'm so happy for Robin.' It was so sweet. So I had some sense that something interesting was happening. And certainly, as a writer, that was a thrill."

What the early critics had missed about the movie were the many layers of resonance it offered to a mass audience. For younger viewers, *Dead Poets Society* presented a stylized vision of a rarefied prep-school experience as it might have been in a different era. For adults, it was a gauzy lens through which to look back on their own educations and coming-of-age experiences, the rebellions they fought for and the issues that seemed to matter to them in their idealistic youths. Viewers felt compelled to reflect on their lives and wonder who had been their Mr. Keating — that person who had provided crucial instruction or encouragement at an impressionable age, helping to make them the person that they became — or to await the arrival of such a figure at some future time.

The acting work of the Poets was irresistible, establishing a new generation of young heartthrobs and starting several of them on long and prosperous careers. But at the film's center was Robin's warm, understated, and carefully distributed performance as Keating, which balanced the actor's energy and intellect in perfect proportion and ended with the character's unexpected defeat.

In its opening weekend, in just eight theaters, *Dead Poets Society* took in about $340,000. The following weekend, it was expanded to nearly seven hundred theaters and the box office rose to more than $7.5 million, enough to place third behind *Star Trek V* and *Indiana Jones and the Last Crusade.* The movie played all summer long, growing to more than a thousand theaters at its peak, until by mid-September it had taken in almost $90 million, becoming one of the ten highest-grossing films of the year and the second most lucrative that Disney had released. (The studio's top earner was the Rick Moranis comedy *Honey, I Shrunk the Kids,* which Schulman also helped to write.)

As with *Good Morning, Vietnam,* Robin found himself inundated with praise for his performance from admirers all over the country, including the usual retinue of Hollywood figures. He also heard from people who had no connection to him, yet who felt as if they knew him from his compassionate portrayal of Keating. Among the more unexpected letters of congratulations was one from Fred Rogers, the gentle broadcaster and educator who hosted the PBS children's program *Mister Rogers' Neighborhood.* His note to Robin read:

> This afternoon — all by myself — I went to see "Dead Poets Society." It's a fine film and your performance in it is superb. I admire you greatly and I thank you for enriching the lives of so many through your art. You certainly contribute many verses as "the power of the play goes on."
> Gratefully,
> Fred Rogers

While Robin savored these appreciations, he would soon be celebrating another joyous milestone. On July 31, Marsha gave birth to a daughter they named Zelda Rae. In a gesture of conciliation, and a reminder of the threads that ran through the extended Williams family, her name had been picked out in advance by Zak, her half brother. By now, Valerie was in a new relationship with the journalist and author David Sheff, who had a young son of his own, Nic, a year older than Zak. The two boys regarded each other as siblings and, like most children of the era, spent countless hours playing Nintendo games, a hobby that Robin shared. As Marsha's due date approached, the boys began to brainstorm names for the baby. If it's a boy, Nic proposed, he should be named Mario, after *Super Mario Bros.* Zak, inspired by *The Legend of Zelda,* suggested that Zelda would be a good name for a girl — and it stuck.

"Family is what you make of it," Zak said years later. "For us, it's the people who you love and trust and are around you. I did play a role in Zelda's name, and she has very much embraced it as part of her identity. As one does with their name."

Six days after Zelda's birth, Robin sat with Barbara Walters for an ABC television interview, taking Marsha and their new baby girl, who was dressed in a black bow tie dotted with white hearts, out for her first horse-drawn carriage ride in Central Park. Speaking to Walters back in his apartment, Robin excitedly gushed about the joy that Zelda had already brought into his life. "She's nine pounds, seven ounces," he said. "Actually, a friend said we gave birth to a woman. She had shoes and a bag." Though Robin had experienced the elation of first-time fatherhood when Zak was born, he was no less ecstatic to have it happen a second time. "It was amazing to go through it again," he said. "Just as amazing the second time. Just to look at her is better than any videotape. You can sit and watch this: [he quickly cycled through several contorted baby faces] She checks me out and goes, 'Will you be buying me things?' "

His long-term plan for Marsha and Zelda was to move back to San Francisco, where they could begin a proper domestic family life. But he was committed to making several more films in New York that would take him nearly a year to complete. The first of these projects was *Cadillac Man,* a farcical comedy that cast Robin as its overextended, womanizing title character: a fast-talking used-car salesman who, while saddled with alimony payments to an ex-wife and an unpaid Mafia loan, splits his romantic interest between two mistresses, played by Fran Drescher and Lori Petty; then, during a two-day stretch when he's been told he must sell twelve cars or lose his job, he is taken hostage by a gun-wielding motorcyclist (Tim Robbins). For the character, anyway, getting a buyer into a car or a woman into bed are just different forms of seduction.

The movie, which was filmed in part at a working car lot in Queens, held a certain appeal to Robin because the character reminded him of his father and his frenzied, frustrating years in the automobile industry. It was lighter, less substantial fare than some of the other films he'd been making lately, and its director, Roger Donaldson, allowed him to improvise in his scenes with Robbins. He regarded it as "an interesting ensemble piece" but was left frustrated by the feeling that Orion Pictures, the studio behind it, had taken the edginess out of the film in postproduction, well after he had shot his scenes. "They tried it out on test audiences and decided to soften it up," Robin said, "changing the tone more towards comedy, but that's the studio's right. When it's drama and comedy, they get confused on how to sell it and what audiences will respond to." Asked point-blank if he should have made *Cadillac Man,* Robin answered, "I don't know."

That was Robin's spring and summer; in the fall, he moved on to another film, *Awakenings,* a comedy-drama adapted from the 1973 nonfiction book by the distinguished neurologist Oliver Sacks. Sacks had written *Awakenings* based on his work at Beth Abraham Hospital in the Bronx, where he treated patients who had survived a pandemic of encephalitis lethargica, a disease that froze them physically in catatonic states but left them conscious as their brains continued to function. By giving these patients l-dopa, a drug used to treat Parkinson's disease, Sacks was able to revive them, resulting in what he called "an astonishing, festive 'awakening' . . . as they burst into explosive life after having been almost inanimate for decades."

The *Awakenings* screenplay, written by Steven Zaillian, deviated in many ways from the factual record. It replaced Sacks with a character named Dr. Malcolm Sayer, a soft-spoken, bumbling, but brilliant physician, and focused on his relationship with a patient, Leonard Lowe, who contracted the disease while still a child and is resuscitated decades later to find that he has become a grown man. The film was directed by Penny Marshall, Robin's former classmate at the Harvey Lembeck acting workshop and a sister of his *Mork & Mindy* benefactor Garry Marshall. Robert De Niro, whose path Robin had crossed on the night of John Belushi's death, was sent the *Awakenings* script and offered either the role of Sayer, the doctor, or Lowe, the patient; he chose the patient, whom Marshall considered "the glitzy role," so she turned to Robin to play the buttoned-down doctor.

"He's not thought of as a dramatic actor," Marshall said, "but I like to juggle things around. I see things that aren't always apparent." Robin, of course, had no trouble with roles that straddled the boundary between mirth and sincerity, but he had concerns about appearing with De Niro, who could be a stoic and impenetrable figure when the cameras weren't rolling and a force of nature when they were turned on. "He was afraid Bobby was going to blow him off the screen," Marshall recalled. "I said, 'I won't let that happen.' "

Shooting for *Awakenings* began in October 1989 at the Kingsboro Psychiatric Center, a functioning but underfunded public hospital in Brooklyn that could be a dismal place to visit on a voluntary basis. "It's depressing," Robin said of the environs. "Everything is caged. Even the sun room is a big cage." Many of its patients, including people who had Tourette's syndrome and schizophrenia, were used as background actors, and Robin could not help but feel like an inmate himself sometimes. "There's a lot of doors and only five keys," he said.

What helped make the experience more bearable was the opportunity to work closely with Sacks, who served as a consultant on the film, and whose erudite, gentlemanly writing style did not fully prepare Robin for the man he was to meet. Sacks, who grew up in London and received his medical degree from Oxford, was also a motorbike aficionado, a well-traveled hitchhiker, and a sometime weight lifter. He stood about six feet tall and, as Robin would later describe him, "He's like a combination of Arnold Schwarzenegger and Albert Schweitzer. He also looks like Santa Claus, because he's got this big beard, and usually there's food in it, that he's forgotten is there. And the amazing thing is, as big as he is and as strong as he is, he's this very gentle and compassionate man, who is brilliant."

Sacks allowed Robin to study the personal film footage he had made while treating the encephalitis patients, and Robin found it extremely moving to see these people come out of their catatonic states, even temporarily. As he later said, it was like watching "something that seems apparently dead, but yet the human mind and spirit shines through that. They would be like this" — here he affected the frozen face of one such patient — "and he'd say, 'Watch,' and all of a sudden they would come back, and you could see they were there. And then they would go out again. . . . He said he was only going on that faith, that they were there."

Sacks also brought Robin with him on his rounds at Bronx State Hospital, where he cared for geriatric patients. Though Sacks had previously helped Dustin Hoffman prepare for his role as an autistic savant in *Rain Man,* he saw Robin as a unique case study unto himself, unlike anyone he'd encountered in the realms of medicine or art. After one hospital visit where he let Robin meet with a group of disturbed patients, Sacks observed afterward, "He had absorbed all the different voices and conversations and held them in his mind with total recall, and now he was reproducing them, or, almost, being possessed by them." Robin, he said, had an "instant power of apprehension and playback,

431

a power for which 'mimicry' is too feeble a word (for they were imitations full of sensitivity, humor and creativity)."

A few weeks later, Sacks was talking with Robin, having bent himself into a pensive pose, when he noticed that Robin was mirroring his stature. "He was not imitating me; he had become me, in a sense," Sacks said. "It was like suddenly acquiring a younger twin. This disquieted both of us a bit, and we decided that there needed to be some space between us so that he could create a character of his own — based on me, perhaps, but with a life and personality of its own."

Sacks could not help but talk about Robin in neurological and somewhat esoteric terms. "Robin has an almost instant access to parts of the mind — dreamlike parts, with phantasmagoric associations — that most of us don't," he said. He compared Robin to Theodore Hook, a nineteenth-century British writer and artist whose talents included the ability to improvise entire operas in which he would sing all the roles. "For Hook, as for Robin, the demand never let up," Sacks said. "But Hook never had a chance for quiet inwardness — he drank heavily, and he died in his fifties. Robin's brilliance, however, is considerably controlled. He's not in its grip."

Over the five-month shoot, which stretched into the winter of 1990, Robin learned not to be intimidated by the intensity of De Niro, who he said with a single gaze could "clear an eye-line all the way to Tasmania." When De Niro recoiled in revulsion at a scene that called for an insect to crawl across his table, Robin settled his costar's nerves by wrapping pipe cleaners around his own ears and pretending to be a cockroach. Their collaboration remained harmonious even when, while shooting a scene where Dr. Sayer had to restrain Leonard during a seizure, Robin's elbow slipped and caught De Niro in the face, breaking his nose. "My elbow went *BAM*!" Robin explained, "and it made a noise like a chicken bone breaking. And all of a sudden the entire crew went, 'I gotta go now.' " De Niro, unbothered, said the accident corrected a similar injury he'd sustained on *Raging Bull.* "The thing is, my nose was broken once before, and he knocked it back in the other direction — straightened it out. It looks better than it did before."

Marshall, too, found her own way of relating to Robin and reining him in, having concluded that one of her most important duties was "to keep Robin from being funny." As she observed, "Robin could make Bob laugh so hard his face got all red, and Bob was supposed to be, you know, *sick.*" She developed a shorthand signal on set, to indicate to Robin when his ad-libbing was getting too shticky: she would curl her hand into a fist and hold it against her crotch. "It meant 'More balls,' " Marshall explained.

Shooting wrapped in February and the film would not be released for several months. In the meantime, Robin remained in close contact with Sacks, who wrote to say how much he appreciated the actor's semi-portrayal of him: "You have created a quite new, wholly credible, and very moving figure," Sacks said in one letter, "and I think you made a perfect twosome with Bob, an odd couple, an improbable coupling, which becomes completely right."

In another letter, Sacks rhapsodized about the magic of filmmaking, which he had never seen in quite such vivid detail before, writing to Robin:

> you — as actors, as dramatists — are also making worlds; and though these are 'illusions', they are also full of truth. I have never known any actors before; nor have I been much of a theater- or film-goer; but I think these experiences have changed me . . . (or will).

Just before the conclusion of the *Awakenings* shoot, Robin learned that his performance in *Dead Poets Society* had earned him another Academy Award nomination for Best Actor, the second of his career. He would again be facing formidable competition in his category, up against Tom Cruise (*Born on the*

Fourth of July), Morgan Freeman (*Driving Miss Daisy*), Kenneth Branagh (*Henry V*), and Daniel Day-Lewis (*My Left Foot*), but the fact that he had been recognized once more was itself a significant achievement to him — a sign that the first nomination had not been a fluke, that he was here to stay. When he learned of the honor, he sounded his own barbaric yawp over the roofs of New York, stepping outside to shout a satisfied "Yes!"

Dead Poets Society had been nominated for four Oscars in total, including one for Schulman's screenplay, one for Weir's directing, and one for Best Picture. A large contingent from the *Dead Poets* team was dispatched to the Academy Awards ceremony on March 26, including Robin and Marsha, who brought Robin's mother, Laurie, and Steven Haft, the film's producer, and his wife, Lisa Birnbach. It was also the first Oscars show to be hosted by Billy Crystal, who was riding high on the success of *When Harry Met Sally . . . ,* and his presence lent an intimate, family feeling to the festivities — one that was further enhanced by the presence of Zelda, who was then almost eight months old, and Haft and Birnbach's baby daughter, Maisie, who was born just twelve days earlier.

The extended clan started its morning at the Hotel Bel-Air in Los Angeles, then moved to the Omni Los Angeles Hotel in the afternoon to be near the Dorothy Chandler Pavilion prior to the start of the ceremony. "The whole idea," Birnbach said, "was that we were going to leave the Bel-Air in the morning, have some huge suite and spend the day there, with my twelve-day-old, with Zelda, with baby nurses, with parents, with hairdressers, with makeup artists, with stylists, with Billy and Janice Crystal and Laurie Williams. It was a pinch-me day."

While the babies were getting their last feedings of the day and the adults were preparing to head out, Laurie was enjoying a final touch-up. "She was not scared of being theatrical," Birnbach said of Robin's mother, an avid runner and tennis player who, a few months earlier, had been featured in *Silver Foxes II,* an exercise video for people over sixty, hosted by the parents of Hollywood celebrities. "She wore hats, she wore turbans, she wore a lot of makeup," Birnbach said. "She had her hair done and her face done. And then, as she put a kind of turban-snood thing over her gray hair, her last words, before we left to go the Dorothy Chandler were, 'Let's be Cuban!' It was like something Lana Turner would say. I thought that was so charming and so her."

The evening showed some early promise for *Dead Poets Society,* when Schulman won the Oscar for Best Original Screenplay, prevailing over the likes of Nora Ephron

(*When Harry Met Sally . . .*), Spike Lee (*Do the Right Thing*), Steven Soderbergh (*sex, lies and videotape*), and Woody Allen (*Crimes and Misdemeanors*). "Every writer should have the kind of support that I had during the making of this movie," Schulman said in his acceptance speech, going on to thank Robin by name. But that was the only award *Dead Poets Society* would win that night: to the surprise of many, the Best Actor trophy went to Daniel Day-Lewis, a dark horse, for playing Christy Brown, a writer and artist with cerebral palsy, in *My Left Foot.* On the television broadcast, Robin was placed in the center of the screen as the nominees were announced for the final time; he could be seen to flinch, ever so slightly, when Day-Lewis's name was called, then broke into fervent applause for his triumphant rival.

Following the ceremony, Robin, Marsha, Haft, and Birnbach joined Schulman and his wife, Miriam, at the annual after-party at Spago, hosted by the talent agent Swifty Lazar. The exclusive soiree was open to guests who had won Oscars, making Schulman the A-lister of the entourage and Robin merely a hanger-on. Then, once inside the restaurant, the *Dead Poets* team was seated with Roger Ebert, who had lambasted the film. "He passionately hated it," Birnbach said. "He hated it so much that he would remind viewers how much he hated it when he was reviewing other movies. Like, 'This one's good — unlike that piece of shit, *Dead Poets Society.*' And then we're seated with him." Marsha spent much of the evening running interference to prevent the critic from talking to her husband. "She was a very protective wife," Birnbach said.

Marsha, Robin said, was teaching him to separate his life from his work, "like church and state. Marsha makes me happy — she's an amazing woman, a gentle, great soul, with a deep intelligence. Look how she's helped my career. Now I have too much work and she's helping me learn to say 'No' — the most provocative word in Hollywood."

Those lessons did not arrive in time for *Cadillac Man,* which opened on May 18 to dismal reviews and petered out at the box office. Worse, some critics treated Robin's celebrated performances in *Good Morning, Vietnam* and *Dead Poets Society* as if they somehow stood outside his body of work; well executed as they were, they did not really represent who he was at his core. As the *Detroit Free Press* wrote in its dismissal of the film, "Robin Williams has a secret dream. He wants to be an actor. He wants to win an Oscar. He wants to *not* be Robin Williams." The cuttingly perceptive critique went on to say:

It must goad him to be in his current Catch-22 situation. Playing intensive or modulated versions of himself in *Good Morning, Vietnam* and *Dead Poets Society* won him two Best Actor nominations. But they didn't lead to Oscars because the Academy won't give them to actors who are playing themselves.

Williams is trapped by his own marvelousness. When people go to see his movies, they want to see Williams as Williams. They don't want to see him slipping three-fourths of the way under the skin of some other character.

A few months earlier, Robin and Marsha had purchased a house in San Francisco that they meant to be their new family sanctuary and base of operations, and Marsha and Zelda had already started living in a garden apartment in the city that spring as they waited for work on the house to be completed. But Robin had yet to resume his full-time residence in the Bay Area; he still had one more movie to make in New York.

Terry Gilliam, the anarchic American member of Monty Python, had known Robin through their mutual friend, Eric Idle, and worked with him for a short time on Gilliam's 1988 fantasy film, *The Adventures of Baron Munchausen*. The movie, about an eighteenth-century nobleman with a propensity for tall tales, had run into financing problems that could be assuaged if Gilliam secured a recognizable Hollywood name to play the small role of the King of the Moon, a monarch who exists as a floating head on a silver platter. With Idle's help, Gilliam convinced Robin to do the role (bumping out Michael Palin, another of his Monty Python collaborators).

"It did rescue the film," Gilliam said of Robin's generous performance. "At least half of his dialogue, if not more, was him ad-libbing. It's a small part, but it's such an essential part." It was also a role that Robin accepted over the objection of his managers: "At the time," Gilliam said, "his managers, I don't think really were overjoyed to have him jumping out of other, higher-paid jobs to do this." The compromise they reached was that Robin would not be billed in the movie under his own name; instead, he would go by the pseudonym Ray D. Tutto, a play on the character's name, which in Italian can be translated as "king of everything." The awkward bargain, Gilliam said, "was his managers saying, 'We don't want you pimping his ass.' They thought we would sell the film on Robin Williams's name. That's what they were frightened of. And we never, ever advertised Robin. Had more people known he was in it, it probably would have done better business when it came out."

For his next film, Gilliam had chosen *The Fisher King,* a script by the writer Richard LaGravenese that blended medieval Arthurian fantasy with the self-regarding reality of America at the dawn of the 1990s — at once a whimsical comedy about unlikely buddies and a heartbreaking tragedy about personal loss. It told the story of Jack Lucas, an outrageous radio shock-jock who is driven from the airwaves after goading one of his listeners into committing a mass shooting; and the awkward but genuine friendship he forms with a street vagabond named Parry, who believes it is his duty to seek the Holy Grail, and who hallucinates that he is being stalked by a sinister red knight. Eventually, Lucas learns that Parry is, in fact, a former teacher named Henry Sagan, who lost his mind and created his identity as Parry after his wife was murdered in the shooting incident that Lucas provoked.

LaGravenese said he wrote the screenplay as a reflection on the rampant selfishness he saw in the Reagan era. "I thought the '80s were an awful period in New York, and pretty much the country too," he said. "By the '80s, everyone went, 'Well, fuck it — we're just going to make money.' I wanted to write a story about a narcissistic man who, by the end of the story, commits a selfless act." He also took inspiration from a book by Robert A. Johnson called *He: Understanding Masculine*

441

Psychology, in which the author, a Jungian analyst, explores the male mind through mythological figures like the Fisher King: a character who has been mortally injured but cannot die, and is told that he will be healed when an innocent fool arrives in his court and asks a specific question.

As they search for meaning in the world, LaGravenese explained, "Men in our society do that through high-paying jobs or women or cars or power. What they don't do is go inward, to the archetype of the fool — the part of ourselves that will leap into the unknown, that will take the journey, that will lead to the grail." With men, especially, LaGravenese said, "We lose that innocent part of ourselves, that just takes risks and leaps forward with faith that we'll find our way, as opposed to being sick with experience — being paralyzed by knowing too much how things work."

It was obvious to Terry Gilliam that Robin should play the role of the wildly imaginative but deeply wounded Parry; it made sense on face value, and was further confirmed by an experience Gilliam had with him during the making of *Baron Munchausen.* One night, while the two of them were out to dinner, Robin began to slip into one of his spontaneous characters: he spoke in a Southern rustler's accent and started off calmly, speaking of what a good, loving person he was —

"And then there was the time in the bathtub — well, I held a person underwater a little bit — and uh, okay, I mean they died — but it wasn't my fault."

"He was, in fact, a total, psychotic, probably serial killer," Gilliam said. "But he was the most sweet, charming, voluble character you'd ever want to talk to. I just was in tears, it was so funny." A couple of days later, he and Robin were again having dinner, this time in a larger group that included Marsha and Eric Idle. At one point, Gilliam asked if he could conjure up the character from the earlier meal: "I said, 'Rob, can you bring that guy to the table again, the one we did the other night?' " Gilliam recalled. "And he started doing it, but it had changed. He had already edited the jokes but dropped the residual parts of the character." In one sense, Gilliam said, Robin was just doing what a stand-up comedian does: "He ad-libs a lot of stuff, and then immediately says, 'That worked, that's a good joke,' and files them away. But to me, it wasn't as wonderful as the complete character he had done with me a couple of nights earlier. It was just jokes, as opposed to a brilliant character realized. Those are two different things."

The appeal of *The Fisher King* was undeniable to Robin: he was eager for another opportunity to collaborate with Gilliam, and he understood clearly why the material resonated with him. "It is about damaged people, trying to find redemption and connection," Robin said. Playing a character as broken as Parry gave him permission to explore a very dark but valid part of himself as an actor and performer: the side that creates falsehoods — however fanciful — to shroud yourself from harsh truths.

"If you have to think of something so horrifying, and then if you wanted to totally deny something, how would you create that?" Robin said. "Which I did for a little while. Performing and doing all these things, we never acknowledge anything negative — and if you do, it gets very violent. . . . It is freeing to create that character because you can really explore where you've been, and the aspects of why you would want to deny. Performing for the sake of avoiding."

Through his work on Comic Relief and his visits to homeless shelters, Robin had already encountered many people who were very much like Parry and had been badly hurt in their own ways. "Not that there aren't moments that, for them, are funny," he said. "But you see that it's pretty painful stuff. And also people, most — a large majority in major cities are former mental patients. They come someplace with some severe problems." In the days before shooting started, Robin immersed himself in research, as he often did for his more multifaceted roles; he pored over

Bulfinch's and Malory's retellings of the King Arthur legends and studied portfolios of candid pictures of homeless people around New York City.

What the film also needed was an anchoring actor to play Lucas — "the one who was going to keep Robin and me from floating off into the stratosphere," Gilliam said — and improbably, that person turned out to be Jeff Bridges, the carefree Hollywood scion and actor who was, by this point, a three-time Oscar nominee for *The Last Picture Show, Thunderbolt and Lightfoot,* and *Starman.* The big, bearish, likable Bridges "was the thing that pulled Robin back," said Gilliam, "because Robin was so in love with Jeff, and admired him so much for being such a wondrous actor. And that really was the key to it. It allowed Robin not to carry the whole weight of the film on his shoulders."

Bridges, who knew Robin only from his wild comedy work, was equally endeared to him but also noted his intensity. "He had maybe a touch of a dire, dour quality to him," Bridges said. "But he was very gracious and open at the same time. As I got to know him, I saw that this zany quality, the comic end, was really just a tool he had in his kit bag. He was a trained actor who approached the part with that seriousness, and of course he had that wonderful comedic brain in him that he used at will. But he knew what was up."

The making of *The Fisher King,* which began in May 1990 and ran through early August, was sometimes a strangely serendipitous experience. Its filming locations around New York were often visited by Radioman, a good-natured vagrant who roamed the city with a boom box, hoping to encounter celebrities and talk his way into cameo roles on their movies. With his pointed nose, narrow eyes, wide smile, and thick beard, Radioman was a dead ringer for Robin, particularly when the actor was in character as Parry, and on several occasions he was allowed to wander the set freely before anyone realized he wasn't Robin.

Robin was often beset by crises of confidence during the project. "His problem was — and this would happen once a week, probably — he was feeling his fans were going to be let down, because they weren't getting the full, comic Robin," Gilliam said. "And I would have to keep reassuring him that, no, that's not what we're doing. This is better. The script is much lighter, in many ways, than the finished film. I just knew it had to be as painful as it is, for the character to become what he had become."

Gilliam did not need to push Robin hard, if at all, for the scenes in which Parry breaks down and becomes disconnected from reality. In one sequence that was filmed in a series of overnight shoots, Parry believes he is being chased by the red knight and sprints through the streets of Manhattan, where he finally collapses on a tenement doorstep. "That's where he pushed and pushed, further and further," Gilliam said. "I did this shot where his face splits in the bevel of the glass in the door. And then he just — *ahhhh!* — bent over in this horrible agony. Robin was grasping a bit too closely to his own heart, I thought, but he was going for it."

Other portions of that sequence — close-ups on Robin's face sweating and limbs pumping as he fled — were filmed at a studio where he ran on a treadmill, forcing himself to match or exceed the energy he had put forward in the location shoot. "Again, it was late and he kept running and running," Gilliam said. "He wanted to do more, and I said, 'Rob — you've peaked. You peaked about five minutes ago. And now you're just pushing it. It's not real.' 'I know it is real, and there's more, there's more here, I know. There's more pain I can show' — that's what he was saying to me. And I said, 'We've got to stop, come on. This is bad for you.'"

By the time he completed this part of the film, Robin was riled up, exhausted, and surging with adrenaline. As he headed into the final portion of the sequence — in which Parry, who believes that he is surrendering himself to the red knight, is stabbed and beaten by a gang of street toughs — Robin came to feel that he was being rushed through the scene and denied the time he needed to focus his performance, and he exploded with uncharacteristic fury.

"He felt that, in the course of having to shoot a lot of other stuff at night, we had somehow not allowed enough time for the most important moment for the character," Gilliam said. "The stuntman and the first A.D. couldn't even approach Robin — the anger coming off him just frightened them. I had to do it. I had to go hold him and say, 'Robin, come on, trust me. If it doesn't work now, we will do it again. But I'm not going to steal that from you.' The muscles inside his body were all so tense."

Despite these outbursts, Gilliam felt that Robin should be allowed the freedom and flexibility that he needed for the role. "It touched something inside him," Gilliam said. "He's a comic, and all comics want to be Hamlet, come on. You want to show that you're not just a clown — that inside that clown is a profundity, a deepness, a darkness. You suffer. And I think all comics always end up writing their autobiography, and trying to show how much pain they went through in their life."

Bridges had entered into *The Fisher King* expecting Robin to be an incorrigible cut-up, and he appreciated the tenderness and sensitivity that his costar showed in Lucas's most sensitive moments. In one such scene, Bridges had to deliver a monologue to Robin's character as he lies comatose in a hospital bed, recovering from the earlier beating he sustained. "Before I knew him better, I thought, oh, shit, here's this crazy comic," Bridges said. "While I've got this serious monologue, he's going to try to crack me up and wink at me. And it turned out to be the antithesis of that. He had no words or anything. He just gave me this quiet, meditative support, the way you imagine someone who you love being in a coma, and you're talking to them. You imagine that, in some way, you know they can hear you."

Not every day of filming on *The Fisher King* resulted in Robin's complete physical and emotional depletion. Some days he got to strip off his clothes and run around naked. In early June, the production traveled to the Sheep Meadow in Central Park for a pair of scenes in which Parry goes nude: once by himself, as a lesson to Lucas, urging him to share in the same freedom that he enjoys; and once for the film's closing shot, in which both he and Bridges go au naturel. Though Robin was somewhat nervous about these scenes — not because of the nudity, per se, but because he was so hairy — he also discovered a certain power in baring it all.

"He was turned around so his back's to the camera, so he's wiggling his ass and there's the whole skyline of New York there. He's flashing the entire city!" Gilliam said with a satisfied cackle. "He could be so ecstatic. Richard had written some wonderful stuff, but Robin took the ecstasy to even a higher point. If you're going to have to go to that dark, like Parry did, it was great that Robin could go in the other direction, to that joyous innocence, to escape Parry's nightmare."

Bridges found these scenes — the first of which was shot late at night, and the latter at daybreak — somewhat hectic: "We got started late and had a lot of work to do in a small amount of time," he said. "Then there's this weird guy on a bicycle that was circling our crew and wouldn't let us get the shot. That was maddening." But in that frenzy, Bridges said, "Robin came up with some of his great improvs, like rubbing his ass on the grass. 'You know why dogs do this? Because it feels good!' And then 'Let the little guy flap in the breeze,' shaking his dick in the wind. He had this wonderful freedom, of just letting his hairy body be exposed to all the elements and all the people. He was brave in doing that."

And then sometimes, when Robin and Bridges were at their weariest, the universe would open up to them in ways they could never imagine. After working overnight on a scene under a bridge, the two utterly exhausted actors were at last allowed to step away from the cameras at around four a.m. "We were fucking bushed, man," Bridges said. "It was very hard to smile, and any jokes that were coming out of Robin were dim. I look over and I see a couple of crates under this bridge. And I tap Robin and motion to him, and we sit on these crates. And as soon as our asses hit the crates, a whole bevy of pigeons — there must have been about twenty of 'em up there on the bridge — decide to just unload on us. They shit all over us. And it goes on and on. And then it goes on a little bit more. That was it. And we just looked at each other, and we didn't smile or laugh. It was like fucking Jack Benny, man. We both looked straight ahead, covered in pigeon shit.

"It's a weird comment to make, but the universe just kind of trumped Robin on this," Bridges said. It was, he added, "the only time that I remember Robin being at a loss for words."

13
FATHER MAN

Robin and Marsha took their slow dances wherever they could fit them in. And if one had to happen in the middle of a downtown Manhattan photo studio, to the sounds of the blaring funk music that was supposed to be motivating Robin for another *Rolling Stone* cover shoot, so be it. While a studio crew was immersed in preparations — fiddling with equipment, popping flashes, refreshing the supply of complimentary sushi — husband and wife were a portrait of serenity. They were all they needed in this world. But what Robin wanted more than anything else was time: time to appreciate the fruits of his labor, time to enjoy the home he had back in San Francisco, time to be with Marsha, Zak, and Zelda.

"You have to pull back and recharge," Robin told the magazine. "You have to meet people outside the movies — there's a whole other world. Not everybody is promoting a script. Not everybody is worrying about grosses and points." When you're immersed in the entertainment industry, he said, "you're confronted by your career every five minutes." But when you're living real life, he said, "you're confronted by other things — like no heating. The furnace breaks, and I become Father Man, the man who goes down and changes the fuse, and it *still* fucks up." Maybe if he could just slow down the pace of his life enough, there might even be time for another baby. Only with this one, some new rules would have to be observed. "Marsha says if we have another child, it's no more Zs," he explained. "We're going to another letter."

This was Robin's chance to get things right, an ambition he yearned to fulfill even more so now that he was being honest with himself about how he'd brought down his first marriage. When he was with Valerie, he said, "I'd go off and run around because I didn't know what the fuck I wanted. I'd be a schmuck, and she'd respond in kind. And then we'd try to stop and deal with it, and it wouldn't work. Finally, I had to say, 'I can't do this to myself anymore.' "

"And then," he said, "I became involved with Marsha."

Marsha dismissed the idea that she had somehow been Robin's savior. Still, she said, "He needed stability. I think most people need one person in their life that they *know* they can rely upon. I'm Robin's safety net.

He knows I'm strong."

Robin, however, was categorical about how she had changed him for the better: "I stopped running around with all this madness," he said. "I started to go, 'Wait, I can live a life. I don't have to live and die in my own sweat.' I slowly pulled myself up. I started to create and to work — kind of like the phoenix that rises out of its own ass."

The only obstacles standing in Robin's way were his commitments to the work he had already done and to all the new work he had agreed to take on.

Awakenings opened in limited release on December 22, 1990, and the response was a disappointing contrast to Robin's experience making the film. The reviews were generally unwelcoming and especially hostile to Robin's performance. In the *Chicago Tribune,* Dave Kehr wrote that *Awakenings* "takes a powerful subject and, by reducing it to a series of insistent emotional climaxes, betrays it almost completely." Robin, he wrote, was "an immediate problem, pushing himself forward in an ingratiating, showbiz manner that completely undermines the supposed shyness of his character." Over the span of *Good Morning, Vietnam, Dead Poets Society,* and now this film, Robin, he said, "has become our contemporary embodiment of the beating heart of humanity, whose appeal rests on his ability to project his own sensitivity, his own compassion — at which point those qualities turn into demagoguery."

On the other hand, Roger Ebert, who had trashed *Dead Poets Society,* was much more amenable to *Awakenings.* He gave it four stars and called it "one of Robin Williams' best performances, pure and uncluttered, without the ebullient distractions he sometimes adds — the shtick where none is called for."

The film did brisk business when it went into wide release in January and earned about $52 million. Robin received a Golden Globe nomination for Best Actor in a Motion Picture Drama, though the award went to Jeremy Irons for his role as Claus von Bülow in *Reversal of Fortune.* But when the Academy Award nominations were announced, Robin was overlooked, even as De Niro, his costar, received a nod in the Best Actor category.

Terry Gilliam had warned Robin early on that he was likely to be neglected for *Awakenings.* "He was so proud of his performance in that," Gilliam recalled. "I said, 'But Rob, you're not going to win. You don't have any of the tics and twists and jerks that De Niro has. The guys with the most tics, they're the ones that win.' "

Robin returned to Los Angeles that winter to start filming *Hook,* an ambitious fantasy film that Steven Spielberg had wanted to make for several years. The director had chased the idea of a motion picture about an adult Peter Pan, one that would have starred Michael Jackson as the grown-up incarnation of the boy who could never grow up and Dustin Hoffman as his pirate nemesis, Captain James Hook. But Spielberg had abandoned the project when his son Max was born, fearing that its complex technical requirements would impose on his family time: "I wanted to be home as a dad, not a surrogate dad," he explained.

Spielberg came back to the Peter Pan film in 1990, at which point it had been worked on by another director and several screenwriters. Hoffman was still attached, and now so was Robin, who would play Peter Banning, a yuppie lawyer who is neglectful of his wife and children and has forgotten entirely about his youthful past as Peter Pan. "He's very representative of a lot of people today who race headlong into the future, nodding hello and goodbye to their families," Spielberg said of the character. "I'm part of a generation that is extremely motivated by career, and I've caught myself in the unenviable position of *being* Peter Banning from time to time."

Robin saw himself in the character, too, thinking back to the period of intensive emotional repair he underwent when he was breaking up with Valerie while still trying to be present for Zak. "I had a therapist say,

'Basically the only therapy I can offer you right now is to play with your child,' because I had been using work as a buffer," he explained. *Hook* also provided Robin with his first opportunity to work with Spielberg and Hoffman (from whom he had inherited film roles in *Popeye, The World According to Garp,* and *Dead Poets Society*), as well as a supporting cast that included Julia Roberts as the fairy Tinker Bell. But those big names, and a lavish production that called for a full-scale pirate ship and sets that spread across the soundstages of two studio back lots, came at a steep cost. The budget for *Hook* was estimated at $35 to $50 million (some reports put it at $60 million or more), a steep figure that would have been even larger if Robin, Spielberg, and Hoffman had not agreed to forgo their upfront salaries and instead share 40 percent of the film's gross ticket sales.

The previous fall, Robin had been sent a tantalizing dossier of storyboards for the film, visualizing the pirate ship and a climactic battle sequence between Peter Pan and Captain Hook, among other scenes, along with a note from Bruce Cohen, an associate producer and assistant director, advising him, "We will need to measure you for your flying rig in early January, so the closer you are to your 'flying weight' by then the better." By the time filming began, Robin was twenty pounds lighter than he had been during the making of *The Fisher King.*

Robin spent a month between mid-February and mid-March 1991 making *Hook* at Universal Studios, and then another fifty-seven filming days between March and June on the Columbia lot, with blue-screen special effects work still to come. He shared his screen time with the eccentric Hoffman, who started each morning by eating a bowlful of hot onions and garlic for what he said were health reasons. Hoffman had decided to base his portrayal of Captain Hook in part on William F. Buckley Jr., whose clenched, effete voice was a longtime staple of Robin's routine. "He's bright and educated, but there's something scary there," Hoffman said of Buckley.

As the film's production spilled into late July, the costars developed a feisty working relationship full of one-upmanship and competitive taunts. When Hoffman called for a scene to be halted because he'd lost his motivation, Robin hit him with a retort that had supposedly been flung at him by Laurence Olivier on the set of *Marathon Man:* "When all else fails, try acting." So when Robin later stumbled over his own lines, Hoffman peered into the camera and asked, "What can you expect from Mork?" After nailing the next take, Robin responded, "*Ishtar* is on television tonight."

Robin's real nemesis, however, was the harness he wore in his flying scenes, which caught him squarely in a sensitive area of his body. "It was very hard work, but when you get to fly — whew!" Robin later explained. "To be sixty feet up, flying a hundred and fifty feet over a giant pirate ship, that's a nice day." Pointing at his crotch, he added, "It is a little painful because of the rig," but at least he had gained a new understanding of the Peter Pan role. "I know why a lot of women have played the part," he said.

This was just Robin's day job. On the other side of the San Fernando Valley, in a collection of trailers in Glendale, Walt Disney Pictures was undergoing a renaissance. The animated movies that were once the core of the studio's family-friendly brand had gradually lost favor to live-action features, and it produced only five cartoon films over the span of the 1980s. But in 1989, the last of these releases, *The Little Mermaid,* had been a bona fide smash, grossing more than $84 million and encouraging Disney to develop more of these films.

Among the first of these follow-ups was a cartoon musical set within the Arabic folklore of *One Thousand and One Nights.* The studio's chairman, Jeffrey Katzenberg, had wanted a swashbuckling adventure in the vein of *The Thief of Baghdad,* but the film's directors, Ron Clements and John Musker, and its lead composer, Alan Menken, were able to steer him toward a more intimate retelling of the story of Aladdin. Naturally, one of the most important characters would be the Genie, the all-powerful creature the hero releases from captivity in an oil lamp: in this version, the creative team envisioned a lovable, shape-shifting song-and-dance man modeled on the African American musicians of the Jazz Age.

"The idea of the Genie was, he was black and had an earring," Menken said. "We thought he could be a hipster, à la Fats Waller and Cab Calloway. Growing up, I loved playing Fats Waller songs: 'Your feet's too big, oh my.' That became the vocabulary."

Katzenberg, however, had a different approach: he wanted the Genie to be played by a well-known Hollywood performer, and he had his eye on Robin, his protean leading man from *Good Morning, Vietnam* and *Dead Poets Society*. The use of a celebrity was unusual in feature animation, where the characters, rather than the voices, were supposed to be the stars; and Katzenberg's insistence on choosing Robin in particular ran against the traditions of his filmmakers, who did not like to hire their vocal talent sight unseen. "There was a policy that you really had to audition, or you wouldn't be in the movie," Clements said. But, as Musker explained, "When you're a big-name star like Robin, you don't audition. You have to hire them."

460

Actually, *Aladdin* would end up auditioning for Robin: Disney hired the artist and animator Eric Goldberg to create some test footage using vocal tracks from Robin's stand-up comedy albums. Then Robin was brought for a visit to the studio trailers, where he was shown this footage as well as the storyboards for several of the film's planned musical numbers, including a big, brassy set piece for the Genie called "Friend Like Me," where he pledges his loyalty to his new master.

Robin's participation in *Aladdin* was never really in question: he was a lifelong fan of cartoons, and he often cited the legendary Warner Bros. animator Chuck Jones as a source of inspiration. He had also recently had a positive experience on *FernGully: The Last Rainforest,* an animated film with an environmentally conscious message, which had cast him as a rapping bat named Batty Koda and allowed him to freely improvise his dialogue. But what almost certainly sealed the deal for him was seeing the bits of his wild and boundary-free comedy routine turned into a bona fide cartoon. "I think what probably sold him," Goldberg recalled, "was the one where he says, 'Tonight, let's talk about the serious subject of schizophrenia — No, it doesn't! — Shut up, let him talk!' What I did is animate the Genie growing another head to argue with himself, and Robin just laughed. He could see the potential of what the character could be. I'm sure it wasn't the only factor, but then he signed the dotted line."

That March, while Robin was immersed in the filming of *Hook,* Disney sent him a file full of Goldberg's character designs for the Genie, a friendly, blue-skinned apparition of indeterminate ethnicity, with a tuft of hair, a sly goatee, and the fluidity and lightness of an Al Hirschfeld caricature. These illustrations showed him in a variety of moods and poses — making happy and sad faces, holding Aladdin by the scruff of his vest — but also taking on the physical attributes of the people and things he imitated: in a maître d' outfit, with a ventriloquist's dummy on his arm, becoming Arnold Schwarzenegger, Ed Sullivan, Groucho Marx, a harem girl, a rabbit, a ghoul, an army sergeant. The limitless possibilities of the character were right there on the page.

But not long after this, *Aladdin* suffered several creative setbacks. Howard Ashman, who had been Menken's longtime librettist and had written the lyrics for songs like "Friend Like Me," died from complications of AIDS on March 14. In April, Katzenberg rejected a storyboarded version of the film presented to him by Musker and Clements. Two additional writers, Ted Elliott and Terry Rossio, were brought on to the film, and large sections of the story were rewritten while other scenes and musical numbers were excised entirely. Robin had yet to record any of his tracks.

A preliminary version of the *Aladdin* script, from January 22 of that year, described the Genie as a "hip, hyper, mercurial Robin Williams type, full of exuberance, with a childlike vulnerability." On the page, the character's dialogue was written to sound like Robin, anticipating the many opportunities he might take to break character and ad-lib. As Musker explained, "We wrote the script with Robin and his shifting persona in mind" — but with the full understanding that any and all of it could go out the window when his recording sessions started later that spring. With each take, Musker said, "He performed it as we had written it, like seven or eight times, and then we'd say, 'Okay, wing it.' So then he'd do it another eight times, each time bringing it up even more. On that first scene, we were done after those seven or eight more takes. We said, 'That's great.' He'd say, 'Well, let me just try a few other things.' We wound up with twenty-five different takes of his introduction."

Clements added, "Each take of a two-minute scene was like ten minutes long. And we thought, how the heck are we going to figure out what to use?"

"He would be going to the stratosphere," Musker said, "and we would be trying to find where he was."

A production script dated September 18 added more songs for the character, including "Prince Ali," in which the Genie provides a razzle-dazzle introduction for Aladdin, who is disguised as a make-believe sovereign; and the film's sweeping opening number, "Arabian Nights," which was so vocally demanding that it had to be sung by the Broadway actor Bruce Adler. Robin, who was staying at the Los Angeles home of Barry Levinson, would come back from a long day of shooting on *Hook,* having had his midsection yanked around on wires and pulleys for twelve hours. Then he would spend the evening seated at a piano rehearsing his songs with Menken and David Friedman, the *Aladdin* musical director, or running through new dialogue with Musker and Clements.

Meanwhile, the animators were hard at work trying to decode Robin's auditory output and translate it for a visual medium. In one scene, Goldberg said, "One of Robin's riffs was the Genie didn't believe that Aladdin was going to use his third wish to set him free, so he goes, 'Uh, yeah, right. *Booo-wooop.*' John and Ron didn't know what *Booo-wooop* was. So I said, 'Well, that's Robin's shorthand for telling a lie. It's Pinocchio's nose growing. Can I turn the Genie's head into Pinocchio? We own the character.'

And so we did!"

Katzenberg himself devised a strategy for recording the film's prologue, in which Robin, playing the role of an Arabian street peddler, tries to sell the audience on various worthless wares before offering up the oil lamp that sets the story in motion. He told his filmmakers, "When Robin records this, bring in a bunch of props and put a blanket over it, and then remove the blanket and he'll never have seen them, and then he's just going to go off on each one." That approach — deliberately modeled on Jonathan Winters and his style of improv comedy — was exactly what the directors did when Robin recorded the scene. Among the riffs that made it into the movie were his observations on a faulty water pipe ("a combination hookah and coffee maker — it also makes julienne fries!") and a mysterious plastic box. ("I have never seen one of these intact before. This is the famous Dead Sea Tupperware.")

Other improvised lines would remain on the cutting-room floor, like Robin's reaction to discovering a brassiere. "He looks at it and goes, 'Look at this, it's a double slingshot,' " Goldberg said. " 'Look at this, it's a double yarmulke.' And then he turns and he goes, 'Mmm, I should have called her.' I took some subversive pleasure in realizing as we were working on it that nobody had ever seen this kind of humor in a Disney film before. You

465

feel a little bit naughty: 'Ooo, I wonder if we're going to get away with this.' "

By the end of the summer of 1991, Robin had finished his work on both *Aladdin* and *Hook*. As a parting gift to Spielberg, he gave the director a painting of Peter Pan by the artist Greg Hildebrandt and a book of his illustrations, and Spielberg returned the gesture with a grateful farewell letter. "Your work in HOOK is flogging brilliant!" the director wrote. "There is a consistency of character development from the bookish and selfish Peter Banning to the explosively optimistic and liberated Peter Pan that can only be described as one watches the movie. I don't think I've ever met in my life any actor, producer or other director who is as dedicated, as involved, as passionate, and as hardworking as you have been on HOOK . . . it has been an honor working with you. MOSCOW ON THE HUDSON was no fluke — you have done nothing but grow and explode out of that comic canister into one of the best actors in America today."

Meanwhile, *The Fisher King* came out in limited release on September 20, after a delay from a planned May opening, in the hope that a later date might keep it out of competition with flashier summer entertainments and would better position it for year-end awards consideration. The reviews were largely positive, and so enthusiastically disposed to the film itself, that it was easy to miss the praise for Robin's performance. In *Newsweek,* David Ansen called *The Fisher King* "a wild, vital stew of a movie, an attempt to translate the myth of the Holy Grail to the harsh urban realities of contemporary New York." In passing, he mentioned that Robin "puts all his mercurial comic brilliance in the service of his character (well, almost all)." A *New York Times* review by Janet Maslin praised the film for being "capable of great charm whenever its taste for chaos is kept in check." Robin, in the role of "a gentle soul who has been left homeless and driven half-mad by grief, is allowed to chatter aimlessly, cavort naked in Central Park and generally go overboard." But when he is not "off on any of his various tangents," she said he "brings a disarming warmth and gentleness to the fiendishly comic Parry."

Glenn Close, Robin's costar from *The World According to Garp* and one of many celebrity visitors to the set of *Hook* (where she made a cameo as a pirate), wrote to Robin to tell him how moved she had been by his work in *The Fisher King.* "You held my heart in the palm of your hand — broke it — and then put it back together better than before," she said in her letter. "It is a truly healing movie . . . and we're all in such desperate need for healing things." For the first three weekends of its wider release, *The Fisher King* was number one at the U.S. box office.

Robin made his last promotional appearances for the film at the end of September, and with those commitments fulfilled, he had finally earned his freedom to go home to San Francisco and assume the role he'd been wanting to play for months, as Father Man. It was just in time, too: on November 25, Marsha gave birth to their second child, a son they named Cody Alan.

During the final weeks of Marsha's pregnancy, Robin sat for a series of conversations with *Playboy,* later published in the magazine as a single interview, in which he took stock of his career to this point. He saw that he now had the leverage to pick projects that could keep him closer to home, to be nearer to his family, and to have Marsha involved in his work as deeply as possible. "She makes sure everything runs," he said. "Not that I have a huge entourage. . . . I mean, she's not an entourage. [As interviewer] 'How many in your entourage?' [Pompously] 'Well, the family. Zelda, who I can write off as a roadie.' [As the child Zelda] 'Daddy, can't carry bags, bags heavy.' "

Asked whether he regarded his life or his work as more important to him, Robin answered that he desired "a balance of the two. Time is really this delicate thing. Work-

468

ing your tits off during the week, then find time to come home at night and not be so self-involved. 'So, enough about me. Now, what do you think about me?' "

In that same interview, Robin drew a striking comparison between himself and Jerzy Kosinski, the author of *Being There*, who had committed suicide the previous spring, months after suffering a seizure that he feared might be the harbinger of a debilitating stroke. As Robin explained it, he could almost understand the author's thought process:

> Jerzy Kosinski killed himself; supposedly, the reason was that he just didn't want to become a vegetable, he didn't want to lose his sharpness. There's that fear — if I felt like I was becoming not just dull but a rock, that I still couldn't spark, still fire off or talk about things, if I'd start to worry or got too afraid to say something. As long as you still keep taking the chances and you're not afraid to play Peter Pan. . . . What if it fails? "I don't care, I'm having a great fucking time." If I stop trying, I'd get afraid.

But Robin would not be allowed to drift so easily into domesticity. In November, a San Francisco Superior Court judge denied a motion by his lawyers to dismiss the long-festering lawsuit brought against him by Michelle Tish Carter, the woman with whom

469

he'd had an affair while he was still married to Valerie. With his legal options dwindling, it was increasingly likely that Robin would have to face a trial the following year. The further progress of the case raised the uncomfortable prospect that Robin might be required to testify in court about the details of his personal life and answer questions about whether he and Carter had discussed the subject of sexually transmitted diseases. And it ensured that the lawsuit would remain in the news as Robin was trying to fortify his reputation as a family-friendly entertainer.

As the year-end release of *Hook* approached, the drumbeat of anticipation for the movie unexpectedly gave way to a din of antipathy. A week before the film officially opened on December 11, word began to spread of a dismal screening in Los Angeles for professional critics; it was said that the film was too long, too sentimental, and too burdened by the clichés of self-help psychology. "Chaotic, leaden and only sporadically appealing," one early review read. "This tale of middle-age male loss, redemption and rejuvenation is one we've already seen many times this year." The assessments published at its opening were no better; the *Los Angeles Times* described it as a film in which "arrogant spectacle smothers gentle magic" and "its very excessiveness squeezes the life and joy out of far too much of *Hook.*"

Still, *Hook* opened in first place at the box office and remained there for four straight weekends, going on to take in nearly $120 million — a figure that was considered underwhelming in relation to its exorbitant cost and the months of hype that had preceded it. Robin, who was guaranteed a portion of the first $50 million of its gross, would still be paid handsomely.

Though Spielberg had fitfully tried to knock down reports that he was distancing himself from the film, he wrote a letter to Robin in January 1992, apologizing for his absence from promotional efforts and for having been out of contact for several weeks. The director, who had been so contagiously buoyant the previous summer, now sounded deflated; in the letter, which he addressed to "My faithful, compassionate friend and the true Prince of Pans," Spielberg confessed, "Right now I'm in my 'I don't want to know' phase." He said he had been ignoring all reviews, news reports, and business messages, avoiding any TV or magazines, and spending time only with his wife, Kate Capshaw, and their four children.

This kind of willful evasion, Spielberg wrote, "has good and bad results. For one thing, it makes most of my friends mad at me, because they take my running for shelter very personally. But it's sometimes what I need to do to survive the experience. It's how

I take care of myself, as perverse or unusual as it might seem.

"The pressure that was on me for the last 18 months was at times intolerable," he continued. "It must have been for anyone human." But no matter what, Spielberg assured Robin, the experience of *Hook* had made them lifelong friends. "I'll be out of my bomb shelter very soon," he wrote. "And whether there is still a subdivision up there or not won't make any difference. We will live on, raising our kids, being good friends and making our movies."

Robin gave a teasing acknowledgment to his *Hook* collaborators when he won a Golden Globe Award for his performance in *The Fisher King* later that month. Nearing the end of a discursive acceptance speech, he said, "I'm just thanking everybody now — it's just like [goes into an *Exorcist*-like convulsion] spewing out, 'Dustin! I'd like to thank Steven! No, wrong movie!' " Then, with greater sincerity, he added: "Most of all, I think I would like to thank a woman who is my muse, who is my flame, Marsha, my wife." On-screen, at that moment, she could be seen mouthing "I love you" back to him. And in February, Robin received the third Oscar nomination of his career, once again in the category of Best Actor, for his performance in *The Fisher King.*

The film was up for five Academy Awards

in all, including nominations for Richard La-Gravenese's screenplay and the performance of Mercedes Ruehl, who played the love interest for Jeff Bridges's character. The 1992 Oscars show was one of Billy Crystal's best, beginning with an homage to *Silence of the Lambs* in which he was wheeled onstage in a Hannibal Lecter–style face mask, and serving him with an irresistible running gag when his *City Slickers* costar Jack Palance began doing one-armed push-ups in the middle of his acceptance speech.

Ruehl was an early winner for Best Supporting Actress, but it was the only trophy *The Fisher King* would take home. *The Silence of the Lambs* swept the major awards categories, and Robin lost to its villainous leading man, Anthony Hopkins, despite Terry Gilliam's prediction that he might actually prevail that year. "I said, 'You've got a good chance this time, Rob,' " Gilliam recalled. "It was a pity, because I do think his performance is so good. Maybe for a lot of people, they just felt it was too much like the real Robin Williams. I don't know what they think. I've never understood the mentality of who votes for what in the awards."

In an earlier era, it had taken Robin years to land his debut booking on Johnny Carson's *Tonight Show*. But in the spring of 1992, in a powerful confirmation of Robin's status as a comic and as an actor, Carson chose him to be one of his final guests before he retired from a thirty-year career in late-night television. On May 21, the last night when any guests were booked on the program, Robin was the first of two celebrity visitors to sit across from him on his fabled couch.

Carson introduced Robin with a solemnity and seriousness he did not often exhibit on the air, saying, "In this business, there are comedians, there are comics, and once in a while, rarely, somebody rises above and supersedes that and becomes a comic persona unto themselves. I never ceased to be amazed at the versatility and the wonderful work that Robin Williams does." Robin, who was wearing the platinum blond hair of the character he was playing in a new Barry Levinson movie called *Toys,* entered with a rocking chair that he offered to Carson as a gag gift, and spent much of his segment making fun of the season's aspiring presidential candidates, to the host's delight. Carson responded in kind, joking that Jerry Brown's problem was that — as opposed to Bill Clinton — he never exhaled.

Robin let out a long and satisfied laugh, to which Carson said, "You like that?"

"I *love* that," Robin replied.

"Thank you," Carson said.

Robin also spoke publicly about his new son, Cody, for the first time, marveling at the size of the six-month-old child's testicles. "We're out of here tomorrow night, what do I care?" an unabashed Carson responded.

The night's other guest was Bette Midler, who serenaded Carson with a satirical version of "You Made Me Love You," and then with an achingly sincere performance of "One for My Baby (and One More for the Road)" that brought visible tears to the host's eyes. Robin, who initially had been chiming in with his own jokes while Midler and Carson bantered, gradually went quiet as the segment played on. Marc Shaiman, the composer and songwriter who was Midler's piano accompanist that night, noticed Robin's uncharacteristic silence as well. "If you watch the show, he at first is jumping in a bit, here and there, the way he normally would," Shaiman said. "But he became quickly cognizant of the magical thing that was happening between Bette and Johnny Carson that night. Even Robin — which says a lot — knew to step back. Don't try to add to this. It's not something you saw a lot of, but he was sensitive enough to know: don't be Robin Williams for twenty minutes." Midler later won an Emmy Award for her appearance on the show.

That August, Robin and Michelle Tish Carter finally settled their long-standing lawsuits against each other, only a week before the case was to go to trial, with Robin paying an undisclosed amount to his ex-girlfriend. In the short term it was an embarrassing resolution to an awkward situation, the sewing-up of a wound that was entirely self-inflicted, but a recognition, too, that any circumstance where Robin might have to answer invasive questions about his sex life, publicly and under oath, would be far worse in the long run. In the fall, Robin, Marsha, and the children went to Rabat, Morocco, so that he could work on the film *Being Human,* an assignment that would keep him globetrotting from the North African coast to London to New York and back to San Francisco at a time when he especially sought to escape unwanted attention.

It was during this time that Disney released *Aladdin* — in limited release on November 11 and widely on November 25 — and Robin's cartoon performance turned out to be one of his quintessential roles. The medium of animation was perhaps the only one that could keep pace with the quickness of his imagination while enhancing his improvisations; untethered from physical constraints, and free to focus on his words and their delivery, Robin was as loose, as relaxed, and as charming as he'd been in any bodily performance. For once, there was no such thing as overdoing it: every silly voice and stock accent he had in his arsenal, every celebrity impression in his repertoire, was welcome and necessary for the whole proposition to succeed.

The critics agreed. Janet Maslin of the *New York Times* praised Robin in particular, along with the animators and composers, for making the Genie

a visual correlative to the rapid-fire Williams wit, so that kaleidoscopic visions of Groucho Marx, Arnold Schwarzenegger, William F. Buckley Jr., Travis Bickle and dozens of other characters flash frantically across the screen to accompany the star's speedy delivery. Much of this occurs to the tune of "Friend Like Me," a cake-walking, show-stopping musical number with the mischievous wit that has been a hallmark of Disney's animated triumphs.

The film was an instant smash at the box office, skyrocketing to number one and remaining there for the first several weeks of 1993, and grossing more than $217 million by the end of its initial run.

The same could not be said for *Toys,* which came out a month later and proved a disappointing cinematic reunion for Robin and Barry Levinson, his director on *Good Morning, Vietnam.* Anticipation for the film had been unexpectedly stoked by a brilliant teaser trailer Levinson shot that showed Robin standing in what appears to be a grassy wheat field, speaking straight to the camera and largely undermining any notion of what a movie preview is supposed to accomplish. "I don't know about you," Robin tells the audience, "but that *last* trailer, huh, I've seen it. You know, fast cutting, big music [sings an orchestra fanfare] — what about a different kind of trailer?" He imagined aloud what he thought the finished trailer might look like, then did so again in a kind of pidgin Japanese, even mocked Fox's efforts to market it. ("Studio executives in their great insight said, 'You've got a movie about toys — when's a good time to bring it out? Rosh Hashanah?' ") Perhaps the only thing he didn't do was leave viewers with the slightest clue of what the movie was about.

Moviegoers were left baffled and underwhelmed by what they ultimately saw. *Toys* told the stylized story of Leslie Zevo, a childlike and gently peculiar man attired like a Magritte painting, who seeks to wrest control of his family's toy factory from his nefarious uncle (Michael Gambon), a general who wants to use it to build implements of war. It was full of story elements that appealed to Robin on a fundamental level. "He loved video games," Levinson said. "He loved toy soldiers. It had all those things that would make him want to do the movie. He was much more comfortable at that point in time, because it wasn't like, 'This is my last chance,' which is the way he thought of *Good Morning,*

Vietnam. By then, it was like, 'Okay, I'm established and I can relax a little bit.' " But the vivid palette of its production design concealed more complicated feelings that viewers largely weren't prepared for. "To me, it was a black comedy that was bright," said Levinson. "It seemed so primary colored, and light and sweet. All of that was the facade of it. It's what was underneath it. So, it just got completely misunderstood at the time."

Rolling Stone called *Toys* "a gimmicky, obvious and pious bore, not to mention overproduced and overlong." It awarded zero stars to the film and added, "No amount of brilliant production design . . . can disguise the smug hypocrisy of an antiwar tract that decries the killing games of vid-age children and then offers up a climactic battle between hawk toys and dove toys for their movie delectation."

Robin did his share of press to help support *Toys,* but it still flopped. And he had largely sat out of the promotional rounds for *Aladdin,* a choice he attributed at the time to his commitment to *Toys.* However, he later acknowledged that his decision not to help its campaign had stemmed from a growing frustration with Disney. At the time he signed up to play the Genie — a role for which he was paid only scale wages and not his usual multimillion-dollar salary — he believed the studio had agreed not to use his voice in the

479

marketing or merchandising of the film. So it came as a shock when he heard himself talking back in *Aladdin* commercials and toys.

"All of a sudden, they release an advertisement — one part was the movie, the second part was where they used the movie to sell stuff," Robin explained. "Not only did they use my voice, they took a character I did and overdubbed it to sell stuff. That was the one thing I said: 'I don't do that.' That was the one thing where they crossed the line." Disney countered that it had vetted all of the film's marketing materials with Robin and Marsha, and that nothing it had done violated the studio's contractual agreement with him.

Simply put, Robin said, "I don't want to sell stuff. It's the one thing I don't do. In *Mork & Mindy,* they did Mork dolls — I didn't mind the dolls; the image is theirs. But the voice, that's *me;* I gave them my *self.* When it happened, I said, 'You *know* I don't do that.' And they apologized; they said it was done by other people."

What he meant by this was: There was only so much Robin to go around. But, Robin being Robin, he had to make the point in his own particular style. So, he invoked a dubious tale about the silent-age film director Erich von Stroheim and a moment when he was supposedly caught getting a blow job on the set.

As Robin told the tale, "Suddenly he notices

that all the crew members are watching. He looks down and he goes, 'What are you doing, you nasty girl!' The Disney thing was like that: 'I swear I didn't know what my right hand was doing.' "

14
HOT FLASHES

There seemed to be children everywhere you went in the old house at 2640 Steiner Street, one of the elegant Victorian residences that stood squarely on this slanted San Francisco block. The street and its surroundings were filled with exuberant young extras who had come to take advantage of the mobile petting zoo that had been hired for the opening scene of *Mrs. Doubtfire,* a new comedy that Robin was shooting here. There were also the three child actors starring in the film with him, who played the offspring of a modern couple — thriving white-collar mom, temporarily down-on-his-luck dad — caught in a tug-of-war as their parents headed for divorce. And then there were Robin's own kids: Zak, now ten years old, who visited on days when his dad had custody of him, alongside Zelda, nearly four, and Cody, one and a half, who, along with Eleanor Columbus, the three-and-a-half-year-old daughter of the film's director, Chris Columbus, conspired to make the set their playground.

Mrs. Doubtfire, in which Robin played a struggling, soon-to-be single father who assumes the disguise of a golden-haired female housekeeper so he can spend more time with his children, was perhaps the perfect distillation of his life up to that point. It was the cinematic embodiment of the philosophy he'd learned from his own upbringing, through two marriages, and now his own experiences as a husband and father: family is where you find it; all are welcome and no one ever loses their membership. Beneath the movie's farcical, cross-dressing premise, *Mrs. Doubtfire* exemplified how intensely Robin loved his family — his children, especially — and the lengths he would go for them.

"A man is losing contact with his kids, and he seizes upon an opportunity to see them more," said Randi Mayem Singer, the film's lead screenwriter. "It has the universal theme of a parent's love for their children. There are ugly, mean, nasty divorces. Your marriage may not have worked out, but if you have kids, you have to co-parent them for the rest of their lives. And it's harmful to them to not do it amicably."

More than that, the film solidified the special relationship that Robin and Marsha had as personal and professional partners. *Mrs. Doubtfire* was a project that Marsha had helped to identify and refine until it was just right for Robin; she worked on it as a producer and was involved in every aspect of its creation, while she also drove Zelda to school and ballet classes and toted Cody to the Marina and the Exploratorium in a canvas papoose. The eventual success of *Mrs. Doubtfire* demonstrated just how well she knew her husband's tastes and how moviegoing audiences wanted to see him. And its success was staggering: it became, and remained for many years, his highest-grossing film — no other movie in which he played a leading role would surpass it — and it paid him considerable dividends, both the kind that went toward his standing in Hollywood and those that went straight into his pocket. It was a pinnacle that, once he reached it, he would never see again.

By the time filming began in the spring of 1993, Robin had all the usual apparatus in place needed to run a prosperous film-acting career. To replace Marsha as his full-time assistant, he had hired Rebecca Erwin Spencer, a friend and fellow comedy aspirant at the Holy City Zoo, which she had managed during the 1980s. He had three prominent agents at CAA, Michael Marcus, Michael Menchel, and Michael Ovitz, known collectively as "the Mikes"; and he had his longtime team of Rollins Joffe managers, simply nicknamed "the boys," whose configuration had changed considerably since they started representing him in the 1970s. Jack Rollins, the cofounder of the company, had sold his stake to its junior associates; now the firm and its clients were the responsibility of Buddy Morra, Larry Brezner, David Steinberg, and a new partner, Stephen Tenenbaum, who had joined the group at the start of 1993. As independent producers, Morra, Brezner, Steinberg & Tenenbaum (often abbreviated MBST) had a first-look deal with 20th Century Fox and offices on the studio lot, where the company developed its own slate of film and television projects.

Robin and Marsha had their own production company now, too. The couple hired Cyndi McHale, the wife of Robin's lawyer Gerald Margolis, to be Marsha's assistant and run this new company, which they called Blue Wolf. As to why they chose that name, all the knowledgeable sources were somewhat cryptic on the subject. "Use your imagination," McHale said. "And remember Robin's sense of humor, which was rather dirty." At the time of the company's founding, Marsha said simply, "It's him, because he's the blue wolf." "I'm hairy," Robin explained. *"Furry,"* Marsha added.

The most basic goal of Blue Wolf was to harness Robin and Marsha's voracious cultural appetites and allow them "to pursue things that were of interest to them, as opposed to just the studio blockbusters," Mc-

Hale said. As the couple saw it, they were formalizing a relationship that had existed as far back as *Good Morning, Vietnam,* where Marsha read the scripts Robin was considering and offered her opinions on them, though he was of course free to choose or pass on what he wanted. "She has the patience to discuss a problem for hours and hours," Robin said. "I have to be busy preparing for my part. Anyway, I tend to be direct. I'll just say, 'That sucks!' "

The arrangement gave Marsha a further degree of oversight to protect Robin, largely from himself. Sometimes his intense desire to work led to bad choices; if he couldn't get started on a project right away, or knew deep down that he would have to let a good script go, he could drive himself to unhealthy fixations. "He can sometimes obsess over something he would have liked to have done but couldn't because he had a conflict," she said. "This way, if we have control and I know a project was developed for Robin, I don't have any secret agendas for him — and frankly, I'm probably the only person in his life who is just for him. It doesn't have anything to do with any of the other things that can get in the way. I can say, 'We'll wait a year and a half.' "

As Robin explained, "Sometimes I have this kind of sentimental side that will go for — 'Oh, it's about a puppy' or 'Ahhh, the nice lady died, and the kids . . .' and she'd look at it and go, 'No, it doesn't work.' That's why I need her opinion."

"You don't need to be a latter-day Christ figure," she told him.

Their first official collaboration as a husband-and-wife producing team began with *Alias Madame Doubtfire,* the 1988 children's novel by Anne Fine. The book tells the story of Daniel Hillard, a divorcé who, by inventing the title persona, is able to slip under the watchful eye of his ex-wife — though not past his observant children, who agree to keep his secret for him. As a father, Daniel is fiercely loyal to his kids and pleads his case to them that he has just as much right to them as their mother does.

"You're not just *her* children, you know," he tells them:

You're mine, too. She has no right to treat us this way. I was an adequate father. . . . No, I'd go further than that. I was a very *good* father. I made sure she remembered her vitamin tablets when she was pregnant. I fed her good, wholesome food and made her stop smoking. I did all the heavy shopping, and cheered her up, and brought her endless cups of tea. And whenever she lost her nerve and said that the last thing in the world she wanted was a baby, I promised to take you to the nearest orphanage the moment you were born, and leave you on the doorstep in a box. What man could do more?

The film rights to Fine's novel had been acquired by the producers Matthew Rushton and Frank Levy, who brought it to Elizabeth Gabler, then an executive at United Artists; when Gabler left that studio to work at Fox, she brought the property with her. It was at Fox that Marsha first learned about the project, in a conversation with Robin's managers; she liked the novel but not an early draft of the screenplay, which she felt was too broad. Fox offered her a producing role, and she supervised the rewriting process, sifting through revisions of the script in the predawn hours when she rose with Cody in the earliest months of her son's life. When Christopher Columbus, the screenwriter of *Gremlins* and *The Goonies* and director of the *Home Alone* franchise, became available to direct the movie, Robin and Marsha were told they had a green light.

The appeal of *Mrs. Doubtfire* was simple to Marsha, residing almost entirely in the premise of Robin having to portray a believable female character. "I liked the idea that a man would have to play a woman and do it well enough to pass," she said. "I looked at things, at that point, more in terms of the range that it would require of Robin as an actor, and I figured that we could make the rest work around that. I was just purely interested in the idea of Robin playing this woman, more than anything."

For Robin, the joy of the role was getting to play "someone totally unlike myself," he said. "It isn't just drag. It's the fact that it was like, to be, to have this character that really had a life of her own. No longer does it look anything like myself, and you're free to be this woman, and create her and to make her as funny as you can, but yet still be in character." Yes, there were certain unfamiliar boundaries that came with "this sweet, blue-mouthed old woman," Robin said. "And sometimes I would cross over them. But most of the time I could stay within her, who she was."

Columbus said that what he and Robin both connected to in the material was the guilt they felt at having to be away from their families in order to do their jobs. "In our hearts, we'd love to be Robin's character in the movie — to be the ultimate father twelve hours a day, to stay home and play with the kids," the director said.

But at the time he signed on to make the film, Columbus still had misgivings about the script, which he felt lacked humor and heart, and especially about its conclusion. "The biggest problem was Daniel Hillard and Miranda got back together at the end of the picture," he said.

Marsha agreed that an ending in which Daniel and Miranda patched up their marriage would make *Mrs. Doubtfire* "a Cinderella kind of story" and would "take it away from what we feel is the reality in the world, and in the country, in terms of divorcing families and what ultimately happens."

Their vision of the film, which would end with the characters on good terms but nonetheless accepting that their marriage was over, was one that Robin and Marsha had to fight for. "Everybody — our managers, our agents, people at the studio — said that the audience would want Daniel and Miranda to get back together or, at least, to leave their situation up in the air," Marsha said. More pointedly, she added, "When two people are harmful and wrong for each other, they do not belong together."

Robin had addressed some of these issues in therapy when his marriage to Valerie was unraveling, and he felt especially strongly that it would ring false to reunite the film's parents. "That's the one fantasy most psychiatrists will tell you is perpetuated by children of divorce who are in therapy — and it's the one thing that professionals don't want to perpetuate," he said. "They'll ask kids, 'Ever have a memory of your mom and dad together?' The kids say no, but it's the

490

grand concept. 'They're together.' Sold to you by Norman Rockwell. The family, at the table . . . even though they're all armed."

Mrs. Doubtfire, he argued, should be "about *real* family values. After a divorce, how many fathers just give up? The tendency is to say, 'I love my son,' and then pull away. If you're lucky, the father becomes an uncle. But the weird thing is, he needs his kids as much as they need him."

Over the course of making the movie, which spanned the late winter, spring, and early summer of 1993, Robin spent forty-one shooting days in the camouflage of Euphegenia Doubtfire, a sweet but no-nonsense widow with a Scottish lilt in her voice and a recognizable gleam in her blue eyes. On these occasions, Robin got two entries on the call sheets: the first (1) for Daniel Hillard and the second (1A) for Mrs. Doubtfire.

Transforming Robin's face into hers — a mask made from eight overlapping pieces of foam-latex appliances created by the makeup effects artist Greg Cannom and decorated with multiple layers of pink- and flesh-colored paint and makeup — took about four hours. (As production continued and the artists became more practiced at it, the process was shortened to about three hours.) More makeup was then applied to Robin's hands and he was zipped into a body suit made of "spandex and beans," as he described it, that made him feel "like a walking bean bag chair."

In the earliest on-camera makeup test of the character, on March 8, Robin is seen playing with his pantyhose and garter even before the scene starts, scratching at his leg and the strange garments he's been asked to wear, then looking at the camera as if he's been caught in the act. He is not yet wearing the oversize eyeglasses that would become part of Mrs. Doubtfire's look, and her face appears bloated and severe. Robin starts to speak in an accent that is softer and more authentic (that is, less cartoonish) than he would ultimately use: "Helloooo," he declares. "Nice to meet you. I'm Euphegenia Doubtfire and I'm very — excuse me —" at which point his dentures fall out of his mouth.

Robin improvised short scenes with the actors playing his children and with Sally Field, the Academy Award–winning actress who played Daniel's estranged wife, Miranda. He also claimed to have taken the character out for a test drive in a San Francisco sex shop. "I tried to buy a double-headed dildo," Robin said. "I was going, 'That one, right there, the big one. Do you have anything without veins?' . . . Finally the guy realized it was me, and went, 'Get out of here, Robin, you asshole!' "

As Robin later explained, "I started doing a voice that sounded like Margaret Thatcher, and I realized that would scare the shit out of a kid. 'Go to bed or mommy's going to fire a cruise missile.' " Drawing on recent and immediate experiences, he began to borrow vocal traits from Marit Allen, his soft-spoken costume designer on *Mrs. Doubtfire,* and Bill Forsyth, the Scottish filmmaker who directed him in *Being Human,* to arrive at the character's familiar tone.

This was all the preparation Robin needed to fashion an alter ego that could fool even Marsha, who sensed how completely invested he was in the character. "He's instilled with the spirit of a sixty-five-year-old woman, that's all I can say," she explained. "He no longer becomes the person I know. He becomes this woman. I really feel like I'm not talking to him anymore, even when he uses his own voice." The illusion, however, did not pass muster with Robin's youngest child: as the journalist Lillian Ross wrote of one of her visits to the *Mrs. Doubtfire* set: "With the mysteriously accurate perception of infants, one-and-a-half-year-old Cody Williams would respond to Mrs. Doubtfire's accent and greet his father with a loud 'Da-da' of recognition."

Naturally, Robin made ample use of his freedom to ad-lib on the film, both as Mrs. Doubtfire and as Daniel Hillard. He tried more than a dozen different takes of a scene where Daniel, in trying to clear a path for Mrs. Doubtfire to be hired, calls Miranda

493

while pretending to be a series of increasingly unacceptable candidates for the nanny position ("I was in a band called Bloodlust, and after that I worked for a tattoo artist on Market Street"; "I used to work for a pharmaceutical company. If your kids have trouble sleeping, I've got things to help them"; "I was an embalmer for a while, and after that I was a lady wrestler"). He also tried a few different punch lines for a scene where, in his ignorance of female anatomy, he accidentally sets fire to Mrs. Doubtfire's padded chest while leaning over a stove: "I burnt my funbags." "I should change my name to Mrs. Catchfire." Then, finally, the line that stuck: "My first day as a woman and I'm getting hot flashes."

Robin reworked the script in places, making its language more natural for his voice and its themes more reflective of his feelings. Near the end of the film, Miranda confronts Daniel in court after his deception as Mrs. Doubtfire has been exposed, arguing that he should now forfeit even his once-a-week visitation rights. As a portion of Daniel's response reads in the script,

I wish I could tell you I was sorry for my behavior. I really do. But they're my kids.

Robin made an annotation to delete the lines that immediately followed:

I mean. I was never an obsessive type about anything, you know? But then all of a sudden there's this child. And it's like somebody tears out your heart, and puts it in a bassinet.

Then, in his own handwriting, he jotted a few fragmentary ideas, adding, "I plead insanity with an explanation," that his children were an "addiction" on which "I was hooked the moment they were born" and that he was "crazy about them from the day they were born."

His speech continued:

I was the one who changed their diapers, untangled their mobiles, iced their birthday cakes. I was the Mommy in the "Mommy and Me's." I was the one who sat through those tedious, gossip-infested neighborhood playgroups. I took them to the dentist. Held them down when they got stitches.

Robin cut the word *damned* from the next line, "I was the damned tooth fairy," and wrote a few possible alternate phrases for himself, contending that he "stayed up with them all night when they had the flu" and "I would have breastfed them but they would have gotten hair balls."

In the script, this portion of the scene called for Daniel to say, in a "heartfelt" tone, "I beg of you. Please. Don't take them away from me." To which Robin added: "They need me as much as I need them."

Robin became a kind of surrogate father to his on-screen children; he laughed knowingly when Mara Wilson, the precocious five-year-old who played his younger daughter, boasted to him that she knew what sex was; and he wrote a passionate letter on behalf of Lisa Jakub, who played his older daughter, when she was expelled from her high school for spending too much time making the film. "A student of her caliber and talent should be encouraged to go out into the world and learn through her work," Robin wrote. The school's principal hung the letter in his office but he did not allow Lisa to return.

Into even the tiniest cracks of *Mrs. Doubtfire*, Robin and Marsha slipped their friends and relatives, turning the movie into a personal Rosetta stone, if you knew where to look. Behind the scenes, the film employed Marsha's niece Jennifer Garces as a production assistant, while on camera, Dan Spencer, the husband of Robin's assistant, Rebecca, appeared as a chef; Rick Overton, a stand-up comedian and actor pal of Robin's since the 1980s, played a maître d'; and Robin's half brother Todd popped up in a bit role as a poolside bartender, getting billed in the closing credits under the pseudonym "Dr. Toad."

After each ten-hour day of filming wrapped and another hour was spent removing Robin's mask pieces and makeup, he and Marsha returned home, where Zelda and Cody awaited them. The living room of their rental house was populated with a menagerie of pet rabbits, guinea pigs, an iguana, and a chameleon, and furnished with miniature upholstered couches for the kids. Its dining-room table was covered in catalogs and construction-paper projects, while the den had been taken over by a giant plastic children's fort, with some space set aside for a computer console where Robin would play flight simulators and other video games when Zak visited. Robin's personal study had been turned into a shrine for the collection of toy soldiers and action figures he now gathered as an adult, a plastic and metallic horde of spacemen, samurai, knights, and robots. This grown-ups' playroom was also where Robin kept his *Hook* pinball table, a personal gift from Steven Spielberg, on which Marsha held the top score of 175 million points.

These well-lived-in quarters were only a temporary measure until later that year, when the family could finally move into the home that Robin and Marsha had purchased two years earlier, a twelve-thousand-square-foot stucco house on the San Francisco Bay, with a tiled roof, an exercise room, a media den, and a master bedroom whose panoramic view stretched from the Golden Gate Bridge to the Pacific Ocean. Its ongoing remodeling was a project that Marsha had planned and executed in tandem with her duties on *Mrs. Doubtfire*, much to Robin's astonishment. "It's going to have what she calls 'all of your stuff and all of my stuff' right in it," he said. "It's a warm, interesting home."

One piece of decor that Robin and Marsha could not quite figure out what to do with was a Picasso painting — a self-portrait of the artist in which he depicted himself as a one-eared Vincent van Gogh — that they had reluctantly hung in the living room but whose garishness, they sensed, felt out of place there. The unusual painting, valued at more than $1 million at the time, had been a gift from the Walt Disney company, which was still trying to make amends with Robin after his frustration at how he had been used in the promotion of *Aladdin.* The studio was also trying to lure him back for other projects, including a direct-to-video *Aladdin* sequel in which it was hoped he would reprise the role of the Genie, but Robin steadfastly refused these offers. When Joe Roth, the former Fox chairman who had greenlit *Toys* and *Mrs. Doubtfire,* approached Robin about a new film that Disney was planning to finance, Robin sent back the script, unread, with a polite note that explained he had a problem with Disney.

In the meantime, the Picasso presented a vexing problem for Robin, who did not know if he should have accepted it, let alone be displaying it. His friend Eric Idle semi-jokingly suggested he should destroy it in a public display. "If you're pissed off, go on TV, say it, and torch the Picasso — everybody's wanted to see that," Idle said. "He said, 'No I'll have it copied and burn the copy.' " (When Robin later aired some of his grievances with Disney in a cover story in *New York* magazine that November, Jeffrey Katzenberg, the studio's motion picture chief, wrote him a contrite letter saying, "Thank you for not 'whacking' me. I can't tell you *how* much I appreciate your generosity in this difficult + uncomfortable set of circumstances.")

Though Robin had always intended to come back to San Francisco, this was the first significant stretch of time in several years that he had been able to spend in the city, and he found that it suited him. "Having grown up here, in San Francisco, it was very much a quiet place for him," Zak later said. "He appreciated the privacy that it afforded him, and everyone knew to give him his space. He could spend time with his family and not be harassed. He could run, go on long bike rides, do things he loved." Even if they could not be together every day, Zak felt Robin's presence in his life in a way that he had not before. "The childhood that he afforded me was a really great one," Zak said. "He always made time — not just in terms of providing material things, the clothes on my back — but as a dad he was very present. He always spent time and energy. I always knew that. I felt connected to him."

But not everyone felt included in this arrangement. Valerie, who shared custody of Zak with Robin, did not believe that she was afforded the status of a full-fledged family member, an estrangement that she said was created by Marsha's desire to keep Robin and the children to herself. "Marsha just did not want me around, period," she said. "Just didn't want me around. And created a schism between me and my son and created a schism between Robin and me."

"She took my son, and wanted my son part of her family," Valerie said. "And very much, it was the three of them." Robin, she said, was "*her* husband."

Valerie still had her own time with Zak, but when he was with Robin and Marsha, she felt she was not invited to participate. Even on those occasions when she went to Robin and Marsha's home to pick up Zak, Valerie said, "I wasn't allowed in the house. I just did what I was told. I had another family. And poor Zak. It just wasn't pleasant. I don't feel like spewing poison. I just knew that if I were to just disappear, it would have been easier for everybody. So I disappeared. And for a very long time."

Mrs. Doubtfire was released on November 24, 1993, the day before Thanksgiving, and its reviews were consistent for the now-established genre known as the Robin Williams comedy. The *Detroit Free Press* was among the publications that gave the movie an outright rave, writing that where Robin's early movies gave him either "too free a rein with his improvisations, letting his manic energy rocket him into dizzy and exhausting orbit, or corseted him in nobility or pathos, leeching out his subversive wit," *Mrs. Doubtfire* "makes neither mistake." The paper said the film "indulges his talent for mimicry" while requiring him to perform "an impression that keeps a lid on his antics — that of a prim but bighearted old maid, Mary Poppins on estrogen replacement therapy. . . . The tension between Williams' natural exuberance and the constraints of his drag creation gives *Mrs. Doubtfire* an edgy, tipsy charge."

But the broader range of responses more closely reflected those of the *New York Times,* which praised Robin's performance but was left cold by the movie. "If this film creates as good a showcase for the Williams zaniness as anything short of *Aladdin,* it also spends too much time making nice. And not enough time making sense," wrote Janet Maslin.

Roger Ebert said that *Mrs. Doubtfire* could not stand up to films like *Tootsie*, the 1982 comedy that starred Dustin Hoffman as an underemployed actor who cross-dresses to land a role on a TV soap opera. *Tootsie*, he wrote in a two-and-a-half-star review, was "more believable, more intelligent and funnier. *Tootsie* grew out of real wit and insight; *Mrs. Doubtfire* has the values and depth of a sitcom. Hoffman as an actor was able to successfully play a woman. Williams, who is also a good actor, seems more to be playing himself playing a woman."

These nuances did not discourage audiences from turning out to see *Mrs. Doubtfire* in the largest numbers that any of Robin's films had enjoyed. The film opened at number one and remained in first or second place for the next ten weeks, taking in $100 million even before the year was over, $200 million by the end of February 1994, and nearly $220 million by the end of its initial run.

As producers of the movie, Robin and Marsha were entitled to a portion of the royalties it earned, and these came quickly and abundantly. That May, Peter Chernin, the chairman of 20th Century Fox, wrote to thank them for the film's accomplishments and for the enjoyable working experience: "I have no doubt that the movie would not have been as good, would not have gone so smoothly and would not have been as much fun without your involvement as producers." Enclosed with the letter was a check for $2 million, profits that Chernin said might not be payable for another year, if not several years, but which he wanted the couple to have immediately. "It's too quiet around here without both of you," he said. "Let's find something to get you back here soon."

Within a few weeks, Chernin wrote to Robin again. "In recent memory," he said, "I can think of no actor who was so singularly responsible for the success of his or her film as you were." He added, "You are completely deserving of these advances and we couldn't be happier sending them to you." This time the enclosed check was for $8 million.

The runaway box-office returns of *Mrs. Doubtfire* had shown the studios that Robin was a hot commodity again, and Fox was hardly the only one competing for his services. Walt Disney had unwisely gone ahead with its home-video *Aladdin* sequel, in which he had been replaced as the voice of the Genie by the *Simpsons* actor Dan Castellaneta; sales were strong but reviews were dismal, and audiences just did not accept any other performer as the character. But a reconciliation between Robin and Disney became possible that fall, when Jeffrey Katzenberg left the company and was replaced at its motion-picture division by Joe Roth, who had been Robin's benefactor at

Fox. Among his first official acts at Disney, Roth apologized to Robin, publicly and unequivocally, for how the company had treated him in the *Aladdin* dispute. "Robin complained that we took advantage of his performance as the Genie in the film, exploiting him to promote some other businesses inside the company," Roth said. "We had a specific understanding with Robin that we wouldn't do that. [Nevertheless] we did that. We apologize for it."

Robin accepted Roth's apology, calling it "a decent thing." "It's like a country re-establishing diplomatic relations," Robin said. "It's a good feeling because I've done good things there. I wasn't trying to shake anybody down." He and Disney promptly set about discussing new projects for him, including a direct-to-video *Aladdin* sequel in which he would return to the role of the Genie.

Not all of Robin's movies from this period were received as warmly as *Mrs. Doubtfire.* Two years earlier, he had filmed *Being Human,* a fantasy drama in which he played a man — a soul, really — who is reincarnated in five different eras of history, from the rudimentary existence of a caveman to the overdetermined life of a divorcé in modern-day New York, while at each stage trying to reunite with his wife and children from that time. It was an ambitious effort from the film's Scottish writer-director, Bill Forsyth, who was better known for small-scale, independent comedy-dramas (*Gregory's Girl, Local Hero*) and had never made a studio motion picture before. In this case, Warner Bros., which financed the movie, quickly asserted itself when Forsyth's overlong rough cut received poor responses at test screenings, and ordered him to shorten the film, add voice-over narration, and change its ending.

These alterations wreaked havoc on the film, and the reviews were catastrophic: *Entertainment Weekly* gave it a grade of F, asking, "Is there anything in movies more precious — and less convincing — than Robin Williams, with his little downturned mouth, trying to act mild and sheepish and vaguely unhappy?" In its first weekend of release, in May 1994, the film grossed only $764,000 and crashed in thirteenth place. The biggest hit of Robin's career had just been followed by his biggest bomb.

Still, the disastrous results of *Being Human* were largely papered over by the mammoth success of *Mrs. Doubtfire,* and Robin had long since moved on to other, more unexpected, and more satisfying opportunities. Earlier that year, he appeared in his first proper television role in more than a decade, this time in a dramatic series. He had been recruited to appear on the NBC crime drama *Homicide: Life on the Street* by Barry

Levinson, who served as one of its executive producers. The show, a police procedural set in crime-ridden Baltimore, had struggled to find an audience in its first year and NBC had renewed it for a second season of only four episodes, after which the network would decide whether to move ahead with further installments; it was hoped that Robin's star power would increase the likelihood of a third-season renewal.

The show's second-season premiere, which aired on January 6, 1995, and was titled "Bop Gun," focused on a family of four visiting the city, who are accosted by a stickup crew who shoots the mother dead at point-blank range. Robin was cast as the family's father, who variously spends the episode grieving the death of his wife, tending to his two young children, suffering the bureaucratic indignities that befall the survivor of such a crime, and coping with his feelings of cowardice after having been unable to prevent his wife's murder.

David Simon, the *Baltimore Sun* crime reporter from whose book the series was adapted, and who wrote the "Bop Gun" episode with David Mills, happened to be visiting the set when Robin was filming some of his scenes at the city morgue. From their first glancing interaction, Simon said that Robin was hardly the person that his work suggested: "The crazed, manic stand-up routines, the machine-gun witticisms and impersonations — all of it was on hold as he tried to live in the shattered soul of a husband and father who had just lost his wife to sudden, implacable violence." And yet, Simon observed, "He was, I found, the most in-character actor on that film set."

Simon gave Robin an impromptu tour of an unsettling exhibit at the morgue called the Nutshell Studies, a collection of crime-scene dioramas built on the miniature scale of dollhouses. Simon watched as Robin analyzed each of the displays and tried to deduce the ghastly crimes they depicted. "He guessed at a seemingly accidental death that was in fact a murder, then guessed again at a kitchen suicide by a young girl that seemed at first glance to be a stabbing," Simon said. "I could offer solutions to most of the displays only because I'd learned the answers, years before. The actor took it all in, clicking the buttons to light each diorama and then staring at all of the morbid goings-on until the P.A. told him he was needed back on set."

Robin, as always, passed time between takes entertaining the cast and crew members with brief, impromptu stand-up routines: he "readied himself to shoot another painful scene of grief and guilt, and then, in manic desperation, reached out for as much human comedy as ten minutes will allow," Simon wrote.

Before Simon left the set, he caught sight of Robin in a hallway, "using the few remaining minutes before filming to face the wall and reacquaint himself with whatever horror he was trying to channel. He was sweating, too, as if it had taken all he had to rise to that warm summit and provoke such laughter. To my great surprise, his face was that of an unhappy man, and I retreated, saddened and surprised by the thought."

Robin's other appearances that year included small roles in *Nine Months,* a romantic comedy by his *Mrs. Doubtfire* director Chris Columbus, in which Robin portrayed an antsy Russian obstetrician; and in *To Wong Foo, Thanks for Everything! Julie Newmar,* which cast him as the extravagant patron to a trio of drag queens. But perhaps the most significant part Robin would play was one that took place beyond the view of any cameras.

Over the Memorial Day holiday in 1995, his friend Christopher Reeve traveled to Culpeper, Virginia, to ride his horse, Eastern Express, in a combined training event. He was well practiced at equestrian sports for nearly a decade, ever since he learned to ride a horse for a 1985 TV-film adaptation of *Anna Karenina,* and he had carefully mapped out his route for the cross-country course that awaited him. That Saturday afternoon, Reeve was riding Eastern Express during a warm-up when the horse approached a fence and prepared to jump it, then stopped without warning. Reeve was sent tumbling off the horse and landed on his head, breaking the first and second vertebrae in his neck. The accident left him paralyzed in all four limbs and unable to breathe without the help of a respirator.

As Reeve recovered in the intensive care unit of the University of Virginia Medical Center and awaited a highly risky operation to reattach his skull to the top of his spine, he was surrounded by his family — his wife, Dana, sons Will and Matthew, and daughter Alexandra — as well as extended family members and a handful of close friends. One visitor, in particular, stuck out in his mind from this harrowing period. As Reeve recounted:

At an especially bleak moment, the door flew open and in hurried a squat fellow with a blue scrub hat and a yellow surgical gown and glasses, speaking in a Russian accent. He announced that he was my proctologist, and that he had to examine me immediately. My first reaction was that either I was on way too many drugs or I was in fact brain damaged. But it was Robin Williams. He and his wife, Marsha, had materialized from who knows where. And for the first time since the accident, I laughed. My old friend had helped me know that somehow I was going to be okay.

Robin described his private routine for Reeve slightly differently. Slipping into his Russian accent, he recalled, "I said, 'If you don't mind, I'm going to have to put on a rubber glove and examine your internal organ.' And I said, 'Oh, look at the size of this baby.' "

Regardless, the performance had achieved its desired effect: to remind Reeve that no matter how dire his circumstances may have seemed, he still had people in his life worth holding on to and a capacity to experience joy that was undiminished. "I saw he started to laugh because his eyes lit up and he knew it was me," Robin said. "He said that was one of the things that made him realize he wanted to try and stick around. That, his wife, his children and laughter, and all the other things that make it worthwhile. He's got a great sense of humor about it. You have to. . . . That's how you survive in those situations."

There was no question that Robin was going to do everything he could in return for the man who had been his ally since their days together at Juilliard, and a constant source of moral support throughout their careers — the friend he called Brother Reeve, and who in return called him Brother Rab-inowitz. "When Chris got hurt, right away, he and Marsha were on the plane, taking things to his hospital room," said Cyndi McHale, who ran the Blue Wolf company. While Reeve remained in the hospital, Robin and Marsha provided him with interesting and varied visuals to focus his attention on, "since he couldn't look around," McHale said. "Whatever they could put in his line of sight. They would buy him a nice piece of artwork or something. Just very thoughtful and considerate."

Robin and Marsha helped the Reeves pay for the costly medical equipment that Christopher would now need to use for the rest of his life, and installed an elevator in their Napa ranch home for his use whenever he came to visit. This was just one facet of the philanthropy Robin sought to provide for the people closest to him, and he could do so more easily as his personal wealth grew. "They had a driver, nannies, housekeepers," McHale explained, "and they would put their kids through school, because public schools in San Francisco are terrible. They would actually pay for their employees' kids to go to school. Sometimes it would just be a friend — it wasn't just family members, although they did that as well."

When Reeve wanted to travel to New York just five months after his accident, to participate in a fund-raising event for the Creative Coalition (an arts advocacy group he had helped found) and present an award to Robin for his involvement in Comic Relief, Robin gave Reeve the use of his own private security staff for the visit. And when Robin took the stage at the Pierre Hotel to receive his honor from Reeve, who was transporting himself in a wheelchair he controlled with a careful system of sips and breaths, he joked that Reeve should use his new chair for a tractor pull and quipped, "He's on a roll, literally." For Reeve, the good-natured teasing and taunting he took from Robin was just what he needed. "He took the curse off the wheel-chair," he later said.

The following summer, when the Reeve family traveled to Puerto Rico for one of its first vacations since Christopher's injury, Robin went on the trip, too, to keep his friend entertained and in good spirits. "The week-end would have been so much harder for me without you there," Reeve wrote to him afterward. "Everybody got a great tan from your sunshine."

These displays of support would give rise to an apocryphal and often-repeated tale of a secret pact that Robin and Reeve had sup-posedly made during their Juilliard days, that whoever found fame first would take care of the other. But Robin denied that there was any truth to this story and said it was only natural to help a friend in need. "It's not like we said years ago, 'If one of us shall not make it, the other shall be there — where shall we write it in blood?'" he explained, affecting a mock medieval tone.

"This whole idea that I'm going to take care of him — it's kind of demeaning to him to think he might not be able to take care of himself," Robin said. "I'll be there for him, but he's got plans to be able to sustain himself, to find ways to work and be a functioning person."

Robin's last film of 1995 was *Jumanji*, the director Joe Johnston's adaptation of Chris Van Allsburg's picture book about a children's board game that comes to life and overruns a family's home with wild animals and jungle pitfalls. Robin played the film's protagonist, Alan Parrish, a boy who was sucked into the game in 1969 and emerges twenty-six years later as a full-grown man with a long mane of hair and a feral beard. Of the film's $65 million budget, $15 million went to Robin's salary, but he said he was drawn to the movie because it reminded him of his lonely, mansion-bound childhood in Bloomfield Hills, and because he believed that it was a necessary film at a time when brutality had become too commonplace in entertainment and in real life.

"The world frightens me a lot, the world as it exists," he said. "This is an action movie, it has a certain type of violence, but I can't do a movie where all of a sudden I'll blow things away and make a joke about it. Because we live in a world where that's a reality." As a performer, and one with a family, Robin said he had a special obligation to think about how he was portrayed on-screen and to choose films that reflected his values. "You have a responsibility to yourself, whatever your level of consciousness is, about what you do," he explained. "Would you show this to your own children? What are you putting out there? What do you want to say?" That said, *Jumanji* proved to be too scary for Cody, who had just turned four at the time of the film's release.

The role was not that much of a stretch for Robin; it fell neatly within an archetype he had played before: savvy and self-educated but sensitive; denied a proper childhood and forced too hastily into an unfamiliar adult world; a man-child who yearns to be a father and still needs one himself. And the reviews for *Jumanji* seized upon its failure to innovate or challenge its leading man: in the *Baltimore Sun,* Stephen Hunter wrote that the film "represents a typical movie victory, the triumph of literalism over interference, the conviction that more is always much better than less, the crushing idea that spectacle trumps imagination every time." Its creators, he said, took Van Allsburg's peculiar gothic

514

story and "turned it into a sprawling, vulgar, bloviated mess designed skill-lessly to frighten the young and bore the old. They've managed something quite amazing: They've made Robin Williams uninteresting."

Not that Robin was in any way penalized for it at the box office. *Jumanji* opened at number one and went on to gross more than $100 million domestically during its release, making the film another milestone for Robin and one due largely to his involvement. He was as big a star as he had ever been, and he seemed untouchable.

In *Good Morning, Vietnam*, Robin played Adrian Cronauer, the rebellious disc jockey who upends the monotonous military radio station where he has been posted. The film, directed by Barry Levinson and released in 1987, provided Robin with a perfect blend of quiet drama and ad-libbed comedy, yielding his first number-one box-office hit and his first Academy Award nomination.

Dead Poets Society, set at a regimented boarding school in 1959, recalled Robin's own coming-of-age at a similarly conservative academy. Written by Tom Schulman and directed by Peter Weir, the 1989 film cast Robin as the inspirational and irrepressible teacher John Keating; it offered him limited opportunities for improvisation but resulted in another indelible role and a second Oscar nomination.

Awakenings, adapted from Oliver Sacks's nonfiction book about his treatment of people in catatonic states, cast Robin as the Sacks-like character Dr. Malcolm Sayer and Robert De Niro as one of his resuscitated patients. At its release in 1990, the film, directed by Penny Marshall, was not as successful as Robin hoped it would be, but it led to a long friendship with Sacks, who regarded him as his "younger twin."

Robin earned his third Academy Award nomination for *The Fisher King*, a phantasmagorical morality tale in which he played Parry, a street vagabond who strikes up an unusual friendship with a radio shock-jock played by Jeff Bridges. Bridges came to love Robin, as did the film's director, Terry Gilliam, who saw how the role of Parry stirred something deep inside him: "He's a comic, and all comics want to be Hamlet."

Marsha Garces, seen here with Robin at the 1991 Golden Globe Awards, entered the Williams household as a nanny to Zak and later became an assistant to Robin. It was not until after Robin's marriage to Valerie collapsed that he and Marsha struck up a romantic relationship, and when they married in 1989, she became an indispensable part of his career. As Robin said of her, "She's helping me learn to say 'No'—the most provocative word in Hollywood."

Robin was one of just two celebrities, along with Bette Midler, to be featured on the penultimate broadcast of *The Tonight Show Starring Johnny Carson* on May 21, 1992. Though Robin had never been booked on *The Tonight Show* as a stand-up in the 1970s, his visits to Carson's couch in the '80s were reliably outrageous and collegial. Carson hailed Robin as among those who had transcended their field and had become "a comic persona unto themselves."

©BUENA VISTA PICTURES / COURTESY EVERETT COLLECTION

As the singing, shape-shifting Genie in Walt Disney's 1992 animated adaptation of *Aladdin*, Robin was finally provided with a character and a medium that could keep pace with his rapid-fire imagination. For once, there was no such thing as overdoing it: every silly voice and stock accent he had in his arsenal, every celebrity impression in his repertoire, was necessary for the proposition to succeed.

20TH CENTURY-FOX / GETTY IMAGES

When an unemployed and soon-to-be-divorced father is desperate to spend time with his three children any way he can, he assumes the alter ego of a matronly Scottish housekeeper. *Mrs. Doubtfire*, directed by Chris Columbus and for which Marsha served as a producer, was a perfect synthesis of her and Robin's lives as spouses, parents, and creative partners, and it became the most lucrative film of Robin's career to that point.

Robin as Dr. Sean Maguire, the therapist who comes to care for Matt Damon, the title character in *Good Will Hunting*. The 1997 film's screenplay, written by Damon and Ben Affleck, was engineered to jumpstart their acting careers, and it included the mournful Maguire as a supporting role specifically intended for a more bankable, name-brand star. (The authors imagined a rugged A-lister like Robert De Niro, Robert Duvall, Ed Harris, or Morgan Freeman.)

On his fourth nomination—his first as a supporting actor—Robin won his Academy Award for his performance in *Good Will Hunting*. He brought Marsha and Laurie to the Oscars ceremony on March 23, 1998, and in his acceptance speech, he hoisted his trophy skyward to thank "my father, up there, the man who, when I said I wanted to be an actor, he said, wonderful, just have a backup profession like welding."

RICHARD CORKERY / NY DAILY NEWS ARCHIVE VIA GETTY IMAGES

When a 1995 horse-riding accident left his friend Christopher Reeve paralyzed, Robin never wavered in his financial or emotional support. Here, Robin gives Reeve a tender greeting at a May 2004 screening, watched by Reeve's son Will and his wife, Dana. Reeve died that October and Robin was devastated. "There was a part of him that just seemed so indestructible," Robin said.

KEVIN WINTER / GETTY IMAGES

The Williams family in a joyous moment on the red carpet at the 2006 Golden Globe Awards. From left: Alex Mallick (Zak's girlfriend, later his wife), Zak, Cody, Robin, Marsha, and Zelda. But behind the scenes, the family was in crisis—after some twenty years of sobriety, Robin had started drinking again, to dangerous excess, and the people around him knew it. He and Marsha filed for divorce in 2008, citing irreconcilable differences.

Robin entertaining troops at Baghdad International Airport on a USO tour, one of several that he would make. As the son of a veteran—and as an actor whose most beloved roles included one particularly unruly airman— Robin said he wanted "to let them know people at home haven't forgotten them and also, when I get back, to tell people don't forget the people there."

LISA M. ZUNZANYIKA / U.S. AIR FORCE VIA GETTY IMAGES

JAY PAUL / THE NEW YORK TIMES

Robin in a pensive moment before a performance of *Weapons of Self Destruction*, the 2009 stand-up show that would be his final comedy tour. Even before the tour was halted so that Robin could undergo emergency heart surgery, it was already a candid and intensely personal set in which he talked about his relapse into alcoholism and his divorce from Marsha. "How much more can you give?" Robin wondered. "Other than, literally, open heart surgery onstage?"

JASON MERRITT / GETTY IMAGES

Robin moved quickly in his courtship of Susan Schneider, a graphic artist and designer he met in 2007, and the two were married in 2011. Some of Robin's friends regarded Susan, who was herself a recovering alcoholic, as a positive influence in his life, but unlike Marsha, she was more focused on her own work and was not interested in being Robin's professional collaborator or managing him on a day-to-day basis.

It was not until 2011 that Robin made his Broadway debut as the title character in *Bengal Tiger at the Baghdad Zoo*, the playwright Rajiv Joseph's existential comedy-drama set in Iraq after the U.S.-led invasion. Robin earned strong reviews for his performance as the Tiger, who wanders the play as a sarcastic ghost, but the production's brief run and Robin's failure to receive a Tony Award nomination were bitter disappointments.

Robin's death on August 11, 2014, shocked and saddened the world, and the tragic news was rapidly disseminated on the internet. Not knowing quite how to process the loss, some fans poured their hearts out in social media posts; others created makeshift memorials at locations that had featured prominently in Robin's career, as here at the house in Boulder, Colorado, where his character lived on *Mork & Mindy*.

Zak Williams, right, celebrates as Zelda and Cody watch him throw out the ceremonial first pitch of Game 5 of the 2014 World Series at AT&T Park in San Francisco on October 26, 2014. As Zak said of Robin at his father's memorial service, "He was at once so superhuman and yet so very human. But I don't think he ever felt he was anything special."

■ ■ ■ ■

PART THREE:
SUPERNOVA

■ ■ ■ ■

15
THE GOLDEN DUDE

In *Deconstructing Harry,* a Woody Allen movie released at the end of 1997, Robin played the small but memorable role of an actor whose name is given only as Mel. When we meet him, he is running through a movie scene at Bethesda Fountain in Central Park, while a befuddled crew tries to film him.

The cinematographer peers into the camera and angrily declares, "This goddamn lens — there's something wrong with it."

A camera assistant is surprised to hear this. "This one too?" he asks. "I changed lenses."

"What are you talking about?" the cinematographer snaps back. "The focus is off."

More crew members inspect the equipment, unsure of why they cannot produce a clear picture of Mel. Then they look at him — with their own eyes, not through the camera — and realize that Mel himself is out of focus. The world around him is crisp and defined, but he is blurry. "You're soft," his director tells him, before sending him home.

His wife wonders if he ate anything strange at lunch; his daughter is concerned; his son taunts him: "Daddy's out of focus!"

When Allen wrote to Robin several months earlier in hopes of persuading him to take the part, he said, "I can think of no one who could make the character of Mel funnier in this little skit within my movie. It depends on the actor's ingenuity plus a special effect added later. If you hate it, no problem — we'll do something else one day but I do think this bit — and a payoff bit later in the finale is special." (The punch line being that, while Mel's family members must all wear prescription glasses to see him correctly, he is not required to adjust his life or behavior in any way.)

Allen just wanted an actor who would have some fun with the role, but he had chosen aptly: Robin *was* out of focus. Something was off with him, and its cause could not be easily diagnosed. His family life was happy and harmonious, and his career was in the best shape it had ever been. His movies were making money, and he, in turn, was making more money from them. He was on the verge of a crowning achievement, one that he'd spent years striving for, and which he believed would validate all the work he'd done up to that point, ensuring his longevity, prosperity, and admiration in the motion picture industry. For a time, it did. And then nearly everything he'd built just seemed to evaporate.

Robin's first movie of 1996 was *The Birdcage,* an Americanized remake of the French film *La Cage aux Folles.* In that 1978 comedy (adapted from the Jean Poiret play), a gay couple — one, the star performer at a popular drag nightclub, and the other, its owner — are drawn into a series of farcical scenarios when they meet the conservative parents of their son's fiancée. Written by Elaine May and directed by Mike Nichols, *The Birdcage* was the heralded comic twosome's first creative reunion since they split in the 1960s and pursued separate careers. Nichols, who had previously directed Robin in his stage version of *Waiting for Godot,* cast him as Armand, the proprietor of the Birdcage nightclub in Miami's South Beach; the role of Albert, the flamboyant drag performer who is Armand's live-in lover, went to Nathan Lane, a Tony Award–winning Broadway star. May's script reconceived the fiancée's conservative father as a Republican US senator (played by Gene Hackman) whose moralizing legislative coalition is threatened when another of its members dies in bed with an underage prostitute. Even so, Nichols contended that the film's message was ultimately one of unity and reconciliation: "Reconciling a family, a country, right and left," he said.

"People are more alike than everybody thinks."

Robin relished the idea that *The Birdcage* was pushing back against the sort of reactionary demagogues he so despised in national politics. "Every so often, that sense of righteous indignation gets blown apart when some of these guys are found wearing rubber panties or something," he said. "You know, they say, 'I was just diving.' " With a presidential election on the horizon that year, Robin said, "There's again this whole issue of trying to deny the existence of a whole group of people. This movie tries to equalize that a little and get through to Middle America."

The confluence of a Democratic president, Robin's long-standing reputation as an outspoken liberal, and the extraordinary wealth he was now reaping from his hit movies had made him an increasingly desirable figure in Washington circles and provided him with access to some of its most powerful players. He and Marsha had been personally invited to President Bill Clinton's first inauguration in 1993, and Robin had performed a stand-up set for the Clintons at Steven Spielberg's home in Los Angeles when the president visited California in the spring of 1995. "You were in the tippiest top form," Kate Capshaw, the director's wife, wrote to Robin in a thank-you note. "Your mojo was 'big and hard, baby.' "

On his birthday each July, Robin could look forward to a dutiful congratulatory letter from the White House. "Hillary and I send our best wishes for a joyous celebration and a year filled with great happiness and good health," the president wrote to him in 1996. And when heavy hitters like Al Gore or John Kerry were planning fund-raising events, they would invariably ask Robin for his participation, or simply his money.

Not every elected official saw Robin merely as a motormouthed checkbook. Ann Richards, the Democratic firebrand and former governor of Texas, continued to write affectionate letters to Robin and Marsha even after she was voted out of office, thanking them for their kindness and generosity. "I am working like a field hand," she told them in one dispatch from 1995. "One of these years I am going to get out of this hamster wheel but no time soon." In another letter a few months later, she wrote, "Life for me is good and I am ranting and raving against the right wing wherever they will provide a podium."

Robin's devotion to liberal causes stemmed not from a desire to ingratiate himself with politicians but from a personal sense of community. Being a longtime San Franciscan made him acutely aware of the ongoing challenges faced by gay people and, he thought, gave him a particular insight into their world. He had been attached to play Harvey Milk, the openly gay San Francisco politician, in a biopic called *The Mayor of Castro Street,* though the project did not come to fruition. And he could cite by name the gender-bending members of the Sisters of Perpetual Indulgence, the city's campy, street-performance protest group. He had lived in the Castro district when he and Marsha started their relationship, and, as Robin said, "It's a neighborhood. Yeah, there are a lot of gay men and gay women, but it has the same values as your neighborhood. They want peace and quiet. They want to live their lives, and they do have children — [here he slipped into his redneck voice] *'It's a frightening thing. Tell me no!'* — from previous marriages, artificial insemination, a hundred different ways. It is family-oriented. People don't acknowledge it, but that's the reality."

For *The Birdcage,* Robin had originally been approached to play Albert, the more manic half of the gay couple, but he felt he had already done his share of cross-dressing in *Mrs. Doubtfire.* Lane, his costar, said that during the first few weeks of filming, it dawned on Robin that there was another actor able to go even wilder than he could. "It was hard for him to watch me go off," Lane said. "But then he said he found the comedy in his character. I think we understand each other very well. I remember, at one point, the two of us standing there and saying to [Nichols], 'Can we, can we do it again? Can we, can we try that again?' And I said, 'We are the two most insecure, neediest people I've ever seen in my life.' "

Nichols also appreciated the challenge for Robin in playing what he called "the relatively still center" of the picture. "I knew there would be great humor in suppressing his desire to shriek," the director explained. He does a lot of real acting here in which the comedy is in the small things, not the madness."

Though people did not expect stillness from him, Robin had a quiet side, too, and he said it should not be mistaken for sadness. "When people see me that way, they think something's wrong," he said. "No. 'You're on something.' No. I'm just recharging. In down times I do things like go for a long bike ride or run. The other thing I'm doing in that quiet time is just observing."

He was like this in his home life, too, where in moments when he might have seemed silent and withdrawn, he was actually in a highly receptive, information-seeking mode. "You'd just be talking to him over the breakfast table — 'what's going on in the world?' — and he absorbed things," said Cyndi McHale. "I'd be reading the *New York Times*, and he'd ask a couple questions. And then that night, all that would come out onstage in his stand-up. I'm struggling to get through the story and he, meanwhile, that night, nails it completely onstage without even reading it."

Peter Asher, the musician, producer, and husband of Robin's friend Wendy Asher, became close with Robin and Marsha in this period. He observed, as many of Robin's friends did, that there were "multiple Robins." "Yes, you would see the quiet, intellectual, curious Robin," Peter Asher said. "And then occasionally, you'd be at a dinner and he'd morph into the genius comic commentator, inventor of words and situations and people, which was a whole other animal. They both coexisted and shared the same voracious and stunningly fast intellect."

When their schedules overlapped, Robin and Asher spent their free time doing nothing more taxing than going to a movie or shopping for loud clothing. "We both liked the kind of clothes that you would see in the window and go, 'Who would wear that suit?' — and the answer was, 'We would,'" said Asher. "Of course, he was always the one who'd get a big discount, because they knew he might wear it on *The Tonight Show* or something. So I would end up slipping him some suit I wanted to buy and saying, 'You buy it — I'll pay it back.' Because that way he'd get the celebrity discount."

Sometimes he and Robin would have "heart-to-heart" conversations, but, Asher explained, "when I say heart-to-heart, I don't mean, sharing your innermost feelings. I mean *male* heart-to-heart conversations," he said with a laugh. "Which is, did you read the science section of the paper this morning? Because the answer would always be yes, we both had. We would have conversations about *stuff*. Not about *us*, more likely."

And when Robin feared that his mile-a-minute imagination had gotten too far out of his control and had trampled on someone else's feelings, he was quick to make amends. "When he'd make fun of you, it was always really nice," said Wendy Asher, who had been Robin's friend since the 1970s. "We'd be out to dinner, and he'd thought he'd said something wrong, and he'd have Marsha call up and say, 'Oh, Robin thinks that he upset someone,' and we'd all go, 'No!' He really was caring. It was really more that he wanted to entertain everyone."

Robin's insecurities about his comic talents ran much deeper. He continued to see a therapist and continued to fear that his position in the comedy world could be usurped at any moment by a younger, up-and-coming star. "He was a great appreciator of people's work," Billy Crystal said. "But I think there was a chipping-away, sometimes, and he would feel like he was losing his reign. If, suddenly, there was a new guy, he would be the first to say how great they were. But I could sense the driving question was, 'What about me? That's *my* thing.' "

Lately, Robin had been fixated on Jim Carrey, the stand-up comic and actor who had attained some fame for the panoply of wacky characters he played on the TV sketch show *In Living Color* and was finding unexpected success in films like *Ace Ventura: Pet Detective.* After boasting publicly that he expected to play the villainous Riddler in an upcoming *Batman* sequel and then passing on the role, Robin was chagrined to find that the part had gone to Carrey. When he and his children saw *Dumb and Dumber* (a massive hit for Carrey that grossed more than $127 million) on a Christmas vacation in Hawaii, Robin paid a series of compliments — some sincere, and some backhanded — to the actor, whom he called "funny in a physical" way.

"He chose the thing to do and he's the master of it," Robin said of Carrey. "To do that just straight out. When it works, it just hits you." More acerbically, he added, "But when he starts being honored in France, we'll know we have to worry."

But Robin's concerns ran deeper than he let on. Cheri Minns, a makeup artist who began working regularly with Robin on *The Birdcage,* said that he "got completely freaked out about Jim Carrey, that he was going to take over. Marsha had to step in and tell him,

'There's room for other people. You don't have to freak out. There's room.' Because he was having a complete mental breakdown about it. Robin had more talent in his little finger than Jim Carrey ever had. But Jim Carrey started making big movies and making a good salary, and then Robin was like, 'Oh my God.' Robin did that to himself. He just got himself consumed with worry about things like that. It was total consumption with his career."

When *The Birdcage* was released in March 1996, it received some appreciative reviews. The *Washington Post* noted how unusual it was for Robin not to play "the white-hot center of a picture. Armand is the subdued one of this couple, and, for the most part, Williams plays straight man (if that's the word) to Lane's inspired hormonal spritzing."

The film drew praise from advocacy groups like the Gay & Lesbian Alliance Against Defamation, which said that it went "beyond the stereotypes to see the characters' depth and humanity," but other viewers were troubled that it seemed to indulge many negative clichés of gay people, portraying them as mincing, effeminate transvestites. The gay critic Bruce Bawer called *The Birdcage* a prime example of how "homosexuality continues to bring out the worst aspects of the [film] industry: its timidity, banality

529

and subjection to formula." Watching Robin's and Lane's characters trying to make themselves more palatable to Hackman's, he said, "It is chilling to see Armand and Albert debase themselves before this stand-in for Pat Buchanan, to see Armand sweating bullets in terror of blowing his cover, and to see Albert, finally unmasked as a man, obsequiously offering reassurances that he believes in family values."

From his earliest days as a stand-up, Robin had included a stock gay character in his act, and he believed his history in San Francisco gave him permission to do so. "I used to do a choreographer character on Comic Relief," he said, "and some people loved it and some were offended by it," he said. "People who knew choreographers like him said, 'That's it!' and others said, 'That's a cliché and a stereotype.' It wasn't done out of anger." The criticism he took for doing essentially the same thing in *The Birdcage* caught him off guard, though Robin tried to meet his detractors halfway. "It's not a homophobic thing. But I understand their feelings," he said. *The Birdcage* was another commercial smash for Robin, ranking number one at the box office for the first month of its release and grossing nearly $125 million. But the debate around it had exposed a vulnerability: the times were starting to change and Robin wasn't keeping up with them.

He was shown little mercy for his next film, *Jack,* an improbable comedy-drama in which Robin played a boy with a condition that causes his body to grow at four times the normal rate; at age ten, he already has the developed physique (though not the mature mind) of a forty-year-old man. Despite its offering Robin an opportunity to work with the director Francis Ford Coppola, *Jack* was the most banal iteration of a character he'd played several times before, not to mention a knockoff of the hit Tom Hanks comedy *Big.* "Someone deserves a timeout for letting this mawkish misfire get to the screen," *USA Today* said in a half-star review. "Bad movies happen. But when bad movies happen to good people, it's worse."

At the close of the year, Robin was one of the prominent American actors to appear with the estimable British cast of Kenneth Branagh's *Hamlet,* a lavish, four-hour film adaptation of the Shakespeare tragedy in which the director himself played the melancholy Prince of Denmark. The film, which harked back to the classical training that Robin had received at Juilliard (and which he often flaunted in his stand-up act), cast him as Osric, a minor character who arranges the fateful duel between Hamlet and his rival, Laertes. His great friend Billy Crystal also appeared briefly as the sardonic First Grave-digger, who reacquaints Hamlet with the skull of his old jester Yorick, "a fellow of infinite jest, of most excellent fancy," but he and Robin did not share any scenes together.

For that opportunity, audiences would have to wait until the following spring. It was astonishing, in a sense, that the two comedians had never starred together in a film before. They were among the best known and most admired wisecrackers in the country, they were pals and confidants whose families vacationed together, they had the same management team, and they each had their own piece of the zeitgeist: Robin had his diverse range of film comedies and dramas, and Crystal had his regular gig as the smart-aleck emcee of the Academy Awards. Their annual Comic Relief specials with Whoopi Goldberg were rare opportunities to see what happened when their funny and facile minds were set against each other: usually, Robin would take a joke too far and Crystal would merrily bring it back within safe boundaries.

Comic Relief played a crucial role in establishing the personas they played opposite each other. As Crystal described them, they were "bad boy and daddy. . . . He'll look at me and say, 'Dad, have I been bad?' 'Yes.' " (Robin jokingly said that explanation sounded like a phone-sex hotline.) They were their generation's answer to Bob Hope and Bing Crosby, or Dean Martin and Jerry Lewis, but with a twist: a double act with no straight man, where each competed to outdo the other, a give-and-take-and-give-and-take that could keep going right into the stratosphere.

An opportunity presented itself with the 1983 French film *Les Compères,* about two mismatched men who team up to search for the son of a former lover, each believing that he is the boy's father. Their remake, called *Fathers' Day,* directed by Ivan Reitman and written by Crystal's frequent collaborators Lowell Ganz and Babaloo Mandel, had been engineered for Crystal to play one of the prospective dads, a cynical lawyer, and for Robin to play the other, a suicidal writer.

It was not a movie that Robin was eager to do, though he felt loyal to Crystal and was excited to work with him. But Robin also felt torn between the need to earn a living and the desire to work on movies that were meaningful to him. Steven Haft, his producer on *Dead Poets Society,* explained, "Some actors see themselves doing what they refer to as, 'one for them, one for me.' That place actors get where they're stuck between the opportunity to make millions of dollars doing a commercial film, and wanting to do meaningful work, but realizing that the stuff that pays them the big bucks doesn't get them Oscars." In Robin's case, Haft said, "There was always a script — *always* — on his desk that would have made him two to many millions at any given moment, and he didn't always take them."

Often, the instances when Robin passed on those lucrative opportunities were signs of a quiet tug-of-war for control of his career. On one side stood his managers, who had been present for nearly every significant entry on his résumé going back to *Mork & Mindy* and who saw him principally as a commercial comedy star. On the other side was Marsha, who had become substantially intertwined in his decision-making process and who had a very different vision for her husband. Riding the momentum of *Mrs. Doubtfire,* she was setting up new films for Robin in which he would play less conventional, more noble characters; one of the projects she was pursuing for him would have cast Robin as Father Damien, the Catholic priest who treated lepers on Molokai.

"He depended on her," said their friend Lisa Birnbach. "Anything indie, basically, was something that she recommended he do. Marsha had his back in every way. It also made Marsha have to play the tough guy with everyone who wasn't family. There were times *I* was a little scared of Marsha. And she was very protective."

Some friends of the couple said that, when push came to shove, Marsha just had better instincts than Robin's own managers did. As Wendy Asher succinctly put it, "Every bad film he did, she told him not to do."

The making of *Fathers' Day* proceeded like a comedy of contrasts for its two top-billed clowns, a real-life *Odd Couple* where Crystal's fastidiousness came into frequent conflict with Robin's unmannerly habits. Cheri Minns, Robin's makeup artist, said that often in their trailers, "Billy would bring in some food, and put it down on the counter, and Robin would go over and pick something out with his fingers, and eat some of the food. Which was a Robin trait, but it drove Billy to distraction. Billy would go, 'That's *my* food.' And Robin would say, 'Oh, whatever — it's okay, here.' And Billy says, 'No, I don't want it now. You have it.' "

While filming on the Warner Bros. studio lot, the actors would react very differently when spotted by the tour groups that whizzed by on golf carts. "If Robin saw them, he'd run out to greet the tourists and say hi and sign autographs," Minns recalled. "Billy said, 'Oh, crap. Now I have to go over there and talk to those people, or I'm going to look like an asshole.' " Crystal recalled the making of the movie as a frustratingly ad hoc process. "It was not a great experience, because the script was never really ready to shoot," he said. "But because of everyone's schedules, we had to make it at a certain time, and we were rewriting as we were going. I wasn't sure that Ivan knew what to make of us sometimes, or how to get the best out of us."

To promote the film's release in May 1997, Robin and Crystal were awkwardly shoe-horned into an episode of *Friends*, doing shtick on a coffee-shop couch while the sitcom's principal cast members looked on. They also made a joint appearance on *The Tonight Show*, where the host, Jay Leno, broke into laughter as he described the plot of *Fathers' Day* to his audience. "It's so stupid," Leno said, before catching himself. "But it really works." His faint praise made little difference: *Fathers' Day* was slaughtered by the critics — in the *Wall Street Journal*, Joe Morgenstern called it "a movie of implacable un-funniness" — and it ended up a box-office bomb, grossing only about $29 million.

By that time, Robin was already on to his next project, a unique script that had taken an unusual path to reach him. For several years, Matt Damon and Ben Affleck, two young actors and childhood friends, had been working on a screenplay that they hoped would jump-start their careers. Drawing liberally from their upbringings in Cambridge, Massachusetts, their script, called *Good Will Hunting*, told the story of a disaffected young man from South Boston who, while working as a janitor in the corridors of the Massachusetts Institute of Technology, is discovered to be a self-taught math prodigy. The novice screenwriters had always intended to star in the film themselves — Damon as Will, the title protagonist, and Affleck as his sarcastic Southie sidekick, Chuckie — but to do so, they knew they needed to include a supporting role for which they could cast a more bankable, name-brand star. For that purpose they created the character of Dr. Sean Maguire, a therapist mourning his dead wife, who comes to treat Will and, in doing so, is drawn out of his own loneliness. Though they had no specific actor in mind to play him, Affleck and Damon tried to write Maguire for a rugged A-lister like Robert De Niro, Robert Duvall, Ed Harris, or Morgan Freeman.

Good Will Hunting was first acquired by Castle Rock Entertainment, then picked up by Miramax, the independent studio run by Bob and Harvey Weinstein. There, it caught the interest of the director Gus Van Sant, who had made low-budget hits like *Drugstore Cowboy, My Own Private Idaho,* and *To Die For* — films about drug abusers, male prostitutes, and a murderous meteorologist — and who saw Affleck and Damon's script as possessing more mainstream appeal. Van Sant knew Robin from their abortive efforts to make *The Mayor of Castro Street* and thought he could play the role of Dr. Maguire; Robin also got strong endorsements on the script from his CAA agents and from Marsha's niece Jennifer, who was working as a production assistant on *The Rainmaker,* a legal thriller where she'd befriended Damon.

Robin signed on to *Good Will Hunting* that March. He later described the screenplay as "layered and very moving, but in a very simple way," and said that he saw the repressed Dr. Maguire, who at times gets so wound up that he threatens and even assaults Will, as a conduit for a type of rage he could not release in other roles. "It was great to tap into that anger with him and go, 'Would I hurt him? Yeah. If you keep going,' " Robin explained. " 'You want to work? You want to really deal with who you are? Let's talk. Or you want to sit here and spray musk all day? You can do that, but I don't want to be around it.' . . . It felt good to get the *cojones* to do that."

Robin's time commitment to the project was brief, just a few weeks of filming in Boston and Toronto that May and June; for the film, which was budgeted at about $16 million total, he was paid about $3 million in salary — a steep cut from his usual asking price that was offset with a portion of the movie's profits, if it earned any. He prepared thoroughly for the role, working closely with a dialect coach to learn the nuances of the working-class South Boston Irish accent and to master the mysterious vowel sound described in his notes as "a sound half-way between the *a* of 'FAT' and the *ah* of 'FATHER.' "

When Robin first traveled to Boston to begin rehearsals, Van Sant had the now-commonplace discovery that the actor was very different from the man he had expected. "He assumed this personality, which I'm not sure wasn't always part of him, which was very down," the director said. "He wasn't Mr. Stand Up and Tell a Joke. And I thought that when we were doing the film, that there would be a lot more of that." In fact, Van Sant said Robin could be needy for his approval once shooting started, and he never allowed rampant buffoonery to overwhelm his work.

"He would go, 'Yeah, yeah, boss. Was that not good?' " Van Sant recalled. "And I would say, 'No, that was great. That was really great.' And then we'd move on. And I would never really encourage him to go beyond. I never said, 'But Robin, I thought you were *really* going to let it go, like *Good Morning, Vietnam* — like, let it go, baby!' Because I thought maybe that would be the wrong thing to point him towards. Because it was really working, the way he was doing it."

Affleck and Damon had provided the Maguire character with a couple of emotional, award-baiting monologues. In one, delivered on a bench in the Boston Public Garden, he tells Will that his book learning is no substitute for Maguire's life experience. ("I'd ask you about love, you'd probably quote me a sonnet. But you've never looked at a woman and been totally vulnerable.") In another, set in his office, Maguire excitedly reenacts Carlton Fisk's twelfth-inning walk-off home run from Game 6 of the 1975 World Series, only to reveal that he missed the game so he could strike up a conversation with the woman who became his wife. "I gotta see about a girl," as he put it.

Robin performed these scenes with gusto, and, where he could, he added his own improvisational spins. When Maguire lovingly describes to Will the idiosyncratic qualities about his late wife that he did not expect to miss, it was Robin who came up with the detail that she used to fart in her sleep. That joke drew a laugh from Damon, so of course Robin kept going with it. "At one point — it's not in the movie, they started laughing — he said, 'I used to have to wake up and light a match,' " Affleck said. "And then Matt said, 'Is that how she died?' That's what they're laughing at, uproariously." The finished film used Robin's and Damon's authentic reactions to this ad-libbed bit, though much of the dialogue that followed was not exactly appropriate for the scene. "At a certain point we were so far afield," Damon said. "We went on this riff about farting that just got so insane that I think we were doing ourselves a disservice by the end of the day."

Robin also showed an unexpected intensity in a scene where he threatens Damon's character not to disrespect his dead wife and, in doing so, forcefully grabs him by the throat. The actors performed the sequence so many times that, in the final takes (including the one used in the film), makeup had to be applied to Damon's neck to cover the skin left raw and bloodied from Robin's repeated chokeholds. "Robin really got upset for this moment," Damon said. "I don't know what he was thinking about. But he couldn't stop grabbing me really hard."

In a more serendipitous moment, Robin supplied the film with what became its final spoken line, on one of his last days of shooting in Boston. For the scene, which would precede the closing shot of Will driving off to California to pursue his girlfriend Skylar (Minnie Driver), Robin was merely supposed to open his letterbox and discover Will's farewell note, which concludes, "I gotta see about a girl." As Damon recalled that day's shoot, "We must have done twenty takes. He went into the house, folded the letter up, put it back in the letterbox, shut the door. And on one of the takes, in the middle, he said, 'Son of a bitch stole my line.' And went back in the house. I remember grabbing Gus, like, 'Holy shit! Fuck — what did he just — that is great!' And then he did like ten more and he never repeated that line again."

Robin had a shaky start to his fall movie season in 1997, starting with the November release of *Flubber,* a remake of Disney's *The Absent-minded Professor* in which he played the Fred MacMurray role and which he'd filmed close to home at the former Naval Station Treasure Island in San Francisco Bay. The reviews were pitiful, even for a children's movie ("overproduced, mechanical and resoundingly unfunny," the *San Francisco Chronicle* wrote).

Good Will Hunting, which received a limited release in December and opened nationally the following January, was greeted with mixed responses, both wildly enthusiastic and negative, sometimes in the same review. Though critical attention focused largely on Damon and Affleck, the photogenic young stars making a capable screenwriting debut, there was often blame as well as praise for Robin that followed. The Associated Press wrote that the film "isn't terrible," and that Robin "isn't at his best when he tries to be sincere," dismissing the Maguire character as "just a saltier version of the do-gooders Williams played in *Awakenings* and *Dead Poets Society.*" In the *Los Angeles Times,* Kenneth Turan wrote that Affleck and Damon "lack the craft" to give Maguire "speeches that aren't so fake-sensitive it's amazing Will doesn't laugh the healer out of the room." Robin, the critic wrote, "has played a conventionally understanding if eccentric mentor so often that his presence in a film like this has become a tip-off that it's going to be unremittingly middle of the road. The practice has made Williams better at the part, but his is still the most stodgy and unconvincing aspect of an otherwise lively film."

Then there were publications like the *New York Times,* where Janet Maslin wrote that Damon and Affleck had crafted themselves "a smart and touching screenplay, then seen it directed with style, shrewdness and clarity" by Van Sant; in doing so, they had created for Robin "the rare serious role that takes full advantage of his talents," one in which he was "wonderfully strong and substantial." Joe Morgenstern of the *Wall Street Journal* said flat-out that it was "the finest performance" of Robin's career. Billy Crystal personally regarded it as his favorite of all of Robin's screen roles. "I don't see him in that part — I just see that guy, Maguire," Crystal said. "Robin, for all of his joy, had this built-in loneliness about him at the same time that made him so appealing in parts like that. That strength, with a little bit of weakness underneath it."

For a time that winter, there were three different movies featuring Robin (the last was *Deconstructing Harry,* which opened the week after *Good Will Hunting*) all competing for audiences' attention — no easy feat when the James Cameron juggernaut *Titanic* was dominating the box office. Yet even at a significantly smaller scale than that legendary ocean liner, *Good Will Hunting* proved to be a sturdy, stalwart vehicle. From its first weekend in wide release, *Good Will Hunting* would spend two months in the number two, three, or four slot at the box office, taking in more than $50 million by the end of January and $100 million by the end of March. It concluded its run in the spring of 1998 having sold more than $133 million in tickets, which meant that Robin, with his profit participation in the movie, was likely to earn as much as $15 million to $20 million from it.

Very quickly, the film and Robin's performance emerged as formidable contenders for several prestigious awards. At the end of December, he was nominated for a Golden Globe for Best Supporting Actor, though he lost to Burt Reynolds, who played the ornery father figure to a menagerie of porn-movie stars in *Boogie Nights.* (Robin still managed a memorable appearance at the Golden Globe ceremony when Christine Lahti, a winner for the TV series *Chicago Hope,* was in the bathroom when her name was called, so he crashed the stage and began to riff in mock-Spanish.) In February, *Good Will Hunting* was nominated for nine Academy Awards, including one for Best Picture; one for Van Sant as director; one for Affleck and Damon's screenplay; one for Damon as Best Actor; and one for Robin as Best Supporting Actor, the first time he'd been nominated in that category. Then in March, two weeks before the Oscars ceremony, Robin won the Screen Actors Guild Award, and odds-makers believed the Academy Award race was a neck-and-neck competition between Reynolds and him.

On March 23, 1998, the night of the Oscars ceremony, Robin was seated two rows from the stage of the Shrine Auditorium, on the aisle, with Marsha to his right and his mother, Laurie, one seat to the right of her. Crystal, hosting the program for his sixth time, gave Robin a musical shout-out in an opening song that poked fun at Damon and Affleck's youth ("You're a hit, it's clear to see / and you haven't yet hit puberty"), but Robin barely reacted; his face was frozen in a thin smile of geniality and nervousness as he waited to hear whether he'd prevail on his fourth nomination in ten years.

If the anticipation was unbearable, the resolution was swift: in one of the first awards bestowed that night, Mira Sorvino, the presenter for Best Supporting Actor, opened the envelope and announced, "And the Oscar goes to . . . Robin Williams in *Good Will Hunting*!" With his customary speed, Robin sprang to his feet, kissed Marsha, kissed Laurie, went one row forward to embrace Damon and Affleck in a three-man bear hug, then bounded up to the stage to receive his trophy and make the acceptance speech he'd wanted to give for a decade or more.

He put his hand to his heart, blew a couple of kisses to the audience, then began:

Thank you. Oh, man. This might be the one time I'm speechless. Oh, ah — thank you so much for this incredible honor. Thank you for putting me in a category with these four extraordinary men. Thank you, Ben and Matt, I still want to see some ID. Thank you, Gus Van Sant, for being so subtle you were almost subliminal. I want to thank the cast and crew, especially the people of South Boston, you're a can of corn, you're the best. I want to thank the *mishpucha* Weinstein, mazel tov.

Robin started to choke up as he continued:

And I want to thank Marsha for being the woman who lights my soul on fire every morning, God bless you. [Here, a TV camera found Marsha in her seat, a tear streaming down her cheek.] And most of all, I want to — I want to thank my father, up there, the man who, when I said I wanted to be an actor, he said, wonderful, just have a backup profession like welding. Thank you. God bless you.

From the side of the stage, Crystal came over to Robin and they shared an affectionate embrace. "He saw me and he made this sound, like, 'Oooooohhhh,' " Crystal recalled. "It was as if I had won, I was so happy for him." Then Robin crouched low and did his best Groucho Marx–style duckwalk into the wings. A couple of quips, a large helping of sincerity, and that was it: the moment was over.

As rapidly as these events seemed to transpire in real time, Robin was experiencing them as if the record of his life was playing at half-speed. As he later explained, "Everything goes into this weird [here he made slow-motion noises] and you look around you and you see people you know. I remember seeing Burt Reynolds and he didn't look happy. . . . I was like, sorry, dude, I didn't know. And you go up there, and the next thing you know, you're holding it." He was so discombobulated that he neglected to mention Laurie in his acceptance speech. "I forgot to thank my mother, and she was there," he said. "Even Freud would go, *You must work on zis.*"

Backstage, a euphoric Robin bantered playfully with reporters who held up numbered paddles to indicate they wished to ask him a question ("What am I bid?" he asked, pretending to be a haughty auctioneer. "We will pick 229, 229 . . . Who won the Volvo? Number 1523, yes"), then reflected on what the award meant to him. "It's extraordinary," he said. "It's like, the golden dude. I've been here three times before and lost. . . . Basically, my odds before were the same as the Jamaican bobsled team winning." But now that he had finally crossed that threshold, Robin said, "I'm sailing. Much cheaper than Prozac."

Back at the ceremony, Robin got to see Affleck and Damon win their screenwriting Oscar; he mingled with Jack Nicholson, that night's Best Actor winner (for *As Good as It Gets*), whom he'd often poked fun at in his stand-up but whom he regarded, deep down, as a godlike and nearly unapproachable presence; and he was able to join in an onstage portrait that gathered seventy living actors who'd received Academy Awards for their work. He found himself standing one tier in front of Shirley Temple Black, who leaned over and said, "Call me," which so surprised Robin he could only think to respond, "Sure!" It was just a friendly gesture, but it made Robin realize he was truly part of something now, a pantheon of performers that was synonymous with Hollywood. The occasion bestowed legitimacy upon him and was a moment for reflection and reevaluation — an opportunity to forget about past missteps and wonder if some of his more maligned work was simply underappreciated. Even Kenneth Turan, the *Los Angeles Times* critic who had not especially enjoyed *Good Will Hunting,* wrote in the aftermath of the show that Robin was "as well-liked a figure as today's Hollywood has" and wondered why — even at a moment of maximum accomplishment — he was not being better served by the industry.

"For those who admire Williams' unequaled genius as a comedian and are frustrated by the middle-of-the-road, tree-hugger roles he invariably takes in film," his Oscar victory, Turan wrote, was an occasion for mixed emotions. "On the one hand, it was impossible not to appreciate and share in the pleasure Williams took in winning the Oscar, as well as the pleasure the film community felt in finally giving him one after three previous losses. But seeing the moments of manic comic brilliance . . . reinforced how unfortunate it is that that side of his ability rarely makes it on screen."

Robin spent the night celebrating with Marsha, Laurie, and his new statuette at a party hosted by *Vanity Fair.* Arthur Grace, a photographer who followed him for the evening, later said that Robin "never let his Oscar out of his right hand, sometimes clutching it, sometimes cradling it, occasionally turning it, but mostly holding it firmly by his side." He warmly received the good wishes of longtime friends and colleagues like Eric Idle and Jay Leno, and he accepted the awkward attention he got from hangers-on who just wanted to touch his trophy and the clothing executive who brazenly placed a brand-name beret atop Robin's head.

After stopping at the annual Oscars party of the Hollywood socialite Dani Janssen to rub elbows with Jack Nicholson, Warren Beatty, and Michael Douglas, Robin returned to his room at the Hotel Bel-Air and plopped his award down next to a deli bag from Junior's. A nine-page log of congratulatory phone calls awaited him, received throughout the night from the babysitter who'd been watching Cody and Zelda (and who said they "jumped off the couch" and were "screaming and hugging"); from Valerie, Christopher Reeve, Chris Columbus, Pam Dawber, Steven Spielberg, Steve Jobs, Barry Bonds, Richard Lewis, Rick Overton, Richard Dreyfuss, his local post office, the veterinary hospital, and his auto mechanic. More personal notes came in the next day from Eric Idle ("What a joy to see you in full tears in full shot. Have no fears — all of America was crying too"), George Lucas, Francis Ford Coppola, Anthony Hopkins, Oliver Sacks, and Ted Kennedy (who said that *Good Will Hunting* was "a favorite film of mine — and not entirely coincidentally because of its Boston connection").

Sally Field wrote to say, "Every now and again the Oscar goes to the right person. You are one of those very *right* recipients." And in a handwritten note, rendered in loopy cursive, Jeff Bridges said, "Dear Rob, Man!!! You won!! How fuckin' great. I haven't seen it yet (lost the video), but the clips look great."

When it was over, the experience had been something like a wedding and a wake, all rolled into one. Every living person he cared about had sung his praises, paid their respects to him, and confirmed he was great at what he did. And then they moved on. What came next? For Robin, those next steps had been mapped out well in advance.

From the Bel-Air, Robin and Marsha went north, straight to the set of Robin's new movie, on the campus of the University of California, Berkeley. Outside a lecture hall, Alan Curtiss, the film's first assistant director, was sent to intercept Robin before he could enter. "He had the Oscar in his hand," Curtiss recalled, "and he said, 'Alan, I want you to meet a new little friend of mine. I promised him I would give him a nice home.' I said, 'Robin, we're just going to do a little rehearsal and then we won't actually have to shoot until after lunch.' He goes, 'Okay.' " Then they stepped into the building, and the choir of the Glide Memorial Church in San Francisco, whose members had been brought there just for the day, streamed into the room and began singing joyful gospel songs while the cast and crew celebrated with Robin.

"Tears came to his eyes," Curtiss said. "It was a big, tiered lecture hall that went up like a stadium. He was down at the bottom, looking at everybody. I just remember seeing that smile and the glistening of his eyes, the tears of joy. We had a long lunch, everybody took a few deep breaths, and then he went back to work that afternoon."

That film was *Patch Adams,* a comedy-drama based on the doctor and founder of the Gesundheit! Institute, a hospital that combines humor and clowning with traditional medicine. The film was a commercial success when it was released that Christmas, but it was savaged by critics and disowned by the real-life Adams. ("I hate that movie," he once told Roger Ebert.) For Robin, it was just one more sentimental feel-good role on a rap sheet that hardly needed any more of them. He had gone from a personal pinnacle back to rock bottom.

16
FADE TO WHITE

It was hardly what you'd call a synagogue,
just a small room, about thirty feet by ten
feet, off a dirt parking lot in the Polish city of
Piotrkow. There was nothing on its outside to
give away its identity except perhaps the
spray-painted swastika on the door that was
removed every few days, yet which always
seemed to replace itself by the following
morning. Inside the chamber stood a simple
table and an unpainted, unvarnished cabinet
that served as an ark, around which were
gathered some forty worshippers attending
their Yom Kippur services. The faithful, who
read from photocopied prayer books sent
from distant congregations in Ohio and
Argentina, were a range of ages, from the
youths who were just learning why they
should not tell their neighbors they were Jewish, to the elderly who still bore the numbers
that had been forcibly tattooed onto their
arms. At the end of their High Holidays
celebration in the fall of 1997, they were

joined by a small group of American film-makers and actors, including Robin, who had come to make a movie about the Holocaust.

A few months before Robin would return to America to reap the benefits of *Good Will Hunting* and win his Academy Award, he was here in this former Jewish ghetto to make *Jakob the Liar.* The film, adapted from the novel by Jurek Becker, tells of a Jewish shopkeeper living in Poland under Nazi occupation, who tries to rally his townspeople with fantastical, falsified tales of a radio he says he has and whose broadcasts predict their imminent rescue by a Soviet invasion force. It was by no means a comic subject; the story allowed only a certain kind of fatalistic humor, requiring Robin to keep most of his inventive impulses in check. This was not the kind of movie that anyone expected him to make, nor, as time would bear out, was it a movie he should have made for the good of his career. But it was one he felt he needed to make, and a case study in why he made the decisions that he did.

When audiences considered the highlight reel of Robin's best-known roles, they saw doctors, teachers, fathers, helpers, and healers. "What everybody saw was Robin's humanity," said Steven Haft, his producer on *Dead Poets Society* and *Jakob the Liar.* "But that humanity was also a kind of ideology for him. Insofar as Robin could channel everything from a right-wing American president to a homeless guy in the street, he embraced the world in that way. All people, cultures — humanity as a kind of religion." When Robin chose a part, there was usually something irresistibly personal about it. "It played to his humanity in one form or another," Haft said, and in doing so, "he became very close with the character."

"People expected too much of him," Billy Crystal said. "They wanted him to plug that burst, that comet, into every movie, and it just wasn't fair. Then, when he would do a more sentimental piece they would just crucify him as sappy, and it would crush him. He took that personally.

"When Robin chose to do something," Crystal added, "he chose it for a particular reason. It was never a money decision, he had plenty of that. It was: Did it connect with his heart?"

On face value, there might seem to be little common ground shared by an impoverished, Jewish Holocaust victim and the Episcopalian son of a wealthy Midwestern automobile executive. But in his mind, Robin could justify it: he had grown up around Jews, worked with them, and embraced them as some of his closest friends; he liked to boast that he knew so much Yiddish, "people tend to think I'm Jewish." He was fascinated with the otherness of Jews, admired them for their tenacity, and was furious with how they'd been treated by history. "He realized that Jews had come out of this crime against humanity," Haft said, "and 'crime against humanity' is precisely the sort of thing that could reach deeply in Robin's heart. You add it all up and there is a kind of, barely explicable, Jewish consciousness in this goy guy."

Until now, there had been no compelling reason to call these instincts into question. Robin's run of films from *Mrs. Doubtfire* to *Good Will Hunting* — occasionally acclaimed, usually successful — had bought him the breathing room to make one like *Jakob the Liar* every now and again. But his personal compass was about to lead him to some very despairing places, and to a series of characters who were increasingly hopeless, suffering, maladapted, even homicidal. In one far-flung science-fiction film from this period, called *The Final Cut,* he played a man who uses computers to edit postmortem memories, subjecting himself to lifetime after lifetime of other people's acts of cruelty, infidelity, and violence. "It's the way the world looks to me," his character explains. "The way I see it." But, as another character tells him, "You were meant to live your own life, too."

What would be the cumulative effect on a sensitive, deeply attuned actor like Robin when each successive role brought him to further depths of anguish? "Was it following him down a wormhole of personal angst?" Haft wondered. Never mind what effect it had on his bankability or his bottom line — what did it do to his soul?

As Robin said of one such part he would play in this period, he was not interested in purely good or bad guys. He wanted to take on figures of elastic morality and see how much further he could stretch it. "It's not black and white," he explained. "There is this gray, going on constantly. A confusion, a doubt. A conscience being tweaked and pushed, back and forth. A man making a decision, going against his conscience and, in the end, hoping that he can find his way back."

The first of Robin's films to follow *Good Will Hunting* into theaters, almost a full year later, was a supernatural romance called *What Dreams May Come*. Adapted from a novel by the fantasy writer Richard Matheson, it told the story of Chris, a pediatrician (played by Robin), who helps his wife, Annie (Annabella Sciorra), a painter, overcome her depression after their children are killed in a car crash. But when Chris later dies in another car accident, Annie becomes despondent and commits suicide. Though Chris's altruism gets him sent to heaven — a visually sumptuous afterlife that mirrors the paintings that Annie created — he learns that his wife has been condemned to hell for her suicide, and he sets out to rescue her.

Directed by Vincent Ward, a New Zealand filmmaker with a hallucinatory cinematic style, *What Dreams May Come* had been a costly undertaking, budgeted at $70 million, and the production traveled up and down California, to Venezuela, and to Glacier National Park in Montana during the summer and fall of 1997. Its creators believed that the film would counter a mood of existential uncertainty with optimism and a touch of the divine, offering what its producer Stephen Simon said was an "antidote" to a "millennium consciousness" that was "generally negative and fear-based. People are really looking for some hope and empowerment that can lift them beyond their fears." Though the film was careful not to include or exclude God in its depiction of the hereafter, it offered Robin an opportunity to contemplate what role spirituality played in his life and what kind of judgment might await him at the end of it. "Do I attend church every Sunday?" he said. "No. Do I try and lead a fairly Christian life? Yes. Have I ever had any inappropriate behavior? Yes, years ago." With a ribald reference to Bill Clinton and Monica Lewinsky, he added, "Have I messed up any dresses? No."

These jokes were a way for Robin to deflect some very real pain he had felt in making the movie, a story of separation, loss, suicide, and actual hell. "It was an emotional film and he had to reach some places that were difficult for him," said Cheri Minns, his makeup artist. The material extracted a psychic toll on his costars, too, and Robin often found it easier to attend to their pain than to his own. "What he would tend to do," Minns said, "is he would go into a protective mode for them, and lose his own difficulties in the process. He would champion Annabella and coddle her and try to make everything good for her, and it would lessen what he was going through, because he would give so much energy over to that. That's how he was."

What Dreams May Come, which opened in October 1998, worked for some critics and not others, but few failed to observe that it fit into a pattern Robin had established over the past decade. Carrie Rickey of the *Philadelphia Inquirer* had some skepticism about the film — "If it doesn't choke you with emotion, it will choke you with atmosphere," she wrote — but praised Robin's performance as part of a larger continuum. "From *The Fisher King* through *Mrs. Doubtfire* and *Good Will Hunting,* the actor has vividly dramatized various ways of working through loss," she said. In *What Dreams May Come,* he was something like a modern-day Dante, "guiding us mortals through the rings of hell" in a story where "death and loss make his characters belatedly understand the gift of life."

Kenneth Turan, the *Los Angeles Times* critic who had never fully come around on *Good Will Hunting,* was even more dismissive, writing that Robin had turned in "one of his trademark lachrymose performances," and, despite his recent accomplishments, "the awkward truth is that he is a brilliant comedian who is no more than a passable actor and whose determination to indulge a personal sweet tooth for schmaltz represents one of the most visible wastes of genius around."

The film did poorly, but Robin was unbowed. "I don't need the coin," he said. "I keep working because projects are interesting or very bizarre, which I like. I'm exploring, finding humanity. I'm trying to play characters that allow us to look at who and what we are as a species."

He pointed ahead just a few weeks to the impending release of *Patch Adams,* though he was at a loss to explain why it was the fifth film he'd made in eight years in which he played a physician. "Maybe it's because I want to help people that I play so many doctors. And I like to put on rubber gloves."

Patch Adams, whose production had bookended Robin's Oscar-night triumph, elicited one of the most brutal critical responses of his career, and its title became a notorious shorthand not only for the bottom rung of

Robin's cinematic résumé but for the most misguided of any comic actor's attempts to balance humor and pathos. To this day it is regarded as one of the worst films of its year and decade, and derided, as one typical assessment reads, for pandering "so shamelessly in an effort to manipulate every conceivable human emotion" as it "trots out every hoary plot device, no matter how improbable, exploitative or downright moronic." Even the industry trade paper *Variety* called it "shamelessly sappy and emotionally manipulative" and said that it "pulls out all the stops in a lead role that gives him carte blanche to careen between extremes of silliness and sentimentality." "Even so," its review cautioned, "it's unwise to underestimate the appeal of a popular star doing crowd-pleasing shtick in slickly packaged Hollywood hokum."

Sure enough, *Patch Adams* was a number one film at the box office when it opened on Christmas Day 1998, but the damage was done. At the start of 1999, Robin discharged CAA, the Hollywood firm whose agents had represented him for many years, to follow Michael Ovitz and Michael Menchel to their new talent company, Artists Management Group, though David Steinberg and his partners at Morra, Brezner, Steinberg & Tenenbaum would stay on as his managers.

The theatrical release of *Jakob the Liar* followed a year later. Peter Kassovitz, the film's Hungarian director and co-screenwriter, had survived World War II after being given refuge by a Catholic family and had been reunited with his parents after their release from a concentration camp. Much of its crew had been handpicked by Marsha, who was a credited producer on the project, and several of them were alumni of *Schindler's List* who had been recommended by Steven Spielberg. This was payback of a sort from Spielberg, who had often phoned Robin during the making of *Schindler's List* when his spirits needed lifting.

Haft, who had also been brought on at the Williamses' request, saw the project as one that would simultaneously satisfy Robin's desires to make a picture that was emotionally nourishing and commercially viable. "He and Marsha were looking for things that tamed the beast and touched his soul," Haft said.

Thinking back to *Dead Poets Society,* Haft said that something was different about Robin during the making of *Jakob the Liar.* "There was a certain looseness to the guy that I knew on *Dead Poets* — an awareness of everything going on around him, from the morning news to the kind of personal encounters he had in life that he would carry around with him," Haft said. On this picture "there was something more," which Haft could only characterize as sadness. "The sadness did work in the role and contribute to it," he said. "Robin could have done anything and yet he developed this project. And this project had a lot of resonance for him that was quite sad."

But an unexpected development had complicated matters between the production of *Jakob the Liar* in the fall of 1997 and its opening in September 1999: the film had been eclipsed by *Life Is Beautiful,* an Italian comedy-drama directed by and starring Roberto Benigni. In this thoughtful and almost unerringly precise work of slapstick, Benigni played a Jewish man who during World War II is sent with his young son to a Nazi concentration camp. To shield his son from the horrors of their circumstances and keep them both alive, he convinces the boy that the camp is in fact an elaborate contest whose winner will receive a tank.

After *Life Is Beautiful* won the Grand Prix at the 1998 Cannes Film Festival, it had a well-received theatrical release in America, and the following March it won three Academy Awards, including one for best foreign film and one for Benigni as Best Actor. Benigni, who was largely unknown to American audiences, clowned his way into their hearts by climbing atop the seats of the Dorothy Chandler Pavilion en route to the stage to receive his first statuette. The media, striving for a metaphor that would make him more familiar, dubbed him "the Italian Robin Williams."

The creators of *Jakob the Liar* said they had no idea about *Life Is Beautiful* at the time they were making their movie, and Robin — who had been one of the well-wishers who shook Benigni's hand when he rushed down the aisle to pick up his second Oscar — tried none too convincingly to dismiss speculation that the success of *Life Is Beautiful* was bad for *Jakob the Liar.* "People say they've seen this before," he said, just prior to his film's release. "But how many police movies do we see every year? How many exploding asteroids? People can tolerate that, but they say, 'Oh God, another Holocaust film. Can't have that! Seen that!' "

His argument found little favor in the press, where comparisons to *Life Is Beautiful* ran rampant; one reviewer, who was giving *Jakob the Liar* a positive write-up, even called Robin "the American Roberto Benigni." Kenneth Turan had now lost all patience with him; his pitiless evaluation began: "Robin Williams, enough already. Enough with the compassionate roles, the humanitarian roles, the caring and concerned roles. Enough with the good deeds, for pity's sake. Remember being funny? Maybe you could try that again. How hard could it be?" The film was a crushing failure at the box office, taking in less than

$5 million over a monthlong theatrical run.

The year was still not quite done with him. Just before Christmas, Robin starred in *Bicentennial Man,* a science-fiction movie in which he played an android who lives two hundred years in a quest to become fully human. The film (adapted from two novels, one by Isaac Asimov and the other by Asimov and Robert Silverberg) reunited Robin with Chris Columbus, who had directed him so capably in *Mrs. Doubtfire;* it was also astonishingly expensive, to the point that Disney had to put the project on a months-long pause when its budget hit $100 million. It was resuscitated when Columbia Pictures struck a deal with Disney to jointly finance, distribute, and market the movie.

The results, once again, were dissatisfying — so much so that critics were calling Robin's entire oeuvre into question, even the past films that they'd previously given glowing appraisals. For one reviewer, *Bicentennial Man* illustrated how, over the past twenty years, Robin had carved out a genre of movies all to himself — an observation that was hardly meant as a compliment: "Call it hand-wringing drama in which the high-minded pathos never compensates for submerging Williams' comic talents." *Bicentennial Man* was another bust, bringing in just $58 million.

Robin knew he was alienating his fan base;

he knew which movies in particular were driving the crowds away and which ones audiences hoped to see him replicate. But knowing this brought him no closer to solving the problem; as he saw it, he was at the mercy of the material that was being offered to him. "People keep saying, 'Why don't you do another *Fisher King* or *Mrs. Doubtfire*?' " he said. "But they don't come along every day. I guess they wanted me to stop the touchy-feely movies after *Awakenings.* Then I did *What Dreams May Come,* which so many people really hated. And I can tell you making that movie was like having open-heart surgery with a spoon every day, so the reaction was dispiriting."

His fans felt particularly empowered to tell him exactly how they felt and what they expected from him. "People will come up to you and say, 'If you ever make another movie like that, I'll hurt you,' " he said. "This is interesting feedback. Does it make me deny the validity of what I've done? No. Does it make me want to look for other things? Yes."

But where others saw a calculated pattern of maudlin film roles, Robin explained that he was simply taking what was available to him. And on the level at which he operated, there was no option not to work at all. "I have been working straight for five years, only ever with a couple of months off in between," he said. "It's probably time to take more time off but then things come up and I do them because I feel there's a challenge."

In the winter of 2000, David Letterman, the late-night host, discovered that he had a severely blocked coronary artery and underwent quintuple bypass heart surgery. After several weeks of convalescence, Letterman returned to his desk at CBS's *Late Show* for a celebratory, welcome-home broadcast; he brought out the team of surgeons and nurses who had tended to him and thanked them for their attentive care. Then, once that segment was over, there was only one celebrity entertainer that Letterman wanted to share his stage with on his first night back on television: Robin Williams.

Robin, who had flown out from San Francisco specifically to appear on the program, ran onto the stage dressed in surgical scrubs and rubber gloves, carrying an ice chest and a defibrillator. He accosted one of the stage managers, telling the man to turn his head and cough, then announced to Letterman's studio audience, "Students, before we begin the penile reduction . . ." Finally he took his seat next to the host, who looked thin and delicate but had lost none of his acerbic wit. "It's just nice to have you back," Robin told him. "That'll wear off," Letterman replied.

"Are you all right?" Letterman asked him. "You seem like a pretty healthy guy." With mock paranoia, Robin responded, "God, if it can happen to you, I'm next, I guess. I guess I'll have to go in now, too."

Letterman had needed some cheering up and concluded there was no one better qualified to provide it. "It was stressful and I was tired," the host later said of the occasion. "I think people were worried: what if he has to be taken out mid-show? We don't want him to have a heart attack and die. We were looking for something that I could curate rather than actually participate in. And it worked. Looking back on it — and God bless him for doing that — I don't remember a single show where Robin didn't end up with a standing ovation."

But Robin needed that appearance as much as Letterman did; it had been a long time since he had been allowed to cut loose and laugh at himself, and to be appreciated for it.

As Robin saw it, there were only two movies he'd made up until now in which he'd played characters who could be classified as dark or villainous: one, a discredited ex-psychiatrist reduced to working as a grocery clerk in Kenneth Branagh's 1991 film noir *Dead Again;* the other, a dapper, placid, bomb-building mastermind known only as the Assassin in Christopher Hampton's 1996 adaptation of Joseph Conrad's *The Secret Agent.* Both were small, unbilled roles he'd taken for the simple pleasure of playing against the expectations of audiences — and the film industry — that considered him a milquetoast. "The idea of me doing this already starts people going, 'Wait a minute,' " he explained. "I've only done warm, nice people, and already it puts people in an interesting mode — off-balance, which was great."

Then in quick succession, he made three movies that he would call his "triptych of evil," all of which would ask him to plumb his deepest, murkiest recesses. The first, *One Hour Photo*, which he filmed in the fall of 2000, was the feature directing and screenwriting debut of Mark Romanek, who had previously directed bleak, stylized music videos for Nine Inch Nails and Johnny Cash. The project was Romanek's homage to the paranoid character pieces of the 1970s he'd grown up admiring, like *Taxi Driver, The Conversation,* and *The Tenant;* these films focused his imagination on the setting of a generic, suburban big-box retail store, awash in white fluorescent light, and the character of Seymour "Sy" Parrish, an isolated photo-lab employee who becomes dangerously fixated on a family whose pictures he develops.

Robin was intrigued by the possibility that he could cast aside the pressures that came with his usual, antic self and instead play someone so lacking in magnetism. "They're no longer bound by the laws of likability," he said. "You have a character that can be so normal — hyper-normal, and banal in many ways, that you no longer have to be charismatic." Prior to the start of filming, which took place primarily at a closed-down Office Depot store in the Canoga Park section of Los Angeles, he trained one-on-one with a photo technician to learn to cut and print film. He watched taped interviews of convicted serial killers, and he consulted with a psychiatrist to learn about the distinguishing characteristics of mental conditions like autism and Asperger's syndrome, whose symptoms, his notes indicated, include "a lack of spontaneous seeking to share enjoyment, interests, or achievements with other people."

Romanek and Cheri Minns, Robin's makeup artist, worked together to create a signature look for the Sy Parrish character, which included dyeing Robin's hair blond, thinning it out, shaving back his hairline, and dressing him in large eyeglasses, to make him look older and more inconspicuous. Robin would later claim to be flattered by moviegoers who said that they didn't recognize him in the role, but Minns said the opposite was true, that the anonymity of the character sometimes frustrated him. On one of the first days of the shoot, Minns said, "We're walking to the set, in public. So we walked by a few people, and no one recognized him. Then it disturbed him. So the next people that walked by, he's like, 'Hi! How are you! Hi!' 'It's me, it's Robin Williams!' He wouldn't say *that,* but that's basically what he was doing. He'd be like, 'Hi!' I'd say, 'Jesus, Robin, you can't stand it that two people don't know who you are?' It just really freaked him out, that people didn't recognize him."

At the start of 2001, Robin moved on to the second film in his unlikely trilogy, a pitch-black comedy called *Death to Smoochy.* Directed by Danny DeVito and set in a hypercompetitive pastiche of the children's television industry, it cast Robin as Rainbow Randolph, the gaudy, singing, dancing, bowler-hatted host of his own top-rated kids' TV show — who, behind the scenes, is Randolph Smiley, a cruel, cosseted, insecure celebrity who lives in a Manhattan penthouse, drinks heavily, spends profligately, and accepts bribes from parents who seek to get their eager moppets on his program. Having grown impatient with Randolph's disgraceful ways, the president of his TV network (Jon Stewart) hits upon a low-cost solution: to replace him with Smoochy, a purple rhinoceros played by Sheldon Mopes (Edward Norton), a virtuous entertainer plying his trade in a Coney Island methadone clinic. As Robin's character descends into anger, degradation, and revenge scenarios, the film handily earned its R rating with scenes in which he yells at a baby: "Hello, little nipplenibbler, the rhino's a Nazi!"; and tricks Mopes, on air, into serving children a batch of cookies shaped like penises. ("Welcome to Fatty Arbuckle land," he grumbles to himself.) Robin called it "a wonderful, nasty movie."

For the third and final film in this sequence, Robin traveled to British Columbia, Canada, to make the thriller *Insomnia*. Directed by Christopher Nolan, who had earned universal acclaim for his nonlinear murder mystery *Memento,* and adapted from a 1997 Norwegian film, *Insomnia* starred Al Pacino as Will Dormer, a Los Angeles police detective who is brought to an Alaskan town to help investigate the murder of a teenage girl. Even before Dormer's investigations lead him to a prime suspect — a pulp novelist named Walter Finch, played by Robin — Finch taunts the detective with anonymous phone calls, delivered in a calm monotone, in which he alternately shares factual details and deliberate misinformation about the crime.

Nolan, who would later achieve blockbuster status with his Dark Knight franchise of Batman movies, felt that Robin's outward congeniality would make him a more seductive murderer. "He presents the logic and the rationalization of the character in such a straightforward manner that you want to believe him for a while," he said. "Dormer is in such a state by this point, you don't quite know who to believe, and a lot of what Robin is saying makes a kind of sense, because he does it in this very straightforward and logical manner."

Robin was again able to draw upon the serial-killer research he had used for *One Hour Photo,* particularly a documentary he had watched about Jeffrey Dahmer. As he recalled, "They asked him, 'When you started cutting up the bodies, what did you do?' And he said, 'I stored them in a case, exactly like that camera case right there.' And you could see the interviewer go, [seizes up] 'Okay, let's cut. That's it for today. Thank you.'"

When it comes to playing an unbalanced person, Robin said, "The more normal and regular it seems, the creepier it is."

Crucial to *Insomnia* is its setting of a secluded fishing village where the sun does not set, and Robin filmed many of his scenes in the spring and early summer of 2001 in Port Alberni, a small city on Vancouver Island, and in tiny Alaskan towns on the Canadian border. Though the settings were beautiful, he also found them lonesome and limited in the kinds of stimulation they could offer. "There's a lot of log rolling" and "a couple of bars," he said.

He could eat only so many catered on-set meals before his attention and his appetite turned elsewhere. Explaining a local custom in which a bartender serves a shot of powerful grain alcohol and lights the leftover portion with a match, he said, "We had these wild parties in Alaska" where "they 'Hyderize' you there which is 175–180 proof. Do the math, that's a lot of alcohol."

Robin turned fifty years old on July 21, 2001, a milestone he celebrated with his family and friends on his ranch in Napa. He saw the moment as a dividing line in his career, and when he went past it, his days as a cinematic leading man were numbered. "Once I hit fifty," he said, "I'm looking for characters. The romantic parts are over. 'Mr. Pitt, he gonna take it now.' " With more sincerity, he said that he had "hit this phase where you look at stuff. The time is changing, you're on the clock now. It's like, 'This is it.' You want to maximize what you do."

If there was a lesson he had learned from his work up to this point, he said, it was "not to rush off and do things. If I have to wait for something, I'll wait. There have been times when I rushed into things. Sometimes it was pure greed, sometimes it was, 'we'll make it better.' I don't believe 'we'll fix it' anymore. Don't ever go that way."

When his father, Rob, had died, it was both abrupt and slow — the unexpected onset of illness followed by a gradual decline that left Robin just enough time to make peace with him before he passed away. His mother, Laurie, had remained a continual presence in his life every day since, a reliable companion for Sunday brunches, teatimes, and tennis matches, an enthusiastic exerciser and an inveterate pack rat. Then, suddenly, she was gone, too: she died in her Tiburon home on September 4, 2001, at the age of seventy-eight. The official cause given was heart failure. Zak, her grandson, later said that she had lived a full life, one in which "she wore mini-skirts till the day she died."

In a remembrance she shared shortly before her death, Laurie said she enjoyed being both social and solitary. "I enjoy my own company," she explained. "I get along very well with me. I don't like being alone on a constant basis. I'm not a recluse. I love parties and being with people. And then I love getting home. It's like being in your castle, crossing the moat and pulling up the drawbridge." Though she had seen some difficulties in her life, "all in all, it's been a kick in the shorts," she said. "I really think we were put on earth to know great joy."

Robin had learned many memorable verses from Laurie over the years, and her obituary in the *San Francisco Chronicle* contained a poem said to be one that he'd written for her.

Think young and you'll never grow old,
The years will pass you by,
Birthdays are for merrymaking,
Present giving and birthday caking,

Age is the state of your mind
As the days of your years unfold,
Don't live in the past,
Right up to the last
Think young and you'll never grow old

Like her husband before her, Laurie's body was cremated and the ashes were scattered off the coast of Marin County. The family had only a few days to mourn before the terrorist attacks of September 11, 2001, an event that the entire world would grieve and whose full impact on Robin would not reveal itself immediately.

For several years, Robin had been vowing an official return to stand-up comedy; aside from the sporadic unannounced club pop-in, Comic Relief special, or talk-show appearance — which was usually more of a one-man whirlwind than a formal, practiced routine — he had not put out a stand-up TV special or record album since his storied Metropolitan Opera show in 1986. His explanation for what finally got him back into the game varied from telling to telling. Perhaps it was the thrill of participating in a tribute to Whoopi Goldberg when she received the Mark Twain Prize at the Kennedy Center, which had helped shake off a post-9/11 delirium: "People treated it like we had just lifted the siege of Richmond," he later said of the tribute event. "People were just like, 'Wow,' and it was like they had not had any entertainment. . . . People needed it." Or perhaps it had taken this long to find a six-month stretch on his calendar that he could devote to the endeavor. In any case, it was a homecoming he had been promising publicly for at least three years, and some of his colleagues sensed that his desire to do it ran deeper and had been brewing longer.

Eddie Izzard, the British comedian, monologuist, and actor, had met Robin in 1996 when they worked together on *The Secret Agent.* He considered Robin an idol and an influence; the two became friends, and Robin and Marsha helped produce Izzard's show *Dress to Kill* when he brought it to San Francisco in 1998. Despite their mutual passion for stand-up, Izzard said he and Robin didn't share notes or discuss technique. The championship pugilist was far from his fighting weight.

"I was surprised he didn't go back and do more stand-up," Izzard said. "He got into that place, that multimillion-dollar film place, but then I don't think he wanted to be there. It's when you get stuck in that place where you have to do something for the finances." When you're performing on a regular basis, Izzard said, "you develop systems of how to create new shows, which might have been difficult for him. Because it is quite tricky when you have your fifth, sixth, seventh, eighth show.

The trouble of repeating, the trouble of going through areas that interest you but you might have attacked before — you can go into those same subjects but you've got to go into them a different way. I think everyone must have this problem, and I've spent a lot of time trying to work out how to do it."

In December 2001, Robin played a series of shows at Bimbo's 365 Club, a small, sit-down nightspot in San Francisco, where he tried out a new set that could sometimes run two hours or more and which he eventually pared down to about ninety minutes. Then, during the first half of 2002, he took the set on a national tour where, at each stop, he and David Steinberg fine-tuned the material while Peter Asher recorded the performances for an album. The set was customized only slightly from city to city: "He would do ten minutes about wherever he was," Asher said, "which was information he would glean on arrival from the limo driver, from the baggage guy at the hotel, from people at the desk. He would find out about the local sports scandal or the mayor who'd been indicted, whatever the big stories in town were, and incorporate them into a whole new bit."

Early assessments of the tour were not encouraging. Checking in on a performance in Philadelphia, one critic wrote, "To say Robin Williams' act . . . was all over the place would be an understatement." Though the review praised Robin's "timing and wildcat energy," it also observed that his "African American and Latino characters were occasionally cringe-inducing (especially in front of a lily-white audience)." The review concluded, "Two hours with him is exhausting, but his style has a distinct advantage: By the time you realize the last joke wasn't funny, Williams has told two more."

Death to Smoochy was similarly savaged when it opened on March 29, 2002. The *Washington Post* called it Robin's penance for every "earnest, life-affirming movie he's done in the past decade" and "a particularly toxic little bonbon, palatable to only a chosen and very jaundiced few." It was a colossal bomb, grossing slightly more than $8 million, and after barely three years with Artists Management Group, the talent firm his agents Ovitz and Menchel had founded, Robin left the company and rehired CAA to represent him.

Insomnia fared better when it was released on May 24, and though it was regarded principally as a tour de force for Pacino, Robin also received widespread praise. "Robin Williams is a shockingly effective counterweight," said *Slate*. "The key is what he doesn't do: Those rubber features remain rigid, that madcap energy harnessed."

By the time he came onstage at the Broadway Theatre in New York on July 14 for a live

HBO broadcast of his stand-up show, Robin was in a combative mood. He had something to prove. He wore a short-sleeve Southwestern-style shirt, and the set was sparsely decorated, with a table full of water bottles that he would constantly gulp from. An image of one of his eyes hovered over everything. Despite the setting, Robin told the audience, "This is not going to be your normal night of *the-a-tuh.* This will be Shakespeare with a strap-on." What followed was an angry, scattershot performance, uncharacteristic in its lack of focus and its absence of charity.

He shouted his way through sarcastic criticism of President George W. Bush ("Him talking about business ethics is kind of like having a leper give you a facial — it doesn't really work") and recycled one of his old lines about Ronald and Nancy Reagan to say that "W. doesn't speak while Cheney's drinking water." There were predictable potshots at Bill Gates, Martha Stewart, Mike Tyson, and the New York Yankees, though he praised women in general for dressing skimpily in the warm weather: "The titties are out today."

His observations about the aftermath of 9/11 had uncomfortable strains of anti-Arab and anti-Islamic sentiment, as when he joked that "you can't bomb the Afghanis back to the Stone Age, because they'll go, 'Upgrade!' " Proposing a plan to share

Jerusalem among religious groups, Robin said, "Jews will get Hanukkah, Passover. Christians will get Christmas and Easter. And Muslims will have Ramadan and that other holiday, Kaboom." Even an anecdote he told about an unexpectedly intimate encounter he shared with Koko, a silverback gorilla who communicates in sign language, felt cynical and harsh. As Robin recounted their embrace, "When an eight-hundred-pound gorilla's got you by the tits, you listen."

Nonetheless, the record that Asher produced from the tour, *Robin Williams Live 2002*, would go on to win a Grammy; as he held his latest trophy up to his ear, Robin declared, "Oh my God, listen! You can actually hear careers ending." The album included a bonus track that Robin and Asher created, called "The Grim Rapper," in which Robin, playing the personification of Death, delivered rhymes like:

You've lost all your fluids, your vital sap
It's time to get ready for the big dirt nap

Critics identified a similar strain of morbidity in *One Hour Photo*, which finally opened at the end of the summer, but somehow it seemed to suit Robin. "Oddly, when he's playing serious roles, he tends to trust the audiences more than when he's doing comic work," Elvis Mitchell wrote in the *New York*

Times. "He's not sweating to ingratiate himself through the damp excesses that can mark some of his other work." In *One Hour Photo,* Mitchell said, Robin "is so good here it's almost painful to watch."

By then, Robin was not really chasing positive reviews or constructive feedback. In October, with no fanfare, he turned up at Bagram Air Base in Afghanistan, flying into the country on a thunderous C-130 turboprop transport plane, and crossing long expanses of dusty, treacherous desert to arrive at the protective shelter of the base. Once there, on an itinerary arranged by the USO, he roamed the grounds in a backward baseball cap, Oakley sunglasses, and cargo shorts; offered encouragement, photos, and autographs to the soldiers; and bellowed at the top of his lungs, as they surely hoped to hear, "GOOO-OOOOD MORNING, BAGRAM!"

As the son of a veteran, and as an actor whose most beloved roles included one particularly unruly airman, Robin felt an obligation to support his country's fighting forces in whatever ways he could. "I wanted to go over there specifically to Afghanistan and to those bases, to let them know people at home haven't forgotten them and also, when I get back, to tell people don't forget the people there," he explained.

It was his first visit to an active battlefield,

and while it did not change his feelings about the moral grotesqueness of war, when he saw the people who volunteered to wage it, he was struck by how young they were. "You go and you see this youth," he said, "and that's why you think, 'war — how insane.' This youth, these people, and this incredible energy and intelligence and dedication is getting chewed up."

He traveled light, accompanied only by his assistant, Rebecca Erwin Spencer, and when he felt like performing some stand-up comedy, all he needed was a riser, a microphone, an amplifier or two, and a roomful of grateful soldiers, which was never hard to come by. These were quick and dirty — *very* dirty — sets, ten or fifteen minutes at a clip, full of jokes about masturbation, Viagra, getting drunk off only two beers, and his undiminished distaste for President Bush. ("Things are still the same at home," he told the troops. "George is learning to speak. We're trying to help him.")

Many of the same qualities that had made his live Broadway set so off-putting — the vulgarity, the fatalism — played perfectly in front of battle-weary troops who had no use for delicacy or euphemism. "I know that this isn't the end of the world," Robin told one crowd, "but you can fuckin' see it from here."

This was just the first of many trips that Robin would make to the Middle East with the USO over the next several years. He traveled to Afghanistan again in 2003 and made his first visit to Iraq that December, just in time for the capture of Saddam Hussein. He returned to both front lines in 2004, added Kuwait to his itinerary in 2007, and made a grand circuit of Iraq, Pakistan, Afghanistan, and Bahrain in 2010. But that initial tour of Bagram, and the astonishing freedom it offered, would always be special to him. "There were no restrictions," he said. "The shows were the shows. And it was just me. . . . In terms of a performance, it's some of the best audiences you'll ever get in your life."

There was something about the atmosphere of pervasive, maximum danger, where the threat of death was so omnipresent that you just had to laugh at it, that Robin needed to see for himself. On that maiden trip to Bagram, his plane had to make combat landings and takeoffs — a perilously steep descent or ascent, to avoid possible enemy fire — which he described as feeling "like a weird ride except you realize the consequence of the ride is if someone shoots at you that maybe you go down." Making that fateful first landing, he recalled, "You start seeing the whole flight crew strapping in Kevlar and helmets and guys getting up by the doors. . . . The moment you get off the plane, they say, 'Please sir, stay on the path.' 'Why? What's on the other side?' 'It's still mined.' I went,

'Thank you.' "

Robin seemed to be oscillating from one blinding wilderness to the next, from blazing hot sand to freezing cold snow, and he found himself north of the border again in the spring of 2004 to make *The Big White.* It was a modestly budgeted independent movie, nothing like the big studio features he'd been accustomed to, about a down-on-his-luck travel agent who tries to cash in his missing brother's million-dollar insurance policy using a dead body he found in a dumpster. The production was based in Winnipeg, Canada, with intermittent expeditions into Alaska and Yukon, and Robin, who had traveled there only with Spencer, his assistant, and Minns, his makeup artist, found the emptiness of these locales unsettling.

"Winnipeg is one of the most dismal places, as far as I'm concerned," Minns said. "There's nothing to do there. Nothing. Robin would say, 'You can just ride your bike forever. You can watch your dog run away for a week.' "

One day, for lack of anything better to do, Minns and Spencer decided to attend the grand opening of a local drugstore, and when Robin got wind of their plans, he pleaded to go with them. On the drive over, Minns noticed a curious phenomenon: sometimes, when their car was stopped in traffic, pedestrians and passengers in other cars would look over, recognize Robin and get extremely excited; at other times, people seemed not to notice him at all.

"What's going on?" Minns asked Robin. "He says, 'I turn it on, and I can turn it off. I can make them see me, or I can make them not see me.' It was kind of bizarre, but it was really funny, because then I said, 'Show me.' So he would do it, and I would be like, 'Oh, my God, those people totally looked right at you and they didn't see that it was you.' And then the next car would be like, 'Robin Williams, oh my God!' It was too funny."

By now, it was no secret to these two close coworkers that Robin had started drinking again. It had never been entirely possible for Spencer or Minns to babysit Robin on his location shoots, and the task became a lost cause when he would decide to go out at night, on his own, and make a guest appearance at a comedy club. After these shows, Robin would be left to his own devices, when his intense likability was his most valuable asset and his greatest danger.

"He makes everyone around him feel like they're his best friend," Minns said. "So when people see him — and, of course, know him and know that he's so fucking funny — they want to hang out, they feel like they can. Because Robin makes them feel that way. He makes a total stranger feel that way. It's like, 'Oh, yeah, I'm with Robin.' No, you're not with Robin. We were doing that constantly. Rebecca and I had a thing that we'd say: 'Ugh, his new best friend.' 'Oh, there's another new best friend.' And we'd have to get rid of them. He just didn't want people not to like him."

Usually in these encounters, Minns said, "He was getting drinks. They're offering him every drug imaginable. Everything, and if he wasn't sober, he was taking anybody he could up on what they were offering. It was awful."

Then it all went off the rails. "He was drinking in a big way on *The Big White*," Minns said, "He was drinking big-time. That's his touch-stone of where he fell off the wagon. He had to have fallen off the wagon before that. But that's when he started doing it out in the open and didn't care who saw it."

In Robin's own recounting, his first misstep on the sober path he'd successfully walked for nearly two decades occurred while the production was in Skagway, Alaska. Having nothing but time and empty space to contemplate, Robin had retreated into an unhealthy obsession with his own résumé, revisiting loss after loss, tallying up failure after failure, and convincing himself that this time he was done for good. "My film career was not going too well," he later recalled. "One day I walked into a store and saw a little bottle of Jack Daniel's. And then that voice — I call it the lower power — goes: 'Hey. Just a taste. Just one.' I drank it, and there was that brief moment of 'Oh, I'm okay!' "

The instant he took that first sip, he said, "You feel warm and kind of wonderful. And then the next thing you know, it's a problem, and you're isolated."

"Within a week," Robin said, "I was buying so many bottles I sounded like a wind chime walking down the street."

Sometimes Robin cracked jokes because they helped defuse uncomfortable situations. Sometimes he resorted to them when he was angry. And sometimes he told them because he was terrified.

17

WEAPONS OF SELF DESTRUCTION

For all the awards that Robin had won in his career, this time was different. When he was presented with the Cecil B. DeMille Award — a lifetime achievement prize, bestowed on him at the age of fifty-three — at the Golden Globes, on January 16, 2005, he'd had time to prepare his speech. He started out in a fake foreign accent, offering his appreciation to the Hollywood Foreign Press Association in various languages and thanking them "for, number one, having an open bar"; he gave an on-the-spot assessment of his new statuette "with the little nipply thing on the top," then held it to his chest, pointed outward, and called himself Janet Jackson.

Then, with more sincerity, Robin acknowledged his three children, all of whom were with him that night. He thanked Cody, now thirteen, whom he called "the ninja poet"; Zelda, fifteen, "photographer, actress, big fan of Hello Kitty"; and Zak, twenty-one, "the linguist . . . he's going to open up a syntax repair shop." Each of them abided their brief on-camera moment with a kind of *aw-dad* humility, wanting to support their father while seeming to wish they could be anywhere but there. Robin went on: "I also want to share this award," he said, "with a very special woman — a wife-time achievement award — with Marsha. I would like to give you the Croix de Guerre for living with a comedian. It's an interesting job, isn't it? We're a tad moody. . . . We're a little rough. But thank you for offering me a shelter in the midst of schadenfreude."

Marsha kissed her fingertips and waved them at Robin. But something about her gaze seemed intense; she had been through a lot of pain, and only a few other people in that room knew its full extent. This was a family in crisis, and it was not going to make it through the ordeal intact.

Robin was drinking again, and they knew it, not that he was making much effort to disguise it from them anymore. Even as he tried to persuade himself that he could avoid the pitfalls of excess if he wanted to, he knew just how bad things had gotten. "You keep thinking, 'I can handle this — I got this under control,' " he later explained. "Yeah, for a day. You go a week. And I didn't drink for a week and then *bang.* And then the next week I'd be back at it. And then the next."

Robin thought he had dealt long ago with

his dependencies on alcohol and drugs, back when *Mork & Mindy* was canceled and Zak was born, and that he had kicked these addictions completely. But having done so with no special help or treatment, without ever considering the underlying factors that might have steered him toward substance abuse, perhaps made it worse for him when he fell back on bad habits. "I went twenty years clean," he said. "But there was still, in the background, this voice like, 'Psst.' So when I relapsed, I went back hard."

Robin knew, too, that his drinking was doing real and lasting damage to his relationship with his family, the kind that would not be healed even if he got sober again and made amends for his wrongdoing. "I was shameful," he said, "and you do stuff that causes disgust, and that's hard to recover from. You can say, 'I forgive you' and all that stuff, but it's not the same as recovering from it. It's not coming back."

By this time, his movie career had run aground in the way he always feared it would. Nothing had come of *The Final Cut,* which was used as an early experiment in digital distribution and released in only about 115 theaters before it vanished. He was given a critical drubbing for *House of D,* a 1970s-era period piece written and directed by David Duchovny, in which Robin played a mentally handicapped janitor ("another of his almost sickeningly lovable weirdos," one reviewer said) and Zelda had a small supporting role. *The Big White,* the film whose creation had provided a bleak arctic backdrop for him to squander his sobriety, disappeared just as hurriedly. The MBST firm, the latest incarnation of the management company that had been guiding his career for nearly three decades, was acquired in July 2005 by CKX, Inc., an entertainment conglomerate that owned, among other properties, the name and likeness of Elvis Presley, the Graceland estate, and the *American Idol* TV series. Robin remained an MBST client, but to CKX he was just one more asset in its portfolio.

Amid the misery, though, his wicked sense of delight about the world — that ability to take mischievous pleasure in things that polite people were not supposed to find funny — had not been snuffed out; he just had to find different outlets for it. After Ronald Reagan died in the summer of 2004, Billy Crystal was watching a television broadcast of the funeral services. His phone rang, and on the other end was Robin, speaking not as himself but in Reagan's dry whisper, as if calling from the afterlife. Crystal just went with it. "We started doing these weird interviews," he recalled. "I said, is it beautiful up there? And he would go, 'Well, yes, but it's awfully hot.' It's not supposed to be hot. 'Oh. Maybe that's why Nixon's balls are on my nose.' It went on and on and on. It was so funny. We'd talk about going into a studio and just letting it go with the dirty side of both of us."

But then the losses in Robin's life became more personal and devastating, and they just kept coming. His dear friend Christopher Reeve died on October 10, 2004, after slipping into a coma and succumbing to a particularly severe type of pressure wound that affects people in wheelchairs. In the nine years since the riding accident that had paralyzed him, Reeve had never given up hope that he would walk again someday, and as he gradually reclaimed control of regions of his body — an index finger; his lungs — he had represented to Robin an embodiment of hope, heroism, and the power of the human brain.

For Robin, who had often seen Reeve contend with and recover from complications of his paralysis, his death was sudden and shocking, a blow that would be compounded several months later when Reeve's wife, Dana, was diagnosed with lung cancer; she died in 2006. But what hit Robin hardest, even after Reeve had been robbed of so much of his strength and vitality, was accepting that his friend's unyielding determination could not defeat his injuries.

"I never knew he was on borrowed time," Robin said after Reeve's death. "Many people told me he lived a lot longer than they thought possible, and I said I never knew he was on the clock — other than the same clock we're all on. There was a part of him that just seemed so indestructible."

Then, a year later, Richard Pryor was gone — Robin's comedy mentor, his unattainable benchmark for onstage candor, and a cautionary example of what happened when that single-minded passion is taken too far. Pryor had been debilitated by open-heart surgery in 1991 and the years-long onset of multiple sclerosis. He died on December 10, 2005, after a heart attack, another personal idol with whom Robin had remained close through a long, degenerative process.

As Robin recalled, "It was tough to see him near the end, with MS, where he was there, but slowly but surely, the body was shutting down on him. That was fucked up, that was the hardest part in the world to see, knowing that he's in there. But even then he'd kind of joke about it. He's the type of guy that would talk about his addictions, the crack pipe going, 'Richard, they don't know you like I know you.' He was brutal that way."

It would have been easy and understandable for Robin to say that his heartache had driven him back to drinking, but he denied that this was the case. "It's more selfish than that. It's just literally being afraid. And you think, oh, this will ease the fear. And it doesn't." His list of fears consisted of a single entry: "Everything," he said. "It's just a general all-round *arggghhh.* It's fearfulness and anxiety."

There had been a Thanksgiving dinner with his family in 2005 where Robin had gotten so drunk that he had to be brought upstairs and put to bed. But that was not enough to get him to change his ways. Then there had been the AIDS charity dinner that Robin attended at the Cannes Film Festival in the spring of 2006, looking ruddy and wobbly, his eyes hidden behind a pair of designer sunglasses, where he paid $80,000 for a performance by Wyclef Jean and another $40,000 for an Armani diamond necklace. ("I just bought a $40,000 coke vial," Williams said at the time.) That day, Robin thought for sure his personal humiliation was about to be exposed to the entire world: "I realized I was pretty baked," he said, "and I look out and I see, all of a sudden, a wall of paparazzi. And I go, 'Oh well, I guess it's out now.' " But that had not convinced him that he needed to seriously reevaluate his life, either.

When he finally did hit rock bottom, Robin contemplated taking his own life — but only for an instant, at which point he immediately talked himself out of it. He later recounted this moment for Marc Maron, the podcaster and a fellow comedian, in a darkly comic scene he depicted as a conversation between himself and his conscience:

When I was drinking, there was only one time, even for a moment, where I thought, "Oh, fuck life." Then even my conscious brain went, *Did you honestly just say, 'Fuck life?'* I went, *You know you have a pretty good life as it is right now. Have you noticed the two houses?* Yes. *Have you noticed the girlfriend?* Yes. *Have you noticed that things are pretty good, even though you may not be working right now?* Yes. *Okay, let's put the suicide over here, on 'discussable.' Let's leave that over here, in the discussion area. We'll talk about that. First of all, you don't have the balls to do it. I'm not going to say it out loud. I mean, have you thought about buying a gun?* No. *What were you going to do, cut your wrist with a Waterpik?* Maybe. *So that's erosion. What are you thinking about that? So, can I put that over here in the 'What the Fuck' category?* Yes, let's put that over here in 'What the Fuck.' *Because — can I ask you what you're doing right now? You're sitting naked in a hotel room with a bottle of Jack Daniel's.* Yes. *Is this maybe influencing your decision?* Possibly. *Okay, we're going to put that over here. . . . Possibly for therapy, if you want to talk about that in therapy, or maybe a podcast two years from now.*

And then, as his family members saw it,

Robin sunk even lower still. "It got to a point where he wasn't really functioning anymore, on any meaningful level," Zak said. "Honestly, it wouldn't have taken long for things to get really bad, really quick." It required an intervention — really, an ultimatum — from the other members of his family for Robin to accept that he needed help for his alcohol addiction, and that it was more than any of them could provide. He would have to check into a residential treatment facility and get clean there.

Robin later took ownership for this decision, saying, "It was me, but it was also everyone in the family saying, 'You've got to go.' I went, 'You're right. I can't bullshit you. I know I need help.' Thanks to family and friends, you go."

But some of Robin's friends felt that they had not been allowed to see the full extent of his problem until it had already reached a dangerous stage. "He kept things from me," Billy Crystal said. "Then he broke down and told me about the drinking and that he had started again. He explained that he had screwed up and hurt everybody and that he was going to go into a place to recover. It was very hard for him to accept the rage that was coming toward him at that time, but he understood that he had just shattered something and that's the price you pay."

Crystal said it was never a question that he

would be there to lift Robin up when he fell down. "A sickness is a sickness, which is what his alcoholism was," he said. "It's not excusing it. And we were there for Marsha and the kids, too."

"It was a test of our friendship," Crystal added. "We loved the family, we loved the kids, and they got hurt. That was the darkest time."

In the summer of 2006, Robin began a stay at a Hazelden Foundation center in Newberg, Oregon, a peaceful campus where he lived soberly while detoxing under a doctor's care and attending support meetings with other recovering addicts. "You've got to sit back and go, okay, you're separated, with others," Robin said. "You start going, 'Oh fuck.' You think, 'I'm fucked up. I'm a badass.' And there are stories you hear in rehab that make you go, shit, I'm a little Catholic girl."

Still, he tried to find comedy where he could. As he said a fellow patient told him, "He tried to commit suicide, and he put a little tube in his car to pump the fumes in. But only had a quarter tank of gas. It's a bit of a gallows humor."

In his sessions at Hazelden, Robin was taught for the first time to follow the tenets of the twelve-step program, which directs its followers to accept that their addictions have taken control of their lives, to turn themselves over to a higher power, to acknowledge how they have wronged other people, and to make amends for this behavior. For Robin it proved to be a comforting and potent philosophy, requiring him to reevaluate every aspect of how he lived his life. As Zak, who had known several other friends and loved ones who had previously been to rehab programs, said, "Unless you fully give yourself over, it's not going to be successful — people are all keen on the bottoming-out aspect. For different people that means different things."

Cruelly, details of Robin's rehab stay were published in the *National Enquirer* even before he had finished the program, a violation of the center's anonymity policy that forced him to make a public announcement that he was undergoing treatment. But he just took it in stride. "When I was in rehab," he explained, "somebody got out of rehab, and shared what I had told to a tabloid. Which was fucked up, and everybody in rehab got angry. I went, 'Hey man. It's out there. Somebody's going to make money off that shit.' But it was weird."

After he checked out of Hazelden that fall, Robin spent several subsequent weeks in a sober-living home, a transitional step between rehab and returning to his day-to-day life with Marsha and his children. A long road of Alcoholics Anonymous meetings and a con-stant self-scrutiny of his behavior lay ahead for him, but, as Zak pointed out, Robin also had a ready-made support system of fellow comedians waiting for him. "It's my estimation that community is really important in the recovery process, and comics — at least in my experience — are disproportionately more prone to using substances, and then recovering," Zak said. "He has a huge community of sober and active people, the comic community, there to support him."

Equipped with a new set of guiding principles, Robin was a changed man, but not entirely for the better. His relationship with Marsha could never be the same again: his return to drinking, which he had kept secret, was a fundamental deception — a catastrophic breach of faith inflicted by the person she was supposed to be able to trust completely and who was supposed to keep no secrets from her. The revelation of his relapse poisoned their marriage and caused her to question everything she knew and took for granted about him. If he could lie to her about this, what else could he lie to her about? After Robin's drinking was out in the open, and his episodes of blatant drunkenness were called out for what they were, Marsha was left to feel that the bond between them was a fragile tether he could break again if it suited him.

"I've had various friends who have fallen off the wagon in dramatic ways, and he was one of them," said Peter Asher. "For whatever reason, Robin was one of those people who, when he fell off the wagon, did it quite dramatically. And also, of course, you have the problem that if you're a celebrity, inevitably, you end up doing it publicly. You can't get away with away with a regrettable night on the town without it becoming a thing. Which must be very annoying. We all have indiscretions and they don't all get blasted all over the place."

For his part, Robin wasn't sure that he wanted things to go back to the way they used to be. Marsha was intertwined in every aspect of his life: she managed their household, attended to Zelda and Cody, ran their social calendar, helped choose his movies and the people he worked with, decided who got past her filter and who was kept away — maybe he saw himself differently than she did and desired other things for himself.

What he wanted, Zak surmised, was just to explore: "He had been married most of his adult life and wanted to just explore other things out there," he said. Perhaps this stagnant phase of his career was not an entirely bad thing; Robin could use this opportunity to take stock of himself in a way he hadn't been able to for a very long time. "When fame hit, it hit really hard," Zak said. "It was nonstop from twenty-seven years old, onward. It was just a ride. It's only when things slowed a little bit that he could assess the situation."

The decision that Robin and Marsha reached — gradually, over a period of many months, and with considerable reluctance — was that they should split up. They separated at the end of 2007.

It was how Robin had been taught to live since childhood: nothing is permanent, transition is constant. Anywhere can be home and anyone can be family, and you can always start over again in new places, with new people. Though it might seem a strange, even insensitive attitude to some, it reflected the essential way Robin saw the world. Reality was a medium that he could shape and manipulate, not some fixed and rigid thing; the temperament that made him spontaneous and capable of astonishing comic insight also made him unconcerned with traditional boundaries and accepted norms. In the words of the journalist Lillian Ross, who wrote extensively about Robin for the *New Yorker* and befriended him and became close with his family, "Robin was a genius, and genius doesn't produce normal men next door who are good family men and look after their wives and children. Genius requires its own way of looking at and living in the world, and it isn't always compatible with conventional ways of living."

Robin's choices had profound consequences for the people closest to him, and his separation from Marsha felt like another wound to a family that had already been hurt so much, the culmination to a series of problems that he alone had caused. Alex Mallick-Williams, who was Zak's girlfriend at the time and would marry him in 2008, said that in the years prior, "We were all in this warm glow of Marsha. She made everything perfect and beautiful. And when he fell off the wagon, it was almost like the light was turned out and went away."

His films from this period were unremarkable, an illustration of just how divergent and disconnected the strands of his career had become. Some were big, broad studio movies that paid him million-dollar salaries, like *RV*, a comedy that cast him as the head of a family on a slapstick cross-country journey; others were lower-budget dramas like *The Night Listener*, based on Armistead Maupin's novel about a radio host searching for a young memoirist who may or may not exist. None of these films was working, critically or commercially; even *Man of the Year*, a satire in which Robin played a comedian who is persuaded to run for president, and which marked his third collaboration with Barry Levinson, was a dud.

A lone exception was the last movie he had made before entering rehab, the family-oriented adventure *Night at the Museum*, which starred Ben Stiller as a watchman at the American Museum of Natural History, where the exhibits and models come magically to life after hours. Robin played an animated statue of Theodore Roosevelt, who roams the hallways on horseback and punctuates his pronouncements with shouts of "Bully!" Released at Christmas in 2006, *Night at the Museum* took in more than $250 million in the United States, surpassing *Mrs. Doubtfire* as the highest-grossing film that Robin had ever made. But it was hardly a project that owed its success to Robin's involvement, or that could be considered a starring vehicle for him; it was just another role, and he was merely a player in the ensemble.

Robin had given his assurance, in the weeks before his treatment started, that he would join Billy Crystal and Whoopi Goldberg in a 2006 edition of Comic Relief; it was the first time that the comedy benefit was being held since 1998 and it would now raise funds to aid the victims of Hurricane Katrina, which had struck New Orleans the year before. With the event scheduled for November 18, there were some concerns, around late September, that Robin might not attend, having only just completed his rehab stay. But sure enough, he was there to help kick off the show at Caesars Palace in Las Vegas, looking slightly diminished in a harlequin costume as he sang

"When the Saints Go Marching In" and danced with a Mardi Gras parade. At the end of the trio's traditional opening remarks, Crystal began to introduce the show's first stand-up performer, Ray Romano: "He's tall, he's white, he's Italian, everybody loves him —"

"Is it pinot grigio?" Robin asked. ("You're close," Crystal said, under his breath.) "You know, it's so great to get out of rehab and come right to Las Vegas," Robin continued. "Highballs and hookers and strippers, oh my."

"But it must be comforting to know that there really is an Eiffel Tower," Crystal told him.

"That's really good, I'm not hallucinating," Robin said in a mock-quavering voice.

Even after months of inactivity for Robin, his reliable give-and-take with Crystal had not lost its velocity, and he showed no hesitation about turning his personal difficulties into grist for their routine. But the rest of the show focused largely on a new generation of comics — Jon Stewart, Stephen Colbert, Sarah Silverman — who did not take any particular inspiration from Robin, Crystal, or Goldberg, and whose voices were better attuned to a cynical, self-aware moment. It was the last Comic Relief special that Robin would participate in.

Having put his career on pause so he could

attend rehab, Robin had to take what films were available to him when he started working again. These included trifling comedies like *License to Wed,* in which he played an overenthusiastic reverend advising a young couple who are about to get married; and *August Rush,* a drama that cast him as a Fagin-like figure who trains young homeless musicians in Washington Square Park. It was a sign of just how far Robin had fallen professionally, and how toxic his name had become, that critics felt no hesitation dismissing these movies with maximum scorn. One writer said of *License to Wed,* "There are few things that can make some viewers run screaming from a comedy faster than footage of Robin Williams hamming it up"; another said that Robin "is at his most annoying here."

The summer 2007 release of *License to Wed* coincided with the one-year anniversary of Robin's sobriety (at which point, he joked, "You get a small chip redeemable for one drink"), and he welcomed the occasion to promote the film and answer questions about his rehab experience. He fully accepted that his addiction would remain a lifelong responsibility and that he would never be able to say he had completely overcome it: "It's always there," Robin explained. "You'll always have a little bit of fear. You have to just keep at it."

He was understandably less forthcoming

about what was happening behind the scenes between him and Marsha, while they were still grappling with the question of whether they could keep their partnership alive. When one TV host innocuously asked him what the secret was to maintaining an eighteen-year marriage, Robin answered, "A wonderful wife. As a comedian, it's always difficult to say — a wife who's not afraid of me being free-range, in terms of having to perform so much. And also who's just extraordinary. Without that, I would be doomed. I think she is a gift." Asked later in the same interview to name someone who did not find him funny, Robin reflexively answered, "My wife."

What might have been a summer of renewal and reflection was overcast with sadness when Robin's half brother Todd died of heart failure on August 14. He was sixty-nine years old and had stood in Robin's mind as an adventurous, larger-than-life, seemingly immortal figure; as one of his colleagues at the winery he ran said of him, "The man essentially drove his life at ninety miles an hour until it went off a cliff. He enjoyed every minute he had on earth, and he's probably in heaven right now having a BLT with extra bacon and laughing his head off." Robin agreed, saying that Todd, a conspicuously heavy drinker in his day, was a man who "left a big footprint with a cork, or as a friend said, he left a great trail." For days and weeks afterward, Robin received letters of condolence from old friends of Todd's who knew him from the various bars he'd tended, and even from Valerie, who remembered Todd as someone "who loved sucking the juice out of life." She told Robin, "I hope you are enjoying your life more now that the addiction beast is at bay."

At the end of the year, Robin moved out of the San Francisco home that Marsha had helped design for the two of them. Zelda, who had turned eighteen the previous summer, was already living in Los Angeles while pursuing an acting career; Cody, who was sixteen, remained with Marsha. On March 21, 2008, a few days after the family returned from a final trip to Paris together, Marsha filed for divorce from Robin, citing irreconcilable differences.

They broke up their Blue Wolf production company, which, by this point, "was pretty much just an entity with nothing going on," said Cyndi McHale, who ran the company. "We had already closed the L.A. office, and then I closed the San Francisco office. They had fifty bins of joint storage, so I just weeded my way through that." Even as these connections between Robin and Marsha were being dissolved, McHale said, "They were still on good terms and they would still have lunch together. I think that they both were missing what they had. They were very supportive of each other, and they still did have a great deal of affection for each other."

In some part of Robin's mind, their marriage was not yet a lost cause. That summer, when he traveled to New York to make *Old Dogs* — another corny studio comedy in which he and John Travolta played business partners trying to raise twin children that Robin's character has only just learned that he fathered — he continued to call Marsha in San Francisco, in hopes of reconciling. "He was still wanting to come home," said Alex Mallick-Williams. "He was still wanting to go back to Marsha. Obviously, we wanted them to get back. But it was too much."

Even the hope that their divorce would be completed quickly and with as little acrimony as possible was dashed when Gerald Margolis, the Williams family's attorney, who had been Robin's lawyer since the dawn of his career, died from complications of pneumonia that September; he had been diagnosed with progressive muscular atrophy, a degenerative neurological disease, some years earlier. "He was going to mediate because they both trusted him, and they each had their own lawyer," said McHale, Margolis's widow. "And then he died and everything fell apart for about a year."

So Robin returned to Tiburon, where he'd started over once before some forty years earlier. It was where everyone knew him and knew also to give him his space, to let him run or ride his bike in peace, to treat him like an ordinary human being, even if their first impulse was to regard him as anything but. He bought himself a house on Paradise Cay, a small waterfront community where many of the homes have their own docks and the yachts to go with them; his residence, on a quiet stretch of road undocumented on Google Maps, was a comparatively simple, single-level dwelling marked only by a black fence, behind which sat a pair of comical simian gargoyles, one playing a panpipe and the other a flute.

As with many of Robin's past homes, its most cherished feature was hidden from view. As his friend Lisa Birnbach described it, "He had a huge room that was like a safe room — a bunker, no windows — with the most meticulously kept collections of soldiers from every war that soldiers were made. Historic ones. Glass ones. Metal ones. Gold ones. Lead ones. From Japan, from Germany. From the Boer War, the Spanish-American War. And then a lot of *Star Wars*-y stuff, too. I don't think he let people in that room much. And it was spotless. I think if you moved a soldier at all, he would know it. People wondered, why is he collecting them, still? But I think they were his friends."

In the serene surroundings, Robin attended his regular AA meetings and performed stand-up occasionally at the Throckmorton Theatre, a charmingly tumbledown three-hundred-seat space in nearby Mill Valley that offered him an island of visibility in a sea of anonymity. "When he dropped by, it's because he felt like going on or he just felt like hanging out, so we never put pressure on him to do a performance," said Mark Pitta, who had been a comedian with Robin in San Francisco in the 1970s and now hosted a weekly Tuesday night stand-up showcase at the theater. "Sometimes Robin would be in the green room hanging out, and we would love for him to go on. Lucy Mercer, who runs the theater, would always go, 'Would you like a Coca-Cola?' Just to get him some caffeine. And then when the headliner was about ten minutes from ending, I would say to him: 'Do you feel like playing today?' That's how casual it was."

It didn't take long for the community to become aware of Robin's affinity for the Throckmorton, and for theatergoers to turn out for the chance of catching one of his surprise appearances. One evening after ending his weekly show, Pitta recalled, "I said, 'Thanks, good night,' and the audience left, and I go in the wings and Robin is standing there. He goes, 'Can I play?' And I'm like, 'Oh, sure.' And I didn't reintroduce him. He just walked out and the audience started coming back in. Afterward, he said, 'You know, I needed that.' Sometimes he'd get his creative juices out just by holding court in the green room. But sometimes he needed to be onstage. Like we all do."

At the Throckmorton and at the Napa Valley Opera House near his ranch home, Robin started developing a new stand-up set that would consolidate all the suffering and woe he had lately experienced into a single, cleansing monologue; as if there were any doubt about who he held responsible for his spate of troubles, he titled the show *Weapons of Self Destruction.* He made no secret of the fact that a new tour would also help him fulfill the fiscal commitments of his day-to-day operations and to the two ex-wives he was now pledged to support. "Initially," Robin said, "I was going to call the tour *Remember the Alimony.* And they went, 'Maybe not.' "

"It was a financial thing of going, no movies are on the horizon, so I'll go back and make money the old-fashioned way — just go back out," he explained. "As a comic, it's one tool I have that I can use. And I'm not strapped. So much was happening, it was like, you're coming through some hardcore shit. When times are scary or weird, go and have a good laugh."

The national tour was announced in the summer of 2008 and got under way in the fall, but it did not get very far. At the start of

2009, as Robin reached Florida, he was hounded by a nagging cough he could not seem to shake; it grew worse, and, more worryingly, he also began experiencing spells of dizziness. With help from his manager David Steinberg, who was with him on the road, Robin was brought to a series of doctors in Miami who determined he had an irregular heartbeat, a damaged mitral valve in need of repair, and a broken aortic valve that would have to be replaced.

"I kept thinking it was a pulmonary thing," Robin recounted. "I had one doctor thinking it was a respiratory thing. I took these respiratory tests, I went no. And then when they finally did the angiogram, the angiogram just showed this valve that was like, *pfffffft,*" he said, making a raspberry noise. "It was just blown. It was crazy-ass. And then, what do we do?"

"They said, 'Ho, ho ho, he's not leaving here. Just hold on, we're going to operate tomorrow,' " Steinberg recalled. "I said, 'Relax. This is a pretty big decision. You don't just hop into it.' "

Robin also wanted to take a moment to consider his options before undertaking the dangerous but necessary procedure. "It wasn't like when Letterman went in with five blocked arteries, they said we have to do this tomorrow," he explained. "It was more like, you have time, but you don't want to push it.

You don't want to gamble."

Friends said that while Robin was weighing his options, he was also reckoning with just how close he had come to dying and how very near to him this terrifying possibility still lingered. A few days before he arrived in Florida, Robin had been in Austin, biking with Lance Armstrong, the champion cyclist. "We went for a short, easy, flat ride," Armstrong said. "He mentioned to me that he hadn't been riding that much, and wasn't in great shape. But he was really struggling on the bike. I just chalked it up to, he hadn't been on a bike in a while. Then a couple days went by, and he had those other symptoms that led him to the doctor, and then they found the bigger issue.

"It's pretty scary to think about," Armstrong said, "that you've got a bad valve, you're out on a ride and anything can happen out there. You wait a day or two and you come across that really stressful moment, either physically or emotionally, or a combination of all that, and it's over. You literally fall down, and if you're not around someone who can help, you're done. And that is a very profound thing to think about, and it changes you. There's just no telling, on a day like that, what would I have done? I'm not trained. It would have been — ugh." He did not finish the thought.

Dana Carvey, who had undergone multiple

angioplasties and a double bypass operation to unblock a coronary artery in the late 1990s, said that Robin reached out to him from Miami, seeking his advice. "He was extremely vulnerable that night he called me," Carvey said, "which is totally understandable, because he wasn't on his home turf. He was on tour and he's being told all these things. I was glad to talk to him. It was cathartic for me, I knew exactly where he was, emotionally, that night. Like, what's going on? And I was glad to be, like, no, this is an area I really know a lot about, and I have great context for it." After consultation with Carvey and his heart surgeon, P. K. Shah, Robin flew to the Cleveland Clinic in Ohio to make his final decision about the valve replacement.

"They said, 'Okay, here's the drill,' " Robin recalled. " 'You can go with a bovine valve, which we may have to replace, maybe not, in twenty years. Or if you get a mechanical heart, you never have to replace the valve, but you have to take a blood thinner, and if you don't get the dosage right, it can cause clotting.' Okay, I'll go bovine valve. I'll take door number one, Bobby, bovine."

Asked whether he considered the possibility that the surgery itself might be fatal, Robin replied, "I don't think you have time. If that's there, it's so deep in the back. It didn't really come up." Then, slipping into a booming, God-like voice: "*Hey, this may not go well.* Once you've made the decision, it's pretty much full-speed."

But friends said Robin was grappling with a fear they'd never seen him express before. "He was really wobbly and getting scared," Crystal said. "When he got to Cleveland for the surgery, we had these talks. He told me what the repairs were, and it was much more complicated than just doing a bypass. I said to him, this is like when astronauts go on the far side of the moon and they lose communication for like forty minutes. You want to make sure that they come back around the other side, and then you hear the static, and then, 'Hello, Houston.' So, I'll be Houston. When you come back from the far side, I'll be there."

From across the country, Robin's family members gathered at the hospital to be with him before the operation on March 13, 2009. Marsha, in the midst of the divorce proceedings, flew out from San Francisco; Zelda and Cody came, too, as did Zak and his wife, Alex, even though they felt they had been discouraged by Robin's managers. "His people were like, 'No, you shouldn't come,' " Alex said. "And we were like, 'Of course, we're going to come. We're not going to *not* be there if he needs heart surgery.' " No one was trying to prevent her and Zak from seeing Robin, she said, but the confusion was symptomatic of a power struggle that was always happening around Robin and which had grown more acute as the risks to his health intensified. "People always wanted to be Robin's Number One," she said. "I mean, I get it. He's a magnetic man. You would want to be his Number One. But he has a family, guys."

McLaurin Smith-Williams, Robin's surviving half brother, also came to Cleveland from his home in Memphis. One night before Robin's operation, the two of them went to dinner at a popular barbecue restaurant called Hot Sauce Williams — the name alone was irresistible — where Robin's unexpected presence quickly created a stir. "I think they must have called every cousin and relative in the city, because pretty soon the place filled up," McLaurin said. "One of the ladies in there, who was apparently a family member, she comes over to Robin and said, 'I'm going to be in the operating room — I'm one of the surgical nurses. I'll be there with you when they cut you open!' "

Even though Robin and Marsha's divorce was not yet finalized, his family knew that he had started dating other women again. They knew and had met his girlfriend Charlotte Filbert, a twenty-seven-year-old artist from New York whose paintings he had bought; and at the Cleveland Clinic, they were introduced to Susan Schneider, a forty-four-year-old artist and graphic designer who had been on tour with him when his heart problems became apparent. Susan had met Robin in October 2007 at an Apple Store in Marin, spotting him in camouflage clothing but, of course, immediately recognizing who he was. "How's the camo working for ya?" she teasingly asked him.

"Not too good," Robin answered.

"Oh, that's too bad," she said.

"Not really," he replied. "You found me."

As they spoke, Robin learned that Susan was a lifelong Marin resident who had earned a design degree from California College of the Arts in Oakland, and had two young sons, Peter and Casey, from a previous marriage that had ended in 2001. She was also a recovering alcoholic with twenty-three years' sobriety; he joked to her, using the falsetto child's voice from his comedy act, that she must have been an "alcotot" when she was in kindergarten. Eventually they started attending twelve-step meetings together.

Other members of Robin's family believed that he and Susan had already known each other from Alcoholics Anonymous before they had their Apple Store encounter. "I knew that they had met at AA," Zak said. "I learned that they met because Dad told me. They might not have spoken directly prior but I do know that they had attended the same meetings. And I knew that they moved very quickly in terms of their relationship."

Amid the anxiety and uncertainty of whether Robin would even survive the surgery or his recovery from it, his children were concerned that Susan was monopolizing their father. In a particularly awkward moment, Robin's surgeons offered his family a pager to hold on to during the procedure, which could be used to summon them on a moment's notice if any problems occurred. While Zak and Cody hesitated, each expecting the other to take the pager, they were startled when Susan claimed it for herself.

"We were hurt, as a family, that we weren't able to spend time with Dad," Zak later said. "As far as we knew, he wasn't going to make it out of heart surgery. It would be her last time with him as well. But we were worried and we had met her for the first time, and she had explicitly expressed a disinterest in getting to know us as people. Which is hard, because we're really into being supportive of family and community."

All of this was transpiring without Robin's awareness. When he woke up from his surgery, he was in the intensive care unit, attached to machines. Looking down at his shaved chest, he could see electric wires sprouting up as bountifully as the hair that previously grew there. He spent the next ten days connected to these various devices, including a morphine drip that he, a recovering alcoholic and drug addict, could activate whenever he was in pain — but only up to a point. "They do have a cut-off," he said, "so you can't just fall asleep going, ahhhhh. You can't just start wanking yourself." His intake of pain medications for his recovery would also have to be carefully monitored. "A lot of the drugs they give you are opiates," he said, "and your body goes, 'I know this shit. Let's go back on the train.' And you have to go, 'No.' "

For many years, Robin and Crystal had a custom of calling each other in various characters and guises and doing long riffs over the phone. "They used to be restricted to late at night, when he knew I was up, because we're both registered insomniacs," Crystal explained.

It was a tradition that Crystal modified slightly for Robin's recovery period. "I started leaving these messages as a guy named Vinny," he said, adopting a Brooklyn accent. " 'I'm Vinny, the valve guy. I've got your valve. I hope it's the right valve. Because the order number, I couldn't make out if it was a 652-C or a 652-G, so I brought both. Let me know what you need.' [beep] 'Hey, I haven't heard back from you. It's Vinny, the valve guy.' So that when he woke up, he'd have ten or twelve messages from Vinny the valve guy."

"Once he got out of all the anesthesia," Crystal said, "I got a call from him, just crying with laughter. 'My ribs hurt, boss, but oh my God, the valve guy.' "

He could already sense how his friend had emerged from the ordeal a new man. "When you go through a death scare," Crystal said, "you realize what he's realized: how short things are. They're not clichés, they're real. When you experience that, it just changes your point of view about life." In Robin's case, Crystal said it made him "be so much more attentive to friends and the kids, and needing that more. And wanting it more."

Once Robin was discharged from intensive care and returned home for further convalescence, he realized he felt different, too. What he desired most of all was human interaction, in whatever form he could receive it. "That's the weird thing after the heart surgery is, you appreciate every fucking connection with a person," he said. "It's so fucking amazing. Human contact after you've had heart surgery is pretty fucking valuable. You appreciate little things, like walks on the beach with a defibrillator."

18
THE TIGER IN WINTER

When David Letterman was recuperating from his quintuple bypass operation in 2000 and needed a prescription-strength dose of levity, Robin was the comedian he turned to. Nine years later, it was Letterman's time to return the favor, bringing him onto the *Late Show* for his first major post-surgery appearance. Robin was ostensibly there to promote his appearance in the comedy sequel *Night at the Museum: Battle of the Smithsonian,* but really, he wanted the world to see him healthy, restored, and exuberantly embracing existence. Dashing onto the stage of the Ed Sullivan Theater on the evening of May 12, 2009, in a neat gray suit, Robin threw open the jacket to reveal underneath a black T-shirt with a large white heart drawn on it. He playfully thanked Letterman "for the ambulance ride" and observed that they were both now members of the "brotherhood of the zipper chest," then broke into tears as he thanked by name the doctors who had overseen his surgery.

As they swapped war stories about their recoveries, Letterman started to say to Robin, "It's sort of thrilling to have that project, to bring yourself back." But Robin found his inspiration in something simpler: "To be alive!" During a commercial break, the host turned to Robin and privately asked him, "You ever get emotional after the open-heart surgery?" Robin felt his eyes welling up with tears once again as he answered, "Fuck yeah."

"It was very much like shorthand between two survivors," Robin later said. "You really do get weepy, like, 'Oh, a kitten.' 'Oh my God, did you see that flower?' Butch up, motherfucker."

He could only speculate as to why he was more receptive and sentimental in his post-surgical state. "I think, literally, because you have cracked the chest," he said, explaining that men, in particular, clad themselves in a layer of armor, but once it is pierced — here he mimed his rib cage being broken open — "It's like, 'Babies! My babies!' You are vulnerable, totally, for the first time since birth. You're heavily medicated and the only thing you're missing is a tit. If they had that after surgery, a lot more people would go, yeah. 'You want more drugs?' No, a tit."

Friends like Eric Idle and Bobcat Goldthwait, who spent portions of the summer visiting Robin at his Napa ranch while he rested and regained his strength, felt they saw a new spirit sweep over him. Comedy had never been a mere occupation for Robin; it was always an expression of some inner need to spread joy and please people. But now it had become even more important; it was a mechanism for survival, to remind himself that he was lucky to have survived and that he should savor every moment of his latest act.

"Comedy is life-affirming," Idle explained. "Better to be here and funny than not. It's all inevitable, so it's about optimism in the face of inevitable disaster." Robin, he said, "was back, but he was calmer, it seemed to me. He wasn't frenetic. He was mellower."

Goldthwait agreed he had seen "a bit of a rebirth in Robin" and that his friend seemed "the happiest I've seen him in years." "I guess almost dying will give you a sense of gratitude," he said.

"Most comedians are wired with a sense of self-loathing," Goldthwait said, and what he and Robin had in common was that neither of them could readily accept "that we are enough that people will be happy with that. We always have to be on, or working. And people are happy when he's *not* on, which, with the amount of self-loathing we have, is really hard for us to accept."

Given the spate of suffering that Robin had

experienced in recent years — the descent into alcoholism, the divorce from Marsha, the open-heart surgery — Idle said, "If you come out, you realize you've been given a gift, and that it can't all be about you. He's always been a good dad, a loving dad, tried hard to be a good father, a good husband. It's not easy."

One of Robin's next post-recovery appearances was in a movie that Goldthwait wrote and directed called *World's Greatest Dad,* whose title was hardly intended as a compliment. In this scathing black comedy, Robin portrayed Lance, a high school English teacher with frustrated literary ambitions and a monstrous teenage son. When his son accidentally dies by hanging himself in an act of autoerotic asphyxiation gone awry, Lance forges a suicide note to cover up the circumstances of his death. That note, once obtained by the students and faculty at Lance's school, becomes a kind of viral sensation, and Lance gains the opportunity to build a prosperous writing career with further forgeries published under his dead son's name — so long as he never reveals that he is the true author of these works.

World's Greatest Dad was the first movie Robin had made with Goldthwait since *Shakes the Clown,* Goldthwait's 1991 directorial debut about a down-on-his-luck birthday party entertainer, in which Robin had a cameo as an aggressive mime instructor. Like its predecessor, *World's Greatest Dad* was a low-budget independent feature — one shot before the halted *Weapons of Self Destruction* tour, and which would receive only a limited theatrical release in the summer of 2009 — and Robin's decision to take the lead role was one that Goldthwait interpreted as a significant gesture of trust and friendship. "He's always acted like we're peers, which, clearly, we're not," Goldthwait said.

As far as Robin was concerned, he was simply supporting an artist he respected and a script he genuinely responded to. "I wanted to play it," he said. "It was not like, 'Oh, this'll be a favor — help little Bobby.' No, it's actually a part that I went, 'I like this.' I joked with him after the movie, it's like *Dead Penis Society.* I liked the fact that it deals with the relationship between a boy and a single father. Their relationship is so strained, and everything that the parent does isn't working."

Naturally Robin could not help but take the opportunity to reflect on his relationships with his own children, all of whom were now young adults. He did not deny that these bonds had been tested at times, but he believed that his sobriety had strengthened them. "Sometimes it's *Lord of the Flies* and other times it's, 'Ooh, they're angels,' " he said. "There have been phases with all of them where it's been rough, and they come through it. I'm totally a work in progress. I'm learning and trying. But right now I'm at a point where I can go, 'Yeah, I love them. Everything about them. The good and the bad.' I think they say the same about me. As an alcoholic, that's a great gift."

Zak, who was now twenty-six years old, in the first year of his marriage to Alex and living in New York, felt connected to Robin in ways he never had before — less like a traditional parent and child than like peers who could apply an unsparing eye to each other's lives and offer candid advice.

"There's no expectation for you to be a father figure," Zak would tell him. "You're relinquished of your duties as such. I'm here as your friend."

At times, Zak found himself playing the role of guardian and caregiver to Robin, offering him support and encouragement in his moments of insecurity. "Dad's happiness was correlated very much to how he was doing, career-wise," Zak said. "When there were films that would be less successful, he took it very personally. He took it as a personal attack. That was really hard for us to see."

Robin was afraid of disapproval and rejection, and at a certain point his need for acceptance led to a prohibitive excess of caution.

"I think it was hard to take a leap into

things, because validation was so important for him," Zak said. "There's a challenge there, when people validating the projects know what they want for you, and that leads to a specific way in which your business gets done. His team was great at giving him latitude to work on the projects he wanted to work on. But the industry was changing. I used to joke with Dad, 'Al Pacino wouldn't make it as a celebrity today. A small, mousy Italian?' "

Robin also recognized that "he was no longer the leading role that he wanted to be," Zak said, but his fears that he couldn't navigate the complexities of contemporary entertainment inhibited him from branching out into other disciplines.

"Dad was extraordinarily intimidated by the business side of the biz," Zak said. "That broke my heart. Because he was brilliant. He was a polymath. He could put things together. He could do anything. But I think that he felt that there was a side to the movie business that he didn't want to touch, that kept him in front of the camera. That was challenging for me, because I always wanted to push him to do more things: Write, direct, produce. He felt that it wasn't for him. He was an entertainer at heart."

By the fall of 2009, Robin was ready to resume the *Weapons of Self Destruction* tour he'd had to postpone, with an itinerary that revisited all the cities he'd missed, running from September 30 in Bloomington, Indiana, through December 5 in Las Vegas. His Washington, DC, performances on November 20 and 21 would be taped for an HBO special to air in December.

Robin seemed to be motivated by an urgent need to talk to audiences about everything he'd experienced. "It would be insane *not* to talk about it," he said. " 'So what happened?' 'Nothing.' It's what's happened, and everyone knows."

Billy Crystal saw this compulsion in him, too. "From our intense conversations and experiences over the last couple of years, especially with his divorce and the illness, and the pain that he's gone through, his brain is the one thing that's kept him buoyant," he said of Robin. "I think he needs the stand-up in a different way than he did before. It's still a safe place for him to be, but he can talk about things and make himself feel better, not just everybody else."

In truth, the ninety-minute set, whose central onstage image was a photograph of Robin's face with a piece of tape across his mouth labeled "DANGER," still featured a fair amount of shtick. From its opening, in which Robin, dressed entirely in black, would take the stage to the thunderous rumble of the aggressive Kid Rock anthem "Bawitdaba," the performance retained much of the truculence and coarseness of his 2002 tour; the stock voices he used for gay, black, Jewish, Asian, and Southern people were still flaunted like faded college T-shirts; and there were one-liners about Barack Obama, Joe Biden, Sarah Palin, and George W. Bush, attempts at topicality that still felt alien to Robin's act, but which could be easily revised and interchanged from show to show.

As David Steinberg, his manager, explained, all he had to do was glance at a newspaper or TV show, feed Robin a headline, and the material practically wrote itself. "I lob him softballs, and then he makes them Robin," Steinberg said. "It's a pretty good job."

Occasionally, Robin made use of other writers, including Mason Steinberg, David Steinberg's son, a resource that some members of his team did not feel he necessarily needed. Cyndi McHale, who had been in charge of Blue Wolf and worked as a travel coordinator on *Weapons of Self Destruction,* said that David Steinberg persuaded Robin to bring Mason on board by leaning on Robin's fear of irrelevance. "He got that by saying, 'You're not reaching out to kids, the younger generation. They're just not getting it. You need fresh, new material,' " she explained. "And then he installed his son to do it. To me, Robin never needed a writer. He's brilliant. How do you tell Robin what to say or do? You leave him alone and let him. He's just a genius. But everybody comes at it from their own perspective."

Beneath its calcified outer shell, however, the show contained an inner core of confession, a deeper layer of truthfulness that Robin was trying to work into his act. As he later said, he had faith that an audience well versed in his recent woes would turn out for the resuscitated tour, just to see if he was still standing. "And you're alive," he said, with a satisfied laugh, "and you're not like, [pretending to speak through an electrolarynx] 'Thank you for coming. Nice to be here. Wonderful audience.' It's a bit of that, and then, 'Whaddaya got? What's new?' "

Beyond that, Robin wondered, "How much more can you give? Other than, literally, open-heart surgery onstage? Not much. That's about it. But it is actually cool to talk about this shit."

About fifteen minutes into the set, Robin offered the first real window into his life, with a long riff on his open-heart surgery. He talked about the symptoms and examinations that led up to it: "An angiogram is where they go through your groin to your heart," he explained, "and who knew that the way to a man's heart was through his groin? Many women are going, we've known that forever." And he explained why he had been tempted to choose a porcine replacement valve: "Because you're already inoculated for swine flu. And one of the side effects is you can find truffles, which is kind of cool."

He was clear-eyed, too, about the many missteps he'd made lately in his film career, joking in a bit about his car's GPS system: "I was driving across the Golden Gate Bridge. I was halfway across, and all of a sudden, the car went, 'Take a right turn.' What? No can do, HAL. Not that depressed, really. And the car went, 'Really, Robin? I saw *Bicentennial Man.*' Shut the fuck up! Damn you."

He was more circumspect about making reference to his divorce, never mentioning Marsha by name and quipping only obliquely, "In marriage, I've learned this: There's penalties for early withdrawal and depositing in another account. Remember that."

But when, at the show's one-hour mark, Robin turned to the subject of alcoholism, he went in with a vengeance, delivering a fiery comic jeremiad that made an angry mockery of the kind of misbehavior he'd engaged in at the height of his addiction. He ridiculed the wanton selfishness of the compulsive drinker and gave a brief but vehement recitation of the warning signs of alcoholism, such as, "After a night of heavy drinking, you wake up fully clothed, going, 'Hey, somebody shit in my pants!'"

"There's a voice that tells alcoholics that we can drink," Robin said in the routine. "It's the same voice that you hear if you go up to the top of a very large building, and you look over the side — there's a little voice that goes, [small, squeaky sound] 'Jump! You can fly!' " Even the tour's promotional materials featured self-flagellating jokes that sounded as if they'd come straight from a twelve-step meeting, like his one-liner, printed across the official *Weapons of Self Destruction* tour program, that describes an alcoholic as someone who "violates their standards faster than they can lower them."

Under closer examination, these were not routines where Robin actually talked about himself. "It's *like* me," he explained, "but not totally me. It's based on what happened, but is it the actual incident? No. To protect others? Maybe. I haven't had the balls to talk about it full-out. In a room full of alcoholics, I can."

Robin was especially pleased with one bit, clearly based on personal experience, in which he talked about the process of bottoming out. Alcoholics, he said, "can't wait to shit on everybody, family, friends." Throwing up his middle fingers like they were sharpened blades, he exclaimed, "We'll be like, 'Fuck you! Fuck you! Fuck you! Fuck you! Go fuck yourself! Fuck you! Fuck you!" Then, unexpectedly, he pointed his middle fingers back at himself. In a quieter tone, he said, "I'm fucked."

After having performed that scene a number

of times on the road and hearing it silence his crowds, Robin later explained, "There was a moment where the whole audience went, 'Ohhh.' And I went, *that's* the moment."

In his experience, Robin said, "You have to give up. That's the time when you finally do have hope. That's that weird thing when you're totally fucking alone. That's the moment when the help begins."

The honesty that Robin expressed onstage inspired a mutual openness in his fans, like the one who gave him a hand-written note after a performance in Atlanta that read:

> *Thank you for saving me.* You are a great person and you give so much of yourself to others. My son died of cancer and without you I would not have made it thru.
>
> Just remember I would go to Hell to bring you back. If you need me. I love you!! I know you hear this all the time — But you were there for me.

That kind of adoration flattered Robin, but it frightened him, too — not that he worried these people would want too much from him, but that he would inevitably let them down. "What's your credibility?" he asked himself, after letting out a loud, delighted cackle. "Why are you looking to me for advice? You come to me? Isn't there someone more qualified?"

It made him reflect on his friend Richard Pryor, whose personal suffering he could perhaps finally match but whose truthfulness he could never seem to equal. "The most honest person I ever knew in comedy was Pryor," he said. "He literally would talk about dying, being in the hospital after burning himself alive. He's covered in ice, steam is coming off of him, and he's got an orderly going, 'Hey, Richard, how about that last autograph?' He basically made fun of the fact that he died and came back from it."

Honesty could also be a danger, as Robin knew: "Relentlessly honest people, they're almost frightening to be around," he said. " 'You're fat.' Thank you." But as he continued to chart a course back to sobriety and integrity, he felt he had to embrace a policy of total candor: "That's the only cure you have right now, is the honesty of going, 'This is who you are.' I know who I am."

As the *Weapons of Self Destruction* tour reached its conclusion at the end of 2009, Robin seemed to have found a new sense of calmness and order. Even though his movies were entering and exiting theaters with little notice or impact, he was happy in Tiburon and able to reconnect with people who had been absent from his life for many years. "Our relationship started up again after he divorced Marsha," said Valerie. "And we had a rich texting relationship. It was very sweet, but guarded, in that there was no romance. There was just a deep love and caring. He could let the love flow again, I guess, which is a hippie way of putting it."

He remained a fixture at the Throckmorton Theatre in Mill Valley, where sometimes he'd go out and perform comedy if the mood struck him, or just sit up in the lighting booth and make quiet whistling noises to himself and his pals as he watched other stand-ups fumble their way through their sets. "I'd be onstage and he'd be up in one of the boxes," said Marc Maron. "Any time a joke would not do as well as I anticipated, I'd hear him up there, going, 'Ohohohohoho.' "

"Even if you were trying out new stuff and the crowd stared at you, they liked you," said Steven Pearl, another Throckmorton regular. "And even Robin got stared at there. He'd do some joke, it wouldn't go over — 'Ooh, needs work. Needs work.' But the crowd, they're just good, friendly people."

Though his star had dimmed, Robin was still a vastly more recognizable performer than the journeyman comics who played there regularly; they treated him like an equal and tried not to be awed by his celebrity, but deep down they knew that his presence there was special. "His face was as known as the Coca-Cola logo, and he had zillions of dollars," said Pearl. "It was like Muddy Waters walking into a blues club in Chicago. 'Hey,

636

the old man's here!' "

Robin didn't come to the Throckmorton to be idolized, but he did benefit emotionally from his visits. When he was at the theater, Pearl said, "He was one of the guys. We were just a bunch of crazy people hanging out and making each other laugh. And that's what it was. He was like any of my other friends — I didn't love him any more or any less."

Many of the Throckmorton comics were also introduced to Susan Schneider, who was now in a serious committed relationship with Robin; they saw her as a positive, healing influence in his life. "I met Susan in the green room," said Mark Pitta. "For three months I called her Cindy and she never corrected me. I thought that was cute. When she was out of the room, I would tell him, 'Man, she's like a bright light when she walks in here. So tall and smiley. She had really good energy.' One time, when she came back in the room, Robin looked at her and he says, 'He says you're a bright light!' But that was sweet."

Other longtime friends of Robin's, who had known him through his nearly twenty years of marriage to Marsha, saw Susan as a very different woman from his second wife. She was more focused on her own art and not interested in being Robin's professional col- laborator, which was perhaps what Robin needed at that moment. "She loved taking him to her yoga studio for her gallery openings and things like that," said Cyndi Mc-Hale. "Susan was warm and friendly and inclusive for quite a while. She didn't want anything to do with his business. She just wanted to paint."

"Robin wasn't a guy that entertained," Billy Crystal said. "As a couple, Marsha did all that — Thanksgivings and big functions — so it was different with Susan. It was an adjustment to get to know her, because we were and still are so close with Marsha. What do you do in those situations? We got to know her a little bit."

Marsha had first come into Robin's life as an employee before she was his romantic partner or spouse, but Susan did not have the same preparation, and she approached their relationship differently. As Wendy Asher explained, "Marsha worked for him for a while. Before they were even together, she knew Robin really well. She traveled with him. So she knew exactly what she was getting into. And she also knew how to take care of Robin. Robin needed someone to take care of him, and it wasn't that difficult, if you're aware of things. Marsha organized every single thing. She's an organizer. And Susan wanted people to take care of her. Things were just not the same."

Privately, Robin told Susan that he had been diagnosed with depression and was taking medication to treat it; as he put it to her, he had been on enough Effexor "to cheer up a whole army of elephants." But he was also working with a psychiatrist to get off of prescription drugs, and over time, she said, "I watched a happy man emerge."

But as Robin stopped using antidepressants, Susan also became familiar with the fuller spectrum of his emotions and the fears he had about his professional standing. "The line of work he was in bred anxiety and self-centered concerns," she said. "He would always say, 'You're only as good as your last performance.' Some insecurities were just hard-wired into him from childhood, or genetic, or he'd picked them up in reaction to bad experiences in life."

McLaurin, his half brother, had been making occasional trips to the Bay Area from his home in Memphis to spend more time with Robin. They talked about science, math, and military history and visited bookstores: Robin gave him gifts of rare and antique editions that included experimental proofs of Sir Isaac Newton's *Philosophy* from 1721 and an original edition of Mark Twain's *Sketches New and Old* from 1875. McLaurin, too, saw Robin grapple with a fluctuating sense of his self-worth. "He was very modest about his career," McLaurin said. "We were having lunch somewhere and he said, 'You know, that waiter, he has as much talent as I do.' He said, 'I just had a bunch of breaks.' And that was his attitude: I don't know why I'm so famous. I don't do anything particularly special. He actually thought that."

In the spring of 2009, David Steinberg learned from his wife about a play she had seen at the Kirk Douglas Theatre in Culver City called *Bengal Tiger at the Baghdad Zoo.* Written by Rajiv Joseph, it was a bleak, existential comedy-drama set in Iraq during the early, chaotic days following the US-led invasion and overthrow of Saddam Hussein in 2003. Its principal characters included the Tiger, who in the first scene is shot to death by American soldiers after he bites off a Marine's hand. He wanders as a ghost through the rest of the play, offering sarcastic commentary on the nature of being and not being; when he sees his own dead body from the outside, he muses:

> So that's what I look like. You go your whole life never knowing how you look. And then there you are. You get hungry, you get stupid, you get shot and die. And you get this quick glimpse at how you look, to those around you, to the world. It's never what you thought. And then it's over. Curtains. Ka-boom.

Later in the play, when another character joins him in the afterlife and asks him what happens next, the Tiger responds, "I'll tell

640

you what happens: God leans down just close enough and whispers into your ear: *Go fuck yourself.* And then He's gone."

The Tiger is portrayed by an actor who walks upright and wears no special costume; as an author's note from Joseph indicates, "The Tiger can be any age, although ideally he is older, scrappy, past his prime, yet still tough. He can be any race except Middle-Eastern. His language is loose, casual; his profanity is second nature." In 2010, *Bengal Tiger at the Baghdad Zoo* was named a finalist for the Pulitzer Prize, and a Broadway transfer was put in motion; when an established star was needed to play the title role in this production, Robin's name was at the top of that wish list.

The play had Steinberg's approval and soon Robin's as well. Once he was able to review the script for himself, Robin said, "It just hit me hard, it was so powerful." He responded to what he called "the Buddhist nature" of the story: "It's all these ghosts wandering around, talking and gaining more consciousness as they continue through the play." (And, he said, "I'm hairy enough to be a tiger, so that's good.") In an acting career that spanned more than three decades, he had yet to make his Broadway debut (his 2002 stand-up performance notwithstanding); the closest he had previously come was his role in the problematic 1988 run of *Waiting for Godot* with Steve Martin. By comparison, Robin said *Bengal Tiger at the Baghdad Zoo* was "like Beckett but even darker, which is hard to do."

Moisés Kaufman, who had directed the play's productions in 2009 and 2010 and would direct it on Broadway, introduced himself to Robin in a telephone call. Kaufman had grown up in Venezuela watching dubbed reruns of the popular sitcom *Mork y Mindy,* and he expected to be intimidated by Robin but found him humble, open-minded, and eager to get to work. "Before I hung up," Kaufman recalled, "he said, 'Okay, boss. I'll read the play again, let's meet and we'll talk.' He called me boss. It was very moving." In a face-to-face conversation at his home in Tiburon, Robin explained to Kaufman that his USO trips to the Middle East had strongly influenced his decision to take on the role. "He had been spending a lot of time with soldiers," Kaufman said. "He would go and perform for them, and he would see what these kids were going through. And he felt that this is the only piece of writing he had seen that spoke to him about the experience of the kids over there. Because these characters both suffered so much."

Robyn Goodman, a lead producer of the Broadway production, had also gotten to know Robin and Susan in the process of recruiting him, and she believed his interests in the play ran even deeper. What Robin connected with, Goodman said, were its underlying themes: "the pressures of war, which are a little bit like the pressures of mortality, or exactly like it, in some cases. The play was about defining your moral constructs under pressure, and I think Robin always felt under pressure. There was something in that play, and that part, that was asking the big questions about why we're alive and how we behave, morally, in situations." Now that Robin had his sobriety, his heart surgery, and Susan, "finally he was making good choices in life," said Goodman. "He was taking care of himself."

Goodman came to feel that Susan was an essential match for Robin at this stage of his life — a friend, a fellow traveler, and a creative talent in her own right. She found Susan's paintings so fascinating that Goodman eventually bought one for herself, an oil work that Goodman described as a "very tumultuous, dark setting of a sea and a storm. There was something wild about it that I really loved. There's an emotion in her painting that I respond to."

The play was a risky proposition for Robin: it required a commitment of at least five months in New York, from rehearsals to opening to its hopeful inclusion in the Tony

Awards, during which time he could not make a movie or appear in other projects that required substantial amounts of his time. There was a chance the play could run longer if it succeeded and much shorter if it failed; despite his Juilliard training, he knew nothing about the business of theater, particularly as it was practiced on Broadway in 2011.

But accepting the challenge gave him clarity about what he wanted to be doing as an actor, what he wanted his life to look like going forward, and the people he wanted around him. Knowing that he and Susan would be separated for much of the time he was in New York, he proposed to her just before he left Tiburon; they did not immediately set a wedding date but planned for Susan to come out and visit him every week while he did the play.

That February, Robin began his work in earnest. As Kaufman recalled, "When the costume designer came in, as he was taking his measurements, Robin said to him, 'Okay, thank you, boss.' I was like, 'Dude, you call *everybody* boss! There's nothing special about boss!' I always teased him. I said, 'I'm going to call you boss, too.' It became a running joke."

In the rehearsal room, the director and the cast observed that the Robin who showed up was not a self-important superstar but a curious craftsman who was eager to put in the hours. "He was interested in the beat of the play and very collaborative," Kaufman said. "Any note that I gave him, the first words out of his mouth were, 'It sounds very interesting. Let me try it.' That didn't mean he always agreed! But we had conversations about it, and we were both on a journey of discovery. He was so willing to try anything and so excited by the process. He was having the life of a working actor and that gave him so much joy."

When previews of the play started at the Richard Rodgers Theatre on March 11, Robin was ready and off-book, with his ad-libbing impulses bound and gagged for the duration of the run. "He never improvised," Kaufman said. "It was always the text that Rajiv wrote. Every single word. There was never any question of improvisation. That was never even discussed. He always did the text, and he always did it perfectly, to the letter." Susan, who watched him work rigorous eight-show weeks with two performances each on Wednesdays and Saturdays, was astonished by his capacity to assimilate and retain the material. "He was always on top of it," she said. "The show schedule was intense and his memory skills herculean."

Little by little, Robin began to open up to his costars, including Arian Moayed, who played an Iraqi translator who works for the US soldiers, and whose dressing room was opposite Robin's. During intermissions, Robin would occasionally slip into his room, close the door only partway, "and he'd be like, 'How do you think it's going tonight, boss?' " Moayed recalled. "And I was like, 'Good.' 'Did you notice something I was trying in that first scene?' " Eventually, Moayed realized what Robin was really asking for in these moments: "I was like, of course, he's just like us — he needs the validation," he said. "In the grand scheme of the audience, if you saw this show two times, back to back, you would not notice the difference. But for us, it's monumental. Those small, minute things are what we all try to do in the game of making art. We try to perfect and perfect and perfect. And it's never perfect."

As performances continued, Moayed gained glimpses into Robin's world beyond his work, and a values system in which sobriety and charity had become inextricably connected. After one show, Moayed said, "a guy came up to me, with tattoos and a Mohawk and he must have been, like, twenty-seven. And I was like, 'Hey.' I didn't know who he was. He was very kind, and I was like, 'How do you know anyone here?' And he's like, 'Oh, yeah, Robin's my sponsor. And he flew me out.' I was like, 'Shut the fuck up.' " Later on, Moayed mentioned this encounter to Robin, who seemed unsurprised by it. "Robin was like, 'Yeah, I had to put him in rehab,' " he said. "I was like, 'Are you fucking kidding me with this right now? *Who are you?*' "

On the play's official opening night of March 31, 2011, Robin was showered with notes of celebration and good wishes, sent by his friends and representatives, that ran the gamut from formal sincerity to inappropriate silliness. His CAA agents passed along a card saying they had symbolically adopted a tiger through the World Wildlife Fund, while his managers sent a phony autographed picture of the stage-magic duo Siegfried and Roy, whose cofounder Roy Horn had been mauled in a 2003 tiger attack. The fake inscription read, "To our big cat, We would love to give you a kiss on your opening, but we are in Las Vegas." It was signed, "Siegfried + What's left of Roy."

The major reviews of the play were exuberantly positive and seemed to promise a healthy commercial run, with plenty of praise directed at Robin for his interpretation of the wisecracking Tiger. The *New York Times,* in an appraisal written by Charles Isherwood, called *Bengal Tiger* a "smart, savagely funny and visionary new work of American theater." Though Isherwood deemed Robin's casting a "standard concession to the celebrity-centric economy of today's theater," he also wrote that "the kinetic comic who has sometimes revealed a marshmallowy streak in movies, never indulges the audience's hunger for displays of humorous invention or pinpricks of poignancy. He gives a performance of focused intelligence and integrity, embodying the animal who becomes the play's questioning conscience with a savage bite that never loosens its grip." The *Hollywood Reporter* had its own unique take: "Think of him as Lenny Bruce meets Friedrich Nietzsche in the body of a man-eating predator."

But *Bengal Tiger* failed to capture the attention of theatergoers. Audience members who were drawn in by Robin's name and the promise of seeing him live onstage were presented with a challenging work, unlike anything he had previously appeared in and not so easy to laugh at. Just look at the marquee of the Richard Rodgers Theatre, Moayed observed: "It says Robin Williams, and then, underneath it, *Bengal Tiger at the Baghdad Zoo.* The title is so funky that it could be the title for a comedy. After the first previews, I'd always go to the ushers and be like, 'What are they saying?' And they're like, 'By intermission, they're like, we thought this was stand-up.' So that was definitely part of the case."

Robyn Goodman, its lead producer, pointed to a fundamental mismatch between the material and what ticket buyers expected of Robin. "If you take a famous singer and you put them in a play where they don't sing, audiences really don't want to see them," she said. "We were still embroiled in Afghanistan and Iraq, and it had the word *Baghdad* in the title. I don't think people wanted to see a play about war at that point."

In a further setback, when nominations for the Tony Awards were announced on May 3, Robin was shut out of the category for Best Performance by an Actor in a Leading Role in a Play. *Bengal Tiger* was not among the contenders for Best Play, either, though Moayed was nominated for Best Performance by an Actor in a Featured Role in a Play. One of the congratulatory phone calls Moayed received after the announcement was from Robin. "He called me that morning," Moayed said, "and I was very uncomfortable. I was sad, but I didn't want to show him that. And I remember saying, 'Robin, I can't believe it. I'm so sorry you didn't get nominated. I feel terrible about it.' And he goes, 'Ah, forget it. Don't worry about it. Hey, what can you do?' " Robin seemed more concerned the play itself had been overlooked. "You could hear it in his voice," said Moayed. "He goes, 'That just doesn't make any sense.' He was feeling what we were feeling."

In a separate conversation with Rajiv Joseph, the playwright, Moayed said, "I just broke down in tears, because I was like, this is not fair. This wasn't the point. Robin is so fucking good in this. I was like, he's a fucking star and he deserves it. When he didn't get nominated, the whole thing felt like a fuck-you, to be quite honest."

Joseph said that the lack of a Tony nomination for Robin was a bitter blow to the show's cast and collaborators. "We wanted him to have an EGOT," Joseph said, referring to the rare show-business achievement of winning an Emmy, a Grammy, an Oscar, and a Tony. "He deserved one. It was a real tough year, but that made me mad, that he didn't get a nomination. I think he deserved one." Despite the snub, Robin dutifully appeared as a presenter at the Tony Awards in June to announce the winners for Best Book of a Musical. ("This is an incredible room," he said to the audience at the Beacon Theatre. "The only beard here is on my face.")

On July 3, *Bengal Tiger* closed, having played just 108 performances. Though this was a disappointment by Broadway standards, producer Robyn Goodman said she did not want Robin to be discouraged by the experience. "I wrote Susan afterwards," she explained, "and I said, 'Please tell Robin not to be angry at Broadway or the audiences or the Tony voters. Sometimes you hit the zeitgeist, and sometimes you're against the zeitgeist. And he was so wonderful that he must at some point come back to Broadway and do a play again. This shouldn't be his last experience.' "

Robin turned sixty on July 21, and while

his journey to this age had hardly been free of grievous injury and physical catastrophe, at least he could say that the past year was markedly healthier than those that had immediately preceded it. About the worst he had suffered physically was the development of a slight, intermittent tremor in his left hand, which he believed was the lingering result of a past shoulder injury. Back in the Bay Area, he celebrated his birthday a few days early, on July 16, at the Cavallo Point luxury hotel and lodge in Sausalito. The invitations were embossed with the silhouette of a hummingbird, an animal whose energy, flightiness, and constant movement seemed to perfectly embody the evening's honoree, and the guest list consisted of almost every valued person who had figured into Robin's life, even the cast members from *Bengal Tiger,* who were flown out to California for the occasion. Robin danced with Susan; he danced with Billy Crystal's wife, Janice; he danced with Crystal.

Throughout the evening, attendees could watch a continuous video loop of birthday testimonials recorded by friends, collaborators, and loved ones, including Susan (who painted him a picture of a cupcake), Steven Spielberg, Larry Brezner, Al Pacino, Barry Levinson, Chris Columbus, Peter and Wendy Asher, Whoopi Goldberg, and Robert De Niro. Even Mort Sahl, the irascible satirist and nightclub comedian of the 1950s and '60s, who had also become a regular at the Throckmorton Theatre and a friend of Robin and Susan's, contributed warm words of encouragement. "Your life is like a movie," Sahl said in his video segment. "And in this movie, you get the girl."

The celebration was something of a dry run for the more intimate event that followed three months later, when Robin and Susan were married on October 22, 2011. The outdoor wedding ceremony was held at the Meadowood Napa Valley resort in front of about 130 guests, including Robin's three children and Susan's two sons; the bride was dressed in a strapless ivory and blush-colored gown with a train, while the groom wore a tuxedo. Robin's best man was Bobcat Goldthwait, who had also put together an unusual bachelor party for him at a Tiburon restaurant. Mark Pitta recalled, "Bobcat decided to get a fat stripper to dress like Charlie Chaplin. I was looking at Mort Sahl like, when is this going to end? I can't eat my food."

The ceremony was officiated by the Reverend Peadar Dalton, a former Catholic priest whom Robin had seen speak at a memorial service. "He said he was particularly touched with my analogy of death being similar to birth," Dalton said. "I had said that when a baby is born they don't know what they are being born into — but they are being born into a fuller experience of life and love with their families. Death is the same. In my opinion we are not dying — we're born into another experience that is greater than ourselves and that is an extension of what it is to love and be loved."

Though the nuptials had been meant to end with the release of trained doves, nature intervened with an earlier display. "This white butterfly appears out of nowhere and goes straight down the aisle and flies over, between them and above them, and flies away," the comedian Rick Overton recalled. "Who pays for that service? Everyone's getting their phones out, looking on Google — who does that? If I'm the dove guy, I'm going, 'Oh, well, fuck me. I've got the whole dove thing and this butterfly shows up?' It just happened. We chose to make that a good omen."

The reception that followed seemed to encapsulate the life of a man who had touched the summit of superstardom but treasured his perception as a man of the people. There was a caricature artist, like the kind that would be found at a street fair; there were the working-stiff comics Robin knew from the Throckmorton; and there were the guests who were so famous they intimidated the other guests. "It was like high school," said Mark Pitta. "There was a clique going on. I was talking to people that I knew, then I look over and there was Billy Crystal and Bobcat and George Lucas, all off to the other side. Like. But Robin was like a host. He said hi to everybody, spent time with people, made sure everything was cool."

The wedding was a more fraught affair for those friends of Robin's who also felt they owed their allegiance to Marsha and were not sure whether to attend the ceremony. Even for Peter and Wendy Asher, it was a divisive proposition; Peter went to the wedding but Wendy did not. As Peter explained, "When people break up and someone has a new girlfriend, and then gets remarried, it's tricky. So one approaches that with a combination of diplomacy and tact, and trying to be as loyal to everyone as possible. It's a tough call. I got to know Susan a bit. I never felt like I knew her particularly well. She seemed very pleasant."

As Robin and his new wife prepared to spend their honeymoon in Paris, all that Susan was concerned with was a long and joyous future together with her husband. "I remember feeling that we had not met too late in life," she said. "We met right on time."

19
GONE

Why?

It was a question that crossed Robin's mind more often these days, now that he had put in roughly thirty-five years as a professional entertainer and more than sixty as a human being. What did he still get out of doing what he was doing, and why did he feel the compulsion to keep doing it? He had already enjoyed nearly all of the accomplishments that one could hope for in his field, tasted the richest successes, won most of the major awards. "He can retire right now, for god's sake," his friend David Letterman said of him during a *Late Show* appearance from this period. "He's going to the hall of fame."

He could hardly believe the speed at which time had flown by, taking him from a hungry newcomer to a champion in his field to, well, whatever he was now. "We were just kids," Robin told the host, "and now we're old and —"

"Irrelevant," Letterman said.

"Incontinent," Robin said. "Incontinent and irrelevant. That sounds like a comedy team. Please welcome Incontinent & Irrelevant."

Every stage of his career had been an adventure into the unknown, an improvisation in its own right, but there was truly no road map for where he was now. Everything came to an end at some point; it was a reality he accepted and confronted so often in his work, even as he tried to outrace it. What would it look like for him, he wondered, when he wrapped things up and told the crowd good night for the last time? How could it be anything other than devastating? He had known few other peers who had made it to this phase of life with their bodies and their reputations intact, and it rarely ended well for any of them.

The work was less abundant than it used to be and nowhere near as lucrative, and so much of it seemed to be focused on finality, particularly in the form of death. In August 2012, he had appeared in an episode of *Louie,* the cable TV comedy written by and starring the comedian Louis C.K., that begins with both men meeting at the grave of a comedy club manager who has recently died, and whom they both privately despised. "When he died I felt nothing," Louie tells Robin. "I didn't care. But I knew, when I pictured him going in the ground and nobody's there, he's alone, it gave me nightmares." Robin replies, "Me too."

On a lark, they visit a seedy strip club frequented by their deceased acquaintance, only to find that everyone else there — the strippers, the DJ — is mourning the loss of the generous man the two comedians never knew. On their way out of the club they turn to each other in understanding.

"Do me a favor?" Robin requests.

"I'll go to yours," Louie answers him.

"Whoever dies first?" Robin asks.

And that's all they need to say to each other.

Later that fall, Robin was in New York making a film called *The Angriest Man in Brooklyn,* another morbid indie comedy, in which he plays its title character, a surly lawyer who is diagnosed with an aneurysm and told he has ninety minutes to live. In one scene, the character jumps off the Brooklyn Bridge into the East River, but he survives, and he is dragged from the water by the doctor who, it turns out, has falsely diagnosed him. When he described the creation of this sequence to Letterman, the host had asked him if he needed a gamma globulin shot, and Robin answered, "I didn't get a shot, and I hope it doesn't end up, twenty years from now, I'm not like Katharine Hepburn, going, [quavering voice] 'E-very-thing's fi-ine.' "

So why did Robin persist in making these films, each one a far cry from the Hollywood features he had once thrived on, and which were lucky to receive even a theatrical release? Why did he continue to fill every free block of time in his schedule with work, whatever work he could find? Yes, he needed the money, especially now that he had two ex-wives and a new spouse he wanted to provide with a comfortable home. "There are bills to pay," he said. "My life has downsized, in a good way. I'm selling the ranch up in Napa. I just can't afford it anymore." He hadn't lost all his money, but, he said, "Lost enough. Divorce is expensive."

Financial pressures did not fully account for Robin's relentlessness; he worked because he enjoyed it, because he got something out of it, because he wanted to. In the spring of 2012, he was given something called the Stand-Up Icon Award at the Comedy Awards in New York — a noncompetitive prize dreamed up by Comedy Central, for a ceremony that the cable channel had held only once before and would never broadcast again. Robin begrudgingly accepted, even though he felt that the whole idea of a comedy awards show was "like a bake-off for bulimics."

Still, when he received the prize at a gala ceremony at the Hammerstein Ballroom on April 28, he was genuinely touched to be able to share a room with hipper, younger comedy stars like Patton Oswalt, Chris Rock, Tina

Fey, and Amy Poehler; elders like Don Rickles; and industry pals like Robert De Niro. Following an introduction from Oswalt, Robin began by holding up his new trophy and saying, "Thank you for this lovely platinum Ambien, this lovely R2-D2 illegitimate child. Thank you." He spotted Susan in the audience and added, "Tonight, my darling Susan, you'll be fucking an icon."

He thanked those comedic forefathers, like Jonathan Winters, who had been his personal inspirations, and those, like Mort Sahl, who had lately become his friends. Given the setting and the circumstances, he could not resist a little retrospective self-deprecation. "You start off doing comedy, and it's a long time ago," he said. "You have an open-mic night. You sign up. You get on late at night. They give you three minutes. Thirty-seven years later, I come on here, I get this [the award] and three minutes. Thank you. Fuck off."

Something to him felt right, or at least familiar, about ending up back at the same place he had started out professionally. "It's like life," Robin said. "You start off in diapers, you end up in diapers. The bottom line is, I am one of the luckiest fucks in show business. I'm so goddamn lucky. The only difference between me and a leprechaun is, I snorted my pot of gold."

Winters, his first real comedy hero and the

one most responsible for influencing the performer that Robin became, died of natural causes the following April, at the age of eighty-seven. Winters had always been grateful for the friendship of the onetime student who had outstripped the master, and for the gifts of toy soldiers that Robin occasionally bestowed on him; Winters could be needy, too, and was ashamed of his own neediness. In one of the many letters he wrote to Robin over the years, he implored his old pal to get together with him soon, "before I take the 'great escalator north!' " After Winters's death, Robin wrote an essay of appreciation for the *New York Times* in which he reflected on his friend's compulsion to joke about everything he had encountered or experienced, even the depression that had shaped his dour, stone-faced demeanor. As Robin wrote:

His car had handicap plates. He once parked in a blue lane and a woman approached him and said, "You don't look handicapped to me."

Jonathan said, "Madam, can you see inside my mind?"

Robin had continued to bounce from one low-budget film to the next; a rare exception in this period was his small role as President Dwight D. Eisenhower in the biographical film *Lee Daniels' The Butler,* a brief appearance that critics simply refused to countenance ("especially egregious," one wrote of the performance). But he finally seemed poised for a professional resurgence when he was cast in *The Crazy Ones,* a new CBS comedy show that would make its debut in September 2013. The series was Robin's first ongoing television role since *Mork & Mindy* ended three decades earlier, casting him as Simon Roberts, the irrepressible, not yet over-the-hill cofounder of a fast-paced Chicago advertising agency he runs with his straitlaced daughter (Sarah Michelle Gellar). When he first met with the series' creator, David E. Kelly, Robin recalled, "He basically sat me down and said, this is my idea for a show. Father-daughter advertising firm, father's kind of an idea man, but he's had an interesting life. Multiple marriages and rehab — I went, 'I've done the research.' The daughter's there to back him up, but the father's trying to get her to be more creative."

The Crazy Ones seemed perfectly calibrated for the older audience cultivated by CBS, which had a track record for giving new lifeblood to bygone TV stars, while the show provided Robin with distinct opportunities to improvise in each episode. It surrounded him with an ensemble of young actors, who helped to offset the fact that Robin was now gaunter and grayer than viewers were accustomed to seeing, and it paid a steady salary of $165,000 an episode — more in a week than he'd earn in a month working for scale on an independent movie.

But there was an even simpler pleasure about *The Crazy Ones.* As Robin explained, "It's a regular job. Day to day, you go to the plant, you put your punch card in, you get out. That's a good job."

In another Letterman appearance that fall, Robin drew parallels between the father-daughter relationship on his show and his real-life relationship with Zak, who by this time had earned an MBA from Columbia University, and who — to hear his father tell it — was hitting his stride while Robin was reaching the end of his usefulness. Slipping into his impersonation of a doddering old man, Robin looked directly into the camera and said, "Where are we going today? 'To take Daddy out by the sidewalk.' "

When the first episode of *The Crazy Ones* aired on September 26, it was met with lukewarm reviews. Unlike *Mork & Mindy,* which had been filmed in front of a live studio audience that responded to his every ad-lib with uproarious laughter, *The Crazy Ones* used a single-camera format that was a poor fit for Robin's talents. The show played like a movie running in an empty theater, and each joke hung awkwardly in the air as it was met with silence. Some critics, at least, were gentle in noting that the Robin of *The Crazy Ones* was no longer the indefatigable dynamo they had come to adore in an earlier era. "Watching Mr. Williams return to the kind of improvisation-style routines that made him famous in the 1970s is bittersweet, like watching Jimmy Connors play tennis again," Alessandra Stanley wrote in the *New York Times.* "They are still impressive, but audiences can't help recalling how much more elastic and powerful they were at their peak." Others were not so diplomatic, like the one who simply wrote, "Williams seems exhausted. So is this show."

The ratings foretold a bleak outlook: the first episode of *The Crazy Ones* was watched by about 15.5 million people, a respectable start that suggested at least a curiosity about the series. But within a month, nearly half that audience had tuned out, and the numbers eroded further with each passing week. It was no *Mork & Mindy;* the magic was gone.

During the making of *The Crazy Ones,* Robin lived in Los Angeles, by himself, in a modestly furnished rental apartment. It was a far cry from when he last starred in a Hollywood sitcom, and an even more scaled-down existence than he had established for himself in Tiburon. He didn't do much socializing off the set, and the visitors he often entertained at work were his comedian pals from the Throckmorton Theatre scene. When his friend Steven Pearl happened to find himself in L.A., he simply called Robin's personal assistant, Rebecca Erwin Spencer, and asked if he and a companion could visit Robin at a location shoot.

"We just hung out, watched him film," Pearl said. "I got to see them shave Robin's arms for some publicity photos. I've never seen anyone get their arms shaved, but that boy was hairy. That boy was Cousin Itt, man."

Robin did not disguise to Pearl his motivations for doing *The Crazy Ones,* any more than Pearl withheld from Robin his true feelings about what he thought was a mediocre show. "He admitted, he was just doing it for the money — 'I'm doing it for the money, I need the money,' " Pearl said. "It was okay. It didn't crack me up or anything. It wasn't horrible. There's stuff on TV that's just total garbage, man. But I was happy he was working. As his friend, I was hoping the show would run for ten years. But it didn't. They never give anything a chance to get better anymore, that's the thing."

Robin's new domestic life with Susan was very different, too. Unlike Marsha, who saw it as her responsibility to decorate and maintain their house, to organize dinner parties and surround him with intellectual friends who kept him stimulated, Susan had been accustomed to living an independent life of her own. She traveled widely by herself and with her sons, and she did not manage Robin's day-to-day affairs and did not always accompany him when he worked out of town.

"Any time he traveled, Marsha was very good at putting him in touch with Oliver Sacks or Salman Rushdie or Bob De Niro, so that he was constantly stimulated," their friend Cyndi McHale explained. "Especially when he was on the road, and away from his family, so that he'd have fun and he'd be engaged. And he wasn't just having dinner every night with his assistant or his hair and makeup person or his stand-in. They're all lovely people, but you need to mix it up, for his brain."

Other friends, like the comedian Rick Overton, believed that Susan played a crucial role for Robin, even when the two of them were hundreds of miles apart. "She made him happy," Overton said. "You could see it in his face. I don't think he had a complete life, but I'm glad that some things were done to give him some comfort."

A year earlier, Zak and his wife, Alex, had moved back to San Francisco so that Zak could take a job for a technology start-up in Mountain View and they could be nearer to Robin. Zak and Alex would make lunch for Robin, hang out with his friends, and watch favorite movies with him, everything from classic Japanese anime to Stanley Kubrick's nuclear Armageddon comedy *Dr. Strangelove.*

As Alex saw it, Robin didn't just enjoy the time he spent with Zak; he depended on his son in a way that he never had before. Growing up, Zak had missed out on crucial time with his father — time that was lost to Robin's career, his divorce, his dependencies and recoveries. Now their restored connection could be fulfilling but also overwhelming. "That's when Robin just really needed him, and he would reach out to Zak," Alex said. "His dad finally was like, 'I need you, I want to be around you, I want to spend time with you.' It was everything Zak always wanted, but not the way he wanted it."

Throughout this time, Zak was often in contact with Rebecca Erwin Spencer and her husband, Dan, who lived in Corte Madera, near Tiburon, and who Zak felt took good care of Robin. "They were very open and did love him very much — they were pretty good about keeping us in the fold," he said. "I think there was inclusivity up until a point when things started getting a little weird."

That moment came around the time when Robin went to Los Angeles to start working on *The Crazy Ones.* "I'm kicking myself for not visiting him during that time," Zak said. "Because I think that was a very lonely period for him. In retrospect, I feel like I should have been there, spending time with him. Because someone who needs support was not getting the support he needed."

Starting in October 2013, Robin began to experience a series of physical ailments, varying in their severity and seemingly unconnected to one another. He had stomach cramps, indigestion, and constipation. He had trouble seeing; he had trouble urinating; he had trouble sleeping. The tremors in his left arm had returned, accompanied by the symptoms of cogwheel rigidity, where the limb would inexplicably stop itself at certain fixed points in its range of motion. His voice had diminished, his posture was stooped, and at times he simply seemed to freeze where he stood.

Susan was used to seeing Robin experience a certain amount of nervousness, but when she spoke to him now, his anxiety levels seemed off the chart. "It was like this endless parade of symptoms, and not all of them would raise their head at once," she said. "It was like playing whack-a-mole. Which symptom is it this month? I thought, is my husband a hypochondriac? We're chasing it and there's no answers, and by now we'd tried everything."

Billy Crystal said that Robin began to reveal some of his discomfort, but only up to a point. "He wasn't feeling well, but he didn't let on to me all that was going on," Crystal said. "As he would say to me, 'I'm a little crispy.' I didn't know what was happening, except he wasn't happy."

In the fall, Crystal and his wife, Janice, invited Robin out to see the Joseph Gordon-Levitt comedy *Don Jon* at a movie theater in Los Angeles. When they met at the parking lot, Crystal said, "I hadn't seen him in about four or five months at the time, and when he got out of the car I was a little taken aback by how he looked. He was thinner and he seemed a little frail."

Over dinner afterward, Crystal said, "He seemed quiet. On occasion, he'd just reach out and hold my shoulder and look at me like he wanted to say something." When the friends said good-bye at the end of the night, Robin burst out with unexpected affection. "He hugged me good-bye, and Janice, and he started crying," Crystal said. "I said, 'What's the matter?' He said, 'Oh, I'm just so happy to see you. It's been too long. You know I love you.' "

On their car ride home, Crystal said he and Janice were barraged by calls from Robin, sounding tentative and expressing his appreciation for the couple. "Everything's fine, I just love you so much, 'bye," went one call. Five minutes later the phone rang again: "Did I get too sappy? Let's see each other soon."

That winter in Los Angeles, Robin was performing with Rick Overton at an improv show called *Set List* at the iO West comedy club on Hollywood Boulevard. Overton

668

described it as "the hottest, bragging-rights, *Top Gun,* black-belt version of stand-up," but also "one of the joys that brought the kid back — that brought the bounce back in his smile." Robin did not initially want to perform at the show, but Overton talked him into it. "I said, 'You're going to look at me with that *oh-man-you-were-right* look — you won't even know how right I am until you do it.' He came back and said, 'You were totally fucking right.' And he felt younger. And I said, 'That's why I do it.' I love that feeling of banging up there like a kid and holding on to the mic stand and wondering what's next."

Outside the club that night, they were stopped by a paparazzo photographer with a video camera. The interaction was fleeting, no more than a minute, and Robin answered only a few cursory questions about what advice he would give to up-and-coming performers. "Find a room like this and go on," he told his ambusher. "This room's amazing." But even in that short conversation, it was unmistakable how gaunt and worn down Robin looked.

Overton came to believe there was something wrong with his friend, even if he did not quite understand what it was. "I saw the eyes dimming," he later said. "And that's the gateway to the soul. Like a rheostat in a dining-room light set. I would see that candle flicker brightly when he would do *Set List,* or come up and do improv. We'd get back to playing like kids. We'd bounce off each other for a little bit, and we'd get access to the old guy again. And then it would start to dim when we'd be hanging out afterwards, at the restaurant. I can't imagine the weight of it. I can't even dream of it. I don't blame him for one damn thing."

Before production wrapped on *The Crazy Ones* in February 2014, its producers made a last-ditch effort to reinvigorate its viewership with a bit of guest casting. Pam Dawber was invited to play a role in one episode, as a possible romantic interest for the Simon Roberts character, marking the first time that she and Robin had performed together since *Mork & Mindy,* and the first screen role that Dawber — who had stepped back from the business to raise her children with the actor Mark Harmon — had taken in fourteen years.

Dawber knew the stunt was something that would only be attempted by a TV series faced with the looming threat of cancellation, but she accepted the role anyway. "I did that show only because I wanted to see Robin," she said. "Not because I thought it was a great show. I thought it was such the wrong show for Robin, and he was working as hard as he could. The couple episodes I saw, I felt so sorry for him, because he was just sweating bullets. He was sweet and wonderful and loving and sensitive. But I would come home and say to my husband, 'Something's wrong. He's *flat.* He's lost the spark. I don't know what it is.' "

Dawber also drew the conclusion that Robin was experiencing serious health problems, but she felt uncomfortable broaching the subject with him. "In general, he was so *not* who I knew him to be," she said. "But I didn't feel right prying, because I hadn't been around him. So I did what I could. 'I hear you have a new marriage.' 'Oh, she's wonderful, she's so sweet.' " Knowing about Robin's valve-replacement surgery, Dawber asked him if he was taking any medication for his heart; he told her he was only taking anti-anxiety medication. "I thought, Hm. Maybe that's why he's flat," she said. "And then he told me he was worried because he was losing all this weight and he didn't know why, and he was having all these tests run. I said, 'Have you had your thyroid checked?' We went into all that stuff. He said, 'I don't know.' "

Robin reached out to Dawber many times over the days that she spent making the episode, thanking her for her involvement. "He was so sweet," she said. "And I felt like he was wanting to make a connection but didn't know how. And I almost didn't know how, because I hadn't talked to him in so long."

Despite its retro-TV reunion hook and the increased promotion it received, Dawber's episode of *The Crazy Ones* did nothing to stop the show's continued ratings slide. Fewer than seven million people watched it — one of the smallest audiences it had drawn to that point — and the next week, its season finale was watched by barely five million people. The following month, CBS canceled the show. Friends like Mark Pitta, who spoke to Robin during this period, believed he was at peace with the network's decision. "I said to him, 'How are you doing?' " Pitta recalled. "And he just volunteered it. He goes, 'Well, my show was canceled.' I said, 'How's that going for you?' He goes, 'Well, bad financially. Good creatively.' I didn't watch it. I didn't like it, so I didn't watch it."

By that time, Robin had already moved on to filming *Night at the Museum: Secret of the Tomb,* the third film in the family comedy franchise. That previous winter, he had shot a portion of the movie in London, and now he was completing the rest of his scenes in Vancouver. Though it was the first big-budget feature that Robin had worked on in some time, it was a project that many people close to him had hoped he would not take — it was clear to them that whatever had been afflicting him was getting worse, and he needed to push the pause button on his career until his mystery illness was brought under control.

"I thought he knew it was bad," said Cheri Minns, his makeup artist, who accompanied him on the *Night at the Museum* set. "I thought he'd wind up taking a year off, and he needed the time to figure out what was going on, because he was not himself."

But what proved more powerful than the pleas from his colleagues and from family members like Zak and Alex to slow things down — even more powerful than Robin's desire to sustain his life with Susan and to be a good earner for his managers and agents — was his own desire to keep working through the pain, the one cure-all that had helped him cope with past troubles.

"I don't think he thought he could blow up what he built for himself," Minns said. "It's like he didn't worry about anything when he worked all the time. He operated on working. That was the true love of his life. Above his children, above everything. If he wasn't working, he was a shell of himself. And when he worked, it was like a lightbulb was turned on."

As for the *Night at the Museum* sequel, Minns said, "That was a nightmare. He shouldn't have done that movie. That's how I feel about it." By the time he reached Vancouver, Robin's weight loss was severe and his motor impairments were growing harder to disguise. Even his once-prodigious memory was rebelling against him; he was having difficulty remembering his lines.

"He wasn't in good shape at all," Minns said. "He was sobbing in my arms at the end of every day. It was horrible. Horrible. But I just didn't know."

Eventually, Minns called Robin's managers and told them that he was hurtling toward a breaking point. "I said to his people, 'I'm a makeup artist — I don't have this capacity to deal with what's happening to him,' " she recalled. "Because he'd come to me and confide in me, but I was afraid I was going to say the wrong thing. At night, I was on my computer, looking up 'How to talk to a paranoid,' so that I wouldn't say the wrong thing. I wanted to be supportive."

Dawber, too, would get phone calls from Robin while he worked on the film. "But it was like, 'Robin, you're sick! You're sick,' " she said. "He just was moving on a fast track. And there just was something not right."

Robin was no longer leaving his hotel room at night, and in April he suffered a panic attack. Minns thought that maybe if he slipped out to a local Vancouver comedy club and performed again, it would lift Robin's spirits and remind him that audiences still loved him. But instead, her gentle suggestion had a devastating effect. "I said, 'Robin, why don't you go and do stand-up?' " she recalled. Robin broke down in tears. "He just cried and said, 'I can't, Cheri.' I said, 'What do you mean, you can't?' He said, 'I don't know how anymore. I don't know how to be funny.' And it was just gut wrenching to hear him admit that, rather than lie to me and say something else. I think that's how troubled he was about all of it."

Susan had remained in California while Robin worked on the movie, but she was in frequent contact with him, too, talking him through his escalating insecurities. Under the supervision of his doctor, Robin started taking different antipsychotic medications, but each prescription only seemed to alleviate some symptoms while making others worse. When Robin finished his work on *Night at the Museum* and returned home to Tiburon in early May, Susan said her husband was "like a 747 airplane coming in with no landing gear."

"Robin was losing his mind and he was aware of it," she said.

Susan said that Robin told her he wanted a "reboot for his brain," but he was stuck in a looping paranoia that would spin around and around in his mind. Every time it seemed as if he had been talked down from the latest obsession, he returned to it all over again, fresh in his mind, as if he were encountering it for the first time.

A few days after he came back from Vancouver, Robin was stirred from a fitful evening of sleep, gripped by the certainty that some grave harm was going to befall Mort Sahl. He kept wanting to drive over to Sahl's apartment in Mill Valley to check on him and make sure he was safe, while Susan had to repeatedly convince him that his friend was not in any danger. They went over it, again and again and again, all night, until they both finally fell asleep at three thirty that morning.

On May 28, 2014, Robin was finally given an explanation for the tangled lattice of sicknesses that had been plaguing him. He was diagnosed with Parkinson's disease, a degenerative disorder that attacks the central nervous system, impairing motor functions and cognition, eventually leading to death. To Robin, it was the realization of one of his most deeply felt and lifelong fears, to be told that he had an illness that would rob him of his faculties, by small, imperceptible increments every day, that would hollow him out and leave behind a depleted husk of a human being. Susan tried to find some small shred of positivity in the ordeal — at least now Robin knew what he had and could focus on treating it. "We had an answer," she said. "My heart swelled with hope. But somehow I knew Robin was not buying it."

In a meeting with a neurologist, Robin asked several questions about his diagnosis. Did he have Alzheimer's disease?, he wanted to know. Did he have dementia? Did he have schizophrenia? In each instance he was told no. Despite the encouragement he was offered, that Parkinson's patients are often able to keep their symptoms in check once they find a medication they respond to, Susan said that Robin seemed unconvinced. "Robin couldn't understand why his brain was out of control while at the same time he was being told, 'We're going to get this Parkinson's managed and you'll have another good ten years,' " she said.

Robin shared the news of his Parkinson's diagnosis with his innermost circle: with his children, with his professional handlers, and with his most intimate friends. Crystal recounted the conversation in which Robin revealed the devastating news to him. "His number comes up on my phone," he said, "and he says, 'Hey, Bill.' His voice was high-pitched. 'I've just been diagnosed with Parkinson's.' I didn't miss a beat. Because of my relationship with Muhammad Ali, I knew a lot of really good Parkinson's research doctors. I said, 'In Phoenix, the research center is great. If you want, we can get you in there. It would be totally anonymous. Do you want me to pursue that?' 'Would you?' "

"I never heard him afraid like that before," Crystal said. "This was the boldest comedian I ever met — the boldest artist I ever met. But this was just a scared man."

Among his associates who knew, there was unease: they were worried, of course, about

Robin's well-being but also concerned about whether he was in a position to receive the assistance he needed. "I don't think the people around him knew how to handle it and how to help him," Cyndi McHale said. "Look, it's the perfect storm. He had a physical condition that was manifesting. He knew there was something wrong with his brain. And two of his best friends — my late husband and Christopher Reeve — ended up paralyzed in a wheelchair. So he's thinking, okay, I'm losing control of my body. There's something going on in my brain. I think he was just trapped."

Robin's children felt that it was now more important than ever to share time with their father. But doing so meant navigating past layer after layer of other people who also had access to him and wanted his attention — Susan; his assistant, Rebecca; his managers — and even this much resistance could discourage them from seeking him out.

"I would always make sure that Zak got time in front of his dad," said his wife, Alex. "Zak would never ask for time — Zak would never push and I wouldn't care if I looked pushy in front of his people. If he wanted to see his dad and have lunch with him, he's going to do that."

Like his father, Zak had a side to himself that was averse to conflict and hesitant to call attention to himself when he needed help.

"That's how Zak and Robin definitely are," Alex said. "They could talk about something awful, but they'll romanticize it. And you're like, 'Whoa, that sounds like a horrible experience.' 'No, it was awesome!' How are you doing? 'I'm great. I'm wonderful.' That's what Robin would always say. And that's what Zak would also say. I feel the sadness. It's like a generational sadness."

It was a quality about the Williams men that Alex could never understand. "It's the with-drawing, private side," she said. "I still don't understand it. It feels like the deepest part of the ocean. It's still a mystery."

When Robin did have time to get together with him, Zak could tell that his father was in anguish, and not only from the strain of his condition. "It was really difficult to see someone suffering so silently," Zak said. "But I think that there were a series of things that stacked, that led to an environment that he felt was one of pain, internal anguish, and one that he couldn't get out of. And the challenge in engaging with him when he was in that mind-set was that he could be soothed, but it's really hard when you then go back into an environment of isolation. Isolation is not good for Dad and people like him. It's actually terrible."

Robin had been depressed for a long time, and Zak, too, had problems with anxiety. "But one of the ways in which we cope was to engage with people," Zak explained. "Which is hard, too, because that can be self-perpetuating with anxiety, if you feel that the interactions aren't going as you want them to go."

Robin's children had always been a dependable source of some of the purest, most natural joy he had experienced. But when he saw them now, they were also a reminder that he had chosen to end his marriage to Marsha and break up their home; it filled him with shame to think that he had inflicted the divorce upon them, and the shame compounded itself as he came to believe he had taken something perfect and corrupted it.

"He had told us numerous times that he had made a terrible decision," Zak said. "That doesn't relate to marriage or anything like that — it relates to separating himself from the day-to-day with his family. We'd say, 'No, we're here for you. We're always here for you and we want to be supportive in whatever it is that you do. That's important for us. At the end of the day, your happiness is what matters to us.' And that was hard for him. Because he felt like he was letting people down. That was really difficult to witness."

Even when his children told him that he had no reason to hold on to his guilt and nothing to apologize for, Zak said, "He couldn't hear it. He could never hear it. And he wasn't able to accept it. He was firm in his conviction that he was letting us down. And that was sad because we all loved him so much and just wanted him to be happy."

At home, Susan saw Robin's condition continue to worsen. When they tried to sleep at night, Robin would thrash around the bed, or more often he would be awake and wanting to talk about whatever new delusion his mind had conjured up. Robin tried many treatments to regain the upper hand over the disease: he continued to see a therapist, work out with a physical trainer, and ride his bike; he even found a specialist at Stanford University who taught him self-hypnosis. But each of these strategies could only do so much. In the meantime, Robin started sleeping in a separate bedroom from Susan.

From his perspective, Zak experienced Robin's decline very differently. When they were not together, his father would often contact him to say that he was being made to spend time with friends of Susan's and that he was deeply suspicious of them. "Dad would actually call me and text me, saying, 'I'm hanging out with these people, I don't even know who they are, and they feel like users,' " Zak recalled. "So that was upsetting to me. We thought the environment to be in was Marin, with his new wife. But when he seemed like he was in a perpetual state of anguish, that didn't bode really well with us."

Dana Carvey, who performed occasionally

at the Throckmorton Theatre, had an unexpected encounter with Robin one evening on the streets of Mill Valley. "I was out on the sidewalk," Carvey said, "and it was kind of misty and dark." He heard a voice calling to him, "Hello? Hello?" The speaker was Robin, who came up to him looking very pained. "He wanted to make amends to me, for taking material from me," said Carvey, who answered that he could not think of anything Robin took from him. "He was really taken aback by that," Carvey said. "For years, people had said to him that the phrase 'Mr. Happy,' referring to his dick, was mine. But I don't think it was. I go, 'Robin, I don't believe that was mine.' And I don't think he ever believed me. So we had kind of an awkward exchange. I said, 'I kind of accept that, but I tried to be *you* for four years.' I realized later, this was not the way it was supposed to go. You're supposed to say: 'Thank you.' "

Eric Idle, who was in London that summer preparing for a Monty Python reunion show, tried unsuccessfully to persuade Robin to fly out there and make a cameo appearance at one of the performances. "And all the time I was getting emails from him, and he was going downhill," Idle recalled. "Then he said he could come, but he didn't want to be onstage. I said, 'I totally get that.' Because he was suffering from severe depression." Through their mutual friend Bobcat Goldthwait, Idle said, "we were in touch, and in the end he said, 'I can't come, I'm sorry, but I love you very much.' We realized afterwards he was saying goodbye."

In June, Robin checked himself into the Dan Anderson Renewal Center in Center City, Minnesota, another Hazelden addiction treatment facility like the one where he had been treated in Oregon in 2006. Publicly, his press representatives said that he was "simply taking the opportunity to fine-tune and focus on his continued commitment, of which he remains extremely proud." In fact, this rehab stay was Robin and Susan's understandably inelegant fix for a problem that had no solution. At the very least, it kept Robin cloistered on a campus where he could receive close supervision, and where he could meditate, do yoga, and focus on further twelve-step work that, it was hoped, would help him manage his illness.

But other friends felt that Robin had no reason to stay at a clinic for drug and alcohol rehabilitation when he was suffering from an unrelated physical disorder. "That was wrong," said Wendy Asher. "Robin was drinking when he went to rehab, and this wasn't that. This was a medical problem. Susan thought everything would be fixed through AA, and it just wasn't true."

"Somebody that's that depressed, and on medication for a medical condition, and the medication can cause depression, you just don't tell them to work the twelve steps," Cyndi McHale said. "He needed much more."

Steven Pearl was one of Robin's first friends to encounter him back in the Bay Area when he returned from Minnesota. Pearl was with his girlfriend, Nina, at a barbecue on July 12, when he saw Robin there with his friend Michael Pritchard, a fellow comedian and motivational speaker. Pearl was immediately struck by how much weight Robin had lost and how he did not seem to know who Nina was. "He always gave her a big hug and a kiss," Pearl said. "He did not recognize her. It took him a minute to recognize me. He didn't say a word. I knew something was really wrong. I asked Michael Pritchard, 'Is he okay?' And he goes, 'No.' And that's all he said. I just thought it was depression and he'd come out of it."

July 21 was Robin's sixty-third birthday, but few of his friends seemed able to reach him and offer their warm wishes on the day. Cyndi McHale, who had the same birth date as Robin and had a regular tradition of speaking to him on the day, could not track him down; "I was on the phone with his managers' assistant," she said, "and she was just like, 'He's not doing well.' That was a common line. Rebecca was just like, 'No, he's not doing well.' I was really worried about him."

McHale had not seen Robin, either, at a recent birthday party for George Lucas, an event that he reliably attended. "When he didn't go to that," she said, "I thought, uh-oh, it's really much worse than anybody is letting on."

On the morning of July 24, Susan was taking a shower when she saw Robin at the bathroom sink, staring intensely at his reflection in the mirror. Looking more carefully at him, she noticed that Robin had a deep cut on his head, which he occasionally wiped at with a hand towel that had become soaked with blood. She realized that Robin had banged his head on the wooden bathroom door and began to scream at him, "Robin, what did you do? What happened?" He answered, "I miscalculated." "He was angry because by now he was so mad at himself for what his body was doing, for what his mind was doing," Susan later explained. "He would sometimes now start standing and being in trance-like states and frozen. He had just done that with me and he was so upset, he was so upset."

The last time that Mark Pitta saw Robin at the Throckmorton Theatre was at the end of July, and the encounter left him cold. "I was scared," Pitta said, "because it wasn't my friend. I said, this has nothing to do with his TV show being canceled. He had a thousand-yard stare going. I just talked to him, I said,

'Man, you're not going to believe this. Somebody ran over my cat, twenty feet in front of my house.' And Robin had absolutely no reaction, at all. I was like, uh-oh."

Later in the theater's green room, Pitta and Robin were mingling with another comedian who had brought his service dog. As Pitta recounted the scene, "I just casually said, 'Another comedian I know has a service dog. The dog wakes her up when she chokes in her sleep.' And Robin *instantly* said, 'Oh, a Heimlich retriever.' It got a huge laugh. He just sat there and had a little smile on his face." When he and Robin left the theater at the end of the evening, Pitta said, "I gave him a hug and I said good-bye. He said good-bye to me three times that night. And he said it exactly the same way. He goes, 'Take care, Marky.' He said it three times, that way. And he was the only guy that called me Marky. No one calls me that."

Zelda turned twenty-five on July 31, and that evening she celebrated her birthday with Marsha and Wendy Asher at a restaurant in Los Angeles. Robin wasn't there, though he sent her a necklace and a card that read, "You will always be a star to me," and everyone at the dinner was deeply concerned for Robin's well-being. "I kept saying I'm really worried," Asher recalled. "Then Marsha and I sat at a bus stop, talking about it, and Marsha was worried about it. I was told, from his managers, not to tell people he was depressed. The truth is, sometimes I wish I would have gone to his real friends and said, 'This is going on.' Maybe if everyone would have rallied around or something — you always think that, don't you?"

One evening in early August, Robin made one of his intermittent visits to Zak and Alex's house in San Francisco, as he did when Susan was out of town. This time she happened to be in Lake Tahoe, and Robin showed up to see his son and daughter-in-law like a meek teenager who realizes he's stayed out past his curfew; he was always welcome there, but he carried himself with mild discomfort, as if he still needed someone else's permission to be in their home. At the end of the night, as Robin was preparing to head back to Tiburon, Zak and Alex asked him what it would take to keep him at their house — would they have to tie him up and throw a bag over him?

"Well, that was a joke," Zak said with a bittersweet laugh. "To be clear, that was a joke. But we didn't want someone who seemed like he was in so much anguish to leave. We wanted him to stay with us. We wanted to take care of him."

It wasn't that Robin was ashamed to accept help from his son, Zak later explained. "I don't think so, no," he said. "He wanted to be independent and be who he was, taking care of himself. I think there was an element that he didn't want to inconvenience us."

On the night of August 10, a Sunday, Robin and Susan were home together in Tiburon when Robin began to fixate on some of the designer wrist watches that he owned and grew fearful that they were in danger of being stolen. He took several of them and stuffed them in a sock, and, at around seven p.m., he drove over to Rebecca and Dan Spencer's house in Corte Madera, about two and a half miles away, to give them the watches for safekeeping. After Robin came home, Susan started getting ready for bed; he affectionately offered her a foot massage, but on this night, she said she was okay and thanked him anyway. "As we always did, we said to each other, 'Goodnight, my love,' " Susan recalled.

Robin went in and out of their bedroom several times, rummaged through its closet, and eventually left with an iPad to do some reading, which Susan interpreted as a good sign; it had been months since she'd seen him read or even watch TV. "He seemed like he was doing better, like he was on the path of something," she later said. "I'm thinking, 'Okay, stuff is working. The medication, he's getting sleep.' " She saw him leave the room at around ten thirty p.m. and head to the separate bedroom he slept in, which was down a long hallway on the opposite side of their house.

When Susan woke up the next morning, Monday, August 11, she noticed that the door to Robin's bedroom was still closed, but she felt relieved that he was finally getting some needed rest. Rebecca and Dan came over to the house, and Rebecca asked how the weekend had gone with Robin; Susan optimistically answered, "I think he's getting better." Susan had been planning to wait for Robin to wake up so that she could meditate with him, but when he wasn't awake by ten thirty a.m., she left the house to run some errands.

By eleven a.m., Rebecca and Dan were concerned that Robin still had not come out of his room. Rebecca slipped a note under the door of Robin's bedroom to ask if he was okay but received no response. At 11:42 a.m., Rebecca texted Susan to say she was going to wake Robin up, and Dan went to find a stepstool to try to look through his bedroom window from the outside of the house. In the meantime, Rebecca used a paper clip to force open the lock to the bedroom door. She entered the room and made a horrifying discovery: Robin had hanged himself with a belt and was dead.

20
EVERYTHING WILL BE OKAY

Susan said good-bye to Robin later that afternoon. In a bedroom that had been furnished for adolescent boys, outfitted with a bunk bed, video game consoles, and school supplies, she stood beside him and spoke to him. "Robin," she said, "I'm not mad at you. I don't blame you at all. Not one bit. You fought so hard and you were so brave. With all my heart, I love you." She stroked his hair, looked over his face, and gave his forehead a final kiss. She and a sheriff's chaplain prayed over his body before it was strapped to a gurney and taken away.

The 911 call had come in at 11:55 a.m. Medics were on the scene by noon, and Robin was pronounced dead shortly after. There were no attempts made to resuscitate him. A sheriff's deputy investigated the scene and found no suicide note; a further search of Robin's cell phone, including phone calls, e-mails, text messages, and Internet history turned up no evidence that he was contemplating suicide or communications to other people that he was preparing to do it. The Web browser on his iPad had a few open tabs, where he had been looking at online discussion groups for medications like Lyrica, which is used to control seizures, and propranolol, a beta-blocker. His laptop, which he rarely used, had nothing significant on it. A toxicology report would later show that the only drugs in Robin's system at the time of his death were Mirtazapine, an antidepressant, and Sinemet, which treats the symptoms of Parkinson's disease.

Susan was asked, in the course of the police investigation, if Robin had ever discussed suicide with her and she said he hadn't, not even after he was given his Parkinson's diagnosis. She had no reason to believe he had ever researched methods of suicide or hanging specifically, though Rebecca and Dan mentioned that the character of Robin's son in his movie *World's Greatest Dad* had also died in a similar — but accidental — manner and that the scene had been very emotional for Robin to film.

Before Robin hanged himself, he had placed a folded towel between the belt and the skin of his neck, possibly to reduce pain. When the deputy examined Robin's body, he found what he described as several "superficial vertical and horizontal cuts" on his left wrist that "had a scant amount of blood present."

There was also dried blood on a pocketknife found in the bedroom, and on a washcloth left in the adjoining bathroom.

Robin was gone, but beyond that inescapable fact, nothing was certain and nothing made sense. Though his recent months had been suffused with anguish, he had given no explicit indication to anyone that he wished to end his life. The scene of his suicide, which he orchestrated and implemented alone, revealed no other indications of why he'd done it — why now, why at all — or what he might have wanted to say in his final communication to the people he loved most. Now his mortality was a police matter and soon to be an issue of public record. Before anyone had time to mourn his passing, let alone process it, or to begin to seek answers to the questions that would surely be asked of them, they had to tell the whole world that Robin Williams was dead.

The first announcement came about three hours after his death, in the form of a news release from the Coroner Division of the Marin County Sheriff's Office. Beneath a banner headline that read "Investigation into Death of Actor Robin Williams," it explained, in clinical, dispassionate language, that an emergency telephone call had been made earlier that morning, reporting "a male adult" who "had been located unconscious and not breathing inside his residence." Emergency personnel were dispatched and the man, "pronounced deceased at 12:02 pm has been identified as Robin McLaurin Williams, a 63 year old resident of unincorporated Tiburon, CA." A second paragraph explained that police were conducting an investigation into his death, though "the Sheriff's Office Coroner Division suspects the death to be a suicide due to asphyxia."

About an hour later, Robin's publicist, Mara Buxbaum, put out a short statement:

Robin Williams passed away this morning. He has been battling severe depression of late.

This is a tragic and sudden loss. The family respectfully asks for their privacy as they grieve during this very difficult time.

Buxbaum also shared a message from Susan:

This morning, I lost my husband and my best friend, while the world lost one of its most beloved artists and beautiful human beings. I am utterly heartbroken. On behalf of Robin's family, we are asking for privacy during our time of profound grief. As he is remembered, it is our hope the focus will not be on Robin's death, but on the countless moments of joy and laughter he gave to millions.

Even in an age of instantaneous information, the news of Robin's death was absorbed and circulated with bewildering speed. The incident offered an unparalleled example of a public figure who was recognized in every part of the globe and whose reputation for joyfulness and humor stood in stark opposition to the shocking and solitary manner in which his life came to an end. The whole world seemed to know, all at once, that he had died and was reacting to the incomprehensible event in unison. As only a few occasions in history are capable of doing, it had cloaked the planet in a shadow of sadness. Everyone who knew him experienced it, wherever they were, and everyone felt as if they knew him.

Rick Overton was stuck in standstill traffic on a Los Angeles highway when he got a phone call from Greg Travis, a friend and fellow comedian. "He goes, 'Oh, man, did you hear about Robin?' " Overton said. "I go, 'What about Robin?' He goes, 'Oh, he just died.' " Overton's first impulse was to dismiss the report as "another one of those Internet clickbait bullshit rumors" — just two years earlier, Robin had been the victim of an Internet hoax that alleged he had fallen to his death while shooting a film in Austria — but as he pulled off the highway, Overton began to notice other cars frozen in place, drivers and passengers with their mouths agape. "My heart needed it to be another fake story," he said. "I was hoping and coaxing the universe to rewrite it that way, because I was going into shock. I didn't want it to be true."

Without yet having heard all the details, Overton already knew the cause of Robin's death. "It was a death of a thousand cuts," he said. "But these were massive cuts. Each was a sword blow. For a guy who's known for his freedom and mobility, to find out he may not have that anymore — his facility of speech may not be his anymore; access to a quick thought might not be his anymore. All his trademark things, everything he has identified his personality with — it's like, holy shit, what are you going to do?

"All of that said," Overton added, "he would not have abandoned his family when in his right mind. He would have endured all of that, unless something shorted out. He wasn't Robin at that point. He stopped being the guy we know. That part shut down."

David Letterman was vacationing on his ranch near Glacier National Park in rural Montana, with a group of friends that included Paul Shaffer, Bill Murray, and the actor and comedian Tim Thomerson, when the news reached him. As a fellow survivor of heart surgery, Letterman said, "It just didn't make any sense to me. After what these guys did for me — they opened me up, they took my heart out, they put me on a heart-lung machine for forty-two minutes. And then they put your heart back in and they stitch you back up. After people have gone to that trouble, the last thing in the world you're going to do is ruin it by killing yourself."

Murray was even more visibly stricken. "He couldn't catch his breath," Letterman said. "He kept hyperventilating. I thought he was going to have a heart attack." When the group was able to calm down somewhat, Murray shared a story from the 2004 Academy Awards, the year he was considered a strong favorite to win the Best Actor trophy for *Lost in Translation* but instead was edged out by Sean Penn, for his performance in *Mystic River.* As Letterman recounted, "He said that later that night, Robin came up to him. They certainly didn't know each other well, and Robin said, 'Bill, please don't worry about this. This will happen for you.' Bill was very touched at this guy, who he did not have that sort of relationship with, who took time to be generous and nice about that."

To Letterman and his friends that day, it seemed unfathomable that a man whose astonishing talents left them feeling inadequate had decided his life no longer had value. "Robin could fly, God damn it," Letterman said. "It was the diametric opposite of what his life was. It was almost like, you're never going to suffocate this energy. And then, at the end, he chose to do so. The suffering must have been inestimable."

That evening in New York, Jeff Bridges was attending the red carpet premiere of *The Giver,* a science-fiction film he'd been trying to get made since the 1990s, but all that anyone in attendance could think about was Robin. "It was just the most bizarre mixture of deep, deep sadness and celebration for this thing that I'd been trying to give birth to for twenty years," Bridges said. "All these emotions are running through my heart and mind, and then we see the movie, and then we go have a party. All of a sudden, I look at the window, and I fucking see Robin. And he's coming towards me. I get out of the car, I can't believe it, and then I realize, no, it's not Robin." Instead, Bridges realized he was looking at Radioman, the transient photographer and film-set loiterer he and Robin had often crossed paths with during the making of *The Fisher King.* The fact that he had encountered Radioman on this particular night, Bridges felt, was a sure sign that Robin was trying to reach out to him from whatever part of the cosmos he now occupied. "Radioman is crying, and I'm crying, and we just hug each other," he said. "Robin's spirit was there with us."

It was now late at night in London, where Terry Gilliam was watching a rerun of the animated TV series *Family Guy,* a willfully outrageous cartoon that often used Robin as a satirical punching bag. In the particular episode that Gilliam happened to catch, the show's protagonist, Peter Griffin, comes to the ironic and uncomplimentary conclusion that Robin is not sufficiently appreciated ("Robin Williams has a manic gift that gladdens a sad world, and all he asks in return is our unceasing attention!" the character declares), and he wishes that everyone could be Robin Williams: a wish that comes true, transforming all his friends and family members into needful, overemoting caricatures of Robin. Gilliam watched the show and went to sleep. Had he stayed up just a few minutes later, he would have caught the BBC's first breaking news reports about Robin's death, but instead he learned about it the next morning, still rattled by the *Family Guy* segment he'd seen the night before.

"I went to bed with that floating around in my head, then woke up in the morning to be told Robin died," Gilliam said. "Robin dealt with forces far greater than most of us understand, and he controlled them in weird ways. In the moment he was thinking, 'Nobody loves me anymore,' another side of his brain was getting *Family Guy* on the air in England, where everybody becomes Robin Williams."

Knowing Robin as well as he did, Gilliam said he could almost appreciate the forces that had driven him to suicide. "Robin had a very big head to be alone in," he said. "I understand it. I stare at my computer screen, when you've got the screensaver going through all the photographs of the world and your life, and it's infinitely intriguing. No thinking. You don't exist anymore. That's the key to it. Anybody with what Robin had, you want to not exist."

Beneath his grief for his fallen friend, Gilliam could not deny the presence of another emotion he had not expected to feel, and that was anger. "I'm really pissed off at Robin," he said, half joking and half serious. "I'm getting more and more angry at him. He's such a selfish bastard, solving his problem, but what about the rest of us?"

Several American late-night shows were still being taped as word of Robin's death circulated, and their hosts felt obliged to share the news with their viewers. In the closing minutes of his Monday night broadcast, a shaken-up Conan O'Brien told his studio audience, "This is unusual and upsetting, but we got some news, during the show, that Robin Williams has passed away." As an audible rumble of confusion passed through the crowd, O'Brien continued, "By the time we air — we tape these shows a few hours early, and by the time you see this now, on TV, I'm sure that you'll know. I'm sorry to anyone in our studio audience, that I'm breaking this news. This is absolutely shocking and horrifying and so upsetting on every level." On *The Tonight Show* the following evening, Jimmy Fallon played footage from Robin's first appearance with Johnny Carson, then stood on his desk and declared, "O Captain, my Captain. You will be missed."

Locations that had featured prominently in Robin's life were turned into makeshift shrines, where fans left flowers, candles, and farewell messages: at his home in Tiburon, at the house in San Francisco where he had filmed *Mrs. Doubtfire,* at his star on the Hollywood Walk of Fame, at the bench in Boston's Public Garden where he and Matt Damon had opened up to each other in *Good Will Hunting,* even at the old Queen Anne mansion in Boulder that had been used for exterior shots on *Mork & Mindy.* Social media and Twitter, especially, were blanketed with posts that reflected the heartache and confusion felt by the population at large, as people felt compelled to recite favorite quotations from Robin's performances or give thanks for what his work had meant to them. His suicide seemed to cast everything he had done previously in a newly foreboding light; the serious roles were suddenly more urgent and the comic roles were now irreparably tinged with melancholy. As the film critic Bilge Ebiri tweeted with uncommon precision that day, "You start off as a kid seeing

Robin Williams as a funny man. You come of age realizing many of his roles are about keeping darkness at bay."

While many celebrities posted about their favorite memories of Robin or shared pictures of themselves with him, other friends shunned this strangely performative aspect of the modern-day mourning ritual. Knowing that many people expected to hear from him, Billy Crystal simply tweeted, "No words."

Crystal and his wife, Janice, had been just a few days into what was meant to be a month-long European vacation when they got the call from David Steinberg, who was Crystal's manager as well as Robin's, telling them that Robin had taken his own life. Immediately, the couple canceled the rest of their trip and prepared to return home to mourn their friend. As they passed through the airport in Rome, Crystal was struck by the tableau presented by the international newsstands, where every cover of every publication bore a picture of Robin's face. "For that moment," Crystal said, "there was no war in Iraq or Afghanistan. There were no terrorist threats. There was no trouble in the world, except that Robin had died. Every paper, every-where, the front page. He was a joyous spirit that people loved and trusted. It didn't make sense."

Among the most widely circulated images posted on social media that day was a bittersweet one of Aladdin embracing the Genie, with the caption "Genie, you're free"; the picture was from the final scene of that Disney movie, when Aladdin has used his final wish to release the Genie from his servitude in the lamp and the magical shape-shifter takes off into the sky. A version of this tweet posted by the Academy of Motion Picture Arts and Sciences was seen online an estimated sixty-nine million times, and though it was simply as a tribute and farewell to an Oscar-winning actor, it seemed to strike the wrong tone — as if Robin's body, if not his very life, was a prison he needed to escape from and suicide the means for his emancipation.

Even as Robin's own friends eulogized him that day, some of them found themselves brimming with a frustration and disbelief for which they could not quite find a place. As the comedian Steven Pearl later said, "I don't count his death as a suicide, because it wasn't him that did it, as far as I'm concerned. It just really angered me that that would happen to someone like him. Why couldn't this happen to an asshole? I know plenty of those. It was like John Lennon getting killed again, except this time we knew John. Come on, Robin. You're supposed to die when I was in my eighties, you son of a bitch."

Steven Haft, who produced *Dead Poets Society* and *Jakob the Liar,* was among those who felt certain that, no matter how much agony Robin was in, he would never have knowingly inflicted such pain on his own children. "I don't, to this day, believe he intended to never see his children again," he said.

On Tuesday evening, August 12, Robin's children made their first public remarks, in three individual statements. Zak wrote, "I would ask those that loved him to remember him by being as gentle, kind, and generous as he would be. Seek to bring joy to the world as he sought." Zelda poignantly joked, "To those he touched who are sending kind words, know that one of his favorite things in the world was to make you all laugh. As for those who are sending negativity, know that some small, giggling part of him is sending a flock of pigeons to your house to poop on your car. Right after you've had it washed. After all, he loved to laugh too." Cody wrote, "I will miss him and take him with me everywhere I go for the rest of my life, and will look forward, forever, to the moment when I get to see him again."

Marsha, who had not spoken to the press about Robin in years, released her own statement; it was brief but full of warmth, understanding, and sorrow. It read, in its entirety:

My heart is split wide open and scattered over the planet with all of you. Please

remember the gentle, loving, generous —
and yes, brilliant and funny — man that was
Robin Williams. My arms are wrapped
around our children as we attempt to
grapple with celebrating the man we love,
while dealing with this immeasurable loss.

By the time these statements were released
to the news media, Robin's body had already
been cremated and, like his parents before
him, his ashes had been scattered in the San
Francisco Bay in a private ceremony earlier
that day. There would be no gravestone or
monument for Robin; as Zak would later say
of him, "Only a passing of state has occurred.
My father's vastness is no longer contained
in his body. But his soul, his being, is everywhere."

Two more days passed, and in the absence
of concrete information, speculation about
the circumstances of Robin's death grew
wilder, more inaccurate, and more irresponsible: he was drunk or high when he died; he
was flat broke and the walls were closing in;
his suicide was a hoax and he was still alive;
he was murdered.

On Thursday, seemingly in response to no
particular report or allegation, Susan put out
another statement to the press. It read:

Robin spent so much of his life helping others. Whether he was entertaining millions

704

on stage, film or television, our troops on the frontlines, or comforting a sick child — Robin wanted us to laugh and to feel less afraid.

Since his passing, all of us who loved Robin have found some solace in the tremendous outpouring of affection and admiration for him from the millions of people whose lives he touched. His greatest legacy, besides his three children, is the joy and happiness he offered to others, particularly to those fighting personal battles.

Robin's sobriety was intact and he was brave as he struggled with his own battles of depression, anxiety as well as early stages of Parkinson's Disease, which he was not yet ready to share publicly.

It is our hope in the wake of Robin's tragic passing, that others will find the strength to seek the care and support they need to treat whatever battles they are facing so they may feel less afraid.

It was the first time anyone outside of Robin's innermost circle had disclosed his Parkinson's diagnosis with the wider world, and Susan's statement appeared to bring clarity to the cloudiest of questions surrounding his death. If it was difficult to countenance the idea of Robin killing himself over financial worries or persistent depression, it became somewhat more comprehensible in the face of a degenerative disease that, even with treatment, would gradually shut down his body and his mind. Horrible as his choice was, at least now it seemed it could be framed as a decision between immediate, terminal pain and an untold lifetime of further torment.

Two weeks later, Robin was singled out for a special acknowledgment at the Emmy Awards, at the end of the show's annual In Memoriam montage. After the pop musician Sara Bareilles sang a somber version of "Smile," Billy Crystal took the stage and shared some favorite anecdotes about his friend: sitting in a broadcast booth at Shea Stadium with Tim McCarver and Robin, who knew nothing about baseball, but suddenly perked up and slipped into character when Crystal suggested, "You know, Tim, we have a great Russian baseball player with us"; or bonding with Crystal's older, immigrant relatives at family events by pretending he had recently arrived in America from a little shtetl in Poland.

Dropping any remaining layer of shtick or irony, Crystal continued with an earnestness he did not often put forward in his performances. "For almost forty years," he said, "he was the brightest star in a comedy galaxy. But while some of the brightest of our celestial bodies are actually extinct now, their energy long since cooled, but miraculously, because they float in the heavens, so far away from us now, their beautiful light will continue to shine on us forever. And the glow will be so bright, it'll warm your heart, it'll make your eyes glisten, and you'll think to yourself: Robin Williams, what a concept."

A selection of Robin's TV appearances followed, ending on a bit from *An Evening at the Met* about the inquisitive, innocently foulmouthed three-year-old Zak, and Robin telling his young son he did not always have the answers to life's questions. "But maybe along the way," Robin says, "you take my hand, tell a few jokes and have some fun. . . . Come on, pal. You're not afraid, are you?" In his child's falsetto he answers himself: "Nah." The final punch line — Zak saying "Fuck it" — could not be aired on network television, so the montage concluded with Robin walking off the Metropolitan Opera stage into darkness, his left hand extended into the air as if holding on to some bigger, invisible figure.

The tribute had been difficult for Crystal to compose, coming so soon after Robin's death, when many of the details were still shrouded in mystery. "It would have been easier if he'd had a heart attack and died," Crystal said. "But the fact that it happened the way it happened, there were so many unanswered questions and these terrible assumptions: he must have been drinking, it must have been drugs. Nobody knew, including myself. I would sit down to write something — 'This sounds like shit' — how can I make it funny and personal, and put him in a perspective that I thought would represent who he was and would always be?"

Crystal had cried his way through a dress rehearsal the day before the *Emmy* broadcast, and on the night of the ceremony he wept in the arms of Jay Leno, who was waiting for him in the wings when he finished his delivery. Yet in other moments he felt an inexplicable sense of serenity. Every morning since he had returned home after Robin's death, Crystal had noticed a small green and yellow bird waiting at his window, trying to get his attention by tapping at the glass with its prominent beak or by flying up and hovering ostentatiously. "It keeps pecking at the window and it wouldn't fly away," Crystal said. "It wasn't scared. And I'd hit the window back and it would do it back to me, and then it would fly up and land on this little leaf. Over and over again. It's weird."

With its familiar physical features and show-off tendencies — not to mention the fact that his best friend had shared his name with a bird — Crystal could only arrive at one explanation for this avian attention-seeker. "Jews have this belief when someone dies," he explained. "The thought is that they have thirty days before the soul settles in heaven. I definitely felt it when my mom died.

You feel a presence, whether it's there or not, and then you feel it go." Using his phone, Crystal recorded a video of the bird and showed it to Robin's son Cody. "I didn't say anything," Crystal recalled, "and Cody looked at it and said, 'Oh, that's my dad.' "

On September 27, hundreds of Robin's friends and colleagues gathered at the Curran Theatre in San Francisco for a memorial service. The event was not open to the public or broadcast in any form, affording some intimacy for guest speakers who hoped their words, offered haltingly and through tears, could conjure Robin one last time and bring some resolution to an otherwise unfinished life. On the back of the program was an illustration of a hummingbird, similar to the one that had adorned the invitation to Robin's sixtieth birthday party, only this one was clad in a suit of armor; inside the pamphlet, opposite the list of speakers, was an inspirational quote from Ralph Waldo Emerson:

To laugh often and much;
to win the respect of intelligent people
and the affection of children;
to earn the appreciation of honest critics
and endure the betrayal of false friends;
to appreciate beauty;
to find the best in others;
to leave the world a bit better

whether by a healthy child,
a garden patch, or a redeemed social
    condition;
to know even one life has breathed easier
because you lived here.
This is to have succeeded.

Following an opening invocation by the Reverend Cecil Williams and a medley of soul and R & B songs performed by the Glide Memorial Choir & Change Band, the first speaker of the day was, of course, Billy Crystal. He shared familiar stories about Robin calling him on the day of Reagan's funeral to impersonate the late president ("that would explain why I'm in a hot tub with Joe Stalin and Nixon's balls are resting on the bridge of my nose") and his being reprimanded at a Comic Relief event by the Democratic presidential nominee Michael Dukakis, after which, Crystal said, "He whispers in my ear: 'No way this mother-fucker wins.' "

It was only in their phone conversations of the past few years that he and Robin were truly opening up to each other, Crystal said, and "you can only do that with someone that you totally trust. And isn't that really the measure of a friend? That he not only rejoices in your success but is there with a shoulder to cry on, when things get a little — as he called it — crispy? I'm sorry, folks. I'm a little lost without him."

Robin always dared to go further than his peers, Crystal said: "He was so fucking brave, and I loved that about him, and I always will." In one of their philosophical conversations about the nature of comedy, Robin explained to him that it was like eating a lobster: "You keep crushing stuff and then, hey, there's something sweet where you didn't expect it to be. That was our dear friend. I'll miss him always."

Bobcat Goldthwait spoke next, observing how, after Robin's death, a portion of his dialogue from *World's Greatest Dad* had become an Internet meme. Reciting the line, he said: "I used to think the worst thing in life is ending up all alone. It isn't. The worst thing in life is ending up with people that make you feel all alone." As Goldthwait now explained, "That was just a movie. That couldn't be farther from the truth in regards to Robin. You loved Robin and he loved you."

"I'm not a doctor," Goldthwait said, "but something happened to Robin a few years back. Again, I am not a doctor. But something affected his brain."

More remembrances followed, from Bing Gordon, the venture capitalist and an executive at the video game publisher Electronic Arts; Bonnie Hunt, Robin's *Jumanji* costar; and his assistant, Rebecca Erwin Spencer.

When it was her turn to speak, Susan tried

to sum up what her handful of years together with Robin had meant to her.

"Robin was not alone as he waged war against the mounting offenses of depression, anxiety and Parkinson's," she said. "With trusted companions and professional help he pressed on. I am so proud of how very hard he worked at gaining ground on the physical, mental, emotional and personal pressures he faced. Spiritually, he was gaining ground, too. But he had so very much to overcome."

Neither Valerie nor Marsha spoke during the ceremony.

Eric Idle, who said he was too overwhelmed to write a proper speech, instead performed a short, Monty Python–esque song in Robin's honor, affectionate and humorous with a tinge of exasperation that he did not try to hide. Its lyrics ran, in part:

Good night, Robin
It's hateful that you've gone
But we're grateful
for that fateful
day you came along

Admiral Mike Mullen, the former chairman of the Joint Chiefs of Staff, talked about Robin's participation in the USO tours, and Mort Sahl looked back on the friendship he had shared with Robin since he'd moved back to Mill Valley. Then an emotional

Whoopi Goldberg reflected on how Robin, as well as Crystal, had treated her like a peer and had given her the space to be herself as they bonded together on the Comic Relief project.

She got choked up as she recounted how Robin would phone her up, unexpectedly, even in periods when she was going through divorces, hoping that she would find happiness, companionship, and contentment. "Now, Robin would call me out of the blue," she said. " 'Are you married?' No, I'd say, no, I'm not going to do it again. 'Are you gay?' I'd say, No no no. He said, 'But you're all right?' I'd say, yeah, I'm all right, man." Robin, she said, "spoke to me when nobody else would."

The final speakers of the day were Robin's children, who took the stage together and at times held each other's hands and hugged one another for support. Cody was the first to talk; he was the youngest, at twenty-two, and the least public of the three, but his oration was articulate and powerful. He spoke of having trouble sleeping from the time he was very young and how his father would try to soothe his insomnia with comic books and science magazines. "He would read me articles about space, robots, nuclear bombs, but they might as well have been fairy tales," Cody said. "I would drift into a universe of dreams and he was the captain of the ship. . . .

He gave my imagination rocket fuel, as he did for so many other people."

He compared Robin's laughter to "a volcano eruption" and described his bright blue eyes as being "like the eyes of a child, his eyes were full of love, curiosity, and bewilderment. Those eyes saw a world which, in many places, had plummeted into darkness, and they made the child in him sad and longing. The man that he was would help anyone and anybody he could. Bottom line. His body would go through the motions and he would rev himself up, and unleash on people, and they would laugh and cry and look at each other. It meant the world to them, and to him as well."

More ruefully, Cody acknowledged that Robin had not always been available to him as he was growing up. "I always wished he would belong more to our family than he did to the world," he said. "But that's a selfish notion, I realize. Folks like him don't just grow on trees. It was only fair for us to share. Everybody deserves to laugh so hard it hurts, and everybody deserves his fairy tales." Speaking directly to his father, he said, "Please rest up, and when you're done resting, go explore a hundred different utopias whose doors were locked until now. Traverse a million different realities and make everyone laugh so hard that their cheeks hurt along the way. I will carry your heart and your dream with me always."

Next was Zelda, who reflected on all the experiences that she and her father would never get to share. "There are only two things I am actually sad that he will miss," she said. "One, that he will not get to walk me down the aisle and make a completely inappropriate speech at my wedding. And two, like he did with my little brother, that he will not get to teach his future grandchildren inappropriate jokes that get them sent to the principal's office. I guess showing them his stand-up too young will have to do."

She closed with a quotation from Antoine de Saint-Exupéry's *The Little Prince,* just before the title character — a wandering, innocent space traveler — allows himself to be bitten by a poisonous snake. A portion of it read:

In one of the stars I shall be living. In one of them I shall be laughing. And so it will be as if all the stars were laughing, when you look at the sky at night. . . . You — only you — will have stars that can laugh!

Zak came last of all, and like his half sister and half brother, he spoke tenderly and honestly about his father, but without romance or illusion. "There's Robin Williams the concept, and then there's Robin Williams the man," Zak began.

I'd like to speak about the man. The beautiful, generous, troubled, wonderful, dear man that I am infinitely proud to call my father. Eater of cold chicken breast, drinker of espresso, lover of bumper stickers. I'd like to speak about the man who was a paradox. The alien. I feel the overwhelming joy he brought millions, and I felt his abject loneliness. He was at once so superhuman and yet so very human. But I don't think he ever felt he was anything special. I can't tell you how many times I just wanted to embrace him and say, "Dad, it's okay. Everything's going to be okay." And when I'd say that, he would look at me and smile and say, "I know."

On what would be their final morning together, Zak recalled, "I said to him, 'Dad, everything's going to be okay.' And he said to me, 'I know.' I'll never see him again. But I do know that he said what he meant. Everything will be okay."

Another month later, on October 26, before Game 5 of the 2014 World Series, Zak, Zelda, and Cody strode onto the field at AT&T Park in San Francisco, dressed in San Francisco Giants baseball caps and jerseys. While Zelda and Cody stood at the edge of the pitcher's mound, their arms around each other, Zak stepped onto the rubber and began practicing his windup. Waiting at home plate was

Billy Crystal, who caught the ceremonial first pitch that Zak threw to him; then, supported by the cheers of some forty-three thousand baseball fans, the four of them hugged and walked off the field together.

Crystal later recalled the scene as one of the first few instances of pleasure that he and Robin's children had been allowed to experience following Robin's death. "If Robin could have been there for that, I'd have told him, 'Hey, listen, Zak threw the pitch — and *I* caught it," Crystal said with mock haughtiness. "I think he would have found an incredible joy in that. I didn't let myself get sad that day." Describing one of his favorite qualities about his friend — a huge, eruptive cackle that Robin would let out when he was especially tickled — Crystal said, "I could hear that Pavarotti laugh."

As they savored the moment, Zak, Zelda, and Cody seemed happy, healing, and ready to move forward. But Robin's story wasn't over yet, and neither was theirs.

21
THE BIG ROOM

Death was supposed to have settled many of the questions that Robin's life could not. The paradox of the man who was both wildly outgoing and painfully introverted, at home in a crowd of strangers and desperately alone with the people he knew best, had finally been resolved. Behind the facade, this was a man who was suffering terrible pain, and whose long-standing fears about the erosion of his career and the decay of his body had come to pass simultaneously. Now it seemed that he had taken his own life in a moment of maximum desolation, almost surely to spare himself the punishment of having to stand by as a spectator while his once agile frame turned against him and calcified into a prison for his singularly inventive mind. If anything positive or constructive had occurred in the aftermath of his death, it had, at least, brought sensitive issues of depression and mental health to the forefront and united Robin's family in an effort to heal and move beyond their devastating loss.

But there was still much more that no one knew.

In November 2014, three months after Robin died, the Marin County Sheriff's Office released his autopsy protocol, a report enumerating all the factors that had contributed to his death. The first category on this list was designated "Hanging," with twenty-five descriptive subentries ("Asphyxia, minutes," "Belt ligature encircling the neck," "Ligature mark with slight furrow of the neck," and so on). The second category was "Incised wounds of left wrist"; the third, "Healing abrasion, right arm"; and the fourth, "Hypertensive, atherosclerotic and valvular cardiovascular disease." Then, there was a fifth category, "Neuropathological diagnoses," whose first subentry read: "Diffuse Lewy body dementia (DLBD, aka diffuse Lewy body disease)."

A separate surgical pathology report, which had been prepared over the previous days and which analyzed portions of Robin's brain tissue that had been preserved before his cremation, expanded on this assessment. Its summary read, "These neuropathologic findings in this case support the diagnosis of Lewy body dementia (aka diffuse Lewy body disease or DLBD) using the most recent guidelines established by the National Institute on Aging/Alzheimer's Disease Association. . . . It is important to note that patients with diffuse Lewy body dementia frequently present with Parkinsonian motor symptoms and a constellations [*sic*] of neuropsychiatric manifestations, including depression and hallucination."

What these reports documented for the first time was the presence of a devastating brain disorder that likely accounted for much of what Robin had been experiencing in his final years, and which had never been fully diagnosed in his lifetime. Lewy body disease, a dementia believed to affect more than 1.3 million people in America — and far more men than women — results from a buildup of protein deposits in the brain. "There's a protein that is normally useful in the brain, and it starts to accumulate abnormally, and it's toxic," said the neurologist Douglas Scharre of the Wexner Medical Center at Ohio State University. "Where it builds up it can cause cell loss and cell death, and therefore that contributes to certain conditions."

The onset of the disease is extremely gradual, Dr. Scharre explained: "The proteins build up very slowly. One day you're normal. Then you're having a little bit of motor problems, then little cognitive issues." Those who suffer from it may first notice memory problems or physical stiffness, but over time they often undergo massive personality changes. They experience sleep problems and, in some cases, hallucinations; they may become increasingly physical, even violent; and their mental acuity can flicker on and off, like a light switch.

"They'll just shut down for an hour a day," Dr. Scharre said. "They're not asleep — they're awake. They're just staring off and not doing much. It's not that they're comatose or anything. But they sit there, and then all of a sudden, they're back with it."

James E. Galvin, a neurologist from the Charles E. Schmidt College of Medicine at Florida Atlantic University, explained further: "People can appear drowsy or sleeping, have staring spells, think illogically and incoherently — and these episodes wax and wane, lasting seconds or minutes or hours. And they're unpredictable."

The symptoms of Lewy body disease are distinct from those of other disorders. Unlike people with Alzheimer's disease, who have difficulty forming memories, people with Lewy body disease can store memories but have difficulty retrieving them. Unlike Parkinson's disease, which damages the motor-control portions of the brain, Lewy body disease goes on to attack parts of the brain that govern visual and spatial control as well as decision making.

Though Robin may have been exhibiting some of the movement problems associated with Parkinson's disease, Dr. Galvin said,

"There was more going on, and that more made it suspicious, and that more was above and beyond Parkinson's."

Because of these overlapping symptoms, though, patients are sometimes diagnosed with other conditions, including Parkinson's disease, before Lewy body disease is properly identified. "I don't fault physicians for misdiagnosing it," Dr. Galvin said. "It's not that easy."

Certain drugs, including medications prescribed for Parkinson's, can help treat some of the symptoms associated with Lewy body disease, such as the movement problems, aberrant behaviors, and sleep disruptions. "The medications help a little bit, but not a whole lot," Dr. Scharre said. "We give them in low doses, but if you go up higher, more often they're going to get side effects, because it causes increased hallucinations if you already have that."

Ultimately, the dementia itself is aggressive, irreversible, and incurable. "There's no way to repair the damage that's been done," Dr. Galvin said. "All you're doing is slowing down the symptoms' progression without changing the underlying disease."

He added, "If you give someone a wrong diagnosis, the family has no ability to plan."

It is also a disease with an associated risk of suicide, particularly when patients are younger and before its most severe effects have set in. "If you're young, if you have insight into what's happening, and you have some of the associated symptoms — like depression and the hallucinations," said Edward Huey, a neuropsychiatrist at Columbia University's College of Physicians and Surgeons. "That's when we think the risk of suicide is highest."

In Robin's case, Dr. Galvin said, a complete and precise diagnosis can never be obtained, because it was not completed while he was alive. "If we could look through the retrospect-o-scope, we might say, 'Oh, sure, that's Lewy body disease.' He may have eventually been diagnosed with it. At the time he was presenting symptoms that might have looked like Parkinson's and that's what they were diagnosing. Over time, it probably would have been more refined."

Still, these new findings about Robin's condition seemed to fill in some of the most perplexing gaps surrounding his death, and they were rapidly embraced by many of his friends and loved ones. "It was not depression that killed Robin," Susan would later say. "Depression was one of let's call it fifty symptoms and it was a small one." The disease that her husband had been facing, she said, "was faster than us and bigger than us. . . . one of the doctors said, 'Robin was very aware that he was losing his mind and there was nothing he could do about it.' "

Eric Idle mourned him as a man "misdiagnosed with Parkinsons" and "an undiagnosed victim of dementia with Lewy bodies," and Bobcat Goldthwait reaffirmed the findings of the autopsy, while ruefully acknowledging the many other hypotheses that had taken hold in the public's imagination and become part of Robin's mythology. "He died from Lewy body dementia," Goldthwait said, "but the world wants it to be about something else, depression, drugs, career, relationships, etc. He had a disease that attacked his brain.

"My own opinion is that that's what actually changed his perception of reality," he said.

But other friends saw a cold, conscious deliberation at work in Robin's final actions. As Billy Crystal explained, "I put myself in his place. Think of it this way: the speed at which the comedy came is the speed at which the terrors came. And all that they described that can happen with this psychosis, if that's the right word — the hallucinations, the images, the terror — coming at the speed his comedy came at, maybe even faster, I can't imagine living like that."

Thinking back to their conversations after Robin was told he had Parkinson's disease, Crystal said, "He did ask me a lot of questions about Muhammad Ali. 'When did he start to get bad?' 'When did he go silent?' 'When did this happen?' He was seeing himself. *This was where I'm going to be.* I don't think he could live with that."

Crystal added, "My heart breaks that he suffered and only saw one way out."

The coroner's findings raised a new mystery about Robin's final hours. Was he cognizant of who he was, and was he aware of what he was doing when he committed suicide? Or could he have been in the grip of a dissociative state brought on by his disease when he took his own life? The official reports held no answers to these questions, and perhaps they were impossible to solve. In the past, Robin's family had put out press releases sharing the information they had, only to see these public statements fuel high-flown and romanticized conjectures about him. This time, they made no comment about the new findings, neither advocating for what they knew to be true nor dispelling what they believed might have been false.

For a year-end edition of *Entertainment Weekly,* Billy Crystal contributed a short comic screenplay imagining Robin's arrival in heaven. Set in a celestial nightclub called the Big Room, the script envisioned Robin's entrance accompanied by a Don Pardo voice-over and an angelic ovation; he riffs on iconic audience members like Abraham Lincoln and Anne Frank ("is it true that being Jews, on Sunday nights you would get Chinese food . . . takeout?"), reunites with deceased

725

mentors like Jonathan Winters and Richard Pryor, and meets his hero Albert Einstein. ("Al, wanna know my theory of relativity? Never lend relatives money 'cause you won't get it back.") The scene ends with Robin receiving pats on the back from Lenny Bruce and George Carlin, nods of acknowledgment from George Burns and Groucho Marx, a blown kiss from Gilda Radner, and a respectful derby tip from Charlie Chaplin. "WE PUSH IN ON ROBIN," the stage directions say. "HE SEEMS AT PEACE . . . HE SMILES . . . FADE OUT."

It was a sweet and sentimental flight of fancy, as much a reflection of Crystal's ribald sense of humor as of Robin's, and the storybook ending that anyone would wish for a fallen hero of comedy. But regardless of its author and his good intentions, it was just another fantasy, and it did not reflect starker realities back on earth.

On the afternoon of December 19, 2014, the Friday before Christmas, Susan's lawyers filed a petition in San Francisco Superior Court, asking for a judge to interpret what they said were ambiguities in the rules governing Robin's estate. In 1989, amid his divorce from Valerie, Robin had created a financial trust to ensure that, in the event of his death, she would continue to receive alimony and child support payments; once his financial obligations to Valerie were met, the trust was updated to make Zak its beneficiary, and, during Robin's divorce from Marsha, it was updated to make further provisions for Zelda and Cody.

About a month before he married Susan in 2011, Robin had entered into a prenuptial agreement with her, and in 2012 he signed a brief legal document, known as a pour-over will, that would leave his estate to his trust, which was operated by his attorneys. Robin also created a separate trust specifically for Susan, which left her their home in Tiburon, valued at about $7 million, as well as its contents, and enough cash or property to cover, for her lifetime, "all costs related to the residence." However, the terms of his trust specified property that was to go to his three children, including all of Robin's "clothing, jewelry, personal photos taken prior to his marriage to Susan," as well as Robin's "memorabilia and awards in the entertainment industry and the tangible personal property" at his Napa ranch.

In their petition, Susan's lawyers outlined troubling claims, alleging that just days after Robin's death, "the co-Trustees, through their agents, unilaterally removed Mr. Williams's personal property and asked for permission from Mrs. Williams after the fact."

The trustees, it said, "insisted on gaining access to Mrs. Williams's home for the purpose of dividing and removing property under the specific gifts of the Trust," noting that the trustees had keys to the house. "Naturally, Mrs. Williams became frightened of the co-Trustees invading her home (where she and her two teen-age sons reside)." It was at this point that Susan hired lawyers of her own, and, in retaliation, the petition suggested, "certain home-related services were canceled."

Susan's lawyers said that Robin's trust instructions were ambiguous about what constituted jewelry; whether he meant memorabilia specifically related to his entertainment career or accumulated over his lifetime; what was memorabilia or home contents; and what should be done with property from the Tiburon house that he kept at the Napa ranch.

Susan acknowledged in the filing that she had no claim to possessions like the suspenders Robin wore on *Mork & Mindy,* because they are "related to Mr. Williams's acting career in the entertainment industry." But she said that she should be entitled to other personal items, like the ring and the tuxedo that he wore at their wedding, as well as "Mr. Williams's personal collections of knick-knacks and other items that are not associated with his famous persona."

There were issues, too, with the reserve fund intended for Susan so she could cover the costs of the Tiburon house. As the petition put it, "The co-Trustees have taken a restrictive interpretation of this provision, despite the broad phrasing of the Trust terms."

That, at least, was how Susan had characterized her recent interactions with Robin's children and the executors of his estate. But Zak, Zelda, and Cody naturally saw things very differently, and about a month later, they filed a court document of their own. In emotionally charged terms, they objected to Susan's petition, and they characterized her as an interloper who was trying to exploit a legal process to gain herself even more than Robin had already promised her.

Their legal filing, dated January 21, 2015, stated that they were "heartbroken" that Susan, "Mr. Williams' wife of less than three years, has acted against his wishes by challenging the plans he so carefully made for his estate. While it is styled as a request for instruction, the Petition in fact appears to be a blatant attempt to alter the disposition of assets Mr. Williams specifically planned and provided for under the terms of the Trust Agreement."

And whatever else Susan might seek to claim from Robin's estate, whether property or money, it came from the share the children were already promised, their filing said, "in a way that would prevent them from receiving what their father wanted them to receive."

Contrary to Susan's claim that the trustees of Robin's estate had intimidated her by suggesting that they would be coming into her home to remove trust property, the Williams children said that the trustees had been denied access to the Tiburon residence for nearly three months, even while she had possessions appraised and conducted a $30,000 renovation of the house. At the time of the filing, they said, "more than five months after their father's death, the Williams Children have not been allowed any access to their father's personal effects in the Tiburon Residence, including family photos, that Mr. Williams clearly intended for his children."

Particularly galling to Zak, Zelda, and Cody was an ill-considered turn of phrase in Susan's petition that described Robin's vast holdings of collectibles and mementos as "collections of knickknacks." It was a misstatement they seized upon to show how, in their estimation, Susan had never truly understood their father, and they rebutted it at length in their filing, which said:

it is important to recognize that Mr. Williams was an avid collector of various items of personal, cultural, or historical interest, including, but not limited to: toys, including but not limited to Japanese anime figurines; watches; rings; pendant necklaces; pendants, brooches and lapel pins; carved figurines, including but not limited to Net-suke figurines; carved boxes; theater masks; rare, first edition and autographed books and related materials; graphic novels; record albums; bicycles; walking sticks; Native American articles; models; movie posters; sports-related memorabilia; Middle East tour-related memorabilia, including but [not] limited to flags and coins; antique and unique weapons, including but not limited to knives; mineral specimens and fossils; and skulls. . . . These collections were carefully amassed by Mr. Williams over his lifetime and were precious to him. As the Williams Children grew, so did their father's collections and they shared in their father's excitement as additions were made to his collections.

As far as Susan's contention that she might need more money than the trust instructions promised her to pay for the upkeep of the house, the children's legal filing said: "It is telling indeed that Petitioner appears to be arguing for additional funds for her trust before her trust has even been funded."

The details of the legal dispute soon spilled out into the press, and as further arguments were waged in the court of public opinion, they turned ugly at times. Jim Wagstaffe, one of Susan's lawyers, said that his client was "not somebody who has any sticky fingers," while he castigated Robin's children for the wealth they inherited at his death. "Mr. Williams wanted his wife to be able to stay in her home and not be disrupted in her life with her children," Wagstaffe said. "Compared to what the Williams children were set to receive from their father, this is a bucket of water in a lake."

These blistering legal exchanges triggered a sensitive fault line on the boundary between Robin's children, who were close-knit and had experienced many years of thick and thin together, and Susan, who was still very much a newcomer to a complicated family. The children were fundamentally private people who wanted no special treatment because of who their father was; Susan had known Robin as a celebrity first. They had all been competing for the limited resource of Robin's attention, and now there was no more of it to give. The man who had bridged the gulf between these camps was gone now, and though there was no way of knowing where he would have stood in this dispute, the very notion of it surely would have made him uncomfortable. "One thing Robin didn't like is, he didn't like conflict, and he wanted people to genuinely be happy," Bobcat Goldthwait said. "He really wanted everybody to be happy."

For some of Robin's friends and colleagues, the estate dispute reinforced for them a long-standing discomfort they had felt about Susan, and whether she fully shared the values of her husband and his family on the proper applications of wealth and celebrity. From the moment she was first introduced to Robin's children, in the days before his open-heart surgery, there were concerns about how smoothly she meshed with the rest of the family — whether she respected Robin's relationships with Zak, Zelda, and Cody, as well as with their mothers, Valerie and Marsha. When Susan decided to pursue the matter in court, they felt their suspicions had been justified.

"I think she just wanted to secure her place as Mrs. Williams — the final Mrs. Williams," said Cheri Minns, Robin's makeup artist. "And to always be that. I can't see that. And none of it really matters. Because he's gone."

The producer Steven Haft echoed the sentiment that while Susan was entitled to share in the grief and sadness that the other members of the family felt, she had overstepped her bounds. "It's interesting when I hear Susan described as the widow Williams," he said. "There are only three people on the planet who can be described as the widow Williams, and Susan isn't one of them. There's Marsha. There's Billy. And there's David [Steinberg, Robin's manager]. I have not heard accounts by which Susan deserves the accolade."

Even Robin's children could not completely deny the frustration they felt. "Susan was under the impression that she had struck gold," Zak said of her. "But for us, we're deeply involved with Dad's life. You can't untether us from the equation. I think that was a little unexpected."

Going forward, the children sought to portray themselves as having come to terms with their father's death, past any anger and accepting the reality of his absence. As Zelda explained, "A lot of people who have been through it and lost someone — the ones that I've found who have gone on to lead very full lives — found that they just had to know that there's no point questioning it, and there's no point blaming everyone else for it, and there's no point blaming yourself or the world or whatever the case may be," she said. "Because it happened, so you have to continue to move and you have to continue to live and manage."

When asked what had driven her father to take his own life, she answered, "It's not important to ask."

It was not until October 2015 that Susan and Robin's children reached a settlement in their standoff. The children kept the vast quantity of their father's personal items, including more than fifty bicycles and eighty-five watches, and his collection of toy soldiers, as well as possessions like Robin's Academy

Award statuette for *Good Will Hunting*, which was never in dispute. Susan was allowed to hold on to possessions that had emotional value for her, including their wedding gifts, a favorite watch of Robin's, and a bicycle they had bought on their honeymoon in Paris. She was also permitted to continue to receive funds for the Tiburon house, in which she would be allowed to stay for the rest of her life.

"While it's hard to speak of this as a win, given it stems from the greatest loss of all, I am deeply grateful to the judge for helping resolve these issues," Susan said in a statement at the time. "I can live in peace knowing that my husband's wishes were honored," she continued. "I feel like Robin's voice has been heard and I can finally grieve in the home we shared together."

The Williams children, through their spokesman, said that "in keeping with their father's desire for privacy, they would not be making any public statements about the case."

With nothing binding them anymore, the two factions of Robin's family moved off in different directions. Susan began to speak out publicly about the last months of Robin's life and the circumstances that preceded his suicide; over the span of a few weeks in November, she gave interviews to ABC News (which were shown on *Good Morning America,*

World News Tonight, Nightline, and *The View*) and to *People* magazine; she also contributed an essay to the *Times* of London. These recollections were told only from her perspective and did not infringe on anyone else's memories of Robin, and though each interview essentially focused on the same set of events — their meeting at the Apple store, their wedding, the onset of Robin's health problems, his Parkinson's diagnosis — it was far more than anyone in the Williams family had said about his decline and death.

In March 2016, the California Department of Transportation officially renamed the tunnel that connects Marin County to the Golden Gate Bridge in Robin's honor; locals had already been referring to it as the Robin Williams Tunnel for many years, because its arching entries and exits were painted with rainbows, evoking the colorful hues of the suspenders he wore on *Mork & Mindy.* In October, the SAG-AFTRA Foundation, operated by the labor union that represents professional film and television actors, christened its Robin Williams Center in New York, an educational space and theater. The space was opened with a gala ceremony where the guests included Zak and Zelda, Billy and Janice Crystal, and Whoopi Goldberg. Susan did not attend the event.

That fall, Susan gave another round of interviews about the end of Robin's life, including an appearance on *CBS This Morning* and an essay in the scientific journal *Neurology* that carried the provocative title "The Terrorist Inside My Husband's Brain." Susan, who had joined the board of directors for the American Brain Foundation, a professional association of scientists and doctors, concluded her essay with a direct appeal to the medical experts she trusted would be reading her contribution. "Hopefully from this sharing of our experience you will be inspired to turn Robin's suffering into something meaningful through your work and wisdom," she wrote. "It is my belief that when healing comes out of Robin's experience, he will not have battled and died in vain."

Among the provisions of Robin's trust that were revealed in the legal dispute between Susan and his children was a curious stipulation that read as follows:

All ownership interest in the right to Settlor's name, voice, signature, photograph, likeness and right of privacy/publicity (sometimes referred to as "right of publicity") to the Windfall Foundation, a California Nonprofit Corporation . . . subject to the restriction that such right of publicity shall not be exploited for a twenty-five (25) year period commencing on the date of Settlor's death.

What this meant in plain English was that

Robin had bequeathed all of his distinguishing qualities — what he looked like; what he sounded like; his signature; his name — to a charitable organization, set up by his attorneys, which would not be allowed to profit off them in any form for twenty-five years. It was an unusually forward-thinking way to contemplate how technology and entertainment might evolve over the next quarter century, optimistic and dystopian in equal proportions. There could be no new movies, TV shows, or advertisements in which he could appear or be digitally inserted; no new stand-up routines that could be created from his voice; no holograms or other as-yet undreamt-of media in which some simulacrum of him could be conjured up and made to perform his best-loved roles and routines — at least not before the year 2039. Until then, the human race would have to be satisfied with the finite amount of Robin Williams content he had produced while he was alive.

Aside from his animated features like *Aladdin* and the *Night at the Museum* franchise, Robin had never made a sequel to any of his movies; with the exceptions of those films and his television series, he had never played the same character more than once — as much as his critics loved to accuse him of playing the same character every single time. To date, none of his live-action movies or TV shows have been remade without him. A stage adaptation of *Dead Poets Society,* starring the comic actor Jason Sudeikis as Mr. Keating, opened to tepid reviews at an off-Broadway theater in New York in the fall of 2016. When Sony Pictures announced a few months earlier that it was producing a sequel to *Jumanji* starring Dwayne (The Rock) Johnson, the resulting outrage from fans who felt that Robin's memory had been disrespected was so great that Johnson had to assure the public, "You have my word, we will honor his name and the character of 'Alan Parrish' will stand alone and be forever immortalized in the world of *Jumanji* in an earnest and cool way. I have an idea of what to do and I think his family will be proud. I also think Robin is somewhere lookin' down and laughing."

For all the different strands of culture that Robin had tied together in his work, and all the people he drew from and celebrated as his influences, there was no actor or comedian who could be considered his protégé or his heir, no performer who tried to do what he did the way he did it. He had admirers but no imitators; no one combined the precise set of talents he had in the same alchemical proportions. Maybe they had the intellect, but not the sheer enthusiasm for the variety that the world could offer; the speed, but not the supernatural ability to invent and surprise; the wonderment, but never the purity of heart that came from a genuine empathy for his fellow man. Robin Williams was once in a lifetime, and his lifetime was now very much over.

EPILOGUE

One Saturday morning in the fall of 2009, Robin Williams called me at my home in New York and asked if I'd like to go shopping for comic books with him. We had been spending time together in the weeks prior for a profile I was writing about him for the *New York Times*, but he didn't extend this particular invitation to generate material for that story. We had discovered earlier, one late night in Robin's luxury hotel room in uptown Atlanta after he'd finished that night's set at the Fox Theatre, that we shared a mutual interest in comics and collectibles. When he mentioned that he'd be coming to New York on a break from the *Weapons of Self Destruction* tour and wanted to take me to one of his favorite comic-book shops when he visited, I thought it was the kind of thing a celebrity says during an interview to butter you up — an offhand pleasantry, with no real intention of following through. Only later did I learn that when Robin made this sort of offer, even to someone he knew only casually, it was a promise he meant to keep. He wasn't trying to influence how I wrote about him and he didn't expect anything more in return from me. If he could give you some of his time to help you enjoy your day or feel better about yourself, he would, and he gave pieces of himself to many people.

Later that afternoon, we met outside Forbidden Planet, a well-stocked shop of geeky offerings in Union Square. Robin traveled by himself, with no entourage, security personnel, or even his assistant. He was dressed in casual clothes and didn't seem to be trying to hide his identity from anyone, forgoing even a pair of sunglasses. The aisles were well populated with customers but he made his way through them freely, with the same excitement of a child who has been told that he can have anything he wants in the toy store. Robin spent the greatest portion of our time poring over a glass case full of expensive statuettes of militaristic robots and suggestively posed heroines. He wasn't necessarily looking for new additions to his personal collection but to see how it measured up to the store's display: "I've got that one at home," he said absently, more to himself than me, as he meandered around the case. "Got that one. Got that."

Naturally, it was an unexpected sight for the employees and other shoppers at the store to see him standing just a few feet away, immersed in the same colorful mementos as they were. He was well past the peak of his career, but he was still Robin Williams, the man they'd seen in *Good Morning, Vietnam* and *Dead Poets Society* and all those comedy routines and, yes, *Mork & Mindy.* He had given performances that they had seen and loved and carried with them in their hearts. He was still one of the biggest stars in the entertainment industry, and now, even in a jaded city not much impressed by celebrity, people were astonished and a little bit intoxicated by his presence.

As he turned a corner in the store, Robin nearly bumped into a middle-aged woman who hadn't previously noticed him there. She had been gazing at the floor, and as she turned her attention upward to take in his smiling face, she realized who she was looking at, and she was flabbergasted.

"It's — it's *you,*" she stammered out.

Now it was Robin's turn to glance downward and shuffle his feet in humility. "Yes it is," he said softly. What else could he say?

Robin still had this effect on people, even after having been in the public eye for decades. They could not believe that he was flesh and blood, like they were, and not just an image on a screen; the notion that he was someone who could be encountered and interacted with was almost too much to comprehend.

This was how Robin had experienced every day of his life for more than thirty years. As much as he might want to, he could never be introduced to someone or make eye contact with a stranger without seeing that shock of recognition in their eyes; he couldn't eliminate the barrier that went up when well-intentioned people wanted to give him special treatment. He could never know what it was like to lead what others considered to be a normal life and never see his own life as anything other than normal. Nor could he ever see himself as others saw him and take pride in the talents they easily recognized in him.

I spoke to Robin for the first time several months earlier, when I was working on a story about Bobcat Goldthwait's film *World's Greatest Dad.* Robin and I talked over the phone, and his voice was serene and almost impossibly relaxed, betraying none of the trademarks of the hyperactive stand-up who would have swung from the chandeliers if he'd been allowed to. "I hear you're going to come out and play with us," he said, having given me permission to follow him for a few days later that year on the *Weapons of Self Destruction* tour, which he was preparing to restart after his heart surgery.

I met him in that Atlanta hotel room,

around midnight, after his Fox Theatre performance. As I would later write about that night, the mechanical key hidden in his back was winding down, and the flow of free associations and zany voices was slowing to a trickle. But he wanted to know as much about me as I did about him — my life, my career, how I'd met my wife — and when I finally got an opening to ask him about his upbringing and his mother, the dim lights in the room began to flicker. Robin played off the moment effortlessly: "Mama, mama, is that you?" he asked with mock trepidation. "What is it you wish to say? Speak more of this, O spirit!"

Over the next several days I would see Robin in many different settings: performing for audiences of thousands of people who were just thrilled to see him alive, happy, and in good health; traveling from city to city in a cushy private plane; reflecting quietly on his recent personal difficulties — his divorce from Marsha, his relapse into alcoholism, his heart surgery — and on the challenges facing his stalled career and the recent loss of mentors like Richard Pryor.

There was one part of Robin's day that I was never allowed to see. When I arrived at the Fox Theatre that evening, prior to his performance, I was told that he was in his dressing room, by himself, immersed in his preshow ritual, and that he would be there for thirty to forty-five minutes. No one was permitted to interrupt him during this time. This was a pattern he repeated at each of the tour stops I followed him to, and I never found out what he did during these periods.

Maybe he used this time to meditate, clear his mind, rehearse his lines, and burn off any remaining anxiety, or maybe he just wanted to create a mystique about himself and keep some portion of his creative process a secret, even as he gave away so much of who he was when he was onstage.

I would see Robin or speak with him several more times in the following years, for articles about new projects he was working on or about people close to him; our final conversation was in the summer of 2013, about a year before he died, when I was writing a profile of Billy Crystal and he was working on what would be the only season of *The Crazy Ones.*

Nearly everyone I have spoken to who knew Robin — and most knew him far better than I did — has described experiencing something akin to what I felt when I wasn't allowed into his dressing room. They believed there was some part of himself that he withheld from them; everyone got a piece of him and a fortunate few got quite a lot of him, but no one got all of him.

Only Robin knew for certain what his world looked like, but he seemed to understand that other people would want to piece together his story and try to make sense of it, and that whatever they came up with would inevitably be incomplete. Back in 1979, he allowed a reporter from *Rolling Stone* to follow him around Hollywood for several days, on the set of *Mork & Mindy,* at his gym workouts in preparation for *Popeye,* backstage at the Comedy Store, at home with Valerie.

When they parted ways for the last time, on a darkened stretch of Los Angeles, Robin turned to the writer and offered this admonition before walking off into the night: "Go, young man, and write your story. In a thousand years, roaches will crawl over your words, their little feelers waving, and say: 'Come on, let's keep crawling.' "

ROBIN WILLIAMS: SELECTED WORKS AND AWARDS

Movies

Can I Do It . . . Til I Need Glasses? (1977)
Popeye (1980)
The World According to Garp (1982)
The Survivors (1983)
Moscow on the Hudson (1984)
The Best of Times (1986)
Club Paradise (1986)
Seize the Day (1986)
Good Morning, Vietnam (1987)
The Adventures of Baron Munchausen (1988) (credited as Ray D. Tutto)
Portrait of a White Marriage (1988) (uncredited)
Dead Poets Society (1989)
Cadillac Man (1990)
Awakenings (1990)
Shakes the Clown (1991) (credited as Marty Fromage)
Dead Again (1991)
The Fisher King (1991)
Hook (1991)

FernGully: The Last Rainforest (1992) (voice)
Aladdin (1992) (voice)
Toys (1992)
Mrs. Doubtfire (1993)
Being Human (1994)
Nine Months (1995)
To Wong Foo, Thanks for Everything! Julie Newmar (1995) (uncredited)
Jumanji (1995)
The Birdcage (1996)
Jack (1996)
Aladdin and the King of Thieves (1996) (voice; direct to video)
The Secret Agent (1996) (uncredited)
Hamlet (1996)
Fathers' Day (1997)
Deconstructing Harry (1997)
Flubber (1997)
Good Will Hunting (1997)
What Dreams May Come (1998)
Patch Adams (1998)
Jakob the Liar (1999)
Bicentennial Man (1999)
A.I. Artificial Intelligence (2001) (voice)
One Hour Photo (2002)
Death to Smoochy (2002)
Insomnia (2002)
The Final Cut (2004)
House of D (2004)
Noel (2004) (uncredited)
Robots (2005) (voice)
The Big White (2005)

The Night Listener (2006)
RV (2006)
Everyone's Hero (2006) (voice; uncredited)
Man of the Year (2006)
Happy Feet (2006) (voice)
Night at the Museum (2006)
License to Wed (2007)
August Rush (2007)
World's Greatest Dad (2009)
Shrink (2009)
Night at the Museum: Battle of the Smithsonian (2009)
Old Dogs (2009)
Happy Feet Two (2011) (voice)
The Big Wedding (2013)
Lee Daniels' The Butler (2013)
The Face of Love (2013)
Boulevard (2014)
The Angriest Man in Brooklyn (2014)
A Merry Friggin' Christmas (2014)
Night at the Museum: Secret of the Tomb (2014)
Absolutely Anything (2015) (voice)

Television
The Richard Pryor Show (1977)
Laugh-In (1977)
Eight Is Enough (1977)
Sorority '62 (1978) (pilot)
America 2-Night (1978)
Happy Days (1978–79)
Mork & Mindy (1978–82)

Out of the Blue (1979)
Shelley Duvall's Faerie Tale Theatre (1982)
SCTV Network (1982)
Saturday Night Live (1984, 1986, 1988) (host)
The Larry Sanders Show (1992, 1994)
Homicide: Life on the Street (1994)
Friends (1997)
L.A. Doctors (1999)
Life with Bonnie (2003)
Law & Order: Special Victims Unit (2008)
SpongeBob SquarePants (2009)
Wilfred (2012)
Louie (2012)
The Crazy Ones (2013–14)

Comedy Specials
The Great American Laugh-Off (1977)
Live at the Roxy (1978)
An Evening with Robin Williams (1982)
Robin Williams: An Evening at the Met (1986)
Carol, Carl, Whoopi and Robin (1987)
Robin Williams: Live on Broadway (2002)
Robin Williams: Weapons of Self Destruction (2010)

Comic Relief
1986
1987–'87
1989–III
1991–IV
1992–V
1994–VI

1995–VII
1998–VIII
2006–2006

Comedy Albums
Reality . . . What a Concept (1979)
Throbbing Python of Love (1982)
A Night at the Met (1986)
Robin Williams — Live 2002 (2002)
Weapons of Self Destruction (2010)

Theater
Waiting for Godot (1988)
Bengal Tiger at the Baghdad Zoo (2011)

Awards and Nominations

Academy Awards
Best Actor (*Good Morning, Vietnam*) (1988) — nominated
Best Actor (*Dead Poets Society*) (1990) — nominated
Best Actor (*The Fisher King*) (1992) — nominated
Best Supporting Actor (*Good Will Hunting*) (1998) — won

BAFTA Awards
Best Actor in a Leading Role (*Good Morning, Vietnam*) (1989) — nominated
Best Actor in a Leading Role (*Dead Poets Society*) (1990) — nominated

Outstanding Performer in an Animated Series (*Great Minds Think for Themselves*) (1998) — nominated

Best Actor — Television Series Musical or Comedy (*Mork & Mindy*) (1979) — won

Best Actor — Television Series Musical or Comedy (*Mork & Mindy*) (1980) — nominated

Best Actor — Motion Picture Musical or Comedy (*Moscow on the Hudson*) (1985) — nominated

Best Actor — Motion Picture Musical or Comedy (*Good Morning, Vietnam*) (1988) — won

Best Actor — Motion Picture Drama (*Dead Poets Society*) (1990) — nominated

Best Actor — Motion Picture Drama (*Awakenings*) (1991) — nominated

Best Actor — Motion Picture Musical or Comedy (*The Fisher King*) (1992) — won

Special Award for Vocal Work (*Aladdin*) (1993)

Best Actor — Motion Picture Musical or Comedy (*Mrs. Doubtfire*) (1994) — won

Best Supporting Actor — Motion Picture Drama (*Good Will Hunting*) (1998) — nominated

Best Actor — Motion Picture Musical or

Comedy (*Patch Adams*) (1999) — nominated

Cecil B. DeMille Award (2005)

Grammy Awards

Best Comedy Album (*Reality . . . What a Concept*) (1980) — won

Best New Artist (1980) — nominated

Best Comedy Album (*Throbbing Python of Love*) (1984) — nominated

Best Comedy Album (*A Night at the Met*) (1988) — won

Best Comedy Album (*Good Morning, Vietnam*) (1989) — won

Best Recording for Children (*Pecos Bill*) (1989) — won

Best Spoken Word Album for Children (*Jumanji*) (1997) — nominated

Best Spoken Comedy Album (*Robin Williams: Live on Broadway*) (2003) — won

Best Comedy Album (*Weapons of Self Destruction*) (2011) — nominated

Prime-Time Emmy Awards

Outstanding Lead Actor in a Comedy Series (*Mork & Mindy*) (1979) — nominated

Outstanding Individual Performance in a Variety or Musical Program (*Carol, Carl, Whoopi and Robin*) (1987) — won

Outstanding Individual Performance in a Variety or Musical Program (*ABC Presents: A*

Royal Gala) (1988) — won

Outstanding Guest Actor in a Drama Series (*Homicide: Life on the Street*) (1994) — nominated

Outstanding Individual Performance in a Variety or Musical Program (*Comic Relief VII*) (1996) — nominated

Outstanding Individual Performance in a Variety or Musical Program (*Robin Williams: Live on Broadway*) (2003) — nominated

Outstanding Writing for a Variety, Music or Comedy Program (*Robin Williams: Live on Broadway*) (2003) — nominated

Outstanding Guest Actor in a Drama Series (*Law & Order: Special Victims Unit*) (2008) — nominated

Outstanding Variety, Music or Comedy Special (*Robin Williams: Weapons of Self Destruction*) (2010) — nominated

Screen Actors Guild Awards

Outstanding Performance by a Cast in a Motion Picture (*The Birdcage*) (1997) — won

Outstanding Performance by a Cast in a Motion Picture (*Good Will Hunting*) (1998) — nominated

Outstanding Performance by a Male Actor in a Supporting Role (*Good Will Hunting*) (1998) — won

Outstanding Performance by a Cast in a Motion Picture (*Lee Daniels' The Butler*) (2014) — nominated

NOTES

Prologue

a Barbary Coast whorehouse: Paul Henninger, "Try Laughing This Show Off," *San Bernardino County (CA) Sun,* October 8, 1977.

Chapter 1. Punky and Lord Posh

on the northeast corner of Opdyke Road and Woodward Avenue: These descriptions are taken from *Bloomfield Legacy* 9, no. 2 (Fall 2014), and from Robin's own remembrances of the house, offered on *Inside the Actors Studio,* June 10, 2001.

It was his exclusive domain: Dotson Rader, "What Really Makes Life Fun," *Parade,* September 20, 1998.

"The craziness comes from my mother": Joan Goodman, "Robin Williams Gets a Tall Order in Popeye," *London Times,* March 18, 1981.

Robin would describe himself as having been an overweight child: *Superstars & Their Moms,* ABC, May 3, 1987.

"Daddy, Daddy, come upstairs": Lawrence Linderman, "Playboy Interview: Robin Williams," *Playboy,* October 1982.

in an eight-year span, he attended six different schools: Don Freeman, "Way Out," *TV Guide,* October 28–November 3, 1978.

"It's the contradiction of what people say about comedy and pain": Nancy Collins, "Robin Williams," *Interview,* August 1986.

a portrait photograph of Rob and Laurie Williams: Kristin Delaplane Conti, *The McLaurin & Williams Family Histories,* p. iii. This book was commissioned by Robin Williams and Marsha Garces Williams for the family's personal reference and self-published in 2002.

"Picture George Burns and Gracie Allen": Linderman, "Playboy Interview: Robin Williams."

Robert Fitz-Gerrell Williams: His middle name is often misspelled as Fitzgerald.

He was born in 1906: Conti, *McLaurin & Williams Family Histories,* p. 59.

"periodic toots": Ibid.

"I don't want you to do this anymore": Ibid.

Rob and his first wife: Kevin Fagan, "Robert Williams Dies — Winemaker, Bar Owner and Bon Vivant," *San Francisco Chronicle,*

August 16, 2007.

a lieutenant commander on the USS *Ticonderoga*: Conti, *McLaurin & Williams Family Histories,* p. 61.

he soon returned to work at Ford: Ibid., pp. 61–62.

Rob met an effervescent young divorcée named Laurie McLaurin Janin: Ibid., p. 35.

"the minute he walked in, people were at attention": Ibid., p. 36.

"He definitely had 'IT' ": Ibid.

When the couple miscommunicated over a canceled date: Ibid.

Laurie was born in 1922: Ibid., p. 9.

her father, Robert Armistead Janin, was Catholic: Ibid., p. 11.

The couple had separated by the time their daughter was five: Ibid., p. 10.

the MacLaren clan of Scotland: Ibid., p. 3.

Laurie's great-grandfather Anselm Joseph McLaurin: Ibid., p. 6.

cut off from this aristocratic heritage: Ibid., p. 12.

"I never knew when I woke up each day": Ibid., p. 13.

"It made me realize that we cannot drink": Ibid., p. 14.

the Great Depression nearly wiped out Robert Smith: Ibid., p. 23.

"we didn't have a colored servant": Ibid., p. 55.

she moved to Pass Christian, Mississippi: Ibid., p. 24.

then back again to New Orleans: Ibid., p. 28.

she performed as an actress in the French Quarter: Ibid., p. 29.

At the start of World War II, she was working for the Weather Bureau: Ibid., p. 30.

she met a young naval officer named William Musgrave: Ibid., p. 31. By coincidence, William Musgrave was also from Evansville, Indiana, where Rob Williams had grown up.

Frank Lloyd Wright and Henry Miller: Ibid.

When the war ended and William Musgrave returned home: Ibid., p. 32.

gave birth to their son, Laurin McLaurin Musgrave: Ibid., p. 33.

a model for the Marshall Field's department store: Ibid., p. 36.

On June 3, 1950, they were wed: Ibid.

an apartment on Chicago's north side: Ibid., p. xii.

On July 21, 1951, Laurie delivered their son: Ibid., p. 37. The hospital has since been absorbed into Northwestern Memorial Hospital.

natural childbirth was "giving birth without makeup": Dotson Rader, "Guess Who's Back on TV," *Parade,* September 15, 2013.

the medical staff there peppered her with questions: Conti, *McLaurin & Williams Family Histories,* p. 37.

Laurie would still unhesitatingly describe

Susie as "colored": Ibid.

"She wouldn't put up with anything": *The Whoopi Goldberg Show,* September 18, 1992.

Shortly after Robin's birth: Conti, *McLaurin & Williams Family Histories,* p. 39.

Rob, an astute negotiator: Ibid.

the family almost never took vacations: Aljean Harmetz, "Robin Williams: Comedy for a Narcissistic Time," *New York Times,* December 28, 1978.

one of his childhood nicknames was "Leprechaun": Ibid.

in at least one such photo, she faces off against him: Conti, *McLaurin & Williams Family Histories,* p. 40.

a beloved sight gag for which she would cut apart a rubber band: As Laurie demonstrates in the *Superstars & Their Moms* TV special.

a book, supposedly written by an English princess: Linderman, "Playboy Interview: Robin Williams."

"Spider crawling on the wall": Ibid.

"I love you in blue": Ibid.

"then I tried to find things to make her laugh": *Inside the Actors Studio,* June 10, 2001.

"the need for that primal connection": Rader, "What Really Makes Life Fun."

"my mother has never met a stranger": Conti,

McLaurin & Williams Family Histories, p. 56.

"Lord Stokesbury, Viceroy to India": Ibid., p. 65.

"Lord Posh": David Ansen, "Funny Man: The Comic Genius of Robin Williams," *Newsweek,* July 7, 1986.

"the Pasha": Rader, "What Really Makes Life Fun."

returning home from school with an envelope: Ellen Hawkes, "The Transformation of Robin Williams," *Reader's Digest,* February 1999.

"It all went in and stayed there": Conti, *McLaurin & Williams Family Histories,* p. 63.

"He's very shy, very quiet": Ibid., p. 70.

After "a couple of cocktails, he got very happy": *Inside the Actors Studio,* June 10, 2001.

Robin was allowed to stay up past his bedtime: Freeman, "Way Out."

"My dad was a sweet man, but not an easy laugh": Robin Williams, "A Madman, but Angelic," *New York Times,* April 15, 2013.

his legendary performance in which the host offered him a stick: *The Jack Paar Program,* April 10, 1964. This memorable routine did not occur on Paar's *Tonight Show* but rather on the prime-time NBC variety series he hosted after stepping down from *Tonight.* Archived at http://bit.ly/2bWgdpy.

When Winters, a US Marine, returned from

combat: Williams, "A Madman, but Angelic."

"He was performing comedic alchemy": Ibid.

Washington Road, in Lake Forest: Susan Carlson, "Lake Forest Remembers Former Resident Robin Williams," NBC Chicago, August 12, 2014.

"a big house, in a neighborhood of fairly big houses": Author interview with Jeff Hodgen.

"We'd go up on the garage roof": Author interview with Jon Welsh.

"We'd take it out on the lawn and tunnel under it": Ibid.

"He had an almost artificial, squared-up, shoulders-back thing": Ibid.

He had grown up with his mother in Versailles, Kentucky: Conti, *McLaurin & Williams Family Histories*, p. 66.

"I played too much. So much for higher education": Ibid.

"I was determined not to like her out of loyalty to my mom": Ibid., p. xi.

"I'd do something bad, Pop would be mad": Ibid.

"I was the other way and just full of hell": Ibid., p. 62.

"Todd always extorted all my money": Linderman, "Playboy Interview: Robin Williams."

"She's their daughter and my mother": Author interview with McLaurin Smith-

Williams.

McLaurin could now decide whether he wished to live: The timeline here is somewhat fuzzy. Robin has said he first became acquainted with his half brothers at the age of ten (see, e.g., Linderman, "Playboy Interview: Robin Williams"), and McLaurin recalls being introduced to him at that age (when McLaurin was about thirteen or fourteen). This would indicate it occurred while the Williamses were living in Lake Forest, Illinois; however, McLaurin says he met Robin when the family lived in Bloomfield Hills, Michigan.

"growing up as a quote-unquote only child": Author interview with McLaurin Smith-Williams.

"We were both very private, solitary-type individuals": Ibid.

"they'd fish the car out of the river": Conti, *McLaurin & Williams Family Histories,* p. 64.

"He had a very strong personality and he would have his own way": Author interview with McLaurin Smith-Williams.

"It was kind of the devil you know versus the devil you don't": Ibid.

"He said, 'They get along so well. I don't understand it' ": Ibid.

"Robin would say, occasionally, that he was brought up as an only child": Author interview with Frankie Williams.

"I always thought he looked a little British":

Author interview with Christie Platt. Her maiden name was Mercer.

"the bullies wanted to put me in my place": Author interview with Jeff Hodgen.

"I started telling jokes in the seventh grade": Linderman, "Playboy Interview: Robin Williams."

"He just wasn't in school. 'Where's Robin?' ": Author interview with Jon Welsh.

"He left without much of a ripple": Author interview with Christie Platt.

"the kids who've been moved from one military post to another": Author interview with Jon Welsh.

"I was always the new boy. This makes you different": Freeman, "Way Out."

"there *were* no other kids in the neighborhood": Linderman, "Playboy Interview: Robin Williams."

Susie . . . John and Johnnie Etchen . . . their son Alfred: Conti, *McLaurin & Williams Family Histories,* p. 41. Alfred Etchen died in 2008.

"I didn't realize how lonely Robin had been": Ibid.

"My world was bounded by thousands of toy soldiers": Harmetz, "Robin Williams: Comedy for a Narcissistic Time."

"My imagination was my friend, my companion": "The Robin Williams Show: Sixty Characters in Search of a Maniac," *Time,* October 2, 1978.

the school's navy and gold colors: Linderman, "Playboy Interview: Robin Williams."

"They'd bring in a busload from an all-girls' school": Ibid.

"some kid from upstate who looked like he was twenty-three and balding": Ibid.

"the chance to take out your aggressions on somebody your own size": Ibid.

"really idealistic, really left-leaning, really believed in democracy": Author interview with Sue Campbell. John Campbell died in 2007.

Robin continued to slip one-liners into otherwise sober speeches: Linderman, "Playboy Interview: Robin Williams."

He was a member of the school's honor roll: *Blue and Gold '68* (yearbook), Detroit Country Day School, Birmingham, Michigan, 1968.

"I was looking forward to a very straight existence": Linderman, "Playboy Interview: Robin Williams."

"I know there are fifteen young hotshot kids in there": Conti, *McLaurin & Williams Family Histories,* p. 62.

He parted ways with the company in 1967: Conti, *McLaurin & Williams Family Histories,* p. 45.

"an elephants' graveyard" with "a lot of old rich people": Ibid.

Rob accepted a job at First National Bank: Ibid., p. 63.

Chapter 2. The Escape Artist

nearing the end of their cross-country car ride; "It scared the piss out of me": Linderman, "Playboy Interview: Robin Williams"; and Michael Caleb Lester, "Robin Williams: 'I'm Just Getting Going . . . ,'" *San Francisco,* July 1983.

"I'd go to church on Wednesday night": Conti, *McLaurin & Williams Family Histories,* pp. 46 and 63.

"Christian Dior Scientist": Author interview with Robin Williams.

"It probably would have been easier for me to move to Mexico": Linderman, "Playboy Interview: Robin Williams."

its students were mostly affluent and mostly white: *Log '69,* Redwood High School, Larkspur, California, 1969.

who called him a geek: Linderman, "Playboy Interview: Robin Williams."

his first Hawaiian shirt: Ibid.

courses in psychology, 16-millimeter filmmaking, and black studies: Ibid.

he boldly ran for senior president at Redwood: "All but the Sophomores Vote Slates," *Daily Independent Journal,* January 28, 1969.

"his only thing that brought him into the groups": Author interview with Douglas Basham.

he did eventually try it on "an astrological

scavenger hunt": Linderman, "Playboy Interview: Robin Williams."

Robin remembered ascending the heights of Mount Tamalpais: Ibid.

male runners keep their hair at a "reasonable length": "Parent Upset over Track Haircut Rules," *Daily Independent Journal,* March 4, 1969.

"These are communists that are doing this": Author interview with Douglas Basham. Basham would briefly lose his job at Redwood High School for refusing to enforce Shaw's haircut rule but was later reinstated and went on to teach and coach there until his retirement in 1995.

a member of the school's honor society: *Log '69,* Redwood High School, Larkspur, California, 1969, pp. 182–83.

a performer in its satirical senior farewell play: Author interview with Phillip Culver.

"He would tell me the conversations that were going on": Ibid.

Todd had recently been discharged from the air force: Conti, *McLaurin & Williams Family Histories,* p. 67.

When Todd revived a San Francisco nightspot called Mother Fletcher's: Linderman, "Playboy Interview: Robin Williams."

where he planned to study to become a foreign-service officer: Ibid. The school is now known as Claremont McKenna College.

"Anybody that went to Claremont was expected": Author interview with Dick Gale.

"a time when everybody was being told: question authority": Author interview with Mary Alette Davis. Her maiden name was Hinderle.

"Like going from Sing Sing to a Gestalt nudist camp": Lawrence Grobel, "Robin Williams: The Playboy Interview," *Playboy,* January 1992.

"We could yell, 'Go Nads!' ": Author interview with Bob Davis. He is the husband of Mary Alette Davis.

"I saw this really cute boy in the stairwell": Author interview with Christie Platt.

"I had one or two steady girlfriends in high school": Collins, "Robin Williams."

"after my first day, I was hooked": Linderman, "Playboy Interview: Robin Williams."

a San Francisco spin-off of Chicago's Second City: "Scripps to Present Improvised Theater," *Pomona (CA) Progress-Bulletin,* October 13, 1971. Among the connective tissue that these theaters shared, they each employed Del Close, the revered actor and director who codified many of the rules still used in contemporary improv.

"not only a way to do theater": Author interview with Bob Davis.

"It's actually quite a good life theory":

Author interview with Paul Tepper.

create Claremont's earliest improv group, known as Karma Pie: Ibid. The group was also sometimes known as Karma Pi, for reasons its own members cannot entirely recall.

A local newspaper critic who attended one of their performances: Joseph H. Firman, "College Actors Have More Fun Than Audience," *Pomona (CA) Progress-Bulletin,* January 16, 1970.

"He was doing it the same way all of us were doing it": Author interview with Bob Davis.

"I've got to say that he doesn't really follow the rules of improv": Author interview with Mary Alette Davis.

Some friends began calling him Ralph Williams: Author interview with Dick Gale.

"People would just start clapping when we came in": Author interview with Christie Platt.

Robin honed his stage skills by performing in campus productions: Author interview with Bob Davis.

"We were trying to build the audience": Author interview with Dick Gale.

"much libation, inhalation and conversation": Dick Gale, "An Evening with Al Dauber," *Myths, Legends and Tall Tales of CMC IV,* Claremont McKenna College.

"when Robin came in, all of a sudden, we

had Topo Gigio": Author interview with Dick Gale.

"We started challenging him. 'Do a bohemian priest' ": Author interview with Al Dauber.

"An Evening with Al Dauber, co-starring Dick Gale & Rob Williams": "CMC Mourns, Remembers Actor and Comedian Robin Williams," https://www.cmc.edu/news/cmc-mourns-remembers-actor-and-comedian-robin-williams.

opened with a parody of To Tell the Truth: Gale, "An Evening with Al Dauber."

"When Robin came, it brought about a holistic change": Author interview with Dick Hale.

the single sentence "I really don't know, sir": Linderman, "Playboy Interview: Robin Williams."

one professor asked at the end of the term, "Who is this man?": Hawkes, "The Transformation of Robin Williams."

driving a golf cart through a dining hall: Steve Harvey, "OK, So After That Donna Shalala Said . . . ," Los Angeles Times, February 20, 1999.

The draft number for his birthdate: Selective Service System, "1971 Random Selection Sequence, by Month and Day." Archived at https://www.sss.gov/Portals/0/PDFs/1971.pdf.

"the Viet Cong had to be coming from

Kansas": *Inside the Actors Studio,* June 10, 2001.

"Listen, war is not *dolce et decorum est*": Rader, "What Really Makes Life Fun."

he'd already discovered his calling: Hawkes, "The Transformation of Robin Williams."

"a course at the local trade school to learn how to weld": Author interview with McLaurin Smith-Williams.

"Mom said, 'Your grandmother would be very proud' ": Linderman, "Playboy Interview: Robin Williams."

drawing favorable comparisons to the American Conservatory Theater: James E. Williams, "Dunn's Collegians Reach New Heights in a World Premiere," *San Rafael (CA) Daily Independent Journal,* May 8, 1971.

James Dunn, a San Rafael native and Marine Corps veteran: Alex Horvath, "Mountain Play Director's Long, Rich Career," *San Francisco Chronicle,* May 16, 2003; and Paul Liberatore, "On His 80th Birthday, Jim Dunn Honored with College of Marin Theater Named After Him," *Marin Independent Journal,* February 28, 2013.

"You couldn't walk across our campus in the daytime": Author interview with James Dunn.

"We had to march. We had to learn how to

salute": Author interview with Dakin Matthews.

"He said, 'I would really like to get into the play' ": Author interview with James Dunn.

"every night it was a different Chasuble": Author interview with Ronald Krempetz.

"Most enjoyable of the hard-working cast was Robin Williams as Mr. Martin": James E. Williams, "Ionesco's 'Soprano' Lightens College's Evening of Absurd," *San Rafael (CA) Daily Independent Journal,* December 4, 1970.

strong marks for his work as Banquo in *Macbeth:* James E. Williams, "Astounding Talent in College Play," *San Rafael (CA) Daily Independent Journal,* July 23, 1971.

"really one of the fine young talents in the college's theatrical stable": James E. Williams, "Sizzling Dialogue Helps Bring Professionalism to Roper Play," *San Rafael (CA) Daily Independent Journal,* July 24, 1972.

among the cast members who "add strength to the musical": James E. Williams, "College 'Fiddler' Roaring Success," *San Rafael (CA) Daily Independent Journal,* April 2, 1973.

"we had a new lighting board and it was doing all kinds of strange things": Author interview with James Dunn.

"Robin Williams as an unforgettable Fagin":

James E. Williams, " 'Oliver!' A Smash Hit for Holiday Season," *San Rafael (CA) Daily Independent Journal,* December 4, 1972.

"Hi, Robin. How are you? Where's my five dollars?": Author interview with Ronald Krempetz.

"He was such a nice guy, such a sweetheart": Author interview with Joel Blum.

a command performance for Princess Margaret: Marin Shakespeare Company, *The Taming of the Shrew,* 2004 production notes. Archived at http://marinshakespeare .org/behind-the-scenes-2005/the-taming-of-the-shrew-2004-production/.

The Caucasian Chalk Circle and in *The Music Man:* David Middlecamp, "Robin Williams Among Notable Alumni of Santa Maria's PCPA," *San Luis Obispo (CA) Tribune,* August 15, 2014.

Danny Kaye's "The Lobby Number" from *Up in Arms:* Archived at https://www.you tube.com/watch?v=TrGd42nj3Zk. See also John M. Miller, *Up in Arms.* Archived at http://www.tcm.com/this-month/article.ht ml?id=544370%7C111405.

"you saw a little figure, which was Jim Dunn": Author interview with Shelly Lipkin.

"We slept in his bedroom but we came in through a back window": Author interview with Bob Davis.

His father reluctantly gave him $50: Harry Harris, "A Spacey Fella, This Guy Mork (Ark! Ark! Ark!)," *Philadelphia Inquirer,* September 29, 1978.

Robin's audition consisted of two monologues: Peter Marks, "There Is Nothing Funny About This Image," *New York Times,* May 12, 2002.

Malvolio's famous soliloquy: William Shakespeare, *Twelfth Night,* act 2, scene 5. Archived at http://shakespeare.mit.edu/twelfth _night/full.html.

"I remember thinking he didn't speak very well": Author interview with Elizabeth Smith.

He was also provided a full scholarship: Lillian Ross, "Workouts," *New Yorker,* April 7, 1986.

"I'd been in danger of becoming terminally mellow": Linderman, "Playboy Interview: Robin Williams."

a few rows ahead of him, he saw a man slump over: Ibid.

Its Drama Division had been established in 1968: Jeremy Gerard, "Juilliard Drama School, at 20, Stresses Versatility," *New York Times,* April 19, 1988.

"It had a very monastic, religious feeling about it": Author interview with Richard Levine.

"Juilliard actors were considered first-rate.

They were also considered pains in the ass": Author interview with Paul Perri.

The four-year curriculum emphasized long days of studio training: Andrea Olmstead, *Juilliard: A History* (Urbana: University of Illinois Press, 1999), p. 229.

This Darwinian system operated under the auspices of Houseman: Marilyn Berger, "John Houseman, Actor and Producer, 86, Dies," *New York Times,* November 1, 1988.

"he said, 'The theater *needs* you' ": Linderman, "Playboy Interview: Robin Williams." This is, not surprisingly, a slight exaggeration. Though Houseman appeared in many commercials (including his famous series of TV spots for the investment firm Smith Barney), his Volvo advertisements did not begin airing until the late 1970s.

"Roman numerals, like royalty and the Super Bowl": Matthew Gurewitsch, "A High-Stakes School for Actors," *New York Times,* January 26, 1997.

a staggeringly tall, boyishly handsome young man: Christopher Reeve, *Still Me* (New York: Ballantine Books, 1999), pp. 167–70.

"a short, stocky long-haired fellow from Marin County": Ibid., p. 171.

"She had no idea what to make of him": Ibid.

"There were neutral masks, which covered the face": Author interview with Margot Harley.

"I used to give him big, heroic poems to

make him breathe": Author interview with Elizabeth Smith.

Robin's delivery "was even funnier than the original": Reeve, *Still Me,* p. 171.

he told Robin, "It looks like *you* were enjoying yourself": Author interview with Michael Kahn.

"You feel fabulous. We see nothing": Ian Gibbs, "Five Things We Learned at . . . Robin Williams's Q&A in the New York Comedy Festival," *Time Out New York,* November 12, 2012.

"He didn't have a basic foundation of how to approach acting": Author interview with Michael Kahn.

Robin was asked to give up his place in Group IV: Margot Harley and Michael Kahn agree on this detail, which is also confirmed by the present-day Juilliard administration.

"classmates related to Robin by doing bits with him": Reeve, *Still Me,* p. 171.

"New York seemed unbearably bleak and lonely": Linderman, "Playboy Interview: Robin Williams."

"Whatever you were doing in your room": Author interview with Frances Conroy.

"You would have to walk with someone else to get home safely": Jeff Muskus, "The Voice Under the (Animated) Cowl," *New York Times,* July 31, 2016. Unpublished interview material. Kevin Conroy and

Frances Conroy are not related.

"he couldn't use the word *funky* anymore": Author interview with Richard Levine.

"He had one girl come and I think she stayed for six months": Author interview. This person asked not to be identified by name.

"He may have even slept in the school some nights": Author interview with Frances Conroy.

"I used to bring him breakfast": Author interview with Margot Harley.

"We were all baby boomers, raised in one of the fattest times": Author interview with Paul Perri.

Nonno, a wheelchair-bound ninety-seven-year-old man: Tennessee Williams, *The Night of the Iguana.* Archived at https://coldreads .files.wordpress.com/2014/08/iguana.pdf.

this performance "immediately silenced the critics": Reeve, *Still Me,* p. 171.

"He was on the floor, projecting himself along with his bottom": Author interview with Margot Harley.

"He did five minutes of just imitating a Coke machine": Author interview with Paul Perri.

"it looked like he was creating in that moment — he wasn't": Muskus, "The Voice Under the (Animated) Cowl." Unpublished interview material.

"many of the students broke off into little groups": Kevin Sessums, Facebook post, August 12, 2014. Archived at https://www

.facebook.com/kevin.sessums.7/posts/
10152672521633708:0.

"His life was absurd": E. L. Doctorow, *Rag-time* (New York: Plume, 1996), p. 6.

"Bouncing down the street comes this guy": Author interview with Todd Oppenheimer.

Robin was doused from above with a sudden splash of water: Author interview with Bennett Tramer.

"The school did have a tendency to want to strip you": Author interview with Richard Levine.

"You never had a serious conversation with Robin": Author interview with Todd Oppenheimer.

Reeve was cast in the popular CBS soap opera *Love of Life:* Reeve, *Still Me,* p. 174.

"a free spirit who thought nothing about walking through tough neighborhoods": Linderman, "Playboy Interview: Robin Williams."

"I really *missed* my lady friend": Ibid.

"He would call me, sometimes at one or two o'clock in the morning": Author interview with Shelly Lipkin.

the mutual agreement that he should withdraw: Statement, the Juilliard School, August 12, 2014.

a persistent urban legend has endured: See, for example, Laurence Maslon and Michael Kantor, *Make 'Em Laugh: The Funny Busi-*

ness of America (New York: Twelve, 2008).

"John was very good about letting people go": Author interview with Margot Harley.

"we all felt it was fine that he left": Author interview with Michael Kahn.

Chapter 3. Legalized Insanity

"She fell into this Marin County thing": Ellen Farley, "On the Mork, Get Set, Go — Williams Live," *Los Angeles Times,* December 3, 1978.

he fell into what he considered a massive depression: Linderman, "Playboy Interview: Robin Williams."

Todd had set up shop in the Marina District: Conti, *McLaurin & Williams Family Histories,* p. 67.

"Marina maggots": Fagan, "Robert Williams Dies — Winemaker, Bar Owner and Bon Vivant."

"There was one guy named Beefy": Ibid.

Del Close, the renegade improv virtuoso: Author interviews with Nick David and Joe Spano.

"the form we were using was too restrictive": Author interview with Joe Spano.

"I don't think it was a matter of his aspirations": Ibid.

she gave him $100 for his wardrobe: David Browne, "Robin Williams," *Rolling Stone,* September 11, 2014.

"Serious was very difficult for Robin": Cynthia "Kiki" Wallace, Facebook post, April 12, 2008. Archived at http://jpgmag.com/photos/197332.

"He had gotten used to getting a laugh": Browne, "Robin Williams."

"Admission cost a dollar and we would split the door": Author interview with Don Novello.

"Well, hike when the energy's right": Linderman, "Playboy Interview: Robin Williams."

"It was such a rush the first time I did it": Collins, "Robin Williams."

"If people started heckling you, you just wade over": *WTF with Marc Maron,* April 26, 2010.

"you did the standard thing where people could kind of lose track": Richard Zoglin, *Comedy at the Edge* (New York: Bloomsbury, 2008), p. 162.

" 'No, Pop, I don't need that check, but thanks' ": Linderman, "Playboy Interview: Robin Williams."

"Robin got up and blew everyone away, but he was meek": John Eskow, "Robin Williams: Full Tilt Bozo," *Rolling Stone,* August 23, 1979.

San Francisco had been a comedy town before: Peter Hartlaub, "Comedy Rises in San Francisco, Without Compromise," *San Francisco Chronicle,* May 30, 2015.

the Savoy Tivoli and the Old Spaghetti Factory: J. L. Pimsleur, "Obituary — Frederik

Walter Kuh," *San Francisco Chronicle,* November 12, 1997.

"He would take your breath away": Author interview with Debi Durst. Her maiden name was Pickell.

"The first time I did improv with him, I couldn't keep up": Author interview with Mark Pitta.

"We just wanted to play, just to practice the art, so to speak": Author interview with Tony DePaul.

"The fourth guy up blew the room away, and it was Robin": Author interview with Dana Carvey.

the Boarding House, a music club in Nob Hill: Eskow, "Robin Williams: Full Tilt Bozo."

a sign that its original owner had found: John Cantu, "A Brief History of a Place That Launched a Thousand Quips." Archived at http://www.johncantu.com/backstagepass/brief-history-holy-city-zoo.html.

a blunt but enthusiastic approach to promoting: Steve Rubenstein, "John Cantu — Passionate Voice for Comics in S.F.," *San Francisco Chronicle,* May 14, 2003.

"If you signed up by eight thirty, they would guarantee you a spot": Author interview with Don Stevens.

Robin was onstage trading quips with Michael Pritchard: Ibid.

"Robin just did a hundred little different

pieces": Author interview with Tony De-Paul.

"He was either very quiet, or he was in a monologue": Author interview with Don Stevens.

"I don't know who was his best friend": Author interview with Bob Sarlatte.

"If you were a comic you pretty much drank for free there": Author interview with Will Durst.

"You could turn on a faucet and cocaine would come out": Author interview with Steven Pearl.

"The only thing I remember is cocaine": Author interview with Dana Carvey.

"He wasn't doing drugs in those days": Author interview with Tony DePaul.

"You could see his acting skill, more than his being anything revolutionary": Author interview with Joshua Raoul Brody.

John Wasserman of the *San Francisco Chronicle* chided him: Hartlaub, "Comedy Rises in San Francisco, Without Compromise."

"It hit me right on the nose": Linderman, "Playboy Interview: Robin Williams."

a rudimentary stand-up contest: Dana Sitar, "Comedians Face Off in Month-Long Competition to Become the Next Robin Williams," *SF Weekly,* January 14, 2013; and Jim Richardson, "How to Win the Next San Francisco Comedy Competition," *San*

Francisco Sunday Examiner and Chronicle, November 11, 1979.

"At that time, people didn't know that much about stand-up": Author interview with Bob Sarlatte.

"He wore a cowboy hat, had a hairy chest and sweated a lot": Zoglin, *Comedy at the Edge,* p. 163.

"he gets about five minutes into his act, and all the lights go out": Author interview with Bob Sarlatte.

"People in the audience were angry he didn't win": Zoglin, *Comedy at the Edge,* p. 163.

"She was this Italian woman, a Napoletana girl": Collins, "Robin Williams."

Robin . . . decided to talk to Valerie in a feigned French accent: Author interview with Valerie Velardi.

he walked up to her and addressed her in a Western twang: Lester, "Robin Williams: 'I'm Just Getting Going . . .'"

"He continued to be delightful in many ways": Author interview with Valerie Velardi.

"he was an only child, as far as I'm concerned": Joyce Wadler, "Robin Williams Heads for the Hills," *Rolling Stone,* September 16, 1982.

"I had come from that way of thinking, that anything is possible": Author interview with Valerie Velardi.

"Twyla Tharp doesn't choreograph the June

Taylor Dancers": Linderman, "Playboy Interview: Robin Williams."

"I might have been a bit of a *noodge* on the subject": Author interview with Valerie Velardi.

Robin arrived in Los Angeles in the fall of 1976: William Knoedelseder, *I'm Dying Up Here: Heartbreak and High Times in Stand-Up Comedy's Golden Era* (New York: PublicAffairs, 2009), p. 91.

The Improv was the marginally more polished establishment: Ibid., pp. 20–21; and author interview with Mark Lonow.

the Comedy Store, sat a few blocks north: Zoglin, *Comedy at the Edge,* pp. 146–48; Knoedelseder, *I'm Dying Up Here,* pp. 32–35; and author interview with Pauly Shore.

"It was a hugely romantic period": Author interview with Jay Leno.

"Word spread in the comedy community": Author interview with Mark Lonow.

the West Hollywood studios of Off the Wall: Author interviews with Wendy Cutler and Andy Goldberg.

"he was brilliant from the get-go": Author interview with Wendy Cutler.

"The guy just showed up, wearing the brown suit and the beret": Author interview with Andy Goldberg.

"I remember being very attracted to Robin's energy": Author interview with Wendy Cutler.

"ROBIN WILLIAMS, born in Chicago": Off the Wall program, undated. Provided by Wendy Cutler.

"I'm not saying it was malicious or intentional or anything like that": Author interview with Andy Goldberg.

"He was eating a tuna sandwich on whole wheat, and I was starving": Author interview with Jamie Masada.

an overstuffed grab bag of outrageous voices and exaggerated characters: Zoglin, *Comedy at the Edge,* p. 163.

"I only had one conversation with Andy where he wasn't talking to me as a character": *WTF with Marc Maron,* April 26, 2010.

"he had the ability to incorporate that as if they'd rehearsed it": Author interview with Bennett Tramer.

When Robin got his chance to audition for the Comedy Store: Knoedelseder, *I'm Dying Up Here,* p. 91.

"We were just guys who stood behind the microphone and told jokes": Author interview with David Letterman.

the Comedy Store Players, the club's in-house ensemble: Eskow, "Robin Williams: Full Tilt Bozo."

"The rules of improvisation were sacrosanct": Author interview with Jim Staahl.

Valerie would often sit in the crowd: Author

interviews with Valerie Velardi and Wendy Cutler.

"It was like an audience for the pope": Zoglin, *Comedy at the Edge,* p. 59.

"You could see the entire audience going, *What?*": *WTF with Marc Maron,* April 26, 2010.

"Coke would get him going": Zoglin, *Comedy at the Edge,* p. 59.

Cocaine had already gained acceptance: Ann Crittenden and Michael Ruby, "Cocaine: The Champagne of Drugs," *New York Times Magazine,* September 1, 1974.

"Some guy just walked up to him with a spoon": Author interview with Bob Davis.

"They give it to you for free": Collins, "Robin Williams."

a tight-knit community of stand-ups and industry figures: Knoedelseder, *I'm Dying Up Here,* p. 129.

a sweeping party circuit — to Canter's Deli on Fairfax: Ibid., p. 52.

Freddie Prinze, the dazzling young comic . . . put a loaded .32-caliber pistol to his head: Jon Nordheimer, "Freddie Prinze, 22, Dies After Shooting," *New York Times,* January 30, 1977; and Theo Wilson, "Prinze Dies as Nurse Cries 'Hang On,' " *New York Sunday News,* January 30, 1977.

he had been keeping himself steady by taking quaaludes: Knoedelseder, *I'm Dying Up*

Here, p. 81

a jury would later rule that it had been an accident: United Press International, "Freddie Prinze Death Ruled an Accident," January 20, 1983.

"He wanted to be with his friends": Author interview with Valerie Velardi.

"One of my friends was going out with him": Author interview with Wendy Asher. Her maiden name was Worth.

after their amicable breakup, she began dating Robin: Knoedelseder, *I'm Dying Up Here,* p. 73.

"I had never been so pursued": Browne, "Robin Williams."

"You had to have a lot going for you, to just get in there": Author interview with Joel Blum.

"I saw the way this dude was dressed": Eskow, "Robin Williams: Full Tilt Bozo."

the singer-songwriter Melissa Manchester: Zoglin, *Comedy at the Edge,* p. 162. The couple divorced in 1980.

"no matter what situation was thrown at him, he never got lost": Eskow, "Robin Williams: Full Tilt Bozo."

"They wanted a strapping six-footer": Phil Berger, "The Business of Comedy," *New York Times Magazine,* June 9, 1985.

Rollins, Joffe, Morra & Brezner was all but a guarantee of prosperity and fame: Ibid.; Robert D. McFadden, "Jack Rollins Dies at

100; Managed Comedy Greats Like Woody Allen," *New York Times,* June 18, 2015; Dennis Hevesi, "Charles H. Joffe, Movie Producer, Is Dead at 78," *New York Times,* July 15, 2008; Billy Crystal, *Still Foolin' 'Em: Where I've Been, Where I'm Going, and Where the Hell Are My Keys?* (New York: Henry Holt, 2013), pp. 56–57; Karen Heller, "The King of Comedy," *Philadelphia Inquirer,* May 29, 1988; and author interviews with Robert Klein and Stu Smiley.

"The talent is endless; the discipline is nil": Harmetz, "Robin Williams: Comedy for a Narcissistic Time."

"I knew he could pirouette on a needle": Author interview with Stu Smiley.

"Robin is a neophyte": Eskow, "Robin Williams: Full Tilt Bozo."

"I wasn't aspiring to anything": Author interview with Valerie Velardi.

Chapter 4. My Favorite Orkan

"you could hear, in the audience, 'Huh-HAAH!' ": Author interview with Jay Leno.

"he was hilarious, and the audience was going nuts": Author interview with Howard Papush.

"If he got a call for a birthday party, he would do it": Author interview with Stu Smiley.

Can I Do It . . . Til I Need Glasses?: Directed I. Robert Levy, 1977. Archived at https://

www.youtube.com/watch?v=iC0_xHp1n
mw.

"Is it true, Mrs. Frisbee, that last summer": Ibid. Archived at https://www.youtube.com/watch?v=wO2vpff0rFk.

"I became absolutely enamored of this young man": Author interview with George Schlatter.

a new incarnation of *Laugh-In:* Robin Williams Collection, Howard Gotlieb Archival Research Center, Boston University (hereafter, RWC), box 4, folder 16. See also https://www.youtube.com/watch?v=8KDX7g0xXP4, https://www.youtube.com/watch?v=1q20Y4VUQxM, and https://www.youtube.com/watch?v=DO6_XgpiyFM.

"the only way is to be the funny boy": Jesse Kornbluth, "Robin Williams's Change of Life," *New York,* November 22, 1993.

"Robin said, 'I'm so excited I could drop a log!' ": Author interview with George Schlatter.

"I was afraid they'd want to fire me": Linderman, "Playboy Interview: Robin Williams."

"The one word you'll need is *no*": Bill Zehme, "Robin Williams: The Rolling Stone Interview," *Rolling Stone,* February 25, 1988.

"I want all my friends from the Comedy Store": Author interview with John Moffitt.

sketches . . . that satirized issues of race and bigotry: *The Richard Pryor Show,* season 1, episode 1, September 13, 1977. Archived at https://www.youtube.com/watch?v=IoHxBmstE-I.

mistakenly refer to him as "Robert Williams": RWC, box 6, folder 1.

a trial similar to the one depicted in *To Kill a Mockingbird: The Richard Pryor Show,* season 1, episode 2, September 20, 1977. Archived at https://www.youtube.com/watch?v=stZc9bjVJ7o.

passengers on a lifeboat from the *Titanic: The Richard Pryor Show,* season 1, episode 4, October 4, 1977. Archived at https://www.youtube.com/watch?v=9Vdmhz6OQmA.

NBC made him eliminate the opening sketch: David S. Silverman, *You Can't Air That: Four Cases of Controversy and Censorship in American Television Programming* (Syracuse, NY: Syracuse University Press, 2007), p. 93.

"there was drama going on every five minutes": Author interview with Sandra Bernhard.

"NBC just betrayed him and all of us": Author interview with John Moffitt.

Robin began with a few familiar jokes: Archived at https://www.youtube.com/watch?v=HZ8nAw4SSpk. His punch line refers to racist remarks uttered by Earl Butz, Nixon's secretary of agriculture, who resigned soon after his remarks were made public.

"he went into it with so much hope": Linderman, "Playboy Interview: Robin Williams."

Laugh-In, which had debuted on NBC: "Picks and Pans Review: Laugh-In," *People,* September 5, 1977.

The Great American Laugh-Off: October 20, 1977. Archived at https://www.youtube .com/watch?v=_JoH75rraLo.

shown on October 20: Vincent Terrace, *Television Specials: 5,336 Entertainment Programs, 1936–2012* (Jefferson, NC: McFarland, 2013).

Eight Is Enough: "The Return of Auntie V," November 30, 1977. Archived at http:// www.dailymotion.com/video/x4utpuk. See also https://www.facebook.com/EightIs EnoughTvShow/photos/a.50693910603 6388.1073741828.5069335536036945/757 650534298576/?type=3&theater.

Sorority '62: "Pilot," January 1978. Archived at https://www.youtube.com/watch?v= 16B9jWgmOWw. See also Vincent Terrace, *Encyclopedia of Television Pilots, 1937–2012* (Jefferson, NC: McFarland, 2013).

"I would sound almost English or Scottish": Zoglin, *Comedy at the Edge,* p. 164.

Robin told him that he was originally from Edinburgh: Author interview with Stu Smiley.

Robin was "an Edinburgh, Scotland native":

Jay Sharbutt, "Robin Williams Lives Show Biz Dream," Associated Press, June 4, 1977.

" 'Let's get Fonzie an alien' ": Author interview with Garry Marshall.

a friendly humanoid alien named Mork, from the planet Ork: *Happy Days,* "My Favorite Orkan," February 28, 1978.

"We got this script that was horrid. Horrible": *Home & Family* interview, November 19, 2014.

John Byner or Dom DeLuise, both of whom passed: Author interview with Garry Marshall.

Jerry Paris, the episode's director, had reached out to Jonathan Winters: Harmetz, "Robin Williams: Comedy for a Narcissistic Time."

Roger Rees, an alumnus of the Royal Shakespeare Company: Natalie Finn and Baker Machado, "How Robin Williams Became Mork from Ork: That Happy Days Episode Was Supposed to Be the 'Biggest Piece of S— t,' " *E! News,* August 13, 2014.

"I can't do this role. He's not a real person": Harmetz, "Robin Williams: Comedy for a Narcissistic Time."

Marshall visited the set and asked his cast: "Does anyone know a funny Martian?": Williams, *Home & Family* interview.

Al Molinaro . . . proposed Robin as a candidate: Margalit Fox, "Al Molinaro, Diner Owner on 'Happy Days,' Dies at 96," *New*

York Times, October 30, 2015.

"He stands on a street corner, does a lot of voices and impressions": Author interview with Garry Marshall.

Robin encountered the comedian Richard Lewis coming out: Robin Williams, *Larry King Live,* July 3, 2007.

"He didn't say, 'Hi, you play golf?' ": Author interview with Garry Marshall. a script that he had marked up with brief notes: RWC, box 4, folder 11.

"the *Happy Days* actors were very secure": Author interview with Garry Marshall.

"if the show was successful, we have a job": Author interview with Henry Winkler.

"I'm not deaf and I'm not blind": Author interview with Garry Marshall.

it was as popular as *Happy Days* had been all season: Associated Press, "ABC Keeps Nielsen's Lead," *Colorado Springs Gazette-Telegraph,* March 8, 1978.

he'd pitched many outlandish characters: RWC, box 8, folder 20.

"after they look through all the pilots, they say, 'We got nothing!' ": Author interview with Garry Marshall.

"We felt it would be a mistake to put him on television at that point": Browne, "Robin Williams."

Robin, in his innocence, screamed excitedly: Author interview with Howard Storm.

Sister Terri, a failed TV pilot: Lee Goldberg, *Unsold Television Pilots, 1955–1989* (Calabasas, CA: Adventures in Television, 2015).

"Whatever you said to them, you sold it": Author interview with Garry Marshall.

"a comedy about a being from the planet Ork": Richard F. Shepard, "ABC's Fall TV Schedule to Retain 84% of Present Prime-Time Shows," *New York Times,* May 2, 1978.

"when my agent reads me what this show's about, I was pi-*issed*": Author interview with Pam Dawber.

"Oh ho ho — he was so brilliant": Ibid.

"He had signed an all-purposes contract with George Schlatter": Author interview with Stu Smiley.

"The deal he was under with George Schlatter was very onerous": Author interview with Cyndi McHale.

Schlatter disputes that he did anything to stand in Robin's way: Author interview with George Schlatter.

this four-hour show, held at the San Francisco Civic Auditorium: Jack McDonough, "Martin Musters Talent Muscle in S.F. Boarding House Benefit," *Billboard,* June 10, 1978.

"John was hilarious, but Robin was fearless": Author interview with Billy Crystal.

"It was like two elks spraying musk": Amy Longsdorf, "Perfect Foils," *Allen-town (PA) Morning Call,* May 9, 1997.

"It was electric, and we all just sat there": Author interview with Billy Crystal.

In his twenty-minute set: Audio recording provided by Tom Lapinski.

"The audience knew him from performing in the clubs there": Author interview with Billy Crystal.

"It was just like, of course we were going to be together": Author interview with Valerie Velardi.

"Hey, what's happening with your career?": Don Stitt, Facebook post, August 11, 2014. Archived at https://www.facebook.com/notes/don-stitt/ a-friend-from-san-francisco/10152635137766683/.

Robin and Valerie were married in an outdoor ceremony: Author interview with Valerie Velardi; photograph provided by Zak Williams.

Rick and Ruby . . . performed at the reception: Author interviews with Brian Seff, Monica Ganas, and Joshua Raoul Brody.

"He had both of them very strongly implanted in him": Author interview with Valerie Velardi.

Robin went to Los Angeles in July: RWC, box 12, folder 7.

a strange alien salutation: "Nanu, nanu": The spelling of this and other Orkan phrases that Mork speaks throughout the course of the series tends to be inconsistent from screenplay to screenplay; the *Mork & Mindy* pilot script renders it as "na-no, na-no."

However, I have chosen "Nanu, nanu" because I like it better.

Mindy helps Mork argue his way out of a legal hearing: *Mork & Mindy,* season 1, episode 1, "Pilot," September 14, 1978.

"Look, if you do the show, do whatever you want to do": Author interview with Dale McRaven.

"I was frightened to death": Author interview with Howard Storm.

"nothing less than uproarious" and "a prime contender for best new comedy of the season": Lee Margulies, "Previewing the New Season," *Los Angeles Times,* September 14, 1978.

"this season's most innovative comedy": Austin Siegemund-Broka and Michael Sugerman, "Read the Hollywood Reporter's 1978 Review of Robin Williams in 'Mork & Mindy,' " *Hollywood Reporter,* August 13, 2014.

Robin "soon may be known as the funniest man on television": William A. Henry 3d, "4 New Shows Worth a Peek," *Boston Globe,* September 10, 1978.

People magazine published a modest feature on Robin: *People,* Outlook (column), September 11, 1978.

the network flew Valerie and him to New Orleans: Author interviews with Valerie Velardi and Bennett Tramer.

It was watched in 19.7 million homes: Associated Press, "ABC Off & Running with Season & Ratings," *Nashville Tennessean,* September 20, 1978.

Chapter 5. The Robin Williams Show

A fledgling comic with ruffled hair: "The Robin Williams Show: Sixty Characters in Search of a Maniac."

the same modest apartment: Freeman, "Way Out."

glided around the Paramount campus: Harmetz, "Robin Williams: Comedy for a Narcissistic Time."

"It was a good show because we were so unlimited": Author interview with Dale McRaven.

he described one of the guests as a hide-and-seek champion: RWC, box 5, folder 12.

"It was about this cheerful little man doing very simple things": Linderman, "Playboy Interview: Robin Williams."

One day it might be Henry Winkler: Author interview with Pam Dawber.

"chosen for their abilities to respond to his improvisations": Ansen, "Funny Man."

"It was the greatest acting class I'd ever had": Author interview with Pam Dawber.

"We could be in the middle of doing a take": Ibid.

"It's about one-third of each show": "Robin Williams: 'Mork' Dumbfounds with Inventive Wit and Nannu, Nannu . . . ," *Newark (NJ) Sunday Star-Ledger,* February 4, 1979.

"would jump from seat to seat": Author interview with Howard Storm.

"Listen, Robin, I know there are two of you": Ibid.

"All sitcoms do changes": Author interview with Dale McRaven.

"the writers sent down a blank script": Author interview with Garry Marshall.

"He goosed her with the cane": Author interview with Howard Storm.

"she would be there, continuing the scene": Author interview with Garry Marshall.

"I had the grossest things done to me": Author interview with Pam Dawber.

the only publications that had not yet featured him: Author interview with Joshua Raoul Brody.

an eight-room, $200,000 house in Topanga Canyon: Lois Armstrong, "Living with Mork," *People,* October 29, 1979.

Told by his landlord that he had witnessed the theft: Eskow, "Robin Williams: Full Tilt Bozo."

"Everybody in the stands ran to right field": Author interview with Howard Storm.

"It was really a happening place": Author interview with Pam Dawber.

a television special: *Robin Williams: Live at the Roxy,* October 27, 1978.

"Are there any Hells Angels here tonight?": As seen, for example, in Robin's set from the 1977 HBO special *The Second Annual Home Box Office Young Comedians Show.* Archived at https://www.youtube.com/watch?v=XEiADVI06G0.

a posse of Hells Angels: Author interview with Stu Smiley.

"Please bring some toys and improvise": RWC, box 8, folder 20.

his first comedy album with Casablanca Records: Liz Smith, column, *New York Daily News,* December 18, 1978.

"Normally, he wouldn't have needed me": Author interview with Bennett Tramer.

a bootleg recording of Jonathan Winters: Archived at https://www.youtube.com/watch?v=b5zlnqv-ka4.

"When I said I had a collection, he really freaked out": Author interview with Bennett Tramer.

Robin won a Golden Globe Award: Lee Grant, "Golden Globe Show Staged," *Los Angeles Times,* January 29, 1979.

Mork & Mindy was hitting number one: Associated Press, "110 Million People Saw 'Roots II,' " *Santa Cruz (CA) Sentinel,* March 2, 1979.

Robin would take home about $35,000: Earl Wilson, Last Night with Earl Wilson (column), *New York Post,* March 5, 1979.

a backdrop of "chrome-and-plaster palm glitz": Dave Hirshey, "In Person, It's Robin Williams (Not Mork)," *New York Daily News,* April 13, 1979.

"It wasn't a work of improvisational genius": Author interview with Joshua Raoul Brody.

"his audience would need a scholastic aptitude test": Hirshey, "In Person, It's Robin Williams (Not Mork)."

"anyone as funny as Robin Williams can also create the impression of being so nice": Janet Maslin, "Cabaret: Robin Williams, Life-Size," *New York Times,* April 13, 1979.

"Mom, meet Andy Warhol": Author interview with Bennett Tramer.

Robin and Warhol went shopping at thrift stores: Author interview with Brian Seff.

"this complete throng that was hanging around Robin": Ibid.

"It was part, 'Isn't that fantastic?' ": Author interview with Bennett Tramer.

"It's like the Big Bang": Author interview with Sonya Sones.

Robin's first album, titled *Reality . . . What a Concept:* Robin Williams, *Reality . . . What a Concept,* Casablanca Record and Film-Works, 1979.

"Robin Williams is like a butterfly in harness": "Picks and Pans Review: *Reality . . . What a Concept,*" *People,* August 20, 1979.

Robin's album was in the Billboard Top 10:

RIAA Certified Records, *Billboard,* September 15, 1979.

Bennett Tramer extended his congratulations to Robin's publicist: Author interview with Bennett Tramer.

Chapter 6. Mork Blows His Cork

"Of course the place goes crazy": Author interview with Rich Shydner.

wearing his rainbow suspenders: Armstrong, "Living with Mork."

atop a gossipy column called The Insider: "Shazbat! Did Milton Berle Come from Ork?" The Insider (column), *Los Angeles* 24, no. 3 (March 1979).

this story was carried to the East Coast: Liz Smith, column, *New York Daily News,* March 2, 1979.

the *Chicago Tribune* weighed in with a lengthy feature story: Larry Kart, "Shazbat! Williams' Act No Joke with Comics," *Chicago Tribune,* April 22, 1979.

"There's no truth in it": Armstrong, "Living with Mork."

"When you're a success, it's the same old charge": Ibid.

"Robin would see something and he'd appreciate it": Author interview with Jim Staahl.

"Robin could take a premise or a joke": Author interview with Richard Lewis.

"Something would be in his head, and then it was like, *pop*": Author interview with Jim Staahl.

"It was rush-hour traffic, so it was a slow cab": Author interview with Joshua Raoul Brody.

"If you hang out in comedy clubs, when I was doing it": *WTF with Marc Maron,* April 26, 2010.

"He had an addictive personality": Author interview with Jamie Masada.

"Valerie is my inspiration": Freeman, "Way Out."

"He was young, and it's a strange thing": Author interview with Bennett Tramer.

"Pretty well, I think. She lives in Louisiana now": "Robin Williams: 'Mork' Dumbfounds with Inventive Wit and Nannu, Nannu . . ."

"He's saying it like it's a hardship": Author interview with Brian Seff.

"Robin was like a giant puppy": Author interview with Jim Staahl.

"Lou Reed lookalikes named Hercules and Raquel": Taylor Negron, "My Name Is Julio: I'm So Bad, I Should Be in Detention," *Lowbrow Reader,* no. 9 (2014).

"People were forever looking for stories and angles": Author interview with Jim Staahl.

preparing for a legal separation: Jack Martin, "Mork's Wife Ready to Call Lawyer over an Earthling," *New York Post,* July 27, 1979.

Robin and Valerie at Studio 54: "Loving Couples Do Their Own Thing," *New York Daily News,* August 10, 1979.

When Robin appeared on the cover of *Rolling Stone:* Eskow, "Robin Williams: Full Tilt Bozo."

a story that asked, "Has MORK blown his cork?": Armstrong, "Living with Mork."

"I just loved that man to pieces": Author interview with Valerie Velardi.

a doubling of his salary, to $30,000 an episode: Jack Martin, "Mork Casts His Spell on ABC — Asks Double Pay," *New York Post,* May 16, 1979.

roughly $3 million over the life of the show: Dave Hirshey, "The Spinach-Eater from Ork," *New York Daily News Sunday Magazine,* December 7, 1980.

"the network felt that the older people were dead weight": Author interview with Dale McRaven.

Carroll O'Connor, who later prevailed over Robin at the Emmy Awards: Associated Press, "Guest Stars Big Winners on Television Emmy Awards," *Carbondale (IL) Southern Illinoisan,* September 10, 1979.

"That screwed up the gist of the show": Author interview with Pam Dawber.

scripts veered into sexualized territory: *Mork & Mindy,* season 2, episodes 11–13, "Mork vs. the Necrotons" and "Hold That Mork,"

November 18 and 25, 1979.

"Shows like those changed us during the second year": Linderman, "Playboy Interview: Robin Williams."

"an invasion of privacy" and "misleading advertising": Marilyn Beck, column, *New York Daily News,* October 31, 1979.

a court later ruled that any banners or ads: "Robin Williams Wins Modification of 'Odious' Copy," *Variety,* November 7, 1979.

"To be funny in print is a real hard thing": Eskow, "Robin Williams: Full Tilt Bozo."

Robin would play multiple characters, like Peter Sellers in *Dr. Strangelove:* Author interview with Bennett Tramer.

its original star, Dustin Hoffman, dropped out: Guy Flatley, "Producer Sets Hoffman's Sail for 'Popeye,' " *New York Times,* October 14, 1977; Liz Smith, column, *New York Daily News,* December 18, 1978.

Popeye: Jerry McCulley, "It Is What It Is (And That's All That It Is)," *Popeye — Deluxe Edition: Music from the Motion Picture,* liner notes, Varese Sarabande Records, 2017.

" 'there's no story here' ": Author interview with Bennett Tramer.

"I thought, this is it, this is *my Superman*": Linderman, "Playboy Interview: Robin Williams."

Robin was paid a salary of $500,000: Armstrong, "Living with Mork."

"Imagine San Quentin on Valium": Ibid.

"Altman loved organized chaos": Author interview with Jules Feiffer.

"nuttin' on board t'eat but carroks": Jules Feiffer, *Popeye,* final draft (dated August 11, 1980). Archived at RWC, box 3, folder 10.

"I thought I had written this as a Popeye and Olive Oyl romance": Author interview with Jules Feiffer.

"Bob said I could ad lib the mumbles": Goodman, "Robin Williams Gets a Tall Order in Popeye."

"I was deeply gloomy and drinking just a little bit": Author interview with Jules Feiffer.

"I wanted it to be his announcement of self": Ibid.

"That was literally where they pulled the plug": Author interview with Robin Williams.

the Grammy Award he had won in absentia: "List of Grammy Winners," *Nashville Tennessean,* February 28, 1980.

"He's a simple man": Hirshey, "The Spinach-Eater from Ork."

the film's gala premiere: Tom Hritz, People (column), *Pittsburgh Post-Gazette,* December 9, 1980.

"People didn't know what to make of it": Author interview with Bennett Tramer.

"a thoroughly charming, immensely appealing mess": Vincent Canby, "A Singing, Dancing, Feifferish Kind of 'Popeye,' " *New York Times,* December 12, 1980.

"an apparent big-budget bomb": Gene Siskel, "First-Rate Fairy Tale for Adults," *Chicago Tribune,* December 12, 1980.

it sold nearly $50 million in tickets: http://www.boxofficemojo.com/movies/?id=popeye.htm.

"a nice fairy tale with a loving spirit to it": Linderman, "Playboy Interview: Robin Williams."

John Lennon was shot and killed: Les Ledbetter, "John Lennon of Beatles Is Killed; Suspect Held in Shooting at Dakota," *New York Times,* December 9, 1980.

"There was some paranoia": Author interview with Brian Seff.

Robin worked through some of these feelings: *Mork & Mindy,* season 3, episode 14, "Mork Meets Robin Williams," February 14, 1981.

Chapter 7. Bungalow 3

"A god at twenty-seven, a washout at twenty-eight": Jack Hicks, "Octopus Cakes, Sushi, Live Mud Eel and Beer-Crazed Antelopes," *TV Guide,* May 3, 1980.

"Quite funny people were being booed off": Author interview with Eric Idle.

"I haven't laughed this hard in years": Author interviews with Bennett Tramer and Eric Idle.

"It was just a simple, effortless thing": Author interview with Eric Idle.

Robin made a spur-of-the-moment trip to Toronto: Martin Short, *I Must Say: My Life as a Humble Comedy Legend* (New York: Harper, 2014).

a precipitous tumble in its third season: Noel Holston, "Happy Days Again for 'Mork and Mindy'?" *Orlando Sentinel,* June 25, 1981.

"The third year was groping": Author interview with Garry Marshall.

Mork proposed to Mindy: *Mork & Mindy,* "Limited Engagement" and "The Wedding," October 8 and 15, 1981.

Mork gave birth, through his navel: *Mork & Mindy,* "Three the Hard Way" and "Mama Mork, Papa Mindy," October 29 and November 5, 1981.

playing Mindy's uncle Dave: *Mork & Mindy,* "Mork and the Family Reunion," April 9, 1981.

" 'What a *pretty* little girl *you* are' ": Author interview with Howard Storm.

"I don't think Jonathan had been doing much": Author interview with Dale McRaven.

"the chance to play alongside Babe Ruth":

Linderman, "Playboy Interview: Robin Williams."

he was also a tragic, wounded figure: Scott Marks, "Dig a Hole: Jonathan Winters," *San Diego Reader,* April 12, 2013; and Carmel Dagan, "Comedian Jonathan Winters Dead at 87," *Variety,* April 12, 2013.

"Humor is the mistress of sorrow": Dennis McLellan, "Jonathan Winters Dies at 87; Comic Genius of Improvisation," *Los Angeles Times,* April 13, 2013.

"a quality that forces us, when in doubt, to lash out": Vernon Scott, "Pixilated Pair Are Masters of Improvisation," United Press International, December 8, 1981.

"He and Jonathan Winters are walking down the street": Author interview with Henry Winkler.

his long-awaited debut on *The Tonight Show*: *The Tonight Show Starring Johnny Carson,* October 14, 1981.

"someone once gave me a Valium": Linderman, "Playboy Interview: Robin Williams."

"come to do the Comedy Store, and then go to the Improv": *WTF with Marc Maron,* April 26, 2010.

"I did cocaine so I wouldn't have to talk to anybody": Zehme, "Robin Williams: The Rolling Stone Interview."

"He was running like a mad man": Author interview with Pam Dawber.

"He hadn't slept all night": Author interview with Howard Storm.

"people would say, 'Oh, pardon me. Refried shit?' ": Wadler, "Robin Williams Heads for the Hills."

"after one night of partying, he was late": Author interview with Jim Staahl.

"He was so good that he could just phone it in": Author interview with Howard Storm.

"He was addicted to performing": Author interview with Dale McRaven.

Valerie's public feuds: E.g., "Mrs. Mork Mixes It Up in Disco," Page Six (column), *New York Post,* November 6, 1981.

"We'd have to say, 'Get her out of here' ": Author interview with Howard Storm.

"We got hit hard by the drugs and the women": Author interview with Valerie Velardi.

a horrible incident in which he'd badly burned himself: Joan Acocella, "Richard Pryor, Flame-Thrower," *New Yorker,* March 4, 2015.

a ranch on a 640-acre plot: Author interview with Valerie Velardi.

"rose-smelling, deep-breathing, waterfall country": Salley Rayl, "So Long Mork," *People,* September 13, 1982.

"Look, that's a flower, asshole": Wadler, "Robin Williams Heads for the Hills."

"if Dante were James Brown": Zehme,

"Robin Williams: The Rolling Stone Interview."

got their drugs from some of the same people: Bob Woodward, *Wired: The Short Life & Fast Times of John Belushi* (New York: Simon & Schuster, 1984), pp. 295 and 343–44.

who had died of a heart attack after falling ill: Lembeck played the part of Ovits, Mearth's Orkan schoolmate, in the episodes "P.S. 2001" (December 17, 1980) and "Pajama Game II" (January 7, 1982).

"They're fifty feet tall and I'm only five foot eight": Woodward, *Wired,* p. 296.

he watched Belushi observe Winters: Rayl, "So Long Mork."

they made vague plans to see each other again soon: Woodward, *Wired,* p. 296.

Belushi was staying in Bungalow 3 at the Chateau Marmont: Ibid., pp. 397–98.

Robin himself denied this: Andrew Epstein, "Williams: At Home on the Ranch," *Los Angeles Times,* July 25, 1982.

he made the drive alone to his home in Topanga Canyon: Woodward, *Wired,* pp. 397–98.

In his sleep, he died of an overdose: Ibid., pp. 399–400; Robert D. McFadden, "John Belushi, Manic Comic of TV and Films, Dies," *New York Times,* March 6, 1982; "Belushi's Death Attributed to Heroin and

Cocaine," *New York Times,* March 11, 1982; and Lynn Elber, "Gone 25 Years, Belushi's Impact Still Felt," Associated Press, March 6, 2007.

"Wow, I was with Belushi last night, and *boy*": Author interview with Pam Dawber.

"a powerful personality and a powerful physical being, too": Collins, "Robin Williams."

he seemed "to be running, if not as intense a circle": Woodward, *Wired,* p. 419.

"that was pretty much the bottom rung": Collins, "Robin Williams."

a reported fee of $15,000: Michael Small, "The Investigation Centers on a Burnt-Out Case, Cathy 'Silverbag' Smith," *People,* July 19, 1982.

a feature story published that summer: Larry Haley and Tony Brenna, "World Exclusive Interview: 'I Killed John Belushi,' " *National Enquirer,* June 29, 1982.

"It was a huge wake-up call": Author interview with Pam Dawber.

more unwanted attention from the tabloids: " 'Mork' Testifies Before Belushi Jury," *New York Daily News,* September 30, 1982.

"I was there for ten minutes and split": Collins, "Robin Williams."

"maybe the old mad energy is gone": Linderman, "Playboy Interview: Robin Williams."

Mork & Mindy had been pulled from ABC's schedule: David Hatfield, " 'Mork &

Mindy' Reeling from Ratings Pummeling," *Tucson, Arizona Daily Star,* February 1, 1982.

pursued by a malevolent Neptunian named Kalnik: *Mork & Mindy,* season 4, "Gotta Run," parts 1–3, May 6, 13, and 20, 1982.

a larger, last-ditch plan to persuade ABC: *Mork & Mindy* video presentation dated April 12, 1982; RWC, box 5, folder 17.

ABC canceled *Mork & Mindy* after four seasons: Mike Hughes, "ABC Wields Big Ax," *Lansing (MI) State Journal,* May 6, 1982.

"I think they tried to call me the day before": Wadler, "Robin Williams Heads for the Hills."

"I was dressed as a frog. It hit me hard": Glen Wilson, "A Conversation Between Ed Norton & Robin Williams," *Interview,* April 2002.

"The end of that show wasn't unexpected": Kornbluth, "Robin Williams's Change of Life."

the plum opportunity to play Hamlet for Joseph Papp: Marilyn Beck, Robin Williams: I'm Mellowing with Age (column), *San Bernardino County (CA) Sun,* July 10, 1983.

Star of the Family, a blue-collar comedy: David Bianculli, "The Stars in Her Eyes Are for Real," *Akron (OH) Beacon Journal,* September 26, 1982.

"Robin was hurt to the quick over that": Author interview with Pam Dawber.

"I was just being an all-around fuckup": Wadler, "Robin Williams Heads for the Hills."

"you can guide people; you can make yourself interesting enough": Ibid.

"Enough. Enough. Enough": Author interview with Valerie Velardi.

Chapter 8. Mr. Happy

On the sunny lawn of a suburban New York home: *The World According to Garp,* directed by George Roy Hill, 1982.

"One really good thing about this film": Rayl, "So Long Mork."

Steinberg, a former publicist: Author interview with David Steinberg. Not to be confused with the comedian, actor, and director of the same name.

At the top of the hierarchy, in Roman numerals: RWC, box 8, file 12.

by the time he played the Royal Oak Music Theater: John Smyntek, "Who Said Robin's Overworked?" *Detroit Free Press,* May 21, 1982.

the tale of T. S. Garp, an aspiring writer: Christopher Lehmann-Haupt, " 'The World According to Garp' by John Irving," Books of the Times (column), *New York Times,* April 13, 1978.

he read the book while making *Popeye:* Bob Thomas, "Robin Williams: 'Garp' Role a Departure for Zany Comic," Associated

Press, August 1, 1982.

"It was like going from Marvel Comics to Tolstoy": Rayl, "So Long Mork."

"I'd seen him in *Popeye* and didn't understand a word he said": William Wolf, "Mork Meets Garp," *New York,* August 31, 1981.

"I thought, okay, you've made your point": Linderman, "Playboy Interview: Robin Williams."

"Oh, looky, our baby has a beard": Rayl, "So Long Mork."

who was paid $300,000 to make *Garp:* Wadler, "Robin Williams Heads for the Hills."

"seventeen lights and fifteen guys and a big boom mike": Ibid.

He even shaved his arms: Marilyn Beck, It'll Be "Laverne Minus Shirley," This Fall (column), *Santa Fe New Mexican,* August 4, 1982.

"Garp was like an oil drilling": Linderman, "Playboy Interview: Robin Williams."

"an appropriate choice for the sometimes bewildered Garp": Betsy Light, " 'Garp' Looks Better as a Book," *Indianapolis Star,* August 1, 1982.

"the rubbery nature of Robin Williams' face": Jack Mathews, "Robin Doesn't Belong in Garp's World," *Detroit Free Press,* July 23, 1982.

Glenn Close would receive an Oscar nomination: Associated Press, "Oscar Nominations," *Asbury Park (NJ) Press,* February

18, 1983. Dustin Hoffman, who instead made *Tootsie,* received a nomination for Best Actor.

they had "waited this long to have a baby": Associated Press, "A Child for Robin Williams," *Carbondale (IL) Southern Illinoisan,* September 26, 1982.

"The actual pregnancy was beautiful": Author interview with Valerie Velardi.

he did not expect much sympathy: "Gator Growl Attracts a Crowd of 64,000," *Palm Beach Post,* October 17, 1982.

"It was the biggest crowd Robin had ever worked with": Author interview with David Steinberg.

the stand-up set he'd been refining since the spring: Showbiz Shorts (column), *Fort Myers (FL) News-Press,* October 12, 1982.

a ninety-minute HBO special that would air the next year: *An Evening with Robin Williams,* March 11, 1983.

The Survivors, a farcical comedy: *The Survivors,* directed by Michael Ritchie, 1983.

Jack Nicholson and James Caan, who were replaced by Joe Bologna and Jerry Reed: Marilyn Beck, Producer's Private Pilot Soars as Casting Director (column), *(Phoenix) Arizona Republic,* November 15, 1982.

replaced by Walter Matthau: Marilyn Beck, Robin Williams May Not Survive "The Survivors" (column), *Battle Creek (MI) En-*

quirer, January 10, 1983.

the production showed up in rural Vermont: Susan Green, "Actors, Film Crew Find There's No Stand-in for Snow," *Burlington (VT) Free Press,* January 15, 1983.

Matthau passed the chilly downtime: Richard Freedman, " 'Survivors' Director Says America Loves Guns," Newhouse News Service, July 15, 1983.

"Now I know what it's like to be a dog": Kate Santich, "Shooting 'Survivors' at Tahoe," *Reno Gazette-Journal,* February 7, 1983.

one more TV appearance, on an HBO special: Robin Williams, *The Comedy Store's 11th Anniversary Show,* HBO. The special was taped on April 8, 1983, and first broadcast on July 10.

it sounded good and "kind of Welsh": Author interview with Zak Williams.

"It was like going through flight training and ending up in a glider": Collins, "Robin Williams."

"suddenly there was a focus, a meaning, a continuity": Robin Williams, eighteenth birthday book for Zak Williams. Provided by Zak Williams.

the infant Zak dressed up in a baby-size tuxedo: Zachary Pym Williams birth announcement. Provided by Zak Williams.

Robin and Valerie took him to New York: Marilyn Beck, Steve Martin Has Another

Wild and Crazy Idea (column), *Rochester (NY) Democrat and Chronicle,* May 12, 1983.

one episode of *The Billy Crystal Comedy Hour:* Fred Rothenberg, "Saturday Prime Time TV Getting Better," Associated Press, February 12, 1982.

the independent jazz label Commodore Records: Crystal, *Still Foolin' 'Em,* p. 16.

"I lost my dad young; he lost his dad younger": Author interview with Billy Crystal.

Crystal was in a dour mood: Author interview with Greg Phillips.

"I was a Dr. Spock fan, and I remembered it": Author interview with Billy Crystal.

"Walter Matthau's soulful deadpan": Sheila Benson, "Matthau, Williams Get Jobbed," *Los Angeles Times,* June 22, 1983.

"one of the most confused and repellent films of the year": Gene Siskel, "Lack of Control Proves Fatal to 'The Survivors,' " *Chicago Tribune,* June 22, 1983.

The Survivors was crushed at the box office, too: Box Office Mojo, http://www.boxoffice mojo.com/movies/?id=survivors.htm.

"I met rear admirals from Leningrad driving taxis": Janet Maslin, At the Movies (column), *New York Times,* April 6, 1984.

"They said I sounded Czech": Luaine Lee, "Robin Williams: New Role Moves Actor

Nearer Mainstream," Knight-Ridder, April 20, 1984.

"He's really very modest": Michael Blowen, "Robin Williams: Inventive Comic Actor Is Never Off," *Boston Globe,* February 13, 1986.

"He had never played a musical instrument": Author interview with Greg Phillips.

Robin and Mazursky went to see the documentary *Unknown Chaplin:* Author interview with Bennett Tramer.

Robin said he felt compelled to make more "strange films": Lee, "Robin Williams: New Role Moves Actor Nearer Mainstream."

"Eddie is ideal — he knows exactly what he does": Collins, "Robin Williams."

"It's Robin — have you seen *Trading Places*?": Author interview with Bennett Tramer.

Robin's second comedy album: Robin Williams, *Throbbing Python of Love,* Casablanca Record and FilmWorks, 1983.

"of the three major comedic talents who matured in the '70s": Lawrence Christon, "Robin Takes It Standing Up," *Los Angeles Times,* May 1, 1983.

It debuted at number 180 on the Billboard sales chart: Billboard 200 chart, April 2, 1983. Archived at http://www.billboard.com/charts/ billboard-200/1983-04-02.

He and Murphy acted opposite each other:

Saturday Night Live, season 9, episode 12, February 11, 1984.

Eddie Murphy: Comedian, not *Throbbing Python of Love:* United Press International, "Grammy Award Winners," *Orlando Sentinel,* March 1, 1984.

Robin and his alter ego were "most engaging characters": Vincent Canby, "Film: Paul Mazursky's 'Moscow on the Hudson,' " *New York Times,* April 6, 1984.

"he has a real character to play, and he's extraordinarily touching": David Denby, "Okay by Me in America," *New York,* April 16, 1984.

the day that Zak took his first steps: Judy Klemesrud, "Robin Williams Dons an Émigré's Guise," *New York Times,* April 15, 1984.

"Get off! You've done too much": *Saturday Night Live,* season 9, episode 12, February 11, 1984.

Marsha, who was in her late twenties: Lillian Ross, *Reporting Always: Writings from* The New Yorker (New York: Scribner, 2015), p. 30.

"I interviewed her at a fish restaurant": Author interview with Valerie Velardi.

Chapter 9. Tough love

"Lust!" Robin Williams intoned: *Robin Williams: An Evening at the Met,* HBO, 1986.

"then it just started again": Author interview with Valerie Velardi.

he caught the attention of Michelle Tish Carter: "Accusation Is No Laughing Matter," *Columbus (IN) Republic,* October 8, 1988; David Hay, "Sleeping with the Enemy," *Melbourne (AU) Age,* March 8, 1992; Frank Walker, "Actor in Herpes Test Case," *Sydney (AU) Morning Herald,* March 15, 1992; "Robin Williams Settles Suit over Herpes," *Orlando Sentinel,* July 30, 1992. Via a manager, Carter declined to speak to me for this book.

"Very attractive women throw themselves at men": Brad Darrach, "A Comic's Crisis of the Heart," *People,* February 22, 1988.

filmed at the start of 1985 in Taft, California: Bruce Cook, "Kurt Russell Praises New Movie as Thought-Provoking, Suspenseful," *(Phoenix) Arizona Republic,* March 8, 1985; and "Film Makes Kurt Russell Sing for His Supper," *(Phoenix) Arizona Republic,* April 12, 1985.

the film's box-office receipts were abysmal: Box Office Mojo, http://www.boxofficemojo .com/movies/?id=bestoftimes.htm.

"What's happened to Robin Williams?": "TV Dialogue," *Alexandria (IN) Times-Tribune,* April 17, 1985.

initially intended for Bill Murray: Dale Pollock, "On 'Razor's Edge' After 'Ghostbusters,' " *Los Angeles Times,* October 21, 1984.

"He's not as quirky as he was": Bob Thomas, "Harold Ramis Is Sought for His Behind-The-Camera Work," Associated Press, July 27, 1986.

"Dear boy, go ahead": Donald Chase, "Comics Find Improv Alive in 'Club Paradise,' " *Los Angeles Times,* June 9, 1985.

a Jamaican soldier who had performed in a parachute jump: William Wolf, "Fans, Critics Give 4 Films Thumbs Up," Gannett News Service, June 30, 1985.

Adolph Caesar died of a heart attack: Robert W. Stewart, "Adolph Caesar: Fatal Heart Attack Fells Actor on Set," *Los Angeles Times,* March 7, 1986.

"It should not be run again": James Burrus, "Robin Williams' New Movie Far from 'Paradise,' " *Chapel Hill (NC) Tar Heel,* July 10, 1986.

"a vacation during which everything goes wrong": William Wolf, " 'Club Paradise' Fizzles Like Bad Vacation," Gannett News Service, July 10, 1986.

"They waved a lot of money at me": Hank Gallo, "A Lucky Seven? Robin Williams Rolls the Dice with 'Good Morning Vietnam,' " *New York Daily News,* December 20, 1987.

"I got suckered into a couple films like that": Zehme, "Robin Williams: The Rolling Stone

Interview."

"God. It's out there somewhere": Collins, "Robin Williams."

At a press conference in Beverly Hills: Dennis McDougal, "Comic Relief Will Give Aid to Homeless in U.S.," *Los Angeles Times,* January 15, 1986.

"Basically, they were under contract": Author interview with John Moffitt. John Moffitt was also Robin's director for the brief run of *The Richard Pryor Show.* (See chapter 4.)

their shenanigans had not been widely seen: A lone exception was *Superstars of Comedy Salute the Improv,* a Showtime special that had aired in 1985. Archived at https://www .youtube.com/watch?v=Sc1szJ7HcHA.

at the Comedy Store in San Diego: *Late Show with David Letterman,* November 6, 2014.

It had taken her nearly another decade to break through: Janet Coleman, "The Many Faces of Whoopi Goldberg," *Vanity Fair,* July 1984; and Marshall Fine, "Whoopi's Not Wild About Broadway," Gannett News Service, March 3, 1985.

"It's hands across the street, boys and girls": Associated Press, Names in the News (column), *Santa Fe New Mexican,* March 14, 1986.

if homeless viewers would have their own opportunity to watch: McDougal, "Comic Relief Will Give Aid to Homeless in U.S."

a 1984 fund-raiser: Lawrence Christon, " 'Night of a Dozen Stars' Falls Flat," *Los Angeles Times,* May 4, 1984.

where Robin and Whoopi Goldberg first re-encountered each other: *The Whoopi Goldberg Show,* September 18, 1992.

"You ever see people, like a family of eight": *Comic Relief: Backstage Pass,* HBO, 1986. Archived at https://www.youtube.com/watch?v=kWcqNXo-dSY.

"the homeless men waited patiently": Associated Press, "Comics Join Forces to Help Homeless," *Salem (OR) Statesman Journal,* February 14, 1986.

"Look, no jokes, you three": Hilary Lewis, "Billy Crystal, Whoopi Goldberg Share Robin Williams Stories at Opening of NYC SAG-AFTRA Foundation Center," *Hollywood Reporter,* October 7, 2016.

he was asked to cohost the Academy Awards: United Press International, "Robin Williams to Co-Host Oscars," *Nashville Tennessean,* February 2, 1986.

five days before the Comic Relief broadcast: 58th Academy Awards, ABC, March 24, 1986.

The full script, encompassing ninety-five different comedy sketches: RWC, box 4, folders 7 and 8.

a product called the Sony Poorman: *Comic Relief: Backstage Pass,* HBO, 1986.

"They each made an entrance": Author interview with John Moffitt.

"We'd make these pretty interesting play-books": Author interview with Billy Crystal.

the trio's rotating character bits: *Comic Relief,* HBO, 1986.

"We all started to cry. We knew we were do-ing something good": Author interview with Billy Crystal.

"We're testing our abilities against each other": Ibid.

"a split-personality problem": John J. O'Con-nor, " 'Comic Relief,' Benefit for the Home-less, on HBO," *New York Times,* March 31, 1986.

nearly $2.5 million in donations: William Plummer, "Backstage at Comic Relief," *People,* April 14, 1986.

jobs for homeless people: Zelda Williams, Twitter post, November 12, 2017.

"I wasn't interested in being sucked dry": Kornbluth, "Robin Williams's Change of Life."

"A time when you didn't want to stop": Ansen, "Funny Man."

He had ended his extramarital relationship with Michelle Tish Carter . . . with consid-erable acrimony: Hay, "Sleeping with the Enemy."

that she had contracted herpes from him: "Starwatch: Marriage on the Ropes," *Pitts-burgh Post-Gazette,* October 8, 1988.

"She's tried to support me as much as possible": Collins, "Robin Williams."

"I'm not a controlling person": Author interview with Valerie Velardi.

"Ultimately, things went astray": Zehme, "Robin Williams: The Rolling Stone Interview."

"You suddenly have a malleable little creature": Stu Schreiberg, "Robin Williams," *USA Weekend,* January 24–26, 1986.

"When you see Robin play with *any* child": Ansen, "Funny Man."

"there's a certain vehemence in my show": Ibid.

"Maybe that's the next step": Ibid.

celebrity guests like Robert De Niro, Sean Penn: Tom Shales, "Williams Barrages Met with Laughs," *Reno (NV) Gazette-Journal,* August 28, 1986.

"There'll be a minor change in the program tonight": *Robin Williams: An Evening at the Met,* HBO, 1986.

"I wasn't too aware of it": Author interview with Zak Williams.

a "virtuoso comedy hour": Andrew Sarris (no article title), *Village Voice,* November 4, 1986.

"it's still likely to be a night in comedy Mecca": Shales, "Williams Barrages Met with Laughs."

"You can do it. You're okay. I love you": Kornbluth, "Robin Williams's Change of Life."

a private agreement, handled out of court: Darrach, "A Comic's Crisis of the Heart."

Chapter 10. Gooooooood Morning

a meager $1.6 million: Eric Pooley, "Geller: The Rain King," *New York,* October 14, 1985.

"You want to be proud?": *Seize the Day,* directed by Fielder Cook, 1986.

"you can't get down any further": Nancy Lipton, "Robin Williams Seizes the Play," *Dial Thirteen,* May 1987.

"a miscasting fiasco": John J. O'Connor, "Robin Williams in 'Seize the Day,' " *New York Times,* May 1, 1987.

"You simply slip down the comedy food chain": Zehme, "Robin Williams: The Rolling Stone Interview."

"this is nice, too, not being hot": Jeff Strickler, "Robin Williams Rechannels His Childlike Energy," *Minneapolis Star and Tribune,* February 2, 1986.

"Saigon was still a sleepy little French colonial town": *Good Morning, Vietnam: Special Edition,* DVD, Touchstone Home Entertainment, 2006.

A later treatment by Cronauer, written as a TV movie: Associated Press, " 'Good Morning Vietnam' Started as a Sitcom," *Asbury Park (NJ) Press,* December 15, 1987; Jim Barthold, "The Real Life of

Adrian Cronauer," *Urgent Communications,* March 1, 2005; and William Kerns, "Cronauer, Inspiration for 'Good Morning, Vietnam,' Will Lecture," *Lubbock Avalanche-Journal,* March 9, 2011.

"I really can't get hemmed into some story here": *Good Morning, Vietnam: Special Edition,* DVD.

At his first appearance, as he deplanes from a flight from Greece: Mitch Markowitz, *Good Morning, Vietnam,* 4th rev. draft (dated March 23, 1987). Archived at RWC, box 1, folder 7.

At his first appearance, as he deplanes from a flight from Greece: Mitch Markowitz, *Good Morning, Vietnam,* 4th rev. draft (dated March 23, 1987). Archived at RWC, box 1, folder 7.

"He looks like Judge Bork": Zehme, "Robin Williams: The Rolling Stone Interview."

He and Robin also shared the services of Michael Ovitz: S. L. Price, "Much Ado About Nothing," *Vanity Fair,* March 2012.

"My intention was to play around with the radio": Author interview with Barry Levinson.

he and Levinson shot some test footage in Los Angeles: *Good Morning, Vietnam: Special Edition,* DVD.

budgeted at just $14 million: Donald Chase, "Vietnam the Comedy," *New York Daily*

News, August 16, 1987.

"Right then and there, it occurred to me that he's going to be fine": Author interview with Barry Levinson.

run up to him on the streets and call him ling: *Good Morning America,* June 17, 1987.

helpful advisories like "last half of this road is dirt": *Good Morning, Vietnam* call sheet, June 14, 1987. Archived at RWC, box 12, folder 7.

"They told us all these horror stories": Chase, "Vietnam the Comedy."

a research file for him, comprised of photocopied pages: RWC, box 13, folder 21.

Together they filled the pages of his notebooks: RWC, box 13, folder 21.

"I wonder if we could just make it a little shorter' ": Author interview with Barry Levinson.

In just a single take seated at the microphone: *Good Morning, Vietnam: Special Edition,* DVD.

"He so wanted to please and for everything to work": Author interview with Mark Johnson.

"He's doing all this free-form spontaneity": Author interview with Barry Levinson.

"Our crew was primarily British and a lot of Thai": Author interview with Mark Johnson.

"once you did it again, they had already heard it": Author interview with Barry

Levinson.

Her mother was Finnish, the youngest of seven children: Ross, *Reporting Always,* p. 29; and "Funeral Notices," *Tucson (AZ) Citizen,* March 15, 2002.

"I grew up in a German community": Ross, *Reporting Always,* p. 30.

"my assistant, friend, confidant": Gallo, "A Lucky Seven?"

"I saw that he was funkier": Zehme, "Robin Williams: The Rolling Stone Interview."

"There was this little man behind the curtain, going, 'Take care of your mother and I love you and I've been very worried about certain things' ": Grobel, "Robin Williams: The Playboy Interview."

Rob, for the first time, told Robin of the challenges, disappointments, and failures he had faced in his own life: Hawkes, "The Transformation of Robin Williams."

"He gave me this depth that helps with acting and even with comedy, saying, 'Fuck it. Do you believe in this?' ": Grobel, "Robin Williams: The Playboy Interview."

Rob Williams died in his sleep on October 18, 1987: United Press International, "Robert Fitzgerald Williams, the Father of Comedian Robin Williams," October 19, 1987.

"She was a little in shock, but she sounded happy in a certain way, if only because he went without pain": Zehme, "Robin Williams: The Rolling Stone Interview."

McLaurin . . . who had changed his name from Smith to Smith-Williams as a Father's Day gift to Rob: Author interview with McLaurin Smith-Williams.

"I had poured the ashes out": Zehme, "Robin Williams: The Rolling Stone Interview."

"Vietnam means soldiers fighting": Chase, "Vietnam the Comedy."

a photo of Robin in an airman's uniform: Advertisement, *Los Angeles Times,* December 20, 1987.

"I think it's going to be good": *The Tonight Show Starring Johnny Carson,* December 18, 1987.

"I don't like that title": Gallo, "A Lucky Seven?"

"Each film has had its endearing moments": Vincent Canby, "Film: 'Good Morning, Vietnam,' " *New York Times,* December 23, 1987.

"so blazingly brilliant that he detonates the center": Michael Wilmington, "Movie Review: Robin Williams Is Solid Gold as the Deejay in 'Good Morning, Vietnam,' " *Los Angeles Times,* December 25, 1987.

"Why don't we just check and see how the movie's doing?": Author interview with Barry Levinson.

Robin had a number one movie: Box Office Mojo, http://www.boxofficemojo.com/

movies/?id=goodmorningvietnam.htm.

"It was a huge relief for him": Author interview with Barry Levinson.

"open-heart surgery in installments": Glenn Collins, "In Robin Williams's World, Delight Is a Many-Sided Thing," *New York Times,* January 25, 1988.

"the type that goes, 'I am now at one with myself' ": Zehme, "Robin Williams: The Rolling Stone Interview."

Oprah Winfrey asked him . . . if he had any insecurities: *The Oprah Winfrey Show,* January 13, 1988.

a future, sixty-year-old version of himself: *Saturday Night Live,* season 13, episode 9, January 23, 1988.

Chapter 11. O Captain!

effusive notes of congratulations: RWC, box 13, folder 3.

Steven Spielberg wrote to thank Robin: RWC, box 13, folder 13.

It remained the number one motion picture at the box office: Box Office Mojo, http://www.boxofficemojo.com/movies/?page=main&id=goodmorning vietnam.htm.

it spent thirty-five weeks on the Billboard chart: *Billboard,* April 2, 1988. Archived at http://www.billboard.com/charts/billboard-200/1988-04-02.

sold more than one million copies: Archived at https://www.riaa.com/gold-platinum/?tab_active=default-award&se=good+morning+vietnam#search_section.

another Grammy Award for Best Comedy Album: Associated Press, "A List of Winning Music-Makers," *Philadelphia Inquirer,* February 23, 1989.

Charles Joffe decided to retire: Heller, "The King of Comedy."

the only Oscar nomination that *Good Morning, Vietnam* would receive: Michael Cieply, "No Oscars for U.S. Directors," *Los Angeles Times,* February 17, 2017.

a feature article in *People* magazine: Darrach, "A Comic's Crisis of the Heart."

"I was so angry and horrified": Grobel, "Robin Williams: The Playboy Interview."

Gene Siskel . . . wrote to him: RWC, box 13, folder 3.

Robin and Valerie publicly announced in a statement: United Press International, "Williams, Wife to End Marriage," *Fort Myers (FL) News-Press,* April 1, 1988.

"That award was so close! All those calls to *Entertainment Tonight*": 60th Academy Awards, ABC, April 11, 1988. Archived at https://www.youtube.com/watch?v=2eZliygf7QI and https://www.youtube.com/watch?v=WhvFVuWVHmQ.

not technically a Broadway show: Though

Lincoln Center's Vivian Beaumont Theater is formally regarded as a Broadway house, *Waiting for Godot* was presented at the facility's Mitzi E. Newhouse Theatre, which is not.

Nichols had met with his two lead actors: Mervyn Rothstein, "Nichols Tries to Put the Fun Back in 'Godot,' " *New York Times,* September 13, 1988.

Nichols wrote to Robin a few weeks later: RWC, box 13, folder 2.

filling his copy with enthusiastic annotations: RWC, box 4, folder 2.

"they asked him, 'What are you doing in this play?' ": Rothstein, "Nichols Tries to Put the Fun Back in 'Godot.' "

"the play has not been abused": Denis Donoghue, "Play It Again, Sam," *New York Review of Books,* December 8, 1988.

George Roy Hill . . . wrote to him to tell him: RWC, box 13, folder 3.

"A brilliant mimic, the actor never runs out of wacky voices": Frank Rich, " 'Godot': The Timeless Relationship of 2 Interdependent Souls," *New York Times,* November 7, 1988.

"during previews, everybody loved us": Patricia Bosworth, "There's a More Somber Side to the 'Wild and Crazy Guy,' " *Fame,* August 1989.

final performance on November 27: Archived

at http://www.lct.org/shows/waiting-for-godot/.

"We were a little shell-shocked": Frank Rizzo, "Seize the Day," *Hartford Courant,* June 9, 1989.

"We put our ass out and got kicked for it": Grobel, "Robin Williams: The Playboy Interview."

The first reports about their two-year relationship: William C. Trott, "Price of Love," United Press International, April 28, 1988; and Morning Report (column), *Los Angeles Times,* April 28, 1988.

Robin filed a legal cross-claim of his own: "Starwatch: Marriage on the Ropes"; and Morning Report (column).

"Oh me! Oh life! of the questions of these recurring": Walt Whitman, "O Me! O Life!" *Leaves of Grass.* Archived at https://www.poetryfoundation.org/poems-and-poets/poems/detail/51568.

"It turns out he has non-Hodgkin's lymphoma": Author interview with Tom Schulman.

"It did more than it was supposed to do": Author interview with Steven Haft.

"I don't know, I might wait on that one": Author interview with Dana Carvey.

"Robin wouldn't say no, but he wouldn't say yes": *Script to Screen,* "Dead Poets Society — Script to Screen," University of California Television, March 11, 2013. Archived at

https://www.youtube.com/watch?v=0rnXaf
N336E.

"As soon as the gates were open": *Dead Poets Society: Special Edition,* DVD, Touchstone Home Entertainment, 2006.

"It talks about something of the heart": Grobel, "Robin Williams: The Playboy Interview."

"It all started going wobbly": Author interview with Steven Haft.

"The first thing you do is, you shoot the script": Author interview with Mark Johnson.

"Peter Weir said to me, 'That's got to go' ": Author interview with Tom Schulman.

The casting of the Poets was started over from scratch: Author interviews with Steven Haft, Dylan Kussman, and Gale Hansen; Mandy Bierly, "Josh Charles Shares 'Dead Poets Society' Memories, 25 Years Later," *Entertainment Weekly,* July 3, 2014.

"He was like, 'We have a lot in common' ": Author interview with Gale Hansen.

"It was a way of deconstructing my own position as director": *Dead Poets Society: Special Edition,* DVD.

Robin started filming on December 12: RWC, box 10, folder 5; and Associated Press, "Disney to Film 'The Dead Poets' Society Entirely in Delaware," *Easton (MD) Star-Democrat,* December 6, 1988.

the first classroom scene: Tom Schulman, *The Dead Poets Society,* draft (dated November 11, 1988). Archived at RWC, box 10, folder 5.

"Uh-uh, this is too much' ": Author interview with Tom Schulman.

"We were able to get about a half day ahead of schedule": Author interview with Alan Curtiss.

"He's a kind of writer, without a pen": *Dead Poets Society: Special Edition,* DVD.

"It just didn't work": Rizzo, "Seize the Day."

the more modest tweaks that he scrawled in his script: RWC, box 10, folder 5.

"They're not that different from you, are they?": Schulman, *The Dead Poets Society,* draft.

"He's not playing on obvious emotions": *Dead Poets Society: Special Edition,* DVD.

"Carpe per diem": Q, CBC Radio, September 11, 2014. Archived at https://www.you tube.com/watch?v=tT4xjhPD9fs.

"I'm going to challenge him": Author interview with Gale Hansen.

a group field trip into New York: Dylan Kussman, "Dead Poets in NYC." Archived at https://www.youtube.com/watch?v=y1eOYkQpifk.

"when I mean act up, I mean not in a bad way": Author interview with Andy Weltman.

"Robin and Marsha at that point were pretty

hot and heavy": Author interview with Tom Schulman.

"She was a sweet, generous person": Author interview with Gale Hansen.

"He and Marsha were very private": Author interview with Lisa Birnbach.

"*Dead* was a bummer, *Poets* was too effete": Author interview with Steven Haft.

" 'they can retitle the movie' ": Author interview with Tom Schulman.

"It was a tremendous bonding experience for us all": Author interview with Lisa Birnbach.

"Keating turns to look at Todd. So does everybody else": Schulman, *The Dead Poets Society,* draft.

Ennio Morricone's main theme from *The Mission:* Bierly, "Josh Charles Shares 'Dead Poets Society' Memories, 25 Years Later."

Chapter 12. Dreamlike Parts, with Phantasmagoric Associations

Robin and Marsha got married on April 30, 1989: Blaise Simpson, "The Insiders Are Out-Of-Towners," *Los Angeles Times,* November 21, 1993.

About thirty people attended the wedding: Ross, *Reporting Always,* p. 31.

"He kept that marriage very separate": Author interview with Zak Williams.

"Zak loves Marsha, and Marsha loves Zak":

Carson Jones, "The Truth He Wants Known," *Redbook,* January 1991.

Marsha and her growing belly: Lisa Grunwald, "Robin Williams Has a Big Premise!" *Esquire,* June 1989.

"I replied, but they said I was too late": Grobel, "Robin Williams: The Playboy Interview."

a "dim, sad" movie: Vincent Canby, "Shaking Up a Boys' School with Poetry," *New York Times,* June 2, 1989.

"the most exciting performer in American movies": Michael Wilmington, " 'Poets Society': A Moving Elegy from Peter Weir," *Los Angeles Times,* June 2, 1989.

"a collection of pious platitudes": Roger Ebert, "Dead Poets Society," June 9, 1989. Archived at http://www.rogerebert.com/reviews/dead-poets-society-1989.

"It was the last scene of the movie": Author interview with Tom Schulman.

by mid-September it had taken in almost $90 million: Box Office Mojo, http://www.boxofficemojo.com/movies/?id=deadpoetssociety.htm.

one from Fred Rogers: RWC, box 13, folder 4.

"Family is what you make of it": Author interview with Zak Williams.

"She's nine pounds, seven ounces": *The Bar-*

bara *Walters Special,* ABC, September 26, 1989.

"They tried it out on test audiences": Donna Rosenthal, " 'Cadillac Man' Finds a New Life," *Los Angeles Times,* May 9, 1990.

"an astonishing, festive 'awakening' ": Oliver Sacks, *On the Move: A Life* (New York: Alfred A. Knopf, 2015).

"He's not thought of as a dramatic actor": Gail Buchalter, "You Just Have to Get Out There," *Parade,* December 16, 1990.

"I won't let that happen": Tad Friend, "The Old Gang," *New Yorker,* August 24, 2014.

"It's depressing. Everything is caged": Lou Cedrone, "Comic Tames Humor for Serious Movie Role," *Baltimore Evening Sun,* January 11, 1991.

"There's a lot of doors and only five keys": *The Tonight Show Starring Johnny Carson,* NBC, January 10, 1991.

"Arnold Schwarzenegger and Albert Schweitzer": Ibid.

"something that seems apparently dead": *Robin Williams Talking with David Frost,* PBS, May 29, 1991.

"He had absorbed all the different voices": Sacks, *On the Move,* p. 306.

"He was not imitating me": Ibid., p. 307.

"an almost instant access to parts of the mind": Kornbluth, "Robin Williams's Change of Life."

"My elbow went *BAM!*": *Robin Williams Un-*

plugged, Nine (Australia), April 10, 1996. Archived at https://www.youtube.com/watch?v=qppqhzjWkn8.

"my nose was broken once before": James Cockington, Today's People (column), *Sydney Morning Herald,* December 18, 1990.

"Robin could make Bob laugh so hard": Friend, "The Old Gang."

"I think you made a perfect twosome with Bob": RWC, box 13, folder 5.

"you — as actors, as dramatists — are also making worlds": RWC, box 13, folder 13.

When he learned of the honor: *The Oprah Winfrey Show,* September 26, 1991.

Silver Foxes II, an exercise video for people over sixty: Beth Ashley, "The Active Life of Robin Williams' Mom," Gannett News Service, August 24, 1989.

"She wore hats, she wore turbans": Author interview with Lisa Birnbach.

"the kind of support that I had": 62nd Academy Awards, ABC, March 26, 1990. Archived at https://www.youtube.com/watch?v=kT6QnJLxWxw.

he could be seen to flinch: 62nd Academy Awards. Archived at https://www.youtube.com/watch?v=-Z1E75hTtCA.

"He passionately hated it": Author interview with Lisa Birnbach.

"like church and state": Rosenthal, " 'Cadillac Man' Finds a New Life."

"Robin Williams has a secret dream": Kathy Huffhines, "Robin Williams Is in Low Gear as 'Cadillac Man,' " *Detroit Free Press,* May 18, 1990.

Robin and Marsha had purchased a house: Donna Rosenthal, "Robin's New Life," *Palm Beach Post,* May 28, 1990; and Marilyn Beck, column, *Fort Myers (FL) News-Press,* July 31, 1990.

"It did rescue the film": Author interview with Terry Gilliam.

mythological figures like the Fisher King: Robert A. Johnson, *He: Understanding Masculine Psychology* (New York: Harper & Row, 1974), pp. 1, 11.

"Men in our society do that": Author interview with Richard LaGravenese.

"He was, in fact, a total, psychotic": Author interview with Terry Gilliam.

"It is about damaged people": *The Oprah Winfrey Show,* September 26, 1991.

Bulfinch's and Malory's retellings of the King Arthur legends: RWC, box 10, folder 12.

"the thing that pulled Robin back": Author interview with Terry Gilliam.

"He had maybe a touch of a dire, dour quality": Author interview with Jeff Bridges.

which began in May 1990 and ran through early August: RWC, box 10, folder 12.

"this would happen once a week, probably": Author interview with Terry Gilliam.

"Before I knew him better": Author interview with Jeff Bridges.

Sheep Meadow in Central Park: RWC, box 10, folder 12.

"his back's to the camera": Author interview with Terry Gilliam.

Chapter 13. Father Man

another *Rolling Stone* cover shoot: Jeff Giles, "Fears of a Clown," *Rolling Stone,* February 21, 1991.

"a series of insistent emotional climaxes": Dave Kehr, " 'Awakenings' Mugs at Our Hearts," *Chicago Tribune,* December 20, 1990.

"pure and uncluttered, without the ebullient distractions": Roger Ebert, "Awakenings," December 20, 1990. Archived at http://www.rogerebert.com/reviews/awakenings-1990.

earned about $52 million: Box Office Mojo, http://www.boxofficemojo.com/movies/?id=awakenings.htm.

the award went to Jeremy Irons: David J. Fox, "A Golden Evening for 'Dances with Wolves,' " *Los Angeles Times,* January 21, 1991.

Robin was overlooked: John Horn, " 'Wolves' Leads Oscar Pack," Associated Press, February 13, 1991.

"He was so proud of his performance in

that": Author interview with Terry Gilliam.

"I wanted to be home as a dad": Joseph McBride, *Steven Spielberg: A Biography* (Jackson: University Press of Mississippi, 2010), p. 409.

"He's very representative of a lot of people today": Ibid.

"play with your child": Judy Gerstel, "Williams Swoops Through 'Hook' Interviews," *Detroit Free Press,* December 6, 1991.

some reports put it at $60 million or more: Jeannie Park, "Ahoy! Neverland!" *People,* December 23, 1991.

share 40 percent of the film's gross ticket sales: Nina J. Easton and Alan Citron, "So Happy Together . . . Then Sony Made Three," *Los Angeles Times,* March 10, 1991.

"We will need to measure you for your flying rig": RWC, box 12, folder 7.

twenty pounds lighter than he had been during the making of *The Fisher King:* Park, "Ahoy! Neverland!"

a month between mid-February and mid-March 1991: RWC, box 12, folder 7.

"there's something scary there": Sean Mitchell, "No-Holds Hoffman," *USA Weekend,* December 6–8, 1991.

the film's production spilled into late July: Marilyn Beck, Vanilla Nice, Says Rapper's Film Producer (column), *White Plains (NY) Journal News,* July 8, 1991.

a feisty working relationship full of one-upmanship: Park, "Ahoy! Neverland!"

"when you get to fly — whew!": *The Oprah Winfrey Show,* September 26, 1991.

a cartoon musical set within the Arabic folklore: Author interviews with Alan Menken, Ron Clements, and John Musker.

"There was a policy that you really had to audition": Ibid.

a positive experience on *FernGully: The Last Rainforest:* Tom Green, "Wild Child: Playful Role Fits the Boyish Soul," *USA Today,* December 18, 1992.

"Tonight, let's talk about the serious subject of schizophrenia": Jeff Labrecque, "The Animator and the Animated," *Time: Robin Williams 1951–2014,* 2014.

a file full of Goldberg's character designs: RWC, box 13, folder 5.

Howard Ashman . . . died from complications of AIDS: Eleanor Blau, "Howard Ashman Is Dead at 40; Writer of 'Little Shop of Horrors,' " *New York Times,* March 15, 1991.

Katzenberg rejected a storyboarded version of the film: Author interviews with Ron Clements and John Musker.

the character's dialogue was written to sound like Robin: Ibid.

A production script dated September 18: RWC, box 1, folder 1.

sung by the Broadway actor Bruce Adler: "Arabian Nights" also contained the controversial lyric, "Where they cut off your ear if they don't like your face," which in home-video releases was changed to "Where it's flat and immense and the heat is intense."

he would spend the evening seated at a piano: Author interviews with Ron Clements and John Musker.

"the Genie didn't believe that Aladdin was going to use his third wish": Labrecque, *Time: Robin Williams 1951–2014.*

Katzenberg himself devised a strategy for recording the film's prologue: Author interviews with Ron Clements and John Musker.

"Look at this, it's a double slingshot": Labrecque, *Time: Robin Williams 1951–2014.*

"Your work in HOOK is flogging brilliant!": RWC, box 13, folder 5.

in limited release on September 20: Bob Thomas, "Summer Sizzle," Associated Press, April 20, 1991.

"a wild, vital stew of a movie": David Ansen, "The Holy Grail in the Unholy City," *Newsweek,* September 22, 1991.

"whenever its taste for chaos is kept in check": Janet Maslin, "Film: A Cynic's Quest for Forgiveness," *New York Times,* September 20, 1991.

"You held my heart in the palm of your

hand": RWC, box 13, folder 13.

the first three weekends of its wider release: Box Office Mojo, http://www.boxofficemojo .com/movies/?id=fisherking.htm.

Marsha gave birth to their second child: Morning Report (column), *Los Angeles Times,* November 28, 1991.

who had committed suicide the previous spring: John Taylor, "The Haunted Bird: The Life and Death of Jerzy Kosinski," *New York,* July 15, 1991.

"he just didn't want to become a vegetable": Grobel, "Robin Williams: The Playboy Interview."

the long-festering lawsuit brought against him by Michelle Tish Carter: Associated Press, "Robin Williams Loses Bid to Dismiss Herpes Lawsuit," *San Bernardino County (CA) Sun,* November 9, 1991; and Lisa Russell, Passages (column), *People,* November 25, 1991.

"Chaotic, leaden, and only sporadically appealing": Judy Gerstel, "Spielberg's 'Hook' May Not Be the Hit Hollywood Wants," *Detroit Free Press,* December 6, 1991.

"arrogant spectacle smothers gentle magic": Kenneth Turan, " 'Hook': In Search of Enchantment," *Los Angeles Times,* December 11, 1991.

Hook opened in first place at the box office: Box Office Mojo, http://www.boxoffice

mojo.com/movies/?page=weekend&id=
hook.htm.

"My faithful, compassionate friend and the true Prince of Pans": RWC, box 13, folder 5.

when he won a Golden Globe Award: 49th Golden Globe Awards, January 18, 1992. Archived at https://www.youtube.com/watch?v=MzTbloaIZQI.

The film was up for five Academy Awards in all: Associated Press, " 'Bugsy' Leads List of Oscar Nominees," *Stevens Point (WI) Journal,* February 19, 1992.

" 'You've got a good chance this time, Rob' ": Author interview with Terry Gilliam.

a solemnity and seriousness he did not often exhibit: *The Tonight Show Starring Johnny Carson,* NBC, May 21, 1992.

"he at first is jumping in a bit, here and there": Author interview with Marc Shaiman.

finally settled their long-standing lawsuits: Associated Press, "Williams' Herpes Lawsuit Settled," *Carbondale (IL) Southern Illinoisan,* August 5, 1992.

Robin, Marsha, and the children went to Rabat: See, e.g., Sam Dreiman, "Robin Williams in Rabat," http://roadsandkingdoms.com/2014/robin-williams-in-rabat/.

"a visual correlative to the rapid-fire Williams wit": Janet Maslin, "Film: Disney Puts Its

Magic Touch on 'Aladdin,' " *New York Times,* November 11, 1992.

The film was an instant smash at the box office: Box Office Mojo, http://www.boxoffice mojo.com/movies/?page=main&id=aladdin .htm.

a brilliant teaser trailer Levinson shot: Archived at https://www.youtube.com/watch? v=OejF72Rp1r4.

"He loved video games": Author interview with Barry Levinson.

"a gimmicky, obvious and pious bore": Peter Travers, "Toys," *Rolling Stone,* December 18, 1992.

he had largely sat out of the promotional rounds for *Aladdin:* Green, "Wild Child: Playful Role Fits the Boyish Soul."

"All of a sudden, they release an advertisement": Robert W. Welkos, "The Genie Has a Gripe with Disney," *Los Angeles Times,* November 25, 1993.

"I don't want to sell stuff. It's the one thing I don't do": Kornbluth, "Robin Williams's Change of Life."

Chapter 14. Hot Flashes

"A man is losing contact with his kids": Author interview with Randi Mayem Singer. She shared screenplay credit on *Mrs. Doubtfire* with Leslie Dixon.

sold his stake to its junior associates: McFadden, "Jack Rollins Dies at 100; Managed Comedy Greats Like Woody Allen."

a first-look deal with 20th Century Fox: Claudia Eller, "Fox Extends Brezner Deal," *Variety,* February 10, 1993.

"remember Robin's sense of humor, which was rather dirty": Author interview with Cyndi McHale.

"It's him, because he's the blue wolf": Simpson, "The Insiders Are Out-Of-Towners."

"to pursue things that were of interest to them": Author interview with Cyndi Mc-Hale.

"She has the patience to discuss a problem for hours and hours": Ross, *Reporting Always,* p. 32.

"Oh, it's about a puppy": Simpson, "The Insiders Are Out-Of-Towners."

"You're not just *her* children, you know": Anne Fine, *Alias Madame Doubtfire* (Boston: Jay Street Books, 1988), p. 39.

It was at Fox that Marsha first learned about the project: Ross, *Reporting Always,* p. 25.

"a man would have to play a woman": *Mrs. Doubtfire: Behind-the-Seams Edition,* "From Man to Mrs.," 20th Century Fox, 2008.

"someone totally unlike myself": Ibid.

"we'd love to be Robin's character in the movie": Kornbluth, "Robin Williams's Change of Life."

"Daniel Hillard and Miranda got back together": *Mrs. Doubtfire: Behind-the-Seams Edition,* "From Man to Mrs."

"a Cinderella kind of story": Ibid.

"the audience would want Daniel and Miranda to get back together": Ross, *Reporting Always,* p. 27.

"That's the one fantasy most psychiatrists will tell you is perpetuated": Kornbluth, "Robin Williams's Change of Life."

forty-one shooting days in the camouflage of Euphegenia Doubtfire: Ibid.

Robin got two entries on the call sheets: RWC, box 11, folder 11.

a body suit made of "spandex and beans": *Mrs. Doubtfire: Behind-the-Seams Edition,* "From Man to Mrs."

The earliest on-camera makeup test of the character, on March 8: Ibid.

short scenes with the actors playing his children and with Sally Field: Ibid.

a test drive in a San Francisco sex shop: SiriusXM Town Hall, September 27, 2013. Archived at https://www.youtube.com/watch?v=ApH30VKTj5U.

"a voice that sounded like Margaret Thatcher": SiriusXM Town Hall, September 27, 2013.

"He's instilled with the spirit of a sixty-five-year-old woman": Ross, *Reporting Always,* p. 28.

He tried more than a dozen different takes:

Mrs. Doubtfire: Behind-the-Seams Edition, "The Improvisation of Mrs. Doubtfire."

Robin reworked the script in places: Randi Mayem Singer and Leslie Dixon, *Mrs. Doubtfire,* screenplay draft dated March 16, 1993. RWC, box 11, folder 11.

Mara Wilson, the precocious five-year-old: Mara Wilson, *Where Am I Now: True Stories of Girlhood and Accidental Fame* (New York: Penguin Books, 2016), p. 11.

a passionate letter on behalf of Lisa Jakub: Lisa Jakub, "Farewell to Robin Williams: A Thank You Note," lisajakub.net, August 11, 2014.

The living room of their rental house: Kornbluth, "Robin Williams's Change of Life."

a shrine for the collection of toy soldiers and action figures: Ross, *Reporting Always,* p. 39.

the home that Robin and Marsha had purchased: Kornbluth, "Robin Williams's Change of Life"; and Ross, *Reporting Always,* p. 37.

" 'all of your stuff and all of my stuff' ": Kornbluth, "Robin Williams's Change of Life."

"Thank you for not 'whacking' me": RWC, box 13, folder 5.

"Having grown up here, in San Francisco": Author interview with Zak Williams.

"Marsha just did not want me around, period": Author interview with Valerie Velardi.

"too free a rein with his improvisations": Frank Bruni, "Robin Williams Makes 'Mrs. Doubtfire' Shine," *Detroit Free Press*, November 24, 1993.

"it also spends too much time making nice": Janet Maslin, "Film: Mrs. Doubtfire; A Wig, a Dress and Voila! Dad Becomes the Nanny," *New York Times*, November 24, 1993.

"*Tootsie* grew out of real wit and insight": Roger Ebert, "Mrs. Doubtfire," November 24, 1993. Archived at http://www.rogerebert .com/reviews/mrs-doubtfire-1993.

taking in $100 million even before the year was over: Box Office Mojo, http://www.box officemojo.com/movies/?id=mrsdoubtfire .htm.

Peter Chernin, the chairman of 20th Century Fox, wrote to thank them: RWC, box 13, folder 6.

Roth apologized to Robin, publicly and unequivocally: Robert W. Welkos, "Abracadabra: Disney, Robin Williams Quit Feud," *Los Angeles Times*, October 24, 1994.

"his little downturned mouth": Owen Gleiberman, "Being Human," *Entertainment Weekly*, May 20, 1994.

the film grossed only $764,000: Box Office Mojo, http://www.boxofficemojo.com/ movies/?id=beinghuman.htm.

"the machine-gun witticisms and impersonations": David Simon, "Robin Williams: A Brief Encounter," *The Audacity of Despair,* August 12, 2014. Archived at http://davidsimon.com/robin-williams-a-brief-encounter/.

Reeve was riding Eastern Express during a warm-up: Reeve, *Still Me,* pp. 4–15; and Lois Romano, "Riding Accident Paralyzes Actor Christopher Reeve," *Washington Post,* June 1, 1995.

"At an especially bleak moment, the door flew open": Reeve, *Still Me,* pp. 27 and 33.

"I'm going to have to put on a rubber glove": *The Oprah Winfrey Show,* March 15, 1996.

who in return called him Brother Rabinowitz: E.g., Christopher Reeve, letter to Robin Williams, June 14, 1996; RWC, box 13, folder 13.

"right away, he and Marsha were on the plane": Author interview with Cyndi McHale.

a fund-raising event for the Creative Coalition: Reeve, *Still Me,* pp. 113–18.

"Everybody got a great tan from your sunshine": RWC, box 13, folder 13.

"where shall we write it in blood?' ": Jonathan Alter, "Robin Williams Uncaged," *USA Weekend,* March 1–3, 1996.

the film's $65 million budget: Richard Natale, "Who Is Box-Office Gold," *Los Angeles Times,* August 7, 1995; and Newsmakers (column), *Palm Beach Post,* June 26, 1995.

"The world frightens me a lot": Karen Hershenson, " 'Jumanji' Role Stretches Robin Williams in New Directions," Knight-Ridder, December 16, 1995.

Jumanji proved to be too scary for Cody: Names & Faces (column), *Orlando Sentinel,* December 17, 1995.

"the triumph of literalism over interference": Stephen Hunter, "Flat Film Takes All the Fun Out of 'Jumanji,' " *Baltimore Sun,* December 15, 1995.

Jumanji opened at number one: Box Office Mojo, http://www.boxofficemojo.com/movies/?id=jumanji.htm.

Chapter 15. The Golden Dude

an actor whose name is given only as Mel: *Deconstructing Harry,* directed by Woody Allen, 1997.

Allen wrote to Robin several months earlier: RWC, box 2, folder 6.

"Reconciling a family, a country, right and left": Alter, "Robin Williams Uncaged."

President Bill Clinton's first inauguration: RWC, box 12, folder 25; and Bernard Weinraub, "This Inaugural Thing Just Irks Hollywood," *New York Times,* January 10, 1993.

"You were in the tippiest top form": RWC, box 12, folder 26.

a dutiful congratulatory letter from the White House: RWC, box 13, folder 13.

heavy hitters like Al Gore or John Kerry: RWC, box 13, folder 6.

"I am working like a field hand": Ibid.

the Sisters of Perpetual Indulgence: Ryan Murphy, "Robin Williams Reassures 'Castro' Filmmakers," *Los Angeles Times,* December 21, 1992.

"it has the same values as your neighborhood": Alter, "Robin Williams Uncaged."

"It was hard for me to watch him go off": Bruce Bibby, "Birds of a Feather," *Premiere,* April 1996.

"the relatively still center": Alter, "Robin Williams Uncaged."

"When people see me that way, they think something's wrong": Ibid.

"You'd just be talking to him over the breakfast table": Author interview with Cyndi McHale.

"multiple Robins": Author interview with Peter Asher.

"When he'd make fun of you, it was always really nice": Author interview with Wendy Asher.

He continued to see a therapist: Alter, "Robin Williams Uncaged."

"He was a great appreciator of people's work": Author interview with Billy Crystal.

he expected to play the villainous Riddler: "Williams Probable Riddler for Long-

Awaited 'Batman III,' " *Orlando Sentinel,* November 19, 1993.

and then passing on the role: Judy Brennan, "Cast Announcement for 'Batman Forever,' " *Entertainment Weekly,* June 3, 1994.

a massive hit for Carrey: Box Office Mojo, http://www.boxofficemojo.com/movies/?id=dumbanddumber.htm.

"He chose the thing to do and he's the master of it": Bibby, "Birds of a Feather."

he "got completely freaked out about Jim Carrey": Author interview with Cheri Minns.

"the white-hot center of a picture": Hal Hinson, " 'The Birdcage': A Wingding of a Show," *Washington Post,* March 8, 1996.

it went "beyond the stereotypes to see the characters' depth and humanity": GLAAD, "GLAAD Applauds 'The Birdcage,' " press release, March 5, 1996. Archived at http://www.qrd.org/qrd/orgs/GLAAD/general.information/1996/applauds.birdcage-03.05.96.

"homosexuality continues to bring out the worst": Bruce Bawer, "Film View: Why Can't Hollywood Get Gay Life Right?" *New York Times,* March 10, 1996.

"I used to do a choreographer character on Comic Relief": Marilyn Beck and Stacy Jenel Smith, Robin Responds to Gay Criticism (column), *Detroit Free Press,* February 13, 1996.

grossing nearly $125 million: Box Office Mojo, http://www.boxofficemojo.com/movies/?id=birdcage.htm.

"Someone deserves a timeout": Susan Wloszczyna, "Sappy 'Jack' Goes Splat!" *USA Today,* August 9, 1996.

a lavish, four-hour film adaptation: *Hamlet,* directed by Kenneth Branagh, 1996.

" 'Dad, have I been bad?' ": John Clark, "Can One Movie Contain These Two?" *Los Angeles Times,* May 8, 1997.

" 'one for them, one for me' ": Author interview with Steven Haft.

Father Damien, the Catholic priest: Wayne Harada, "Robin Williams to Star in Film on Father Damien," *Honolulu Advertiser,* July 28, 1996.

"Anything indie, basically, was something that she recommended he do": Author interview with Lisa Birnbach.

"Every bad film he did, she told him not to do": Author interview with Wendy Asher.

"Billy would bring in some food": Author interview with Cheri Minns.

"It was not a great experience, because the script was never really ready": Author interview with Billy Crystal.

awkwardly shoehorned into an episode of *Friends: Friends,* "The One with the Ultimate Fighting Championship," May 8, 1997.

"It's so stupid. . . . But it really works": *The Tonight Show with Jay Leno,* May 6, 1997.

"a movie of implacable unfunniness": Joe Morgenstern, "Sci-Fi Stunts; Dueling Dads," *Wall Street Journal,* May 9, 1997.

grossing only about $29 million: Box Office Mojo, http://www.boxofficemojo.com/search/?q=fathers%27%20day.

their upbringings in Cambridge, Massachusetts: *Good Will Hunting: 15th Anniversary Edition,* "Reflecting on a Journey," Lionsgate, 2012; *Good Will Hunting: 15th Anniversary Edition,* audio commentary; and Jamie Diamond, "When Visiting the Mainstream Is an Experiment," *New York Times,* November 9, 1997.

Robin signed on to *Good Will Hunting* that March: Movie Buzz (column), *Sioux Falls (SD) Argus-Leader,* March 12, 1997.

"layered and very moving, but in a very simple way": *Good Will Hunting: 15th Anniversary Edition,* "Reflecting on a Journey."

a few weeks of filming in Boston and Toronto: RWC, box 11, folder 1; and Marilyn Beck, Midler Launches Weekly TV Sitcom (column), *Saint Cloud (MN) Times,* June 15, 1997.

about $3 million in salary: James Bates, "Big Profits Raise Profile of the 'Small Movie,' "

Los Angeles Times, March 23, 1998; and "Cashing In on Oscar," *Palm Beach Post,* March 25, 1998.

"half-way between the *a* of 'FAT' and the *ah* of 'FATHER' ": RWC, box 11, folder 1.

"He would go, 'Yeah, yeah, boss. Was that not good?' ": *Good Will Hunting: 15th Anniversary Edition,* audio commentary.

his book learning is no substitute for Maguire's life experience: *Good Will Hunting,* directed by Gus Van Sant, 1997.

"I used to have to wake up and light a match": *Good Will Hunting: 15th Anniversary Edition,* audio commentary.

"Robin got really upset for this moment": Ibid.

"We must have done twenty takes": *Good Will Hunting: 15th Anniversary Edition,* "Reflecting on a Journey."

"overproduced, mechanical and resoundingly unfunny": Edward Guthmann, "The Goo, the Bad and the Ugly," *San Francisco Chronicle,* November 26, 1997.

Robin "isn't at his best when he tries to be sincere": Hillel Italie, " 'Good Will Hunting' Aims for Hipness, Settles for Convention," Associated Press, December 5, 1997.

Affleck and Damon "lack the craft" to give Maguire "speeches that aren't so fake-sensitive": Kenneth Turan, "An Uncertain Match Made in Hollywood," *Los Angeles*

Times, December 5, 1997.

"a smart and touching screenplay": Janet Maslin, "Logarithms and Biorhythms Test a Young Janitor," *New York Times,* December 5, 1997.

"the finest performance" of Robin's career: Joe Morgenstern, "Hunting (and Finding) Goodwill," *Wall Street Journal,* December 5, 1997.

"I don't see him in that part — I just see that guy, Maguire": Author interview with Billy Crystal.

more than $50 million by the end of January: Box Office Mojo, http://www.boxofficemojo.com/movies/?id=goodwillhunting.htm.

likely to earn as much as $15 million to $20 million: Bates, "Big Profits Raise Profile of the 'Small Movie' "; and "Cashing In on Oscar."

nominated for a Golden Globe: Associated Press, " 'Titanic' Sails Away with 8 Golden Globe Nominations," *Bloomington (IL) Pantagraph,* December 19, 1997.

Christine Lahti, a winner for the TV series *Chicago Hope:* Patricia Lowry, "Gushing at the Globes," *Pittsburgh Post-Gazette,* January 20, 1998.

nominated for nine Academy Awards: John Horn, " 'Titanic' Gets 14 Oscar Nominations, Tying Record," Associated Press, February 10, 1998.

Robin won the Screen Actors Guild Award:

Francesca Chapman, Chastity Bono: Ellen's on Gay Overload (column), *Philadelphia Daily News,* March 10, 1998.

a neck-and-neck competition between Reynolds and him: Hap Erstein, "Are the Odds on Burt?" *Palm Beach Post,* March 19, 1998.

Crystal . . . gave Robin a musical shout-out: 70th Academy Awards, March 23, 1998. Archived at https://www.youtube.com/watch?v=xYR2YJhRwTU.

"This might be the one time I'm speechless": 70th Academy Awards, March 23, 1998. Archived at https://www.youtube.com/watch?v=q6Egi5V_jNU.

"He saw me and he made this sound, like, 'Oooooohhhh,' ": Author interview with Billy Crystal.

"you look around you and you see people you know": *Good Will Hunting: 15th Anniversary Edition,* "Reflecting on a Journey."

"It's like, the golden dude": Lynn Elber, "Williams Finally Gets His 'Dude,' " Associated Press, March 26, 1998.

one tier in front of Shirley Temple Black: *Good Will Hunting: 15th Anniversary Edition,* "Reflecting on a Journey."

"as well-liked a figure as today's Hollywood has": Kenneth Turan, "Surprise! Cameron Subdued," *Los Angeles Times,* March 24, 1998.

Robin "never let his Oscar out of his right hand": Arthur Grace, *Robin Williams: A Singular Portrait* (Berkeley, CA: Counterpoint, 2016), pp. 160–61.

A nine-page log of congratulatory phone calls: RWC, box 13, folder 8.

"Every now and again the Oscar goes to the right person": Ibid.

"Dear Rob, Man!!! You won!! How fuckin' great": RWC, box 13, folder 9.

"Alan, I want you to meet a new little friend of mine": Author interview with Alan Curtiss.

"I hate that movie": Roger Ebert, Twitter post, May 28, 2011. Archived at https://twitter.com/ebertchicago/status/74603410325909504.

Chapter 16. Fade to White

It was hardly what you'd call a synagogue: Author interview with Steven Haft.

"People expected too much of him": Author interview with Billy Crystal.

"people tend to think I'm Jewish": Naomi Pfefferman, "So, Nu?" *Jewish Journal,* September 16, 1999.

"It's the way the world looks to me": *The Final Cut,* directed by Omar Naim, 2004.

"Was it following him down a wormhole of personal angst?": Author interview with Steven Haft.

"It's not black and white": *Insomnia,* "Day for Night," Warner Home Video, 2010.

budgeted at $70 million: Jenny Peters, "Death Is but a 'Dream,' " *Stevens Point (WI) Journal,* June 27, 1998.

the production traveled up and down California: "Movie Crews Under Close Scrutiny in Glacier," *Great Falls (MT) Tribune,* July 3, 1997.

"People are really looking for some hope": Amy Wallace, "Movies for the Millennium," *Los Angeles Times,* September 4, 1998.

"Do I attend church every Sunday? No": Chuck Arnold, Chatter (column), *People,* September 21, 1998.

"he had to reach some places that were difficult for him": Author interview with Cheri Minns.

"If it doesn't choke you with emotion": Carrie Rickey, "From Heaven to Hell in Allegory of Marriage," *Philadelphia Inquirer,* October 2, 1998.

"he is a brilliant comedian who is no more than a passable actor": Kenneth Turan, " 'Dream's' Team Falters," *Los Angeles Times,* October 2, 1998.

"I don't need the coin": "Robin Williams Can't Resist Movie Roles," *Bloomington (IL) Pantagraph,* November 10, 1998.

"trots out every hoary plot device": Matt Brunson, "*Batman v Superman, Doctor*

Butcher, M.D., Patch Adams Among New Home Entertainment Titles," *Creative Loafing,* August 10, 2016.

"shamelessly sappy and emotionally manipulative": Joe Leydon, "Review: 'Patch Adams,' " *Variety,* December 13, 1998.

Robin discharged CAA: Claudia Eller, "CAA Loses Agent — and Top Star — to Ovitz," *Los Angeles Times,* January 21, 1999.

Peter Kassovitz . . . had survived World War II: Ginette Vincendeau, *La Haine* (New York: I. B. Tauris, 2005).

Spielberg, who had often phoned Robin: Anthony Breznican, "Laughter 'Sus-tained Him': Directors on the Genius of Robin Williams," *Entertainment Weekly,* August 11, 2014.

"He and Marsha were looking for things that tamed the beast": Author interview with Steven Haft.

climbing atop the seats of the Dorothy Chandler Pavilion: 71st Academy Awards, March 21, 1999. Archived at https://www.youtube.com/watch?v=8cTR6fk8frs.

"the Italian Robin Williams": Pfefferman, "So, Nu?"

they had no idea about *Life Is Beautiful* at the time: Jay Boyar, "Robin Williams Will Head Back to Standup," *Orlando Sentinel,* September 22, 1999.

one of the well-wishers who shook Benigni's hand: 71st Academy Awards, March 21,

1999. Archived at https://www.youtube
.com/watch?v=Ybgg4H4zTHo.

"People say they've seen this before": Pfefferman, "So, Nu?"

"the American Roberto Benigni": Jack Gar-
ner, "Williams' Restrained Performance
Boosts 'Jakob' into 'Must-See' Film," Gannett News Service, September 23, 1999.

"Robin Williams, enough already": Kenneth
Turan, "News Isn't Good as Williams Allies
with Sentimentality Again," *Los Angeles
Times,* September 24, 1999.

taking in less than $5 million: Box Office
Mojo, http://www.boxofficemojo.com/mov
ies/?page =weekend&id=jakobtheliar.htm.

adapted from two novels: Israeli Wins European Contest but Not All Approve (column), *Philadelphia Inquirer,* May 11, 1998.

Disney had to put the project on a months-
long pause: "Williams Film Getting Too
Costly for Disney," *Chicago Tribune,* November 19, 1998.

It was resuscitated when Columbia Pictures
struck a deal with Disney: Amy Wallace,
"Disney, Columbia to Team on 'Bicentennial Man,' " *Los Angeles Times,* March 19,
1999.

"high-minded pathos never compensates for
submerging Williams' comic talents": Bruce
Westbrook, Videoviews (column), *Indiana
(PA) Gazette,* June 25, 2000.

bringing in just $58 million: Box Office Mojo, http://www.boxofficemojo.com/movies/?id=bicentennialman.htm.

" 'Why don't you do another *Fisher King* or *Mrs. Doubtfire*?' ": Phillip McCarthy, "What Nightmares May Come," *Melbourne (AU) Sunday Age,* March 21, 1999.

" 'If you ever make another movie like that, I'll hurt you' ": Kenneth Turan, "It's Thrilling to Be Here, Really," *Los Angeles Times,* January 16, 2002.

"I have been working straight for five years": McCarthy, "What Nightmares May Come."

he had a severely blocked coronary artery: Tina Kelley, "Artery Blocked, Letterman Has Heart Bypass Surgery," *New York Times,* January 15, 2000.

he brought out the team of surgeons and nurses: David Hinckley, "Letterman's Return Is All Heart," *New York Daily News,* February 22, 2000.

dressed in surgical scrubs and rubber gloves: *Late Show with David Letterman,* February 21, 2000. Archived at https://www.youtube.com/watch?v=W2igGFIqpJw.

"It was stressful and I was tired. I think people were worried": Author interview with David Letterman.

filmed in the fall of 2000: RWC, box 11, folder 16.

"They're no longer bound by the laws of likability": *The Charlie Rose Show,* August 21, 2002.

he trained one-on-one with a photo technician: Ibid.

taped interviews of convicted serial killers: Duane Dudek, "Williams Enjoying Stand-Up, Darker Roles," *Milwaukee Journal Sentinel,* March 9, 2002.

"a lack of spontaneous seeking to share enjoyment": RWC, box 11, folder 16.

flattered by moviegoers who said that they didn't recognize him: David Germain, "Robin Williams Turns Menacing in Sundance Thriller," Associated Press, January 17, 2002.

"We're walking to the set, in public": Author interview with Cheri Minns.

"a wonderful, nasty movie": *Late Show with David Letterman,* March 28, 2002.

"He presents the logic and rationalization of the character": *Insomnia,* "180°."

" 'When you started cutting up the bodies, what did you do?' ": *Insomnia,* "Day for Night."

"There's a lot of log rolling" and "a couple of bars": Jim Ferguson, "Insomnia," *Asian Connections,* May 2002.

"We had these wild parties in Alaska": *Insomnia* premiere, May 23, 2002. Archived at http://idpr.tumblr.com/post/118299050

461/an-interview-with-robin-williams-at-the-la.

a milestone he celebrated with his family and friends: John Leland, "On and Off Stage with Robin Williams," *New York Times,* August 1, 2016.

"Once I hit fifty, I'm looking for characters": Turan, "It's Thrilling to Be Here, Really."

she died in her Tiburon home on September 4, 2001: Steve Rubenstein, "Laurie Williams — Comedian's Mother," *San Francisco Chronicle,* September 8, 2001.

"she wore mini-skirts till the day she died": Author interview with Zak Williams.

"I enjoy my own company. I get along very well with me": Conti, *McLaurin & Williams Family Histories,* p. 53.

"all in all, it's been a kick in the shorts": Ibid., p. 55.

"I really think we were put on earth to know great joy": Ibid., p. 56.

"Think young and you'll never grow old": Rubenstein, "Laurie Williams — Comedian's Mother."

Laurie's body was cremated: Nancy Dillon, "Robin Williams' Ashes Scattered in Same Place as His Mother's Remains," *New York Daily News,* August 25, 2014.

"People treated it like we had just lifted the siege of Richmond": *The Charlie Rose Show,* August 21, 2002.

a six-month stretch on his calendar: Boyar, "Robin Williams Will Head Back to Standup."

"He got into that place, that multimillion-dollar film place": Author interview with Eddie Izzard.

"He would do ten minutes about wherever he was": Author interview with Peter Asher.

"all over the place would be an understatement": Dan DeLuca, "Wound-Up Williams Does Stand-Up Again," *Philadelphia Inquirer,* March 9, 2002.

"a particularly toxic little bonbon": Ann Hornaday, " 'Smoochy' Hits Smack in the Kisser," *Washington Post,* March 29, 2002.

slightly more than $8 million: Box Office Mojo, http://www.boxofficemojo.com/movies/?id=deathtosmoochy.htm.

rehired CAA to represent him: Claude Brodesser, "Williams Sheds Vet Rep in Return to Fold at CAA," *Variety,* April 10, 2002.

"Robin Williams is a shockingly effective counterweight": David Edelstein, "Hard Day's Night," *Slate,* May 24, 2002.

Robin was in a combative mood: *Robin Williams: Live on Broadway,* HBO, 2002.

"You can actually hear careers ending": Tom Moon, "The Night Belongs to Norah Jones," *Philadelphia Inquirer,* February 24, 2003.

"The Grim Rapper": Robin Williams, *Robin Williams Live 2002*, Sony Legacy, 2002.

"when he's playing serious roles": Elvis Mitchell, "That Orderly World of Appearances He Lives In? It's About to Explode," *New York Times*, August 21, 2002.

"people at home haven't forgotten them": *On Tour with Robin Williams*, American Forces Network Europe, 2002. Archived at https://www.youtube.com/watch?v=DAaz_FT7 USA.

"that's why you think, 'war — how insane' ": *On Tour with Robin Williams:* Phil Bronstein, "Good Morning, Iraq," *San Francisco Chronicle*, February 9, 2005.

"I know that this isn't the end of the world": American Forces Network Europe.

the first of many trips: Mark Thompson, "The Military Absolutely Loved Robin Williams," *Time*, August 12, 2014; and RWC, box 12, folder 7.

"a weird ride except you realize the consequence of the ride": Bronstein, "Good Morning, Iraq."

Robin, who had traveled there only with Spencer . . . and Minns, found the emptiness unsettling: Author interview with Cheri Minns; and Tim Cook, "Robin Williams and His Connection to Winnipeg," Canadian Press, August 13, 2014.

"Winnipeg is one of the most dismal places,

as far as I'm concerned": Author interview with Cheri Minns.

"My film career was not going too well. One day I walked into a store and saw a little bottle of Jack Daniel's": Rader, "Guess Who's Back on TV."

"You feel warm and kind of wonderful": Decca Aitkenhead, "Robin Williams: The G2 Interview," *Guardian,* September 20, 2010.

"I sounded like a wind chime walking down the street": Rader, "Guess Who's Back on TV."

Chapter 17. Weapons of Self Destruction

presented with the Cecil B. DeMille Award: 62nd Golden Globe Awards, January 16, 2005. Archived at https://www.youtube.com/watch?v=j0hYctu65yw.

"You keep thinking, 'I can handle this' ": Author interview with Robin Williams.

"you do stuff that causes disgust": Aitkenhead, "Robin Williams: The G2 Interview."

an early experiment in digital distribution: " 'Final Cut' Goes Out Digitally," *Los Angeles Times,* October 1, 2004.

"another of his almost sickeningly lovable weirdos": "Coming Attractions," *Hartford Courant,* April 24, 2005.

The MBST firm . . . was acquired in July 2005: "Leading Hollywood Management

Firm Joins CKX," press release, July 27, 2005. Archived at http://www.prnewswire.com/news-releases/leading-hollywood-management-firm-joins-ckx-54768512.html.

"We started doing these weird interviews": Author interview with Billy Crystal.

Christopher Reeve died on October 10, 2004: Douglas Martin, "Christopher Reeve, 52, Symbol of Courage, Dies," *New York Times,* October 12, 2004.

Reeve's wife, Dana, was diagnosed with lung cancer: Nadine Brozan, "Dana Reeve, Devoted Caretaker and Advocate, Is Dead at 44," *New York Times,* March 8, 2006.

"I never knew he was on borrowed time": Joanne Nathan, "Christopher Reeve: We Pay Tribute to a Hero," *Hello!,* October 26, 2004.

He died on December 10, 2005: Mel Watkins, "Richard Pryor, Iconoclastic Comedian, Dies at 65," *New York Times,* December 11, 2005.

"It was tough to see him near the end, with MS": Author interview with Robin Williams.

"It's more selfish than that": Aitkenhead, "Robin Williams: The G2 Interview."

a Thanksgiving dinner with his family in 2005: Rader, "Guess Who's Back on TV."

"I just bought a $40,000 coke vial": Courtney Rubin, "Sharon Stone Promotes a

Good Cause at Cannes," *People,* May 26, 2006.

"I realized I was pretty baked": Aitkenhead, "Robin Williams: The G2 Interview."

"When I was drinking, there was only one time": *WTF with Marc Maron,* April 26, 2010.

"It got to a point where he wasn't really functioning anymore": Author interview with Zak Williams.

"It was me, but it was also everyone in the family": Author interview with Robin Williams.

"He kept things from me": Author interview with Billy Crystal.

a Hazelden Foundation center in Newberg, Oregon: The Hazelden Foundation has since merged with the Betty Ford Center.

"You've got to sit back and go, okay": Author interview with Robin Williams.

"he put a little tube in his car to pump the fumes in": *Larry King Live,* July 3, 2007.

details of Robin's rehab stay were published in the *National Enquirer:* "Enquirer Exclusive: Robin Williams in Alcohol Rehab," *National Enquirer,* August 9, 2006.

he was undergoing treatment: "Robin Williams Enters Rehab for Alcohol," *People,* August 9, 2006.

"somebody got out of rehab, and shared what I had told": Author interview with Robin Williams.

"community is really important in the recovery process": Author interview with Zak Williams.

"I've had various friends who have fallen off the wagon in dramatic ways, and he was one of them": Author interview with Peter Asher.

They separated at the end of 2007: Diane Clehane, Mark Dagostino, Peter Mikelbank, and Andrea Orr, "Robin Williams Surprise Split," *People,* April 14, 2008.

"Robin was a genius": Author interview with Lillian Ross.

"We were all in this warm glow of Marsha": Author interview with Alex Mallick-Williams.

took in more than $250 million: Box Office Mojo, http://www.boxofficemojo.com/movies/?id=nightatthemuseum.htm.

Robin might not attend: Marilyn Beck, Organizer Excited About Comic Relief (column), *Poughkeepsie (NY) Journal,* September 28, 2006.

he was there to help kick off the show: Comic Relief 2006, November 18, 2006. Archived at https://www.youtube.com/watch?v=3gCJ2hXP-eo.

"footage of Robin Williams hamming it up": Robert Benziker, Pasa Pics (column), *Santa Fe New Mexican,* June 29–July 5, 2007.

Robin "is at his most annoying here": James Ward, "You'll Want to Revoke Lame 'License to Wed,' " *Nashville Tennessean,* July 3, 2007.

"You get a small chip redeemable for one drink": *Rove Live,* July 15, 2007.

"It's always there": *Larry King Live,* July 3, 2007.

"a wife who's not afraid of me being free range": *Rove Live,* July 15, 2007.

a man who "left a big footprint with a cork": Fagan, "Robert Williams Dies — Winemaker, Bar Owner and Bon Vivant."

someone "who loved sucking the juice out of life": RWC, box 12, folder 24.

Marsha filed for divorce: Clehane, Dagostino, Mikelbank, and Orr, "Robin Williams Surprise Split."

"We had already closed the L.A. office": Author interview with Cyndi McHale.

"He was still wanting to come home": Author interview with Alex Mallick-Williams.

Gerald Margolis, the Williams family's attorney: Valerie J. Nelson, "L.A. Attorney Counseled Rolling Stones, R. Kelly," *Los Angeles Times,* September 25, 2008.

"He was going to mediate because they both trusted him": Author interview with Cyndi McHale.

"He had a huge room that was like a safe room": Author interview with Lisa Birnbach.

"When he dropped by, it's because he felt

like going on": Author interview with Mark Pitta.

"I was going to call the tour *Remember the Alimony*": *WTF with Marc Maron,* April 26, 2010.

"It was a financial thing of going, no movies are on the horizon": Author interview with Robin Williams.

"I kept thinking it was a pulmonary thing": Ibid.

"They said, 'Ho, ho, ho, he's not leaving here' ": Author interview with David Steinberg.

"It wasn't like when Letterman went in with five blocked arteries": Author interview with Robin Williams.

"We went for a short, easy, flat ride": Author interview with Lance Armstrong. Armstrong's Tour de France titles and other victories were later voided when he confessed to some allegations of doping.

Carvey, who had undergone multiple angioplasties: Mike Falcon, "Heart Operation No Laugh for Dana Carvey," *USA Today,* November 5, 2001.

"He was extremely vulnerable that night": Author interview with Dana Carvey.

"They said, 'Okay, here's the drill' ": Author interview with Robin Williams.

"He was really wobbly and getting scared": Author interview with Billy Crystal.

"No, you shouldn't come": Author interview

with Alex Mallick-Williams.

"called every cousin and relative in the city": Author interview with McLaurin Smith-Williams.

a twenty-seven-year-old artist from New York: Jessica Flint, "Charlotte Filbert's Colorful World," *Vanity Fair,* July 2009.

Susan had met Robin in October 2007: Susan Williams, "Remembering Robin Williams," *London Times,* November 28, 2015. Susan Williams did not respond to multiple interview requests for this book.

a lifelong Marin resident: Ryan Parker, Steven Zeitchik, and Lauren Raab, "Robin Williams Dies in Apparent Suicide; Actor, Comic Was 63," *Los Angeles Times,* August 11, 2014.

a previous marriage that had ended in 2001: Marin County Superior Court, Case FL 011397.

a recovering alcoholic with twenty-three years' sobriety: Susan Williams, "Remembering Robin Williams."

"I knew that they had met at AA": Author interview with Zak Williams.

"They do have a cut-off": Author interview with Robin Williams.

"They used to be restricted to late at night, when he knew I was up": Author interview with Billy Crystal.

"That's the weird thing after the heart

surgery": Author interview with Robin Williams.

Chapter 18. The Tiger in Winter

Letterman's time to return the favor: *Late Show with David Letterman,* May 12, 2009.

"shorthand between two survivors": Author interview with Robin Williams.

"Comedy is life-affirming": Author interview with Eric Idle.

"almost dying will give you a sense of gratitude": Author interview with Bobcat Goldthwait.

"you realize you've been given a gift": Author interview with Eric Idle.

"He's always acted like we're peers": Author interview with Bobcat Goldthwait.

"I wanted to play it": Author interview with Robin Williams.

"There's no expectation for you to be a father figure": Author interview with Zak Williams.

revisited all the cities he'd missed: RWC, box 12, folder 10.

"It would be insane *not* to talk about it": Author interview with Robin Williams.

"From our intense conversations and experiences": Author interview with Billy Crystal.

"I lob him softballs and then he makes them Robin": Author interview with David Steinberg.

" 'You're not reaching out to kids, the younger generation' ": Author interview with Cyndi McHale.

"How much more can you give?": Author interview with Robin Williams.

Robin offered the first real window into his life: *Robin Williams: Weapons of Self Destruction,* HBO, 2009.

"It's *like* me . . . but not totally me": Author interview with Robin Williams.

one bit clearly based on personal experience: *Robin Williams: Weapons of Self Destruction,* HBO, 2009.

"Thank you for saving me": RWC, box 13, folder 11.

"What's your credibility?": Author interview with Robin Williams.

"Our relationship started up again": Author interview with Valerie Velardi.

"I'd be onstage and he'd be up in one of the boxes": Author interview with Mark Maron.

"Even if you were trying out new stuff": Author interview with Steven Pearl.

"I met Susan in the green room": Author interview with Mark Pitta.

"She loved taking him to her yoga studio": Author interview with Cyndi McHale.

"Robin wasn't a guy that entertained": Author interview with Billy Crystal.

"Marsha worked for him for a while": Author interview with Wendy Asher.

enough Effexor "to cheer up a whole army of elephants": Susan Williams, "Remembering Robin Williams."

"He was very modest about his career": Author interview with McLaurin Smith-Williams.

"So that's what I look like": Rajiv Joseph, *Bengal Tiger at the Baghdad Zoo* (New York: Dramatists Play Service, 2012).

"It just hit me hard, it was so powerful": Author interview with Robin Williams.

"Before I hung up, he said, 'Okay, boss' ": Author interview with Moisés Kaufman.

"a little bit like the pressures of mortality, or exactly like it": Author interview with Robyn Goodman.

he proposed to her just before he left Tiburon: Susan Williams, "Remembering Robin Williams."

"Robin said to him, 'Okay, thank you, boss' ": Author interview with Moisés Kaufman.

"He was always on top of it": Susan Williams, "Remembering Robin Williams."

" 'How do you think it's going tonight, boss?' ": Author interview with Arian Moayed.

a card saying they had symbolically adopted a tiger: RWC, box 12, folder 20.

"smart, savagely funny and visionary": Charles Isherwood, "Ghostly Beast Burning Bright in Iraq," *New York Times,* March 31, 2011.

"Lenny Bruce meets Friedrich Nietzsche": David Rooney, "Bengal Tiger at the Baghdad Zoo," *Hollywood Reporter,* March 31, 2011.

"The title is so funky": Author interview with Arian Moayed.

"audiences really don't want to see them": Author interview with Robyn Goodman.

"I was very uncomfortable": Author interview with Arian Moayed.

"We wanted him to have an EGOT": Author interview with Rajiv Joseph.

"The only beard here is on my face": 65th Tony Awards, June 12, 2011.

"Please tell Robin not to be angry at Broadway": Author interview with Robyn Goodman.

a slight, intermittent tremor in his left hand: Matthew D. Wood and Eric J. Huang, Surgical Pathology Report, October 20, 2014; and Susan Schneider Williams, "The Terrorist Inside My Husband's Brain," *Neurology,* September 27, 2016.

a continuous video loop of birthday testimonials: Robin Williams sixtieth birthday video.

The outdoor wedding ceremony: Marla Lehner, "All About Robin Williams's Wine Country Wedding," *People,* October 26, 2011.

"Bobcat decided to get a fat stripper": Author interview with Mark Pitta.

"He said he was particularly touched": Ryan Parry and James Robertson, " 'No Glamor, No Glitz, but Great Joy': Minister Who Married Robin Williams and Wife Susan," *Daily Mail,* August 15, 2014.

"This white butterfly appears out of nowhere": Author interview with Rick Overton.

"It was like high school": Author interview with Mark Pitta.

"When people break up and someone has a new girlfriend": Author interview with Peter Asher.

"we had not met too late in life": Susan Williams, "Remembering Robin Williams."

Chapter 19. Gone

"He can retire right now": *Late Show with David Letterman,* April 26, 2012.

both men meeting at the grave: *Louie,* "Barney/Never," season 3, episode 6. August 2, 2012.

"I didn't get a shot": *Late Show with David Letterman,* November 8, 2012.

"There are bills to pay": Rader, "Guess Who's Back on TV."

"like a bake-off for bulimics": *Late Show with David Letterman,* April 26, 2012.

a gala ceremony at the Hammerstein Ballroom: The Comedy Awards, April 28, 2012 (broadcast May 6, 2012).

Winters . . . died of natural causes: William Grimes, "Jonathan Winters, Unpredictable Comic and Master of Improvisation, Dies at 87," *New York Times,* April 12, 2013.

"before I take the 'great escalator north' ": RWC, box 13, folder 6.

"His car had handicap plates": Robin Williams, "A Madman, but Angelic."

"especially egregious": Steven Rea, "Daniels 'Butler" Serves a Big Slice of American History," *Philadelphia Inquirer,* August 16, 2013.

The Crazy Ones, a new CBS comedy: CBS, "CBS Announces 2013–2014 Prime Time Schedule," press release, May 15, 2013.

a steady salary of $165,000 an episode: John Kapetaneas, "The Business of Robin Williams, by the Numbers," ABC News, August 12, 2014.

"It's a regular job. Day to day": *Late Show with David Letterman,* September 25, 2013.

"the kind of improvisation-style routines that made him famous in the 1970s": Alessandra Stanley, "Children Examine Fathers, and They See Trouble," *New York Times,* September 24, 2013.

"Williams seems exhausted. So is this show": Mark A. Perigard, "No Triumphant Return; Fox, Williams Stumble in New Sitcoms," *Boston Herald,* September 26, 2013.

watched by about 15.5 million people: *TV by*

the Numbers, "Thursday Final Ratings," September 27, 2013.

within a month, nearly half that audience had tuned out: *TV by the Numbers,* "Thursday Final Ratings," November 8, 2013.

"We just hung out, watched him film": Author interview with Steven Pearl.

"Marsha was very good at putting him in touch": Author interview with Cyndi Mc-Hale.

"She made him happy": Author interview with Rick Overton.

Zak and Alex would make lunch for Robin: Author interview with Alex Mallick-Williams.

"That's when Robin just really needed him": Ibid.

"They were very open and did love him very much": Author interview with Zak Williams.

a series of physical ailments, varying in their severity: Susan Williams, "Remembering Robin Williams."

his anxiety levels seemed off the chart: Susan Schneider Williams, "The Terrorist Inside My Husband's Brain."

"It was like this endless parade of symptoms": *Good Morning America,* November 3, 2015.

"He wasn't feeling well, but he didn't let on to me all that was going on": Author interview with Billy Crystal.

"The hottest, bragging-rights, *Top Gun,*

black-belt version of stand-up": Author interview with Rick Overton.

a paparazzo photographer with a video camera: Silver Screen PR, "Robin Williams and Rick Overton on Hollywood Blvd Talking About Comedy."

"I saw the eyes dimming": Author interview with Rick Overton.

"I did that show only because I wanted to see Robin": Author interview with Pam Dawber.

Fewer than seven million people watched it: *TV by the Numbers,* "Thursday Final Ratings," April 11, 2014.

its season finale was watched by barely five million people: *TV by the Numbers,* "Thursday Final Ratings," April 18, 2014.

CBS canceled the show: Scott Collins, "CBS Cancels Robin Williams Comedy 'The Crazy Ones,' " *Los Angeles Times,* May 10, 2014.

"I said to him, 'How are you doing?' ": Author interview with Mark Pitta.

"I thought he knew it was bad": Author interview with Cheri Minns.

"But it was like, 'Robin, you're sick! You're sick!' ": Author interview with Pam Dawber.

"Robin, why don't you go and do stand-up?": Author interview with Cheri Minns.

"like a 747 airplane coming in with no landing gear": Susan Schneider Williams, "The

Terrorist Inside My Husband's Brain."

some grave harm was going to befall Mort Sahl: Susan Williams, "Remembering Robin Williams."

He was diagnosed with Parkinson's disease: Susan Schneider Williams, "The Terrorist Inside My Husband's Brain."

" 'We're going to get this Parkinson's managed' ": Susan Williams, "Remembering Robin Williams."

"His number comes up on my phone, and he says, 'Hey, Bill' ": Author interview with Billy Crystal.

"I don't think the people around him knew how to handle it": Author interview with Cyndi McHale.

"Zak would never ask for time — Zak would never push": Author interview with Alex Mallick-Williams.

"It was really difficult to see someone suffering so silently": Author interview with Zak Williams.

Susan saw Robin's condition continue to worsen: Susan Williams, "Remembering Robin Williams."

Robin tried many treatments to regain the upper hand: Susan Schneider Williams, "The Terrorist Inside My Husband's Brain."

Robin started sleeping in a separate bedroom: Darrell Harris, "Coroner Investigative Report in the Matter of the Death of Robin

McLaurin Williams," Coroner Division — Marin County Sheriff's Office, October 29, 2014.

"I don't even know who they are": Author interview with Zak Williams.

"I was out on the sidewalk": Author interview with Dana Carvey.

"I was getting emails from him, and he was going downhill": Clark Collis, "Monty Python Reunion: Eric Idle on His Late Friend Robin Williams," *Entertainment Weekly,* November 11, 2014.

Dan Anderson Renewal Center in Center City: Cavan Sieczkowski, "Robin Williams Checks into Rehab for Continued Sobriety," *Huffington Post,* July 1, 2014.

meditate, do yoga, and focus on further twelve-step work: Susan Schneider Williams, "The Terrorist Inside My Husband's Brain."

"Robin was drinking when he went to rehab, and this wasn't that": Author interview with Wendy Asher.

"Somebody that's that depressed, and on medication": Author interview with Cyndi McHale.

"He always gave her a big hug and a kiss": Author interview with Steven Pearl.

"I was on the phone with his managers' assistant": Author interview with Cyndi McHale.

Susan was taking a shower when she saw

Robin: Kara Warner, "Robin Williams Heartbreaking Final Months," *People,* November 6, 2015.

"I was scared, because it wasn't my friend": Author interview with Mark Pitta.

"I kept saying I'm really worried": Author interview with Wendy Asher.

"To be clear, that was a joke": Author interview with Zak Williams.

Robin and Susan were home together in Tiburon: Harris, "Coroner Investigative Report."

Susan started getting ready for bed: Susan Williams, "Remembering Robin Williams."

Robin went in and out of their bedroom several times: Harris, "Coroner Investigative Report."

"He seemed like he was doing better": Warner, "Robin Williams Heartbreaking Final Months."

She saw him leave the room at around ten thirty p.m.: Harris, "Coroner Investigative Report."

the door to Robin's bedroom was still closed: Ibid.

he was finally getting some needed rest: Susan Williams, "Remembering Robin Williams."

Rebecca and Dan came over to the house: Harris, "Coroner Investigative Report."

Susan optimistically answered, "I think he's getting better": Susan Williams, "Remembering Robin Williams."

she left the house to run some errands: Harris, "Coroner Investigative Report." In other interviews (e.g., Susan Williams, "Remembering Robin Williams"), Susan has said she left to meet with a person she was sponsoring in Alcoholics Anonymous.

Robin still had not come out of his room: Harris, "Coroner Investigative Report."

Chapter 20. Everything Will Be Okay

Susan said good-bye to Robin: Harris, "Coroner Investigative Report."

"I'm not mad at you": Susan Williams, "Remembering Robin Williams."

The 911 call had come in at 11:55 a.m.: Harris, "Coroner Investigative Report."

Mirtazapine, an antidepressant, and Sinemet: Lee M. Blum, "Williams Robin M— Postmortem Toxicology," August 12, 2014.

if Robin had ever discussed suicide with her: Harris, "Coroner Investigative Report."

a news release from the Coroner Division: Keith Boyd, "Investigation into Death of Actor Robin Williams," Marin County Sheriff's Office Coroner Division, August 11, 2014.

"Robin Williams passed away this morning": Mara Buxbaum and Susan Schneider, statements, August 11, 2014.

"Oh, man, did you hear about Robin?":

Author interview with Rick Overton.

Robin had been the victim of an Internet hoax: Peter Gicas, "Robin Williams Is Dead (or Not) — What Does Goldie Hawn Have to Do with It?" *E! News,* May 21, 2012.

"It just didn't make any sense to me": Author interview with David Letterman.

"It was just the most bizarre mixture": Author interview with Jeff Bridges.

the ironic and uncomplimentary conclusion that Robin is not sufficiently appreciated: *Family Guy,* "Family Guy Viewer Mail #2," May 20, 2012.

"I went to bed with that floating around in my head": Author interview with Terry Gilliam.

"This is unusual and upsetting, but we got some news": *Conan,* August 11, 2014.

Jimmy Fallon played footage from Robin's first appearance: *The Tonight Show Starring Jimmy Fallon,* August 12, 2014.

"You start off as a kid seeing Robin Williams": Bilge Ebiri, Twitter post, August 11, 2014.

"No words": Billy Crystal, Twitter post, August 11, 2014.

"For that moment, there was no war in Iraq or Afghanistan": Author interview with Billy Crystal.

seen online an estimated sixty-nine million times: Tim Gray, "Academy's Robin Williams Tweet Criticized by Suicide Prevention Group," *Variety,* August 13, 2014.

"I don't count his death as a suicide": Author interview with Steven Pearl.

"I don't, to this day, believe he never intended to see his children again": Author interview with Steven Haft.

"Seek to bring joy to the world as he sought": Zak Williams, Zelda Williams, Cody Williams, and Marsha Garces Williams, statements, August 12, 2014.

Robin's body had already been cremated: Michael Miller, "Robin Williams Laid to Rest, Ashes Scattered in San Francisco Bay," *People,* August 21, 2014.

"Only a passing of state has occurred": Zak Williams, remarks at Robin Williams memorial service, September 27, 2014.

"Robin spent so much of his life helping others": Susan Schneider, statement, August 14, 2014.

Sara Bareilles sang a somber version of "Smile": 66th Emmy Awards, August 25, 2014.

"It would have been easier if he'd had a heart attack and died": Author interview with Billy Crystal.

an illustration of a hummingbird: Program, *Celebrating Robin Williams,* Curran Theatre, September 27, 2014.

"isn't that really the measure of a friend?" Billy Crystal, remarks at Robin Williams memorial service, September 27, 2014.

"I used to think the worst thing in life is ending up all alone": Bobcat Goldthwait, remarks at Robin Williams memorial service, September 27, 2014.

"Robin was not alone as he waged war": Susan Williams, remarks at Robin Williams memorial service, September 27, 2014.

"Good night, Robin / It's hateful that you've gone": Eric Idle, remarks at Robin Williams memorial service, September 27, 2014.

"Now, Robin would call me out of the blue": Whoopi Goldberg, remarks at Robin Williams memorial service, September 27, 2014.

"He would read me articles about space": Cody Williams, remarks at Robin Williams memorial service, September 27, 2014.

"he will not get to walk me down the aisle": Zelda Williams, remarks at Robin Williams memorial service, September 27, 2014.

"There's Robin Williams the concept": Zak Williams, remarks at Robin Williams memorial service, September 27, 2014.

before Game 5 of the 2014 World Series: MLB.com, "WS2014 Gm5: Robin Williams' kids throw to Crystal." Archived at https://www.youtube.com/watch?v=NbG4f Rkxck0.

"If Robin could have been there for that, I'd have told him": Author interview with Billy Crystal.

a report enumerating all the factors that had contributed to his death: Joseph I. Cohen, Autopsy Protocol, Robin McLaurin Williams, October 31, 2014.

A separate surgical pathology report: Joseph I. Cohen, Surgical Pathology Report, John Doe, October 20, 2014.

"There's a protein that is normally useful in the brain": Author interview with Douglas Scharre.

"People can appear drowsy or sleeping": Paula Span, "A Form of Dementia That Is Often Misdiagnosed," *New York Times,* September 25, 2012.

"There was more going on, and that more made it suspicious": Author interview with James E. Galvin.

"The medications help a little bit": Author interview with Douglas Scharre.

"There's no way to repair the damage that's been done": Span, "A Form of Dementia That Is Often Misdiagnosed."

"If you're young, if you have insight into what's happening": Dave Itzkoff and Benedict Carey, "Robin Williams's Widow Points to Dementia as a Suicide Cause," *New York Times,* November 3, 2015.

"If we could look through the retrospect-o-scope": Author interview with James E. Galvin.

"It was not depression that killed Robin": Kara Warner, "It Was Not Depression That Killed Robin," *People,* November 3, 2015.

"an undiagnosed victim of dementia with Lewy bodies": Eric Idle, Twitter post, August 11, 2015.

"He died from Lewy body dementia": Author interview with Bobcat Goldthwait.

"I put myself in his place. Think of it this way": Author interview with Billy Crystal.

Robin's arrival in heaven, set in a celestial nightclub: Billy Crystal, "Billy Crystal Imagines Robin Williams in Heaven," *Entertainment Weekly,* December 12, 2014.

Susan's lawyers filed a petition in San Francisco Superior Court: James M. Wagstaffe et al., "In the Matter of the Robin Williams Trust, Beneficiary's Petition for Instructions," Superior Court of the State of California, County of San Francisco, December 19, 2014.

Robin had created a financial trust: Melissa Cronin, "A Lasting Legacy," RadarOnline.com, August 13, 2014.

a brief legal document, known as a pour-over will: Arnold D. Kassoy and Joel Faden, "In the Matter of the Robin Williams Trust, Petition for Order Confirming Trust Asset," Superior Court of the State of California, County of San Francisco, January 7, 2015. At the time of Robin's death, Joel Faden and Robin's comanager Stephen Tenen-

897

baum served as cotrustees of his trust. On September 13, 2014, Tenenbaum resigned as a cotrustee and was succeeded by Arnold Kassoy.

a separate trust specifically for Susan: Wagstaffe et al., "In the Matter of the Robin Williams Trust, Beneficiary's Petition for Instructions."

Zak, Zelda, and Cody . . . filed a court document of their own: Meredith R. Bushnell and Rebecca L. D. Gordon, "In the Matter of the Robin Williams Trust, Objections to Beneficiary's Petition for Instructions," Superior Court of the State of California, County of San Francisco, January 21, 2015.

"not be disrupted in her life with her children": Dave Itzkoff, "Robin Williams's Widow and Children Tangle over Estate," *New York Times,* February 2, 2015.

"One thing Robin didn't like is, he didn't like conflict": Author interview with Bobcat Goldthwait.

"she just wanted to secure her place as Mrs. Williams": Author interview with Cheri Minns.

"I hear Susan described as the widow Williams": Author interview with Steven Haft.

"Susan was under the impression that she had struck gold": Author interview with Zak Williams.

"A lot of people who have been through it and lost someone": Eun Kyung Kim,

"Robin Williams' Daughter Zelda on Life Without Dad, Continuing His Charity Work," Today.com, February 26, 2015.

"While it's hard to speak of this as a win": Susan Williams, statement, October 2, 2015.

"they would not be making any public statements": Allan Mayer, statement, October 3, 2015.

the tunnel that connects Marin County to the Golden Gate Bridge: Alyssa Pereira, "Robin Williams Tunnel Officially Gets New Signs," *San Francisco Chronicle,* March 2, 2016.

its Robin Williams Center in New York: Ross McDonagh, "Zelda Williams Joins Brother Zachary Pym for Grand Opening of Robin Williams Center," *Daily Mail,* October 5, 2016.

"you will be inspired to turn Robin's suffering into something meaningful": Susan Schneider Williams, "The Terrorist Inside My Husband's Brain."

"All ownership in the right to Settlor's name": Wagstaffe et al., "In the Matter of the Robin Williams Trust, Beneficiary's Petition for Instructions."

"You have my word, we will honor his name": Dwayne Johnson, Instagram post, May 9, 2016.

Epilogue

"Go, young man, and write your story": Eskow, "Robin Williams: Full Tilt Bozo."

ACKNOWLEDGMENTS

From the rainy day in 1980 when I watched *Popeye* twice in back-to-back showings, Robin Williams has been a hero of mine, and getting to tell his story has been a singular privilege. It is a goal I could never have fulfilled without the help of many people, to whom I am deeply indebted.

I cannot sufficiently convey my gratitude to Zak Williams and Alex Mallick-Williams, who were unfailingly generous with their time, candor, and hospitality. Their openness and kindness contributed immensely to my understanding of Robin, the Williams family, and its history. I hope that I have lived up to the trust they placed in me, and that the portrait of Robin I have provided here reflects the man that they, Marsha, Zelda, and Cody knew.

I would also like to offer my most sincere thanks and appreciation to Valerie Velardi, McLaurin Smith-Williams, and Frankie Williams for graciously agreeing to speak with me and reflect on their lives with Robin.

Billy Crystal was open, honest, and welcoming beyond my expectations. This book would have been incomplete without his caring, thoughtful contributions, and I'm so fortunate to have them.

Lisa Birnbach was not only a valuable interview subject but a dependable sounding board and a bottomless well of insight, wit, and parenting advice, and my work and life are immeasurably better for knowing her.

It has been a joy to get to know Bennett Tramer and Sonya Sones, who provided many wonderful anecdotes and necessary pep throughout the making of this book.

For offering their memories of Robin or participating in interviews for this book, I thank: F. Murray Abraham, Peter Asher, Wendy Asher, Douglas Basham, Sandra Bernhard, Lewis Black, Joel Blum, Jeff Bridges, Joshua Raoul Brody, Sue Campbell, Dana Carvey, Ron Clements, Frances Conroy, Phillip Culver, Alan Curtiss, Wendy Cutler, Al Dauber, Nick David, Bob Davis, Mary Alette Davis, Pam Dawber, Tony De Paul, Mike Dugan, James Dunn, Debi Durst, Will Durst, Jules Feiffer, Dick Gale, James E. Galvin, Monica Ganas, Terry Gilliam, Andy Goldberg, Robyn Goodman, Steven Haft, Gale Hansen, Margot Harley, Jeff Hodgen, Mark Johnson, Rajiv Joseph, Michael Kahn, Moisés Kaufman, Robert Klein, Ronald Krempetz, Dylan Kussman, Richard LaGravenese, Jeff Land, Norman Lear, Pat Lee, Jay Leno, David Letterman, Richard Levine, Barry Levinson, Richard Lewis, Shelly Lipkin, Mark Lonow, Marc Maron, Garry Marshall, Jamie Masada, Dakin Matthews, Cyndi McHale, Dale McRaven, Alan Menken, Cheri Minns, Arian Moayed, John Moffitt, John Musker, Don Novello, Todd Oppenheimer, Rick Overton, Howard Papush, Steven Pearl, Paul Perri, Philippe Petit, Greg Phillips, Mark Pitta, Christie Platt, Lillian Ross, Bob Sarlatte, Douglas Scharre, George Schlatter, Tom Schulman, Brian Seff, Marc Shaiman, Pauly Shore, Rich Shydner, Randi Mayem Singer, Stu Smiley, Elizabeth Smith, Joe Spano, Jim Staahl, Don Stevens, Howard Storm, Paul Tepper, Bruce Vilanch, Greg Jon Welsh, Andy Weltman, Henry Winkler, and Robert Wuhl.

For arranging interviews, connecting me to sources, and sharing ideas and materials, thank you also: Steven Beeman, Maggie Biggar, Paul Bloch, Howard Bragman, Benedict Carey, Nicole Cruz, Derek Del Rossi, Molly Devaney, Ro Diamond, Olivia Dupuis, Kim Foulger, Harry Gold, Gloria Gottschalk, Isaac Grossman, Jess Guinivan, Dick Guttman, Heather Hall, Ron Hoffman, Heather Jackson, Rachel Karten, Judy Katz, Tom Keaney, Matt Labov, Tom Lapinski, Suzanne Ledbetter, Mark Malkoff, Carly Morgan,

Susan Morrison, Lisa Morse, Jeff Muskus, Kliph Nesteroff, Kathy O'Donnell, Marilee Rogers, Sam Rudy, Heidi Schaeffer, Bryan Schneider, Glenn Schwartz, Jean Sievers, James Sliman, Marc Thibodeau, Biff Thiele, Ina Treciokas, and Marina Zenovich.

The Robin Williams collection at the Howard Gotlieb Archival Research Center of Boston University was an invaluable resource in the creation of this book, and I would like to thank Ryan J. Hendrickson, J. C. Johnson, Laura Russo, and Tom Testa there in particular for their assistance.

I am grateful to Christopher C. Child and Jim Power Jr. at the New England Historic Genealogical Society for helping to confirm details of Williams and McLaurin family lineage.

The Billy Rose Theatre Division of the New York Public Library for the Performing Arts, Dorothy and Lewis B. Cullman Center has reliably offered me a launching pad for projects such as this; it is a one-of-a-kind resource and I hope it remains a second home for years to come.

For furnishing additional research materials, I would also like to thank the Langson Library at University of California, Irvine; Newspapers.com; and Music Video Resource.

I am particularly obliged to my extraordinary colleagues at the *New York Times,* where I was first given the opportunity to write about Robin Williams, and I would especially like to recognize my editors Stephanie Goodman, Patrick Healy, Lorne Manly, Sia Michel, Scott Veale, and Alex Ward for those opportunities. Emma G. Fitzsimmons, Peter Keepnews, and Bruce Weber were crucial collaborators on the terrible day we had to write Robin's obituary.

Stephen Rubin had an inexplicable faith that I could deliver on a project of this scope and magnitude long before I found it in myself. Paul Golob, my most valued editor, remained a loyal and patient guide at every step of this process, and I would stand on a desk for him without hesitation. I am especially grateful for the help of their colleagues at Henry Holt and Company, including Gillian Blake, Patricia Eisemann, Fiona Lowenstein, Maggie Richards, and Caroline Wray.

Daniel Greenberg has been my agent and my tireless advocate, and the care that he and the staff at Levine Greenberg Rostan have offered means the world to me.

All my love to my family, especially to Amy, who read every word I wrote, abided all my heartaches and bellyaches, and offered me more tenderness and patience than I deserve, and to Max, who has not yet known a day in his life when I wasn't working on this book. Someday, when you're older, I'll tell you all about me.

ABOUT THE AUTHOR

Dave Itzkoff is the author of *Mad as Hell, Cocaine's Son,* and *Lads.* He is a culture reporter at the *New York Times,* where he writes regularly about film, television, theater, music, and popular culture. He has previously worked at *Spin, Maxim,* and *Details,* and his work has appeared in *GQ, Vanity Fair, Wired,* and other publications. He lives in New York City.

The employees of Thorndike Press hope you have enjoyed this Large Print book. All our Thorndike, Wheeler, and Kennebec Large Print titles are designed for easy reading, and all our books are made to last. Other Thorndike Press Large Print books are available at your library, through selected bookstores, or directly from us.

For information about titles, please call:
  (800) 223-1244

or visit our website at:
  gale.com/thorndike

To share your comments, please write:
  Publisher
  Thorndike Press
  10 Water St., Suite 310
  Waterville, ME 04901